City Life

City Life

EDITED BY

Oscar Shoenfeld AND *Helene MacLean*

Grossman Publishers, New York

1 9 6 9

ACKNOWLEDGMENTS

Excerpt from *The Education of Henry Adams* by Henry Adams. By permission of
Houghton Mifflin Company.

Excerpt from *Twenty Years at Hull House* by Jane Addams. Copyright 1910 by The
Macmillan Company, renewed 1938 by James W. Linn. By permission of The Macmillan
Company.

"Vehicles Out of the Ordinary" by George Ade. From *The Stories of the Streets and of
the Town,* appeared in *The Chicago Record* 1893–1900. By permission of the *Chicago
Daily News.*

"Knoxville: Summer 1915" by James Agee. From *A Death in the Family* by James Agee.
Copyright © 1957 by James Agee Trust. First published in *Partisan Review* (August-
September 1938, Vol. 5, No. 3). By permission of Grosset & Dunlap, Inc.

"My Father's Grocery Store" by Paul M. Angle. Copyright © 1963 by American Heritage
Publishing Co., Inc. (August 1963 *American Heritage*). By permission of American Heritage Publishing Co., Inc.

Excerpt from *Those Days* of Hamilton Fish Armstrong. Copyright © 1963 by Hamilton
Fish Armstrong. By permission of Harper & Row, Publishers.

"Storyville Days and Nights" by Louis Armstrong. From *Satchmo:* My Life in New
Orleans by Louis Armstrong. Copyright © 1954 by Louis Armstrong. By permission of
Prentice-Hall, Inc.

"A New Orleans Childhood: The House on Decatur Street" by Hamilton Basso. Copyright © 1954 by The New Yorker Magazine, Inc. By premission of *The New Yorker.*

Excerpt from *The Worcester Account* by S. N. Behrman. Copyright 1954 by S. N. Behrman. By permission of Random House, Inc.

Excerpt from *My Life* by Claude Bowers. Copyright © 1962 by Patricia Bowers. By permission of Simon & Schuster.

"A House on the Heights" by Truman Capote. From *Selected Writings* by Truman
Capote. Copyright © 1959 by The Curtis Publishing Company. By permission of Random House, Inc.

Excerpt from *Carp's Washington* by Frank G. Carpenter. Copyright © 1960 by Frances
Carpenter Huntington. By permission of McGraw-Hill.

Preface

The city is the teacher of the man.
Plutarch

From ancient times to the present, the city has been the repository of
man's finest accomplishments and his most challenging experiences. *City
Life* is an attempt to recapture the urban past in all its depth and
variety. The sources for the selections that follow are as different from
one another as Edith Wharton was from Richard Wright. The periods
and places are as remote from one another as the post-Civil War Boston
of Henry Adams's boyhood is from the San Francisco of World War II
described by John Dos Passos.

In some ways, this anthology is a "once-upon-a-time" book in which
the city of the past emerges as the magic terrain of childhood. Young
explorers like Harpo Marx and Hamilton Fish Armstrong—born the
same year into totally different worlds—recall the glorious days of their
wanderings in the streets of New York. James Agee endows Knoxville
with a serenity that seems immutable, and Ralph Ellison pays tribute to
the richly assorted sights and sounds of his Oklahoma City boyhood in
the 1920s as the abiding inspiration for his adult accomplishments.

Like other old cities with a crowded past, Philadelphia at the turn of
the century was a place where polarities existed side by side. Elizabeth
Robins Pennell could go her sober way on Spruce Street, secure in the
knowledge that her days were laid out by a prescribed social and moral
pattern. Yet in the nearby back alleys in the "bloody Eighth Ward,"
where Ethel Waters spent part of her childhood running errands for a
brothel, all was improvisation and disorder. Although they were young
contemporaries in the same city, Hamilton Basso's New Orleans is a
world away from the raffish, roistering Negro section of town where
Louis Armstrong was creating the early patterns of jazz.

Among those most poignantly aware of the contrasts in American life
were the immigrants, the twenty million who came to this country in the
years between 1880 and 1902 looking for new opportunities in a stable
world. S. N. Behrman recalls the years in Worcester, Massachusetts, when

he was emerging from his family's European orthodoxy. Ernest Meyer describes his boyhood in Milwaukee when that city was practically a German transplant. And in Chicago, Jane Addams made of Hull House a haven for the Poles, Italians, Hungarians, and Russians who swarmed into the South Side at the turn of the century.

The hopeful and ambitious came to the cities not only from across the ocean, but from across the country as well, from small New England villages, isolated farms, and cotton fields. Mary Ellen Chase left the little schoolhouse in Maine and made her way to Chicago, Edna Ferber shook the Appleton dust off her shoes and got a job as a newspaper reporter in Milwaukee, and many Negro writers flocked to the Harlem of the 20s described by Langston Hughes.

Migrations from one part of the country to another continue. Los Angeles is now a major magnet, and although it is a comparative new-comer to the urban scene, it is growing at an unprecedented rate. With its industries of the future, its comfortable climate, and its unusual physical possibilities for expansion, Los Angeles may well be the model for the new Megalopolis.

The changes in urban America can be charted in this book: from coast to coast, and from one century to another; from Henry Adams's Boston, with which we begin, to Christopher Rand's Ultimate City—Los Angeles.

Contents

The South

The West

New England

BOSTON

Perhaps a clue to Boston's character may be found in the very diversity of selections that follow. Henry Adams writes about a patrician boyhood in the 1850s and Malcolm X, almost a hundred years later, re-creates for us the fascination the big city held for a thirteen-year-old Negro boy, fresh from small-town life in the Middle West.

While Adams and Malcolm X may represent the two extremes in time, in class origins and viewpoint, other contributors to this section also present a wide divergence of social outlook. But for all their differences, it becomes clear that Boston had room for them all; room for growing and thinking. Perhaps the distinction of the city, in the past at least, has been that it could and did provide a rich and tolerant background which stimulated eager minds to realize their full potential.

Norbert Wiener's selection on Cambridge is included in this section because to separate Boston from Cambridge is unthinkable. Cambridge grew and developed out of that special richness of Boston, the true capital of the country of New England.

Henry Adams

Henry Adams (1838–1918), descendant of two Presidents, grew up in Boston before the Civil War. The period described in *The Education of Henry Adams* is the earliest in point of time in this anthology, but the Boston of his boyhood has a peculiar contemporary relevance. Both the issues and the atmosphere sound very modern indeed. Adams is remembered today chiefly for his autobiography, from which the following selection is taken, and for *Mont-Saint-Michel* and *Chartres*.

from The Education of Henry Adams

One of the commonest boy-games of winter, inherited directly from the eighteenth-century, was a game of war on Boston Common. In old days the two hostile forces were called North-Enders and South-Enders. In 1850 the North-Enders still survived as a legend, but in practice it was a battle of the Latin School against all comers, and the Latin School, for snowball, included all the boys of the West End. Whenever, on a half-holiday, the weather was soft enough to soften the snow, the Common was apt to be the scene of a fight, which began in daylight with the Latin School in force, rushing their opponents down to Tremont Street, and which generally ended at dark by the Latin School dwindling in numbers and disappearing. As the Latin School grew weak, the roughs and young blackguards grew strong. As long as snowballs were the only weapon, no one was much hurt, but a stone may be put in a snowball, and in the dark a stick or a slungshot in the hands of a boy is as effective as a knife. One afternoon the fight had been long and exhausting. The boy Henry, following, as his habit was, his bigger brother Charles, had taken part in the battle, and had felt his courage much depressed by seeing one of his trustiest leaders, Henry Higginson—"Bully Hig," his school name—struck by a stone over the eye, and led off the field bleeding in rather a ghastly manner. As night came on, the Latin School was steadily forced back to the Beacon Street Mall where they could retreat no further without disbanding, and by that time only a small band was left, headed by two heroes, Savage and Marvin. A dark mass of figures could be seen below, making ready for the last rush, and rumor said that a swarm of blackguards from the slums, led by a grisly terror called Conky Daniels, with a club and a hideous reputation, was going to put an end to the Beacon

3

Street cowards forever. Henry wanted to run away with the others, but his brother was too big to run away, so they stood still and waited immolation. The dark mass set up a shout, and rushed forward. The Beacon Street boys turned and fled up the steps, except Savage and Marvin and the few champions who would not run. The terrible Conky Daniels swaggered up, stopped a moment with his body-guard to swear a few oaths at Marvin, and then swept on and chased the flyers, leaving the few boys untouched who stood their ground. The obvious moral taught that blackguards were not so black as they were painted; but the boy Henry had passed through as much terror as though he were Turenne or Henri IV, and ten or twelve years afterwards when these same boys were fighting and falling on all the battle-fields of Virginia and Maryland, he wondered whether their education on Boston Common had taught Savage and Marvin how to die.

If violence were a part of complete education, Boston was not incomplete. The idea of violence was familiar to the anti-slavery leaders as well as to their followers. Most of them suffered from it. Mobs were always possible. Henry never happened to be actually concerned in a mob, but he, like every other boy, was sure to be on hand wherever a mob was expected, and whenever he heard Garrison or Wendell Phillips speak, he looked for trouble. Wendell Phillips on a platform was a model dangerous for youth. Theodore Parker in his pulpit was not much safer. Worst of all, the execution of the Fugitive Slave Law in Boston—the sight of Court Square packed with bayonets, and his own friends obliged to line the streets under arms as State militia, in order to return a negro to slavery—wrought frenzy in the brain of a fifteen-year-old, eighteenth-century boy from Quincy, who wanted to miss no reasonable chance of mischief.

One lived in the atmosphere of the Stamp Act, the Tea Tax, and the Boston Massacre. Within Boston, a boy was first an eighteenth-century politician, and afterwards only a possibility; beyond Boston the first step led only further into politics.

Arthur Train

During the 1920s Arthur Train's (1875–1945) literary lawyer, Ephraim Tutt, was as real and vivid to many as was Sherlock Holmes. Train, born in Boston, was a practicing lawyer himself until the success of his Tutt stories, which first appeared in *The Saturday Evening Post*, induced him to give up law for literature. He was a great storyteller and this autobiographical memoir, which was written for *Scribner's* Magazine in 1930, evokes the Boston of his youth with the same clarity that brought Ephraim Tutt to life for so many readers.

from The Puritan Shadow

I was born in the city of Boston in 1875, ninety-two years after the birth of my grandfather in 1783, and fifty-eight years after that of my father in 1817. It was an era of gas, sulphur matches, fixed wooden bathtubs lined with tin, nightgowns, chewing-tobacco, and the Republican party. The Civil War had apparently been fought only the day before yesterday. One had friends who had lost uncles and brothers at Shiloh and Gettysburg— saw, met, and sat on the knees of war governors and generals at the Union Club on Park Street.

There were, of course, no telephones, no electric lights, no safety-matches, no motors or motor-launches, no golf or country clubs, and on transatlantic steamers sidewheels had only recently given place to propellers.

We had bananas, but no grapefruit. Divorce was a social disgrace, irrespective of the guilt of either party, and usually led to social ostracism. Ready-made shoes of good quality could be bought for from $2 up, and ready-made "Plymouth Rock" pants for $3. They were advertised thus:

> *"When the pant hunter pantless is panting for pants,*
> *And pants for the best pants the pant market grants,*
> *He panteth unpanted until he implants*
> *Himself in a pair of our 'Plymouth Rock' pants."*

Senators, generals, and ministers of the Gospel publicly indorsed patent medicines. "Rogers' Groups" were to be found in every "parlor." The bustle was omnipresent. Women wore their hair in "water waves," "bangs," and ringlets; men used bear's grease. "Votes for women" and "women's rights" in general were jokes, and the ladies who aped men's

5

clothing were treated not only as freaks but as of doubtful virtue. It was still eminently respectable to be a Sunday-school superintendent or United States senator, and clergymen were universally objects of admiration to the ladies.

No profanity was permitted upon the stage, and it was nearly twenty years later before the first outspoken "damn" sent a shiver down the backs of the startled audience, although presently, once the "customers" had become properly acclimated to such daring expletives, they inevitably and for many years received them with "sure-fire" applause and laughter. Not until 1900 did the first "God damn" appear under the imprint of a respectable publisher:—not until nearly quarter of a century thereafter was it heard across the footlights. The stage—except for the classics and old English comedies—was still looked upon askance; most actors and actresses were classed with harlots, saloon-keepers, and gamblers. Novels were decried as frivolous and often harmful. "Comic operas," even if advertised as "phantasmas," were not attended by the best people. The mother-in-law joke was still regarded as funny, and black-face minstrels played to packed houses everywhere.

There were hitching-posts and horse-blocks on the residential streets of New York, Philadelphia, and Boston, and a common sight on Beacon Street in the latter city was a herd of several hundred cattle mooing, bellowing, and shoving each other across the sidewalks and even up the steps of the houses, while nurse-maids and pedestrians sought refuge in the vestibules. The Union Pacific Railroad had been completed only a short time, every farmer had his buffalo-robe, and Custer had just made his "last stand." Indians—real, live, dangerous ones in war-paint and feathers —still swarmed the Western plains and were the most popular subject of juvenile literature. That a woman should smoke or ride astride was almost as unthinkable as that she should appear in the streets totally nude, and would have excited as much of a riot. Cigarettes were not widely used and were viewed as decadent, "nasty" and in some occult way as suggestive of obscenity. This last was perhaps due to the lure of giving away with each box a photograph of some Amazonian stage favorite with the exuberant pulchritude so much admired by lewd fellows of the baser sort at that period. The annual circus parade was in effect a local holiday even in cities as large as Boston.

Everybody wore gloves to everything. At dinner-parties, and this was still true down into the twentieth century, men wore white gloves when shaking hands with their host and hostess and peeled them off before going to the table. It may have been that the hands got harder use then than now and gloves helped to conceal reddened joints and broken, blackened nails.

In those days there was nothing invidious in the terms "upper and lower classes," and they were used without embarrassment or apprehension that the speaker might be regarded as either snobbish or unchristian. It was not considered undemocratic to recognize the fact that God had been pleased to call people to different "estates of life" where they should order themselves humbly and reverently to "their betters." At least the betters had no doubt about it. There was enormous respect for anything "established." There was no "muck-raking," the cities were as yet unashamed, no historic character had been debunked. That George Washington could not tell a lie and did it "with his little hatchet" was as certain as that God made cherry-trees. Nobody questioned the literal interpretation of the Scriptures or the divine origin of capitalism. To advocate membership in a trade-union was to read oneself out of respectable society. Everybody went to church or, if not, concealed themselves in the rear of the house, and, except just before morning service, the streets on Sundays were practically deserted.

Darwin's theory of the survival of the fittest was considered a huge, if impious, joke, which Gladstone had supposedly annihilated in his "Impregnable Rock of Holy Scripture" by proving to the satisfaction of almost everybody that the word "day" used in Genesis in the account of God's making of the world, if properly translated, meant really "period of time." Just how he disposed of Methuselah's nine hundred odd years, I forget. Any deviation from established conventions was an indication of either insanity or sin. New England still adhered frigidly to the belief that whatever made for joy or gaiety must be in essence evil.

Life was still lived with Puritan frugality. Even among the well-to-do there were practically no male house domestics. Few people kept more than two servants, who were inevitably female Irish immigrants recently landed. We paid Bridget, our cook, $4 and the "second girl" (there was no first girl) $2.50 per week. The second girl swept off the steps in the morning, washed out the vestibule, waited on table, answered the bell, and helped with the family wash. In winter any peripatetic choreman who happened by shovelled the snow off the sidewalk for twenty-five cents. My father and the cook together managed the furnace, and my mother did much of the dusting. We had beef on Sundays and little meat the rest of the time. There was no "dinner" except on Sundays, its place being taken at night by a nondescript meal of minced fish or fowl, hot breads, pies, cookies, applesauce and corn-meal (or "Indian") "mush."

Boston society in the 70's was the same sort of family affair as exists to-day in those comfortable mid-western towns originally founded by New Englanders who trekked there in covered wagons during the early years of the nineteenth century. When people returned home in the late after-noon they stayed there, and, apart from an occasional political banquet, my father never dined out. In fact I do not think that he possessed such a thing as a dress suit, although he owned a blue "claw-hammer" with tails and brass buttons.

Existence was simple and methodical. Every morning at precisely half past eight o'clock each front door opened and the owner of the house, wearing a tan-colored "reefer," as the short box-coat of those days was locally called, and carrying a green baize bag supposedly holding papers, descended to the sidewalk and started to walk "down-town." At six, or six-thirty, in the evening he reappeared and, ascending the steps once more, disappeared for another ten hours. The ladies "went down-town" about ten o'clock, after having helped one of the "Bridgets" with the lighter housekeeping. On rainy days they took the horse-cars, whose warning tinkle could be heard for several blocks. Indeed, one could "watch out for the horse-car" from the bay window and still have plenty of time to cross the street and signal for it to stop. The drivers and conductors were fam-ily friends, often taking part in the conversations between passengers.

One was aroused each morning by the seven-o'clock car—"Jingle-clup-jingle-ingle-ingle-clup-clup. Whoa!—Clatter!—Giddap!—Clupitty!—Jin-gle-jingle-clup-clup—jingle-jingle-ingle-clupitty-jingle—"

How deep the snow was in those days! How huge the mounds piled along the curbs; higher even than one's head! And what a thud *The Transcript* made when the paper-carrier hurled it into the front vestibule against the door! There is no such snow, no such strong man now! I used to find all kinds of strange loot in that dusty vestibule which had accumu-lated in my absence—sample packages of starch and oatmeal, tiny bottles containing salving ointments and health-giving pills, and wonderful col-ored advertisements of all kinds, some containing the most side-splitting jokes, which were immediately taken away from me by my watchful mama.

Although my father was an Episcopalian—a sect to which still adhered a faint flavor of Popery in its inordinate celebrations of Christmas and Easter—and my mother a Unitarian—or in other words hardly a Chris-tian at all—I was not permitted to indulge in any form of amusement upon the Lord's day, when even a walk must be a mild promenade with no unseemly outcries or cavortings. I was allowed on the Sabbath to read only the Bible and certain selected Sunday-school books bound in red and blue and tooled in gold; to talk only about spiritual or supposedly spiritual things.

At church I was cooped up in a high-backed pew during long, dreary hours, without occupation except to draw surreptitious pictures of the minister in the back of my prayer-book. . . .

As for the other six days in the week certain concessions were made toward liberalism by allowing attendance at Papanti's dancing school on Saturday mornings and, once or twice a winter, at some "operetta" given at the old Boston Museum, where I was hurried past the pickled mermaids and foetuses by my anxious guardian, and where in later years I revelled in old English comedy given by a stock company composed, among others, of Junius Brutus Booth, Jr., Edgar Fawcett, George Wilson, Mrs. Vincent, Annie Clark, Edgar Davenport, John Mason, and, for a time, Richard Mansfield.

It was through such cracks in the wall that I first gained the knowledge that there were other worlds possessed of other standards where, by some curious paradox, people were not damned for doing the very same things that would have damned them in Boston and which, strangely enough, Bostonians were willing to pay to see portrayed upon the stage. From these plays I gathered that there was a thing called "love," not mentioned at home. That this had anything to do with sex was unsuspected and no doubt would have been stoutly denied by those in authority. But that obvious naughtiness might be rather charming, and that parents could even go so far as to laugh at it, aroused the first suspicions in my mind that the line between right and wrong might not be so clearly defined as I had been led to believe. Secretly I pondered and, pondering upon the nature of God, became at nine, as I believed, an atheist. Once upon the skids, my whole intellectual cosmos toppled with a crash.

It was a bookish period and, outside the family connection, the people my father knew were of the literary tradition. Indeed, although I have never cared for the Boston accent, I am grateful for the accurate English I heard as a child. I suppose to-day we would have passed as a distinctly "highbrow" bunch. Even the tradespeople, I feel sure, would seem "literary" to me now, if I should meet them again.

My first lesson in the meticulous use of words occurred in connection with a series of burglaries in the neighborhood. Just behind us on Exeter Street lived a well-known Boston spinster, Miss Ella Day by name. One moonlight night, when I was about ten years old, I was aroused by the noise of a watchman's rattle and hurried to the window hoping to catch sight of the burglar leaping over the back-yard fences. Although I could see no burglar, I did see Miss Day's attenuated right arm projecting from her window with the rattle, which she was vigorously whirling, at the end of it. Thoroughly thrilled, I shouted across to her:

"Miss Day! Miss Day! What is it—robbers?"

Even now I can hear her thin, shaking voice with its slightly condescending acerbity:

"No—*burglars!*"

In those days Boston was Boston.

I pause for an instant to wonder a little whether that example of purism was not worth more to me than all the English courses I later slouched through at Harvard. No doubt, Miss Day would have refused to call a burglar a robber even at a pistol's point. Women have died for less! Yet my mother always said "You was," and my uncle habitually used "shew" for "showed"—which may demonstrate either our illiteracy or our antiquity.

Nancy Hale

There can be few people with Nancy Hale's credentials for writing about Boston. Miss Hale's grandfather was Edward Everett Hale, who wrote *The Man without a Country*, and her great-aunt was Lucretia Peabody Hale, who wrote *The Peterkin Papers*. Edward Everett Hale was for a time Chaplain of the United States Senate, and it was he who when asked whether he prayed for the Senate, replied, "No, I look at the Senators and pray for the people." As the many readers of her numerous magazine articles know, Miss Nancy Hale does not suffer any lack of the same sharp, dry wit. The selection below is taken from *The Empress's Ring*, 1955.

The Copley-Plaza

I see by an advertisement in a year-old magazine I came across cleaning out my Virginia cellar that a big hotel chain has bought the old Copley-Plaza in Boston and renamed it the Sheraton-Plaza. This seems to me absurd. It was called the Copley-Plaza because it is on Copley Square. My own early life was so bound up with the Copley-Plaza that I feel now very much as if someone insisted that I call my mother Mrs. Sheraton.

My earliest Copley-Plaza memory is, I think, of Miss Macomber's dancing class, to which I went when I was about twelve. No, from even before that there are echoes; whispers of the small stringed orchestra playing among the palms as I sit with my feet dangling above the marble floor and am treated to an ice—raspberry or orange—and something called *petits fours*. I have been taken to a matinée to see, from a box, John Craig and Mary Young do *Romeo and Juliet* at the Arlington Street Theatre. The orchestra is playing a waltz called "Les Patineurs," and the *petits fours* are beautiful—green, pink, and white; diamond-shaped and square —but why "fours"? Because there are four corners, or what? I sit comfortably munching, and looking with favor at the palmy scene before me: this, then, is the great world, and very nice.

But by the time I began to go to Miss Macomber's some faint glaze of social comparisons had obscured my consciousness, and I was aware that Miss Macomber's was not the last word in Boston dancing classes. The last word was Foster's classes, held at the Somerset, out on Commonwealth Avenue.

Was it this that lent such a poignant, somehow heartbreaking quality

11

to those late afternoons? Outside, the street lights are being turned on in
the early-falling dusk along Dartmouth Street, Huntington Avenue, St.
James Avenue. Inside the vast, marble, worldly Copley-Plaza, the little
girls are having their pink taffeta and blue satin sashes retied in the dressing room down the corridor from the ballroom. The moment comes, and
we edge out into the corridor, where the boys wait in their blue serge
suits. With somebody (who?) directing us, we form couples to march up
the steps and into the smaller ballroom, where Miss Macomber stands
awaiting us in a peacock-blue taffeta dress and bronze kid slippers. The
lady at the piano is playing "Won't You Wait Till the Cows Come
Home?" We mince or shamble across the shining parquet; the boys bow,
the girls curtsy, and then we hurry, with relief, away to reassemble strictly
according to sex on the gilt chairs along the wall, until Miss Macomber
gives the order "Boys, choose partners for the Slide Polka." At one end of
the room, a few mothers sit—my mother among them—in their furs, their
dark-blue suits neatly fitted over the bust, their plumed hats. Because of
the tragic, romantic air of the whole thing, it is a relief to me when it is
over and I am taken across Dartmouth Street, on our way home, to S. S.
Pierce's, its lights blazing out in the Back Bay twilight, where I can walk
round and round the circular display counter covered with party favors
while my mother sits ordering California pea beans and a five-pound
stone crock of strawberry jam at the grocery counter.

But the memories of that dancing class are not all tragic in atmosphere.
There was the afternoon that I won the Elimination Prize with, as partner, a boy named Sidney Shurtleff (who is now a landscape architect and
has changed *his* name to Shurcliff). The Elimination Contest was a part of
the cotillion that marked the last dancing class of the season. Favors were
given out, to be handed, grudgingly, to the girls by the boys; I think the
last figure in the cotillion was the Elimination Contest. In principle, it
was like musical chairs. Each couple was given a number, and we all
danced—the fox trot, the one-step, the slide polka—and then abruptly
the music would cease, and Miss Macomber would call out a few numbers
drawn from a hat and the couples holding those numbers sat down. The
last couple left dancing won. Sidney and I were the last couple left dancing, and side by side we marched the length of the small ballroom to
receive our prizes. I do not remember what the prizes were. I remember
the tune the lady at the piano was playing as we danced all alone the full
circuit of the ballroom, as victors—a tune from the First World War
called "Babes in the Wood." That last clumsily danced circuit—for we
had not won our prize because of any talent, any superiority whatsoever,

only by chance—was the high point of my life up to then. I tasted triumph.

The next set of memories I bear of the Copley-Plaza are very different from these in mood. I must have been fourteen. I had begun going to Miss Winsor's School, out in Longwood, and I found it hard to make friends; as far as I could figure at that age, my total inability to play basketball or field hockey was the cause of my unpopularity. Some sort of instinct, right or wrong, caused me to begin stopping in at the Copley-Plaza on my way home from school, in search of a kind of comfort, in search of a kind of distraction.

For here I would sit, in the main lobby, opposite to the huge marble desk, dressed in my thick, untidy school clothes, my galoshes, with my plaid schoolbag huddled into the thronelike chair with me, and watch what seemed to me the worldly and wealthy conducting their fascinating lives at the Copley-Plaza. In from the Dartmouth Street entrance would hurry a bellboy, or two bellboys, laden down with expensive luggage, followed by a blond woman in a fur coat, or a close-shaven man in a check waistcoat, or a dark, romantic-looking lady all in black and attended by what seemed to be a governess with two or three rich, well-dressed children—important children, children with lives.

Occasionally I would get up and go down the corridor to the ladies' room, not so much because I needed to as that there I found myself not two feet away from beautiful, expensively dressed women who talked to each other busily about their approaching engagements. I would wash my hands, taking a long time about it, and listen to some lovely girl saying, "We're going to Paris Friday, on the *Ile*. . . ." Then I would go back to my throne in the lobby to watch some more people make their entrances. All the time, the stringed orchestra would be playing waltzes, behind in the palm court—fast and sweet and queerly nostalgic. It was almost as if this were the only life I had.

The final stage of my relationship with the Copley-Plaza takes up where "Babes in the Wood" left off—on a note of triumph. I am a Boston débutante—a *popular* Boston débutante—going to those larger balls which are held here, and which, compared with the dances at the Somerset, somehow never seem quite quite. The Somerset is definitely quite quite. But now I go to all those dances, too. My triumph is almost complete; I have not had to *do* anything to achieve it, it just came, as I grew older and had my hair shingled and began being told I danced well and that I looked like Greta Garbo. I feel a little superior toward balls at the Copley-Plaza.

Back in the old dressing room again. Now it is thronged with girls: girls in knee-length evening dresses, girls with rigid gold slave necklaces around their slender, immature throats, girls in silver kid slippers and ostrich *leis* and Chanel bracelets and pearls—pearls twisted once close around the neck and left swinging down almost to the waist. The most beautiful girl of our year is in black velvet, with a flesh chiffon bosom; she gazes as though sightlessly into the big mirror as she applies eyeshadow to those fabulous eyelids. Someone says, "I hear you made the Vincent. Congrats."

Mixed through the crowd, as though for their own protection, are the pills—the girls with glasses, the girls in pink taffeta dresses, the girls who played field hockey so terribly well at Miss Winsor's. Later in the evening they will retire here to the dressing room after a few too many circlings of the ballroom in the same man's arms, to wait alone until they summon courage to issue forth once more. And here, like birds of a feather, chattering together of Sherry's and the Meadowbrook, are the New York girls —a little taller than anyone else, more glamorous, more unattainable, because they come from New York. They all make the same joke—"The best thing about Beantown is the Merchants Limited going home." New York! It is the as yet unconquered, the next world.

We drift out, dégagé, a little blasé, to find the Harvard men with whom we came. Tails, they wore in those days. The small ballroom and the big ballroom are thrown open together to me now, and Billy Lossez's orchestra is playing. He has a banjo man who is supposed to be hot stuff and who has written a song, called "Afraid of You," that is rumored to have been inspired by one of the débutantes. *Which?* But the great Lossez specialty is "J'ai Pas Su Y Faire," delicate, a little melancholy; you sing it, in your best low, hoarse voice, into your partner's ear in the moment before the next man cuts in. "Do you belong to the Spee or the A.D.?" "Isn't Hope divine?" "How about coming tea dancing with me here tomorrow?" Tea dancing at the Copley-Plaza—that was another facet of this coming-out diamond. But tonight is a ball, given by one of the hunting people out at Myopia for their lumpy daughter. The great thing is to be able to dance in a corner, with your own private stag line. The New York boys are the best dancers—they are snaky. But you are nice to everybody; it pays. One dismal, damp-palmed pipsqueak always says the same thing as he cuts in—"Greetings!" My friends and I call him Greetings.

This is a really smooth dance, they are serving supper *throughout*, with champagne continuously. We débutantes are only allowed to drink champagne. But some of the boys carry hip flasks, and the girls who are wild accept a sip from the flask when they go to sit out. That is another category of girl—the girls who go the limit. There are only a few of them and they are mentioned with bated breath.

I have met a new man. He is tall and rather an awkward dancer, but I know all about him; he is a big man in the Porcellian. After cutting back several times, he asks me if I would like to sit out, and I am delighted to.

We go to one of the small writing rooms; the girls with their beaux wander in and out. "Hello, Sarah." "Uh, hello." "Hello, Lily, Joe."

The hour is timeless. Outside, the Back Bay is fast asleep. Down the street, Childs is drowsing, we will go there for pancakes later. Only here is life going on, to the tune of "J'ai Pas Su Y Faire." "Darling, are you coming to my dance the twelfth?" "I wouldn't miss it." There are three dances on the twelfth—at the Somerset, here, and at the Women's Republican Club.

My new beau says, "Have you ever seen a loof?"

I say, "Never actually, but I've always imagined what one must look like."

"There must be hundreds of them," he says. "So many people seem to be aloof."

At one of the writing desks, we take turns, there in the sitting-out room at half-past two in the morning, at drawing a loof. It has three eyes, a pointed head; its tongue sticks out permanently.

"Aren't you ever going to come back on the floor?" some man passing asks me, but I say "I'm busy drawing a loof." "A *what?*" We laugh, and here my memories fade away, and end.

It is these memories that make the Copley-Plaza seem to me like a showy, faintly second-rate, meretricious mother that nonetheless did give me a kind of life. You can't make my mother into somebody different by suddenly beginning to call her Mrs. Sheraton.

But, if I know the Bostonians, they will keep right on calling the old hotel the Copley-Plaza anyway.

Cambridge

◆

Norbert Wiener

Norbert Wiener (1894–1964) has been called the father of automation, and it was he who invented the term "cybernetics" to describe the new field. Wiener was an "infant prodigy," entering college at eleven and obtaining his Bachelor's degree before he was fifteen. *Ex-Prodigy*, from which this selection is taken, contains a fascinating account of Wiener's intellectual development. The setting is Cambridge, where his father taught at Harvard, and Wiener succeeds in catching the atmosphere of the intellectual community before World War I, when it was dominated by such giants as William James, George Santayana, Ralph Barton Perry, and Josiah Royce.

from Ex-Prodigy

To a person who has seen the intervening stages of its development and decadence, it is difficult to compare the American Cambridge of today with the Cambridge of the beginning of the century. It is only by imperceptible steps that the houses have become grimier, that the traffic has become heavier, that the vacant lots have vanished, and that a community which in 1900 preserved much of the atmosphere of the country town has grown into a great, dirty, commercial city.

On Avon Street in Cambridge we took a moderately old but pleasant house, with an ell behind and a little below the level of the main house. It had ground and cut-glass front doors, a library and living room in front, and a small but adequate study for my father. The upstairs rooms were large and sunny, and the little upper story of the ell housed our nursery. There was a fairly large back yard for my sister and me to play in.

When I was a child, there were those who still spoke of Massachusetts Avenue by its old name, North Avenue; and it was lined by the inartistic but attractive and comfortable mansions of well-to-do businessmen. They are still standing, but fallen from glory. Their *porte-cocheres* shelter no coaches, and the elaborate wood carving of their porches is rotting away. They were inhabited by families with four or five children, and were ruled from the kitchen by a competent and masterful servant girl. The

16

children had ample yards to play in, and the trees which shaded them had not yet been reduced to sickly pallor by the smoke of the East Cambridge factories.

The vacant lots of Cambridge bloomed with dandelions in the spring, buttercups in the summer, and the bluish blossom of chicory in the fall. The streets were, for the most part, unpaved; and when it rained, they were deeply rutted by the wheels of the horse-drawn delivery trucks. In the season of snow, the wagons were replaced by sleighs and sledges, and it was a favorite pastime of the youngsters to tie their sleds behind the delivery sleighs then known as pungs. On the hilly streets there was coasting, not only on the small sleds which one rode belly-bump but on large double-runners made up of two such sleds, a plank, and a steering wheel. There was an abundance of frozen puddles on which one could skate, and it was always possible to go to Jarvis Field and watch the Harvard hockey team at practice.

As I have said, my father was an enthusiastic amateur mycologist; and under his guidance, I toured vacant lots in search of morels in the spring and field agarics in the fall. The morels were confined to a few well-known spots, and the Harvard mycologists considered that they had duly staked their claims on these spots. It was a frequent cause of bad feeling when one of them stole a march on a colleague and reaped the little clump that the latter had considered his private property. Stands of field agarics were less subject to this test of ownership, and coprinus was too common to be considered a property at all.

These additions to our kitchen were supplemented by an occasional lepiota or a batch of elm mushroom. Every now and again we would find a clump of clavaria or hydnum, and even a few rarer delicacies; but these were mostly reserved for our summer vacations. Part of the fun was the fact that one might just possibly confuse these edible fungi with an amanita, or at least an emetic russula; and the knowledge that one would have to wait some twelve hours before the symptoms became obvious was a source of more than one sleepless night to my parents and to myself.

I have botanical memories beyond these stray fruits of the field. I can never forget the little maple keys taking root in the soil, nor the tiny trees which started from them. The smell of fresh earth, of maple bark, of the gum of cherry trees, and of newly mowed grass all belonged to my youth, with the drawl of the lawn mower and the pattering of water from the spray which kept our grass green. In the fall it was always delightful to trudge through the crisp heaps of fallen leaves in the gutter or to smell their aromatic smoke as they burned. In my childhood recollection, these are supplemented by the resinous perfume of freshly cut pinewood and the various builders' smells of linseed oil and new cement.

The whole frame of our lives has changed between that day and this. Wood then was so cheap that we used to knock up for firewood the boxes in which our groceries were delivered, and our butter came in wooden tubs or in neatly dovetailed wooden boxes with sliding lids. The chief token of those ampler days was, however, the ease with which one could secure servant girls. Mother never had less than two, a cook and a children's maid, together with the services of a laundress, and yet my father was only an impecunious instructor or assistant professor, with no promise of tenure for some time to come. For a large part of our time on Avon Street I nearly worshipped our maid, Hildreth Maloney, an intelligent, loyal and competent young woman, who was later to improve her position in the world. I do not remember our cook, but our laundress was a faithful and hard-working woman by the name of Maggy, to which we added the soubriquet, "The Buttonbreaker."

. . .

However, my life was one of play as well as work. My parents entered me as a member of a playground which had been set up in a vacant lot next to the Peabody School. We had to show a card to get in and to allow us to use the services of the playground teacher as well as to crawl through the jungle gym and to coast down the slide or to employ such other devices as were there for our use and our exercise. I spent much time there talking with the policeman on the beat. Patrolman Murray lived opposite us and he loved to tease me with tall tales of police service.

We had all sorts of fights in those days, from snowball fights to a serious gang affair in which two armies of boys met on Avon Hill Street and pelted one another with stones. Our parents soon broke this up. In one snowball fight a companion of mine, who suffered from a high degree of nearsightedness, incurred a detached retina and lost the sight of one eye.

I have said that I, too, was a myope, and I suppose it was this snowball accident as much as anything else that led my parents to punish me for fighting and otherwise discouraged fighting at all costs. I never would have made a good fighter, as the effect of any severe emotion was to paralyze me with such weakness of fear that I could scarcely utter a word, let alone strike a blow. I suppose the reason was as much physiological as psychological, as I have always gone into fits of weakness when my blood sugar was low.

I took a sufficient part in the sports of the children of my age. I helped to make snow forts for snowball battles, as well as the snow prisons in which we immured our captives and in which I occasionally got immured myself. I jumped on behind the delivery sleighs or "pungs" which traversed the yellow slush-covered streets of the winter Cambridge of those days. I scaled the back fences with the best of them, and ruined my clothes when I fell off. I tried to skate on a child's double-runner skates, but my ankles were weak and lax, and I never graduated to the more efficient single runners. I coasted down Avon Hill Street and would try to persuade my seniors and betters to give me a ride on their swifter double-runner sleds. In the spring I searched the pavements and the yards for little pebbles which I could grind up with spittle to make a crude sort of paint, and I would chalk the pavements to make hopscotch courts on which my comrades and I could play. I walked over to North Cambridge to get comic valentines or Christmas cards from the stationery shops, according to the time of year, as well as cheap candies and the other delightful trifles of extreme youth.

Roxbury

Malcolm X

> Perhaps Malcolm X will be remembered longest for his moving
> *Autobiography,* from which this selection comes. Born in Omaha in
> 1925 and shot down in New York City forty years later for reasons
> not yet clear, Malcolm X was, together with Martin Luther King, the
> most dramatic and significant Negro leader to emerge in the United
> States after World War II. Unlike King, Malcolm X was still evolv-
> ing a personal and political philosophy at the time of his death.
> These few pages of vivid writing describe a Boston utterly unknown
> to the other contributors to this section.

from The Autobiography of Malcolm X

So I went gawking around the neighborhood—the Waumbeck and Hum-
boldt Avenue Hill section of Roxbury, which is something like Harlem's
Sugar Hill, where I'd later live. I saw those Roxbury Negroes acting and
living differently from any black people I'd ever dreamed of in my life.
This was the snooty-black neighborhood; they called themselves the
"Four Hundred," and looked down their noses at the Negroes of the black
ghetto, or so-called "town" section where Mary, my other half-sister, lived.

What I thought I was seeing there in Roxbury were high-class, educated, important Negroes, living well, working in big jobs and positions.
Their quiet homes sat back in their mowed yards. These Negroes walked
along the sidewalks looking haughty and dignified, on their way to work,
to shop, to visit, to church. I know now, of course, that what I was really
seeing was only a big-city version of those "successful" Negro bootblacks
and janitors back in Lansing. The only difference was that the ones in
Boston had been brainwashed even more thoroughly. They prided themselves on being incomparably more "cultured," "cultivated," "dignified,"
and better off than their black brethren down in the ghetto, which was no
further away than you could throw a rock. Under the pitiful misappre-
hension that it would make them "better," these Hill Negroes were breaking their backs trying to imitate white people.

Any black family that had been around Boston long enough to own the home they lived in was considered among the Hill elite. It didn't make any difference that they had to rent out rooms to make ends meet. Then the native-born New Englanders among them looked down upon recently migrated Southern home-owners who lived next door, like Ella. And a big percentage of the Hill dwellers were in Ella's category—Southern strivers and scramblers, and West Indian Negroes, whom both the New Englanders and the Southerners called "Black Jews." Usually it was the Southerners and the West Indians who not only managed to own the places where they lived, but also at least one other house which they rented as income property. The snooty New Englanders usually owned less than they.

In those days on the Hill, any who could claim "professional" status—teachers, preachers, practical nurses—also considered themselves superior. Foreign diplomats could have modeled their conduct on the way the Negro postmen, Pullman porters, and dining car waiters of Roxbury acted, striding around as if they were wearing top hats and cutaways.

I'd guess that eight out of ten of the Hill Negroes of Roxbury, despite the impressive-sounding job titles they affected, actually worked as menials and servants. "He's in banking," or "He's in securities." It sounded as though they were discussing a Rockefeller or a Mellon—and not some gray-headed, dignity-posturing bank janitor, or bond-house messenger. "I'm with an old family" was the euphemism used to dignify the professions of white folks' cooks and maids who talked so affectedly among their own kind in Roxbury that you couldn't even understand them. I don't know how many forty- and fifty-year-old errand boys went down the Hill dressed like ambassadors in black suits and white collars, to downtown jobs "in government," "in finance," or "in law." It has never ceased to amaze me how so many Negroes, then and now, could stand the indignity of that kind of self-delusion.

Soon I ranged out of Roxbury and began to explore Boston proper. Historic buildings everywhere I turned, and plaques and markers and statues for famous events and men. One statue in the Boston Commons astonished me: a Negro named Crispus Attucks, who had been the first man to fall in the Boston Massacre. I had never known anything like that.

I roamed everywhere. In one direction, I walked as far as Boston University. Another day, I took my first subway ride. When most of the people got off, I followed. It was Cambridge, and I circled all around in the Harvard University campus. Somewhere, I had already heard of Harvard—though I didn't know much more about it. Nobody that day could have told me I would give an address before the Harvard Law School Forum some twenty years later.

I also did a lot of exploring downtown. Why a city would have *two* big railroad stations—North Station and South Station—I couldn't understand. At both of the stations, I stood around and watched people arrive and leave. And I did the same thing at the bus station where Ella had met me. My wanderings even led me down along the piers and docks where I read plaques telling about the old sailing ships that used to put into port there.

In a letter to Wilfred, Hilda, Philbert, and Reginald back in Lansing, I told them about all this, and about the winding, narrow, cobblestoned streets, and the houses that jammed up against each other. Downtown Boston, I wrote them, had the biggest stores I'd ever seen, and white people's restaurants and hotels. I made up my mind that I was going to see every movie that came to the fine, air-conditioned theaters.

On Massachusetts Avenue, next door to one of them, the Loew's State Theater, was the huge, exciting Roseland State Ballroom. Big posters out in front advertised the nationally famous bands, white and Negro, that had played there. "COMING NEXT WEEK," when I went by that first time, was Glenn Miller. I remember thinking how nearly the whole evening's music at Mason High School dances had been Glenn Miller's records. What wouldn't that crowd have given, I wondered, to be standing where Glenn Miller's band was actually going to play? I didn't know how familiar with Roseland I was going to become.

Ella began to grow concerned, because even when I had finally had enough sight-seeing, I didn't stick around very much on the Hill. She kept dropping hints that I ought to mingle with the "nice young people my age" who were to be seen in the Townsend Drugstore two blocks from her house, and a couple of other places. But even before I came to Boston, I had always felt and acted toward anyone my age as if they were in the "kid" class, like my younger brother Reginald. They had always looked up to me as if I were considerably older. On weekends back in Lansing where I'd go to get away from the white people in Mason, I'd hung around in the Negro part of town with Wilfred's and Philbert's set. Though all of them were several years older than me, I was bigger, and I actually looked older than most of them.

I didn't want to disappoint or upset Ella, but despite her advice, I began going down into the town ghetto section. That world of grocery stores, walk-up flats, cheap restaurants, poolrooms, bars, storefront churches, and pawnshops seemed to hold a natural lure for me.

Not only was this part of Roxbury much more exciting, but I felt more relaxed among Negroes who were being their natural selves and not putting on airs. Even though I did live on the Hill, my instincts were never—and still aren't—to feel myself any better than any other Negro.

I spent my first month in town with my mouth hanging open. The sharp-dressed young "cats" who hung on the corners and in the poolrooms, bars and restaurants, and who obviously didn't work anywhere, completely entranced me. I couldn't get over marveling at how their hair was straight and shiny like white men's hair; Ella told me this was called a "conk." I had never tasted a sip of liquor, never even smoked a cigarette, and here I saw little black children, ten and twelve years old, shooting craps, playing cards, fighting, getting grown-ups to put a penny or a nickel on their number for them, things like that. And these children threw around swear words I'd never heard before, even, and slang expressions that were just as new to me, such as "stud" and "cat" and "chick" and "cool" and "hip." Every night as I lay in bed I turned these new words over in my mind. It was shocking to me that in town, especially after dark, you'd occasionally see a white girl and a Negro man strolling arm in arm along the sidewalk, and mixed couples drinking in the neon-lighted bars—not slipping off to some dark corner, as in Lansing. I wrote Wilfred and Philbert about that, too.

I wanted to find a job myself, to surprise Ella. One afternoon, something told me to go inside a poolroom whose window I was looking through. I had looked through that window many times. I wasn't yearning to play pool; in fact, I had never held a cue stick. But I was drawn by the sight of the cool-looking "cats" standing around inside, bending over the big, green, felt-topped tables, making bets and shooting the bright-colored balls into the holes. As I stared through the window this particular afternoon, something made me decide to venture inside and talk to a dark, stubby, conk-headed fellow who racked up balls for the pool-players, whom I'd heard called "Shorty." One day he had come outside and seen me standing there and said "Hi, Red," so that made me figure he was friendly.

As inconspicuously as I could, I slipped inside the door and around the side of the poolroom, avoiding people, and on to the back, where Shorty was filling an aluminum can with the powder that pool players dust on their hands. He looked up at me. Later on, Shorty would enjoy teasing me about how with that first glance he knew my whole story. "Man, that cat still *smelled* country!" he'd say, laughing. "Cat's legs was so long and his pants so short his knees showed—an' his head looked like a briar patch!"

But that afternoon Shorty didn't let it show in his face how "country" I appeared when I told him I'd appreciate it if he'd tell me how could somebody go about getting a job like his.

"If you mean racking up balls," said Shorty, "I don't know of no pool joints around here needing anybody. You mean you just want any slave you can find?" A "slave" meant work, a job.

He asked what kind of work I had done. I told him that I'd washed restaurant dishes in Mason, Michigan. He nearly dropped the powder can. "My homeboy! Man, gimme some skin! I'm from Lansing!"

I never told Shorty—and he never suspected—that he was about ten years older than I. He took us to be about the same age. At first I would have been embarrassed to tell him, later I just never bothered. Shorty had dropped out of first-year high school in Lansing, lived a while with an uncle and aunt in Detroit, and had spent the last six years living with his cousin in Roxbury. But when I mentioned the names of Lansing people and places, he remembered many, and pretty soon we sounded as if we had been raised in the same block. I could sense Shorty's genuine gladness, and I don't have to say how lucky I felt to find a friend as hip as he obviously was.

"Man, this is a swinging town if you dig it," Shorty said. "You're my homeboy—I'm going to school you to the happenings." I stood there and grinned like a fool. "You got to go anywhere now? Well, stick around until I get off."

One thing I liked immediately about Shorty was his frankness. When I told him where I lived, he said what I already knew—that nobody in town could stand the Hill Negroes. But he thought a sister who gave me a "pad," not charging me rent, not even running me out to find "some slave," couldn't be all bad. Shorty's slave in the poolroom, he said, was just to keep ends together while he learned his horn. A couple of years before, he'd hit the numbers and bought a saxophone. "Got it right in there in the closet now, for my lesson tonight." Shorty was taking lessons "with some other studs," and he intended one day to organize his own small band. "There's a lot of bread to be made gigging right around here in Roxbury," Shorty explained to me. "I don't dig joining some big band, one-nighting all over just to say I played with Count or Duke or somebody." I thought that was smart. I wished I had studied a horn; but I never had been exposed to one.

All afternoon, between trips up front to rack balls, Shorty talked to me out of the corner of his mouth: which hustlers—standing around, or playing at this or that table—sold "reefers," or had just come out of prison, or were "second-story men." Shorty told me that he played at least a dollar a day on the numbers. He said as soon as he hit a number, he would use the winnings to organize his band.

I was ashamed to have to admit that I had never played the numbers. "Well, you ain't never had nothing to play with," he said, excusing me, "but you start when you get a slave, and if you hit, you got a stake for something."

He pointed out some gamblers and some pimps. Some of them had white whores, he whispered. "I ain't going to lie—I dig them two-dollar white chicks," Shorty said. "There's a lot of that action around here, nights: you'll see it." I said I already had seen some. "You ever had one?" he asked.

My embarrassment at my inexperience showed. "Hell, man," he said, "don't be ashamed. I had a few before I left Lansing—them Polack chicks that used to come over the bridge. Here, they're mostly Italians and Irish. But it don't matter what kind, they're something else! Ain't no different nowhere—there's nothing they love better than a black stud."

Through the afternoon, Shorty introduced me to players and loungers. "My homeboy," he'd say, "he's looking for a slave if you hear anything." They all said they'd look out.

At seven o'clock, when the night ball-racker came on, Shorty told me he had to hurry to his saxophone lesson. But before he left, he held out to me the six or seven dollars he had collected that day in nickel and dime tips. "You got enough bread, homeboy?"

I was okay, I told him—I had two dollars. But Shorty made me take three more. "Little fattening for your pocket," he said. Before we went out, he opened his saxophone case and showed me the horn. It was gleaming brass against the green velvet, an alto sax. He said, "Keep cool, homeboy, and come back tomorrow. Some of the cats will turn you up a slave."

When I got home, Ella said there had been a telephone call from somebody named Shorty. He had left a message that over at the Roseland State Ballroom, the shoeshine boy was quitting that night, and Shorty had told him to hold the job for me.

"Malcolm, you haven't had any experience shining shoes," Ella said. Her expression and tone of voice told me she wasn't happy about my taking that job. I didn't particularly care, because I was already speechless thinking about being somewhere close to the greatest bands in the world. I didn't even wait to eat any dinner.

The ballroom was all lighted when I got there. A man at the front door was letting in members of Benny Goodman's band. I told him I wanted to see the shoeshine boy, Freddie.

"You're going to be the new one?" he asked. I said I thought I was, and he laughed, "Well, maybe you'll hit the numbers and get a Cadillac, too." He told me that I'd find Freddie upstairs in the men's room on the second floor.

But downstairs before I went up, I stepped over and snatched a glimpse inside the ballroom. I just couldn't believe the size of that waxed floor! At the far end, under the soft, rose-colored lights, was the bandstand with the Benny Goodman musicians moving around, laughing and talking, arranging their horns and stands.

A wiry, brown-skinned, conked fellow upstairs in the men's room greeted me. "You Shorty's homeboy?" I said I was, and he said he was Freddie. "Good old boy," he said. "He called me, he just heard I hit the big number, and he figured right I'd be quitting." I told Freddie what the man at the front door had said about a Cadillac. He laughed and said, "Burns them white cats up when you get yourself something. Yeah, I told them I was going to get me one—just to bug them."

Freddie then said for me to pay close attention, that he was going to be busy and for me to watch but not get in the way, and he'd try to get me ready to take over at the next dance, a couple of nights later.

As Freddie busied himself setting up the shoeshine stand, he told me, "Get here early . . . your shoeshine rags and brushes by this footstand . . . your polish bottles, paste wax, suede brushes over here . . . everything in place, you get rushed, you never need to waste motion. . . ."

While you shined shoes, I learned, you also kept watch on customers inside, leaving the urinals. You darted over and offered a small white hand towel. "A lot of cats who ain't planning to wash their hands, sometimes you can run up with a towel and shame them. Your towels are really your best hustle in here. Cost you a penny apiece to launder—you always get at least a nickel tip."

The shoeshine customers, and any from the inside rest room who took a towel, you whiskbroomed a couple of licks. "A nickel or a dime tip, just give 'em that," Freddie said. "But for two bits, Uncle Tom a little—white cats especially like that. I've had them to come back two, three times a dance."

From down below, the sound of the music had begun floating up. I guess I stood transfixed. "You never seen a big dance?" asked Freddie. "Run on awhile, and watch."

There were a few couples already dancing under the rose-colored lights. But even more exciting to me was the crowd thronging in. The most glamorous-looking white women I'd ever seen—young ones, old ones, white cats buying tickets at the window, sticking big wads of green bills back into their pockets, checking the women's coats, and taking their arms and squiring them inside.

Freddie had some early customers when I got back upstairs. Between the shoeshine stand and thrusting towels to me just as they approached the wash basin, Freddie seemed to be doing four things at once. "Here, you can take over the whiskbroom," he said, "just two or three licks—but let 'em feel it."

When things slowed a little, he said, "You ain't seen nothing tonight. You wait until you see a spooks' dance! Man, our own people carry *on!*" Whenever he had a moment, he kept schooling me. "Shoelaces, this drawer here. You just starting out, I'm going to make these to you as a present. Buy them for a nickel a pair, tell cats they need laces if they do, and charge two bits."

Every Benny Goodman record I'd ever heard in my life, it seemed, was filtering faintly into where we were. During another customer lull, Freddie let me slip back outside again to listen. Peggy Lee was at the mike singing. Beautiful! She had just joined the band and she was from North Dakota and had been singing with a group in Chicago when Mrs. Benny Goodman discovered her, we had heard some customers say. She finished the song and the crowd burst into applause. She was a big hit.

"It knocked me out, too, when I first broke in here," Freddie said, grinning, when I went back in there. "But, look, you ever shined any shoes?" He laughed when I said I hadn't, excepting my own. "Well, let's get to work. I never had neither." Freddie got on the stand and went to work on his own shoes. Brush, liquid polish, brush, paste wax, shine rag, lacquer sole dressing . . . step by step, Freddie showed me what to do.

"But you got to get a whole lot faster. You can't waste time!" Freddie showed me how fast on my own shoes. Then, because business was tapering off, he had time to give me a demonstration of how to make the shine rag pop like a firecracker. "Dig the action?" he asked. He did it in slow motion. I got down and tried it on his shoes. I had the principle of it. "Just got to do it faster," Freddie said. "It's a jive noise, that's all. Cats tip better, they figure you're knocking yourself out!"

By the end of the dance, Freddie had let me shine the shoes of three or four stray drunks he talked into having shines, and I had practiced picking up my speed on Freddie's shoes until they looked like mirrors. After we had helped the janitors to clean up the ballroom after the dance, throwing out all the paper and cigarette butts and empty liquor bottles, Freddie was nice enough to drive me all the way home to Ella's on the Hill in the second-hand maroon Buick he said he was going to trade in on his Cadillac. He talked to me all the way. "I guess it's all right if I tell you, pick up a couple of dozen packs of rubbers, two-bits apiece. You notice some of those cats that came up to me around the end of the dance? Well, when some have new chicks going right, they'll come asking you for rubbers. Charge a dollar, generally you'll get an extra tip."

He looked across at me. "Some hustles you're too new for. Cats will ask you for liquor, some will want reefers. But you don't need to have nothing except rubbers—until you can dig who's a cop.

"You can make ten, twelve dollars a dance for yourself if you work everything right," Freddie said, before I got out of the car in front of Ella's. "The main thing you got to remember is that everything in the world is a hustle. So long, Red."

The next time I ran into Freddie I was downtown one night a few weeks later. He was parked in his pearl gray Cadillac, sharp as a tack, "cooling it."

"Man, you sure schooled me!" I said, and he laughed; he knew what I meant. It hadn't taken me long on the job to find out that Freddie had done less shoeshining and towel-hustling than selling liquor and reefers, and putting white "Johns" in touch with Negro whores. I also learned that white girls always flocked to the Negro dances—some of them whores whose pimps brought them to mix business and pleasure, others who came with their black boy friends, and some who came in alone, for a little freelance lusting among a plentiful availability of enthusiastic Negro men.

At the white dances, of course, nothing black was allowed, and that's where the black whores' pimps soon showed a new shoeshine boy what he could pick up on the side by slipping a phone number or address to the white Johns who came around the end of the dance looking for "black chicks."

WORCESTER

◆━◆

Many immigrant families came to Worcester, Massachusetts at the turn of the century—in 1910 one-third of its population was foreign-born—and found work in its thriving tool factories and woolen mills. Bright Jewish boys like Sam Behrman didn't live in one of the splendid houses on the hill, but they could look forward to going to the recently established Clark University, which then had 15 instructors and 103 students.

It was a leisurely life for the young who roamed the rolling acres of the city's many fine parks or settled down for a soda in one of the popular ice-cream parlors. But who would have expected that such an establishment would be owned by the notorious anarchists Emma Goldman and Alexander Berkman? In the selection below, compiled from The Worcester Account, *published in 1954, S. N. Behrman describes a clash of ideologies between the orthodoxy of his Jewish household and the "free thought" of the rebels who hoped to change the world.*

S. N. Behrman

S. N. Behrman was born in Worcester in 1893 and studied drama at Clark University, Harvard, and Columbia. In addition to his distinguished work for the theater, he is the author of two successful biographies: *Duveen,* the life of the art dealer, and *Portrait of Max,* an affectionate tribute to the satirist Max Beerbohm with whom Behrman has much in common as a stylist.

from The Worcester Account

We lived, when I was a child and until I left Worcester, in a triple-decker tenement a quarter way up the long hill that was Providence Street. The street belonged to a few Irish, to a few Poles, and to us. The Messrs. Graton and Knight had occupied, when I was very young, two white houses at the opposite corners of Waverly and Providence Streets; these had been the residual islands of a lovely, tree-shaded New England street. Mr. Graton and Mr. Knight were the last of the "Yankees" who lived on the hill. (It seems strange to me now that my immigrant elders always referred to the native New Englanders as "Yankees," as if they themselves were Southern aristocrats!) As the "Yankees," no longer able to afford the maintenance of their large places, moved away, an enterprising real-estate man bought up their properties and put up the triple-deckers.

These triple-deckers, which straggled up our hill, were mostly sadly in need of paint jobs and their mass appearance was somewhat depressing. But in many other respects they were not so bad. They had balconies, front and back, which we called piazzas. The yards in the back had fruit trees—cherry and pear and apple. We had more pear trees in our back yard at 31 Providence Street than Mr. Carnegie had in his at 91st and Fifth! Once, standing on our back piazza, I overheard my young cousin, then about eleven—my family, including my grandmother and two aunts, occupied three of the six flats at 31—improvising an ode to one of the blossoming pear trees; "Oh, you elegant tree!" she began. But then she caught my eye and the rhapsody was aborted. The contemplative and withdrawn could sit on the back piazzas and look at the fruit trees; the urban and the worldly could sit on the front piazzas and survey the passing scene.

I remember Providence Street best in the clear twilight of evenings in

30

early summer. We boys had probably been for a swim at Jerry Daly's bath-house on Lake Quinsigamond. The long trudge back from the lake along Shrewsbury Street was easier than the walk to the lake; most of the four miles was downhill, for one thing. At the bottom of Shrewsbury was the old Union Station, with its gray stone campanile tower. Past the grade crossing on Grafton Street we were practically home; the short length of Grafton Street led into Grafton Square at the base of Providence Street hill. On Grafton Square was Elkind's drug store; we would have a look in there on the chance that someone—an uncle or an older brother—would treat us to a soda.

Elkind's was smartly fitted up. It had tables with glass cases for tops; these cases contained boxes of Page and Shaw's chocolates to tempt us with solid sweets while we were imbibing liquid ones. During my child-hood, Elkind's was the place we made for when we could beg, borrow or steal a nickel. What the country stores were in the early part of the nine-teenth century, the drug stores became at the end of it in towns the size of Worcester; what the pubs are in English villages, Elkind's was for us. (Hard drinking was practically unknown on Providence Street; we boasted one drunk, and he was treated with a tolerant pity.) Elkind's was the forum for political, financial and social gossip; it was tavern, debating society, and even exchange. My uncles, who styled themselves "woolen merchants"—they were actually jobbers—went to the mills in such dis-tant, fabulous places as Woonsocket and Providence and bought up rem-nants, odd lots, and damaged goods, and sold them in their shops on Winter Street. The manufacturers from New York would come up to buy from them and they sometimes sealed their bargains with a bumper at Elkind's.

Very near the bottom of the hill, on the right, was Cassie McMahon's house. She was an adorable young girl; her loveliness took your breath away. But she lived in a private house, a house all to herself and her parents, and this made her automatically unapproachable. She was sweet; she nodded and smiled at us, and then went back into her private house. She had no neighbors—that is to say, no other families living in her house to whom we could get close in order to get close to Cassie. She was iso-lated, which she didn't seem to mind; but we were isolated too, and this was grievous. For many decades I have promised myself that I would go back to find Cassie, but I have never done so. It is still on my unwritten psychic agenda.

Opposite Cassie's, on the left side, was the Providence Street school—

our winter prison. And a little above that was the fire house. In summer
we passed it with dim, luxurious memories of blizzardy winter mornings
when we would lie in bed waiting for the "no-school" bells from the fire
house. That sound induced a joy that no symphonic masterpiece of later
years could possibly rival. But now it was early summer; long days of
leisure stretched ahead of us into infinity and we were independent of
school, independent of the fire house.

On the right, a little above Cassie's, was the first of Providence Street's
two synagogues. This was a shabby wooden building. It was called the
Balbirishocker Schul; its congregation was composed of emigrants from a
town called, I suppose, Balbirishock. None of us—my father's set—ever
went into it; our synagogue was august and made of brick with white
limestone facings and was altogether more imposing than the humble
little Balbirishocker Schul. Why Providence Street needed two synagogues
I never knew. Not long ago I heard a story which, for the first time, made
me understand why. It concerned a deeply religious man who was
wrecked on an island off Tierra del Fuego. For eighteen years he lived
alone on this island. Every morning he went to the shore and waved a
white cloth in the hope of rescue. One morning he actually did signal a
ship. The captain came ashore and the castaway showed him around the
island. At one end was a quite substantial wooden building with a turret.
"That," said the proud islander, "is the synagogue. I built it with my own
hands!" They continued their tour. At the other end of the island, some
miles away, the sightseeing captain saw another building, a replica of the
first. "I built that too," said the castaway. "What on earth is it?" asked the
captain. "That," said the pious craftsman loftily, "is the synagogue I
don't go to!" We—the congregation of the Providence Street Synagogue—
had the distinction of *not* going to the Balbirishocker Schul; the congregation of the latter could pride themselves on not going to ours. I suppose
it gave each of the two factions a feeling of exclusiveness and privacy in
their approach to God. Variety in worship adds, I suppose, to the color of
life and is harmless if kept this side of slaughter; on Providence Street it
usually was.

In summer the Providence Street car was open; when it was crowded, as
it generally was at about the time we would be walking home from the
lake, we could hitch a ride on it easily. We jumped on the runningboard
and held on to one of the varnished posts and leaned far out into the
whipped-up breeze. When the conductor saw us, we would drop off nonchalantly at the next stop as if we had just remembered an important

engagement. If he didn't see us, we stayed on, though we were already late for supper: past all the intersecting streets; past the Polish Catholic Church at Waverly; past Jefferson, where stood the concrete mansion of the Croesus of the hill, Mr. Wolfson—the house with the stained-glass window; up and up to the crest of the hill, where Lovers Lane began. There the car-line stopped and we got off. We got off in another world.

Providence Street was crested with castles. One of these was the twelve-acre estate of the Cromptons. It was surrounded by a gray stone wall. Just inside the wall was an unbroken line of tall hemlocks. Above the trees we could see the great central tower of the mansion. The Crompton house was one of the first Elizabethan houses to be built in this country. Its wall braked the teeming life of our street, which came to a dead halt there. After the death of George Crompton, his sisters lived in the house, but no one ever saw them. The place was still; no sound ever came from it. But walking back home, brushing the wall as we passed it, stopping at the gates to look through the grill at the tree-lined walk that led to the great, many-windowed house, we could populate it at will from the story books we had been reading in and out of school.

A little below the Cromptons', across the street, was a walled town—a vast enclosure with fascinating, improbable, chocolate-colored turrets. This was the Worcester Academy. Inside the Crompton wall was one castle; inside the Academy walls were many, and they all seemed to us equally fabulous. The Academy was a private school which attracted students from all over the United States—mythical young men who could pay for their secondary educations. What manner of young men were these? What cities and families did they come from? We saw them—those of them who were on the Academy football and baseball teams were our heroes—but they were not real; they did not inhabit an actual world; they were as remote as the invisible inhabitants of the Crompton mansion. We even knew by sight the President of the Academy, Dr. Daniel Webster Abercrombie, who was one of the leading classical scholars in the country. But as far as being real to us was concerned, he might as well have lived in the Parthenon. He did, in fact, although it was called Davis Hall.

There was one other great demesne at the top of the hill—St. Vincent's Hospital. St. Vincent's was not walled. The great central red-brick building was set in a park. We saw the nuns scurrying about in this park and they were very friendly. My mother was always being hospitalized in St. Vincent's and she died there. She never could say enough in praise of the nuns. Though my mother spoke very little English, she managed to become firm friends with many of them. Whenever she came, they welcomed her. It was a charming consideration on the part of the nuns that they veiled the holy pictures on the walls—the Virgins and the Crucifixions—to spare the religious sensibilities of their orthodox Jewish patients.

One day, when I was still very young, Providence Street began to come alive with rumors and horrid allegations about the proprietors of a new ice-cream parlor that had been opened in our neighborhood. We children were forbidden to patronize the anathematized parlor, and it was a long time before I dared to defy the ban. Since the new entrepreneurs were Emma Goldman and Alexander Berkman (whom Miss Goldman called Sasha), some people might have disapproved of them on political grounds; the hatred of the Providence Street parents was founded on religious ones. A dread word was applied to Miss Goldman—for somehow most of the vituperation focussed on her instead of on her consort and partner, Berkman, to whom, Providence Street whispered, she was not even married! Some idea of the virulence of the term used to describe Miss Goldman may be gathered from the fact that after the utterance of it the other accusation—that she and Berkman were not married—took on an aspect not so much of derogation as of amiable gossip. The epithet was the word *"apikorista,"* a word that to my elders connoted the ultimate in human depravity. An *apikoros*—*apikorista* was the feminine Yiddish form of this Hebrew word—was a renegade from the Jewish religion, but the word had the even deeper and more sinister connotation of treachery not merely to the Jewish religion but to God himself. That there existed such a person as an *apikorista* scarcely bore thinking about, and I remember distinctly the horror I felt when I heard the word used to describe a tangible, visible person who actually lived in and was doing business in our midst. I knew that there must be people who had defied God, because how otherwise could the word have come into existence, but here it was applied to a person whom one saw on the streets and who actually had a store within walking distance of one of the stricter synagogues. . . . To be an *apikorista* was no laughing matter; the word carried such a weight of obloquy that it was applied only to those guilty of the most monstrous of human delinquencies. Providence Street first heard merely that Miss Goldman was an Anarchist, and we children repeated the news with scoffing ribaldry. I did not know what "Anarchist" meant, exactly, and to me the word had no more than a pleasant reverberation of wickedness.

Even to my elders, it seemed to make Emma simply a figure of fun, for as a cult Anarchism had no adherents on Providence Street. But now my elders were calling her an *apikorista* as well, and where God was involved, the orthodox of Providence Street permitted no latitude.

I remember that before I ever saw Miss Goldman, I used to lie awake at night thinking about her fearfully and trying to imagine her appearance, which I am sure I must have invested with the traditional properties of diabolism. The thought that I might one day see her—pass her in the street—filled me with terror; I hoped that such a disastrous accident would not occur. She was an acute bogy, and even after she and Berkman left Worcester, impelled by their solemn decision to shoot Henry Clay Frick (which Emma describes in her autobiography, *Living My Life,* with that extraordinary, humorless intensity characteristic of saints and fanatics), her legend was perpetuated. The Providence Street parents cited her to us constantly, using her name somewhat as English parents used Napoleon's in the first decades of the nineteenth century, to frighten and to admonish. For the orthodox elders of the Providence Street synagogues, Alexander Berkman's attempt to assassinate Frick was a miraculous piece of luck. "What could you expect?" they demanded of us children, as if we were somehow subtly involved in the *attentat,* and as if they took it for granted we were all potential agnostics. (*"Attentat"* is a favorite word of Emma's, by the way, and it recurs throughout her autobiography. Webster defines it as "an attempt, especially an unsuccessful one, to commit a crime of violence.") "What could you expect of people who don't believe in God?" said our elders. "Naturally, such people are murderers!"

Finally, I met Emma Goldman. . . .

One day when I was grubbing in the cinders of the empty lot next to the Crompton & Knowles factory, on Winter Street, where I used to hunt for bits of glass and metal, I was picked up and walked home by Allie London. He was several years older than I, and I trudged along happily beside him.

"Where do you think I've been?" said Allie, with a kind of glowing, suppressed bravado.

I guessed the lake. I guessed Bancroft Tower.

Allie smiled at these conventional guesses. "I have just had a college ice"—late-nineteenth-century for sundae—"at Emma Goldman's," he announced sturdily.

I was aghast. I couldn't believe it. I stared at Allie, expecting that his appearance would have been somehow altered by the dread contact. Had there been incipient horns sprouting from his forehead, I would not have been surprised. But Allie looked about the same.

"How was it?" I finally managed to stammer.

"Wonderful!" said Allie enthusiastically. "She gives you a double helping for the same money. I'm not going to Elkind's any more."

"But I mean"—I could not bring myself to say the name—"*she?*"

Allie, an extrovert and already emancipated from orthodoxy, was impatient. "I tell you she gives you double. I asked for vanilla and she put on a scoop of strawberry, too. Same money.

I walked along beside Allie in a turmoil, convinced that by the necromancy of the extra scoop Emma had already begun to draw him into her coils.

"Did you see her?" I asked finally.

"Sure I saw her. She served me. Saw her feller, too. They had a fight. I could hear 'em in the back room. They're not married, you know. They had a whale of a fight."

This startled me. Up to then, I had thought that only married people fought. Under the circumstances, it seemed almost unfair for the Goldman-Berkman ménage to assume this prerogative of respectability.

A few days later, Allie again interrupted my excavations in Crompton & Knowles' cinder yard. "Want a treat?" he shouted cheerily.

Of course I did, but as I trotted along beside him, I was suddenly assailed by fear. "You taking me to Elkind's?" I asked hopefully.

"Not using Elkind's any more, I told you. I'm taking you to Goldman's. She gives you double. Don't know how she makes it pay, but that's her lookout."

It was also mine. I felt that my immortal soul hung in the balance. I whimpered. "Suppose my folks hear about it?"

"You don't believe that stuff, do you?" said Allie masterfully.

I have carried all my life a vivid impression of the subsequent scene in the ice-cream parlor. Berkman I do not seem to remember at all except for his voice, but I have always retained a clear picture of Miss Goldman—of her look of ineluctable benevolence, of her great mop of unruly red-blond hair, of her smile, and of her eyes, which I have always been sure were blue. I remember the shock of discovering that she was not frightening; it was my introduction, I have always believed, to the tangled world of reality, in which even the despised, the criminal, the fanatically wrongheaded, the hopelessly perverted may yet have a certain charm.

The counter was neat, and the benevolent deity stood behind it. When

Allie asked me what I wanted, I was tongue-tied; I fully expected some emanation from the *apikorista* to pulverize me. Did she say, to temper Allie's impatience, "Take your time, my boy, there's no hurry"? I have always believed so. I managed finally to articulate a desire for chocolate. When it came—double scoop, twice what you would have got at Elkind's —Allie gave me the triumphant side glance of the successful prospector.

Miss Goldman left us, and we sat at the counter and ate. Soon, from the back room, came the lifted voices—Emma's and Berkman's. Allie looked at me significantly. "Fighting again," he whispered.

I have always flattered myself that I was more discerning than Allie that day. Though the voices were lifted, I sensed that it was not in anger or recrimination. The language they spoke was neither English nor Yiddish; the Yiddish I spoke at home and the English I spoke on the streets and in school were the two languages I knew, so I could not know that those loud words were Russian. But I sensed that there was no anger in the intonation; the discussion had the volume and the intensity of a quarrel but no animus. It was even sorrowful. I wondered. I wondered deeply.

When I got home, my sense of guilt was so profound that I was sure my mother would immediately see that I had done something wrong. But she didn't. I went to sleep that night with the pleasurable, lawless feeling that this was, after all, a world in which crime could go undetected. After that, I went to Emma's whenever Allie asked me. There were few excursions that could satisfy, simultaneously and so fully, a boy's natural instincts for the illicit and for the wholesome. It was like comfortably spooning up delicious ice cream in the Inferno. Nickels didn't come my way very often, and when I was not invited by Allie, I fell into the habit of wandering by the forbidden ice-cream parlor in the hope that something would turn up. Nothing ever did. I even remember wondering whether, since Emma gave you a double scoop for one nickel, she might not be so quixotic as to give you one scoop for nothing. I never tested it out.

But whenever I did go into Emma's baleful precincts, I always heard the eternal chain argument from the back room. It went on and on, the voices rising and falling, intense without bitterness, violent without anger. One day, I got a nickel of my own, the gift of a prodigal uncle, and with it clutched in my palm I made at once for Emma's. To my consternation, the place was closed. I peered inside. The room was dismantled— chairs heaped one on top of the other. The kindly Devil and her voluble consort were gone. I turned away disconsolate. Without Mme. Mephistopheles, Worcester seemed less like Heaven than usual.

I discussed the vanished couple with Allie. His uncle was a friend of

their landlord. Allie told me that to the landlord the sudden decision of
his tenants to give up the parlor had seemed an act of pure insanity, for the
place had been doing a land-office business in spite of the disapproval of
Providence Street. Evidently the double scoops of ice cream had paid off,
for the profits were fabulous; they sometimes, said the landlord, came to
fifty dollars a week. (The standards of affluence in those days were fairly
modest; I remember that an uncle of mine who was not on speaking terms
with one of his brothers denounced him to me one day, capping his long
complaint with the bitter remark "And with all this he is a Croesus!"
This surprised me; the Croesus seemed as shabby and ineffectual as my
other uncles. I expressed my doubt. "Why," shouted my uncle, "in the
real estate alone he has four hundred dollars!") To give up a thriving
business for no reason, in the full tide of success, was unheard of on Providence Street. "But what can you expect?" the landlord said to Allie's
uncle in final summary, shrugging his shoulders. "What can you expect of
an *apikorista* who isn't even married?"

The East

PHILADELPHIA

———❖———

After the turbulent years of its revolutionary youth, Philadelphia settled into a Quaker quiet and righteousness. The old families upheld their traditions with the assurance that their ways were the right ways—that their city was the only city worth living in.

This was the atmosphere that shaped the childhood of Elizabeth Robins Pennell soon after the Civil War. But even the sequestered little girl of the 1870s was aware of another world very different from her own. At the end of the selection below, she remarks that nothing disturbed "the calm of Spruce Street save the Sunday afternoon invasion of the colored people in their Sunday clothes from every near alley."

It was to an alley in "The Bloody Eighth Ward" that Ethel Waters came to live when she was six years old. In 1906, when prostitution was legal in the City of Brotherly Love, the child who was to become one of the country's greatest Negro performers spent a year in the red-light district on Clifton Street, where murder, rape, and police raids were as traditional as the serenity on Spruce Street.

Elizabeth Robins Pennell

Elizabeth Robins Pennell (1855–1936) was the wife and collaborator of the Philadelphia-born artist Joseph Pennell. She wrote the text and he provided illustrations for many books on American and English life. One of their joint efforts was *Our Philadelphia* (1914), from which the following selection is taken.

from Our Philadelphia

Naturally, I could not live in Spruce Street and not believe, as every Philadelphian should and once did, that no other kind of a house except the Spruce Street house was fit for a Philadelphian to live in. The Philadelphian, from infancy, was convinced by his surroundings and bringing-up that there was but one way of doing things decently and respectably and that was the Philadelphia way, nor can ꞏꞏy prolonged exile relieve me from the sense of crime at times when I catch myself doing things not just as Philadelphians used to do them.

I was safe from any such crime in my Grandfather's house. All Philadelphia might have been let in without fear. Had skeletons been concealed in the capacious cupboards, they would have been of the approved Philadelphia pattern. My Grandfather was not at all of Montaigne's opinion that order in the management of life is sottish, but looked upon it rather as "Heaven's first law." His day's programme was the same as in every red brick house with white marble steps and a back-yard full of roses and shrubs and Johnny-jump-ups. Everything at Eleventh and Spruce was done according to the same Philadelphia rules at the same hour, from the washing of the family linen on Monday, when Sunday's beef was eaten cold for dinner, to the washing of the front on Saturday morning, when Philadelphia streets from end to end were all mops and maids, rivers and lakes.

When my Grandfather, with his family on their knees around him, began the day by reading morning prayers in the back-building dining-room, he could have had the satisfaction of knowing that every other Philadelphia head of a family was engaged in the same edifying duty, but I hope, for every other Philadelphia family's sake, with a trifle less awe-inspiring solemnity. After being present once at my Grandfather's prayers, nobody needed to be assured that life was earnest.

He did not shed his solemnity when he rose from his knees, nor when

41

he had finished his breakfast of scrapple and buckwheat cakes and left the breakfast table. He was as solemn in his progress through the streets to the Philadelphia Bank, at Fourth and Chestnut, of which he was President, and having said so much perhaps I might as well add his name, Thomas Robins, for in his day he was widely known and it is a satisfaction to remember, as widely appreciated both in and out of Philadelphia. His clothes were always of the most admirable cut and fit and of a fashion becoming to his years, he carried a substantial cane with a gold top, his stock was never laid aside for a frivolous modern cravat, his silk hat was as indispensable, and his slow walk had a dignity royalty might have envied. He was a handsome old man and a noticeable figure even in Philadelphia streets at the hour when John Welsh from the corner, and Biddles and Cadwalladers and Whartons and Peppers and Lewises and a host of other handsome old Philadelphians with good Philadelphia names from the near neighborhood, were starting downtown in clothes as irreproachable and with a gait no less dignified. The foreigner's idea of the American is of a slouchy, free-and-easy man for ever cracking jokes. But slouchiness and jokes had no place in the dictionary or the deportment of my Grandfather and his contemporaries, at a period when Philadelphia supplied men like John Welsh for its country to send as representatives abroad and there carry on the traditions of Franklin and John Adams and Jefferson. My Father—Edward Robins—inherited more than his share of this old-fashioned Philadelphia manner, making a ceremony of the morning walk to his office and the Sunday walk to church. But it has been lost by younger generations, more's the pity. In memory I would not have my Grandfather a shade less solemn, though at the time his solemnity put me on anything but easy terms with him.

The respectful bang of the front door upon my Grandfather's dignified back after breakfast was the signal for the family to relax. The cloth was at once cleared, my Grandmother and my Aunts—like all Philadelphia mothers and daughters—brought their work-baskets into the dining-room and sat and gossiped there until it was time for my Grandmother to go and see the butcher and the provision dealer, or for my Aunts to make those formal calls for which the morning then was the unpardonable hour.

It seems to me, in looking back, as if my Gandmother could never have gone out of the house except on an errand to the provision man, such an important part did it play in her daily round of duties. She never went to market. That was not the Philadelphia woman's business, it was the Philadelphia man's. My Grandfather, at the time of which I write, must have grown too old for the task, which was no light one, for it meant getting up at unholy hours every Wednesday and every Saturday, leaving the rest of the family in their comfortable beds, and being back again in time for prayers and eight o'clock breakfast. I cannot say how this division of daily labour was brought about. The century before, a short time as things go in Philadelphia, it was the other way round and the young Philadelphia woman at her marketing was one of the sights strangers in the town were taken to see. But in my time it was so much the man's right that as a child I believed there was something essentially masculine in going to market, just as there was in making the mayonnaise for the salad at dinner. A Philadelphia man valued his salad too highly to trust its preparation to a woman. It was almost a shock to me when my Father allowed my motherly little Aunt to relieve him of the responsibility in the Spruce Street house. And later on, when he re-married and again lived in a house of his own, and my Step-Mother made a mayonnaise quite equal to his or to any mere man's, not even to her would he shift the early marketing,—his presence in the Twelfth Street Market as essential on Wednesday and Saturday mornings as in the Stock Exchange every day—and his conscientiousness was the more astonishing as his genius was by no means for domesticity. Philadelphia women respected man's duties and rights in domestic, as in all, matters. I remember an elderly Philadelphian, who was stopping at Blossom's Hotel in Chester, where all Americans thirty years ago began their English tour, telling me the many sauces on the side table had looked so good she would have liked to try them and, on my asking her why in the world she had not, saying they had not been offered to her and she thought perhaps they were for the gentlemen. Only a Philadelphian among Americans could have given that answer.

Towards three o'clock in the Spruce Street house, my Grandmother would be found, her cap carefully removed, stretched full-length upon the sofa in the dining-room. The picture would not be complete if I left out my Father's rage because the dining-room was used for her before-dinner nap as for almost every purpose of domestic life by the women of the family. I have often wondered where he got such an un-Philadelphia idea. In every house where there was a Grandmother, she was taking her nap at the same hour on the same sofa in the same dining-room. I could never see the harm. It was the most comfortable room in the house, without the isolation of the bed-room or the formality of the parlours.

At four, my Grandfather returned from his day's work, the family re-assembled, holding him in sufficient awe never to be late, and dinner was

served. The hour was part of the leisurely life of Philadelphia as ordered
in Spruce Street. Philadelphians had dined at four during a hundred
years and more, and my Grandfather, who rarely condescended to the
frivolity of change, continued to dine at four, as he continued to wear a
stock, until the end of his life. It was no doubt because of the contrast with
Convent fare that the dinner in my recollection remains the most wonderful and elaborate I have ever eaten, though I rack my brains in vain to
recall any of its special features except the figs and prunes on the high
dessert dishes, altogether the most luscious figs and prunes ever grown and
dried, and the decanter at my Grandfather's place from which he dropped
into his glass the few drops of brandy he drank with his water while
everybody else drank their water undiluted. When friends came to dinner, I recall also the Philadelphia decanter of Madeira, though otherwise
no greater ceremony. Dinner was always as solemn an affair in my Grandfather's house as morning prayers or any act of daily life over which he
presided, the whole house, at all times when he left it, relapsing into
dressing gown and slippered ease after the full-dress decorum his presence
required of it.

The eight o'clock tea is a more definite function in my memory, perhaps because the hours of waiting for it crept by so slowly. After dinner,
the Aunts, my Father, the one Uncle who lived at home, vanished I never
knew where, though no doubt Philadelphia supplied some amusement or
occupation for the forlorn wreck four o'clock dinner made of the afternoon. But the interval was spent by my Grandfather and Grandmother at
one of the front parlour windows, the old-fashioned Philadelphia afghan
over their knees, their hands folded, while I, alone, my Sister having had
the independence to vanish with the grown-ups, sat at the other, not daring to break the silence in which they looked out into the drowsy street
for the people who seldom came and the events that never happened;
nothing disturbing the calm of Spruce Street save the Sunday afternoon
invasion of the colored people in their Sunday clothes from every near
alley. It gives me a pang now to pass and see the window empty that once
was always filled, in the hour before twilight, by those two dear grey
heads.

Ethel Waters

Ethel Waters was one of the first Negro performers to see her name in lights on Broadway as the star of DuBose Heyward's *Mamba's Daughters* in 1939. She was born in Chester, Pennsylvania in 1900, and her early years were spent as a vaudeville and club singer. She had a second dramatic triumph in *Member of the Wedding,* the play and film adapted from Carson McCullers' novel. Miss Waters has made many recordings, some of which have recently been reissued. The selection that follows is taken from her autobiography, *His Eye Is on the Sparrow,* published in 1950.

from His Eye Is on the Sparrow

I did have one childhood home for more than a few weeks. It was a three-room shanty in an alley just off Clifton Street. Prostitution was legal in Philadelphia then, and Clifton Street, located in the old Bloody Eighth Ward, lay in the heart of the red-light district.

There was always something interesting to watch in that lively neighborhood. Every night the whores, black and white, paraded up and down Clifton Street. They all wore the same outfit, a regular uniform consisting of a voile skirt with taffeta underneath, cork-heeled shoes, a black velvet neckband, and big whores' hoop earrings. Of course their unmistakable trade-mark was their hip-wriggling walk.

I was not yet six years old when we moved there and seven when we left, but I had one hell of a time for myself in that plague spot of vice and crime. I came to know well the street whores, the ladies in the sporting houses, their pimps, the pickpockets, shoplifters, and other thieves who lived all around us. I played with the thieves' children and the sporting women's trick babies. It was they who taught me how to steal.

Things at home didn't change much, but I remember that little alley home as the heaven on earth of my childhood. For once we were all together in a whole house—Vi, Ching, Charlie, me, Mom on her days off. And after a while Louise also came to live with us.

We stayed in Clifton Street for fifteen months. That was the only time I could feel that I had a family that wasn't continually disrupting and belonged in one neighborhood. My family kept on squabbling, but I lived more in the street than at home.

All of us dead-end kids ran errands for the whores. Some of them were good for as much as fifteen, twenty, or twenty-five cents in tips. We spent most of our earnings on candy and food. You could buy a frankfurter for three cents at a street stand, yat-gaw-mein cost a nickel in the Chinese joints, and for a dime you could get a whole plate of fish and French-fried potatoes at a food stand called See Willie's.

A bunch of us would often sleep all night out on the street, over the warm iron gratings of bakeries or laundries. Our families didn't care where we were, and these nesting places, when you put your coat under you, were no more uncomfortable than the broken-down beds with treacherous springs or the bedbug-infested pallets we had at home. Being so large for my age, I was accepted as an equal by older boys and girls. My biggest asset as a street child in the tenderloin was my ability to keep my mouth shut.

Along with a few other Clifton Street youngsters I acted as a semi-official lookout girl for the sporting houses. Though prostitution was a legalized business, there were occasional police raids. These came when church groups bore down heavily on the authorities or after one body too many, stabbed, shot, or cut up very untidily, had been found in some dark alley.

Any of us slum children could smell out a cop even though he was a John, a plain-clothes man. These brilliant sleuths never suspicioned that we were tipsters for the whole whoring industry. Usually we'd be playing some singing game on the street when we spotted a cop, a game like Here Come Two Dudes A-Riding or the one that begins:

> *"King William was King James's son,*
> *Upon his breast he wore a star,*
> *And that was called . . ."*

On smelling out the common enemy, we boys and girls in the know would start to shout the songs, accenting certain phrases. If we happened to be playing a singing game we'd whistle the agreed-on tune. The other kids, even those who weren't lookouts, would innocently imitate us, and in no time at all the whole neighborhood would be alerted. The street women would disappear, the lights would go out, and the doors would be locked in the sporting houses.

Some of the friendlier policemen tried to be nice to us, but that got them nowhere. It was an unwritten law among us not to accept candy from cops or have anything to do with them. It was the only law that was never broken on Clifton Street.

The Bloody Eighth at that time was not exclusively a Negro slum. We had plenty of white neighbors, Hunkies and Jews, and some Chinese. The few respectable families, white and black, forced by circumstances to live in that slum kept to themselves as much as possible.

I didn't know much about color then. There was no racial prejudice at all in that big melting pot running over with vice and crime, violence, poverty, and corruption. I never was made to feel like an outcast on Clifton Street. All of us, whites, blacks, and yellows, were outcasts there together and having a fine time among ourselves.

Anyway, racial prejudice couldn't have existed in that neighborhood where vice was the most important business. The white and Negro street whores worked together, lived and slept together. The two men who owned and protected most of them were Lovey Joe and Rosebud, both of them Negroes. It was not considered unusual for a colored prostitute to have a trick baby white as a lily.

I've always had great respect for whores. The many I've known were kind and generous. Some of them supported whole families and kept at their trade for years to send their trick babies through college. I never knew a prostitute who did harm to anyone but herself. I except, of course, the whores who are real criminals and use knockout drops and bring men to their rooms to be robbed, beaten, and blackmailed.

No woman in my immediate family ever turned to prostitution. Neither were they saints. Sometimes they lived with men they weren't married to. This is true of my mother and my two aunts, Vi and Ching. And they never saw anything wrong in getting what presents they could from their men—shoes for themselves or for me, clothes, or money.

My grandmother hated the idea of my growing up in the red-light district and strongly disapproved of prostitution. But there was nothing she could do about it. The alley shanty was the best home she could find or afford.

ROCHESTER

❧

*"Rochester was a big country town in what I may be al-
lowed to call the 'teen-age years' of the present century,"
says Robert Coates, recalling his boyhood in upper New
York State. The city had a population of about 220,000
then; the affluent lived in rambling houses on the quiet
tree-lined avenues, and even the more modest homes on the
side streets had porches where boys and girls could sing
songs like "Sympathy" in time to the swing of the glider.
Like many young people of his time, Coates grew up with
the automobile, and in the selection below from his memoir* The View from Here, *published in 1960, he recalls an
activity that was a Rochester specialty: the use of the family car as a "jitney bus" to compete for passengers with the
snail-paced trolley cars.*

Robert Coates

Robert Coates was born in New Haven in 1897, went to Yale, and during the 1920s lived in the south of France. During his years abroad he was active in the expatriate world of *avant-garde* magazines, and on his return to the United States, his friend James Thurber helped him get a job on *The New Yorker,* where he enjoyed a long career as art critic. He is the author of many short stories and several novels.

from The View from Here

I have a host of other random recollections about the early automobiles and me. Though the fact may be almost forgotten now, we *named* our cars in the old days, for they were not then the bleak, interchangeable units from an endless assembly line they are now; instead, they had—or they seemed to us to have—the proud, individual character of yachts, and it was in that sense that we named them. Lately, I've been casting about in my own mind, and probing those of such friends as I can get at, to resurrect a few examples of early nomenclature.

Odd though some of them may seem, I prefer them to the examples of ready-made nomenclature, often chromium-inscribed on the fender or trunk lid—"Star-Flite," "Jet-Flite," "Impala," and so on—that the automobile manufacturers now pin on their products.

Our Stoddard-Dayton, because of its color, was always called "Brownie," and the Paige that came after it—owing, I think, to some defect in its headlights—was christened "Blinky." The Chrysler that followed *it* marked, obviously, the change from the sentimental to the purely practical era, for, as far as I can recall, we had no name for it at all.

To give you an idea of the extent to which sentiment entered in, a friend of mine, prodded by me in the course of these researches, has suddenly recalled that when his family sold their first car—an Overland, named, fairly allusively, "The Scout"—and, the deal consummated, the new owner was driving it away, my friend's mother, standing on their front porch, watching, abruptly burst into tears.

"I hope he takes good care of it!" she wailed, with all the poignance that accompanies a parting with a good friend or servitor after years of faithful companionship. We had something of the same feeling after we'd traded our Paige for the Chrysler, for the older car was bought soon after-

49

ward by a junkman, who cut off the after part of the body and converted it, rather ramshackledly, into a truck. We used to hang our heads guiltily whenever we saw our old friend, thus mutilated, going by.

Our friends the Schaeffers' old Cadillac was called, affectionately, "The Ark," and another family we knew had a Rambler they nicknamed, I suppose with some vague reference to vagabondage, "Dusty." Another fellow I knew recalls that *his* family's car was called, more poetically, "Hot Spur," while another confesses shyly that their first car, a Franklin, was christened "Daisy." This really does seem to be a pretty long reach in search of allusiveness—but, as I said at first, if you think of a car in the same context as a yacht, or even a family cruiser, it becomes a good deal less startling. After all, no one laughs at even a sixteen-footer named "Rosabelle," "Princess," or "Wanderer III."

So far, I notice, I seem to have described most of our excursions as occurring in sunny weather, and I suppose on the theory that one tends to remember the pleasant things rather than the unpleasant, this is only natural. We did run into rain, though, on occasion, and my most vivid memories about that have to do with the moments before the downpour came, when a ritual called "beating the storm" was enacted by every motorist worthy of the name.

This, of course, is unknown in these modern days of cars that are either totally enclosed or have tops, motor-operated, which go up at the touch of a button. The early tops, however, were the one feature of the old motorcars that I remember with distaste. Big, clumsy, broad-beamed affairs, with their heavy wooden ribs and billowing canvas, they were a direct descendant of the bowed top of the prairie schooner, which they much resembled, and they were as difficult to get up as they were to put down and stow away again. Is it any wonder that, when a storm loomed suddenly, the slow, peaceful traffic along the highway would be turned into a mad scramble, as everyone stepped on the gas and did his damnedest to get away from it?

I should add, too, that my own excursions weren't all family affairs, either. I hope I offend no Rochesterian, of either my own or other generations, by saying that Rochester was a big country town in what I may be allowed to call the "teen-age years" of the present century. So it was, though, or so I see it, but it was so in the pleasantest sense imaginable— the sense, to be explicit, that its streets were broad, shady, and uncrowded, the houses lining them comfortable and well-appointed, set in ample grounds, and the life itself easy, confident, and unhurried.

To complete the picture, I must add that the Rochester girls, in keeping with the town's general atmosphere, were almost without exception healthy, cheerful, fresh-skinned, and, frequently, very pretty. And I was just in my middle teens at the time, at the age when a boy is beginning to realize, even if a little reluctantly, that girls have a place in the world, too, along with tennis, boxing, baseball, and such other masculine employments—that even, mysteriously, there is a peculiar, indescribable pleasure to be found in just teaching a girl how, say, to hold a tennis racket in one of those slim, soft, unmuscular hands, and how to swing it.

And the very easygoingness and the semirusticity of the life of Rochester were a help in this development. Winters, there was skating on Kondolf's Pond or one of the many park lakes (the boy kneeling gallantly to put on the girl's skates for her, with, usually, a bonfire roaring on the bank nearby) or bobsledding on Cobb's Hill—and always hot chocolate and cookies waiting later at someone's family's home, set out in the big basement playroom, Rochester's precocious version of what later acquired the sorry name of "rumpus room."

There were basketball games and school dances, hay rides on the big farm sledges that were still available; and, quite frequently, little impromptu dances at homes, where the girls would make fudge or Welsh rarebit, thus displaying their talents for domesticity.

In the summertime, whenever one fellow or another could borrow his family's car, there were outings—swimming parties out at someone's cottage on Lake Ontario or at camps in the Finger Lakes region—and here again the girls had a chance to show their cooking skills, for these usually included a picnic, but a more impromptu one than the adult variety.

This, perhaps, because we were never quite sure (parents are so unaccountable) until the last minute if the car would really be available; at any rate, what we did was to bring our supplies along raw, in a manner of speaking, and prepare them on the spot.

Best of all, in my recollection, was a dish, or concoction, called the "bacon bat." I don't know if it was peculiar to Rochester or was common elsewhere. But, in any case, all you need is a few husky boys to gather wood for an open fire and get it going; some pretty girls, with makeshift aprons over their dresses and their faces flushed with the heat of the flames; a big frying pan, and some bread, eggs, bacon, and tomatoes.

After that, the procedure is simple. You just fry the bacon in the pan, scramble the eggs in the bacon fat, spread these out, with some thick tomato slices, between large hunks of bread—and there you are, the bacon bat. You eat the sandwiches standing, of course, and preferably over the fire itself, for drippings and other debris are prodigious. But, given the right circumstances, I can think of nothing else more delicious.

Afterward, we would sit around the fire for a while, watching the dying embers. Then, bundled cozily together in the open car, we would drive home, singing; and, to my mind, an open touring car, top down on a summer night, with the breeze rippling in around the windshield, and the trees rustling transitorily in the welcoming way they have, their leaves set in motion by the very rush of your passage, is still about as pleasant a means of transportation as anyone could ask for.

"Moonlight Bay" we'd sing, certainly, for it was particularly appropriate with the lake water stretching off, rippling, and, by now, possibly, even moonlit, beside us; and we all loved the wonderfully wistful effect one got when the boys, in their deeper voices, echoed the end of each line after the girls had sung it: "We were sailing along (*We were sailing along*) on Moonlight Bay (*on Moonlight Bay*), I could hear the voices ringing. . . ."

And then also there were others, like "Sympathy" ("I need sy-*im*-pa-thy"), "Sayonara" ("Sweet Good-by"), and "On the Banks of the Saskatchewah" (from a play called *The Pink Lady,* starring an actress named Hazel Dawn, whom I had fallen in love with as soon as I saw her, on the stage of the Seneca Theatre). If we felt especially ambitious, we might try a few rounds: "There is a boat/Hails to the ferry," or "Big Tom is cast," or, of course, the perennial favorite, "Row, row, row your boat/Gently down the stream/Merrily, merrily, merrily, merrily/Life is but a dream."

There might have been a certain amount of hand-holding, accompanied by flashing sidelong glances, and even a discreet bit of cuddling, earlier. But a touring car makes for camaraderie rather than for romance, and a cool night breeze makes for drowsiness; if the trip was at all long, even the songs, eventually, would die. Half asleep, if not actually wholly so—all, that is, except the driver—we'd arrive home at last.

I'd learned about girls in another way, too, by means of the motorcar. I don't know if anyone else remembers the "jitney bus" era any more. I'm not even sure how localized the phenomenon was, and, hence, if it was confined to the general region of western New York State or if it spread elsewhere. All I know is that some time around 1915 or 1916, in Rochester, private cars operating like miniature buses, in competition with the trolleys, began appearing on the streets.

They lined up along the curb at the principal intersections downtown —State and Main, Main and Genesee Avenue, and so on—each with a little hand-lettered sign on the windshield stating the route it followed;

the charge was a "jitney," a nickel, the same as the trolleys, and, until the novelty wore off—and until the streetcar company, after some hasty lobbying, got laws passed regarding licensing, insurance requirements, route schedules, and so on: all, till then, disregarded in those free and easy times—they were literally everywhere.

At the start, the drivers were men, but when the summer vacation came on, all the boys who could wangle the family car even part of the time got in on it as well. I was one. I don't recall how my father got to and from his office downtown, unless he rode the jitneys, too, and it must have been an inconvenience all round. But I suppose my parents figured it was good for me, since it showed enterprise, and for a couple of weeks or so, or until disillusionment set in, I drove our car as a jitney bus on the Lake Avenue line.

I had chosen Lake Avenue partly because it passed fairly near our house and was a well-traveled thoroughfare besides. But it was a handsome street, too, broad and, once one got outside the center of the city, lined with large, substantial houses. In much the same way that I suppose a man opening a stationery store takes pride in the fact that it's in a good neighborhood rather than a poor one, I took a slightly snobbish pleasure in the feeling that, if I was in business at all, it was with the best kind of people.

And I was in business, make no mistake about it. To be sure, a number of my passengers were people I knew, or my family did, and I felt at first a certain embarrassment in taking money from them. But they, as adults, laughed that aside, and I soon learned to do so, too. And I suppose there should have been a certain tedium in driving the same route over and over—down Lake Avenue to State Street and on to the intersection at Main; turn to join the line at the curb and wait there till I had my quota of passengers, and then up State to Lake and out again.

I didn't feel it, though. I was out in the world, on my own at last, and I can still see myself, and—in that odd sort of double vision that one gets with remembering—*be* myself, too, driving back and forth, back and forth, as gravely serious about my business responsibilities as only a boy of seventeen or so can be, and at the same time intensely curious, watching what went on about me.

As a matter of fact, I had very few signal adventures. There were the brushes with the trolley-car motormen, who, of course, hated us, and who, if they saw some possible passenger waiting at a corner ahead, would put on full speed in an effort to get there ahead of us. But an automobile, even then, had a quicker pickup than a trolley, and we usually got there first; even if we didn't, half the time the customer would wait for the jitney. Just riding in an automobile in those days, for a good many people, was still something of an adventure—as a plane trip now is, as compared to one on an express train. And my choice of the Lake Avenue route turned out to be a fortunate one, for it ran out to the big Eastman Kodak plant, in a parklike area of its own on the outskirts of town, and where, of course, at closing time, there were hundreds of workers looking for transportation.

I was beginning to think I had fallen on a bonanza when one day, at the plant, a remarkably pretty girl hopped into the seat beside me. (The front seat, in a jitney bus, was comparable in its attractiveness to the seat behind the motorman in an open trolley.) She was dark-haired, dark-eyed, plump, high-colored; and, pretty as she undeniably was, she was also a little frightening, for she was at least a couple of years older than I was— an intimidating thing for a fellow of seventeen—and obviously much more experienced. And instead of wrapping herself in the stiff, suspicious silence I'd already got used to in most of my other feminine passengers, she was almost alarmingly approachable. Yet for all that, I soon found myself getting along wonderfully well with her.

She was demure at first, of course, but even then there was a hint that the demureness was only external, a barrier that could easily be broken through, and when I tried out my "line" on her (as I recall, and I don't much like to, it was a mixture of jokes that were meant to be faintly risqué, mannish talk about tennis and other sports I engaged in, and dark hints about petting parties I'd been out on; and it went over pretty well with girls of my own age), she melted considerably. By the time we reached the street corner where she got off, it had somehow come to be understood that she'd ride with me regularly from then on.

I believe she paid her fare the first couple of times, though I was probably too entranced to notice. If so, it wasn't more than a few days later that it turned out she'd forgotten her purse, somehow, and was nickel-less.

"That's all right," I assured her gallantly.

"Do you mean it?" she asked. I said, sure, and from then on there was no more nonsense about paying. Clearly, she had—mistakenly, of course —taken my waiving the fare that one day to mean that I was willing to forego it forever, and I was in no state to correct her. I didn't much mind, either.

I always had three or four paying passengers in the back seat to give me some sense of profit. Besides, I felt I was beginning to make headway with her, though I was a little uncertain in what direction. I never tried to make a date with her. I had a feeling she'd be far too worldly for me, for one thing; for another, she was a factory girl, and in the middle-class morality of those times, that automatically made her a little bit suspect.

Factory girls were considered to be "wild," and I was afraid that if I got too involved with her, I might "get beyond my depth," in some way. Who knows, I might even have to marry her! Yet I was still fascinated with her, and I would gladly have ferried her home from work all summer, for free, if she hadn't started ringing her friends in on me.

Only a day or so later, she turned up with another girl. The new one was not so pretty, either, but since they got off together I could hardly collect the fare from one and not from the other. And the next day—having thus felt the ground out, I suppose—she appeared with a whole clutch of them; and when *they* got off, again all together, it turned out that none of them expected to pay, either. To be sure, one did start to reach for her purse, but my girl put a stop to that immediately.

"Oh, he doesn't let *us* pay!" she cried. "Do you, babe?" I grinned weakly, I guess, and with that they all ran off up the street. I suppose I might even have let that pass, I was so bemused, if a couple of them, a few steps away, hadn't laughed. And I was at that age when a boy is peculiarly sensitive to the sound of girls laughing, mysteriously, anywhere around him.

For all I know, they may have been laughing at something utterly unrelated to me, though I doubt it. But in my mind that laugh struck home, and in a flash I saw myself as I was sure they must see me—a poor, callow, young fool, boastful with nothing to boast of (I remembered I'd been telling them, in great detail, only a few minutes before, how I'd almost won the West High School tennis championship that spring), and a snobbish little twerp, too, for the matter of that, though I don't think the full realization of that came until later—now left grinning stupidly in my father's car, while they made a mock of me.

I had been in a slightly similar mess before, when things had gotten out of hand with a woman, only that time the woman had been my mother. She and I were on a streetcar, riding home from some shopping trip downtown, and on boarding it I had absent-mindedly slid into the favored seat by the window, leaving her to take the one on the aisle. I had hardly got settled there before I realized I had put myself in a position no true gentleman should ever be found in—since a gentleman, unfailingly, always saw his lady seated, and in the most comfortable condition, before himself sitting down.

I solved that problem by simply withdrawing from it. Or, rather, I withdrew, for the duration of the journey, from my mother. In a sense, I dematerialized her. I pretended she just wasn't there, or if she was, I wasn't acquainted with her, and I spent the rest of the trip, and it was a fairly long one, staring fixedly out the window.

The only trouble was, I had no way of conveying this new attitude of mine to my mother, and it puzzled her. We'd been talking fairly animatedly before, and this sudden uncommunicativeness on my part confused her completely. "Are you all right? Is anything the matter?" I remember her asking once, and I muttered, from the side of my mouth. "Yes. Yes. I'm all right. Just don't feel like talking, that's all." Finally, bewildered but compliant, she, too, lapsed into silence.

I solved my problem with the Kodak girls in a somewhat similar fashion—by just withdrawing from them, and from jitney-bus driving, entirely. My parents, I remember, were disappointed to see my first business venture ending so abruptly; and since again I couldn't explain the true situation, I'm afraid they took it as just another example of that footlessness I was always being accused of. But I couldn't help it, under the circumstances. I was darned if I was going to be taken in by those girls again —not if I could help it!

NEW YORK

Visit New York for the first time;
walk in any direction
until you're thirsty.
Drop anchor at any bar and grill;
talk to the bartender;
tell him you're a stranger,
never saw the city before.

What will he say?

"You should have seen it
in the old days.

"Take this neighborhood.
None of these big apartment houses then.
Or take the Bronx.
It was a wilderness;
walk a mile to the 'el'
Mouquins, Villepegue's
Shanley's, the old Claremont Inn
and Broadway—
'Give my regards to Broadway.'

"They don't come like that any more.

"I was a kid selling papers
outside of Lüchow's on Fourteenth Street.

*Every night,
this guy with a fur collar on his coat
gives me a dollar for the Globe
and lets me keep the change.*

"They don't come like that any more" *

—Percy Seitlin

* From *That New York,* by Percy Seitlin, whose memoir *Is Anything All Right?* was published in 1969.

New York after the Civil War was a city where all the right people knew each other and paid very little attention to anyone else. The best families lived in the brownstones that bordered Washington Square, or farther uptown near Gramercy Park, or on Murray Hill, and when they weren't at home, they were in Newport or in Europe. In the article below, first published in Harper's Magazine *in March 1938, Edith Wharton describes her childhood in the fashionable world of the 1880s—the overfurnished brownstones, the formal Assemblies, the meagerness of intellectual stimulation, and the excitement of the theater. As she says, her reminiscences "have acquired the historical importance of fragments of dress and furniture dug up in a Babylonian tomb."*

Edith Wharton

Edith Wharton (1862–1937) was a member of an old New York family, and she was bound by its conventions until, bored by her surroundings and disappointed in her marriage, she turned to serious writing. She was a friend and admirer of Henry James and, like him, lived abroad for a large part of her life. Her many short stories and novels examine the international scene as well as the New York world she knew so well. Among her best known works are *The House of Mirth* (1905), *Ethan Frome* (1911), and *The Age of Innocence*, which was awarded the Pulitzer Prize in 1921.

A Little Girl's New York

When four years ago I wrote the closing lines of my reminiscences, *A Backward Glance*, I thought of myself as an old woman laying a handful of rue on the grave of an age which had finished in storm and destruction. Now that I am older by only four years, I realize that my view was that of the sentimentalist watching the slow downward flutter of the first autumn leaves in still blue air, and talking with a shudder of forests stripped by winter gales. For the succeeding years have witnessed such convulsions, social and political, that those earlier disturbances now seem no more than a premonitory tremor; and the change between the customs of my youth and the world of even ten years ago a mere crack in the ground compared with the chasm now dividing that world from the present one.

All elderly people feel the shock of changes barely perceptible to the generation that has had a hand in their making; but even centenarians can seldom have had to look back across such a barrier of new towers of Babel (or their ruins) as divides my contemporaries from the era of the New Deal; and I need no other excuse for beginning my old story over again than the growing mass of these obstructions. Everything that used to form the fabric of our daily life has been torn in shreds, trampled on, destroyed; and hundreds of little incidents, habits, traditions which, when I began to record my past, seemed too insignificant to set down, have acquired the historical importance of fragments of dress and furniture dug up in a Babylonian tomb.

It is these fragments that I should like to assemble and make into a little memorial like the boxes formed of exotic shells which sailors used to fabricate between voyages. And I must forestall my critics by adding that I already foresee how small will be the shells I shall collect, how ordinary their varieties, and the box, when it is made, what a mere joke of a thing —unless one should put one's ear to the shells; but how many will?

In those days the little "brownstone" houses (I never knew the technical name of that geological horror) marched up Fifth Avenue (still called *"the* Fifth Avenue" by purists) in an almost unbroken procession from Washington Square to the Central Park. Between them there passed up and down, in a leisurely double line, every variety of horse-drawn vehicle, from Mrs. Belmont's or Mrs. Astor's C-spring barouche to a shabby little covered cart drawn by a discouraged old horse and labelled in large letters: *Universal Exterminator*—which suggested collecting souls for the *Dies Irae,* but in reality designated a patent appliance for ridding kitchens of cockroaches.

The little brownstone houses, all with Dutch "stoops" (the five or six steps leading to the front door), and all not more than three stories high, marched Parkward in an orderly procession, like a young ladies' boarding school taking its daily exercise. The façades varied in width from twenty to thirty feet, and here and there, but rarely, the line was broken by a brick house with brownstone trimmings; but otherwise they were all so much alike that one could understand how easy it would be for a dinner guest to go to the wrong house—as once befell a timid young girl of eighteen, to whom a vulgar *nouveau-riche* hostess revealed her mistake, turning her out carriageless into the snow—a horrid adventure which was always used to point the rule that one must *never* allow a guest, even totally unknown, to discover such a mistake, but must immediately include him or her in the party. Imagine the danger of entertaining gangsters to which such social rules would expose the modern hostess! But I am probably the last person to remember that Arcadian code of hospitality.

Those were the days—à propos of Fifth Avenue—when my mother used to say: "Society is completely changed nowadays. When I was first married we knew everyone who kept a carriage."

And this tempts me to another digression, sending me forward to my seventeenth year, when there suddenly appeared in Fifth Avenue a very small canary-yellow brougham with dark trimmings, drawn by a big high-stepping bay and driven by a coachman who matched the brougham in size and the high-stepper in style. In this discreet yet brilliant equipage one just caught a glimpse of a lady whom I faintly remember as dark-haired, quietly dressed, and enchantingly pale, with a hat-brim lined with cherry color, which shed a lovely glow on her cheeks. It was an apparition surpassing in elegance and mystery any that Fifth Avenue had ever seen; but when our dark-blue brougham encountered the yellow one, and I cried: "Oh, Mamma, look—what a smart carriage! Do you know the lady?" I was hurriedly drawn back with the stern order not to stare at strange people and to remember that whenever our carriage passed the yellow one I was to turn my head away and look out of the other window.

For the lady in the canary-colored carriage was New York's first fashionable hetaera. Her name and history were known in all the clubs, and the name of her proud proprietor was no secret in New York drawing-rooms. I may add that, being an obedient daughter, I always thereafter *did* look out of the other window when the forbidden brougham passed; but that one and only glimpse of the loveliness within it peopled my imagination with images of enchantment from Broceliande and Shalott (we were all deep in the "Idylls of the King"), and from the Cornwall of Yseult. She was, in short, sweet unsuspecting creature, my first doorway to romance, destined to become for me successively Guinevere and Francesca da Rimini, Beatrix Esmond and the *Dame aux Camélias*. And in the impoverished emotional atmosphere of old New York such a glimpse was like the mirage of palm trees in the desert.

I have often sighed, in looking back at my childhood, to think how pitiful a provision was made for the life of the imagination behind those uniform brownstone façades, and then have concluded that since, for reasons which escape us, the creative mind thrives best on a reduced diet, I probably had the fare best suited to me. But this is not to say that the average well-to-do New Yorker of my childhood was not starved for a sight of the high gods. Beauty, passion, and danger were automatically excluded from his life (for the men were almost as starved as the women); and the average human being deprived of air from the heights is likely to produce other lives equally starved—which was what happened in old New York, where the tepid sameness of the moral-atmosphere resulted in a prolonged immaturity of mind.

But we must return to the brownstone houses, and penetrate from the vestibule (painted in Pompeian red, and frescoed with a frieze of stencilled lotus-leaves, taken from Owen Jones's *Grammar of Ornament*) into the carefully guarded interior. What would the New Yorker of the present day say to those interiors, and the lives lived in them? Both would be equally unintelligible to any New Yorker under fifty.

Beyond the vestibule (in the average house) was a narrow drawing-room. Its tall windows were hung with three layers of curtains: sash-curtains through which no eye from the street could possibly penetrate, and next to these draperies of lace or embroidered tulle, richly beruffled, and looped back under the velvet or damask hangings which were drawn in the evening. This window garniture always seemed to me to symbolize the superimposed layers of under-garments worn by the ladies of the period—and even, alas, by the little girls. They were in fact almost purely a symbol, for in many windows even the inner "sash-curtains" were looped back far enough to give the secluded dwellers a narrow glimpse of the street; but no self-respecting mistress of a house (a brownstone house) could dispense with this triple display of window-lingerie, and among the many things I did which pained and scandalized my Bostonian mother-in-law, she was not least shocked by the banishment from our house in the country of all the thicknesses of muslin which should have intervened between ourselves and the robins on the lawn.

The brownstone drawing-room was likely to be furnished with monumental pieces of modern Dutch marquetry, among which there was almost always a cabinet with glazed doors for the display of "bric-à-brac." Oh, that bric-à-brac! Our mothers, who prided themselves on the contents of these cabinets, really knew about only two artistic productions—old lace and old painted fans. With regard to these the eighteenth-century tradition was still alive, and in nearly every family there were yards and yards of precious old lace and old fans of ivory, chicken-skin, or pale tortoise-shell, exquisitely carved and painted. But as to the other arts a universal ignorance prevailed, and the treasures displayed in the wealthiest houses were no better than those of the average brownstone-dweller.

My mother had a collection of old lace which was famous among her friends, and a few fragments of it still remain to me, piously pinned up in the indigo-blue paper supposed (I have never known why) to be necessary to the preservation of fine lace. But the yards are few, alas; for true to my conviction that what was made to be used should be used, and not locked up, I have outlived many and many a yard of noble *point de Milan,* of stately Venetian point, of shadowy Mechlin, and exquisitely flowered *point de Paris,* not to speak of the delicate Valenciennes which ruffled the tiny handkerchiefs and incrusted and edged the elaborate *lingerie* of my youth. Nor do I regret having worn out what was meant to be worn out. I know few sadder sights than Museum collections of these Arachne-webs that were designed to borrow life and color from the nearness of young flesh and blood. Museums are cemeteries, as unavoidable, no doubt, as the other kind, but just as unrelated to the living beauty of what we have loved.

I have said that the little brown houses, marching up Fifth Avenue like disciplined schoolgirls, now and then gave way to a more important façade, sometimes of their own chocolate hue, but with occasional pleasing alternatives in brick. Many successive Fifth Avenues have since been erected on the site of the one I first knew, and it is hard to remember that none of the "new" millionaire houses which, ten or fifteen years later, were to invade that restless thoroughfare (and all of which long ago joined the earlier layers of ruins) had been dreamed of by the boldest innovator. Even the old families, who were subsequently to join the newcomers in transforming Fifth Avenue into a street of would-be palaces, were still content with plain wide-fronted houses, mostly built in the 'forties or 'fifties. In those simple days one could count on one's two hands the New York houses with ballrooms; to the best of my recollection, only the Goelets, Astors, Butler Duncans, Belmonts, Schermerhorns, and Mason Joneses possessed these frivolous appendages; though a few years later, by the time I made my first curtsy at the "Assemblies," several rich couples, the Mortons, Waterburys, Coleman Draytons, and Francklyns among them, had added ballrooms to their smart establishments.

In the smaller houses a heavy linen called "crash," laid on the floors of two adjoining drawing-rooms, and gilt chairs hired from "old Brown" (the Grace Church sexton, who so oddly combined ecclesiastical and worldly duties) created temporary ballrooms for small dances; but the big balls of the season (from January to Lent) were held at Delmonico's, then, if I am not mistaken, at the corner of Twenty-eighth Street and Fifth Avenue.

The Assemblies were the most important of these big balls—if the word

"big" as now understood could be applied to any social event in our old
New York! There were, I think, three Assemblies in the winter, presided
over by a committee of ladies who delegated three of their number to
receive the guests at the ballroom door. The evening always opened with a
quadrille, in which the ladies of the committee and others designated by
them took part; and there followed other square dances, waltzes and
polkas, which went on until the announcement of supper. A succulent
repast of canvasback ducks, terrapin, foie-gras, and the best champagnes
was served at small tables below stairs, in what was then New York's only
fashionable restaurant; after which we re-ascended to the ballroom (in a
shaky little lift) to begin the complicated maneuvers of the cotillion.

The "Thursday Evening Dances," much smaller and more exclusive,
were managed by a committee of the younger married women—and how
many young and pretty ones there were in our little society! I cannot,
oddly enough, remember where these dances were held—and who is left, I
wonder, to refresh my memory? There was no Sherry's restaurant as yet,
and no Waldorf-Astoria, or any kind of modern hotel with a suite for
entertaining; yet I am fairly sure we did not meet at "Del's" for the
"Thursday Evenings."

At all dances, large or small, a custom prevailed which caused untold
misery to the less popular girls. This was the barbarous rule that if a
young man asked a girl for a dance or, between dances, for a turn about the
ballroom, he was obliged to keep her on his arm until another candidate
replaced him; with the natural result that "to him (or rather *her*) that
hath shall be given," and the wily young men risked themselves only in
the vicinity of young women already provided with attendant swains. To
remedy this embarrassing situation the more tactful girls always requested
their partners, between dances, to bring them back to their mothers or
"chaperons," a somnolent row of stout ladies in velvet and ostrich feathers
enthroned on a row of settees against the ballroom walls.

The custom persisted for some years, and spoilt the enjoyment of many
a "nice" girl not attractive enough to be perpetually surrounded by
young men, and too proud to wish to chain at her side a dancer who
might have risked captivity out of kindness of heart. I do not know when
the fashion changed, and the young men were set free, for we went back
to Europe when I was nineteen, and I had only brief glimpses of New
York until I returned to it as a married woman.

The most conspicuous architectural break in the brownstone procession
occurred where its march ended, at the awkwardly shaped entrance to the
Central Park. Two of my father's cousins, Mrs. Mason Jones and Mrs.

Colford Jones, bought up the last two blocks on the east side of Fifth Avenue, facing the so-called "Plaza" at the Park gates, and built thereon their houses and their children's houses; a bold move which surprised and scandalized society. Fifty-seventh Street was then a desert, and ball-goers anxiously wondered whether even the ubiquitous "Brown coupés" destined to carry home belated dancers would risk themselves so far a-field. But old Mrs. Mason Jones and her submissive cousin laughed at such apprehensions, and presently there rose before our astonished eyes a block of pale-greenish limestone houses (almost uglier than the brownstone ones) for the Colford Jones cousins, adjoining which our audacious Aunt Mary, who had known life at the Court of the Tuileries, erected her own white marble residence and a row of smaller dwellings of the same marble to lodge her progeny. The "Jones blocks" were so revolutionary that I doubt whether any subsequent architectural upheavals along that historic thoroughfare have produced a greater impression. In our little provincial town (without electricity, telephones, taxis, or cab-stands) it had seemed inconceivable that houses or habits should ever change; whereas by the time the new millionaires arrived with their palaces in their pockets Fifth Avenue had become cosmopolitan, and was prepared for anything.

The lives led behind the brownstone fronts were, with few exceptions, as monotonous as their architecture. European travel was growing more frequent, though the annual holiday abroad did not become general until I grew up. In the brownstone era, when one crossed the Atlantic it was for a longer stay; and the returned traveler arrived with a train of luggage too often heavy with works of art and "antiques." Our mothers, not always aware of their aesthetic limitations, seldom restricted their purchases to lace and fans; it was almost a point of honor to bring back an "Old Master" or two and a few monsters in the way of modern Venetian furniture. For the traveler of moderate means, who could not soar to Salvator Rosa, Paul Potter, or Carlo Dolci (prime favorites of the day), facsimiles were turned out by the million by the industrious copyists of Florence, Rome, or Amsterdam; and seldom did the well-to-do New Yorker land from a European tour unaccompanied by a Mary Magdalen cloaked in carefully waved hair, or a swarthy group of plumed and gaitered gamblers doing a young innocent out of his last sequin. One of these "awful warnings," a Domenichino, I think, darkened the walls of our dining room, and Mary Magdalen, minutely reproduced on copper, graced the drawing-room table (which was of Louis Philippe *buhl*, with ornate brass heads at the angles).

In our country houses, collections of faïence, in which our mothers also flattered themselves that they were expert, were thought more suitable than pictures. Urbino, Gubbio, and various Italian luster wares, mostly turned out by the industrious Ginori of Florence, abounded in Newport drawing-rooms. I shall never forget my mother's mortification when some ill-advised friend arranged for a newly arrived Italian Minister—Count Corti, I think—to visit her supposed "collection" of "china" (as all forms of porcelain and pottery were then indifferently called). The diplomatist happened to be a collector of some repute, and after one glance at the Ginori output crowding every cabinet and table, he hurriedly draped his surprise in a flow of compliments which did not for a moment deceive my mother. I still burn with the humiliation inflicted by that salutary visit, which had the happy effect of restricting her subsequent purchases to lace, fans, or old silver—about which, incidentally, she also knew a good deal, partly, no doubt, because she and my father had inherited some very good examples of Colonial silver from their respective forebears.

This fine silver and Sheffield plate may have called her attention, earlier than most people's, to the Colonial furniture that could then be had almost for the asking in New England. At all events, our house at Newport was provided, chiefly through the old Mr. Vernon, the Newport antiquarian, with a fine lot of highboys and lowboys, and with sets of the graceful Colonial Hepplewhite chairs. It is a pity she did not develop this branch of her collecting mania and turn a deaf ear to the purveyors of sham Fra Angelicos and Guido Renis, who besieged the artless traveler from every shop door of the Lungarno and the Via Babuino. But even great critics go notoriously wrong in judging contemporary art and letters, and there was, as far as I know, only one Lord Hertford to gather up the matchless treasures of French eighteenth-century furniture in the arid days of the Empire.

Most of the little brownstone houses in which the Salvator Rosas and Domenichinos gloomed so incongruously on friendly drawing-room walls still possessed the surviving fragments of "a gentleman's library"—that is, the collection of good books, well written, well printed, well bound, with which the aboriginal New Yorkers had beguiled their long and dimly lit leisure. In a world of little music and no painting, there was time to read; and I grieve to think of the fate of the treasures to be found in the "libraries" of my childhood—which still belonged to gentlemen, though no longer, as a rule, to readers. Where have they gone, I wonder, all those good books, so inevitably scattered in a country without entail or primogeniture? The rarest, no doubt, have long since been captured by dealers and resold, at soaring prices, to the bibliophiles of two continents, and unexpurgated Hogarths splendidly bound in crushed Levant are no longer outspread on the nursery floor on rainy days, as they used to be for the delectation of my little Rhinelander cousins and myself. (I may add that, though Hogarth was accessible to infants, *Leaves of Grass,* then just beginning to circulate among the most advanced intellectuals, was kept under lock and key, and brought out, like tobacco, only in the absence of "the ladies," to whom the name of Walt Whitman was unmentionable, if not utterly unknown.)

In our New York house, a full-blown specimen of Second Empire decoration, the creation of the fashionable French upholsterer, Marcotte, the books were easily accommodated in a small room on the ground floor which my father used as his study. This room was lined with low bookcases where, behind glass doors, languished the younger son's meager portion of a fine old family library. The walls were hung with a handsome wallpaper imitating the green damask of the curtains, and as the Walter Scott tradition still lingered, and there was felt to be some obscure (perhaps Faustian) relation between the Middle Ages and culture, this sixteen-foot-square room in a New York house was furnished with a huge oak mantelpiece sustained by vizored knights, who repeated themselves at the angles of a monumental writing table, where I imagine little writing was done except the desperate calculations over which I seem to see my poor father always bent, in the vain effort to squeeze my mother's expenditure into his narrowing income. . . .

We had returned when I was ten years old from a long sojourn in Europe, so that the New York from which I received my most vivid impressions was only that tiny fraction of a big city which came within the survey of a much governessed and guarded little girl—hardly less of a little girl when she "came out" (at seventeen) than when she first arrived on the scene, at ten.

Perhaps the best way of recapturing the atmosphere of my little corner of the metropolis is to try to remember what our principle interests were —I say "our" because, being virtually an only child, since my big brothers had long since gone forth into the world, I shared either directly or indirectly in most of the household goings-on.

My father and mother entertained a great deal and dined out a great deal; but in these diversions I shared only to the extent of hanging over the stair-rail to see the guests sweeping up to our drawing-room or, conversely, my mother sweeping down to her carriage, resplendent in train, aigrette, and opera cloak. But though my parents were much invited, and extremely hospitable, the *tempo* of New York society was so moderate that not infrequently they remained at home in the evening. After-dinner visits were still customary, and on these occasions old family friends would drop in, ceremoniously arrayed in white gloves and white tie, with a tall hat, always carried up to the drawing-room and placed on the floor beside the chair of the caller—who, in due course, was regaled with the ten o'clock cup of tea which followed heavy repast at seven-thirty. On these occasions the lonely little girl that I was remained in the drawing-room later than her usual bedtime, and the kindly whiskered gentlemen encouraged her to join in the mild talk. It was all very simple and friendly, and the conversation ranged safely from Langdons, Van Rensselaers, and Lydigs to Riveses, Duers, and Schermerhorns, with an occasional allusion to the Opera (which there was some talk of transplanting from the old Academy of Music to a "real" Opera House, like Convent Garden or the Scala), or to Mrs. Scott-Siddons's readings from Shakespeare, or Aunt Mary Jones's evening receptions, or my uncle Fred Rhinelander's ambitious dream of a Museum of Art in the Central Park, or cousin John King's difficulty in housing in the exiguous quarters of the New York Historical Society a rather burdensome collection of pictures bequeathed to it by an eccentric young man whose family one did not wish to offend —a collection which Berenson, visiting it many years later, found to be replete with treasures, both French and Italian.

But the events in which I took an active part were going to church— and going to the theater. I venture to group them together because, looking back across the blurred expanse of a long life, I see them standing up side by side, like summits catching the light when all else is in shadow. Going to church on Sunday mornings was, I fear, no more than an unescapable family duty; but in the afternoon my father and I used to return alone together to the second service. Calvary Church, at the corner of Gramercy Park, was our parish church, and probably even in that day of hideous religious edifices, few less aesthetically pleasing could have been found. The service was "low," the music indifferent, and the fuliginous chancel window of the Crucifixion a horror to alienate any imaginative mind from all Episcopal forms of ritual; but the Rector, the Reverend Dr. Washburn, was a man of great learning, and possessed of a singularly beautiful voice—and I fear it was chiefly to hear Dr. Washburn read the

Evening Lessons that my father and I were so regular in our devotions. Certainly it is to Dr. Washburn that I owe the discovery of the matchless beauty of English seventeenth-century prose; and the organ-roll of Isaiah, Job, and above all, of the lament of David over the dead Absalom, always come back to me in the accents of that voice, of which I can only say that it was worthy to interpret the English Bible.

The other great emotion of my childhood was connected with a theater. Not that I was, even at a tender age, an indiscriminate theater-lover. On the contrary, something in me has always resisted the influence of crowds and shows, and I have hardly ever been able to yield myself unreservedly to a spectacle shared with a throng of people. But my distrust of theatrical representation goes deeper than that. I am involuntarily hypercritical of any impersonation of characters already so intensely visible to my imagination that anyone else's conception of them interferes with that inward vision. And this applies not only to plays already familiar to me by reading, but to any stage representation—for, five minutes after I have watched the actors in a new play, I have formed an inner picture of what they ought to look like and speak like, and as I once said, in my rash youth, to someone who had asked me if I enjoyed the theater: "Well, I always want to get up on the stage and show them how they ought to act"—a reply naturally interpreted as a proof of intolerable self-assurance.

However, in spite of my inability to immerse myself in the play, I *did* enjoy the theater in my childhood, partly because it was something new, a window opening on the foam of faëryland (or at least I always hoped to see faëryland through that window), and partly, I still believe, because most of the acting I saw in those early days in New York was really much better than any I have seen since. The principal theaters were, in fact, still in possession of good English companies, of whom the elders had played together for years, and preserved and handed on the great tradition of well-trained repertory companies, versus the evil "star" system which was so soon to crowd them out of business.

At Wallack's Theatre, still ruled by the deeply dyed and undoubtedly absurd Lester Wallack, there were such first-rate actors as old Mrs. Ponisi, Beckett, Harry Montague, and Ada Dyas; and when they deserted the classic repertory (Sheridan, Goldsmith, etc.) for the current drama, the average play they gave was about as good as the same type of play now acted by one or more out-of-focus stars with a fringe of obscure satellites. But our most exciting evenings came when what the Germans call

"guest-players" arrived from London, Berlin, or Rome with good repertory companies. Theater-going, for me, was in fact largely a matter of
listening to voices, and never shall I forget the rapture of first hearing

> *And gentlemen in England now abed*
> *Shall think themselves accursed they were not here,*

in George Rignold's vibrant barytone, when he brought Henry V to New
York.

Again and again my father took me to see (or, I might better say, to
hear) Rignold in Henry V; and it is through listening to him that I discovered the inexhaustible flexibility, the endless metrical resources, of
English blank verse. To hear the great Agincourt speech, where the clar-
ion call of mighty names—

> *Harry the King, Bedford and Exeter,*
> *Warwick and Talbot, Salisbury and Gloucester,*

is succeeded by the impetuous sweep of

> *Be in their flowing cups freshly remembered,*

and that in turn by the low still music of

> *We few, we happy few, we band of brothers—*

was to be initiated once for all into some of the divinest possibilities of
English prosody.

Since those faroff days I have never heard of George Rignold (who was,
I think, a Colonial), and have no reason to suppose that he ever made a
name for himself on the London stage; but I am sure he was a great
interpreter of English verse, and in that play—the only one I ever saw
him in—a great actor.

Only once, on another, later, occasion, did the theater of my childhood
give me an emotional experience of such rare quality; and that was when
a *"Gastspielerin"* from some distinguished German company appeared at
the Amberg Theatre in "Iphigenie auf Tauris," and I heard Iphigenia's
opening speech

> *Heraus in eure Schatten, rege Wipflen*

spoken with the awed simplicity of a priestess addressing the divinity she
served. When, by contrast, I remember the exasperation and disgust with
which I assisted at the Salzburg production of "Faust" for the million, I

can only conclude that the nineteenth century, in spite of its supposed shortcomings, knew more about interpreting poetry than we do.

In the way of other spectacles New York did not as yet provide much. There was in fact only the old Academy of Music, where Campanini, in his prime, warbled to an audience still innocently following the eighteenth-century tradition that the Opera was a social occasion, invented to stimulate conversation; but my recollection of those performances is not clear, for, by the time I was judged old enough to be taken to them, the new Opera House was inaugurated, and with it came Wagner, and with Wagner a cultivated and highly musical German audience in the stalls, which made short work of the chatter in the boxes. I well remember the astonishment with which we learned that it was "bad form" to talk during the acts, and the almost immediate compliance of the box-audience with this new rule of politeness, which thereafter was broken only by two or three thick-skinned newcomers in the social world.

Apart from the Opera, the only popular entertainments I can recall were Barnum's three-ring circus (a sort of modern ocean liner before the letter)—and Moody and Sankey's revivalist meetings. I group the two in no spirit of disrespect to the latter, but because both were new and sensational, and both took place in the old Madison Square Garden, at that time New York's only large auditorium, where prize fights and circuses placidly alternated with religious revivals, without any sign of public disapproval. But I must add that, sincere as no doubt the protagonists were, there was a theatrical element in their call to religion which, in those pre-Eddyan days, deeply offended the taste of many people; and certainly, among the throngs frequenting their meetings many avowedly went for the sake of Sankey's singing rather than of his companion's familiar chats with the Almighty. Though America has always been the chosen field of sensational religious performances, the New York of my childhood was still averse to any sort of pious exhibitionism; but as I was never allowed to assist at the Moody and Sankey meetings, my impression of them is gathered entirely from the comments of my father's friends, from whom I fear Saint Francis of Assisi and Savonarola would have received small encouragement. My mother, at any rate, gave none to the revivalists; and my father and I had to content ourselves with the decorous beauty of Evening Prayer at Calvary Church.

From all this it will be seen that the New York of those days was a place in which external events were few and unexciting, and little girls had mostly to *"be happy and building at home."*

"Yet" (as Stevenson's poem continues)

> *Yet as I saw it, I see it again,*
> *The kirk and the palace, the ships and the men,*
> *And as long as I live, and where'er I may be,*
> *I'll always remember my town by the sea—*

a town full indeed for me of palaces and ships, though the palaces came out of the "Tempest," "Endymion," and "Kubla Khan," and the ships were anchored on the schoolroom floor, ready to spread their dream-sails to all the winds of my imagination.

New York life as recalled by Clarence Day is somewhat less pretentious and rigid than the world of Edith Wharton, but the period is the same—New York in the 1870s, when the Day family occupied a house just below Forty-ninth Street on Madison Avenue, a socially acceptable location right near the Columbia College campus, then located where Rockefeller Center is now.

Clarence Day

The essayist and artist Clarence Day (1874–1935) was born in New York, and although he suffered from ill-health for most of his life, he was a contributor to *The New Yorker* from its beginnings. He created a durable classic in *Life with Father,* from which the following selection is taken. Published in the year of his death, it was turned into a play in 1939 and established a record of 3224 performances.

Father's Home Disappears

Father wanted to buy a home that would be permanent. He had been married five years, and he felt that it was high time to settle down once and for all. The little house at 251 Madison Avenue, which had been all right for a young bride and groom, was getting too small, now that there were boys in the family.

Grandpa Day smiled and told Mother that there was no such thing in New York as permanence, and that he had been forced out of four comfortable homes in his day. Father agreed that this had been so in the old days, and he also admitted that of course the town was bound to keep growing, but he thought that a man who picked the right district could now settle down.

Every respectable citizen in the seventies owned his own house. A decent three- or four-story house, unencumbered by mortgages, and situated within one or possibly two blocks of Fifth Avenue—and it oughtn't to be above Fifty-ninth Street or below Washington Square. Those were the usual requirements.

Father looked around carefully, he got the most expert advice that he could, and then he used his best judgment. As a result, he selected and bought 420 Madison Avenue. This was a sunny house, just below Forty-ninth Street, it was fairly near Central Park, and it was in a new and

73

eligible district for good private residences. Brokers said that "the permanent residential quality of that whole section" was guaranteed by the fine
public edifices which had been built in the neighborhood. St. Luke's Hospital stood on Fifth Avenue, from Fifty-fourth Street to Fifty-fifth,
surrounded by big, shady trees and a broad grassy lawn. St. Patrick's
Cathedral, at Fiftieth Street, had been recently dedicated. And Columbia
College and its campus occupied a whole city block from Forty-ninth
Street to Fiftieth, and from Madison Avenue over to what is Park Avenue
now, but what was then a broad open cut full of locomotives and trains.

In the seventies, there were almost no apartments, and people didn't
move nearly so frequently as they do today. The old saying was that three
moves were as bad as a fire. This move of ours from 251 to 420 bulked as
large in my mind as the flight of the Israelites from Egypt, all except the
Red Sea, and they didn't have to carry such heavy furniture as a Victorian
family.

Mother used to tell us little stories about it for years. As I remember,
the hardest thing to handle was Uncle Hal's clock—the wedding-present
that he and Aunt Addie had given to Mother. At the top of this magnificent structure—which would have been more in place, really, if it had
been erected in Central Park—was seated a robed and amply-built
woman; below her was the clock face, and on each side, lower down, was a
man, one of whom had a hammer, and both of whom looked kind of cross.
I suppose it was an allegory of some sort, but I don't know what about.
The woman seemed to be in favor of harmony, but the two men were not.
To save this massive bronze statuary from injury Mother actually carried
it up in a cab, in her lap, bouncing about on the cobblestones, and then
went back for her five-months-old baby.

Our new home was a four-story brownstone-front house with a stoop,
and it had all the modern conveniences of 1879. It had gas-lights in every
room, even the cook's. We used kerosene lamps in the parlor, but that was
only because the gas chandelier was too high to light without climbing up
on a step-ladder. There was a convenient little gas-jet even in the cellar,
which didn't burn very well to be sure, as it had only a small bluish flame,
but which saved us from bothering with candles, which struggled to light
up the ghostly pillars and dark silent shadows. Another convenience was
that the big kitchen range had a grating in front that slid open, and a
mechanical shaker to let the cook stir the coal fire. There was a round
little Dutch oven for basting besides. In the long white-washed cellar there
was a coal-bin, a wood-bin, a wine-closet, and barrels and barrels of pota-

toes and cider and apples. And there was a fine hot-air furnace that roared and rattled and misbehaved itself wildly, which had to be wrestled with by Margaret, the cook, and probed into by Father. Most of the rooms had fireplaces too, which burned cannel coal or small logs, and gave out a fragrant glow on chilly evenings. The waitress was always lugging a coal scuttle or an armful of logs up the stairs, and until after we boys were older she had no one to help her.

On every floor except the fourth of the new house we had running water, and there were two shining tin bathtubs—one for Father and Mother and one for the rest of the family (three boys, Cousin Julia, an occasional visitor, and later a nurse and new baby). The cook and waitress didn't have a bathtub, but there was a white china water-pitcher and bowl in their bedroom, the same as in mine, and off at one end of the cellar they had a cold little water-closet.

All the plumbing was completely boxed in, of course, except in the cellar. When we opened the great, stately door of Father's bathroom and looked in there, in awe, all we saw was a long dark mahogany case in which his tin bathtub shone, and a forbidding mahogany structure beside it, three feet square and three high, with a solid closed cover on top. All the woodwork and trim of this room was somberly polished, not painted. A pure white Victorian bathrobe on a hook was the one touch of light. The walls were dark and the one little window was up in the high ceiling, where it opened into a narrow interior airshaft. The whole place had a dim, brooding tone, like a crypt in a church.

There wasn't any washstand in the bathroom—that wasn't the custom —but there was one in a box at each end of the passageway between the two bedrooms.

In nearly every room there was a bell-pull which jerked at one of the eight dangling bells that hung in a row in the kitchen. In each of the three upper hallways was a speaking tube too, and as these also connected with the kitchen, Margaret, our cook, had her hands full. The way to use a tube was to blow into it vigorously, ignoring the dust that flew out, until one of these blowings succeeded in working the whistle which was affixed to the mouthpiece below. On hearing this whistle Margaret was supposed to spring to the appropriate tube and shout loudly up it. But Margaret was so short that she had to climb up on a chair before she could do this, and then, if it was the wrong tube, get down again, move the chair, haul up all her petticoats once more to make another climb, and when she had done all this howl up the next tube instead. By that time

Father or Mother had lost patience and begun pulling a bell, and Margaret would clump upstairs to answer it, muttering to herself, "Such a house!"

On the first floor, a little above the street level, were the dining-room, pantry and parlor. On the second were Father's and Mother's rooms. The furniture in Father's room and in the dining-room was dark and severe. In Mother's room and the parlor it was dark but ornamental or rich. In all four of these rooms it was massive.

Our quarters up on the third and fourth floors were more simple. Little beds, light walls, plain hard carpets, and three shelves full of toys. Soldiers, building blocks, marbles, a Punch and Judy show, and five red iron cars. As we were all boys there were no dolls of course, and we had no books by women authors.

Our toys were made for hard wear and tear, and they got plenty of it. It was only at Christmas that any additions were made to our stock. We knew every battered lead soldier, individually, we knew almost every nicked block, we could tell at a glance just which boy every marble belonged to, except those made of clay which we called migs. And each brother had his own sacred place where his own toys were kept, except when the waitress cleaned the room and mixed everything up.

Our books were few but we read and re-read them, *Robinson Crusoe* the most. *Gulliver's Travels, Tanglewood Tales, King Solomon's Mine,* and *Pilgrim's Progress* came next. Christian's adventures were more exciting and real to me than anything in other story-books, and I was especially taken with Apollyon and poor old Giant Despair.

Down below our nursery windows, on the sidewalk, was a little gas lamp-post. A German band of three or four pieces used to come of an evening and stand under its flickering light, reading their music, and tooting away on their horns. We were thirsty for music, there were no phonographs or radios then, and we huddled in the window, squirming ecstatically, and listening to their stirring marches. Sometimes Father would stick his head out of the front door and tell them to go away and be damned, but as soon as we heard him shut it again we'd toss down our pennies, wrapped in twisted bits of paper, so that they could see them, and they'd play one more tune.

Down the murderously dark and steep flight of stairs from the dining-room was the front basement. We boys had our supper there, and sometimes we played games on the floor under Father's big billiard table.

The daylight filtered in through an iron-barred window, which looked out into our "area." Sitting on the broad window seat, we could see the legs and feet of passers-by walking along on the sidewalk above. On days when the postman was in a hurry or when nobody answered the bell, he reached in his hand through the bars, pushed this window up, and tossed in the letters.

On the mantel was a clock of black marble, shaped like a tomb from the Nile. On one wall was an engraving of Rosa Bonheur's rearing horses being led to a fair. Each of us boys had his favorite horse in that cavalcade —in fact I had three. On the opposite wall was an engraving of Landseer's "Stag at Bay." We stood and stared at him in awe. Our other heroes, Crusoe and Christian, and still more of course Gulliver, in spite of all the adventures they had, were somehow at heart pretty humdrum. That stag was quite different. He was tragic and male and magnificent.

On the other side of the room from the stag was Father's brown walnut desk, where he made entries in his ledger of investments, or his household accounts. His mood while he did this was cheerful, if he and the country were prosperous. In bad times he flung up his head in defiance, and looked at bay, like the stag.

The top of the billiard table was kept covered with a grey rubber cloth. On nights when Father went down there after dinner and lit the four hooded gas-lights and took off and folded up that cover, the whole room seemed transformed. The engravings on the walls were in darkness, but the broad top and the gleaming rims of the table were flooded with light. A scarlet ivory ball and two white ones rolled on this rich green expanse, and Father stood studying them in his snowy-white shirt-sleeves, with his polished cue, inlaid with mother-of-pearl, in his hand.

Years later when I read about how artistically the Japanese could arrange single flowers, and how it made mandarins happy to stare at Ming yellow, I thought of this scene in our basement. It was my introduction to beauty.

For the first ten or fifteen years that we lived in 420, the neighborhood got better and better. Father's judgment as to its permanence seemed fully justified. It had become thickly planted with residences in many of which friends of our family were making their homes. We had grown fond of 420 by that time. Birth and death and endless household events had taken place inside its walls, and it had become a part of ourselves.

Then business began invading upper Fifth Avenue and spreading to Madison. A butcher bought a house near us and turned it into a market. We felt he was an impudent person and bought nothing from him for months, until in an emergency Mother sent in there for a rack of lamb chops. We then discovered that this butcher was not only an upstart, he was extremely expensive, and he was catering to the fashionable Fifth Avenue families and didn't care a rap about ours.

More and more of the old houses around us were made into stores. After 1900 some of the best people left, and soon that whole district began steadily sliding downhill.

All these changes didn't at first seem as though they would last. Many owners resisted them, hoping against hope year by year. But the Indians had to give way when the white men arrived, and when a group of gigantic white buildings sprang up into the air at and around Forty-second Street, most of the old brownstone houses in our neighborhood finally disappeared too.

Father held on to his as long as he could. What drove him away at last was the noise of the new street-cars all night. The old horse-cars had had something human about them—they wouldn't have been much out of place even in ancient Rome. In size and appearance they fitted into the old human scale. The new cars were monsters, and the strident and unnatural din they made wrecked Father's sleep. After tossing actively around in his bed for what seemed to him hours, swearing resentfully at the misery they had brought into his life, he sometimes threw off his blankets and strode to the open window, in his bare feet and nightshirt, and shook his fist at them and yelled until he woke Mother up.

She slept in the back. She offered to take his front room instead. He would not give it up. She begged him at least then to stuff his ears full of cotton at night. He said he would not go through such indignities. He seemed to feel that adopting her remedies would be giving in to those street-cars. He said he'd rather move and defy them.

It was years after we left, as it happened, before I went back there. Then one day I had an appointment to keep in an office on the twelfth or thirteenth floor of the sky-scraper which had been put up on that site. We still owned the land and I knew there was now a sky-scraper there, but I hadn't seen it, I'd been living out West for some time, and after getting back I'd been ill. On my way down my mind was preoccupied by other things, and it wasn't until I stepped out of my taxi that I took a look at the street.

My nerves or my brain cells must have been unconsciously full of old memories, for apparently what I expected to find were two rows of short houses, set well back from the sidewalks, with the cheerful rattle of a wagon or two, or a cab, going by. Instead of that, there were what seemed to me immensely high ramparts that I couldn't—from the street—see the tops of. They rose up into the air directly from the inner edge of the sidewalk. I felt them crowding against me. In the street between these ramparts there was a rushing bedlam of sound—boots, roars, grindings, clashing. And on those once quiet sidewalks where we had spun our tops and slid down the railings, I found myself jostled by masses of hurrying people.

On the corner where the three pretty Lyons girls used to live, in a fat little house full of windows, there was a gigantic and grimy white tower heaving up to the sky. The sunny, irregular, red brick buildings which Columbia College once occupied, the lamp-post where the band used to play, even the flagstones were gone.

I went into the new and modern 420 and got into an elevator. Up we shot, past the floor where Father's four-poster and bureau had been, past the level of the nursery and my bedroom, on and on, up and up; and there, suspended almost in the clouds, high above our old life, was the office where I had an appointment. I don't know why I felt dizzy. I had been up in hundreds of sky-scrapers higher than this. I tried not to keep thinking of my childhood home, way down below. I pushed the button and in a moment the man inside opened the door, as casually as though everything were perfectly natural and he were living on solid earth.

The two worlds of Brooklyn Heights in the 1880s—the world below, of the docks and tenements, and the one above, of the fine houses and shipping merchants—are described by Ernest Poole in The Harbor, *from which the selection below was taken. The novel was published in 1915 and went through six editions in one month. It presents a scene very different from the one described by Truman Capote farther along in this section.*

Ernest Poole

Ernest Poole (1880–1950) was born in Chicago. He was graduated from Princeton, and after working in a New York settlement house, became the publicist for the Chicago stockyard workers' strike. As a young journalist, he specialized in articles about tenement life and labor conditions. He was *The Outlook's* correspondent in Russia during the 1905 revolution and was sent to Germany and France as a correspondent for *The Saturday Evening Post* during World War I. His novel *The Family* won the Pulitzer Prize in 1916.

from The Harbor

As I walked home from church with my mother that day the streets seemed as quiet and safe as her eyes. How suddenly tempting it seemed to me, this quiet and this safety, compared to the place where I was going. For I had decided to run away from my home and my mother that afternoon, down to the harbor to see the world. What would become of me 'way down there? What would she do if I never came back? A lump rose in my throat at the thought of her tears. It was terrible.

"All the same I am going to do it," I kept thinking doggedly. And yet suddenly, as we reached our front steps, how near I came to telling her. But no, she would only spoil it all. She wanted me always up in the garden, she wanted me never to have any thrills.

My mother knew me so well. She had seen that when she read stories of fairies, witches and goblins out of my books to Sue and me, while Sue, though two years younger, would sit there like a little dark imp, her black eyes snapping over the fights, I would creep softly out of the room, ashamed and shaken, and would wait in the hall outside till the happy ending was in plain view. So my mother had gradually toned down all the fights and the killings, the witches and the monsters, and much to my disappointment had wholly shut out the gory pirates who were for me the most frightfully fascinating of all. Sometimes I felt vaguely that for this she had her own reason, too—that my mother hated everything that had to do with the ocean, especially my father's dock that made him so gloomy and silent. But of this I could never be quite sure. I would often watch her intently, with a sudden sharp anxiety, for I loved my mother with all my soul and I could not bear to see her unhappy.

"Never on any account," I heard her say to Belle, "are the children to go down the street toward the docks."

"Yes, ma'am," said Belle. "I'll see to it."

At once I wanted to go there. The street in front of our house sloped abruptly down at the next corner two blocks through poorer and smaller houses to a cobblestone space below, over which trucks clattered, plainly on their way to the docks. So I could go down and around by that way. How tempting it all looked down there. Above the roofs of the houses, the elevated railroad made a sharp bend on its way to the Bridge, trains roared by, high over all the Great Bridge swept across the sky. And below all this and more thrilling than all, I caught glimpses of strange, ragged boys. "Micks," Belle sometimes called them, and sometimes, "Finian Mickies." Up here I had no playmates.

From now on, our garden lost its charms. Up the narrow courtway which ran along the side of the house I would slip stealthily to the front gate and often get a good look down the street before Belle sharply called me back. The longest looks, I found, were always on Sunday afternoons, when Belle would sit back there in the garden, close to the bed of red tulips which encircled a small fountain made of two white angels. Belle, who was bony, tall and grim, would sit by the little angels reading her shabby Bible. Her face was wrinkled and almost brown, her eyes now kind, now gloomy. She had a song she would sing now and then. "For beneath the Union Jack we will drive the Finians back"—is all I can remember. She told me of witches in the Scotch hills. At her touch horrible monsters rose in the most surprising places. In the bathtub, for example, when I stayed in the bath too long she would jerk out the stopper, and as from the hole there came a loud gurgle—"It's the Were-shark," Belle would mutter. And I would leap out trembling.

This old "Were-shark" had his home in the very middle of the ocean. In one gulp he could swallow a boy of my size, and this he did three times each day. The boys were brought to him by the "Condor," a perfectly hideous bird as large as a cow and as fierce as a tiger. If ever I dared go down that street and disobey my mother, the Condor would "swoop" down over the roofs, snatch me up in his long yellow beak with the blood of the last boy on it, and with thunder and lightning would carry me off far over the clouds and drop me into the Were-shark's mouth.

Then Belle would sit down to her Bible.

Sunday after Sunday passed, and still in fascinated dread I would steal quietly out to the gate and watch this street forbidden. Pointing to it one day, Belle had declared in awful tones, "Broad is the way that leadeth to destruction." But it was not broad. In that at least she was all wrong. It was in fact so narrow that a Condor as big as a cow might easily bump himself when he "swooped." Besides, there were good strong lamp-posts where a little boy could cling and scream, and almost always somewhere in sight was a policeman so fat and heavy that even two Condors could hardly lift him from the ground. This policeman would come running. My mother had said I must never be scared by policemen, because they were really good kind men. In fact, she said, it was foolish to be scared by anything ever. She never knew of Belle's methods with me.

So at last I had decided to risk it, and now the fearful day had come. I could barely eat my dinner. My courage was fast ebbing away. In the dining-room the sunlight was for a time wiped out by clouds, and I grew suddenly happy. It might rain and then I could not go. But it did not rain nor did anything I hoped for happen to prevent my plan. Belle sat down by the angels and was soon so deep in her Bible that it was plain I could easily slip up the path. Sue never looked up from her sand-pile to say, "Stop Billy! He's running away from home!" With a gulp I passed my mother's window. She did not happen to look out. Now I had reached the very gate. "I can't go! I can't open the gate!" But the old gate opened with one push. "I can't go! There is no policeman!" But yes, there he was on my side of the street slowly walking toward me. My heart thumped, I could hardly breathe. In a moment with a frantic rush I had reached the nearest lamp-post and was clinging breathless. I could not scream, I shut my eyes in sickening fear and waited for the rushing of enormous wings.

But there came no Condor swooping.

Another rush—another post—another and another!

"What's the matter with you, little feller?"

I looked up at the big safe policeman and laughed.

"I'm playing a game," I almost shouted, and ran without touching another post two blocks to the cobblestone space below. I ran blindly around it several times, I bumped into a man who said, "Heigh there!

Look out!" After that I strutted proudly, then turned and ran back with all my might up the street, and into our house and up to my room. And there on my bed to my great surprise I found myself sobbing and sobbing. It was a long time before I could stop. I had had my first adventure.

I made many Sunday trips after that, and on no one of them was I caught. For delighted and proud at what I had done I kept asking Belle to talk of the Condor, gloomily she piled on the terrors, and seeing the awed look in my eyes (awe at my own courage in defying such a bird), she felt so sure of my safety that often she would barely look up from her Bible the whole afternoon. Even on workdays over her sewing she would forget. And so I went "to destruction."

At first I stayed but a little while and never left the cobblestone space, only peering up into the steep little streets that led to the fearsome homes of the "Micks." But then I made the acquaintance of Sam. It happened through a small toy boat which I had taken down there with the purpose of starting it off for "heathen lands." As I headed across the railroad tracks that led to the docks, suddenly Sam and his gang appeared from around a freight car. I stood stock-still. They were certainly "Micks"— ragged and dirty, with holes in their shoes and soot on their faces. Sam was smoking a cigarette.

"Heigh, fellers," he said, "look at Willy's boat."

I clutched my boat tighter and turned to run. But the next moment Sam had me by the arm.

"Look here, young feller," he growled. "You've got the wrong man to do business with this time."

"I don't want to do any business," I gasped.

"Smash him, Sam—smash in his nut for him," piped the smallest Micky cheerfully. And this Sam promptly proceeded to do. It was a wild and painful time. But though Sam was two years older, he was barely any larger than I, and when he and his gang had gone off with my boat, as I stood there breathing hard, I was filled with a grim satisfaction. For once when he tried to wrench the boat from me I had hit him with it right on the face, and I had had a glimpse of a thick red mark across his cheek. I tasted something new in my mouth and spit it out. It was blood. I did this several times, slowly and impressively, till it made a good big spot on the railroad tie at my feet. Then I walked with dignity back across the tracks and up "the way of destruction" home. I walked slowly, planning as I went. At the gate I climbed up on it and swung. Then with a sudden loud cry I fell off and ran back into the garden crying, "I fell off the gate! I fell on my face!" So my cut and swollen lip was explained, and my trips were not discovered.

I felt myself growing older fast. For I knew that I could both fight and tell lies, besides defying the Condor.

In the next years, for weeks at a time my life was centered on Sam and his gang. How we became friends, how often we met, by just what means I evaded my nurse, all these details are vague to me now. I am not even sure I was never caught. But it seems to me that I was not. For as I grew to be eight years old, Belle turned her attention more and more to that impish little sister of mine who was always up to some mischief or other. There was the corner grocer, too, with whom I pretended to be staunch friends. "I'm going to see the grocer," I would say, when I heard Sam's cautious whistle in front of the house—and so presently I would join the gang. I followed Sam with a doglike devotion, giving up my weekly twenty-five cents instead of saving it for Christmas, and in return receiving from him all the world-old wisdom stored in that bullet-shaped head of his which sat so tight on his round little shoulders.

And though I did not realize it then, in my tense crowded childhood, through Sam and his companions I learned something else that was to stand me in good stead years later on. I learned how to make friends with "the slums." I discovered that by making friends with "Micks" and "Dockers" and the like, you find they are no fearful goblins, giants bursting savagely up among the flowers of your life, but people as human as yourself, or rather, much more human, because they live so close to the harbor, close to the deep rough tides of life.

Into these tides I was now drawn down—and it did me some good and a great deal of harm. For I was too little those days for the harbor.

Sam had the most wonderful life in the world. He could go wherever he liked and at any hour day or night. Once, he said, when a "feller" was drowned, he had stayed out on the docks all night. His mother always let him alone. An enormous woman with heavy eyes, I was in awe of her from the first. The place that she kept with Sam's father was called "The Sailor's Harbor." It stood on a corner down by the docks, a long, low wooden building painted white, with twelve tight-shuttered, mysterious windows along the second story, and below them a "Ladies' Entrance." In front was a small blackboard with words in white which Sam could read. "Ten Cent Dinners" stood at the top. Below came, "Coffee and rolls." Next, "Ham and eggs." Then "Bacon and eggs." And then, "To-day"—with a space underneath where Sam's fat father wrote down every morning still more delicious eatables. You got whiffs of these things and they made your mouth water, they made your stomach fairly turn against your nursery supper.

But most of our time we spent on the docks. All were roofed, and exploring the long dock sheds and climbing down into the dark holds of the square-rigged ships called "clippers," we found logs of curious mottled wood, huge baskets of sugar, odorous spices, indigo, camphor, tea, coffee, jute and endless other things. Sam knew their names and the names of the wonder-places they came from—Manila, Calcutta, Bombay, Ceylon. He knew besides such words as "hawser," "bulkhead" and "ebb-tide." And Sam knew how to swear. He swore with a fascinating ease such words as made me shiver and stare. And then he would look at me and chuckle.

"You think I'll go to hell for this, don't you," he asked me once. And my face grew hot with embarrassment, for I thought that he assuredly would.

I asked him what were heathen lands, and he said they were countries where heathen lived. And what were heathen? Cannibals. And what were they?

"Fellers that eat fellers," he said.

"Alive?" I inquired. He turned to the gang:

"Listen to the kid! He wants to know if they eat 'em alive!" Sam spat disgustedly. "Naw," he said. "First they roast 'em like any meat. They roast 'em," he added reflectively, "until their skin gets brown and bubbles out and busts."

One afternoon a carriage brought three travelers for one of the ships, a man, his wife and a little girl with shining yellow pig-tails. "To be et," Sam whispered as we stood close beside them. And then, pointing to some of the half-naked brown men that made the crew of the ship near by— "cannibals," he muttered. For a long time I stared at these eaters, especially at their lean brown stomachs.

"We're safe enough," Sam told me. "They ain't allowed to come ashore." I found this very comforting.

But what a frightful fate lay in store for the little girl with pig-tails. As I watched her I felt worse and worse. Why couldn't somebody warn her in time? At last I decided to do it myself. Procuring a scrap of paper I retired behind a pile of crates and wrote in my large, clumsy hand, "You look out—you are going to be et." Watching my chance, I slipped this into her satchel and hoped that she would read it soon. Then I promptly forgot all about her and ran off into a warehouse where the gang had gone to slide.

These warehouses had cavernous rooms, so dark you could not see to the ends, and there from between the wooden columns the things from the ships loomed out of the dark like so many ghosts. There were strange sweet smells. And from a hole in the ceiling there was a twisting chute of steel down which you could slide with terrific speed. We used to slide by the hour.

Outside were freight cars in long lines, some motionless, some suddenly lurching forward or back, with a grinding and screeching of wheels and a puffing and coughing from engines ahead. Sam taught me how to climb on the cars and how to swing off while they were going. He had learned from watching the brakemen that dangerous backward left-hand swing that lands you stock-still in your tracks. It is a splendid feeling. Only once Sam's left hand caught, I heard a low cry, and after I jumped I found him standing there with a white face. His left hand hung straight down from the wrist and blood was dripping from it.

"Shut up, you damn fool!" he said fiercely.

"I wasn't saying nothing," I gasped.

"Yes, you was—you was startin' to cry! Holy Christ!" He sat down suddenly, then rolled over and lay still. Some one ran for his mother, and after a time he was carried away. I did not see him again for some weeks.

We did things that were bad for a boy of my size, and I saw things that I shouldn't have seen—a docker crushed upon one of the docks and brought out on a stretcher dead, a stoker as drunk as though he were dead being wheeled on a wheelbarrow to a ship by the man called a "crimp," who sold this drunken body for an advance on its future pay. Sam told me in detail of these things. There came a strike, and once in the darkness of a cold November twilight I saw some dockers rush on a "scab," I heard the dull sickening thumps as they beat him.

And one day Sam took me to the door of his father's saloon and pointed out a man in there who had an admiring circle around him.

"He's going to jump from the Bridge on a bet," Sam whispered. I saw the man go. For what seemed to me hours I watched the Great Bridge up there in the sky, with its crawling processions of trolleys and wagons, its whole moving armies of little black men. Suddenly one of these tiny specks shot out and down, I saw it fall below the roofs, I felt Sam's hand like ice in mine. And this was not good for a boy of ten.

But the sight that ended it all for me was not a man, but a woman. It happened one chilly March afternoon when I fell from a dock into water covered with grease and foam, came up spluttering and terrified, was quickly hauled to the dock by a man and then hustled by Sam and the gang to his home, to have my clothes dried and so not get caught by my mother. Scolded by Sam's mother and given something fiery hot to drink, stripped naked and wrapped in an old flannel night-gown and told to sit by the stove in the kitchen—I was then left alone with Sam. And then Sam with a curious light in his eyes took me to a door which he opened just a crack. Through the crack he showed me a small back room full of round iron tables. And at one of these a man, stoker or sailor I don't know which, his face flushed red under dirt and hair, held in his lap a big fat girl half dressed, giggling and queer, quite drunk. And then while Sam whispered on and on about the shuttered rooms upstairs, I felt a rush of such sickening fear and loathing that I wanted to scream—but I turned too faint.

I remember awakening on the floor, Sam's mother furiously slapping Sam, then dressing me quickly, gripping me tight by both my arms and saying,

"You tell a word of this to your pa and we'll come up and kill you!"

That night at home I did not sleep. I lay in my bed and shivered and burned. My first long exciting adventure was over. Ended were all the thrills, the wild fun. It was a spree I had had with the harbor, from the time I was seven until I was ten. It had taken me at seven, a plump sturdy little boy, and at ten it had left me wiry, thin, with quick, nervous movements and often dark shadows under my eyes. And it left a deep scar on my early life. For over all the adventures and over my whole childhood loomed this last thing I had seen, hideous, disgusting. For years after that, when I saw or even thought of the harbor, I felt the taste of foul, greasy water in my mouth and in my soul.

So ended the first lesson.

The Lower East Side produced many world-famous figures, among them, the sculptor Jacob Epstein. Although he spent his boyhood on the swarming streets, his Russian immigrant parents were sufficiently well-off to have Polish servants, young peasant girls who went about the house with kerchiefs on their heads and unshod feet, performing the tasks forbidden to Jews on the Sabbath. To the young artist, the densely packed and racially varied humanity of his neighborhood was an inspiration, and he found plenty of subjects for his early drawings as he roamed around in Manhattan. "The New York of the pre-skyscraper period was my formation ground," he says at the end of the following selection from his autobiography, Let There Be Sculpture, *published in 1940.*

Jacob Epstein

The renowned sculptor Sir Jacob Epstein (1880–1959) went from Hester Street to a knighthood in England in 1954 where he made his home after studying with Rodin in Paris. His work, which caused great controversy because of its emphasis on power rather than prettiness, is to be found in museums throughout the world as well as in public squares. Among his best-known sculptures are *Adam, Eros,* and *Ecce Homo,* as well as portrait busts of Joseph Conrad, George Bernard Shaw, and Winston Churchill.

from Let There Be Sculpture

My earliest recollections are of the teaming East Side where I was born.

This Hester Street and its surrounding streets were the most densely populated of any city on earth; and looking back at it, I realized what I owe to its unique and crowded humanity. Its swarms of Russians, Poles, Italians, Greeks, and Chinese lived as much in the streets as in the crowded tenements; and the sights, sounds, and smells had the vividness and sharp impact of an Oriental city.

From one end to the other Hester Street was an open-air market. The streets were lined with pushcarts and peddlers, and the crowd that packed the sidewalk and roadway compelled one to move slowly.

As a child I had a serious illness that lasted for two years or more. I have vague recollections of this illness and of my being carried about a great deal. I was known as the "sick one." Whether this illness gave me a twist away from ordinary paths, I don't know; but it is possible. Sometimes my parents wondered at my being different from the other children, and would twit me about my lack of interest in a great many matters which perhaps I should have been interested in, but just wasn't. I have never found out that there was in my family an artist or anyone interested in the arts or sciences, and I have never been sufficiently interested in my "family tree" to bother. My father and mother had come to America on one of those great waves of immigration that followed persecution and pogroms in Czarist Russia and Poland. They had prospered, and I can recall that we had Polish Christian servants who still retained peasant habits, speaking no English, wearing kerchiefs, and going about on bare feet. These servants remained with us until my brother Louis, my older brother, began to grow up; and then with the sudden dismissal of the Polish girls, I began to have an inkling of sexual complications. My elder sister, Ida, was a handsome, full-bosomed girl, a brunette; and I can recall a constant coming and going of relatives and their numerous children. This family life I did not share. My reading and drawing drew me away from the ordinary interests, and I lived a great deal in the world of imagination, feeding upon any book that fell into my hands. When I had got hold of a really thick book like Hugo's *Les Misérables* I was happy, and would go off into a corner to devour it.

I cannot recall a period when I did not draw; and at school the studies that were distasteful to me, mathematics and grammar, were retarded by the indulgence of teachers who were proud of my drawing faculties, and passed over my neglect of uncongenial subjects. Literature and history interest me immensely, and whatever was graphic attracted my attention. Later, I went to the Art Students' League uptown and drew from models and painted a little, but my main studies remained in this quarter where I was born and brought up. When my parents moved to a more respectable and duller part of the city, it held no interest whatever for me. I hired a room in Hester Street in a wooden, ramshackle building that seemed to date back at least a hundred years and, from my window overlooking the market, made drawings daily. I could look down upon the moving mass below and watch them making purchases, bartering, and gossiping. Opposite stood carpenters, washerwomen, and day workers, gathered with their tools in readiness to be hired. Every type could be found here, and for the purpose of drawing I would follow a character until his appearance was sufficiently impressed on my mind for me to make a drawing. A character who interested me particularly was a tall, lean, bearded young man, with the ascetic face of a religious fanatic, who wandered through the streets lost in a profound melancholy. His hair grew to his shoulders, and upon this was perched an old bowler hat. He carried a box in one hand, and as he passed the pushcarts, the vendors would put food into his box, here an apple, there a herring. He was a holy man, and I followed him into synagogues, where he brooded and spent his nights and days.

On one occasion I was taken to see the Chief Rabbi, a man of great piety who had been brought from Poland to act as the Chief Rabbi; but, as New York Jews do not acknowledge a central authority, he never attained this position. An attempt to use him to monopolize the Kosher meat industry was indignantly rejected. This sage and holy man lived exactly as he would in a Polish city, with young disciples, in ringlets (*payes*), who attended him as he was very infirm, lifting him into his chair and out of it, and solicitous of his every movement. The patriarchal simplicity of this house much impressed me. The New York Ghetto at that time was a city transplanted from Poland. Parallel with all this was the world of the "intelligentsia," the students, journalists, scholars, advanced people, socialists, anarchists, free thinkers, and even "free lovers." Newspapers in Yiddish, Yiddish theaters, literary societies, clubs of all kinds for educational purposes, night classes abounded; and I helped organize an exhibition of paintings and drawings by young men of the quarter. There existed a sort of industry in enlarging and coloring photographs, working them up in crayon; and there were shops that did a thriving trade in this. I had student friends who, to earn money, put their hands to this hateful work, and by industry could earn enough to go on with more serious studies. I never had to do this, as I could always sell my drawings.

I kept the room on Hester Street until, on returning to it one morning, I found it burned to the ground, and my charred drawings (hundreds of them), floating about in water with dead cats. I had to find another room, this time in a tenement with clothing workers, where I restarted my studies. I never remember giving up this second room; perhaps because of that it has returned to me in dreams with a strange persistence. Even in Paris and in London, in my dreams I find myself in the room as I left it, filled with drawings of the people of the East Side.

The many races in this quarter were prolific. Children by hundreds played upon the hot pavements and in the alleys. Upon the fire escapes and the roofs the tenement-dwellers slept for coolness in summer. I knew well the roof life in New York, where all East Side boys flew kites; I knew the dock life on the East and West sides; I swam in the East River and the Hudson. To reach the river the boys from the Jewish quarter would have to pass through the Irish quarter; and that meant danger and fights with the gangs of that quarter, the children of Irish immigrants.

The Jewish quarter was bounded on one side by the Bowery. At the time, this street was one long line of saloons, crowded at night by visitors to the city, sailors, and prostitutes. As a boy I could watch through the doors at night the strange garish performers, singers and dancers; and the whole turbulent night life was, to my growing eager mind, of never-ending interest. I recall Steve Brodie's saloon with its windows filled with photographs of famous boxers, and the floor inlaid with silver dollars. For a boy a tour along the Bowery was full of excitement. When you reached Chinatown, crooked Mott Street leading to Pell Street, you could buy a stick of sugar cane for one cent and, chewing it, look into the Chinese shop windows, or even go into the temple, all scarlet and gilding, with gilded images. The Chinamen had a curious way of slipping into their houses, suddenly, as into holes; and I used to wonder at the young men with smooth faces like girls. Chinese children were delightful when you saw them, but no Chinese women were to be seen. Along the west front, on the Hudson side, you saw wagons being loaded with large bunches of bananas and great piles of melons. Bananas would drop off the over-loaded wagons; you picked them up, and continued until you came to the open-air swimming baths with delightful sea water. I was a great frequenter of these swimming places, and went there until they shut down in November for the winter.

At this period New York was the city of ships of which Whitman wrote. I haunted the docks and watched the ships from all over the world being loaded and unloaded. Sailors were aloft in the rigging, and along the docks horses and mules drew heavy drays; oyster boats were bringing their loads of oysters and clams; and the shrieks and yells of sirens and the loud cries of overseers made a terrific din. At the Battery, newly arrived immigrants, their shoulders laden with packs, hurried forward; and it must have been with much misgiving that they found their first steps in the New World greeted with the hoots and jeers of hooligans. I can still see them hurrying to gain the Jewish quarter and finding refuge among friends and relatives. I often traveled the great stretch of Brooklyn Bridge, which I crossed hundreds of times on foot, and watched the wonderful bay with its steamers and ferryboats. The New York of the pre-skyscraper period was my formation ground. I knew all its streets and the water-side; I made excursions into the suburbs: Harlem, Yonkers, Long Island; Coney Island I knew well, and Rockaway, where I bathed in the surf. I explored Staten Island, then not yet built upon, and the Palisades with their wild rocks leading down to the Hudson River.

The slums and ghettos of the present are a world away from the Lower East Side at the end of the nineteenth century. Many of the laws that aimed to improve living conditions in the tenements were the result of the crusading activities of Jacob Riis, whose book How the Other Half Lives *inspired Theodore Roosevelt's program of reforms. The selection below originally appeared as an article in the December 1897 issue of* Century Magazine.

Jacob Riis

Jacob Riis (1849–1914) was born in Denmark and came to the United States in 1870 when he was twenty-one years old. As a police reporter for the *New York Tribune,* and later for the *Evening Sun,* he made the Lower East Side his specialty. He was also a gifted photographer, and many of his photographs—of sweatshops, criminal hangouts, and slum interiors—are a document of the horrors he tried to correct. His best-known book is *The Making of an American,* published in 1901.

Merry Christmas in the Tenements

It was just a sprig of holly, with scarlet berries showing against the green, stuck in, by one of the office boys probably, behind the sign that pointed the way up to the editorial rooms. There was no reason why it should have made me start when I came suddenly upon it at the turn of the stairs; but it did. Perhaps it was because that dingy hall, given over to dust and drafts all the days of the year, was the last place in which I expected to meet with any sign of Christmas; perhaps it was because I myself had nearly forgotten the holiday. Whatever the cause, it gave me quite a turn.

I stood, and stared at it. It looked dry, almost withered. Probably it had come a long way. Not much holly grows about Printing-House Square, except in the colored supplements, and that is scarcely of a kind to stir tender memories. Withered and dry, this did. I thought, with a twinge of conscience, of secret little conclaves of my children, of private views of things hidden from mama at the bottom of drawers, of wild flights when papa appeared unbidden in the door, which I had allowed for once to pass unheeded. Absorbed in the business of the office, I had hardly thought of Christmas coming on, until now it was here. And this sprig of holly on the wall that had come to remind me,—come nobody knew how far,—did it grow yet in the beech-wood clearings, as it did when I gathered it as a boy, tracking through the snow? "Christ-thorn" we called it in our Danish tongue. The red berries, to our simple faith, were the drops of blood that fell from the Saviour's brow as it drooped under its cruel crown upon the cross.

Back to the long ago wandered my thoughts: to the moss-grown beech in which I cut my name, and that of a little girl with yellow curls, of blessed memory, with the first jack-knife I ever owned; to the story-book with the little fir-tree that pined because it was small, and because the hare jumped over it, and would not be content though the wind and the sun kissed it, and the dews wept over it, and told it to rejoice in its young life; and that was so proud when, in the second year, the hare had to go round it, because then it knew it was getting big,—Hans Christian Andersen's story, that we loved above all the rest; for we knew the tree right well, and the hare; even the tracks it left in the snow we had seen. Ah, those were the Yule-tide seasons, when the old Domkirke shone with a thousand wax candles on Christmas eve; when all business was laid aside to let the world make merry one whole week; when big red apples were roasted on the stove, and bigger doughnuts were baked within it for the long feast! Never such had been known since. Christmas to-day is but a name, a memory.

A door slammed below, and let in the noises of the street. The holly rustled in the draft. Some one going out said, "A Merry Christmas to you all!" in a big, hearty voice. I awoke from my reverie to find myself back in New York with a glad glow at the heart. It was not true. I had only forgotten. It was myself that had changed, not Christmas. That was here, with the old cheer, the old message of good-will, the old royal road to the heart of mankind. How often had I seen its blessed charity, that never corrupts, make light in the hovels of darkness and despair! how often watched its spirit of self-sacrifice and devotion in those who had, besides themselves, nothing to give! and as often the sight had made whole my faith in human nature. No! Christmas was not of the past, its spirit not dead. The lad who fixed the sprig of holly on the stairs knew it; my reporter's notebook bore witness to it. Witness of my contrition for the wrong I did the gentle spirit of the holiday, here let the book tell the story of one Christmas in the tenements of the poor.

It is evening in Grand street. The shops east and west are pouring forth their swarms of workers. Street and sidewalk are filled with an eager throng of young men and women, chatting gaily, and elbowing the jam of holiday shoppers that linger about the big stores. The street-cars labor along, loaded down to the steps with passengers carrying bundles of every size and odd shape. Along the curb a string of peddlers hawk penny toys in push-carts with noisy clamor, fearless for once of being moved on by the police. Christmas brings a two-weeks' respite from persecution even to the friendless street-fakir. From the window of one brilliantly lighted store a bevy of mature dolls in dishabille stretch forth their arms appealingly to a troop of factoryhands passing by. The young men chaff the girls, who shriek with laughter and run. The policeman on the corner stops beating his hands together to keep warm, and makes a mock attempt to catch them, whereat their shrieks rise shriller than ever. "Them stockin's o' yourn 'll be the death o' Santa Claus!" he shouts after them, as they dodge. And they, looking back, snap saucily, "Mind yer business, freshy!" But their laughter belies their words. "They gin it to ye straight that time," grins the grocer's clerk, come out to snatch a look at the crowds; and the two swap holiday greetings.

At the corner, where two opposing tides of travel form an eddy, the line of push-carts debouches down the darker side-street. In its gloom their torches burn with a fitful glare that wakes black shadows among the trusses of the railroad structure overhead. A woman, with worn shawl drawn tightly about head and shoulders, bargains with a peddler for a monkey on a stick and two cents' worth of flittergold. Five ill-clad young-sters flatten their noses against the frozen pane of the toy-shop, in ecstasy at something there, which proves to be a milk-wagon, with driver, horses, and cans that can be unloaded. It is something their minds can grasp. One comes forth with a penny goldfish of pasteboard clutched lightly in his hand, and casting cautious glances right and left, speeds across the way to the door of a tenement, where a little girl stands waiting. "It 's yer Chris'mas, Kate," he says, and thrusts it into her eager fist. The black doorway swallows them up.

Across the narrow yard, in the basement of the rear house, the lights of a Christmas tree show against the grimy window-pane. The hare would never have gone around it, it is so very small. The two children are busily engaged fixing the goldfish upon one of its branches. Three little candles that burn there shed light upon a scene of utmost desolation. The room is black with smoke and dirt. In the middle of the floor oozes an oil-stove that serves at once to take the raw edge off the cold and to cook the meals by. Half the window-panes are broken, and the holes stuffed with rags. The sleeve of an old coat hangs out of one, and beats drearily upon the sash when the wind sweeps over the fence and rattles the rotten shutters. The family wash, clammy and gray, hangs on a clothes-line stretched across the room. Under it, at a table set with cracked and empty plates, a discouraged woman sits eying the children's show gloomily. It is evident that she has been drinking. The peaked faces of the little ones wear a famished look. There are three—the third an infant, put to bed in what was once a baby-carriage. The two from the street are pulling it around to get the tree in range. The baby sees it, and crows with delight. The boy shakes a branch, and the goldfish leaps and sparkles in the candle-light.

"See, sister!" he pipes; "see Santa Claus!" And they clap their hands in glee. The woman at the table wakes out of her stupor, gazes around her, and bursts into a fit of maudlin weeping.

The door falls to. Five flights up, another opens upon a bare attic room which a patient little woman is setting to rights. There are only three chairs, a box, and a bedstead in the room, but they take a deal of careful arranging. The bed hides the broken plaster in the wall through which the wind came in; each chair-leg stands over a rat-hole, at once to hide it and to keep the rats out. One is left; the box is for that. The plaster of the ceiling is held up with pasteboard patches. I know the story of that attic. It is one of cruel desertion. The woman's husband is even now living in plenty with the creature for whom he forsook her, not a dozen blocks away, while she "keeps the home together for the childer." She sought justice, but the lawyer demanded a retainer; so she gave it up, and went back to her little ones. For this room that barely keeps the winter wind out she pays four dollars a month, and is behind with the rent. There is scarce bread in the house; but the spirit of Christmas has found her attic. Against a broken wall is tacked a hemlock branch, the leavings of the corner grocer's fitting-block; pink string from the packing-counter hangs on it in festoons. A tallow dip on the box furnishes the illumination. The children sit up in bed, and watch it with shining eyes.

"We're having Christmas!" they say.

The lights of the Bowery glow like a myriad twinkling stars upon the ceaseless flood of humanity that surges ever through the great highway of the homeless. They shine upon long rows of lodging-houses, in which hundreds of young men, cast helpless upon the reef of the strange city, are learning their first lessons of utter loneliness; for what desolation is there like that of the careless crowd when all the world rejoices? They shine upon the tempter, setting his snares there, and upon the missionary and the Salvation Army lass, disputing his catch with him; upon the police detective going his rounds with coldly observant eye intent upon the out-

come of the contest; upon the wreck that is past hope, and upon the youth pausing on the verge of the pit in which the other has long ceased to struggle. Sights and sounds of Christmas there are in plenty in the Bowery. Juniper and tamarack and fir stand in groves along the busy thoroughfare, and garlands of green embower mission and dive impartially. Once a year the old street recalls its youth with an effort. It is true that it is largely a commercial effort—that the evergreen, with an instinct that is not of its native hills, haunts saloon-corners by preference; but the smell of the pine-woods is in the air, and—Christmas is not too critical—one is grateful for the effort. It varies with the opportunity. At "Beefsteak John's" it is content with artistically embalming crullers and mince-pies in green cabbage under the window lamp. Over yonder, where the mile-post of the old lane still stands,—in its unhonored old age become the vehicle of publishing the latest "sure cure" to the world,—a florist, whose undenominational zeal for the holiday and trade outstrips alike distinction of creed and property, has transformed the sidewalk and the ugly railroad structure into a veritable bower, spanning it with a canopy of green, under which dwell with him, in neighborly good-will, the Young Men's Christian Association and the Gentile tailor next door.

In the next block a "turkey-shoot" is in progress. Crowds are trying their luck at breaking the glass balls that dance upon tiny jets of water in front of a marine view with the moon rising, yellow and big, out of a silver sea. A man-of-war, with lights burning aloft, labors under a rocky coast. Groggy sailormen, on shore leave, make unsteady attempts upon the dancing balls. One mistakes the moon for the target, but is discovered in season. "Don't shoot that," says the man who loads the guns; "there's a lamp behind it." Three scared birds in the window-recess try vainly to snatch a moment's sleep between shots and the trains that go roaring overhead on the elevated road. Roused by the sharp crack of the rifles, they blink at the lights in the street, and peck moodily at a crust in their bed of shavings.

The dime-museum gong clatters out its noisy warning that "the lecture" is about to begin. From the concert-hall, where men sit drinking beer in clouds of smoke, comes the thin voice of a short-skirted singer warbling, "Do they think of me at home?" The young fellow who sits near the door, abstractedly making figures in the wet track of the "schooners," buries something there with a sudden restless turn, and calls for another beer. Out in the street a band strikes up. A host with banners advances, chanting an unfamiliar hymn. In the ranks marches a cripple on crutches. Newsboys follow, gaping. Under the illuminated clock of the Cooper Institute the procession halts, and the leader, turning his face to the sky, offers a prayer. The passing crowds stop to listen. A few bare their heads. The devoted group, the flapping banners, and the changing torch-light on upturned faces, make a strange, weird picture. Then the drum-beat, and the band files into its barracks across the street. A few of the listeners follow, among them the lad from the concert-hall, who slinks shamefacedly in when he thinks no one is looking.

Down at the foot of the Bowery is the "panhandlers' beat," where the saloons elbow each other at every step, crowding out all other business than that of keeping lodgers to support them. Within call of it, across the square, stands a church which, in the memory of men yet living, was built to shelter the fashionable Baptist audiences of a day when Madison Square was out in the fields, and Harlem had a foreign sound. The fashionable audiences are gone long since. To-day the church, fallen into premature decay, but still handsome in its strong and noble lines, stands as a missionary outpost in the land of the enemy, its builders would have said, doing a greater work than they planned. To-night is the Christmas festival of its English-speaking Sunday-school, and the pews are filled. The banners of United Italy, of modern Hellas, of France and Germany and England, hang side by side with the Chinese dragon and the starry flag—signs of the cosmopolitan character of the congregation. Greek and Roman Catholics, Jews and joss-worshipers, go there; few Protestants, and no Baptists. It is easy to pick out the children in their seats by nationality, and as easy to read the story of poverty and suffering that stands written in more than one mother's haggard face, now beaming with pleasure at the little ones' glee. A gaily decorated Christmas tree has taken the place of the pulpit. At its foot is stacked a mountain of bundles, Santa Claus's gifts to the school. A self-conscious young man with soap-locks has just been allowed to retire, amid tumultuous applause, after blowing "Nearer, my God, to thee" on his horn until his cheeks swelled almost to bursting. A trumpet ever takes the Fourth Ward by storm. A class of little girls is climbing upon the platform. Each wears a capital letter on her breast, and has a piece to speak that begins with the letter; together they spell its lesson. There is momentary consternation: one is missing. As the discovery is made, a child pushes past the doorkeeper, hot and breathless. "I am in "Boundless Love, " she says, and makes for the platform, where her arrival restores confidence and the language.

In the audience the befrocked visitor from up-town sits cheek by jowl with the pigtailed Chinaman and the dark-browed Italian. Up in the gallery, farthest from the preacher's desk and the tree, sits a Jewish mother with her three boys, almost in rags. A dingy and threadbare shawl partly hides her poor calico wrap and patched apron. The woman shrinks in the pew, fearful of being seen; her boys stand upon the benches, and applaud with the rest. She endeavors vainly to restrain them. "Tick, tick!" goes the old clock over the door through which wealth and fashion went out long years ago, and poverty came in.

Loudly ticked the old clock in time with the doxology, the other day, when they cleared the tenants out of Gotham Court down here in Cherry street, and shut the iron doors of Single and Double Alley against them.

Never did the world move faster or surer toward a better day than when the wretched slum was seized by the health officers as a nuisance unfit longer to disgrace a Christian city. The snow lies deep in the deserted passageways, and the vacant floors are given over to evil smells, and to the rats that forage in squads, burrowing in the neglected sewers. The "wall of wrath" still towers above the buildings in the adjoining Alderman's Court, but its wrath at last is wasted.

It was built by a vengeful Quaker, whom the alderman had knocked down in a quarrel over the boundary line, and transmitted its legacy of hate to generations yet unborn; for where it stood it shut out sunlight and air from the tenements of Alderman's Court. And at last it is to go, Gotham Court and all; and to the going the wall of wrath has contributed its share, thus in the end atoning for some of the harm it wrought. Tick! old clock; the world moves. Never yet did Christmas seem less dark on Cherry Hill than since the lights were put out in Gotham Court forever.

In "the Bend" the philanthropist undertaker who "buries for what he can catch on the plate" hails the Yule-tide season with a pyramid of green made of two coffins set on end. It has been a good day, he says cheerfully, putting up the shutters; and his mind is easy. But the "good days" of the Bend are over, too. The Bend itself is all but gone. Where the old pigsty stood, children dance and sing to the strumming of a cracked piano-organ propelled on wheels by an Italian and his wife. The park that has come to take the place of the slum will curtail the undertaker's profits, as it has lessened the work of the police. Murder was the fashion of the day that is past. Scarce a knife has been drawn since the sunlight shone into that evil spot, and grass and green shrubs took the place of the old rookeries. The Christmas gospel of peace and good-will moves in where the slum moves out. It never had a chance before.

The children follow the organ, stepping in the slush to the music,— bareheaded and with torn shoes, but happy,—across the Five Points and through "the Bay,"—known to the directory as Baxter street,—to "the Divide," still Chatham street to its denizens though the alderman have rechristened it Park Row. There other delegations of Greek and Italian children meet and escort the music on its homeward trip. In one of the crooked streets near the river its journey comes to an end. A battered door opens to let it in. A tallow dip burns sleepily on the creaking stairs. The water runs with a loud clatter in the sink: it is to keep it from freezing. There is not a whole window-pane in the hall. Time was when this was a fine house harboring wealth and refinement. It has neither now. In the old parlor down-stairs a knot of hard-faced men and women sit on benches about a deal table, playing cards. They have a jug between them, from which they drink by turns. On the stump of a mantel-shelf a lamp burns before a rude print of the Mother of God. No one pays any heed to the hand-organ man and his wife as they climb to their attic. There is a colony of them up there—three families in four rooms.

"Come in, Antonio," says the tenant of the double flat,—the one with two rooms,—"come and keep Christmas." Antonio enters, cap in hand. In the corner by the dormer-window a "crib" has been fitted up in commemoration of the Nativity. A soapbox and two hemlock branches are the elements. Six tallow candles and a night-light illuminate a singular collection of rarities, set out with much ceremonial show. A doll tightly wrapped in swaddling-clothes represents "the Child." Over it stands a ferocious looking beast, easily recognized as a survival of the last political campaign,—the Tammany tiger,—threatening to swallow it at a gulp if one as much as takes one's eyes off it. A miniature Santa Claus, a pasteboard monkey, and several other articles of bric-à-brac of the kind the tenement affords, complete the outfit. The background is a picture of St. Donato, their village saint, with the Madonna, "whom they worship most." But the incongruity harbors no suggestion of disrespect. The children view the strange show with genuine reverence, bowing and crossing themselves before it. There are five, the oldest a girl of seventeen, who works for a sweater, making three dollars a week. It is all the money that comes in, for the father has been sick and unable to work eight months, and the mother has her hands full: the youngest is a baby in arms. Three of the children go to a charity school, where they are fed, a great help, now the holidays have come to make work slack for sister. The rent is six dollars—two weeks' pay out of the four. The mention of a possible chance of light work for the man brings the daughter with her sewing from the adjoining room, eager to hear. That would be Christmas indeed! "Pietro!" She runs to the neighbors to communicate the joyful tidings. Pietro comes, with his new-born baby, which he is tending while his wife lies ill, to look at the maestro, so powerful and good. He also has been out of work for months, with a family of mouths to fill, and nothing coming in. His children are all small yet, but they speak English.

"What," I say, holding a silver dime up before the oldest, a smart little chap of seven—"What would you do if I gave you this?"

"Get change," he replies promptly. When he is told that it is his own, to buy toys, his eyes open wide with wondering incredulity. By degrees he understands. The father does not. He looks questioningly from one to the other. When told, his respect increases visibly for "the rich gentleman."

They were villagers of the same community in southern Italy, these people and others in the tenements thereabouts, and they moved their patron saint with them. They cluster about his worship here, but the worship is more than an empty form. He typifies to them the old neighborliness of home, the spirit of mutual help, of charity, and of the common cause against the common enemy. The community life survives through their saint in the far city to an unsuspected extent. The sick are cared for; the dreaded hospital is fenced out. There are no Italian evictions. The saint has paid the rent of this attic through two hard months; and here at his shrine the Calabrian village gathers, in the persons of these three, to do him honor on Christmas eve.

Where the old Africa has been made over into a modern Italy, since King Humbert's cohorts struck the up-town trail, three hundred of the little foreigners are having an uproarious time over their Christmas tree in the Children's Aid Society's school. And well they may, for the like has not been seen in Sullivan street in this generation. Christmas trees are rather rarer over here than on the East Side, where the German leavens the lump with his loyalty to home traditions. This is loaded with silver and gold and toys without end, until there is little left of the original green. Santa Claus's sleigh must have been upset in a snow-drift over here, and righted by throwing the cargo overboard, for there is at least a wagon-load of things that can find no room on the tree. The appearance of "teacher" with a double armful of curly-headed dolls in red, yellow, and green Mother-Hubbards, doubtful how to dispose of them, provokes a shout of approval, which is presently quieted by the principal's bell. School is "in" for the preliminary exercises. Afterward there are to be the tree and ice-cream for the good children. In their anxiety to prove their title clear, they sit so straight, with arms folded, that the whole row bends over backward. The lesson is brief, the answers to the point.

"What do we receive at Christmas?" the teacher wants to know. The whole school responds with a shout, "Dolls and toys!" To the question, "Why do we receive them at Christmas?" the answer is not so prompt. But one youngster from Thompson street holds up his hand. He knows. "Because we always get 'em," he says; and the class is convinced: it is a fact. A baby wails because it cannot get the whole tree at once. The "little mother"—herself a child of less than a dozen winters—who has it in charge cooes over it, and soothes its grief with the aid of a surreptitious sponge-cake evolved from the depths of teacher's pocket. Babies are encouraged in these schools, though not originally included in their plan, as often the one condition upon which the older children can be reached. Some one has to mind the baby, with all hands out at work.

The school sings "Santa Lucia" and "Children of the Heavenly King," and baby is lulled to sleep.

"Who is this King?" asks the teacher suddenly, at the end of a verse. Momentary stupefaction. The little minds are on ice-cream just then; the lad nearest the door has telegraphed that it is being carried up in pails. A little fellow on the back seat saves the day. Up goes his brown fist.

"Well, Vito, who is he?"

"McKinley!" shouts the lad, who remembers the election just past; and the school adjourns for ice-cream.

It is a sight to see them eat it. In a score of such schools, from the Hook to Harlem, the sight is enjoyed in Christmas week by the men and women who, out of their own pockets, reimburse Santa Claus for his outlay, and count it a joy—as well they may: for their beneficence sometimes makes the one bright spot in lives that have suffered of all wrongs the most cruel—that of being despoiled of their childhood. Sometimes they are little Bohemians; sometimes the children of refugee Jews; and again, Italians, or the descendants of the Irish stock of Hell's Kitchen and, Poverty Row; always the poorest, the shabbiest, the hungriest—the children Santa Claus loves best to find, if any one will show him the way. Having so much on hand, he has no time, you see, to look them up himself. That must be done for him; and it is done. To the teacher in this Sullivan-street school came one little girl, this last Christmas, with anxious inquiry if it was true that he came around with toys.

"I hanged my stocking last time," she said, "and he did n't come at all." In the front house, indeed, he left a drum and a doll, but no message from him reached the rear house in the alley. "Maybe he could n't find it," she said soberly. Did the teacher think he would come if she wrote to him? She had learned to write.

Together they composed a note to Santa Claus, speaking for a doll and a bell—the bell to play "go to school" with when she was kept home minding the baby. Lest he should by any chance miss the alley in spite of directions, little Rosa was invited to hang her stocking, and her sister's, with the janitor's children's in the school. And lo! on Christmas morning there was a gorgeous doll, and a bell that was a whole curriculum in itself, as good as a year's schooling any day! Faith in Santa Claus is established in that Thompson-street alley for this generation at least; and Santa Claus, got by hook or by crook into an Eighth-Ward alley, is as good as the whole Supreme Court bench, with the Court of Appeals thrown in for backing the Board of Health against the slum.

But the ice-cream! They eat it off the seats, half of them kneeling or squatting on the floor; they blow on it, and put it in their pockets to carry home to baby. Two little shavers discovered to be feeding each other, each watching the smack develop on the other's lips as the acme of his own bliss, are "cousins"; that is why. Of cake there is a double supply. It is a dozen years since "Fighting Mary," the wildest child in the Seventh-Avenue school, taught them a lesson there which they have never forgotten. She was perfectly untamable, fighting everybody in school, the despair of her teacher, till on Thanksgiving, reluctantly included in the general amnesty and mince-pie, she was caught cramming the pie into her pocket, after eying it with a look of pure ecstasy, but refusing to touch it. "For mother" was her explanation, delivered with a defiant look before which the class quailed. It is recorded, but not in the minutes, that the board of managers wept over Fighting Mary, who, all unconscious of having caused such an astonishing "break," was at that moment engaged in maintaining her prestige and reputation by fighting the gang in the next block. The minutes contain merely a formal resolution to the effect that occasions of mince-pie shall carry double rations thenceforth. And the rule has been kept—not only in Seventh-Avenue, but in every industrial school—since. Fighting Mary won the biggest fight of her troubled life that day, without striking a blow.

It was in the Seventh-Avenue school last Christmas that I offered the truant class a four-bladed penknife as a prize for whittling out the truest Maltese cross. It was a class of black sheep, and it was the blackest sheep of the flock that won the prize. "That awful Savarese," said Miss Haight, in despair. I thought of Fighting Mary, and bade her take heart. I regret to say that within a week the hapless Savarese was black-listed for banking up the school door with snow, so that not even the janitor could get out and at him.

Within hail of the Sullivan-street school camps a scattered little band, the Christmas customs of which I had been trying for years to surprise. They are Indians, a handful of Mohawks and Iroquois, whom some ill wind has blown down from their Canadian reservation, and left in these West-Side tenements to eke out such a living as they can weaving mats and baskets, and threading glass pearls on slippers and pincushions, until, one after another, they have died off and gone to happier hunting-grounds than Thompson street. There were as many families as one could count on the fingers of both hands when I first came upon them, at the death of old Tamenund, the basket-maker. Last Christmas there were seven. I had about made up my mind that the only real Americans in New York did not keep the holiday at all, when, one Christmas eve, they showed me how. Just as dark was setting in, old Mrs. Benoit came from her Hudson-street attic—where she was known among the neighbors, as old and poor as she, as Mrs. Ben Wah, and believed to be the relict of a warrior of the name of Benjamin Wah—to the office of the Charity Organization Society, with a bundle for a friend who had helped her over a rough spot—the rent, I suppose. The bundle was done up elaborately in blue cheese-cloth, and contained a lot of little garments which she had made out of the remnants of blankets and cloth of her own from a younger and better day. "For those," she said, in her French patois, "who are poorer than myself"; and hobbled away. I found out, a few days later, when I took her picture weaving mats in her attic room, that she had scarcely food in the house that Christmas day, and not the car-fare to take her to church! Walking was bad, and her old limbs were stiff. She sat by the window through the winter evening, and watched the sun go down behind the western hills, comforted by her pipe. Mrs. Ben Wah, to give her her local name, is not really an Indian; but her husband was one, and she lived all her life with the tribe till she came here. She is a philosopher in her own quaint way. "It is no disgrace to be poor," said she to me, regarding her empty tobacco-pouch; "but it is sometimes a great inconvenience." Not even the recollection of the vote of censure that was passed upon me once by the ladies of the Charitable Ten for surreptitiously supplying an aged couple, the special object of their charity, with army plug, could have deterred me from taking the hint.

Very likely, my old friend Miss Sherman, in her Broome-street cellar,—it is always the attic or the cellar,—would object to Mrs. Ben Wah's claim to being the only real American in my note-book. She is from down East, and says "stun" for stone. In her youth she was lady's-maid to a general's wife, the recollection of which military career equally condones the cellar and prevents her holding any sort of communication with her common neighbors, who add to the offense of being foreigners the unpardonable one of being mostly men. Eight cats bear her steady company, and keep alive her starved affections. I found them on last Christmas eve behind barricaded doors; for the cold that had locked the water-pipes had brought the neighbors down to the cellar, where Miss Sherman's cunning had kept them from freezing. Their tin pans and buckets were even then banging against her door. "They're a miserable lot," said the old maid, fondling her cats defiantly; "but let 'em. It 's Christmas. Ah!" she added, as one of the eight stood up in her lap and rubbed its cheek against hers, "they 're innocent. It is n't poor little animals that does the harm. It 's men and women that does it to each other." I don't know whether it was just philosophy, like Mrs. Ben Wah's, or a glimpse of her story. If she had one, she kept it for her cats.

In a hundred places all over the city, when Christmas comes, as many open-air fairs spring suddenly into life. A kind of Gentile Feast of the Tabernacles possesses the tenement districts especially. Green-embowered booths stand in rows at the curb, and the voice of the tin trumpet is heard in the land. The common source of all the show is down by the North River, in the district known as "the Farm." Down there Santa Claus establishes headquarters early in December and until past New Year. The broad quay looks then more like a clearing in a pine-forest than a busy section of the metropolis. The steamers discharge their loads of fir-trees at the piers until they stand stacked mountain high, with foot-hills of holly and ground-ivy trailing off toward the land side. An armytrain of wagons is engaged in carting them away from early morning till late at night; but the green forest grows, in spite of it all, until in places it shuts the shipping out of sight altogether. The air is redolent with the smell of balsam and pine. After nightfall, when the lights are burning in the busy market, and the homeward-bound crowds with baskets and heavy burdens of Christmas greens jostle each other with goodnatured banter,—nobody is ever cross down here in the holiday season,—it is good to take a stroll through the Farm, if one has a spot in his heart faithful yet to the hills and the woods in spite of the latter-day city. But it is when the moonlight is upon the water and upon the dark phantom forest, when the heavy breathing of some passing steamer is the only sound that breaks the stillness of the night, and the watchman smokes his lonely pipe on the bulwark, that the Farm has a mood and an atmosphere all its own, full of poetry, which some day a painter's brush will catch and hold.

Into the ugliest tenement street Christmas brings something of picturesqueness as of cheer. Its message was ever to the poor and the heavy-laden, and by them it is understood with an instinctive yearning to do it honor. In the stiff dignity of the brownstone streets up-town there may be scarce a hint of it. In the homes of the poor it blossoms on stoop and fire-escape, looks out of the front window, and makes the unsightly barber-pole to sprout overnight like an Aaron's rod. Poor indeed is the home that has not its sign of peace over the hearth, be it but a single sprig of green. A little color creeps with it even into rabbinical Hester street, and shows in the shop-windows and in the children's faces. The very feather-dusters in the peddler's stock take on brighter hues for the occasion, and the big knives in the cutler's shop gleam with a lively anticipation of the impend-ing goose "with fixin's"—a concession, perhaps, to the commercial rather than the religious holiday. Business comes then, if ever. A crowd of raga-muffins camp out at a window where Santa Claus and his wife stand in state, embodiment of the domestic ideal that has not yet gone out of fash-ion in these tenements, gazing hungrily at the announcement that "A silver present will be given to every purchaser by a real Santa Claus.—M. Levitsky." Across the way, in a hole in the wall, two cobblers are pegging away under on oozy lamp that makes a yellow splurge on the inky black-ness about them, revealing to the passer-by their bearded faces, but noth-ing of the environment save a single sprig of holly suspended from the lamp. From what forgotten brake it came with a message of cheer, a thought of wife and children across the sea waiting their summons, God knows. The shop is their house and home. It was once the hall of the tenement; but to save space, enough has been walled in to make room for their bench and bed. The tenants go through the next house. No matter if they are cramped; by and by they will have room. By and by comes the spring, and with it the steamer. Does not the green branch speak of spring and of hope? The policeman on the beat hears their hammers beat a joyous tattoo past midnight, far into Christmas morning. Who shall say its message has not reached even them in their slum?

Where the noisy trains speed over the iron highway past the second-story windows of Allen street, a cellar-door yawns darkly in the shadow of one of the pillars that half block the narrow sidewalk. A dull gleam be-hind the cobweb-shrouded windowpane supplements the sign over the door, in Yiddish and English: "Old Brasses." Four crooked and moldy steps lead to utter darkness, with no friendly voice to guide the hapless customer. Fumbling along the dank wall, he is left to find the door of the shop as best he can. Not a likely place to encounter the fastidious from the Avenue! Yet ladies in furs and silk find this door and the grim old smith within it. Now and then an artist stumbles upon them, and exults exceedingly in his find. Two holiday shoppers are even now haggling with the coppersmith over the price of a pair of curiously wrought brass candlesticks. The old man has turned from the forge, at which he was working, unmindful of his callers roving among the dusty shelves. Standing there, erect and sturdy, in his shiny leather apron, hammer in hand, with the firelight upon his venerable head, strong arms bared to the elbow, and the square paper cap pushed back from a thoughtful, knotty brow, he stirs strange fancies. One half expects to see him fashioning a gorget or a sword on his anvil. But his is a more peaceful craft. Nothing more warlike is in sight than a row of brass shields, destined for ornament, not for battle. Dark shadows chase each other by the flickering light among copper kettles of ruddy glow, old-fashioned samovars, and massive andirons of tarnished brass. The bargaining goes on. Overhead the nineteenth century speeds by with rattle and roar; in here linger the shadows of the centuries long dead. The boy at the anvil listens open-mouthed, clutching the bellows-rope.

In Liberty Hall a Jewish wedding is in progress. Liberty! Strange how the word echoes through these sweaters' tenements, where starvation is at home half the time. It is an all-consuming passion with these people, whose spirit a thousand years of bondage have not availed to daunt. It breaks out in strikes, when to strike is to hunger and die. Not until I stood by a striking cloak-maker whose last cent was gone, with not a crust in the house to feed seven hungry mouths, yet who had voted vehemently in the meeting that day to keep up the strike to the bitter end,—bitter indeed, nor far distant,—and heard him at sunset recite the prayer of his fathers: "Blessed art thou, O Lord our God, King of the world, that thou hast redeemed us as thou didst redeem our fathers, hast delivered us from bondage to liberty, and from servile dependence to redemption!"—not until then did I know what of sacrifice the word might mean, and how utterly we of another day had forgotten. But for once shop and tenement are left behind. Whatever other days may have in store, this is their day of play. The ceremony is over, and they sit at the long tables by squads and tribes. Those who belong together sit together. There is no attempt at pairing off for conversation or mutual entertainment at speechmaking or toasting. The business in hand is to eat, and it is attended to. The bridegroom, at the head of the table, with his shiny silk hat on, sets the example; and the guests emulate it with zeal, the men smoking big, strong cigars between mouthfuls. "Gosh! ain't it fine?" is the grateful comment of one curly-headed youngster, bravely attacking his third plate of chicken-stew. "Fine as silk," nods his neighbor in knickerbockers. Christmas, for once, means something to them that they can understand. The crowd of hurrying waiters make room for one bearing aloft a small turkey adorned with much tinsel and many paper flowers. It is for the bride, the one thing not to be touched until the next day—one day off from the drudgery of housekeeping; she, too, can keep Christmas.

A group of bearded, dark-browed men sit apart, the rabbi among them. They are the orthodox, who cannot break bread with the rest, for fear, though the food be kosher, the plates have been defiled. They brought their own to the feast, and sit at their own table, stern and justified. Did they but know what depravity is harbored in the impish mind of the girl yonder, who plans to hang her stocking overnight by the window! There is no fireplace in the tenement. Queer things happen over here, in the strife between the old and the new. The girls of the College Settlement, last summer, felt compelled to explain that the holiday in the country which they offered some of these children was to be spent in an Episcopal clergyman's house, where they had prayers every morning. "Oh," was the indulgent answer, "they know it isn't true, so it won't hurt them."

The bell of a neighboring church-tower strikes the vesper hour. A man in working-clothes uncovers his head reverently, and passes on. Through the vista of green bowers formed of the grocer's stock of Christmas trees a passing glimpse of flaring torches in the distant square is caught. They touch with flame the gilt cross towering high above the "White Garden," as the German residents call Tompkins Square. On the sidewalk the holy-eve fair is in its busiest hour. In the pine-board booths stand rows of staring toy dogs alternately with plaster saints. Red apples and candy are hawked from carts. Peddlers offer colored candles with shrill outcry. A huckster feeding his horse by the curb scatters, unseen, a share for the sparrows. The cross flashes white against the dark sky.

In one of the side-streets near the East River has stood for thirty years a little mission church, called Hope Chapel by its founders, in the brave spirit in which they built it. It has had plenty of use for the spirit since. Of the kind of problems that beset its pastor I caught a glimpse the other day when, as I entered his room, a rough-looking man went out.

"One of my cares," said Mr. Devins, looking after him with contracted brow. "He has spent two Christmas days of twenty-three out of jail. He is a burglar, or was. His daughter has brought him round. She is a seam-stress. For three months, now, she has been keeping him and the home, working nights. If I could only get him a job! He won't stay honest long without it; but who wants a burglar for a watchman? And how can I recommend him?"

A few doors from the chapel an alley runs into the block. We halted at the mouth of it.

"Come in," said Mr. Devins, "and wish Blind Jennie a merry Christmas." We went in, in single file; there was not room for two. As we climbed the creaking stairs of the rear tenement, a chorus of children's shrill voices burst into song somewhere above.

"This is her class," said the pastor of Hope Chapel, as he stopped on the landing. "They are all kinds. We never could hope to reach them; Jennie can. They fetch her the papers given out in the Sunday-school, and read to her what is printed under the pictures; and she tells them the story of it. There is nothing Jennie doesn't know about the Bible."

The door opened upon a low-ceiled room, where the evening shades lay deep. The red glow from the kitchen stove discovered a jam of children, young girls mostly, perched on the table, the chairs, in each other's laps, or squatting on the floor; in the middle of them, a little old woman with heavily veiled face, and wan, wrinkled hands folded in her lap. The singing ceased as we stepped across the threshold.

"Be welcome," piped a harsh voice with a singular note of cheerfulness in it. "Whose step is that with you, pastor? I don't know it. He is welcome in Jennie's house, whoever he be. Girls, make him to home." The girls moved up to make room.

"Jennie has not seen since she was a child," said the clergyman, gently, "but she knows a friend without it. Some day she shall see the great Friend in his glory, and then she shall be Blind Jennie no more."

The little woman raised the veil from a face shockingly disfigured, and touched the eyeless sockets. "Some day," she repeated, "Jennie shall see. Not long now—not long!" The pastor patted her hand. The silence of the dark room was broken by Blind Jennie's voice, rising cracked and quavering: "Alas! and did my Saviour bleed?" The shrill chorus burst in:

> *It was there by faith I received my sight,*
> *And now I am happy all the day.*

The light that falls from the windows of the Neighborhood Guild, in Delancey street, makes a white path across the asphalt pavement. Within there is mirth and laughter. The Tenth Ward Social Reform Club is having its Christmas festival. Its members, poor mothers, scrubwomen,—the president is the janitress of a tenement near by,—have brought their little ones, a few their husbands, to share in the fun. One little girl has to be dragged up to the grab-bag. She cries at the sight of Santa Claus. The baby has drawn a woolly horse. He kisses the toy with a look of ecstatic bliss, and toddles away. At the far end of the hall a game of blindman's-buff is starting up. The aged grand-mother, who has watched it with growing excitement, bids one of the settlement workers hold her grand-child, that she may join in; and she does join in, with all the pent-up hunger of fifty joyless years. The worker, looking on, smiles; one has been reached. Thus is the battle against the slum waged and won with the child's play.

Tramp! tramp! comes to-morrow upon the stage. Two hundred and fifty pairs of little feet, keeping step, are marching to dinner in the News-boys' Lodging-house. Five hundred pairs more are restlessly awaiting their turn upstairs. In prison, hospital, and almshouse to-night the city is host, and gives of her plenty. Here an unknown friend has spread a generous repast for the waifs who all the rest of the days shift for themselves as best they can. Turkey, coffee, and pie, with "vegetubles" to fill in. As the file of eagle-eyed youngsters passes down the long tables, there are swift move-ments of grimy hands, and shirt-waists bulge, ragged coats sag at the pock-ets. Hardly is the file seated when the plaint rises: "I ain't got no pie! It got swiped on me." Seven despoiled ones hold up their hands.

The superintendent laughs—it is Christmas eve. He taps one tenta-tively on the bulging shirt. "What have you here, my lad?"

"Me pie," responds he, with an innocent look; "I wuz scart it would get stole."

A little fellow who has been eying one of the visitors attentively takes his knife out of his mouth, and points it at him with conviction.

"I know you," he pipes. "You 're a p'lice commissioner. I seen yer picter in the papers. You're Teddy Roosevelt!"

The clatter of knives and forks ceases suddenly. Seven pies creep stealthily over the edge of the table, and are replaced on as many plates. The visitors laugh. It was a case of mistaken identity.

Farthest down-town, where the island narrows toward the Battery, and warehouses crowd the few remaining tenements, the somber-hued colony of Syrians is astir with preparation for the holiday. How comes it that in the only settlement of the real Christmas people in New York the corner saloon appropriates to itself all the outward signs of it? Even the floral cross that is nailed over the door of the orthodox church is long withered and dead: it has been there since Easter, and it is yet twelve days to Christmas by the belated reckoning of the Greek Church. But if the houses show no sign of the holiday, within there is nothing lacking. The whole colony is gone a-visiting. There are enough of the unorthodox to set the fashion, and the rest follow the custom of the country. The men go from house to house, laugh, shake hands, and kiss each other on both cheeks, with the salutation, "Every year and you are safe," as the Syrian guide renders it into English; and a nonprofessional interpreter amends it: "May you grow happier year by year." Arrack made from grapes and flavored with aniseed, and candy baked in little white balls like marbles, are served with the indispensable cigarette; for long callers, the pipe.

In a top-floor room of one of the darkest of the dilapidated tenements, the dusty window-panes of which the last glow in the winter sky is tinging faintly with red, a dance is in progress. The guests, most of them fresh from the hillsides of Mount Lebanon, squat about the room. A reed-pipe and a tambourine furnish the music. One has the center of the floor. With a beer-jug filled to the brim on his head, he skips and sways, bending, twisting, kneeling, gesturing, and keeping time, while the men clap their hands. He lies down and turns over, but not a drop is spilled. Another succeeds him, stepping proudly, gracefully, furling and unfurling a hand- kerchief like a banner. As he sits down, and the beer goes around, one in the corner, who looks like a shepherd fresh from his pasture, strikes up a song—a far-off, lonesome, plaintive lay. " 'Far as the hills,' " says the guide; "a song of the old days and the old people, now seldom heard." All together croon the refrain. The host delivers himself of an epic about his love across the seas, with the most agonizing expression, and in a shock- ingly bad voice. He is the worst singer I ever heard; but his companions greet his effort with approving shouts of "Yi! yi!" They look so fierce, and yet are so childishly happy, that at the thought of their exile and of the dark tenement the question arises, "Why all this joy?" The guide answers it with a look of surprise. "They sing," he says, "because they are glad they are free. Did you not know?"

The bells in old Trinity chime the midnight hour. From dark hallways men and women pour forth and hasten to the Maronite church. In the loft of the dingy old warehouse wax candles burn before an altar of brass. The priest, in a white robe with a huge gold cross worked on the back, chants the ritual. The people respond. The women kneel in the aisles, shrouding their heads in their shawls; the surpliced acolyte swings his censer; the heavy perfume of burning incense fills the hall.

The band at the anarchists' ball is tuning up for the last dance. Young and old float to the happy strains, forgetting injustice, oppression, hatred. Children slide upon the waxed floor, weaving fearlessly in and out be- tween the couples—between fierce, bearded men and short-haired women with crimson-bordered kerchiefs. A Punch-and-Judy show in the corner evokes shouts of laughter.

Outside the snow is falling. It sifts silently into each nook and corner, softens all the hard and ugly lines, and throws the spotless mantle of charity over the blemishes, the shortcomings. Christmas morning will dawn pure and white.

New Yorkers who kept an eye on the activities of the social world in the 1930s will remember news photos of an imposing woman who turned up at opera openings with a wide band across her forehead. That was Mrs. Cornelius Vanderbilt II, reigning dowager of society and the subject of her son's tribute, Queen of the Golden Age, *published in 1956, from which the selection below is taken.*

Cornelius Vanderbilt, Jr.

Cornelius Vanderbilt Jr., great-grandson of the financier and railroad executive, was born in New York in 1898. He was educated here and abroad and has variously been a reporter for the *Herald Tribune,* a Washington correspondent for the *Times,* and the editor and publisher of newspapers in Los Angeles, San Francisco, and Miami.

from Queen of the Golden Age

If I close my eyes, I can see her now against the pale satin walls of her Fifth Avenue palace, a tall, slender, excitingly beautiful woman in a gold lamé gown by Worth.

Above Grace Vanderbilt's famous drawing room were wardrobes filled with hundreds of other Worth and Pacquin creations, many of them so laden with jet and pearls and embroidery that they could not be hung up, but lay in clouds of blue tissue paper on twelve-foot shelves. There were closets just for hats, for parasols, for shoes—five hundred pairs of shoes, with as many handbags to match. Her jewels—including a rose the size of a peony, fashioned entirely of diamonds and platinum—were said to be worth more than a million. "What do you have that's new and beautiful today?" she would ask the clerks at Tiffany's as they hurried up to her with deferential smiles.

Thirty-three servants, imported from ducal and princely households abroad, kept her mansions on Fifth Avenue in New York and on Bellevue Avenue in Newport running to perfection. She entertained every British monarch from Victoria to George VI, as well as King Albert of Belgium, the King and Queen of Spain, the crowned heads of Scandinavia and the Netherlands, and the King of Siam, to mention but a few of her royal friends. On her ocean-going yacht, the *North Star,* she wined and dined German princes and grand dukes, the Emperor Wilhelm of Germany, and the ill-fated Czar and Czarina of Russia.

Theodore Roosevelt, General Pershing, Mark Twain, Lord Rosebery, and Winston Churchill all added their luster to the brilliance of her after-dinner salons. Rubinstein practiced daily in her many-mirrored music room, the finest in New York. Melba and Caruso and the De Reszkes came to sing for her.

When distinguished visitors from abroad arrived in New York, they paid their respects to Mrs. Vanderbilt before driving to City Hall. The number of her Fifth Avenue home, 640, was almost as well-known on the Continent as 10 Downing Street is today.

To friends, she was known as the Queen or Her Grace. Spiteful tongues called her the Dowager Duchess or Kingfisher. There has never been a hostess like her. It is hard to believe there will ever be another. In a single year (and that was during the Depression) she entertained 37,000 guests. Her sway over society began in the gaslit red velvet parlors of the turn of the century and—outlasting two major wars, the Crash, bathtub gin, flappers, and café society—survived for fifty dazzling years.

One of the greatest chroniclers of life in New York was O. Henry who called his chosen city "Baghdad-on-the-Subway," and celebrated its people and places in hundreds of short stories. The hopeful occupants of rooming houses, the saloon wits, the pretentious rich, the young lovers whose parlor is Central Park, the streets and buildings as they were around 1900 are permanently present in The Four Million, *a collection of tales published in 1906 from which the following is taken.*

O. Henry

O. Henry (1862–1910) was the pen-name of William Sydney Porter, who was born in North Carolina, was a newspaperman in Texas, and tried banana culture in Central America. His career as a writer was well-launched when he became involved in an embezzling charge that resulted in his spending more than three years in a Federal prison. He continued writing under his chosen name while he was in jail, and on his release, he came to New York in 1901 where he soon achieved a reputation as one of America's great story-tellers.

Mammon and the Archer

Old Anthony Rockwall, retired manufacturer and proprietor of Rockwall's Eureka Soap, looked out the library window of his Fifth Avenue mansion and grinned. His neighbour to the right—the aristocratic clubman, G. Van Schuylight Suffolk-Jones—came out to his waiting motorcar, wrinkling a contumelious nostril, as usual, at the Italian renaissance sculpture of the soap palace's front elevation.

"Stuck-up old statuette of nothing doing!" commented the ex-Soap King. "The Eden Musée'll get that old frozen Nesselrode yet if he don't watch out. I'll have this house painted red, white, and blue next summer and see if that'll make his Dutch nose turn up any higher."

And then Anthony Rockwall, who never cared for bells, went to the door of his library and shouted "Mike!" in the same voice that had once chipped off pieces of the welkin on the Kansas prairies.

"Tell my son," said Anthony to the answering menial, "to come in here before he leaves the house."

When young Rockwall entered the library the old man laid aside his newspaper, looked at him with a kindly grimness on his big, smooth,

115

ruddy countenance, rumpled his mop of white hair with one hand and rattled the keys in his pocket with the other.

"Richard," said Anthony Rockwall, "what do you pay for the soap that you use?"

Richard, only six months home from college, was startled a little. He had not yet taken the measure of this sire of his, who was as full of unexpectedness as a girl at her first party.

"Six dollars a dozen, I think, dad."

"And your clothes?"

"I suppose about sixty dollars, as a rule."

"You're a gentleman," said Anthony, decidedly. "I've heard of these young bloods spending $24 a dozen for soap, and going over the hundred mark for clothes. You've got as much money to waste as any of 'em, and yet you stick to what's decent and moderate. Now I use the old Eureka—not only for sentiment, but it's the purest soap made. Whenever you pay more than 10 cents a cake for soap you buy bad perfumes and labels. But 50 cents is doing very well for a young man in your generation, position and condition. As I said, you're a gentleman. They say it takes three generations to make one. They're off. Money'll do it as slick as soap grease. It's made you one. By hokey! it's almost made one of me. I'm nearly as impolite and disagreeable and ill-mannered as these two old knickerbocker gents on each side of me that can't sleep of nights because I bought in between 'em."

"There are some things that money can't accomplish," remarked young Rockwall, rather gloomily.

"Now, don't say that," said old Anthony, shocked. "I bet my money on money every time. I've been through the encyclopædia down to Y looking for something you can't buy with it; and I expect to have to take up the appendix next week. I'm for money against the field. Tell me something money won't buy."

"For one thing," answered Richard, rankling a little, "it won't buy one into the exclusive circles of society."

"Oho! won't it?" thundered the champion of the root of evil. "You tell me where your exclusive circles would be if the first Astor hadn't had the money to pay for his steerage passage over?"

Richard sighed.

"And that's what I was coming to," said the old man, less boisterously. "That's why I asked you to come in. There's something going wrong with you, boy. I've been noticing it for two weeks. Out with it. I guess I could lay my hands on eleven millions within twenty-four hours, besides the real estate. If it's your liver, there's the *Rambler* down in the bay, coaled, and ready to steam down to the Bahamas in two days."

"Not a bad guess, dad; you haven't missed it far."

"Ah," said Anthony, keenly; "what's her name?"

Richard began to walk up and down the library floor. There was enough comradeship and sympathy in this crude old father of his to draw his confidence.

"Why don't you ask her?" demanded old Anthony. "She'll jump at you. You've got the money and the looks, and you're a decent boy. Your hands are clean. You've got no Eureka soap on 'em. You've been to college, but she'll overlook that."

"I haven't had a chance," said Richard.

"Make one," said Anthony. "Take her for a walk in the park, or a straw ride, or walk home with her from church. Chance! Pshaw!"

"You don't know the social mill, dad. She's part of the stream that turns it. Every hour and minute of her time is arranged for days in advance. I must have that girl, dad, or this town is a blackjack swamp forevermore. And I can't write it—I can't do that."

"Tut!" said the old man. "Do you mean to tell me that with all the money I've got you can't get an hour or two of a girl's time for yourself?"

"I've put it off too late. She's going to sail for Europe at noon day after to-morrow for a two years' stay. I'm to see her alone to-morrow evening for a few minutes. She's at Larchmont now at her aunt's. I can't go there. But I'm allowed to meet her with a cab at the Grand Central Station to-morrow evening at the 8:30 train. We drive down Broadway to Wallack's at a gallop, where her mother and a box party will be waiting for us in the lobby. Do you think she would listen to a declaration from me during that six or eight minutes under those circumstances? No. And what chance would I have in the theatre or afterward? None. No, dad, this is one tangle that your money can't unravel. We can't buy one minute of time with cash; if we could, rich people would live longer. There's no hope of getting a talk with Miss Lantry before she sails."

"All right, Richard, my boy," said old Anthony, cheerfully. "You may run along down to your club now. I'm glad it ain't your liver. But don't forget to burn a few punk sticks in the joss house to the great god Mazuma from time to time. You say money won't buy time? Well, of course, you can't order eternity wrapped up and delivered at your residence for a price, but I've seen Father Time get pretty bad stone bruises on his heels when he walked through the gold diggings."

That night came Aunt Ellen, gentle, sentimental, wrinkled, sighing, oppressed by wealth, in to Brother Anthony at his evening paper, and began discourse on the subject of lovers' woes.

"He told me all about it," said Brother Anthony, yawning. "I told him my bank account was at his service. And then he began to knock money. Said money couldn't help. Said the rules of society couldn't be bucked for a yard by a team of ten-millionaires."

"Oh, Anthony," sighed Aunt Ellen, "I wish you would not think so much of money. Wealth is nothing where a true affection is concerned. Love is all-powerful. If he only had spoken earlier! She could not have refused our Richard. But now I fear it is too late. He will have no opportunity to address her. All your gold cannot bring happiness to your son."

At eight o'clock the next evening Aunt Ellen took a quaint old gold ring from a moth-eaten case and gave it to Richard.

"Wear it to-night, nephew," she begged. "Your mother gave it to me. Good luck in love she said it brought. She asked me to give it to you when you had found the one you loved."

Young Rockwall took the ring reverently and tried it on his smallest finger. It slipped as far as the second joint and stopped. He took it off and stuffed it into his vest pocket, after the manner of man. And then he 'phoned for his cab.

At the station he captured Miss Lantry out of the gabbing mob at eight thirty-two.

"We mustn't keep mamma and the others waiting," said she.

"To Wallack's Theatre as fast as you can drive!" said Richard, loyally.

They whirled up Forty-second to Broadway, and then down the white-starred lane that leads from the soft meadows of sunset to the rocky hills of morning.

At Thirty-fourth Street young Richard quickly thrust up the trap and ordered the cabman to stop.

"I've dropped a ring," he apologized, as he climbed out. "It was my mother's, and I'd hate to lose it. I won't detain you a minute—I saw where it fell."

In less than a minute he was back in the cab with the ring.

But within that minute a crosstown car had stopped directly in front of the cab. The cab-man tried to pass to the left, but a heavy express wagon cut him off. He tried the right and had to back away from a furniture van that had no business to be there. He tried to back out, but dropped his reins and swore dutifully. He was blockaded in a tangled mess of vehicles and horses.

One of those street blockades had occurred that sometimes tie up commerce and movement quite suddenly in the big city.

"Why don't you drive on?" said Miss Lantry impatiently. "We'll be late."

Richard stood up in the cab and looked around. He saw a congested flood of wagons, trucks, cabs, vans and street cars filling the vast space where Broadway, Sixth Avenue, and Thirty-fourth Street cross one another as a twenty-six inch maiden fills her twenty-two inch girdle. And still from all the cross streets they were hurrying and rattling toward the converging point at full speed, and hurling themselves into the straggling mass, locking wheels and adding their drivers' imprecations to the clamor. The entire traffic of Manhattan seemed to have jammed itself around them. The oldest New Yorker among the thousands of spectators that lined the sidewalks had not witnessed a street blockade of the proportions of this one.

"I'm very sorry," said Richard, as he resumed his seat, "but it looks as if we are stuck. They won't get this jumble loosened up in an hour. It was my fault. If I hadn't dropped the ring we—"

"Let me see the ring," said Miss Lantry. "Now that it can't be helped, I don't care. I think theatres are stupid, anyway."

At 11 o'clock that night somebody tapped lightly on Anthony Rockwall's door.

"Come in," shouted Anthony, who was in a red dressing-gown, reading a book of piratical adventures.

Somebody was Aunt Ellen, looking like a gray-haired angel that had been left on earth by mistake.

"They're engaged, Anthony," she said, softly. "She has promised to marry our Richard. On their way to the theatre there was a street blockade, and it was two hours before their cab could get out of it.

"And oh, Brother Anthony, don't ever boast of the power of money again. A little emblem of true love—a little ring that symbolized unending and unmercenary affection—was the cause of our Richard finding his happiness. He dropped it in the street, and got out to recover it. And before they could continue the blockade occurred. He spoke to his love and won her there while the cab was hemmed in. Money is dross compared with true love, Anthony."

"All right," said old Anthony. "I'm glad the boy has got what he wanted. I told him I wouldn't spare any expense in the matter if—"

"But, Brother Anthony, what good could your money have done?"

"Sister," said Anthony Rockwall. "I've got my pirate in a devil of a scrape. His ship has just been scuttled, and he's too good a judge of the value of money to let drown. I wish you would let me go on with this chapter."

The story should end here. I wish it would as heartily as you who read it wish it did. But we must go to the bottom of the well for truth.

The next day a person with red hands and a blue polka-dot necktie, who called himself Kelly, called at Anthony Rockwall's house, and was at once received in the library.

"Well," said Anthony, reaching for his check-book, "it was a good bilin' of soap. Let's see—you had $5,000 in cash."

"I paid out $300 more of my own," said Kelly. "I had to go a little above the estimate. I got the express wagons and cabs mostly for $5; but the trucks and two-horse teams mostly raised me to $10. The motormen wanted $10, and some of the loaded teams $20. The cops struck me hardest—$50 I paid two, and the rest $20 and $25. But didn't it work beautiful, Mr. Rockwall? I'm glad William A. Brady wasn't onto that little outdoor vehicle mob scene. I wouldn't want William to break his heart with jealousy. And never a rehearsal, either! The boys was on time to the fraction of a second. It was two hours before a snake could get below Greeley's statue."

"Thirteen hundred—there you are, Kelly," said Anthony, tearing off a check. "Your thousand, and the $300 you were out. You don't despise money, do you, Kelly?"

"Me?" said Kelly. "I can lick the man that invented poverty."

Anthony called Kelly when he was at the door.

"You didn't notice," said he, "anywhere in the tie-up, a kind of a fat boy without any clothes on shooting arrows around with a bow, did you?"

"Why, no," said Kelly, mystified. "I didn't. If he was like you say, maybe the cops pinched him before I got there."

"I thought the little rascal wouldn't be on hand," chuckled Anthony. "Good-by, Kelly."

In the early 1900s, the city moved north, and with each new building boom, a new wave of immigrant families settled uptown. In what is now Spanish Harlem on East Ninety-third Street, boys from Jewish, Irish, German, and Italian families were staking their territories and setting up their gangs. One of these boys was Harpo Marx, who with his brothers lived the exciting life of the streets, wandered around in Central Park, and watched the baseball games "for free" from a promontory behind the Polo Grounds. He described some of his adventures in the following selection from his autobiography, Harpo Speaks, *published in 1961.*

Harpo Marx

Harpo Marx (1893–1964) with his eloquent silences, his childlike grin, and his fine musicianship, created a great screen personality as a member of the Marx Brothers, whose films continue to enchant not only a following that has seen them many times over, but also a young, new audience to whom they are a happy revelation. Harpo was the great favorite of a group of artists and writers, and there is a wonderful portrait of him by Dali in the collection of the Museum of Modern Art.

from Harpo Speaks

In a short time, my brother Chico was far out of my class as a sporting blood. I wasn't wise enough or nervy enough to keep up with him. Chico settled into a routine, dividing his working day between cigar store and poolroom, and latching onto floating games in his spare time, and I drifted into the streets.

Life in the streets was a tremendous obstacle course for an undersized kid like me. The toughest obstacles were kids of other nationalities. The upper East Side was subdivided into Jewish blocks (the smallest area), Irish blocks, and German blocks, with a couple of Independent Italian states thrown in for good measure. That is, the cross streets were subdivided. The north-and-south Avenues—First, Second, Third and Lexington—belonged more to the city than the neighborhood. They were neutral zones. But there was open season on strangers in the cross streets.

If you were caught trying to sneak through a foreign block, the first

121

thing the Irishers or Germans would ask was, "Hey, kid! What Streeter?"
I learned it saved time and trouble to tell the truth. I was a 93rd Streeter,
I would confess.

"Yeah? What block 93rd Streeter?"

"Ninety-third between Third and Lex." That pinned me down. I was a
Jew.

The worst thing you could do was run from Other Streeters. But if you
didn't have anything to fork over for ransom you were just as dead. I
learned never to leave my block without some kind of boodle in my
pocket—a dead tennis ball, an empty thread spool, a penny, anything. It
didn't cost much to buy your freedom; the gesture was the important
thing.

It was all part of the endless fight for recognition of foreigners in the
process of becoming Americans. Every Irish kid who made a Jewish kid
knuckle under was made to say "Uncle" by an Italian, who got his lumps
from a German kid, who got his insides kicked out by his old man for
street fighting and then went out and beat up an Irish kid to heal his
wounds. "I'll teach *you!*" was the threat they passed along, Irisher to Jew
to Italian to German. Everybody was trying to teach everybody else, all
down the line. This is still what I think of when I hear the term "progressive education."

There was no such character as "the kindly cop on the beat" in New
York in those days. The cops were sworn enemies. By the same token we,
the street kids, were the biggest source of trouble for the police. Individually and in gangs we accounted for most of the petty thievery and destruction of property on the upper East Side. And since we couldn't afford to
pay off the cops in the proper, respectable Tammany manner, they
hounded us, harassed us, chased us, and every chance they got, happily
beat the hell out of us.

One way, the only way, that all of us kids stuck together regardless of
nationality was in our cop-warning system. Much as I loathed and feared
the Mickie gang or the Bohunk gang, I'd never hesitate to give them the
highsign if I spotted a copper headed their way. They'd do the same for
me and the other 93rd Streeters.

The cops had their system, too. If a patrolman came upon a gang fight
or a front-stoop crap game and needed reinforcements in a hurry, he'd
bang his nightstick on the curb. This made a sharp *whoinnng* that could
be heard by cops on other beats throughout the precinct, and they'd come
a-running from all directions, closing in a net around the point the warning came from.

In my time I was grabbed, nabbed, chewed out and shin-whacked by the cops, but never arrested. This may sound miraculous, considering all the kinds of trouble I was able to get into, but it wasn't. My Uncle Sam the auctioneer, don't forget, was a wheel in Tammany Hall. Nephews of men in the Organization did not get arrested.

For another thing, the cops went mostly for the gangs, the most conspicuous targets, and I was not a gang boy. I was a lone wolf. This made me, in turn, more conspicuous to the gangs. Gang boys couldn't tolerate loners. They called me a "queer" and worse. Today, I guess, a kid like me would get all kinds of special attention from the authorities. They'd call me an "antisocial nonconformist"—and worse.

So my pleasures had to be secret ones. I couldn't even fly pigeons from the roof of my own house. Every time I set out a baited cage to catch some birds, the cage would be smashed or stolen. I wanted desperately to have a pet. Once I brought home a stray puppy, and fixed a nest for him in the basement of 179. I had him for exactly a week. As soon as he got used to his new home he felt frisky and began to bark. Some kids heard him and promptly stole him.

The janitor of our tenement, an elderly Bavarian plagued with corns and carbuncles, wouldn't protect my pets. He had a running feud with my family because our garbage pails were full of holes. Every time they went down the dumbwaiter for him to dump, the janitor would mutter and curse and yell up the shaft, "Hey, up dere! Hey! Dem's got *leaks* on!"

I took to spending a lot of time in Central Park, four blocks to the west, the park being a friendly foreign country. It was safe territory for lone wolves, no matter what Streeters we were.

Summers I hung around the tennis courts. I loved to watch the game, and there was always the chance I could hustle myself a tennis ball. In the wintertime the park was not so inviting, unless there's been a snowfall or a good freeze. When there was snow on the ground I'd hustle a dishpan somewhere ("hustle" being a polite word for steal), and go sliding in the park. This was a risky pleasure. A dishpan in good condition was worth five cents cash from a West Side junk dealer, and I had more than one pan swiped out from under me by bigger kids.

After a freeze they would hoist the Ice Flag in Central Park, which told the city the pond was okay for skating. Nobody was happier to see the flag than I was. I was probably the best single-foot skater in New York City.

Our family's total sports equipment was one ice skate, which had belonged to Grandma, and which Grandpa kept as a memento, like the old harp. And as the harp had no strings, the skate had no straps. I had to improvise with twine, rope, old suspenders, elastic bands, whatever I could find.

I spent many hours on the frozen pond in Central Park, skating gimpily around the edge of the ice on my one left-foot skate. I spent many more hours sitting on the ice, freezing my bottom where my pants weren't patched, tying and splicing and winding, in the endless struggle to keep the skate lashed to my foot.

Oddly enough, winter had fewer hardships for me than summer did. I could always find a warm spot somewhere when it was cold. But when the city was hot, it was hot through and through, and there was no cool spot to be found.

The only relief was temporary, like a chunk of ice from the loading platform of the ice works. That was a blessing to hold and suck on, but it didn't last long. What to do then? Only one thing to do then—go for a swim in the East River. But the way we had to swim, off the docks, was exhausting and we couldn't stay very long in the water.

You can always spot a guy who grew up poor on the East Side by watching him go for a swim. When he gets in a pool he will automatically start off with a shallow kind of breast stroke, as if he were pushing away some invisible, floating object. This was a stroke you had to use when you jumped in the East River. It was the only way you could keep the sewage and garbage out of your face.

One way of keeping your mind off the heat was making horsehair rings. We used to sneak into the brewery stables and cut big hanks of hair from the horses' tails, then braid them into rings. Horsehair rings were not only snazzy accessories to wear, three or four to a finger, but they were also negotiable. They could be swapped for marbles or Grover Cleveland buttons, and they were handy as ransom when you were ambushed by an enemy gang.

Then, suddenly one summer, rings and marbles became kid stuff to me. I found out how to use the city transportation system for free, and I was no longer a prisoner of the neighborhood. My life had new horizons. I, a mere mortal, could now go forth and behold the Gods in Valhalla—which is to say, the New York Giants in the Polo Grounds.

Trolleys were the easiest way to travel without paying. You just hopped on board after a car had started up, and kept dodging the ticket taker. If the ticket taker caught up with you, you got off and hopped on the next trolley to come along. It was more sporting to hang on the outside of the car, but you took a chance of being swatted off by a cop.

It wasn't so easy with elevated trains. You couldn't get on an El train without giving a ticket or transfer to the ticket chopper at the platform gate. To swindle the ticket chopper took a good deal of ingenuity, involving old transfers, chewing-gum cards (which happened to be the same size as tickets), some fancy forgery—and for me, thanks to Grandpa's training —sleight of hand.

Once a year the city would change its system of tickets and transfers, trying to cut down on the number of free riders. But they never came up with a system that couldn't somehow be solved by us kids.

Thus I was now a man-about-town. In my travels I found out, in the summer of 1903, how to watch the Giants play for free. That was the only sure way to beat the heat in New York. When John J. McGraw and his noble warriors took the field in the Polo Grounds, all the pains and complaints of the loyal fan faded away, and he sweltered in blissful contentment.

I was a loyal fan but I could never afford, naturally, the price of admission to the Polo Grounds. Then I discovered a spot on Coogan's Bluff, a high promontory behind the Polo Grounds, from which there was a clear view of the ballpark. Well, a clear view—yes, but clear only of the outside wall of the grandstand, a section of the bleachers, and one narrow, tantalizing wedge of the playing field.

So to tell the truth, I didn't really watch the Giants. I watched a Giant—the left fielder.

When the ball came looping or bounding into my corner of the field, I saw real live big-league baseball. The rest of the time—which was most of the time—I watched a tiny man in a white or gray uniform standing motionless on a faraway patch of grass.

Other kids collected pictures of Giants such as McGraw, McGinnitty and Matthewson. Not me. I was forever faithful to Sam Mertes, undistinguished left fielder, the only New York Giant I ever saw play baseball.

Eventually I came to forgive Sam for all the hours he stood around, waiting for the action to come his way. It must have been just as frustrating for him down on the field as it was for me up on the bluff. It was easy for pitchers or shortstops to look flashy. They took lots of chances. My heart was with the guy who was given the fewest chances to take, the guy whose hope and patience never dimmed. Sam Mertes, I salute you! In whatever Valhalla you're playing now, I pray that only right-handed pull-hitters come to bat, and the ball comes sailing your way three times in every inning.

Much as I ran away from it every chance I got, the home neighborhood was not altogether a dreary slum. It had its share of giants too, men and women who belonged to the Outside World, who brought glitter and excitement into the lives of the rest of us East Siders.

Such a luminary was Mr. Jergens, who ran the ice-cream parlor around the corner on Third Avenue. Mr. Jergens built and operated the first automobile in the neighborhood, a jaunty little electric runabout. When the runabout came cruising through our street, older kids would jump up and down and throw their caps under the car, yelling, "Get a horse!"

If Mr. Jergens was disturbed by the jeering mobs, he never showed it. He drove straight on, leaning over the tiller, which he held with a death grip, squinting at the horizon of Lexington Avenue like Christopher Columbus sailing for the New World.

I was one of the privileged few in the neighborhood who got to touch the runabout. Mr. Jergens had ordered a suit from Frenchie, and I went along when he delivered it. Mr. Jergens saw me admiring the car, in the alley behind the ice-cream parlor. He grinned at me and promised to take me for a ride. Boy oh boy oh boy! I had heard that the runabout could zoom down the brewery hill at a speed of fifteen miles an hour!

But I never got my ride in the automobile. After making his promise to me, Mr. Jergens went upstairs and tried on his new suit and it was years before he ever spoke to me or my father again.

There were two true aristocrats in our neighborhood, Mr. Ruppert and Mr. Ehret, the owners of the big breweries. Jake Ruppert's mansion was on the corner of 93rd and Park Avenue. This was a fabulous place to me, for the principal reason that Ruppert's garden contained a row of peach trees, which once a year bore lovely, luscious peaches.

Ruppert's garden also contained two huge watchdogs who ranged along the inside of the iron spiked fence, on the alert for peach poachers. It was the theory of Ruppert's caretaker that the dogs would be more vicious if they were kept hungry. This theory backfired. I used to hustle a bag of fat and meat scraps from a butcher, feed the starving dogs through the fence until they got friendly and sleepy, then shinny over the spikes and fill my shirt with ripe peaches.

No fruit ever tasted so sweet as stolen fruit, which was about the only kind I ever had until I became, at the age of eleven, a full-time working man.

There was a spectacular pageant on our street, every weekday of the year. The show went on at nine in the morning, and was repeated at six in the evening. This was the passing of Mr. Ehret through 93rd Street, to and from the Ehret Brewery.

Mr. Ehret rode in a dazzling black carriage, pulled by a team of prize black stallions. A footman and a coachman, in regal uniforms of blue and gold, sat on top of the carriage. The eastern half of our block sloped downhill toward the East River and when the brewer's carriage reached the top of the slope, in the morning, the coachman would stand up and shake the reins and the stallions would charge down the hill in full gallop.

When they passed our house, the stallions were wild-eyed and foaming at their bits, and the cobblestones rang like anvils. When they returned at night, straining against the rise, you could see the sparks fly up from their pounding hooves.

Thunder and lightning. Pomp and circumstance. Glory and magnificence. I wonder how a poor kid who never watched a brewer ride to his brewery, who never shivered with goose bumps when the coachman rose to start the downhill gallop, could ever know that there was another kind of life, the Good Life.

Thanks for the show, Mr. Ehret. Thanks for the peaches, Mr. Ruppert. Sorry I never liked beer.

Then there were the Brownstone People. They weren't as high and mighty as the brewers, but I think they furthered my education about the outside world just as much.

We lived on the tenement side of 93rd Street, the north side. Facing us, on the south, was a row of one-family brownstone town houses. They were not cluttered in front with ugly fire escapes, like the tenements. They were decorated with ivy and window-boxes full of flowers.

What went on inside those elegant houses was something I found impossible to imagine, like the sound of harp music. While other kids wondered about life on Mars or the Moon, I used to wonder about life across the street. For hours at a time, I watched the brownstones and saw the Brownstone People come and go. There were two whom I watched and waited for in particular.

One was a dashing young lady named Marie Wagner, who was a well-known tennis player of the day. I took to following Miss Wagner to Central Park to the courts, where I became her self-appointed ball retriever. The courts had no backstops, and I ran myself ragged chasing down ten-

nis balls. But it was worth it. For an afternoon's work, Miss Wagner
would reward me with an old ball.

I couldn't expect to own a tennis ball for longer than a day or two
before it got swiped by some older kid, so whenever Miss Wagner paid me
off I'd sprint for home and get in as many licks as I could before the
bandits turned up. I was conducting a sort of one-man Olympics, compet-
ing against myself for new world's records in Tennis Ball Bouncing
Against the Stoop of 179 East 93rd Street, New York City.

I kept hoping that one afternoon I'd still be bouncing and catching the
ball when Miss Wagner came home. Then she might see me from across
the street, and know that I wasn't using the trophy she'd given me in any
childish, ungrateful way. I was improving my game.

But she never saw me in action. This was a lingering, cruel disappointment. I had quite a crush on the dashing Miss Wagner.

I regret to confess that the time I set the All-Time Stoop Bouncing
World's Record of 341 without a miss, I didn't use a ball of Marie Wagner's. By that time I had become a pretty worldly fellow. I still hung
around the tennis courts in the park, but I had turned pro. I retrieved for
anybody and everybody, not for love, but strictly for the loot.

My other idol of the brownstones was a gentleman named Mr. Burns, a
retired attorney. Mr. Burns was as elegant as his house. When he stepped
forth for his daily stroll to Central Park he wore a derby hat, a trim,
faintly striped suit, suede gloves, and narrow patent-leather shoes. When
the sun shone he carried a walking stick with a silver top. When it looked
like rain he swung a long, furled umbrella with a silver handle.

Once I asked Frenchie if Mr. Burns was rich and famous. Frenchie's
answer baffled me. He nodded and said, mysteriously, "British cut."

The most astonishing thing about Mr. Burns, however, was the tipping
of his hat. On the street he tipped his hat to everybody. He even tipped
his hat to kids! I used to lurk on the corner of 93rd and Lex, waiting for
Mr. Burns to start his daily walk. When he came briskly by, headed for
the park, he never appeared to see me. But as he passed he never failed to
switch his stick or umbrella from right hand to left and tip his derby.

This was a grand and satisfying moment in the life of a lone-wolf,
friendless kid.

In my daydreams I knew now what it was going to be like on the abso-
lute pinnacle of worldly success. I would be riding down Third Avenue in
my black carriage pulled by four black stallions, munching on ripe, red
peaches from the bushel on the seat beside me. As I tipped my derby to
people on the streets, right and left, I saw them smile with gratitude, and

I could hear the cop saying as he held back the crowd, "Stand back, now! Make way for Mr. Marx, the famous tennis star and left-fielder with the silver handle on his walking stick!" When I passed a peaked-face, shaggy-top kid with horsehair rings on his fingers, I tossed him a peach and a brand-new tennis ball. The kid said, "Bless you, sir!" and a great shout went up from the crowd, and the cop, grinning from ear to ear, saluted me with his nightstick.

I tipped my derby again, to the north and to the south, and ordered my coachman to start the gallop.

At Christmastime, the brownstones across the street were even more remote from my tenement world. Wreaths of holly appeared on the doors and in the windows, and at night I could see Christmas trees inside, glowing with the lights of candles.

The one thing I remembered that Miss Flatto had taught me, in P. S. 86, was the legend of Santa Claus. I was entranced by it, but being a young cynic, I told myself it was all a bunch of Irish malarkey. The only time anybody got presents in our family was when Uncle Al came to visit or when Frenchie happened to get paid for two suits at a crack.

Nevertheless, on the night of December 24, a month after my ninth birthday, I decided to give Santa Claus a chance to make good. I hung one of my stockings in the airshaft, pinned under the window. The airshaft, I figured, was the nearest thing to a chimney in our house. Maybe even better. A lot more room for a fat and jolly old guy to shinny down.

On Christmas morning, my stocking was still empty. I didn't tell anybody about it. I was too ashamed of being played for a sucker.

Yet, a year later, when I saw the holly on the brownstones, and the candles flickering on the Christmas trees, I swallowed my pride and hung my stocking again. This time, to bolster my faith, I confessed to Chico that night what I had done. Chico wasn't scornful, or even surprised. He knew all about the Christmas stocking deal. "But," he said, "you got to figure the odds. Figure how many airshafts on 93rd Street, let alone in the rest of the city, Sandy Claus has to shinny down in one night. Then you figure he's got to take care of the Irishers and Bohunks and Eyetalians before he gets around to the Jews. Right? So what kind of odds is that?"

Chico was being sensible and convincing as usual. Still, it was a question of faith versus mathematics. A stubborn glimmer of faith still burned inside me. I left my stocking in the airshaft.

Next morning Chico surprised me. He got to the stocking before I did. When he found it empty, he was disappointed and he was sore. He wadded up the stocking and threw it at me. "When are you going to learn?" he said. "When are you going to learn you can't go against the odds?"

Then he got even madder and called me some pretty unbrotherly names. This was the earliest Chico had ever gotten out of bed, and he had just remembered that the poolroom didn't open until noon on holidays.

The only holidays we shared as a family were the excursions we took, once every summer, to the beach. We couldn't afford to go as far as the ocean, out at Coney Island. We took the cheaper excursion boat from the dock at 96th Street, the one that paddled up through Hell Gate to North Beach, in the Bronx.

At North Beach we had a marvelous time, basking in the sweet air of freedom. We were where no free-loading relatives or rent agents or disgruntled customers of Frenchie's could ever find us. Minnie told jokes and sang songs with Groucho, Frenchie snoozed on the sand, smiling even in his sleep, and Chico would wander off looking for some action. I was supposed to mind Gummo and Zeppo, but I ducked away every chance I got to see if I could hustle a charlotte russe or a hunk of watermelon off some kid smaller than me.

Our feast for the holiday would be a stack of sandwiches, liverpaste and cheese on stiff pumpernickel bread. The cheese was green, and so hard it had to be spread with a paint scraper, but it was delectable.

We would stretch the day to the last possible minute, running—along with the rest of the crowd—to catch the last boat home. By the time the warped old tub chugged back into the East River, all the passengers would be on one side, leaning wearily toward home, and the boat would list until you could reach your hand over the rail and skim the scum off the river. It was a miracle every time it made the dock and got itself hitched to the piles and pulled up level before capsizing.

It was always a melancholy homecoming. For most of us on board, the one-day excursion was the only vacation we would have from a year of hard work and misery. The blind man who played the concertina knew there wasn't another nickel or penny left for his tin cup amongst the whole crowd, but he played on, and sang homesick Italian ballads.

In the boat's saloon there was a piano, bolted with iron straps to the deck. Its keyboard was locked. The piano must have been left over from the boat's palmier days, when the passengers wore white flannels and linens, and there was an orchestra for dancing. Nobody ever played the piano on our excursions, and that was the sad part of the holiday for me.

.   .   .

There was one supreme holiday every two years, and there was nothing sad about it. This was not a family affair. It belonged to everybody. The poorest kid in town had as much a share in it as the mayor himself.

This was Election Day.

Months ahead, I started, like every other kid, collecting and stashing fuel for the election bonfire. Having quit school, I could put in a lot of extra hours at it. I had a homemade wagon, a real deluxe job. Most kids greased their axles with suet begged or pinched off a butcher shop, but I was fancier. I scraped genuine axle grease off the hubs of beer wagons, working the brewery circuit from Ehret's to Ruppert's to Ringling's.

I hauled staves, slats, laths, basket-lids, busted carriage spokes, any loose debris that would burn, and piled it all in a corner of our basement. This was one thing the janitor helped me with. The Election Day bonfire was a tradition nobody dared to break. If you were anti-bonfire you were anti-Tammany and life could become pretty grim without handouts from the Organization. Worse than that, the cops could invent all kinds of trouble to get you into. So around election time, there were no complaints up the dumbwaiter shaft about the leaks in our garbage cans.

The great holiday lasted a full thirty hours. On election eve, the Tammany forces marched up and down the avenues by torchlight, with bugles blaring and drums booming. There was free beer for the men, and free firecrackers and punk for the kids, and nobody slept that night.

When the Day itself dawned, the city closed up shop and had itself a big social time—visiting with itself, renewing old acquaintances, kicking up old arguments—and voted.

*Born into the world of Edith Wharton's novels, Hamilton
Fish Armstrong grew up a few blocks from Washington
Square. As a boy on his own, he explored the more colorful
parts of the city—the docks, the markets, the exotic neighborhoods far from home—sometimes traveling as much as
ten miles a day on his roller skates. His boyhood coincided
with Harpo's, and in spite of the differences in their backgrounds, they might both have played in Central Park on
the same days. The reminiscences below come from Armstrong's* Those Days, *published in 1963.*

Hamilton Fish Armstrong

Hamilton Fish Armstrong was born in New York in 1893, graduated from Princeton, and for many years edited the influential journal *Foreign Affairs*. He has been an adviser to several U.S. Presidents
and is the author of many books and articles on international politics.

from Those Days

I had learnt the geography of polite neighborhoods long ago, when my
mother would take me along in the carriage which in winter she had once
a week to pay calls on her friends—Washington Square, Gramercy Park,
Stuyvesant Square (almost every house there full of relatives), up to Murray Hill and as far as the forties and fifties. The custom of New Year's
calls was dying out, although a few old-fashioned gentlemen still held to
it and appeared at the houses of their relatives and close friends to drink a
cup of the hot milk punch that tradition demanded should be ready that
day from eleven o'clock on. They left their overcoats and sticks in the
front hall, but brought their silk hats into the parlor, placing their gloves
in them before they laid them on a table, presumably to signify that this
was to be a short appearance and not a real visit. Each gentleman wished
to make as full a round as possible, and I have been told that by acting
with great dispatch though proper ceremony he could pack in as many as
fifteen calls. Though this custom was vanishing, there still existed the
institution of the "day," when the ladies of a certain neighborhood were
expected to be at home.

In the Washington Square neighborhood the "day" was Friday, and I
was stationed in the front hall to lead in visitors by the hand. At the age

132

of three or four I took this duty seriously. There would be tea and hot chocolate in the dining room, as well as bouillon in a silver urn, also glazed importés and other little cakes from Dean's and such very small, very thin watercress sandwiches that they hardly seemed worth the trouble of eating. When my mother went to return calls on other "days" and took me with her I would sit conversing with the Irish coachman while she went inside briefly, for here too the idea was to get in a considerable number of calls.

I got to know the shopping districts too. Nearby on Broadway were Wanamaker's and Daniel's (Sons and Sons, why not grandsons?), Fleischmann's and Dean's; on Union Square were Brentano's and Tiffany's; and a bit further up on Broadway were the department stores and Purcell's and Huyler's (on a cold day there might be hot chocolate, but not if it was Lent). Fleischmann's bakery, next to Grace Church, was the place to stop at the right seasons for hot cross buns, election cake, Christmas cinnamon stars and New Year's cookies with caraway seeds, and at any season for little square sponge cakes; not for rolls—these were delivered fresh before breakfast, advancing civilization not having as yet required that they be picked up in a supermarket, limp in their cellophane. Bread was baked at home every other day and tasted like it. Fleischmann's bakery and sidewalk café were very animated in the daytime, but by nightfall a shabby queue stretched around the corner, where at the close of business the day's unsold bakings were distributed to the hungry. Brooks was on Broadway near Twenty-second Street, having by that date covered half of its northward migration from the corner of Catherine and Cherry streets. When my father was my age he had been taken to the old store far downtown for his first New York suit. Seventy years later he was able to describe it in detail: "The trousers were light grey, with a stripe down the side of dark grey, the jacket a blue roundabout with brass navy buttons." With it went red-topped boots into which he stuffed his trousers. When I was ten Brooks would have been surprised if my mother had brought me in for a blue roundabout. As it was, she took me to Best's or Stern's, and because such visits entailed trying on things I did my best to divert her into doing errands at other stores where I could wait outside, sitting on the steps and looking at life.

Now that I had my skates I was able to explore much further afield, at first the maze of small streets in Greenwich Village (this was before the Village swallowed up Washington Square), but soon ranging from Washington Market north along the waterfront to where the Atlantic liners came in. On Saturday mornings when a ship was about to sail I would hide my skates on the dock and go aboard. I got to know them all, the *Lorraine* and the *Savoie*, the old four-stack *Mauretania* and her competitor the *Deutschland*, the *Carmania* and the *Celtic*. The *Kaiser Wilhelm der Grosse* first came into port in the spring of 1906 and immediately became known as the "Rolling Willie." (As I walked nonchalantly up her gangplank, pretending I had come to see off a real departing friend, I had no idea of course that I would make a winter crossing in her as the transport *Agamemnon*, rolling just as nastily under her wartime name.) Each ship had its own ornate decor, its own band playing the right national tunes and its pleasant or cross library steward who would or would not give me the ship's postcards. Only the smell was generic—part grease, part linoleum, part fresh paint, part stale coffee, part leather and nicotine exhaled from the smoking room. I identified it then with the romance of the sea and only later learnt the mistake. Once romance came photograhically near. Mary Garden summoned me to her side as a supernumerary in a going-away scene on the top deck—"a young admirer," the newspapers said the next day. She had just created the part of Mélisande, and everyone was talking about whether her voice was up to her looks; her looks, it was agreed, were stunning. Clasping me to her side, she assured me she was going to play games with me all across the Atlantic. I grinned inwardly even more than I did for the photographers.

My trips to Sunday school were hazardous, as bands of Micks used to lie in wait in the long crosstown blocks for the figure of fun I made in an Eton suit on roller skates. How better could they have used their time after Mass on a Sunday morning than in trying to keep a dirty little Protestant away from his heathen church? By varying my route, but thanks even more to my speed, I was able to arrive intact and without using the hockey stick I carried "just in case." I rather liked Sunday school, partly because getting there was a game, but more because my teachers were two soft and warm-hearted young girls, Dorothea and Ruth Draper. Ruth treasured my rendering of the First Commandment: "I am the Lord thy God. You'll never have another like me."

When I was nine the time came for me to go to a "real" school uptown, and unless it was pouring rain or snowing I went, of course, on skates. When the weather ruled this out I used the Fifth Avenue stage or the Sixth Avenue El.

On the stage I rode by choice on the outside, either perched up behind the driver or, if I was lucky, alongside him. You mounted to this vantage point by the hub and two widely spaced iron footholds. Thence, as the stage rumbled heavily along, New York unrolled before you. First came the sedate brownstone houses of lower Fifth Avenue; then the Flatiron Building, to some a thing of soaring beauty, to others an architectural monstrosity, but in everyone's eyes, including those on the top of the stage, a continuing wonder (height, 307 feet); then Madison Square with the Farragut of Saint-Gaudens, one of his best, conspicuous for all the passing traffic to see (until relegated by Mr. Moses to obscurity among the trees in the middle of the park); and the Worth Monument opposite, marking the burial place of the Mexican War hero, since invaded by a marble comfort station which hopefully does not disturb the general's bones. Then came the Holland House and the Brunswick Hotel, where in spring there might be a four-in-hand coach drawn up, making ready to tool up to Claremont or Pelham or out to Tuxedo, grooms holding the horses, while on top several feather-bedecked ladies preened themselves before a group of dazzled onlookers. On you went past the Waldorf up Murray Hill and along the old reservoir resembling an Egyptian tomb, afterwards replaced by the Public Library guarded by the two lions with Horace Greeley faces.

If you secured the seat beside the driver you took care not to interfere with a leather strap attached to his leg, for it performed an important function. Passing through an aperture under the seat, it led along the ceiling of the stage to the top of the rear door; and by it the driver controlled the door's opening and closing. When he stopped to take on passengers he moved his leg back, allowing the door to swing open by its own weight; then he would slide his leg forward, banging the door to, and start his horses off again. If you had to ride inside, where in winter it was stuffy and smelt of the stable, with a touch of kerosene added after dusk from the flickering lamp, the procedure was to wriggle your way forward and deposit your nickel in a box situated under the driver's seat. He could peer down through a small window and verify that your fare had been paid; if you were slow about it, he would mortify you by angrily thumping. If you needed change, you attracted his attention by ringing a bell and passing your money up to him through a small sliding panel; and he would hand the change back to you in an envelope colored according to the amount involved. Often there was much bowing by gentlemen offering to pass along the money for ladies, and sometimes an argument, in which everyone joined, as to whether or not a certain fare had been paid. When you wanted to get off you gave notice via the driver's leg by jerking the strap on the ceiling.

His various duties kept the driver busy, especially in winter when an extra horse was needed to help scale the slippery slope of Murray Hill.

Gradually I became intimate with certain drivers, who let me help with handing down envelopes; and when the stage was full I would wave grandly to groups waiting on the corners to signify that we couldn't stop.

My station for the Sixth Avenue El was at Eighth Street. When I reached the corner of Tenth Street and saw a train just rounding the curve from Bleecker Street I knew exactly whether or not it was worth while sprinting the two blocks and tearing up the long iron stairs to try to make it. If only the first car was in view I could catch it quite surely; if two or three cars, it would be a close shave; more than that, hopeless, and I could save my breath and leave my oatmeal and Postum untroubled in my innards. Sometimes, against all rules, the friendly ticket chopper would let me save a vital second or two by pushing my nickel into his hands rather than stopping for a ticket at the little wicket.

The El stations have been described as "Renaissance-Gothic in style, like a Swiss chalet on stilts." In winter, the atmosphere in the tightly sealed waiting room was semi-solid; the pot-bellied stove, with a mushroom top to spread the heat, mingled its coal fumes with the smell of tobacco juice from the spittoons and the powerful antiseptic from the "retiring rooms." When spring came, the colored-glass windows of the stations were reluctantly opened up, and on the trains you rode breezily on the car platforms, although there you missed the latest jingles of Phoebe Snow, the pleadings of the Gold Dust twins to let them do your work, Sapolio's report on the doings of the mayor, the butcher and other happy workers in Spotless Town, and the threats of the balding-headed man, "Going!—Going!!—Gone!! Too Late for Herpicide!!!"

The beginning of school uptown coincided with my introduction to the dance, if attendance at Miss Benjamin's class can properly be said to have had much to do with dancing. Miss Benjamin, short and agile, wore a tight black bodice and a black silk pleated skirt, brief for those days, which made the black stockinged legs very prominent. Miss Winchester, younger, plump, in ruffles, was "at the piano," as they say in concert announcements. The pupils were ranged in two rows facing each other, boys on one side, girls (more of them) on the other.

"Never the twain shall meet" was the rule all winter. At Miss Benjamin's signal, Miss Winchester struck a reverberating chord, and simultaneously Miss Benjamin called out, "Advance right foot." A paused ensued, until the slowest-witted girl and the most reluctant boy had managed to do as directed. Miss Benjamin nodded, Miss Winchester struck another chord and Miss Benjamin called, "Bring up left foot." Then the directions were repeated, beginning with the left foot, and with explanations about turning step-by-step sideways, until each had come stiffly back to his or her original position. Nobody had the slightest inkling, of course, what it might feel like to do all this in rhythm and with a partner of the opposite sex.

My closest friend in the neighborhood, Giraud de Rham, was condemned also to go to Miss Benjamin's. To give each other encouragement, we went together; this had the added advantage that we could then be late and each alternately blame the other for having been delayed at home in starting. One afternoon when we arrived we heard Miss Benjamin already at work inside. There in the hall stood a row of fur bootees, lined neatly up by the little girls' nannies; and there, conveniently near, stood a water cooler. Unhesitatingly Giraud put a glassful of water in each bootee. For some reason the crime was not traced to him, and as he did not have quite the nerve to confess, his scheme to be expelled from the class came to nothing.

In the spring the twain met. The event was looked forward to with dread, and properly. Each was assigned a partner, and doubtless the young lady found the strange boy who now advanced to meet her as repulsive as he found her. You were instructed to hold your partner at arm's length; this meant, if by good luck she wore a sash, that you grasped it to steady yourself and also in order to keep her from gradually drifting away into space. Rhythm was present only in theory, since Miss Winchester was continually being halted by Miss Benjamin in order to give time for someone to bring up that other foot. In those intervals the rest of the class held their pose, as though they were playing "Still pond, no more moving." Needless to say, I did not master the dance at Miss Benjamin's; nor did I until, much later, one of Marion's kind friends took me out by main force onto the floor of the Canoe Club at North Hatley and danced me around and around until I stopped counting, indeed stopped thinking at all about my feet, and simply waltzed.

The de Rhams lived in a "swell-front" house on the corner of Fifth Avenue and Ninth Street, built, I believe, by the Brevoort family. Outside, it was painted mouse color; inside, the spacious rooms and halls were mostly a greenish café-au-lait or chocolate. These rather depressing hues could not diminish the establishment's vast merits in my eyes. Not only did it possess a large garden on Fifth Avenue, with lilacs, roses of Sharon and forsythia; in the rear, opening onto Ninth Street, was a stable, not a disused stable turned into a studio as has happened now to the remaining stables in the neighborhood, but a stable with a pair of smart horses in it, a victoria for good weather, a coupé for use in winter, an Irish coachman full of anecdotes and amiability, and, above, a large loft with hay and straw, excellent for roughhousing and games. In the spring when we were not roller-skating together we played in the yard; in the winter we played in the stable loft.

Giraud died at St. Mark's the year before it became time for me to go to boarding school also. I sat through the funeral at Grace Church, the first funeral of a friend, in a daze of misery. No explanation was possible as to how it could be that someone so manly and buoyant was snatched away, and I left.

During two winters, on two afternoons a week, I went up on my skates to the Seventh Regiment Armory, there to drill in the wavering lines of the Knickerbocker Greys with other unfortunates of assorted sizes. Two miles up in the morning to the Allen-Stevenson School, then on Forty-ninth Street, and two back; three miles up to the Armory, and three back; that made ten miles. But the skating part I loved and it never seemed long. I couldn't say as much for the drills. I suppose my parents thought it might be good for me to experience a sort of discipline I did not have at home; perhaps there was no more to it than the fact that one of the Shippen nephews had outgrown his uniform and I was able to inherit it. If it was the discipline, I resisted it; if it was the uniform, I in turn outgrew it. The trips in uniform were painfully conspicuous. However, this military interlude was so short that I never reached officer's status (which seemed to come automatically if one held on long enough) and thus mercifully was spared the encumbrance of a sword, which would have been much less useful in opening a way through unfriendly onlookers than my usual hockey stick.

A ritual of my daily skatings to school was to keep an exact record of the elapsed time of each trip. This I did in a small blue book which was always in my jacket pocket. It would have been no more fun to cheat about even a matter of seconds than it would be to cheat oneself at solitaire. The notebook is lost, but my recollection is that the best trips varied between fourteen and fifteen minutes. I was always trying, of course, to better my record. In those days very few traffic policemen were needed on Fifth Avenue, but there were two that played a big part in my life. One—tall, thin, dark, reserved—was stationed at Twenty-third Street, the other—robust, rosy-cheeked, smiling—a block higher up, where the Avenue crosses Broadway. They understood the importance of the record I was trying to set, and when they heard the toot of the whistle which I carried on a string around my neck they would hold up traffic so as not to delay me an unnecessary second.

I loved those two policemen, really loved them, especially my friend at Twenty-fourth Street. I made presents for him for Christmas at the same time I was making presents for my father, perhaps a packet of tissue paper to use in shaving, cut with nail scissors into a fat heart, held between highly ornamented cardboard covers, with a ribbon to hang it up with; or perhaps a pincushion made out of the toe of a red sock, stuffed with sawdust (procured from the butcher in Jefferson Market), sewn across the top by one of my sisters, and likewise suspended from a ribbon. On February 14 I would pause on my dash uptown to give him a home-made valentine, profusely decorated with pasted-on flowers and suitably inscribed. On St. Patrick's Day he got a knot of green ribbon, which he apologized for not being able to pin onto his uniform. Following my first trip abroad I went off to boarding school, so no longer saw him daily. However, it was a continuous preoccupation with me on that trip to find the right present to bring home to him, until in Venice I settled on a small picture frame in blue and pink mosaic. He always said he liked my presents, which he stuffed inside his helmet, and I never doubted my good taste.

In my goings and comings on skates I moved with agility; on foot, annoyed at being slow, I was forever bumping into something, barking my shins, raising a bump on my forehead, squashing a finger in a gate. It wasn't so much that I was awkward as that I was in a hurry. I have always liked to be here or there, not in between. The treatment for cuts was first soap and water, then water with carbolic. I was detached enough to recognize and appreciate the smell even while writhing under the sting. But I wasn't really strong and courageous, simply durable.

As a young journalist in Greenwich Village, Mary Heaton Vorse wrote about the New York scene as she knew it before World War I. It was a time when movie theaters were springing up all over town, and in the article below, which originally appeared in The Outlook, *June 24, 1911, she describes an assortment of audiences. The Houston Street population has changed since then, but many Italian families remain on Bleecker Street and continue to worship at the Church of Our Lady of Pompeii.*

Mary Heaton Vorse

Mary Heaton Vorse (1884–1966) was a well-known radical reporter of the 1920s and 30s who wrote about most of the major strikes of the period from first-hand experience. She was shot at and physically attacked, but she continued to write articles and books that dealt with the militant activities of the labor movement. Born in New York in the 1880s, she lived most of her life in Provincetown, where she was one of the founders of the Provincetown Players.

Some Picture Show Audiences

You cannot go to any one of the picture shows in New York without having a series of touching little adventures with the people who sit near you, without overhearing chance words of a *naïveté* and appreciation that make you bless the living picture book that has brought so much into the lives of the people who work.

Houston Street, on the East Side, of an afternoon is always more crowded than Broadway. Push-carts line the street. The faces that you see are almost all Jewish—Jews of many different types; swarthy little men, most of them, looking undersized according to the Anglo-Saxon standard. Here and there a deep-chested mother of Israel sails along, majestic in *shietel* and shawl. These are the toilers—garment-makers, a great many of them—people who work "by pants," as they say. A long and terrible workday they have to keep body and soul together. Their distractions are the streets, and the bargaining off the push-carts, and the show. For a continual trickle of people detaches itself from the crowded streets and goes into the good-sized hall; and around the entrance, too, wait little boys—eager-eyed little boys—with their tickets in their hands, trying to decoy those

140

who enter into taking them in with them as guardians, because the city ordinances do not allow a child under sixteen to go in unaccompanied by an older person.

In the half-light the faces of the audience detach themselves into little pallid ovals, and, as you will always find in the city, it is an audience largely of men.

Behind us sat a woman with her escort. So rapt and entranced was she with what was happening on the stage that her voice accompanied all that happened—a little unconscious and lilting *obbligato*. It was the voice of a person unconscious that she spoke—speaking from the depths of emotion; a low voice, but perfectly clear, and the unconsciously spoken words dropped with the sweetness of running water. She spoke in German. One would judge her to be from some part of Austria. She herself was lovely in person and young, level-browed and clear-eyed, deep-chested; a beneficent and lovely woman one guessed her to be. And she had never seen Indians before; perhaps never heard of them.

The drama being enacted was the rescue from the bear pit of Yellow Wing, the lovely Indian maiden, by Dick the Trapper; his capture by the tribe, his escape with the connivance of Yellow Wing, who goes to warn him in his log house, their siege by the Indians, and final rescue by a splendid charge of the United States cavalry; these one saw riding with splendid abandon over hill and dale, and the marriage then and there of Yellow Wing and Dick by the gallant chaplain. A guileless and sentimental dime novel, most ingeniously performed; a work of art; beautiful, too, because one had glimpses of stately forests, sunlight shifting through leaves, wild, dancing forms of Indians, the beautiful swift rushing of horses. One must have had a heart of stone not to follow the adventures of Yellow Wing and Dick the Trapper with passionate interest.

But to the woman behind it was reality at its highest. She was there in a fabled country full of painted savages. The rapidly unfolding drama was to her no make-believe arrangement ingeniously fitted together by actors and picture-makers. It had happened; it was happening for her now.

"Oh!" she murmured. "That wild and terrible people! Oh, boy, take care, take care! Those wild and awful people will get you!" *"Das wildes und grausames Volk,"* she called them. "Now—now—she comes to save her beloved!" This as Yellow Wing hears the chief plotting an attack on Dick the Trapper, and then flies fleet-foot through the forest. "Surely, surely, she will save her beloved!" It was almost a prayer; in the woman's simple mind there was no foregone conclusion of a happy ending. She saw no step ahead, since she lived the present moment so intensely.

When Yellow Wing and Dick were besieged within and Dick's hand was wounded—

"The poor child! how can she bear it? To see the *geliebte* wounded before one's very eyes!"

And when the cavalry thundered through the forest—

"God give that they arrive swiftly—to be in time they must arrive swiftly!" she exclaimed to herself.

Outside the iron city roared; before the door of the show the push-cart venders bargained and trafficked with customers. Who in that audience remembered it? They had found the door of escape. For the moment they were in the depths of the forest following the loves of Yellow Wing and Dick. The woman's voice, so like the voice of a spirit talking to itself, unconscious of time and place, was their voice. There they were, a strange company of aliens—Jews, almost all; haggard and battered and bearded men, young girls with their beaus, spruce and dapper youngsters beginning to make their way. In that humble playhouse one ran the gamut of the East Side. The American-born sat next to the emigrant who arrived but a week before. A strange and romantic people cast into the welter of the terrible city of New York, each of them with the overwhelming problem of battling with strange conditions and an alien civilization. And for the moment they were permitted to drink deep of oblivion of all the trouble in the world. Life holds some compensation, after all. The keener your intellectual capacity, the higher your artistic sensibilities are developed, just so much more difficult it is to find this total forgetfulness—a thing that for the spirit is as life-giving as sleep.

And all through the afternoon and evening this company of tired workers, overburdened men and women, fills the little halls scattered throughout the city and throughout the land.

There are motion-picture shows in New York that are as intensely local to the audience as to the audience of a Tuscan hill town. Down on Bleecker Street is the Church of Our Lady of Pompeii. Here women, on their way to work or to their brief marketing, drop in to say their prayers before their favorite saints in exactly the same fashion as though it were a little church in their own parish. Towards evening women with their brood of children go in; the children frolic and play subdued tag in the aisles, for church with them is an every-day affair, not a starched-up matter of Sunday only. Then, prayers finished, you may see a mother sorting out her own babies and moving on serenely to the picture show down the road—prayers first and amusement afterwards, after the good old Latin fashion.

It is on Saturday nights down here that the picture show reaches its high moment. The whole neighborhood seems to be waiting for a chance to go in. Every woman has a baby in her arms and at least two children clinging to her skirts. Indeed, so universal is this custom that a woman who goes there unaccompanied by a baby feels out of place, as if she were not properly dressed. A baby seems as much a matter-of-course adjunct to one's toilet on Bleecker Street as a picture hat would be on Broadway.

Every one seems to know everyone else. As a new woman joins the throng other women cry out to her, gayly:

"Ah, good-evening, Concetta. How is Giuseppi's tooth?"

"Through at last," she answers. "And where are your twins?"

The first woman makes a gesture indicating that they are somewhere swallowed up in the crowd.

This talk all goes on in good North Italian, for the people on Bleecker Street are the Tuscan colony. There are many from Venice also, and from Milan and from Genoa. The South Italian lives on the East Side.

Then, as the crowd becomes denser, as the moment for the show approaches, they sway together, pushed on by those on the outskirts of the crowd. And yet every one is good-tempered. It is—

"Not so hard there, boy!"

"Mind for the baby!"

"Look out!"

Though indeed it doesn't seem any place for a baby at all and much less so for the youngsters who aren't in their mothers' arms but are perilously engulfed in the swaying mass of people. But the situation is saved by Latin good temper and the fact that every one is out for a holiday.

By the time one has stood in this crowd twenty minutes and talked with the women and the babies, one has made friends, given an account of one's self, told how it was one happened to speak a little Italian, and where it was in Italy one had lived, for all the world as one gives an account of one's self when traveling through Italian hamlets. One answers the questions that Italian women love to ask:

"Are you married?"

"Have you children?"

"Then why aren't they at the picture show with you?"

This audience was an amused and an amusing audience; ready to laugh, ready to applaud. The young man next to me had an ethical point of view. He was a serious, dark-haired fellow, and took his moving pictures seriously. He and his companion argued the case of the cowboy who stole because of his sick wife.

"He shouldn't have done it," he maintained.

"His wife was dying, *poveretta*," his companion defended.

"His wife was a nice girl," said the serious young man. "You saw for yourself how nice a girl. One has but to look at her to see how good she is." He spoke as though of a real person he had met. "She would rather have died than have her husband disgrace himself."

"It turned out happily; through the theft she found her father again. He wasn't even arrested."

"It makes no difference," said the serious youth; "he had luck, that is all. He shouldn't have stolen. When she knows about it, it will break her heart."

Ethics were his strong point, evidently. He had something to say again about the old man who, in the Franco-Prussian War, shot a soldier and allowed a young man to suffer the death penalty in his stead. It was true that the old man's son had been shot and that there was no one else to care for the little grandson, and, while the critic admitted that that made a difference, he didn't like the idea. The dramas appealed to him from a philosophical standpoint; one gathered that he and his companion might pass an evening discussing whether, when a man is a soldier, and therefore pledged to fight for his country, he has a right to give up his life to save that of an old man, even though he is the guardian of a child.

Throughout the whole show, throughout the discussion going on beside me, there was one face that I turned to again and again. It was that of an eager little girl of ten or eleven, whose lovely profile stood out in violent relief from the dingy wall. So rapt was she, so spellbound, that she couldn't laugh, couldn't clap her hands with the others. She was in a state of emotion beyond any outward manifestation of it.

In the Bowery you get a different kind of audience. None of your neighborhood spirit here. Even in what is called the "dago show"—that is, the show where the occasional vaudeville numbers are Italian singers—the people seem chance-met; the audience is almost entirely composed of men, only an occasional woman.

It was here that I met the moving-picture show expert, the connoisseur, for he told me that he went to a moving-picture show every night. It was the best way that he knew of spending your evenings in New York, and one gathered that he had tried many different ways. He was in his early twenties, with a tough and honest countenance, and he spoke the dialect of the city of New York with greater richness than I have ever heard it spoken. He was ashamed of being caught by a compatriot in a "dago show."

"Say," he said, "dis is a bum joint. I don't know how I come to toin in here. You don't un'erstan' what that skoit's singin', do you? You betcher I don't!"

Not for worlds would he have understood a word of the inferior Italian tongue.

"I don't never come to dago moving-picter shows," he hastened to assure me. "Say, if youse wanter see a real show, beat it down to Grand Street. Dat's de real t'ing. Dese dago shows ain't got no good films. You hardly ever see a travel film; w'en I goes to a show, I likes to see the woild. I'd like travelin' if I could afford it, but I can't; that's why I like a good travel film. A good comic's all right, but a good travel film or an a'rio-plane race or a battle-ship review—dat's de real t'ing! You don't get none here. I don't know what made me come here," he repeated. He was sincerely displeased with himself at being caught with the goods by his compatriots in a place that had no class, and the only way he could defend himself was by showing his fine scorn of the inferior race.

You see what it means to them; it means Opportunity—a chance to glimpse the beautiful and strange things in the world that you haven't in your life; the gratification of the higher side of your nature; opportunity which, except for the big moving picture book, would be forever closed to you. You understand still more how much it means opportunity if you happen to live in a little country place where the whole town goes to every change of films and where the new films are gravely discussed. Down here it is that you find the people who agree with my friend of the Bowery —that "travel films is de real t'ing." For those people who would like to travel they make films of pilgrims going to Mecca; films of the great religious processions in the holy city of Jerusalem; of walrus fights in the far North. It has even gone so far that in Melilla there was an order for the troops to start out; they sprang to their places, trumpets blew, and the men fell into line and marched off—all for the moving-picture show. They were angry—the troops—but the people in Spain saw how their armies acted.

In all the countries of the earth—in Sicily, and out in the desert of Arizona, and in the deep woods of America, and on the olive terraces of Italy—they are making more films, inventing new dramas with new and beautiful backgrounds, for the poor man's theater. In his own little town, in some far-off fishing village, he can sit and see the coronation, and the burial of a king, or the great pageant of the Roman Church.

It is no wonder that it is a great business with a capitalization of millions of dollars, since it gives to the people who need it most laughter and drama and beauty and a chance for once to look at the strange places of the earth.

Philosopher and professor, Irwin Edman grew up on Morningside Avenue in Harlem, which at the turn of the century had the character of a small village populated by proper middle-class families. Scarcely a Negro was seen on those streets at the time, and the broad avenues had an idyllic charm quite unlike the hurly-burly of Manhattan farther south. Harlem had its own fine shops, fancy restaurants, and theaters for vaudeville and stock companies. Directly above the house where Edman lived as a boy was Morningside Park—wonderful for sledding and coasting— and above that was the new Columbia campus, to which the University had moved from Forty-ninth Street in 1890.

Irwin Edman

Irwin Edman (1896–1954) spent practically his entire life in the neighborhood where he grew up. He was an undergraduate at Columbia and became one of its most popular professors. He wrote several books of philosophy and memoirs. The selection below comes from his *Philosopher's Holiday,* published in 1938.

from Philosopher's Holiday

Every philosophy is expressed by a philosopher and, though all philosophers inhabit the same earth and live under the same sky, the local nook in which each grew up inevitably affects the cadence and the contour of his thought. . . . As a humble worker in the same spiritual vineyard I may be pardoned for not outgrowing my own corner of the universe. For despite any ambition to see things, Spinoza-like, under the form of eternity, I am reminded always of the forms of living which will seem to me most intimate simply because I grew up in a certain section of Manhattan in the first decade of the twentieth century. Any vision of timeless things I shall ever have will inevitably be coloured by a childhood spent in a little older New York.

Everyone, I suppose, who has had even a relatively happy childhood, grows nostalgic about it. Doubtless, Johnny, the fourteen-year-old son of my college classmate, James Marshall, will look back thirty years from now on the days when one put up with old-fashioned, sightless radio, when hardly anyone owned a private aeroplane, when most apartments did not have air-conditioning, when manners were easy and informal, when children did what they pleased and spelled as they pleased in progressive schools, and there was exciting news in the papers about China and Spain. But, seen through a sentimental haze or not, the New York of thirty to forty years ago seems to me now a very much simpler and more liveable and lovable place than the one the New Yorker lives in today. Older people confirm me in the remembered impressions of a child. I recall a simpler and more friendly Manhattan: the Manhattan of bicycling even in the centre of town, of seeing with disdainful amusement the first horseless carriages, of sitting in the open-air German beer gardens with their hedges of potted plants (the word German in those days had a genial sound), of boarding the open trolley cars which marked, more than flowers, the advent of spring, and of chatting with the friendly neighbours across the hall. There was no radio; there was only the ancient horned phonograph; but there was Schumann heard on the neighbour's piano or by one's sister on that of one's own family. There was no subway, but there were, to a boy, delightful rides on the elevated when one sat opposite the motorman's box watching his casual expertness with the controller and the airbrake, and the neat way he slowed for the curve at Fifty-Third Street, or coasted from Ninety-Third to Eighty-First. One had heard tales of the dead man's handle; the way the train would come to a halt if the motorman should suddenly die and his hand fall from the control. I used to watch in the morbid hope that that might happen sometime before my very eyes as I watched the motorman through the transparent glass window of his little cabin.

My family lived most of the time I went to school and high school on Morningside Avenue, just below Morningside Park. It was a quiet, bourgeois neighbourhood, though neither I nor anybody else knew the word much then. Harlem meant not the world of Negroes or of "swing" but of middle-class domesticity. Indeed, some of the pleasantest streets in the city were, and are, those up in the One Hundred and Thirties, one of them still with beautiful shade trees. Morningside Avenue was extremely quiet; there were no autos, though by the time I was fifteen one began to see a few. Harlem had a life of its own, a kind of village duplicate of downtown. There was "Koch's," the highly respectable department store on One Hundred and Twenty-Fifth Street. There was the West End Theatre on One Hundred and Twenty-Fifth Street just off Morningside Avenue, where the New York hits used to come late in the season or the next season for a week's stand. As a child you were taken (by the time you were fourteen or fifteen, you went alone or with a friend) on Saturday afternoon to see, a season late, *The Girl of the Golden West,* David Warfield in *The Return of Peter Grimm,* or *The Wizard of Oz.* A little further east, just off Eighth Avenue, was the Penny Arcade, where you could have a view of Palestine or the Wild West for a penny, a brief moving picture; or try your strength with weights; or get weighed; or have your fortune told; or hear sung by various sopranos the ballads of the day: "In the Shade of the Old Apple Tree," "Down by the Old Mill Stream," and that rousing music-hall song, "Tarara Boom-di-ay." Still further east, around the corner on Seventh Avenue, was the Alhambra Theatre, one of the once nation-wide chain of Keith vaudeville theatres, also filled with children of the neighbourhood on Saturday afternoons. It was a changeless routine. First the acrobat, then a comedy turn, then a song and dance team, then a monologist, working up to some comedy star such as Eva Tanguay with her mad reckless song, "I Don't Care," or some famous "legitimate" actress appearing at a climactic moment, just before intermission, in one of her famous scenes or in a one-act play. I am not sure Ethel Barrymore came to the Alhambra—at least in my time—but I think she did. And I believe her "vehicle" was Barrie's *The Twelve-Pound Look,* with her famous line: "That's all there is; there isn't any more," delivered in her deep, dignified contralto that half hid a wise laughter.

Still further east, 'way across town, near Lexington Avenue, was the Harlem Opera House, which, when I knew it, had a stock company that every week played a different play for twelve performances, two each day. I must have seen two dozen plays or so there, but the only two I remember are *The Old Homestead* and *Sherlock Holmes.* Each in its way was typical of the repertoire and the acting, which I thought superb. It was not, I suppose, but greater acting has seldom since produced in me so complete and wonderfully compelling an illusion.

And it was a great treat afterwards to go into Childs—the original neolithic Childs, with white-topped tables—and to eat, as I wish I were still competent to do today, griddle cakes.

But life to a boy in Harlem in the nineteen-tens was not all Saturday afternoon theatres and griddle cakes. Even apart from school there were other amusements. The streetcars—at least to some of us—played the same role of adventure and speed that an auto might have for youngsters of today, possibly more. You went alone or with your family all the way up Amsterdam Avenue on a Saturday afternoon in spring, when the theatre season was over, to Fort George, where there was a miniature Coney Island. The ride was almost as much fun as the Ferris wheels, the merry-go-rounds, the popcorn at the end of it, especially as in the open

trolleys with their cross seats you could sit up in front by the motorman
and watch him clang his footbell, as the car blazed along at what seemed
terrific speed once it got into the region of open lots, and woodland even,
and farmland beyond One Hundred and Forty-Fifth Street. For a more
ambitious trip there was, of course, Coney Island. That you were not
allowed—at least till you were fifteen or sixteen—to do alone. In the first
place it was a long and arduous trip. One had to start early, for there was
the lengthy and interesting journey down to Brooklyn Bridge. Since the
trip was part of the fun and time was not of the essence, one might even
go by trolley instead of by elevated down to Brooklyn Bridge. The best
way of going was to take the horse car, the Dinkey Car we called it—one
of the few remaining ones in the city—down St. Nicholas Avenue across to
One Hundred and Tenth Street and Madison Avenue; then on the Madison Avenue trolley, a matter of about fifty-five minutes, to Brooklyn
Bridge. It was exciting to watch the changes in neighbourhoods and to-
pography, and to admire the way the car took the stiff grade up past the
armoury at Ninety-Fifth Street, to pass through the brownstone elegance,
even then, of the Seventies and Sixties, past our doctor's house, into the
busy Forties, through the shops and crush and trucking—the car began to
move very slowly, and there was considerable clanging—and finally,
under the elevated on the Bowery—still a name to conjure with as a legend—with its toughs and foreigners and saloons. Finally one arrived at
Brooklyn Bridge with its trolleys marked with many strange Brooklyn
destinations, to take another open-air trolley, through miles of country-
looking streets, to Coney Island itself. I seem to remember the trip more
than the destination. One had, I recall, a shore dinner at Feltman's and
did all the concessions at Luna Park and Dreamland before one of them
—I forget which—was burnt down. One had the thrill and the discomfort
of the scenic railway, and at dusk one had the long ride back to Brooklyn
Bridge. By that time one sleepily assented to going home on the speedier
"L."

But it was not necessary to go so far afield for diversion. Right close by,
in Morningside Park, there was coasting in winter, with the added adventure of being possibly interfered with by the "toughs" who lived in the
slummy block between Manhattan and Eighth Avenues, a block east of
the Park. There was "dry" coasting even in spring, when one was very
young. I, for instance, had an Irish Mail, a child's bright red handcar. A
chum used to help me transport it to the top of the park, and as a reward
was allowed to speed with me down the hill that ran around the Park,
sitting backwards, and using his shoes as a brake. That occupation was

finally ended by a policeman who told us we were an obstruction to traffic. There wasn't much traffic to be obstructed. Most of the land at the top of the park was still rocks that is all apartment houses now, and Philosophy Hall, where my office has been for the past twenty years, had not yet been built. Once on one of our rides we were engaged in conversation by a Columbia freshman; we could tell he was a freshman by his small black cap with its white button. We reported for days around the block that we had actually talked with a bona fide Columbia student, but nobody believed us.

There was roller skating, and "cops and robbers," and ball games as well, though my near-sightedness prevented me from participating in the latter. There were indoor games, particularly "Parcheesi," in which one did not need to be an athlete; and there was "collecting." Country boys may collect various interesting things, birds' nests and what not, but I am sure they could not have had more fun than we had collecting streetcar transfers and time-tables. I don't know who started it in our neighbourhood, but I know quite a ritual and set of standards developed. The streetcar lines along the avenues in New York issued red and green transfers: red for south bound, green for north. The crosstown lines issued white ones. By what logic I know not, the red transfers counted ten dollars, the green two dollars, and the crosstown five. The crosstown ones, as a matter of fact, should, by those laws of supply and demand about which I learned myself when I in time became a Columbia student, have counted higher, for it seldom happened that one's friends or relatives took only a crosstown trip without using their transfers. Suburban transfers counted twenty-five, and those of distant cities, like Philadelphia and Boston, one hundred. It was, of course, chiefly through friends and relatives that we acquired transfers. We became a perfect plague to the adults in the neighbourhood. Transfers became for us a kind of currency, and one of the chief things for which we used them was railroad time-tables, which also had relatively established values. The great trunk lines of the East, the Pennsylvania and the New York Central and the B. and O., were worth about a hundred dollars each. Those West and South anywhere up to five hundred, for being further away they were harder to come by. Those of us whose parents travelled much for business or pleasure were in luck. I myself developed into quite a capitalist for a while, for I dragooned my father once into bringing me home from the West the time-tables of the Santa Fe, the Great Northern, the Nickel Plate, the Canadian Pacific. For the last, on the ground that it was from a foreign country, I received a thousand dollars.

One of our group discovered one day by accident something that quite disrupted our financial system and produced a period of inflation for a time while we all aped his discovery. He found that in the offices of some of the New York railroads there were racks containing the time-tables of almost all the railroads in the country. It became quite a game for us to visit the offices and quietly, though tremblingly, denude the racks. If we had any doubts as to whether it was stealing or not, an angry clerk one day made it clear what the railroads thought about it, and time-tables from remote railroads went back to their usual prices.

Our crowd consisted of the boys who lived on Morningside Avenue or on the "nice" blocks of brownstone houses just off it. We were all the sons of middle-class families, and our respectable fathers, many of them, wore top hats on Sunday, a formality which somehow seemed to consort with that simple epoch, like the stiff collars even we small boys wore, and which did not seem to us at all odd.

But just one block east lay another world. There was a row of tenements which poured forth upon the street after school hours the One Hundred and Twentieth Street Gang. They seemed very tough indeed to me, and we all, particularly myself, with our stiff collars and blue suits, seemed mollycoddles to them. I passed through that street afternoons sometimes on my way to the Deutsche Apotheke of Kohler and Wohl. On certain days—Hallowe'en, for instance—it required real physical courage. I knew some of those boys by sight and some to speak to from seeing them at Public School 10. But, without knowing much about Middletown, without having read proletarian novels, I still felt—we all felt—a chasm between us. The sturdier among us on Morningside Avenue rather emulated the toughs' ways and pretended to their sophistication. But I was not one of the sturdier ones, and their voices, their words, and their fists frightened me. I also in some vague way felt sorry for them, especially on hot June evenings when I knew almost all of our crowd would soon be off in the country. But I also had a great moral revulsion: they used bad words, they shouted at each other, they pommelled each other in a way that, in the code on Morningside Avenue, was not considered very nice. Passing to and from Kohler and Wohl's, I could often overhear what they thought of me. Once or twice they looked threatening, but on the whole one came through unscathed, without more than the insults of "Four Eyes" for one's spectacles and "Mamma's Boy" for one's blue suit and "Whitey"—not without good humour—for one's blond hair.

My world and my standards and those of the Hundred and Twentieth Street Gang came to a crucial conflict once. I was on my way from Kohler and Wohl's with some headache powders for my mother. It was growing dark, about five o'clock one crisp October afternoon. The Gang was out in full force. I tried to walk as invisibly as possible. A ragamuffin about my own age suddenly seized me by the shoulder. "Gimme all you got," he said. I was at once frightened and outraged, but fright conquered. I meekly gave him my fountain pen, the new Waterman I had received for my birthday, a batch of transfers amounting to over a thousand dollars, my watch. He tore up the transfers.

"Got any money?" he said.

"Twenty-five cents. What," I said and with some singular surge of moral scruple, "what do you want to do with it?"

"Cigarettes," he said.

Now in our neighbourhood and among my friends a cigarette at that period, even for adults, seemed the last word in moral disintegration. Some reformist zeal overcame my cowardice. "I'll give you the quarter I've got if you'll promise not to spend it on cigarettes," I said.

The tough looked at me strangely. Something in the request puzzled him.

"What's the idea?" he asked in astonishment.

"They're coffin nails," I said; "they're bad for you, and you'll die early. You really oughtn't to smoke, you know."

He eyed me with wonder and compassion.

"Say, you're a good guy," he said, and to my own intense astonishment he restored my watch and my fountain pen, and held out his hand for the quarter I had in my fingers.

"Come and have some pop with me," he said.

Before I could stop the words from coming out of my mouth, I said: "I must bring this package home to my mother."

He looked at me with more wonder and a tinge of contempt. But whenever the toughs beleaguered me thereafter, and he was about, he'd say: "Say, let that guy alone; he's all right."

It's the only moral conquest I can remember making.

For the most part our world on Morningside Avenue and the streets immediately adjacent was a closed and tranquil one. There were a few class distinctions: two of the group went to the Horace Mann School, which seemed to the families of the rest of us a little pretentious. One of us moved away to one of the early elevator apartments over by the river and he warned us to dress up properly when we came to see him. We leagued together not to, and never did. Summer evenings we would sit on the railings of the park, singing the current songs, occasionally go to nickelodeons, the movies in stores, which had just come in, and on summer afternoons ride out on our bicycles to Van Cortlandt Park or the still verdant West Bronx.

The subway opened, the apartment house era began; we grew older. One of us died of appendicitis at sixteen; it seemed like the collapse of a world. Several moved away. The Park Commissioner, I notice, has streamlined Morningside Park. There are bright new railings; the park has been landscaped, the big rock half-way up, from which we used to begin coasting, has been smoothed down. Most of the buildings on Morningside Avenue seem to have been turned into rooming-houses; the whole quarter seems desolate. Kohler and Wohl's, I noticed the other day, has become a chain store, with a lunch counter. The Dinkey Car is no more. And S——, who was the Prince Charming of Morningside Avenue, who used to recite so elegantly on Sunday evenings and was the Beau Brummel of the Morningside crowd, now lives on Park Avenue, and, being a movie magnate, spends most of his time on Broadway. We meet at theatres occasionally, and invariably remind each other nostalgically of a little older New York. Johnny and his friends will doubtless do that forty years from now, reminding each other of the black-and-white movies, the one-man buses, the cumbersome old disk records, and the motor-cars with the motors in front.

I learned to know worlds elsewhere, and certainly the university world I now live in (now, as it was then, just across the park) is a very different one. My realm of values is no longer measured by streetcar transfers; the little older New York is gone, and I think of it seldom. But I suspect that tiny neighbourhood will linger subterraneously in any thinking, however cosmic in its theme, on which I might ambitiously embark.

In twenty years the Harlem that Irwin Edman knew as a boy had been thoroughly transformed into an almost solidly Negro community. The article below, written for Harper's Magazine *in October 1924, describes a period of stirring activities in the Negro world: the New Renaissance in the arts, the agitation by black nationalists such as Marcus Garvey, and the steady stream of new arrivals from the South, which had already swelled the Harlem population to one twelfth of the entire city's. Some of Konrad Bercovici's observations sound oddly dated; others are startlingly contemporary. He was a man who knew the city well, and he reported on this aspect of it with sympathy and affection.*

Konrad Bercovici

Konrad Bercovici (1882–1961) was born in Rumania, came to New York as a young man, and because he was a gifted linguist, he was soon reporting on the foreign quarters for the *New York World* and later, the *Post*. He wrote many novels as well as books about the gypsies, and in 1924 his regular pieces for *The American Mercury* were collected in a book called *Around the World in New York*.

The Black Blocks of Harlem

Until ten years ago Harlem was a district of New York. A suburban section within the city, inhabited by second-generation Germans and German Jews. To-day it is a city in itself—negro town, the heart and the pulse of the colored population of Greater New York. Harlem cannot hold the entire colored population of New York; neither can the older negro district, the 59th street section; nor could Brooklyn. There are obstructions and objections and restrictions everywhere against them. The center of the colored people is in Harlem. Indeed it is the center, the intellectual center, of the colored population of the United States.

There are between three and four hundred thousand colored people in Greater New York. In the last census there were not one tenth that many. But Chicago rioted after St. Louis had gone on a "nigger spree." Atlanta, Georgia, had its dance. Lynchings, burnings, persecutions are the main reasons why colored folk have been flocking in New York, where a "nigger slaughter" is not so frequent an occurrence.

All shades and all sizes. Woolly-haired, immense, half-lumbering Africans as black as pitch. Brown-colored bronzed men and women, mahogany blonds, down through all nuances to the almost white negro, straight haired and blue eyed, whom nobody suspects.

Not all white men of Europe are of the same race, of the same blood, of the same faith. Not all negroes are alike, although most of their ancestors were ravished from Africa. Since their arrival in this country there have been many inmixtures into their blood. I have seen perfectly black negroes of long Spanish faces, with the cruel penetrating eyes of the Moor and the elegant gait of Iberians. I have met red-haired negroes with a wistful Irish smile. I have friends of a lighter shade, from New Orleans, where they have so thoroughly mixed with the French that they are hardly to be distinguished; with all the love of color and softness of one race and the precision of mind and clarity of the other. The Italians have mixed with the negroes, and the Slavs and the English, and the Mexicans and the Indians.

Of these mixtures the ones with Indian blood are the finest—the women especially, with skin like golden bronze dyed in deep red blood. The big gala eyes swim in clear white pools, and the hair is like shavings of ebony, lustrous and rich, plaited down over the trim and beautiful necks. And there are Jewish negroes—Abyssinian Jews, squat and long bearded, hooknosed *falashes*, real Jews—who because of their color are compelled to live among people of an alien faith instead of among their own co-religionists.

Four hundred thousand negroes in New York! There has never been such a number of negroes in any one place, not only on this continent but on any other continent before or now. Every twelfth person in Greater New York is a negro or has negro blood. Four out of five negroes have white blood and are none the better for it. Much of the best the race has achieved is the work of pure-blooded Africans. They have their own life, their own dreams. More isolated in their social relations than any other single group, their dreams and ideals may be sectional but they are their own. Thicker walls separate them from any other population—not only color, but a thousand and one aversions; a thousand and one superstitions; a thousand and one traditions. We have been taught that the negro is a different sort of animal because of his color, because of his particular odor, because of the coarseness of the grain of his skin, because of his speech, because of his tastes for certain foods. Each of our major senses has been prejudiced against them. And yet . . . **four** out of five negroes have white blood. There is at least as much white blood in the American negro race as there is black. And that is so not because of black immorality, but because of white immorality and the inhumanity of our ancestors. The whiter a negro the weaker he is physically. The pure blacks are giants. When slave dealers went to Africa they selected the strongest specimens, for work and breeding. Only the strongest survived transportation on a slave ship.

And yet a great deal of the true native art of this country is of negro origin: folklore, the spirituals, jazz, the dance, and some of our best poetry. They brought that in their souls from Africa. It may be argued that the origin of native American art is African.

Anyone who can keep dry eyes and calm heart during the singing of spirituals by negroes should be avoided for his callousness. Any white man who can gaze into negro eyes without horror for the wrong done them during centuries should be . . . condemned to read the prophet Isaiah's fifth chapter for the rest of his life, mornings and evenings.

Four hundred thousand negroes in one city! They have not increased immorality. They have not increased crime. They have their own proportion of vice and their due percentage of criminals; neither more nor less than any other single group in this city. They have their gambling dens and cabarets and houses of prostitution, and corrupt politicians and swindlers, and saints and institutions and churches, and artists and novelists and musicians, exploiters and exploited—and bankers. Not one quality, not one single vice of modern civilization is missing. They are, as a matter of fact, living as separate from any other group as any other group lives separate from them. The pity of it! For so much lightness, so much gaiety, so much naïve merriment is lost. Nowhere in the city except in the Harlem or in the Brooklyn negro sections does one hear so much frank laughter. Nobody can laugh as engagingly as a negro. It is one of the first things which strikes a visitor. New York is a laughless city. But there is laughter in Harlem, in the Brooklyn negro quarter in Bensonhurst, on 59th Street, and even in the narrow Carmine Street and Minetta Lane, where the congestion is such that one can almost cut the air with a knife. There one finds laughter and song and dance.

A friend of mine recently said to me. "Harlem! The old Harlem is dead. I have lived there all my life until not long ago, when I was squeezed out by the negro population invading the old section. All the *Gemütlichkeit* of it is gone. Gone are the comfortable *Weinstüben* where one could smoke his pipe and peacefully drink his glass of Rhine wine.

Gone is the old *Liedertafel* and the hundred-and-one social organizations and the *Turnvereins* and the singing clubs where one could pass the evening peacefully. They have all moved elsewhere, and the new places do not have the atmosphere of the old ones. It used to be so pleasant to pass a Harlem street on a summer evening. The young ladies were accompanying their *Lieder* with the twanging of the soft zither, and the stirring robust melodies from the Lutheran Churches used to fill the air on a Sunday. It is all gone now."

It is all gone. But in my recent long peregrinations through the Harlem streets I have failed to see the little notice under the *To Let* signs, "No Jews need apply," or the other little notices in German, *"Keine Juden, und keine Hunde."* An American city with such signs on its doors was a shame. The absence of them largely compensates for the absence of the other things my friend so much regretted.

At 138th and 139th Streets, between Edgecombe and Columbus Avenues, are two rows of houses that were designed by Stanford White. Built in pre-negro days, they had been the pride of the neighborhood, homes of fairly well-to-do white people until not very long ago. In my eagerness to see what the negroes have done to Harlem, I visited these streets again. They were still there, the houses, and although inhabited every one of them by negroes, still as beautiful, still as tasteful, still as clean. The little bits of color in the curtains, the flower assortment on the sills and in the cement urns of the broad sidewalks made them more agreeable than ever.

The story of the passing of those houses into negro hands is the story of negro Harlem. Below the surface of that story is the story of the negro migration from the South. When the 59th Street district around Seventh and Eighth Avenues was no longer able to hold, even after they had been sardine-packed, the negro invasion of this city, Harlem was in one of her periodical real-estate slumps. The old-fashioned railroad flats, mostly dark and cold, and uniformly built, were being vacated steadily for the better houses built in the Bronx and elsewhere. Not a house but had several empty apartments. Yet they would not rent to negroes.

In his eagerness to cover his carrying expenses, one of the shoestring landlords rented an apartment in the middle of the block to a mulatto family. By the end of the month the rest of the tenants living in that house had vacated their apartments. By the end of the following month the whole house was occupied by negroes. Before that they had been living packed four and five families in one apartment in the 59th Street negro section. Tenants of houses adjoining, to right and left and across the street, began to abandon the block. Before winter that whole block was a negro block. And as the negroes were not in a position to pay rents as high as the whites who had abandoned them, the houses were soon up for sale. They passed into the hands of negro owners and such owners as did not object to having negro tenants, expecting to increase their rents as soon as conditions permitted. In this respect the negro owner has, like Emperor Jones, learned a thing or two from the white landlord.

The white population fled as if in dread of a contagious disease. Block after block was deserted by the white tenants. Negro real-estate agents, seeing their chance, infiltrated in other blocks by buying a house and going to live in it themselves. No one refused to sell. Dollars were dollars. Some of those who objected most strongly to negroes sold their houses. It was enough that one negro family should come to live in a house for the whole block to be abandoned to them. And because of this invasion, 138th and 139th Streets, and Edgecombe and Columbus Avenues, though distant from the steady biting-in of the infiltering colored population, were being steadily abandoned by white people vacating in advance of the invasion. The beautiful houses designed by Stanford White stood empty for a long time until the bank owning the mortgages, which had been allowed to become defaulted, decided to tear them all down and sell the ground. These houses were a useless burden and a loss on their hands. They could then have been bought for five or six thousand dollars apiece, although they had cost fully five times that amount to build. Upon the advice of Mr. Jacques Nail, a negro student real-estate agent, the houses were sold on small payments to negro tenants instead of being torn down. The invasion, which had till then been only from the south to the north, began to run from the north to the south, until at present hardly a house in that section of Harlem between 120th Street and 140th Street, and Lenox and Amsterdam Avenues, but is inhabited by colored people. Churches, banks, stores, theaters, the power to grant political offices, municipal offices, everything has passed into the hands of negroes. A city in itself—brown-black town—Harlem. And they have not left Harlem as they had found it. A visit to Harlem would help dispel the idea that "niggers" are shiftless—when they have an incentive for their work, something more than corn and sowbelly. But it will also teach how prejudice might, because of enforced congestion, cause one of the most serious holocausts this or any other city has ever experienced. As it is, the infant death rate is just keeping pace with the birth rate among the negroes of Harlem.

The beautiful Abyssinian Baptist Church on 138th Street was designed by a negro architect, built by a negro contractor, with negro labor, and money collected from negroes in the city. Not a thing within the church but was done by negro hands. The pastor, the Reverend Dr. Powell—a tall colored man with a thunderous voice and big curly head of hair— looks very much like the picture of Alexandre Dumas, the celebrated French novelist, who was himself partly of negro blood. I have yet to listen to a better choir than the one directed by the choir leader of that church. I have yet to listen to a better church organist than the colored woman who was treading the pedals and combining the stops of the magnificently voiced organ of that church. This church, like most other negro churches, is really more than a church. It is a social center.

At one of the recent services Doctor Powell announced they were going to have classes conducted by capable physicians for instruction in sex. Children of all ages were urged to come and there were also classes for the parents. So far as I know, it is the first time that such a course has ever been undertaken by a church. Doctor Powell does not hold that ignorance is bliss in all matters. "Why dodge the sex question when the living are a testimony to its existence?" he thundered. "It is because of ignorance that so many diseases have spread."

There are numerous courses and classes within that church. It has an employment bureau, sewing classes, cooking classes, a gymnasium; and Doctor Powell showed me with great pride his home, "Furnished very much as are the best homes on Riverside Drive, so that a colored girl looking for employment in one of the better homes might, by helping to take care of my apartment, learn how to work and earn her wages elsewhere," he explained. "The Southern negro girl on coming here must be helped to become a capable worker."

At the revival meetings, while the hymns and spirituals are sung the old folks "get religion." The women, in shrill, piercing voices, scream out. "Yea, Lord! Yea, Lord! Yea, Lord!" while the droning voices of the multitude moan and wail. Voices break out, self-denunciatory and praying for the Lord to come to their aid and save them and protect them against the evil spirit that is within. The whole congregation joins in prayer, only to be interrupted by a rousing voice citing a whole chapter from the Bible and commenting upon it. Rising to his feet, another man is so moved that he loses complete control of the language he has been speaking and passes on to an incomprehensible gibberish, into a tongue he himself no longer understands, a subconscious language (if one may say so) which has been stirred from centuries past, beyond the time of other days, like under enharmonics of life; the base of all emotions and reactions. Really, these people have religion. They go to church not as an obligatory call, a duty, a formality. It is part of them.

I saw a young white boy of splendid physique and beautiful blond hair and blue eyes distributing literature between hymns. "Surely," I asked Walter White, who was with me, "this young boy is not colored?"

"He is," Walter answered. He himself is blond and blue eyed and fair skinned. "Only one drop of colored blood makes a white man a negro, but nine-tenths of white blood in a colored man does not make him a white man. It has been so decreed. See how white he is. Should he live among white people and should they find out he is of negro ancestry, they would draw away from him as if he were the worst kind of criminal."

There are a hundred little churches housed in apartment ground floors, with little windowpane pictures of saints and gold-lettered wooden signs on the walls. Some of them have the most fantastic names: Eureka Church, the Oasis Church, and similar titles. And services are announced in the quaintest possible language, in removable enameled letters. The reason for these many small churches is to be found in what follows. A colored man after having lived in New York for a little time returns home, South, on a visit. Going to church on Sunday, the brother is asked by the preacher to step up to the front and tell his brethren about the great city. The visiting brother is well dressed, looks prosperous and happy. He generally draws such a glorious picture of the opportunities, the tolerance, and the economic conditions here that the whole community, including minister, doctor, and undertaker, follows him to the city within a week or two. The hardships they encounter could only be braved and vanquished by laughing, gay-hearted folk. Any other kind would succumb.

Within the last year nearly five hundred thousand negroes have migrated from the South. It is because of this that housing conditions are appalling in Harlem and in other negro quarters. Really no one would dare publish the results of investigations into density of population in some Harlem districts; or the Brooklyn districts, for that matter. After these houses had passed into colored hands, rents were raised until they are to-day, relatively speaking, probably the highest in the city. Apartments for which white people had paid forty dollars a month a few years ago are now rented for a hundred dollars or more. Families have doubled up, and tripled up, to pay the exorbitant rents from the wages obtained in such occupations as are open to the negroes. One must not forget that only very few occupations are within their reach. Trades unions long refused them membership. Whenever they have won such privileges it was only for fear lest they be used as strikebreakers during an industrial war. As it is, many trades have barred them from the possibility of earning a living.

There is greater privacy in the low dives and cabarets, in the streets, in dark hallways, in the numerous saloons which flourish in spite of white prohibition, than in the homes. Because of high rents, less than a hundred colored children graduate yearly from the high schools of the city. They must work. There would be starvation in many a negro home if child-labor laws should be strictly enforced. High rents caused by segregation is the reason for black immorality and lawlessness and the blind pigs leaning on the walls of the police stations. The white messenger who collects the protection money has his drinks served in his own cup which he carries in his pocket—and complains of black immorality! Most of the expensive dives in Harlem are supported by white customers who complain of black immorality.

Chris Matthews, formerly one of Harvard's greatest athletes, related to me recently that for a year he had been refused permission by his teammates to eat at the same training table with them. In Annapolis they had drained the water from the pool after he had taken his swim, in spite of the fact that he had been instrumental in winning the championship for his team. I have listened for hours to tales of riots and lynchings, as told by Miller and Lyles, the co-authors of "Shuffle Along" and "Running Wild," and the tales of Walter White and Wendell Johnson; but the tale of the lynching of Matthews' soul seems to me the most tragic one. Though his body still lives, they have killed him.

And in spite of that, and in spite of all the misery they have endured, what joy and gaiety and merriment they are capable of! What full-throated laughter, what spontaneous giggling in which every limb and the whole body takes part in an expression of joy or merriment! Heinrich Heine in one of his essays said that the dance is the song of the limbs. The colored people have made laughter the dance of the inner voices.

There are some six weekly newspapers edited and publishd by colored people for colored people in the city, not to speak of several magazines of more serious import. The professional men of all walks meet and know one another thoroughly. There are numerous lodges and groupments and societies where they come to discuss things. Like the intellectuals in other districts, they also have their coffee houses, where they stay till the wee hours of the morning talking about this and that.

At the Abyssinian Jewish Synagogue, the black-bearded, dusky-faced men affirm that Moses, Jesus, Solomon, and David were Ethiopians like themselves. They point to numerous passages in the Bible, interpreting this way and that to confirm their views and opinions. They sit day after day, night after night, discussing in the old Hebrew the Old Testament, which they have at their finger tips. With that curious separatist spirit so marked in the Orient, the few hundred Abyssinian Jews are split into a hundred factions because of the interpretation of a verse in the Bible. How little color has to do with the marked characteristics of a race or nation! In their studiousness, their professions, their family life, their sad humor and their lack of ability to laugh as loudly and as frankly as the others, they show themselves to be much more Hebrews than the white Hebrews are. And when I asked one of them what he would really wish his condition in New York to be, he told me, "To live among the other Jews." They resent the epithet "negro," and their inability to mingle with their white brethren of the same religion makes them bitter against their privileged co-religionists. One of them told me, "There is no chance of any of us ever crossing the line, for there is no white blood in us."

And his wife stood up in her enormous corpulence and added, "And there shall not be."

To which her husband replied, "Except if a white co-religionist marries into our fold."

They are very poor, for their children are also forced into poorly paid professions because of their color. Most handicrafts are closed to them. The negro is not persecuted in New York. He is segregated and tolerated. Only the poorest paid work is open to him whose skin is not white.

One night I was sitting at a table with two negroes and their wives at one of the "protected" cabarets of the town. There were about a hundred people in the establishment, but I was the only man in street clothes. They were all immaculately dressed. The women were resplendent in gorgeous gowns. Rivers of diamonds were displayed, shining brightly in the subdued lights of the place. They danced, frantically, joyously, with the most sensuous abandon of body and spirit, to the jazz played by a gyrating band, the musicians actually dancing on the platform while they played. The drinks were unusually expensive, and though because of their profession (which I suspected) the visitors should have known better, the only difference in the wine, in spite of the different prices, was the color and the shape of the bottle in which it was served.

My male companions at the table did not wait long to strike up friendship. A tall, corpulent man leaned over to me and questioned gently:

"Your name, please."

I told him. Whereupon he rose and ceremoniously introduced me to the rest of the company. He eyed with displeasure the bottle in which my wine was served, for it was not of the highest priced. It shamed his table. He asked me politely to consent to partake of his wine. When I had consented he spilled my wine in the brass bowl and put the empty container under the table out of sight. As the waiter did not appear quickly enough to suit him, Mr. Smith raised his eyebrows and said:

"Is it not remawkable haow these ma-an servants are procrastinating?"

"They is procrastinating!" the other assented, happy to mouth so high-sounding a word. "Yes, sir, they is procrastinating—yes, sir!"

While the music played and the dancing women exhibited their diamond-studded garters through the bottom slit in their gowns, and the phosphorescent white combs in their hair were gleaming, he inquired of my profession. And then he spoke of his.

"The other gentleman, Mr. Jones, and his partners. I's a sci'ntist and di'tishon and chemist. A sci'ntist, that's what I is, a di'tishon. There are plently of learned folk in Harlem, sir."

"Is that so?"

"Yes, that's what I is. We two, my partner and me, is going to change the color of our race and make it happy. We are going to make 'em white, so they can live everywhere and go everywhere and be even the President of the United States. The only trouble with the colored race is that it ain't white. Not that I say we is inferior! No, sir! Only when you are in Rome you've got to be like Romans, as Lincoln said. So we will make 'em white."

"Is that so?"

"All this straightening-out hair business, permanent wave, is not the thing; ain't near the real thing. The hair is like tassel on corn. To change it you must change the seed. It is not sci'ntific. I am a di'tishon. I believe in doing things fundamentally."

Suddenly he raised his voice and looked to the people about him. People crowded our table now though the music played.

"Why am the Northern people blond? Why am they blond? I asks." And his large belly shook like jelly while his black eyes rolled furiously in the white pools. "I say they am blond because they eats fish: cold-blooded animals they eat, and because of that they have fair skin and blond hair. Color comes from within, and not from outside. That is sci'ntific. But you cannot change the whole colored race into a white race at once. Burbank he ain't done changing the nature of fruit by paintin' it. You've got to do it sci'ntifically. And through the mothers especially. And so when a woman has got sense enough to come to me I look at her and study the grain of her face. Then if she is very black I prescribe a diet of fish with a little vegetables three times a day. And I give her the right kind of face powder. And it's the face powder I's interested in with my partner here." (Mr. Jones puffed at his cigar and bowed in acknowledgment.)

"Still, the business is idealistic, it is. But there ain't no reason in the world why ideals should be losing propositions! No, siree! And if a woman of lighter shade comes up I give her a diet of two-times-a-day-fish and a little more vegetables of a certain kind and give her a different kind of face powder, a little lighter. And if a woman whiter than that comes she gets fish only once a day and the use of a different kind of face powder. There are eight hundred and forty-nine different kinds of face powders to choose from. And I selects the right kind after studying the grain of the face and the hands. I's a di'tishon and a sci'ntist, a chemist."

"And then you think that diet will straighten out a woman's hair?" I asked.

"I ain't interfering with another end of my business; that is hair culture. No, siree! But do you knows the Bible? Do you know the Bible, I asks." He waxed more enthusiastic as he continued. "Do you remember how Jacob got them striped sheep from his father-in-law Laban? He fooled him by putting the half-peeled branches from the trees in front of the water well to which the ewes used to come to drink. And so most of the sheep were born flecked because the ewes looked at them. Well, do you remember it?"

I nodded.

"Well, that am exactly how I do the things. Nothing like the Bible for an honest man. Study the Bible for ideas. I have a woman eat fish and give her the proper shade of face powder, and she'll be looking into the mirror at herself a dozen times a day. Women is that fallacious, vain, and perspicacious. And watch her offspring. That is sci'ntific. Like Laban's lambs got striped, her offspring is gwine to be whiter. It's in the Bible, sir. If you believe in the Bible you can't dispute this here fact, or you is a heathen. For I'se a sci'ntist and di'tishon and benefactor and student."

I told him he was wonderful, whereupon a dozen more gentlemen and ladies, evidently already the clients of the firm of Smith and Jones, crowded our table. And my friend affirmed to them that I had said he was wonderful.

"And this gentleman knows, for he is a celebrated sci'ntist himself and a student of the Bible."

Who will ever imitate the nice jollity and naïveté of the man! The music played and the couples danced and as they passed by the women patted his cheek, assuring him that he was wonderful. And they were getting such tender and sweet glances in return!

There are a hundred, a thousand, different charlatans of his kind in Harlem who want to make the colored people happy by making them look like whites. Every other house on the Avenue has a practitioner of some sort. The colored people are so easily separated from the money. They are naïve and confident. Not only all the sciences, but also all the superstitions flourish in like way. There is a horde of representatives of schools of medicine I have never heard of—spedopractors, manopractors, pedipractors—doctors all of them.

The advent of Marcus Garvey, who styled himself the emperor of the African race a few years ago, has had very much to do with the factionalization of Harlem. The full-blooded negro was taught to feel through Garvey's propaganda that he was better than his brother of lighter skin. The blacker, the greater the pride. And a thousand and one disputes have been going on since Marcus Garvey's advent. Undoubtedly the negro Moses started out as a saint with high ideals, with great love in his heart. His desire to take his people out of this country and lead them back to Africa had a solid emotional background. It was unfortunate that he should have become involved in the financial intrigues which ultimately led him to jail. He was a picturesque and imposing figure with a sad and eloquent voice and magnetic gestures. Somewhat of a *poseur*—yet genuine. There are any number of people to this day in Harlem who still believe he was honest and who cannot be convinced that he had ever swept aside a single penny which they had given him. They have bought shares in the different enterprises that he had started; and the Black Star Line, which was much scoffed at when its lone vessel was confiscated by the Prohibition Agency for carrying whisky, is still something of which they dream. "Garvey was jailed," they say, "because he is colored." They will tell you big interests were behind his persecution. He was the black genius of organization, and therefore dangerous. Some even spoke of him as the Gandhi of the negroes.

Marcus Garvey's influence is still alive in Harlem. It has worked havoc in the relations between the West Indian negro and the native negro. The antagonism breaks out in all fields. It is of frequent occurrence that a West Indian negro should ruin another negro in business. They boycott one another's stores, restaurants, and dancing places. There is no peace between the West Indian negro and the rest of the population. They neither associate nor intermarry, and seldom if ever belong to the same society, lodge, or congregation with the others. It also so happens that the West Indian negro is of more astute commercial makeup than the other negroes. Most of them have become quite wealthy in a very short time. They are not as happy-go-lucky as the native negroes. They save and invest their money in sound ventures, and do not part with their gold for hair-culture salves and the like. They are seldom as profoundly scarred in their emotions as the others are. They take religion more casually. They don't dance as well. They are more satisfied to stay black, are proud of their race. There is less white blood in them than in the native negro.

A most interesting little man is Mr. Roach, the owner of the Renaissance Dancing Hall. A wealthy man and influential in the community, is this Mr. Roach. He confessed to me he had once had literary ambitions, and had drawn for inspiration while serving as cook for Mr. Irving Bacheller. Later on he became a servant to a Miss Watkins whose writings he admired. But it availed him but slight. He had great difficulty. Write as he would, imitating as closely as possible either of his two masters, his stuff did not sell. In despair he became a valet to Mr. Wilton Lackaye, the actor, whereupon he promptly had better luck by selling a moving-picture scenario for sixty-five dollars. This made him think about motion pictures. He owns to-day a screen theater, has invested in a colored production company, and is the proprietor of several buildings and dancing halls. Had any of his stories been accepted he would to-day be a publisher.

A little below the Renaissance, on Lenox Avenue, is the Lafayette Theater, once the home of the Ethiopian Players of which Charles Gilpin, now of national fame, was once a prominent member. The Ethiopian Players have produced a number of negro actors who have won national fame. They have staged Shakespearian plays, plays by Shaw, Oscar Wilde, Ibsen, and plays by local authors, mostly on negro subjects.

Among interesting Harlem figures are men like Doctor Du Bois, the editor of the *Crisis,* and Mr. James Weldon Johnson, the poet, whose commemoration of the fiftieth anniversary of the emancipation of the negro was published in *The New York Times* in 1913. It was one of the most widely commended poems of the year. His poem, "The Young Warrior," set to music by H. T. Burleigh, almost became the national hymn of Italy during the World War. Mr. Johnson has published several books of poetry of his own, and is the editor of *The Book of American Negro Poetry.* Walter F. White, my companion during my Harlem days, is a novelist and one of the best-known figures in Harlem. Welcomed everywhere, known everywhere, a fluent talker and fiery orator, as ready with tears in his eyes as he is with a smile on his lips, he knows Harlem and knows his people. He is for this and many other reasons one of the most valuable assets of the negro race. He has investigated almost every riot and lynching for the past ten years; and should one want a nightmare without going to the trouble of eating Welsh rarebit, he can have it if he meets and listens to Walter White.

Claude McKay, the poet, author of *Harlem Shadows,* though a Jamaica negro, is one of the most pampered poets of Harlem. Young, handsome, and fiery, with undeniable talent, he is loved by everybody, and even his escapades are being recounted with great gusto. McKay is now in Russia, the guest of the Soviet Republic. Another interesting figure was Mrs. Lillie C. Walker, who has become both famous and wealthy from her hair-straightening process. Branches of her parlor are now in operation all over the country, and her bottled preparation is selling in almost every drug store. Mrs. Walker, who in her lifetime made several million dollars through her invention and through shrewd real-estate investments, was also a speaker and a singer, and one of the most race-conscious negroes in the country. She left her estate to her daughter when she died, who, a most handsome amazon as though hewn out of dark bronze, stands fully six feet in her stockings. She is living in great luxury in a palace she has had designed and built for herself by a negro architect, in Irvington, New York, surrounded by social secretaries and all the luxuries of life. A well-traveled and cultured woman, she too is a very proud negro. Her father having been killed in a riot, she is anything but passive on the subject. Rising from her chair as she talked to me, she looked more like an African empress than the offspring of a former slave. Speaking about negroes whose relatives and parents have been killed in riots or in lynchings, her frame trembled, her lips quivered, and her eyes filled with tears. She looked like an avenging nemesis. But white Irvington objects to her living there. She is as isolated as if she lived on an island a thousand miles from shore . . . except when her own people come to visit her.

In general, what one feels very distinctly in Harlem is that it is composed practically of two elements: those whose ambition it is to "cross the line" or have their offspring cross the line to live with the whites as whites; and another, much better element who refuse to live with whites under false pretenses, who want to live as negroes, race conscious, who hope by their achievements to compel the white people surrounding them to recognize them as their equals. And they insist that their best men have been full-blooded negroes. To them, the great numbers of their kind invading Harlem and New York is very agreeable. They have them all together. They can have meetings with larger crowds. They can lecture to them. They can make them race conscious and with their help agitate for such legislation as is favorable to the negro.

People like Mary Burroughs and the crowd of the Association for the Advancement of Colored People are laboring for the education of the negro and making his life more complete, by pointing out to him the values in literature, by making him conscious of a poetry all his own; building a new edifice on an old foundation by pointing out the great arts that have flourished at all times in Africa, in olden times and down to the time when their ancestors were ravished from the coasts of Africa and brought here as slaves. Native song and dance are almost entirely of Negro origin. A visit to musical comedies such as "Shuffle Along" and "Running Wild," which have been tremendous hits on Broadway and in most of the principal cities of the country, prove their contention. These comedies have been written, staged, and executed from first to last by negroes and have a quality all their own. The tunes and dances are both intoxicating and infectious. Not one risqué or obscene joke. And yet the women dancers have been forced into tights by our censors, while the white dancers in revues and follies romp bare-limbed in other theaters. And when a man like H. O. Tanner, the painter, becomes famous, the negroes get angry because he is referred to as an American painter, and not mentioned as a negro, which he is.

How prejudice against negroes has been melted in New York is perhaps best illustrated by the recent enormous success of the singer Roland Hayes. For years and years, this great artist has tried to get an opportunity to show his ability and his great art. It has been refused him only because of his color. Managers raised their brows. No white population would come to hear a negro singer, it was claimed. In despair, Hayes went to England, where in less than a year after his arrival he was summoned to sing before the King. When he returned to New York on a visit to his parents, he found quite a different attitude. His success was overwhelming. I counted one white out of every five people in the audience at some of his concerts. And although he sang very beautifully in several languages, he never reached such heights or depths as when singing the simple spirituals of his race. Even a few who had come to scoff remained to praise and admire.

Hundreds of negroes arrive daily in New York from every Southern state. It is pathetic, the eagerness with which the other negroes, poor and overcrowded as they live, extend hospitality to the newcomers. Yet hundreds find themselves on the street. The Harlem mission, where many are taken care of, is overcrowded nightly with shivering, ragged, hungry creatures who look as though they had just escaped from hell. There is no way to stop the invasion. There is no way to enlarge the houses in which negroes live. Space enclosed by walls is rigid. Segregation breeds immorality and criminality and increases mortality. One-twelfth of the population of a city cannot be restricted to live in one-fortieth of its area harmlessly and be excluded from most decent means of earning its livelihood. Prostitution, bootlegging, and charlatanism are rampant on every corner. The saloons are wide open. So are the gambling dens and the dope joints. I have been accosted by boys under twelve who offered to sell me gin while the policeman on the corner twirled his stick and looked aside. Rents are high. Wages are small. Trade unions are adverse. And yet . . . Harlem goes earlier to work than any other district. Street-cleaners, dishwashers, chauffeurs, elevator men, and the home-sleeping servant girls have to be early at work. And at night ten thousand men, exceedingly well dressed and looking more prosperous than the others, go to their employment, for that many are regularly employed in cabarets and dance halls as musicians.

And yet . . . watch them in the street cars, subways, and the elevated trains. They laugh and giggle. Their eyes sparkle and their white teeth flash, recounting last night's dance, last night's party, last night's meeting, last night's affair at the church. Never do they call one another by Christian names. It is always Mister, Missus. And when one of them recently gave me his visiting card it read: "MR. ELEAZAR GODSON, *Chief Indoor Aviator,* etc., etc." I puzzled long before I discovered "Indoor Aviator" meant elevator man, and that "Of Hygeinist Bureau" meant Street Cleaning Department.

If there should be another such displacement of negroes from the South to the North as took place in 1923, when nearly five hundred thousand abandoned their home states, the day is not far off when there will be a negro population of a million in the city. Their political power is already a considerable one. Political machinery is at work to swing it this way and that in exchange for winked-at liberties and favors. Whether the negroes in New York can be permanently segregated in one particular quarter is very problematical.

And one of them bitterly remarked to me the other day, "They sing our songs, the whites do. They dance to the music we make. They dance our dances. And the bullets made no difference when they killed us in the War, whether we were white or black. And yet when it comes to renting us an apartment they turn up their noses. As soon as I get enough money I shall go to live in France where they don't discriminate against us."

In his autobiography, Langston Hughes recalls Harlem as he knew it in the 1920s. The great names shimmer with glory still: Paul Robeson, Roland Hayes, Ethel Waters, Louis Armstrong, Duke Ellington, Josephine Baker. So many rich whites came uptown to hear them, prices rose so high at the various fashionable night spots, that the ordinary neighborhood Negro couldn't afford places like the Cotton Club. And so the phenomenon of the Harlem rent party began—and continued well into the Depression. The selection below, from The Big Sea, *published in 1940, concludes with samples of printed invitations to such parties.*

Langston Hughes

One of America's most gifted and versatile Negro writers, Langston Hughes (1902–1967) was born in Missouri, went to high school in Cleveland, and attended Columbia University. At various times in his life he was a seaman, a cook in a Montmartre cafe, and a newspaper correspondent. His career as a poet began in 1926 with the publication of *Weary Blues.* He received many Guggenheim grants, wrote for the theater, and translated poetry by Cuban and Haitian writers. His own poems have been translated into many languages and several have been set to music. The newspaper sketches in which he created the enduring character Simple have been collected in *Simple Speaks His Mind* (1950) and *The Best of Simple* (1961). *I Wonder as I Wander* (1956) is a continuation of his autobiography.

When the Negro Was in Vogue

The 1920's were the years of Manhattan's black Renaissance. It began with *Shuffle Along, Running Wild,* and the Charleston. Perhaps some people would say even with *The Emperor Jones,* Charles Gilpin, and the tom-toms at the Provincetown. But certainly it was the musical revue, *Shuffle Along,* that gave a scintillating send-off to that Negro vogue in Manhattan, which reached its peak just before the crash of 1929, the crash that sent Negroes, white folks and all rolling down the hill toward the Works Progress Administration.

Shuffle Along was a honey of a show. Swift, bright, funny, rollicking, and gay, with a dozen danceable, singable tunes. Besides, look who were in it: The now famous choir director, Hall Johnson, and the composer,

172

William Grant Still, were a part of the orchestra. Eubie Blake and Noble Sissle wrote the music and played and acted in the show. Miller and Lyles were the comics. Florence Mills skyrocketed to fame in the second act. Trixie Smith sang "He May Be Your Man But He Comes to See Me Sometimes." And Caterina Jarboro, now a European prima donna, and the internationally celebrated Josephine Baker were merely in the chorus. Everybody was in the audience—including me. People came back to see it innumerable times. It was always packed.

To see *Shuffle Along* was the main reason I wanted to go to Columbia. When I saw it, I was thrilled and delighted. From then on I was in the gallery of the Cort Theatre every time I got a chance. That year, too, I saw Katharine Cornell in *A Bill of Divorcement*, Margaret Wycherly in *The Verge*, Maugham's *The Circle* with Mrs. Leslie Carter, and the Theatre Guild production of Kaiser's *From Morn Till Midnight*. But I remember *Shuffle Along* best of all. It gave just the proper push—a pre-Charleston kick—to that Negro vogue of the 20's, that spread to books, African sculpture, music, and dancing.

Put down the 1920's for the rise of Roland Hayes, who packed Carnegie Hall, the rise of Paul Robeson in New York and London, of Florence Mills over two continents, of Rose McClendon in Broadway parts that never measured up to her, the booming voice of Bessie Smith and the low moan of Clara on thousands of records, and the rise of that grand comedienne of song, Ethel Waters, singing: "Charlie's elected now! He's in right for sure!" Put down the 1920's for Louis Armstrong and Gladys Bentley and Josephine Baker.

White people began to come to Harlem in droves. For several years they packed the expensive Cotton Club on Lenox Avenue. But I was never there, because the Cotton Club was a Jim Crow club for gangsters and monied whites. They were not cordial to Negro patronage, unless you were a celebrity like Bojangles. So Harlem Negroes did not like the Cotton Club and never appreciated its Jim Crow policy in the very heart of their dark community. Nor did ordinary Negroes like the growing influx of whites toward Harlem after sundown, flooding the little cabarets and bars where formerly only colored people laughed and sang, and where now the strangers were given the best ringside tables to sit and stare at the Negro customers—like amusing animals in a zoo.

The Negroes said: "We can't go downtown and sit and stare at you in your clubs. You won't even let us in your clubs." But they didn't say it out loud—for Negroes are practically never rude to white people. So thousands of whites came to Harlem night after night, thinking the Negroes loved to have them there, and firmly believing that all Harlemites left their houses at sundown to sing and dance in cabarets, because most of the whites saw nothing but the cabarets, not the houses.

Some of the owners of Harlem clubs, delighted at the flood of white patronage, made the grievous error of barring their own race, after the manner of the famous Cotton Club. But most of these quickly lost business and folded up, because they failed to realize that a large part of the Harlem attraction for downtown New Yorkers lay in simply watching the colored customers amuse themselves. And the smaller clubs, of course, had no big floor shows or a name band like the Cotton Club, where Duke Ellington usually held forth, so, without black patronage, they were not amusing at all.

Some of the small clubs, however, had people like Gladys Bentley, who was something worth discovering in those days, before she got famous, acquired an accompanist, specially written material, and conscious vulgarity. But for two or three amazing years, Miss Bentley sat, and played a big piano all night long, literally all night, without stopping—singing songs like "The St. James Infirmary," from ten in the evening until dawn, with scarcely a break between the notes, sliding from one song to another, with a powerful and continuous underbeat of jungle rhythm. Miss Bentley was an amazing exhibition of musical energy—a large, dark, masculine lady, whose feet pounded the floor while her fingers pounded the keyboard—a perfect piece of African sculpture, animated by her own rhythm.

But when the place where she played became too well known, she began to sing with an accompanist, became a star, moved to a larger place, then downtown, and is now in Hollywood. The old magic of the woman and the piano and the night and the rhythm being one is gone. But everything goes, one way or another. The '20's are gone and lots of fine things in Harlem night life have disappeared like snow in the sun— since it became utterly commercial, planned for the downtown tourist trade, and therefore dull.

The lindy-hoppers at the Savoy even began to practise acrobatic routines, and to do absurd things for the entertainment of the whites, that probably never would have entered their heads to attempt merely for their own effortless amusement. Some of the lindy-hoppers had cards printed with their names on them and became dance professors teaching the tourists. Then Harlem nights became show nights for the Nordics.

Some critics say that that is what happened to certain Negro writers, too—that they ceased to write to amuse themselves and began to write to amuse and entertain white people, and in so doing distorted and over-colored their material, and left out a great many things they thought would offend their American brothers of a lighter complexion. Maybe—since Negroes have writer-racketeers, as has any other race. But I have known almost all of them, and most of the good ones have tried to be honest, write honestly, and express their world as they saw it.

All of us know that the gay and sparkling life of the so-called Negro Renaissance of the '20's was not so gay and sparkling beneath the surface as it looked. Carl Van Vechten, in the character of Byron in *Nigger Heaven,* captured some of the bitterness and frustration of literary Harlem that Wallace Thurman later so effectively poured into his *Infants of the Spring*—the only novel by a Negro about that fantastic period when Harlem was in vogue.

It was a period when, at almost every Harlem uppercrust dance or party, one would be introduced to various distinguished white celebrities there as guests. It was a period when almost any Harlem Negro of any social importance at all would be likely to say casually: "As I was remarking the other day to Heywood—," meaning Heywood Broun. Or: "As I said to George—," referring to George Gershwin. It was a period when local and visiting royalty were not at all uncommon in Harlem. And when the parties of A'Lelia Walker, the Negro heiress, were filled with guests whose names would turn any Nordic social climber green with envy. It was a period when Harold Jackman, a handsome young Harlem school teacher of modest means, calmly announced one day that he was sailing for the Riviera for a fortnight, to attend Princess Murat's yachting party. It was a period when Charleston preachers opened up shouting churches as sideshows for white tourists. It was a period when at least one charming colored chorus girl, amber enough to pass for a Latin American, was living in a pent house, with all her bills paid by a gentleman whose name was banker's magic on Wall Street. It was a period when every season there was at least one hit play on Broadway acted by a Negro cast. And when books by Negro authors were being published with much greater frequency and much more publicity than ever before or since in history. It was a period when white writers wrote about Negroes more successfully (commercially speaking) than Negroes did about themselves. It was the period (God help us!) when Ethel Barrymore appeared in blackface in *Scarlet Sister Mary!* It was the period when the Negro was in vogue.

I was there. I had a swell time while it lasted. But I thought it wouldn't last long. (I remember the vogue for things Russian, the season the

Chauve-Souris first came to town.) For how could a large and enthusiastic number of people be crazy about Negroes forever? But some Harlemites thought the millennium had come. They thought the race problem had at last been solved through Art plus Gladys Bentley. They were sure the New Negro would lead a new life from then on in green pastures of tolerance created by Countee Cullen, Ethel Waters, Claude McKay, Duke Ellington, Bojangles, and Alain Locke.

I don't know what made any Negroes think that—except that they were mostly intellectuals doing the thinking. The ordinary Negroes hadn't heard of the Negro Renaissance. And if they had, it hadn't raised their wages any. As for all those white folks in the speakeasies and night clubs of Harlem—well, maybe a colored man could find *some* place to have a drink that the tourists hadn't yet discovered.

Then it was that house-rent parties began to flourish—and not always to raise the rent either. But, as often as not to have a get-together of one's own, where you could do the black-bottom with no stranger behind you trying to do it, too. Non-theatrical, non-intellectual Harlem was an unwilling victim of its own vogue. It didn't like to be stared at by white folks. But perhaps the downtowners never knew this—for the cabaret owners, the entertainers, and the speakeasy proprietors treated them fine —as long as they paid.

The Saturday night rent parties that I attended were often more amusing than any night club, in small apartments where God knows who lived —because the guests seldom did—but where the piano would often be augmented by a guitar, or an odd cornet, or somebody with a pair of drums walking in off the street. And where awful bootleg whiskey and good fried fish or steaming chitterling were sold at very low prices. And the dancing and singing and impromptu entertaining went on until dawn came in at the windows.

These parties, often termed whist parties or dances, were usually announced by brightly colored cards stuck in the grille of apartment house elevators. Some of the cards were highly entertaining in themselves:

WE GOT YELLOW GIRLS, WE'VE GOT BLACK AND TAN
WILL YOU HAVE A GOOD TIME?—YEAH MAN!
A SOCIAL WHIST PARTY
—GIVEN BY—
MARY WINSTON
147 WEST 145TH STREET   APT. 5
SATURDAY EVE. MARCH 19TH, 1932
GOOD MUSIC   REFRESHMENTS

HURRAY

COME AND SEE WHAT IS IN STORE FOR YOU AT THE

TEA CUP PARTY

GIVEN BY MRS. VANDERBILT SMITH

AT 409 EDGECOMBE AVENUE

NEW YORK CITY

APARTMENT 10-A

ON THURSDAY EVENING, JANUARY 23RD, 1930

AT 8:30 P.M.

ORIENTAL—GYPSY—SOUTHERN MAMMY—STARLIGHT

AND OTHER READERS WILL BE PRESENT

MUSIC AND TALENT   —   —   REFRESHMENTS SERVED

RIBBONS-MAWS AND TROTTERS A SPECIALTY

FALL IN LINE, AND WATCH YOUR STEP, FOR THERE'LL BE

LOTS OF BROWNS WITH PLENTY OF PEP AT

A SOCIAL WHIST PARTY

GIVEN BY

LUCILLE & MINNIE

149 WEST 117TH STREET, N. Y. GR. FLOOR, W,

SATURDAY EVENING, NOV. 2ND 1929

REFRESHMENTS JUST IT   MUSIC WON'T QUIT

IF SWEET MAMMA IS RUNNING WILD, AND YOU ARE LOOKING

FOR A DO-RIGHT CHILD, JUST COME AROUND AND

LINGER AWHILE AT A

SOCIAL WHIST PARTY

GIVEN BY

PINKNEY & EPPS

260 WEST 129TH STREET   APARTMENT 10

SATURDAY EVENING, JUNE 9, 1928

GOOD MUSIC   REFRESHMENTS

RAILROAD MEN'S BALL

AT CANDY'S PLACE

FRIDAY, SATURDAY & SUNDAY,

APRIL 29–30, MAY 1, 1927

BLACK WAX, SAYS CHANGE YOUR MIND AND SAY THEY

DO AND HE WILL GIVE YOU A HEARING, WHILE MEAT

HOUSE SLIM, LAYING IN THE BIN

KILLING ALL GOOD MEN.

L. A. VAUGH, PRESIDENT

OH BOY   **OH JOY**

THE ELEVEN BROWN SKINS
OF THE
EVENING SHADOW SOCIAL CLUB
ARE GIVING THEIR
SECOND ANNUAL ST. VALENTINE DANCE
SATURDAY EVENING, FEB. 18TH, 1928
AT 129 WEST 136TH STREET, NEW YORK CITY

GOOD MUSIC   REFRESHMENTS SERVED

SUBSCRIPTION   25 CENTS

There was a time when "moving day"—October 1st—was practically an official holiday in New York. In the 1920s and 30s apartments were plentiful, rents were within the realm of the possible for bright young people just starting out, and it was an exciting adventure to move from one part of town to another. Bernadine Kielty Scherman recalls this ritual, as well as others that were part of her New York, in the selection below from her autobiography, Girl from Fitchburg, *published in 1964.*

Bernadine Kielty Scherman

Bernadine Kielty Scherman was born in northern Massachusetts at the turn of the century. She was one of the original editors of *Story Magazine*, a critic for the *Book of the Month Club*, of which her husband, Harry Scherman, was the founder, and is the author of many children's books. She is the mother of the conductor Thomas Scherman.

from Girl from Fitchburg

Moving in New York was regulation. And by moving I mean actually changing the locale of one's home. In those palmy days apartments abounded, and the landlord had to work to get you. He "decorated" for you every year: he whitewashed the ceilings, varnished the floors and slabbered fresh paint on last year's unwashed paint. He papered walls with paper of your own choice provided it came within his price range, which meant that you saw the same paper on the walls of all your friends' apartments. He frequently made concessions, offering one month's free rent, two months' free rent, and leases were rarely for more than one year.

It seemed almost easier to move than to stay. You could skip housecleaning, you told yourself, and avoid having a painter pile up your furniture in the middle of each room for a week and never unpile it. Instead, you argued, you could walk straight into an interesting new apartment, clean and freshly decorated.

Looking for apartments became a popular summer sport. You picked the neighborhood you liked and walked slowly through the streets looking for "For Rent" signs. You asked to see apartments that were way beyond your limit, just for thrills. And the dim closed-up large-roomed apartments, opened up by a shuffling janitor, would be rich with heavy rugs and tapestry-covered furniture, lamps of dark Tiffany glass hanging low over dining-room tables, the stuff of novels. They weren't your style, but they gave a peep into another kind of life. You wondered about the people who were at ease in that stuffy grandeur, and glanced surreptitiously at framed photographs.

Forty dollars was a medium rent. Sixty dollars was big but conceivable. More than sixty denoted a life of which you had no part. So back in your own price range the drama continued, still with accompanying excitement, still with new combinations of rooms to be had, new arrangements for furniture to consider, and the emergence of a slightly aberrant household personality.

During those weeks you thought of little else.

Moving day was practically a New York holiday. From the night of September 30 to the morning of October 2, side streets were lined with vans. Jobbers sometimes moved two and three apartments in the one day. They'd dump your furniture, and disappear to the next job. They were all of a kind, men of brawn and beery breaths, ex-stevedores or bar-bouncers. A week before their arrival the husband-and-wife team spent each evening wrapping newspapers around china and glass, arranging them with utmost care in barrels, in order to withstand the dropping and pushing they were surely going to get.

Nor was the actual moving the primrose path that you tried to tell yourself it would be. The decorating job could be done ahead only if the retiring tenant had in turn found an apartment that he could get into before moving day. Otherwise there would be the clash of your household arriving and his household departing. And once you were installed in new quarters the same wheel once more started to revolve. Curtains had to be lengthened or shortened, and new ones bought for the extra window. The bathroom mats didn't fit. (Once we had a triangular bathroom.) You needed a new table for a chair. A new lamp for the new table. Trips to Macy's began with renewed vigor, all other householders doing the same, the stores as busy and almost as full as before Christmas. You stood behind salesgirls, goods in hand, watching your turn, ready to pounce.

Between 1914 and 1922 we moved six times—into six new apartments of no perceptible difference one from the other.

Instead of matinées we now went to the Polo Grounds on Saturday afternoons to root for the Giants in their striped suits. We watched for Catcher Chief Bender, a full-blooded Indian whom the fans always greeted with the war cry. We saw Connie Mack's Million-Dollar-Infield from Philadelphia (Eddie Collins is the only one whose name I remember), and Ty Cobb at the top of his fame with the Detroit Tigers.

It was at the Polo Grounds that the man from Fitchburg came over to greet my husband and me—the one who told us about my father's baseball prowess. He was an ex-mayor of Fitchburg, not unlike New York's Jimmy Walker (of future date), good-looking, smartly dressed, affable. That the Irish contingent from whom I sprang were on the sporty side, I had accepted with mild disfavor when I lived in New England. But my values were fast changing. From time to time through years of World Series in New York several of these men have turned up, good company, all of them, jaunty, sophisticated, and a revelation to me who really had not known them at all. The ex-mayor also reminded me that Pat Moran, famous manager of the Phillies and later of the pennant-winning Cincinnati Reds, was a cousin of my Moran-Kielty grandmother. This relationship I had accepted vaguely in the past without pride. But when I went to look at Fitchburg once again in 1962, I went out to see the monument erected to Pat Moran in West Fitchburg where he was born, and meditated briefly on what a silly little snob I had once been.

In spring the hurdy-gurdy man—at first with monkey, and later, by rule of the S.P.C.A., without—ground out "Sancta Lucia" and "Funiculi-Funicula" for pennies. For many years it was the same shabby old man with a long drooping mustache. He must have walked many miles every week because I used to see him in all corners of the city. The last of a long, long line, he was finally put off the streets by Mayor La Guardia, who wasn't a man to stand for any nonsense. Since his time we've had no hurdy-gurdies.

On holidays German bands played in the courtyards of apartment houses, loud and, it seemed, deliberately off key. Far from throwing out pennies, we closed the windows.

Frequently in those days we took the subway to Borough Hall, Brooklyn, to visit friends who lived on the Heights, that oasis of wide streets, Civil War houses, dignity and peacefulness. The Heights is still spacious and beautiful, but the approach has changed almost beyond belief. In 1963 we returned to Borough Hall by subway after an absence of many years. Emerging into the daylight, into what used to be a hodgepodge of dark streets, gloomy buildings and an anarchy of traffic, we found ourselves in a vast open plaza, paved in light stone that shone in the midday sun, and for the first time we saw Borough Hall itself in proper perspec-

tive. Once in the old days, our friends told us about watching a rookie
policeman trying to untangle the snarl of traffic at that spot—the worst in
all of Greater New York. Horns tooted, cabbies shouted, cars were at a
standstill. As they watched, our friends saw that the tall young cop was
crying.

There are tricks for re-living the past. One way to recapture that particular small-scale New York is to take a ride on the IRT local subway south
from Grand Central. This is the old section. The stations used to be dim
and now they are flooded with light. The old turnstyles are gone. The
fare has risen. But they *feel* the same. The station names stare out old
and familiar, the insignia in careful tiling, a specific design for each station, far more imaginative than the functional signs used in the "new"
subway. The same kind of people are riding, gum-chewing, tabloid-read-
ing. The clothes are a bit more casual, men's top coats are short (among
subway riders), pants are narrower, shoes are better. There is a mite less
smell than when those Ukrainian peasants from Rivington Street used to
get on at Grand Street—so strong that it carried you right back to the
steppes. Fewer bearded Jews in double-breasted black coats are reading
the worn volume of the Torah. When I was on jury duty not long ago,
taking the local from Fourteenth Street down, I was back in the old days.

Besides the subway, four noisy El lines clattered up and down the city
in those days—on Ninth, Sixth, Third, and Second Avenues. The Ninth
went down Columbus Avenue through Hell's Kitchen, past the lush fragrance of chocolate factories in the Thirties, and on into dark turgid
Greenwich Street, parallel to the docks. Below it, saloons and brothels
beckoned, into which the sailors hurried, and out of which they staggered,
saturated. (Here for a time was the hangout of Eugene O'Neill.) It was
not a pleasant ride.

The Sixth Avenue branched off the Ninth Avenue tracks at Fifty-third
Street and, on its way downtown, skirted the theaters. It was Main Street
for chorus girls, stagehands, waiters. In open windows of three-story flats,
canary cages were hanging. At Forty-third the El passed over Jack's, famous hangout for newsmen and stage folk, immortalized by Samuel Hop-
kins Adams in *Tenderloin*. At Twenty-seventh Street it went over Mou-
quin's, one of the famous old French restaurants, formerly meeting place
of the sporty set, later the rendezvous of the foremost painters of the day,
the so-called Ash Can Group—Maurice Prendergast, William Glackens,
George Luks, John Sloan, Ernest Lawson, and the rest.

The Third Avenue El took you practically into the tenements. Women leaned out over the window sills, children played on fire escapes. When the train slowed up you sometimes witnessed a scene of domestic ferment. Clanging loosely along over the dark cavern of a thoroughfare already spiritually darkened, on its way to the Tombs or City Hall or Brooklyn Bridge, it still was not depressing as was the Ninth Avenue El, not so secret and furtive. It caught the eye of artists. You see it in the paintings of John Sloan at the turn of the century, and of Edward Hopper a generation later. Long after the other lines had folded, the Third Avenue El remained, its stations cozy right up to the end of 1955, Gothic overhangs decorating the roofs, wooden benches with curved backs, and pot-bellied stoves that were kept burning brightly in the winter.

The Third Avenue El sheltered and protected the Bowery and the Bowery bums. Even now, with their dark wing-cover removed, the tattered old men are still there. You see them leaning against the same old buildings, many of which are also still miraculously standing. They ask little of life—nothing more than a place to lie down and a little to eat, for both of which they are willing to queue up for hours, and enough to drink. They don't want jobs. They don't want women, it's said. They're not even what is known generally as "alcoholics." The Bowery bum, they say, is a social drinker. He seldom drinks alone, he'll pass the bottle, and combine with others to get the price of one. Even now, with its shadows brushed away and a plan afoot to modernize and socialize the Bowery, the thin pale men in old clothes continue to resist the light. There are said to be from twelve thousand to twenty thousand of them still around—looking just the same today as the gaunt figures one saw there in 1914, 1915, 1916—and before. We often walked from Grand Street to Chinatown for dinner. Or from Chinatown down Park Row to the Brooklyn Bridge and over the bridge, one of the loveliest walks in New York, then and now. The Bowery men took no notice then. Nor do they now.

A web of streetcars ran all over town in those days, and the Fifth Avenue buses had open tops which made for a perfect view of the city—along windy Riverside Drive, down Fifth Avenue-of-the-mansions, contemptuous then of apartment dwellers, through commercial Fifth Avenue lined with the most elegant shops in the world, and on to Washington Square and Stanford White's beautiful Arch.

Only a few skyscrapers thrust their towers aloft in 1914. The Singer Building (forty-one stories) was the only one I remember from my fairyland visit of 1908. The Woolworth Tower, built a few years later, was breathtaking. People rode down in the subway to City Hall just to get out and stare up at the "Cathedral" of commerce. Designed by Cass Gilbert and inspired by the London Houses of Parliament, it cost $13,500,000 for which it is said that the five-and-ten-cent-store magnate paid cash. The Flatiron Building was always good for a laugh—"twenty-three skiddoo"— girls' skirts ballooning in the wind at its sharp corner. It had no glamor. But opposite it the Metropolitan Life building was a thing of beauty. The Eternal Light caught the imagination, and Madison Square set it off with its big shade trees and the O. Henry characters resting under them.

One of the most striking earmarks of this new life was the interweaving of Jews into the overall pattern. I married a Jew, I was living in a city the background of which was dark-haired, bright-eyed, short-statured, in contrast to the big wide-faced Irish that was Boston. This city screen of New York was Italian as well as Jewish, but from the very first it was the Jews with whom I had a special affiliation. . . . I was always more expert than Harry at picking a Jewish figure in a crowd—the counterpart of some child whose face I had come to know well. I would see the brothers or uncles or cousins of these children in the subway, at the theater, behind delicatessen counters. But more important were the many individual friendships enkindled in those early days. Few people, I claim, have had such a unique opportunity to know so many Jewish figures from so many backgrounds, with such varieties in living, in taste and interests. There they were awaiting me when I emerged from my adolescent cocoon—the Weisses, the wits in George's Little House, school children, housemothers, and now families, friends, shopkeepers—smart intrepid people whom, God forbid, I might never have come to know had I stayed on in Fitchburg. There they were strange to me, here they were my familiars.

We were all so guileless, back there in 1914! Our pleasures were simple and our energies devoted to small immediate needs. If we thought about such a generality at all, we'd say that, yes, we were secure. Politics had little interest for most of us, and Europe was the stuff of novels. When the upheaval of war shook the foundations of our world, we were as unprepared for it as children.

To a young couple just married with a home to make and life in a big city to adjust to, war in Europe was far-off drama. It made fascinating reading, but was hardly more than incidental in daily living. Through that lovely week in midsummer, 1914—I remember the weather vividly— when the first news began to come through, people gathered around newsstands to read the headlines: Austria declaring war on Serbia (July 28);

Germany declaring war on Russia (August 1); Germany declaring war on France (August 3); Belgium overrun and Britain declaring war on Germany (August 2). The air at night was filled with "Extra! Extra!" shouted by newsboys, and everywhere men came down out of their houses, pennies in hand. I was doing social work at that time and saw a fist fight in Yorkville in the bakery where I was having lunch. Pro-Germans around New York were nearly as numerous as Pro-English. People put maps on their walls, and in time, as the war advanced, stuck pins in to show the movement of troops. We trusted Woodrow Wilson "to keep us out of the war." We also wanted the "world made safe for democracy." But none of these slogans touched us emotionally.

Alfred Kazin's parents were Russian immigrants who met in a Lower East Side boarding house similar to those that appalled Jacob Riis at the turn of the century, and like many poor Jews who wanted "better things for the children," they moved to Brooklyn—to Brownsville, where Kazin was born in 1915. Brownsville was to become a Negro slum in the 50s and 60s but during Kazin's boyhood it was almost solidly Jewish with a strong Socialist tradition. At the beginning of A Walker in the City, *published in 1951, Kazin re-creates the Brooklyn of his boyhood with a poetic tenderness tinged with some bitterness.*

Alfred Kazin

Alfred Kazin, a graduate of City College, is one of America's leading critics as well as an editor and teacher. One of his most influential books, a study of American literature titled *On Native Grounds,* was published when he was twenty-seven. He has edited volumes of Emerson and Blake and is the author of a study of F. Scott Fitzgerald. He has continued his autobiography in *Starting Out in the Thirties,* published in 1965.

from A Walker in the City

Every time I go back to Brownsville it is as if I had never been away. From the moment I step off the train at Rockaway Avenue and smell the leak out of the men's room, then the pickles from the stand just below the subway steps, an instant rage comes over me, mixed with dread and some unexpected tenderness. It is over ten years since I left to live in "the city"—everything just out of Brownsville was always "the city." Actually I did not go very far; it was enough that I could leave Brownsville. Yet as I walk those familiarly choked streets at dusk and see the old women sitting in front of the tenements, past and present become each other's faces; I am back where I began.

It is always the old women in their shapeless flowered housedresses and ritual wigs I see first; they give Brownsville back to me. In their soft dumpy bodies and the unbudging way they occupy the tenement stoops, their hands blankly folded in each other as if they had been sitting on these stoops from the beginning of time, I sense again the old foreboding

186

that all my life would be like this. *Urime Yidn. Alfred, what do you want of us poor Jews?*

The early hopelessness burns at my face like fog the minute I get off the subway. I can smell it in the air as soon as I walk down Rockaway Avenue. It hangs over the Negro tenements in the shadows of the El-darkened street, the torn and flapping canvas sign still listing the boys who went to war, the stagnant wells of candy stores and pool parlors, the torches flaring at dusk over the vegetable stands and pushcarts, the neon-blazing fronts of liquor stores, the piles of *Halvah* and chocolate kisses in the windows of the candy stores next to the *News* and *Mirror,* the dusty old drugstores where urns of rose and pink and blue colored water still swing from chains, and where next door Mr. A.'s sign still tells anyone walking down Rockaway Avenue that he has pants to fit any color suit. It is in the faces of the kids, who before they are ten have learned that Brownsville is a nursery of tough guys, and walk with a springy caution, like boxers approaching the center of the ring. Even the Negroes who have moved into the earliest slums deserted by the Jews along Rockaway Avenue have been infected with the damp sadness of the place, and slouch along the railings of their wormy wooden houses like animals in a cage. The Jewish district drains out here, but eddies back again on the next street; *they* have no connection with it. A Gypsy who lives in one of the empty stores is being reproached by a tipsy Negro in a sweater and new pearl-gray fedora who has paid her to tell his fortune. *You promis' me, didnja? Didnja promis', you lousy f . . . ?* His voice fills the street with the empty rattle of a wooden wheel turning over and over.

The smell of damp out of the rotten hallways accompanies me all the way to Blake Avenue. Everything seems so small here now, old, mashed-in, more rundown even than I remember it, but with a heartbreaking familiarity at each door that makes me wonder if I can take in anything new, so strongly do I feel in Brownsville that I am walking in my sleep. I keep bumping awake at harsh intervals, then fall back into my trance again. In the last crazy afternoon light the neons over the delicatessens bathe all their wares in a cosmetic smile, but strip the street of every personal shadow and concealment. The torches over the pushcarts hold in a single breath of yellow flame the acid smell of half-sour pickles and herrings floating in their briny barrels. There is a dry rattle of loose newspaper sheets around the cracked stretched skins of the "chiney" oranges. Through the kitchen windows along every ground floor I can already see the containers of milk, the fresh round poppy-seed evening rolls. Time for

supper, time to go home. The sudden uprooting I always feel at dusk cries
out in a crash of heavy wooden boxes; a dozen crates of old seltzer bottles
come rattling up from the cellar on an iron roller. Seltzer is still the poor
Jew's dinner wine, a mild luxury infinitely prized above the water out of
the faucets; there can be few families in Brownsville that still do not take
a case of it every week. It sparkles, it can be mixed with sweet jellies and
syrups; besides, the water in Europe was often unclean.

In a laundry window off Dumont Avenue a printed poster with a Star
of David at the head proclaims solidarity with *"our magnificent brothers
in Palestine."* A fiery breath of victory has come to Brownsville at last!
Another poster calls for a demonstration against evictions. It is signed by
one of those many subsidiaries of the Communist Party that I could detect
if it were wrapped in twenty layers of disguise. "WORKERS AND PEOPLE OF
BROWNSVILLE . . . !" Looking at that long-endured word *Landlord*, I
feel myself quickening to the old battle cries.

And now I go over the whole route. Brownsville is that road which
every other road in my life has had to cross.

When I was a child I thought we lived at the end of the world. It was the
eternity of the subway ride into the city that first gave me this idea. It
took a long time getting to "New York"; it seemed longer getting back.
Even the I.R.T. got tired by the time it came to us, and ran up into the
open for a breath of air before it got locked into its terminus at New Lots.
As the train left the tunnel to rattle along the elevated tracks, I felt I
was being jostled on a camel past the last way stations in the desert.
Oh that ride from New York! Light came only at Sutter Avenue. First
across the many stations of the Gentiles to the East River. Then clear
across Brooklyn, almost to the brink of the ocean all our fathers crossed.
All those first stations in Brooklyn—Clark, Borough Hall, Hoyt, Nevins,
the junction of the East and West Side express lines—told me only that I
was on the last leg home, though there was always a stirring of my heart at
Hoyt, where the grimy subway platform was suddenly enlivened by
Abraham and Straus's windows of ladies' wear. Atlantic Avenue was
vaguely exciting, a crossroads, the Long Island railroad; I never saw a
soul get in or out at Bergen Street; the Grand Army Plaza, with its
great empty caverns smoky with dust and chewing-gum wrappers, meant
Prospect Park and that stone path beside a meadow where as a child
I ran off from my father one summer twilight just in time to see the
lamplighter go up the path lighting from the end of his pole each gas
mantle suddenly flaring within its corolla of pleated paper—then, that

summer I first strayed off the block for myself, the steps leading up from
the boathouse, the long stalks of grass wound between the steps thick with
the dust and smell of summer—then, that great summer at sixteen, my
discovery in the Brooklyn Museum of Albert Pinkham Ryder's cracked
oily fishing boats drifting under the moon. Franklin Avenue was where
the Jews began—but all middle-class Jews, *alrightniks,* making out "all
right" in the New World, they were still Gentiles to me as they went out
into the wide and tree-lined Eastern Parkway. For us the journey went on
and on—past Nostrand, past Kingston, past Utica, and only then out into
the open at Sutter, overlooking Lincoln Terrace Park, "Tickle-Her" Park,
the zoo of our adolescence, through which no girl could pass on a summer
evening without its being understood forever after that she was "in"; past
the rickety "two-family" private houses built in the fever of Brownsville's
last real-estate boom; and then into Brownsville itself—Saratoga, Rockaway, and home. For those who lived still beyond, in East New York,
there was Junius, there was Pennsylvania, there was Van Siclen, and so at
last into New Lots, where the city goes back to the marsh, and even the
subway ends.

Yet it was not just the long pent-up subway ride that led me to think of
Brownsville as the margin of the city, the last place, the car barns where
they locked up the subway and the trolley cars at night. There were always raw patches of unused city land all around us filled with "monument works" where they cut and stored tombstones, as there were still on
our street farmhouses and the remains of old cobbled driveways down
which chickens came squealing into our punchball games—but most of it
dead land, neither country nor city, with that look of prairie waste I have
so often seen on my walks along the fringes of American cities near the
freight yards. We were nearer the ocean than the city, but our front on
the ocean was Canarsie—in those days the great refuse dump through
which I made my first and grimmest walks into the city—a place so celebrated in New York vaudeville houses for its squalor that the very sound
of the word was always good for a laugh. CAN-NARR-SIE! They fell into the
aisles. But that was the way to the ocean we always took summer evenings
—through silent streets of old broken houses whose smoky red Victorian
fronts looked as if the paint had clotted like blood and had then been
mixed with soot—past infinite weedy lots, the smell of freshly cut boards
in the lumber yards, the junk yards, the marshland eating the pavement,
the truck farms, the bungalows that had lost a window or a door as they
tottered on their poles against the damp and the ocean winds. The place
as I have it in my mind still reeks of the fires burning in the refuse dumps.

Farms that had once been the outposts of settlers in Revolutionary days had crumbled and sunk like wet sand. Canarsie was where they opened the sluice gates to let the city's muck out into the ocean. But at the end was the roar of the Atlantic and the summer house where we stood outside watching through lattices the sports being served with great pitchers of beer foaming onto the red-checked tablecloths. Summer, my summer! Summer!

We were of the city, but somehow not in it. Whenever I went off on my favorite walk to Highland Park in the "American" district to the north, on the border of Queens, and climbed the hill to the old reservoir from which I could look straight across to the skyscrapers of Manhattan, I saw New York as a foreign city. There, brilliant and unreal, the city had its life, as Brownsville was ours. That the two were joined in me I never knew then—not even on those glorious summer nights of my last weeks in high school when, with what an ache, I would come back into Brownsville along Liberty Avenue, and, as soon as I could see blocks ahead of me the Labor Lyceum, the malted milk and Fatima signs over the candy stores, the old women in their housedresses sitting in front of the tenements like priestesses of an ancient cult, knew I was home.

We were the end of the line. We were the children of the immigrants who had camped at the city's back door, in New York's rawest, remotest, cheapest ghetto, enclosed on one side by the Canarsie flats and on the other by the hallowed middle-class districts that showed the way to New York. "New York" was what we put last on our address, but first in thinking of the others around us. *They* were New York, the Gentiles, America; we were Brownsville—*Brunzvil,* as the old folks said—the dust of the earth to all Jews with money, and notoriously a place that measured all success by our skill in getting away from it. So that when poor Jews left, *even* Negroes, as we said, found it easy to settle on the margins of Brownsville, and with the coming of spring, bands of Gypsies, who would rent empty stores, hang their rugs around them like a desert tent, and bring a dusty and faintly sinister air of carnival into our neighborhood.

They have built a housing project deep down the center of Brownsville, from Rockaway to Stone, cutting clean diagonal forms within the onlooking streets, and leaving at one end only the public school I attended as a boy. As I walked past those indistinguishable red prisms of city houses, I kept remembering what they had pulled down to make this *project*—and despite my pleasure in all this space and light in Brownsville, despite even my envious wonder what our own life would have been if *we* had lived, as soon all of New York's masses will live, just like everybody else, still, I could not quite believe that what I saw before me was real. Brownsville in that model quarter looks like an old crone who has had a plastic operation, and to my amazement I miss her old, sly, and withered face. I miss all those ratty little wooden tenements, born with the smell of damp in them, in which there grew up how many schoolteachers, city accountants, rabbis, cancer specialists, functionaries of the revolution, and strong-arm men for Murder, Inc.; I miss that affected squirt who always wore a paste diamond on his left pinky and one unforgotten day, taught me to say *children* for *kids;* I miss the sinister "Coney Island" dives where before, during, and after the school day we all anxiously gobbled down hot dogs soggy in sauerkraut and mustard, and I slid along the sawdust floor fighting to get back the violin the tough guys always stole from my locker for a joke; I miss the poisonous sweetness I used to breathe in from the caramels melting inside the paper cartons every time I passed the candy wholesaler's on my way back from school; I miss the liturgical refrain *Kosher-Bosher* lettered on the windows of the butcher shops; the ducks at Thanksgiving hanging down the doorways of the chicken store; the clouds of white dust that rose up behind the windows of the mattress factory. Above all I miss the fence to the junk yard where I would wait with my store of little red volumes, THE WORLD'S GREATEST SELECTED SHORT STORIES, given us gratis by the *Literary Digest,* hoping for a glimpse of a girl named Deborah. At eleven or twelve I was so agonizedly in love with her, not least because she had been named after a prophetess in Israel, that I would stand at the fence for hours, even creep through the junk yard to be near her windows, with those little red books always in my hand. At home I would recite to myself in triumph the great lines from Judges: *Desolate were the open towns in Israel, they were desolate, until that I arose, Deborah. . . .* But near her I was afraid, and always took along volumes of THE WORLD'S GREATEST SELECTED SHORT STORIES as a gift, to ease my way into her house. She had five sisters, and every one of them always seemed to be home whenever I called. They would look up at me standing in their kitchen with the books in my hand, and laugh. "Look, boychik," the eldest once said to me in a kindly way, "you don't have to *buy* your way in here every time with those damned books just to see Deborah! Come on your own!"

There is something uncanny now about seeing the old vistas rear up at each end of that housing project. Despite those fresh diagonal walks, with their trees and children's sandboxes and Negro faces calmly at home with the white, so many of the old tenements have been left undisturbed on every side of the project, the streets beyond are so obviously just as they were when I grew up in them, that it is as if they had been ripped out of their original pattern and then pasted back again behind the unbelievable miniatures of the future.

To make that housing project they have torn away the lumber yard; the wholesale drygoods store where my dressmaker mother bought the first shirts I ever wore that she did not make herself; how many poolrooms; and that to me sinister shed that was so long a garage, but before that, in the days of the silents, a movie house where every week, while peddlers went up and down the aisles hawking ice-cream bricks and orange squeeze, I feasted in my terror and joy on the "episodes." It was there one afternoon, between the damp coldness in the movie house and the covetous cries of the peddlers, that I was first seized by that bitter guilt I always felt in the movies whenever there was still daylight outside. As I saw Monte Blue being locked into an Iron Maiden, it suddenly came on me that the penalty for my delicious reveries might be just such a death— a death as lonely, as sickeningly remote from all human aid, as the one I saw my hero calmly prepare to face against the yellow shadows of deepest Asia. Though that long-forgotten movie house now comes back on me as a primitive, folksy place—every time the main door was opened to let in peddlers with fresh goods, a hostile mocking wave of daylight fell against the screen, and in the lip-reading silence of the movies I could hear the steady whir and clacking of the machine and the screech of the trolley cars on Rockaway Avenue—I instantly saw in that ominous patch of light the torture box of life-in-death, some reproach calling out the punishment for my sin.

A sin, perhaps, only of my own devising; the sin I recorded against all idle enjoyment, looking on for its own sake alone; but a sin. The daylight was for grimness and labor.

I see that they have also torn out the little clapboard Protestant church that stood so long near the corner of Blake Avenue. It was the only church I ever saw in our neighborhood—the others were the Russian Orthodox meeting-house in East New York, and the Catholic church on East New York Avenue that marked the boundary, as I used to think of it, between us and the Italians stretching down Rockaway and Saratoga to Fulton. That little clapboard church must have been the last of its kind surviving from the days when all that land was owned by Scottish farmers. I remember the hymns that rolled out of the church on Sunday mornings, and how we sniffed as we went by. All those earnest, faded-looking people in their carefully brushed and strangely old-fashioned clothes must have come down there from a long way off. I never saw any of them except on Sunday mornings—the women often surprisingly quite fat, if not so fat as ours, and looking rather timid in their severe dresses and great straw hats with clusters of artificial flowers and wax berries along the brim as they waited for each other on the steps after the service; the men very stiff in their long four-buttoned jackets. They did not belong with us at all; I could never entirely believe that they were really there. One afternoon on my way back from school my curiosity got the better of me despite all my fear of Gentiles, and I stealthily crept in, never having entered a church in my life before, to examine what I was sure would be an exotic and idolatrous horror. It was the plainest thing I had ever seen—not, of course, homey, lived-in, and smelling of sour wine, snuff, and old prayer books, like our little wooden synagogue on Chester Street, but so varnished-clean and empty and austere, like our school auditorium, and so severely reserved above the altar and in the set rows of wooden pews to the service of an enigmatic cult, that the chief impression it made on me, who expected all Christians to be as fantastic as albinos, was that these people were not, apparently, so completely different from us as I had imagined. I was bewildered. What really held me there was the number of things written in English. I had associated God only with a foreign language. Suspended from the ceiling over the altar was a great gold-wood sign on which the black Gothic letters read: I AM THE RESURRECTION AND THE LIFE. I remember standing in the doorway, longing to go all the way up the aisle, then suddenly running away. The distance from that doorway to the altar was the longest gap in space I had ever seen.

All my early life lies open to my eye within five city blocks. When I passed the school, I went sick with all my old fear of it. With its standard New York public-school brown brick courtyard shut in on three sides of the square and the pretentious battlements overlooking that cockpit in which I can still smell the fiery sheen of the rubber ball, it looks like a factory over which has been imposed the façade of a castle. It gave me the shivers to stand up in that courtyard again; I felt as if I had been mustered back into the service of those Friday morning "tests" that were the terror of my childhood.

It was never learning I associated with that school: only the necessity to succeed, to get ahead of the others in the daily struggle to "make a good impression" on our teachers, who grimly, wearily, and often with ill-concealed distaste watched against our relapsing into the natural savagery they expected of Brownsville boys. The white, cool, thinly ruled record book sat over us from their desks all day long, and had remorselessly entered into it each day—in blue ink if we had passed, in red ink if we had not—our attendance, our conduct, our "effort," our merits and demerits; and to the last possible decimal point in calculation, our standing in an unending series of "tests"—surprise tests, daily tests, weekly tests, formal midterm tests, final tests. They never stopped trying to dig out of us whatever small morsel of fact we had managed to get down the night before. We had to prove that we were really alert, ready for anything, always in the race. That white thinly ruled record book figured in my mind as the judgment seat; the very thinness and remote blue lightness of its lines instantly showed its cold authority over me; so much space had been left on each page, columns and columns in which to note down everything about us, implacably and forever. As it lay there on a teacher's desk, I stared at it all day long with such fear and anxious propriety that I had no trouble believing that God, too, did nothing but keep such record books, and that on the final day He would face me with an account in Hebrew letters whose phonetic dots and dashes looked strangely like decimal points counting up my every sinful thought on earth.

All teachers were to be respected like gods, and God Himself was the greatest of all school superintendents. Long after I had ceased to believe that our teachers could see with the back of their heads, it was still understood, by me, that they knew everything. They were the delegates of all visible and invisible power on earth—of the mothers who waited on the stoops every day after three for us to bring home tales of our daily triumphs; of the glacially remote Anglo-Saxon principal, whose very name was King; of the incalculably important Superintendent of Schools who would someday rubberstamp his name to the bottom of our diplomas in grim acknowledgment that we had, at last, given satisfaction to him, to the Board of Superintendents, and to our benefactor the City of New York—and so up and up, to the government of the United States and to the great Lord Jehovah Himself. My belief in teachers' unlimited wisdom and power rested not so much on what I saw in them—how impatient most of them looked, how wary—but on our abysmal humility, at least in those of us who were "good" boys, who proved by our ready compliance and "manners" that we wanted to get on. The road to a professional future would be shown us only as we pleased *them*. *Make a good impression the first day of the term, and they'll help you out. Make a bad impression, and you might as well cut your throat.* This was the first article of school folklore, whispered around the classroom the opening day of each term. You made the "good impression" by sitting firmly at your wooden desk, hands clasped; by silence for the greatest part of the live-long day; by standing up obsequiously when it was so expected of you; by sitting down noiselessly when you had answered a question; by "speaking nicely," which meant reproducing their painfully exact enunciation; by "showing manners," or an ecstatic submissiveness in all things; by outrageous flattery; by bringing little gifts at Christmas, on their birthdays, and at the end of the term—the well-known significance of these gifts being that they came not from us, but from our parents, whose eagerness in this matter showed a high level of social consideration, and thus raised our standing in turn.

It was not just our quickness and memory that were always being tested. Above all, in that word I could never hear without automatically seeing it raised before me in gold-plated letters, it was our *character*. I always felt anxious when I heard the word pronounced. Satisfactory as my "character" was, on the whole, except when I stayed too long in the playground reading; outrageously satisfactory, as I can see now, the very sound of the word as our teachers coldly gave it out from the end of their teeth, with a solemn weight on each dark syllable, immediately struck my heart cold with fear—they could not believe I really had it. Character was never something you had; it had to be trained in you, like a technique. I was never very clear about it. On our side *character* meant demonstrative obedience; but teachers already had it—how else could they have become teachers? They had it; the aloof Anglo-Saxon principal whom we remotely saw only on ceremonial occasions in the assembly was positively encased in it; it glittered off his bald head in spokes of triumphant light; the President of the United States had the greatest conceivable amount of it. Character belonged to great adults. Yet we were constantly being driven onto it; it was the great threshold we had to cross. *Alfred Kazin, having shown proficiency in his course of studies and having displayed satisfactory marks of character* . . . Thus someday the hallowed diploma, passport to my further advancement in high school. But there—I could already feel it in my bones—they would put me through even more doubting tests of character; and after that, if I should be good enough and bright enough, there would be still more. *Character* was a bitter thing, racked with my endless striving to please. The school—from every last stone in the courtyard to the battlements frowning down at me from the walls—was only the stage for a trial. I felt that the very atmosphere of learning that surrounded us was fake—that every lesson, every book, every approving smile was only a pretext for the constant probing and watching of me, that there was not a secret in me that would not be decimally measured into that white record book. All week long I lived for the blessed sound of the dismissal gong at three o'clock on Friday afternoon.

*A Brooklyn boyhood contemporary with Alfred Kazin's but
of a different kind is the subject of Norman Rosten's memoir,* Under the Boardwalk, *published in 1968. As a child
in the 20s, he lived in Coney Island, in a house where every
available space was transformed into lockers rented to bathers who came from all over the city for "a dip in the ocean."
Those were the years when the beaches could scarcely be
seen for the bodies; when Steeplechase and Luna Park were
magic places even to the child who grew up next door to
them.*

Norman Rosten

Poet, playwright, and scriptwriter, Norman Rosten was born in 1914,
was graduated from Brooklyn College, and studied drama at the University of Michigan. He has written several volumes of poetry, numerous magazine articles on Brooklyn, and adapted Joyce Cary's *Mr.
Johnson* for Broadway.

from Under the Boardwalk

Come to Coney! The posters called, and everybody listened. And they
came. On summer weekends a thousand people a minute spilled from the
subway and trolley terminals and down Surf Avenue, some to the beach,
some to the pools, sailors and girls waiting for evening, and the mystery of
the place brocaded with lights and real stars.

Beyond the Amusement Park, over the rim of spires and pennants, just
a block away, the mist was rising from the Atlantic, burning off under a
high sun. It was going to be a good hot weekend. Let it rain Monday
through Thursday, but Friday through Sunday let it stay clear and blue
—this was the prayer of the merchant, and he prayed all summer long.

From the avenue right at the corner I could hear the early morning
barkers trying out their voices: hurry hurry a nickel a nickel hurry a frank
a root beer a nickel hurry potato chip fresh all fresh (fresh last week) and
corn hot fresh (really warm and soggy) try a ride it's a dime take the little
girl along she'll love to be kissed hurry hurry . . .

It was all starting up again, that long humid day of a million people,
and nobody seemed to mind the lies and the sweat, or notice the rundown
houses and streets full of the poor.

The High-Striker bell began to clang. I watched a guy proving his strength to his girl: slamming down the wooden mallet on the rubber pad which sent the slug shimmying up the tight wire, past Weakling past Weak Sister past 1500 past 2000 past Muscle Man and Sally and Lover Boy and Hercules all the way to the top: BONG! A box of candy, a Kewpie doll, souvenir! I flexed my boy's muscle and longed for the day when I could reach Hercules. BONG for the girl, O for a BONG!

Across the horizon, the empty ferris wheel towered, turning on its trial run. The outside gondolas kept an easy balance, while inside the wheel a series of looped overhead tracks allowed other gondolas to drop and swing in tight arcs, rocking until they gently came to rest. At night, a thousand, maybe ten thousand electric bulbs framed the wheel, and on a clear night, when the lights turned, it was as if the nearby stars were turning along with them, you couldn't be sure.

The rides were warming up. Every two or three minutes, a string of cars whooshed and clanked around the curve of the roller coaster, to disappear down the spidery tracks and drop into a dip of great delight before it sped upward again. Soon the screams of girls would be heard on the turns and drops, rising above the clatter of the cars. I knew the girls were locked in their seats and couldn't escape, and on the drops they would freeze and scream, and when you pulled them close they were too busy screaming to fight back if you held their breasts or slid a hand under their dress. I heard all kinds of stories about what went on down those drops but maybe they were lies, too.

You couldn't tell what was real in a place like this. Whenever you thought something was real, the music of a calliope would start up. It was one of the problems in living here. Maybe that's what the signs meant: Come to Coney! Come to the land where you can't tell what's real! Hurry hurry . . .

Each morning as the sun's heat slowly glazed the streets, the garbage truck came by. Its side panels were about six feet high, forming an open box. Inside, the garbage man labored in dungarees, high boots, and a T-shirt. A handkerchief was tightly bound across his forehead, his hands covered with heavy asbestos gloves. The truck moved slowly along, as two other men dragged or rolled the refuse-laden cans from the curb into the street. With a rhythmic grunt-and-lift, together they heaved the can to the lip of the panel, where the man inside seized it, shifted it to his hip, and in a continuing movement spilled the contents into the boxed area. Then, without a pause, he flipped the empty can over the side where waiting hands received it, spinning it to the curb while a partner began rolling another loaded can toward the truck. Together, they repeated their lifting maneuver with a loud *Ho,* while the driver crept along at a slow steady pace.

By the time it reached our house, the truck was almost full, the mounds piled high in the corners. A foul odor, like a haze, hung over it. The man, standing higher now in the center, waist-deep in garbage, was covered with sweat while around his head an army of black flies buzzed. Large, heavy-winged, swarming above the stench, descending in waves, they settled on his arms as though to devour him whole, but the garbage man kept to his rhythm, taking the can, emptying it, tossing it back over the side. When finally the truck passed our house, a gang of waiting boys flung apple rinds, chicken bones, even bottles into it, yelling at the figure balanced on the pile.

"Hey, stinky, here's more garbage!"

"Phew, you stink!"

"Get a horse!"

Someone always had balls of dried horse dung ready, and tossed them like grenades, taunting the man who said nothing, who moved his glistening arms black with flies, until the truck reached the avenue.

I followed. It was time to do my work.

My job at this prenoon hour was to hawk bathers for the locker establishment in our house. In the summer season, we rented locker space to as many people as we could squeeze into it. There were all kinds of "clubs," for example, ten boys and girls, sharing one room on weekends. My mother enjoyed the confusion. She would even allow part of our own apartment to be used if the demand was great. On some weekends we rented the garage (which was really a storeroom). One summer I slept in the hallway on a small folding-cot I carried around most of the time so I'd be sure of having something to lie on. On a holiday, relatives always came to visit and I'd sleep on the beach or under the boardwalk. It was like a camping trip without going anywhere.

Our regular bath lockers (built in our basement because nothing much was going on in that empty basement and my mother liked to have things going on everywhere) could squeeze in over fifty people. Not that there were fifty lockers. My mother had a system of renting each locker several times a day, and hanging the clothes in a storeroom, so that at the end of the day nobody was sure whom he might find dressing in his locker. I remember a lot of screaming and giggling but nobody complained. My mother's place was always a sellout.

I didn't like my job, being thrust this way into a world of strangers, having to call out: *Lockers twenty-five cents hot and cold showers no wait-*

ing. There was always waiting, and I hated to call out lies, but nobody seemed to mind. On a good morning I'd haul in maybe twenty-five and many more would come by themselves.

The avenue was full of suckers that morning, and I got about fifteen customers in less than an hour. I had all sorts of tricks such as grabbing the duffle bag while giving my pitch or if it was a young couple I'd speak my lines to the girl so that the boy would show he could make up his mind and it was easier to say yes. Most people liked yes better than no. My mother taught me these tricks, she made them up one every minute.

My work completed early, I decided to take a swim. I was already in my swim trunks. I raced barefoot over the hot pavement toward the beach a block away, stopping to cool my feet in patches of tree shade.

I had to dash under the boardwalk to get to the beach. Midway under it, I paused to catch my breath. A chill of apprehension touched me with the sudden cold air. A fetid odor rose up from the sand: it seemed to come from a subterranean source, born of sewage seeping in from the ocean and absorbed in the deepest layers of earth.

In this place of half light, sunlight flaked down through the boards, a pattern of gold running straight, then diagonally, then straight again. I chased the filtered light until it unraveled and ended at the concrete pillars. I played games with it: cutting it up, throwing sand on it, catching it in the air with my open mouth, or letting it tremble on my eyelids. Tired of that, I zigzagged between the pillars, my heart pounding, looking up through the thin spacings between the boards in search of ladies who left their underwear home, an Indian stalking his prey.

Under the boardwalk, for miles, stretched a fringe of corrugated metal and wire fence, entrances to locker houses, frayed billboards, rotting wood, and decayed boats alive with rats and mongrel dogs. Some of the Steeplechase rides skirted the area. You could hear, if you were close to the fence, the rustle of water where the gondola glided through the Tunnel of Love. Nearby, in the shadows, men and women loitered, silent, some holding hands, some clinging to each other, a man pressing a girl against the concrete pillar, a girl combing a man's hair, others watching, silent, waiting.

It was spooky under here. I leaped again into the blinding sun where the sand blazed at my feet and the edge of water rose and fell just a little ways ahead. I was glad to be out in the light again. I skipped over legs, arms, and heads, gathering myself for the plunge. The breakers roared in my ears. Skinny, my soul half-formed, I dived over a rim of foam and under the heaving wall of water.

The coolness enfolded me. My lungs ballooned with air. I became a fish, my glazed eyes open to the green world below. I saw glistening legs of swimmers, slowmotion thrashing legs, erotic and muffled in the sea-green meadow. How my heart hungered! I was a fish nibbling at weeds, nudging at limbs, swimming round and round those languorous girls like the ones in the bathing suit ads with their lips smiling and their legs together like fins.

Down I propelled to a colder level. In my ears boomed the faraway hiss of surf—all the way from Europe or Africa! I had no pain or cares, and overhead I knew the world waited with its flowering sun. I was far from my house and my mother's caution. In an instant, I saw my drowning death, the funeral route, my face unsmiling in the open casket. My mother weeping, my father stunned, cousins and uncles and aunts in dreadful black veils, all rushed past my eyes. They'd miss me, they'd suffer. O this power I had!

My feet kicked bottom sand. My lungs tired. I turned my stroke upward, the green became lighter, and I broke into sunlight, gasping for air. I hung onto the rope, breathing hard. The shore seemed to retreat, grow small, the landscape beyond the boardwalk—ferris wheel, parachute drop, loop-the-loop, Steeplechase—becoming a child's cutout.

With short quick strokes I swam to the shore, edging past a grapefruit rind that rode the wave with the ease of a yellow boat.

By now, at noon, the beach was almost filled. Of course, you never can fill up a beach, the whole idea of a beach is that no matter how crowded it gets you can always squeeze another thousand people in. People were stepping over other people, jumping over other people, calling or staring down at other people. Through this jumbled mass, more other people were maneuvering toward the water which you couldn't see because of the density of the crowd. Voices and sounds merged to a hum, the buzzing of an immense hive.

I lay face down on the sand, my bones stretching in the heat, my head turned slightly in the crook of my arm where, as through a keyhole, I could steal forbidden glimpses of this world. Red, white, blue, green, yellow umbrellas. A sudden kiss, a breast revealed, a hand at rest upon a thigh, a gently stroking motion. I watched and dreamed with eyes open.

Then, filtering through the hum, through the haze, a faint sound drifted to my ears. At first I thought it was someone singing. As the sound came closer, I recognized the chant of the pretzel man.

He moved carefully through the sun-baked sand, head bent forward, wearing sneakers, loose trousers, faded sport shirt, and a round straw skullcap. He was an old man, his skin weathered by sun and wind. Supported by rope which cut into his shoulders, a large basket of pretzels hung at his hip. The pretzels were mounted on sticks jutting vertically from the basket. Slowly, accurately, he stepped between the people sprawled everywhere, calling *Pretzels ten cents fresh pretzels.*

Close by, he set the basket on the sand. He wiped the sweat from his face, groaning softly. Then he sat down, took off his sneakers and shook the sand out, thoughtfully, one sneaker at a time. He looked up at the sky. He reached for a small water flask from his pocket and drank. A group of kids rushed by, their heels kicking sand against the basket, and he yelled after them, "Hey, hey, watch out! Gangsters!"

I counted the pretzels on the sticks. I counted at least twenty-five. My mouth hungered. Maybe he'd drop one? A woman alongside of me turned toward him. "How much the pretzels?"

"Ten cents."

"For one?"

"Naturally. Would it be ten cents a dozen?"

"And three?"

"Thirty cents, lady."

"I saw three for a quarter on the boardwalk."

"On the beach it's ten cents."

"At the subway station it's even five cents."

"Go to the station then, if you please."

"Give me one," said the woman.

The pretzel man folded back the white cloth which covered part of the basket, removed one pretzel from the stick, and replaced the cloth. He accepted a coin, reached into his pocket, and made change.

The woman asked, "These are fresh?"

He answered firmly. "Baked fresh this morning."

My mouth was watering. I wondered, if he'd turn his back for a moment, whether I'd have the courage to slip a pretzel off the stick. He would hardly miss one pretzel. He suddenly stiffened and gave a little cry. My eyes followed his gaze. Coming down from the boardwalk stairs, at a slight trot, a policeman moved toward him. He swung the basket to his shoulder and started quickly toward the water.

As he passed me, I reached up and neatly picked a pretzel off the stick and, with the same motion, slid it under my shirt. I fell back to the sand. It was so easy I wanted to laugh—and practically in front of the cop, too! The pretzel smelled good, the pungent dough, the salt. But I wouldn't eat it right away. I wanted to see what would happen first.

I got up and followed the policeman. Onlookers were converging toward him from all directions, anticipating an arrest or, better still, a brawl. The old man had broken into a run, the basket swinging perilously at his side. As he ran, he kicked off his sneakers, tossed away his shirt and, at the water's edge, setting the basket carefully down, he got out of his trousers. He wore swimming trunks underneath. With a mute look at the amused spectators, he plunged into the water, still wearing the straw skullcap, and swam out to the rope.

The policeman came up to the shore, waving his nightstick. "Come out, you!"

The pretzel man, puffing at the rope, bobbing up and down with the mild waves, called back, "What for?"

"I warned you yesterday to get off the beach."

"So I forgot."

"If I catch you around again, y'hear, I'll give you a summons."

"Ha, ha," the old man laughed wildly, adjusting his hat.

The crowd laughed. The policeman flicked his club impatiently. The pretzel man called out, "Come in here and give me a summons, ha, ha!" The policeman pointed at him with his nightstick, shouting, "Keep off the beach. Last warning!" He started to walk away. The voice from the water called after him, "It's against the law to eat, is that right? I have to make a living!" He pulled himself along the rope toward the shore, his voice shrill, "I have to make a living, tell that to the captain. Go put crooks in jail, I'm not a crook. I have a family, a sick wife . . ."

The policeman disappeared. Two kids ran up from nowhere, snatched pretzels off the stick, and darted away. The crowd laughed. The old man scrambled out of the water. He waved to the cop, "Catch them, catch the little gangsters!" He started chasing the kids, but soon gave up. He came back to the basket, reached for his trousers and put them on over his dripping trunks; he found his shirt and his sneakers. He lifted the basket to his shoulder and peered into the crowd. "Come out, you little crooks! I know you're hiding!"

Several youths scooped up handfuls of sand and ran by with Indian whoops, tossing the sand over the pretzels. The old man kicked at them savagely. "Gangsters!" he shouted. Tears sprang to his eyes. He blew the sand from the pretzels, shifted the weight of the basket more evenly on his shoulders, and started off.

I followed him along the beach. I was hungry, but now I couldn't eat the stolen pretzel. The old man kept a wary eye ahead and behind, stopping often to scan the beach for any sign of the law. I stopped when he

did, jogged after him when he started up again. I figured if I got up close,
I could slip the pretzel back on the stick. I closed in on him. As he was
making a sale, I edged toward the basket, at the same time holding the
pretzel ready. Suddenly he looked up and saw me. His body stiffened.
"Here's one of them! You want to steal more?" And he lunged at me. I
stepped back, and easily vanished in the crowd. I heard his voice. "Gang-
ster, let me catch you, if I catch you . . . Where is he?"

I lay on the sand, breathing heavily. Soon he was calling again, going
off, *Pretzels fresh a dime fresh every time.* I rose, and ran a wide circle
ahead of him, then dropped to the sand, waiting for him to pass. The
pretzel, heated by my body, grew sticky under my shirt. This time I
wouldn't try to get it on the stick, but just run by and toss it into the
basket.

Through a lattice of sprawled and passing figures, I watched him approach. He was coming in a straight line, but as he neared me he turned
off in answer to a customer's shout. I figured this was a good time to do
it.

I got up again, pressed toward him, swallowing, because I was hungry
now, real hungry, and it was crazy not to eat the pretzel, but I couldn't
eat it, I knew that, and wanted to get it out of my hands as soon as
possible. I broke into a trot and swerved so that I would cut directly
across his path.

I had just reached him, when he saw me again. His eyes lit up with
surprise. He swung his arm, as if to strike me, and swung the basket behind him so I couldn't toss the pretzel into it. I continued my run past
him and stopped helplessly a little way off.

"I'll catch you, wait!"

"Take your lousy pretzel," I yelled. "I don't want it."

"You want to steal, heh?"

"Listen, I don't want it. Here, take it." I held out the pretzel, looking
very foolish with all the people watching, but all he did was to shout at
me and curse me, so I moved off and disappeared again into the crowd. I
watched him pass me, getting smaller and smaller until he was lost in the
swirling hive, the sun-drenched day. The pretzel was now soggy from my
sweat. I took one bite, then hurled it into the water.

I ran back to the house. I wanted to get the pretzel man out of my
mind. Passing the locker room, I stuck my head into the shower, and the
ladies clucked and screamed like a bunch of chickens.

I felt better already.

During the Depression, Union Square, the small park bordering Fourteenth Street, was the common meeting ground for the soap-box orators of all dissident groups and the starting point of many May Day parades. Radicals of the 30s knew the surrounding streets well—the cafeterias, the movie theater that specialized in Russian films, and the meeting halls that were the scene of political polemics and splits. In his novel Union Square, *published in 1933, Albert Halper satirizes the radicalism to which he later became sympathetic. From that book, a section appears below which captures the shabbiness and noise of the neighborhood of those years. The burlesque houses and the barkers have gone, but bargain-hunters still flock to Klein's and the cut-rate stores.*

Albert Halper

Albert Halper was born on Chicago's West Side in 1904. After a series of jobs that provided him with material for his novels about the working class, he came to New York in 1929, determined to succeed as a writer. After the publication of *Union Square* he received a Guggenheim grant in 1934 on which he wrote *The Foundry*. Later works include *The Chute* (1937), *Sons of the Fathers* (1940), *The Little People* (1942), and *Atlantic Avenue* (1956). He is also the editor of a short-story anthology about his native city, *This Is Chicago*.

from Union Square

The morning broke damp and chill. The gray fog which had settled down during the night did not lift as usual. Traffic swept around the square. Long before the doors of Klein's Dress Store opened, crowds of women and girls had gathered. Private policemen in gray uniforms tried to keep order at about nine-thirty, because at that time all the doors were unlocked and the women swept forward in a powerful surge, grabbing at the dresses on the racks, searching and clawing for bargains. It was cash down here, "on the Square," each woman held her money in her fist.

Near the curbing, along Fourth Avenue, ran the subway grating, with dank heat flowing up. Women did not like to stand there, as the warm draft blew their skirts up, but the men did not seem to mind; there was always a gang of them gaping and grinning and nudging, waiting for unsuspecting dames to walk across the ironwork.

With the first crack of daylight the parade of the Fourteenth Street beggars began. There were legless fellows; blind men who held onto small, faithful dogs; deformed, cleanly shaven fellows who wore army shirts and overseas hats to give a good "ex-service" effect; an old hag with scabby cheeks; a Negro boy who twitched horribly, allowing saliva to dribble over his chin, and all kinds of wrecked bits of humanity.

It was a busy thoroughfare, but there was room for all. The bootblacks —old men and young men—stood two or three yards apart, leaning against the low wall surrounding the square, and as you passed they called out (some briskly, others in a hollow, tired tone of voice) and pointed toward your shoes. "Shine 'em up five cents, shine 'em up five cents," they said. There were also young men and boys who peddled songs printed on big, square sheets of paper, songs that told you all about the silver lining and how to chase the blues away. And further down were the high-pressure boys, the lads who spat and hawked their wares at you, offering, for your consideration, socks, bars of candy, twenty-five-cent neckties ("they're worth two bucks apiece, mister, honest to Christ!") shoelaces, needles for the lady of the house, and little Japanese toys to tickle the kiddies' fancy. But the cleverest lads of all were the fellows who sold worthless watches out of small, black leather bags, one eye out for passing suckers, the other on the policeman down the street.

The noise was terrific, everything was bedlam. Folks crossed the street against the traffic and were shouted at by our vigilant police. Everywhere you turned a vender shoved an object under your nose, yelling, screaming, urging you to buy. Some even clutched you by the arm, others followed you a way with whining voices; and on all sides stood the pretzels, stacked up on long, upright sticks, trundled along by old women and men wheeling mangled baby-buggies.

Barkers stood in front of almost every store, like at a circus, rattling off the bargain prices of fur pieces, shoes and dresses hot from the marts of fashion, pointing to the goods in the windows. In their second-floor windows one of the bigger fur stores had six or seven manikins walking around in small circles, young girls with heavy make-up on their faces, modeling cloaks and fur pieces. A small crowd of idle men stood on the street below and made comments concerning the scenery above.

At ten o'clock most of the movie houses opened up, greeting the citizenry with a burst of electric lights in the box-office windows. Bargain prices were offered before noon, at the "early bird" matinee, and long lines of people, mostly men and girls out of work and a few who had night jobs, shoved their dimes through the "How Many?" window and went inside, into the warmth and the darkness.

Later on, on the corner of Irving Place, which was just a short distance from the square, the barker from the burlesk show swung into action. Every day he donned another costume. He was a small, hook-nosed gent and had a dry, hoarse way of shouting, as if his throat was lined with coal dust. Yesterday he wore a pirate costume, now he stood in a clown's outfit, his cheeks painted a sickly white, his great red grinning mouth standing from his face as raw as a fresh veal cutlet.

"Girls, girls," he shouted, "fifty bee-ootiful girls, men . . . dancing, singing, shaking . . . all young and easy to look at . . . smoking in loges, get along, folks, the show starts soon, you can't afford to miss this great, glittering, stoo-pendous array of bee-ootiful girls . . ."

The damp wind blew through his flimsy costume, he stuck another cough-drop into his mouth. "Girls, girls . . ." and his words go floating toward your back as you pass him by.

Down the street the radio-phonograph feud had already started up, an everyday occurrence. Over the doorways stand horns and from these horns the news and racket from the world goes forth—blaring out upon the street, prize-fight returns, Spanish music, and how to make a pudding out of two cups of flour and a pound of Sonny Boy oatmeal.

This is no place for quarter. Each man steps upon his comrade, some tread lightly, others crush you with their heavy boots. And centered between the sets of car tracks stand the policemen, the officers of the law— big fellows with white gloves on their mitts, their outdoor faces the color of a good grade of juicy beef, and when they raise their regal palms the traffic halts, stands still like a slack conveyor belt, awaiting the sharp slit of the whistle.

Swarm after swarm of heads pass, wave on wave, all kinds of nationalities, the true melting pot of the town. Little dark Cuban women, big black Negresses from Jamaica, tiny little kept women from West Side apartment houses, tall lanky Swedish girls with washed-out faded eyes, sturdy Polish housewives carrying big shopping bags—all crowd into the bargain stores and shove and push and jam near the counters. The salesgirls, kids who get twelve dollars a week, stand tired against the onrush, answering questions about the merchandise with dead, slack mouths, glancing at the clock often, putting on a brisk, alert front whenever the floor manager takes a casual stroll up and down the aisles.

Six days a week the swirl goes on. But within the square itself, it's quiet.

A few bums and seedy unemployed sit huddled on the benches, staring at the cliffs of buildings, gazing at the sea of passing heads. From a cold, gray sky a wind comes sniffing at their bones. 4%, says the sign over the Amalgamated Bank. The flavor lasts.

And the flagpole, like a tremendous carpet tack, sticks its points into the windy sky.

"Little Italy" in lower Manhattan is one of the city's more colorful neighborhoods, with its own festivals, governing bodies, and family traditions. A. J. Liebling, who specialized in off-beat characters and settings in many of his pieces for The New Yorker, *had a fine ear and a sharp eye for the Mulberry Street scene described in the selection below, reprinted from a collection of his work published in the year he died.*

A. J. Liebling

The reporter who made the sins of the press his personal domain, A. J. Liebling (1904–1963) was born in New York. After feature-writing for various newspapers, he joined the staff of *The New Yorker* in 1935. He was a war correspondent in France, where he particularly enjoyed the food and wine. His best-known work has been collected in *The Telephone Booth Indian* (1942), *Mink and Red Herring* (1949), and *The Earl of Louisiana* (1961). At the time of his death he was married to the writer Jean Stafford.

Beginning with the Undertaker

In the middle of any New York block there is likely to be one store that remains open and discreetly lighted all night. This is the undertaker's. The undertaker or an assistant is always in attendance, waiting for something to turn up. Undertakers are sociable men; they welcome company during their unavoidable periods of idleness. High-school boys study for their state Regents' examinations in undertakers' offices on hot June nights. The door is always open, the electric fan soothing, the whole environment more conducive to reflective scholarship than the crowded apartment where the boy lives. Policemen going off duty sometimes drop in for a visit with the undertaker before climbing into the subway for the long trip home to another part of the city.

There is no merchandise in the front part of an undertaker's store. Usually there are a few comfortable chairs for bereaved relatives, and policemen sit in these chairs. During the day, the undertaker acts as a referee in the disputes of children. Housewives tell him their troubles; priests appeal to him to head church committees. Ten to one he becomes the biggest man in the neighborhood, like my friend Mayor Angelo Rizzo of Mulberry Street. Some New York streets have mayors, but they are not elected. A man lives on a street until the mayoralty grows over him, like a patina. To Mayor Rizzo, Elizabeth Street, although but two blocks east of Mulberry, is an alien place. For the feast of San Gennaro, who is the Mulberry Street saint, Mayor Rizzo usually heads at least three committees and festoons his shop front with electric lights. A celebration on Elizabeth Street leaves him unmoved. "Just one of them Sicilian saints," he says.

Once Mayor Rizzo told me he was hard put to keep track of his constituents' baths. "I think I will have to get a secretary," he said, as he improved the taste of a casket salesman's gift cigar with a swig of iced *barbera* wine. He sat in front of 178 Mulberry Street, enthroned upon one of the elegant portable chairs which he is prepared to furnish in any number for correct funerals. "They should call this cigar a La Palooka," he remarked on the side.

"Mrs. Aranciata is getting crazy because she don't remember whether Jimmy has been to Cooney* Island twenty-two times or twenty-three times. So she come to me and said I should tell the kid not to go no more, because maybe that will make it an even number of times and he will get rheumatism. So I said to her, 'But suppose he has been only twenty-two times? Then by keeping him home you will be preventing him getting on the odd number again, and the rheumatism will be your fault.'

" 'Oh, *Madonna mia,*' she says, 'and what will I do?'

"So I says, 'Why don't you forget all about it and purtend this is a new year. Start all over again and when he goes to Cooney tell me, and I will keep track of it on a piece of paper.' So she is delighted and the next thing I know she tells all her friends, and now I got about fourteen women coming in wanting me to keep score how many times the family goes swimming.

"It is like when I feed one cat spaghetti a couple of winters ago and in a week I got a waiting line of five hundred and ninety-eight cats, including a lot of Sicilian cats from Elizabeth Street."

"But what difference does it make how many times you go swimming— at Coney or anyplace else?" I asked.

"What difference does it make?" shouted Mr. Rizzo. "Do you mean to tell me that you, an educated man, do not know that saltwater baths are only good for you if you go an odd number of times? Any old woman on Mulberry Street knows that much."

To prove his point Mayor Rizzo called the cop on the beat.

"You are an Italian," said His Honor. "Which is it lucky to take baths, an odd number or an even number?"

* This is the New York pronunciation of Coney Island. It seems to me as noteworthy as the Texas fashion of saying "Hughston" for Houston.

"Odd number," answered the officer promptly. "My mother-in-law, she keeps count on her fingers. She would never go in the water two times, or four times, in an afternoon, but always three times or five times."

The argument became a little involved here. Some of the folklore hydrotherapists held that each immersion counts as a bath, and if you go in the drink an odd number of times at each visit to the beach, your health will not suffer.

Others maintain that you must keep track of the total number of days' bathing, and be sure to wind up the season on an odd.

"I remember when I was a kid an old lady from Calabria made me go in fifty-one times one summer," said Al Gallichio, the restaurant man.

An antique and gracious lady waddling past with a bag of zucchini was invoked as a superior authority.

"Pardon me, madam," said Mayor Rizzo, "but I would wish to request a word with you."

"Voluntarily," she replied.

"When you are accustomed to go bathing, which is the more auspicious, to go an even or an uneven number of times?"

"Childish," said the dame. "It makes no difference. But once you have begun to go, you must go at least fifteen times, else your bones rot. It is for that reason I have not gone to the sea, this year, because I might not be able to afford fifteen visits."

She was an exception, because the odd-and-even belief, in one or other of its two forms, is prevalent all the way from Bleecker Street down to Park Row.

"It is very important this year," said the Mayor, "because we got no public bath in the neighborhood. There used to be a bathhouse on Center Market Place where the fellow would let you take a shower for a nickel. Of course, even the old timers do not count whether a shower is odd or even. But now the Broome Street Tamanacle* Church has bought the building. A lot of these old houses have no bathtubs even, so the nearest place the people can get a bath is Allen Street, and they figure they might just as well go out to Cooney.

"Do I believe in this odd-and-even business?" he said. "Well, I tell you. I went swimming off the Battery just once, which is an odd number, and a kid pushed my head under and nearly drowned me, so I figured if I went back, that would be an even number and even worse luck and I probably would remain drowned, so now I do all my swimming in a bathtub."

* A regional pronunciation of Tabernacle.

Like many other well-known writers—Walt Whitman, Hart Crane, Arthur Miller, Norman Mailer—Truman Capote has lived in Brooklyn Heights. In the essay below, which is included in his Selected Writings, *published in 1963, he describes his neighborhood historically and as he knew it in the 50s. Both Capote and Knapp's Antiques have since moved to Manhattan, but Brooklyn Heights, now designated a National Historic Landmark by the Federal Government, continues to attract new residents who enjoy its peaceful tree-lined streets and spectacular harbor view.*

Truman Capote

Truman Capote was born in New Orleans in 1924. In 1948, his first novel, *Other Voices, Other Rooms,* appeared. Since then he has gone from one success to another with short stories, novels, essays and plays. *Breakfast at Tiffany's* and *In Cold Blood* were turned into popular films; *The Grass Harp* was produced on Broadway.

A House on the Heights

I live in Brooklyn. By choice.

Those ignorant of its allures are entitled to wonder why. For, taken as a whole, it *is* an uninviting community. A veritable veldt of tawdriness where even the *noms des quartiers* aggravate: Flatbush and Flushing Avenue, Bushwick, Brownsville, Red Hook. Yet, in the greenless grime-gray, oases do occur, splendid contradictions, hearty echoes of healthier days. Of these seeming mirages, the purest example is the neighborhood in which I am situated, an area known as Brooklyn Heights. Heights, because it stands atop a cliff that secures a sea-gull's view of the Manhattan and Brooklyn bridges, of lower Manhattan's tall dazzle and the ship-lane waters, breeding river to bay to ocean, that encircle and seethe past posturing Miss Liberty.

I'm not much acquainted with the proper history of the Heights. However, I *believe* (but please don't trust me) that the oldest house, the oldest still extant and functioning, belongs to our back-yard neighbors, Mr. and Mrs. Philip Broughton. A silvery gray, shingle-wood Colonial shaded by trees robustly leafed, it was built in 1790, the home of a sea captain. Period prints, dated 1830, depict the Heights area as a cozy port bustling with billowed sails; and, indeed, many of the section's finer houses, particularly those of Federal design, were first intended to shelter the families of shipmasters. Cheerfully austere, as elegant and other-era as formal calling cards, these houses bespeak an age of able servants and solid fireside ease; of horses in musical harness (old rose-brick carriage houses abound hereabouts; all now, naturally, transformed into pleasant, if rather doll-pretty, dwellings); invoke specters of bearded seafaring fathers and bonneted stay-at-home wives: devoted parents to great broods of future bankers and fashionable brides. For a century or so that is how it must have been: a time of tree-shrouded streets, lanes limp with willow, August gardens brimming with bumblebees and herbaceous scent, of ship horns on the river, sails in the wind, and a country-green meadow sloping down to the harbor, a cow-grazing, butterflied meadow where children sprawled away breezy summer afternoons, where the slap of sleds resounded on December snows.

Is that how it was? Conceivably I take too Valentine a view. However it be, my Valentine assumes the stricter aspect of a steel engraving as we mosey, hand in hand, with Henry Ward Beecher, whose church once dominated the spiritual life of the Heights, through the latter half of the last century. The great Bridge, opened in 1883, now balanced above the river; and the port, each year expanding becoming a more raucous, big-business matter, chased the children out of the meadow, withered it, entirely whacked it away to make room for black palace-huge warehouses tickly with imported tarantulas and reeking of rotten bananas.

By 1910, the neighborhood, which comprises sly alleys and tucked-away courts and streets that sometimes run straight but also dwindle and bend, had undergone fiercer vicissitudes. Descendants of the Reverend Beecher's stiff-collared flock had begun removing themselves to other pastures; and immigrant tribes, who had first ringed the vicinity, at once infiltrated en masse. Whereupon a majority of what remained of genteel old stock, the sediment in the bottom of the bottle, poured forth from their homes, leaving them to be demolished or converted into eyesore-seedy rooming establishments.

So that, in 1925, Edmund Wilson, allowing a paragraph to what he considered the dead and dying Heights, disgustedly reported: "The pleasant red and pink brick houses still worthily represent the generation of Henry Ward Beecher; but an eternal Sunday is on them now; they seem sunk in a final silence. In the streets one may catch a glimpse of a solitary well-dressed old gentleman moving slowly a long way off; but in general the respectable have disappeared and only the vulgar survive. The empty quiet is broken by the shouts of shrill Italian children and by incessant mechanical pianos in dingy apartment houses, accompanied by human voices that seem almost as mechanical as they. At night, along unlighted streets, one gives a wide berth to drunkards that sprawl out across the pavement from the shadow of darkened doors; and I have known a dead horse to be left in the road—two blocks from the principal post office and not much more from Borough Hall—with no effort made to remove it, for nearly three weeks."

Gothic as this glimpse is, the neighborhood nevertheless continued to possess, cheap rents aside, some certain appeal brigades of the gifted—artists, writers—began to discover. Among those riding in on the initial wave was Hart Crane, whose poet's eye, focusing on his window view, produced *The Bridge*. Later, soon after the success of *Look Homeward, Angel,* Thomas Wolfe, noted prowler of the Brooklyn night, took quarters: an apartment, equipped with the most publicized icebox in literature's archives, which he maintained until his "overgrowed carcass" was carried home to the hills of Carolina. At one time, a stretch of years in the early forties, a single, heaven knows singular, house on Middagh Street boasted a roll call of residents that read: W. H. Auden, Richard Wright, Carson McCullers, Paul and Jane Bowles, the British composer Benjamin Britten, impresario and stage designer Oliver Smith, an authoress of murder entertainments—Miss Gypsy Rose Lee, and a Chimpanzee accompanied by Trainer. Each of the tenants in this ivory-tower boarding house contributed to its upkeep, lights, heat, the wages of a general cook (a former Cotton Club chorine), and all were present at the invitation of the owner, that very original editor, writer, *fantaisiste,* a gentleman with a guillotine tongue, yet benevolent and butter-hearted, the late, the justly lamented George Davis.

Now George is gone; and his house too: the necessities of some absurd civic project caused it to be torn down during the war. Indeed, the war years saw the neighborhood slide to its nadir. Many of the more substantial old houses were requisitioned by the military, as lodgings, as jukebox canteens, and their rural-reared, piney-woods personnel treated them quite as Sherman did those Dixie mansions. Not that it mattered; not that anyone gave a damn. No one did; until, soon after the war, the Heights commenced attracting a bright new clientele, brave pioneers bringing brooms and buckets of paint: urban, ambitious young couples, by and large mid-rung in their Doctor-Lawyer-Wall Street-Whatever careers, eager to restore to the Heights its shattered qualities of circumspect, comfortable charm.

For them, the section had much to offer: roomy big houses ready to be reconverted into private homes suitable for families of old-fashioned size; and such families are what these young people either had made or were making at stepladder rates. A good place to raise children, too, this neighborhood where the traffic is cautious, and the air has clarity, a seaside tartness; where there are gardens for games, quiet stoops for amusing; and where, above all, there is the Esplanade to roller-skate upon. (Forbidden: still the brats do it.) While far from being a butterflied meadow, the Esplanade, a wide terrace-like walk overlooking the harbor, does its contemporary best to approximate that playing pasture of long-gone girls and their brothers.

So, for a decade and longer, the experiment of reviving the Heights has proceeded: to the point where one is tempted to term it a *fait accompli.* Window boxes bloom with geraniums; according to the season, green foliated light falls through the trees or gathered autumn leaves burn at the corner; flower-loaded wagons wheel by while the flower seller sings his wares; in the dawn one occasionally hears a cock crow, for there is a lady with a garden who keeps hens and a rooster. On winter nights, when the wind brings the farewell callings of boats outward bound and carries across rooftops the chimney smoke of evening fires, there is a sense, evanescent but authentic as the firelight's flicker, of time come circle, of ago's sweeter glimmerings recaptured.

Though I'd long been acquainted with the neighborhood, having now and then visited there, my closer association began two years ago when a friend bought a house on Willow Street. One mild May evening he asked me over to inspect it. I was most impressed; exceedingly envious. There were twenty-eight rooms, high-ceilinged, well proportioned, and twenty-eight workable, marble-manteled fireplaces. There was a beautiful staircase floating upward in white, swan-simple curves to a skylight of sunny amber-gold glass. The floors were fine, the real thing, hard lustrous timber; and the walls! In 1820, when the house was built, men knew how to make walls—thick as a buffalo, immune to the mightiest cold, the meanest heat.

French doors led to a spacious rear porch reminiscent of Louisiana. A porch canopied, completely submerged, as though under a lake of leaves, by an ancient but admirably vigorous vine weighty with grapelike bunches of wisteria. Beyond, a garden: a tulip tree, a blossoming pear, a perched black-and-red bird bending a feathery branch of forsythia.

In the twilight, we talked, my friend and I. We sat on the porch con-

sulting Martinis—I urged him to have one more, another. It got to be
quite late, he began to see my point: Yes, twenty-eight rooms *were* rather
a lot; and yes, it seemed only *fair* that I should have some of them.

That is how I came to live in the yellow brick house on Willow Street.

Often a week passes without my "going to town," or "crossing the
bridge," as neighbors call a trip to Manhattan. Mystified friends, suspect-
ing provincial stagnation, inquire: "But what do you *do* over there?" Let
me tell you, life can be pretty exciting around here. Remember Colonel
Rudolf Abel, the Russian secret agent, the biggest spy ever caught in
America, head of the whole damned apparatus? Know where they nabbed
him? Right here! smack on Fulton Street! Trapped him in a building
between David Semple's fine-foods store and Frank Gambuzza's television
repair shop. Frank, grinning as though he'd done the job himself, had his
picture in *Life;* so did the waitress at the Music Box Bar, the colonel's
favorite watering hole. A peevish few of us couldn't fathom why our pictures weren't in *Life* too. Frank, the Music Box Bar girl, they weren't the
only people who knew the colonel. Such a gentleman-like gentleman: one
would never have *supposed.* . . .

I confess, we don't catch spies every day. But most days are supplied
with stimulants: in the harbor some exotic freighter to investigate; a bird
of strange plumage resting among the wisteria; or, and how exhilarating
an occurrence it is, a newly arrived shipment at Knapp's. Knapp's is a set
of shops, really a series of storerooms resembling caverns, clustered together on Fulton near Pineapple Street. The proprietor—that is too modest a designation for so commanding a figure—the czar, the Aga Khan of
these paradisal emporiums is Mr. George Knapp, known to his friends as
Father.

Father is a world traveler. Cards arrive: he is in Seville, now Copenhagen, now Milan, next week Manchester, everywhere and all the while on a
gaudy spending spree. Buying: blue crockery from a Danish castle. Pink
apothecary jars from an old London pharmacy. English brass, Barcelona
lamps, Battersea boxes, French paperweights, Italian witch balls, Greek
icons, Venetian blackamoors, Spanish saints, Korean cabinets; and junk,
glorious junk, a jumble of ragged dolls, broken buttons, a stuffed kanga-
roo, an aviary of owls under a great glass bell, the playing pieces of
obsolete games, the paper moneys of defunct governments, an ivory umbrella cane *sans* umbrella, crested chamber pots and mustache mugs and
irreparable clocks, cracked violins, a sundial that weighs seven hundred
pounds, skulls, snake vertebrae, elephants' hoofs, sleigh bells and Eskimo

carvings and mounted swordfish, medieval milkmaid stools, rusted fire-
arms and flaking waltz-age mirrors.

Then Father comes home to Brooklyn, his treasures trailing after him.
Uncrated, added to the already perilous clutter, the blackamoors prance
in the marvelous gloom, the swordfish glide through the store's Atlantic-
depth dusk. Eventually they will go: fancier *antiquaires,* and anonymous
mere beauty lovers, will come, cart them away. Meanwhile, poke around.
You're certain to find a plum; and it may be a peach. That paperweight—
the one imprisoning a Baccarat dragonfly. If you want it, take it now:
tomorrow, assuredly the day after, will see it on Fifty-Seventh Street at
quintuple the tariff.

Father has a partner, his wife Florence. She is from Panama, is handsome, fresh-colored and tall, trim enough to look well in the trousers she
affects, a woman of proud posture and, vis-à-vis customers, of nearly eccentric curtness, take-it-or-go disdain—but then, poor soul, she is under
the discipline of not being herself permitted to sell, even quote a price.
Only Father, with his Macaulayan memory, his dazzling ability to immediately lay hold of any item in the dizzying maze, is so allowed. Brooklyn-
born, waterfront-bred, always hatted and usually wearing a wet cold
cigar, a stout, short, round powerhouse with one arm, with a strutting
walk, a rough-guy voice, shy nervous sensitive eyes that blink when irrita-
tion makes him stutter, Father is nevertheless an aesthete. A tough aesthete who takes no guff, will not quibble over his evaluations, just declares: "Put it down!" and, "Get it Manhattan half the money, I give it
yuh free." They are an excellent couple, the Knapps. I explore their museum several times a week, and toward October, when a Franklin stove in
the shape of a witch hut warms the air and Florence serves cider accompanied by a damp delicious date-nut bread she bakes in discarded coffee-
cans, never miss a day. Occasionally, on these festive afternoons, Father
will gaze about him, blink-blink his eyes with vague disbelief, then, as
though his romantic accumulations were closing round him in a manner
menacing, observe: "I got to be crazy. Putting my heart in a fruitcake
business like this. And the *investment.* The money alone! Honest, in your
honest opinion, wouldn't you say I'm crazy?"

Certainly not. If, however, Mrs. Cornelius Oosthuizen were to beg the
question—

It seems improbable that someone of Mrs. Oosthuizen's elevation
should have condescended to distinguish me with her acquaintance. I owe
it all to a pound of dog meat. What happened was: the butcher's boy

delivered a purchase of mine which, by error, included hamburger meant to go to Mrs. O. Recognizing her name on the order slip, and having often remarked her house, a garnet-colored château in mood remindful of the old Schwab mansion on Manhattan's Riverside Drive, I thought of taking round the package myself, not dreaming to meet the fine lady, but, at most, ambitious for a moment's glance into her fortunate preserve. Fortunate, for it boasted, so I'd had confided to me, a butler and staff of six. Not that this is the Height's sole *maison de luxe:* we are blessed with several exponents of limousine life—but unarguably, Mrs. O. is *la regina di tutti.*

Approaching her property, I noticed a person in Persian lamb very vexedly punching the bell, pounding a brass knocker. "God damn you, Mabel," she said to the door; then turned, glared at me as I climbed the steps—a tall intimidating replica of frail unforbidding Miss Marianne Moore (who, it may be recalled, is a Brooklyn lady too). Pale lashless eyes, razor lips, hair a silver fuzz. "Ah, *you.* I know you," she accused me, as behind her the door was opened by an Irish crone wearing an ankle-length apron. "So. I suppose you've come to sign the petition? Very good of you, I'm sure." Mumbling an explanation, muttering servile civilities, I conveyed the butcher's parcel from my hands to hers; she, as though I'd tossed her a rather rotten fish, dangled it gingerly until the maid remarked: "Ma'am, 'tis Miss Mary's meat the good lad's brought."

"Indeed. Then don't stand there, Mabel. Take it." And, regarding me with a lessening astonishment that I could not, in her behalf, reciprocate: "Wipe your boots, come in. We will discuss the petition. Mabel, send Murphy with some Bristol and biscuit. . . . Oh? At the dentist's! When I *asked* him *not* to tamper with that tooth. What hellish nonsense," she swore, as we passed into a hatrack-vestibule. "Why didn't he go to the hypnotist, as I told him? Mary! Mary! Mary," she said when now appeared a friendly nice dog of cruel pedigree: a spaniel *cum* chow attached to the legs of a dachshund, "I believe Mabel has your lunch. Mabel, take Miss Mary to the kitchen. And we will have our biscuits in the Red Room."

The room, in which red could be discerned only in a bowl of porcelain roses and a basket of marzipan strawberries, contained velvet-swagged windows that commanded a pulse-quickening prospect: sky, skyline, far away a wooded slice of Staten Island. In other respects, the room, a heavy confection, cumbersome, humorless, a hunk of Beidermeier pastry, did not recommend itself. "It was my grandmother's bedroom; my father preferred it as a parlor. Cornelius, Mr. Oosthuizen, died here. Very suddenly:

while listening at the radio to the Roosevelt person. An attack. Brought
on by anger and cigars. I'm sure you won't ask permission to smoke. Sit
down. . . . Not there. There, by the window. Now here, it *should* be
here, somewhere, in this drawer? Could it be upstairs? Damn Murphy,
horrid man always meddling with my—no, I have it: the petition."

The document stated, and objected to, the plans of a certain minor
religious sect that had acquired a half-block of houses on the Heights
which they planned to flatten and replace with a dormitory building for
the benefit of their Believers. Appended to it were some dozen protesting
signatures; the Misses Seeley had signed, and Mr. Arthur Veere Vinson,
Mrs. K. Mackaye Brownlowe—descendants of the children in the
meadow, the old-guard survivors of *their* neighborhood's evilest hours,
those happy few who regularly attended Mrs. O.'s black-tie-sit-downs. She
wasted no eloquence on the considerable merit of their complaint; simply, "Sign it," she ordered, a Lady Catherine de Brough instructing a Mr.
Collins.

Sherry came; and with it an assembly of cats. Scarred battlers with lep-
rous fur and punch-drunk eyes. Mrs. O., motioning toward the least respectable of these, a tiger-striped marauder, told me: "This is the one you
may take home. He's been with us a month, we've put him in splendid
condition, I'm sure you'll be devoted. Dogs? What *sort* of dogs have you?
Well, I don't approve the pure breeds. Anyone will give *them* a home. I
took Miss Mary off the street. And Lovely Louise, Mouse and Sweet William—my dogs, all my cats, too, came off the streets. Look below, there in
the garden. Under the heaven tree. Those markings: graves are what you
see, some as old as my childhood. The seashells are goldfish. The yellow
coral, canaries. That white stone is a rabbit; that cross of pebbles: my
favorite, the first Mary—angel girl, went bathing in the river and caught
a fatal chill. I used to tease Cornelius, Mr. Oosthuizen, told him, ha-ha,
told him I planned to put him there with the rest of my darlings. Ha-ha,
he wasn't amused, not at all. So, I mean to say, your having dogs doesn't
signify: Billy here has such spirit, *he* can hold his own. No, I insist you
have him. For I can't keep him much longer, he's a disturbing influence;
and if I let him loose, he'll run back to his bad old life in the St. George
alley. I wouldn't want *that* on my conscience if I were you."

Her persuasions failed; in consequence our parting was cool. Yet at
Christmas she sent me a card, a Cartier engraving of the heaven tree protecting the bones in its sad care. And once, encountering her at the bakery, where we both were buying brownies, we discussed the impudent
disregard her petition had received: alas, the wreckers had wrecked, the

brethren were building. On the same occasion, she shame-on-you informed me that Billy the cat, released from her patronage, had indeed returned to the sinful ways of the St. George alley.

The St. George alley, adjoining a small cinema, is a shadowy shelter for vagrants: wino derelicts wandered over the bridge from Chinatown and the Bowery share it with other orphaned, gone-wild creatures: cats, as many as minnows in a stream, who gather in their greatest numbers toward nightfall; for then, as darkness happens, strange-eyed women, not unlike those black-clothed fanatics who haunt the cat arenas in Rome, go stealing through the alley with caressing hisses and sacks of crumbled salmon. (Which isn't to suggest that Mrs. O. is one who indulges in this somehow unhealthy hobby: regarding animals, her actions, while perhaps a bit overboard, are kindly meant, and not untypical of the Heights, where a high percentage of the pet population has been adopted off the streets. Astonishing, really, the amount of lost strays who roam their way into the neighborhood, as though instinct informed them they'd find someone here who couldn't abide being followed through the rain, but would, instead, lead them home, boil milk, and call Dr. Wasserman, Bernie, our smart-as-they-come young vet whose immaculate hospital resounds with the music of Bach concertos and the barkings of mending beasts.)

Just now, in connection with these notes, I was hunting through a hieroglyphic shambles I call my journal. Odd, indeed the oddest, jottings—a majority of which conceal from me their meanings. God knows what "Thunder on Cobra Street" refers to. Or "A diarrhea of platitudes in seventeen tongues." Unless it is intended to describe a most tiresome local person, a linguist terribly talkative in many languages though articulate in none. However, "Took T&G to G&T" does make sense.

The first initials represent two friends, the latter a restaurant not far away. You must have heard of it, Gage & Tollner. Like Kolb's and Antoine's in New Orleans, Gage & Tollner is a last-century enterprise that has kept in large degree its founding character. The shaky dance of its gaslight chandeliers is not a period-piece hoax; nor do the good plain marble-topped tables, the magnificent array of gold-edged mirrors, seem sentimental affectations—rather, it is a testament to the seriousness of the proprietors, who have obliged us by letting the place stay much as it was that opening day in 1874. One mightn't suppose it, for in the atmosphere there is none of the briny falderal familiar to such aquariums, but the specialty is sea food. The best. Chowders the doughtiest down-Easter must approve. Lobsters that would appease Nero. Myself, I am a soft-shelled-crab *aficionado:* a plate of sautéed crabs, a halved lemon, a glass of chilled Chablis: most satisfactory. The waiters, too, dignified but swift-to-smile Negroes who take pride in their work, contribute to the goodness of Gage & Tollner; on the sleeves of their very laundered jackets they sport military-style chevrons awarded according to the number of years each has served; and, *were* this the Army, some would be generals.

Nearby, there is another restaurant, a fraction less distinguished, but of similar vintage and virtually the same menu: Joe's—Joe being, by the way, an attractive young lady. On the far fringes of the Heights, just before Brooklyn becomes Brooklyn again, there is a street of Gypsies with Gypsy cafés (have your future foretold and be tattooed while sipping tankards of Moorish tea); there is also an Arab-Armenian quarter sprinkled with spice-saturated restaurants where one can buy, hot from the oven, a crusty sort of pancake frosted with sesame seed—once in a while I carry mine down to the waterfront, intending to share with the gulls; but, gobbling as I go, none is ever left. On a summer's evening a stroll across the bridge, with cool winds singing through the steel shrouds, with stars moving about above and ships below, can be intoxicating, particularly if you are headed toward the roasting-pork, sweet-and-sour aromas of Chinatown.

Another journal notation reads, "At last a face in the ghost hotel!" Which means: after months of observation, in all climates at all hours, I'd sighted someone in a window of a haunted-seeming riverfront building that stands on Water Street at the foot of the Heights. A lonely hotel I often make the destination of my walks: because I think it romantic, in aggravated moments imagine retiring there, for it is as secluded as Mt. Athos, remoter than the Krak Chevalier in the mountains of wildest Syria. Daytimes the location, a dead-end Chiricoesque piazza facing the river, is little disturbed; at night, not at all: not a sound, except foghorns and a distant traffic whisper from the bridge which bulks above. Peace, and the shivering glow of gliding-by tugs and ferries.

The hotel is three-storied. Sunstruck scraps of reflected river-shine, and broken, jigsaw images of the bridge waver across the windows; but beyond the glass nothing stirs: the rooms, despite contradictory evidence, milk bottles on sills, a hat on a hook, unmade beds and burning bulbs, appear unoccupied: never a soul to be seen. Like the sailors of the *Marie Celeste,* the guests, hearing a knock, must have opened their doors to a stranger who swallowed them whole. Could it be, perhaps it *was,* the stranger himself that I saw?—"At last a face in the ghost hotel!" I glimpsed him just the once, one April afternoon one cloudless blue day; and he, a balding man in an undershirt, hurled up a window, flexed hairy arms, yawned hugely, hugely inhaled the river breeze—was gone. No, on careful second thought, I will never set foot in that hotel. For I should either be devoured or have my mystery dispelled. As children we are sensitive to mystery: locked boxes, whisperings behind closed doors, the what-thing that lurks yonder in the trees waits in every stretch between street lamps; but as we grow older all is too explainable, the capacity to invent pleasurable alarm recedes: too bad, a pity—throughout our lives we ought to believe in ghost hotels.

Close by the hotel begins a road that leads along the river. Silent miles of warehouses with shuttered wooden windows, docks resting on the water like sea spiders. From May through September, *la saison pour la plage,* these docks are diving boards for husky ragamuffins—while perfumed apes, potentates of the waterfront but once dock-divers themselves, cruise by steering two-toned (banana-tomato) car concoctions. Crane-carried tractors and cotton bales and unhappy cattle sway above the holds of ships bound for Bahia, for Bremen, for ports spelling their names in Oriental calligraphy. Provided one has made waterfront friends, it is sometimes possible to board the freighters, carouse and sun yourself: you may even be asked to lunch—and I, for one, am always quick to accept, embarrassingly so if the hosts are Scandinavian: they always set a superior table from larders brimming with smoked "taste thrills" and iced aquavit. Avoid the Greek ships, however: very poor cuisine, no liquor served except *ouzo,* a sickly licorice syrup; and, at least in the opinion of this panhandler, the grub on French freighters by no means meets the standards one might reasonably expect.

The tugboat people are usually good for a cup of coffee, and in wintry weather, when the river is tossing surf, what joy to take refuge in a stove-heated tug cabin and thaw out with a mug of the blackest Java. Now and again along the route minuscule beaches occur, and once, it was around sunset on a quiet Sunday, I saw on one of them something that made me look twice, and twice more: still it seemed a vision. Every kind of sailor is common enough here, even saronged East Indians, even the giant Senegalese, their onyx arms afire with blue, with yellow tattooed flowers, with saucy torsos and garish *graffitti* (Je t'aime, Hard Luck, Mimi Chang, Adios Amigo). Runty Russians, too—one sees them about, flap-flapping in their pajama-like costumes. But the barefooted sailors on the beach, the three I saw reclining there, profiles set against the sundown, seemed mythical as mermen: more exactly, mermaids—for their hair, striped with albino streaks, was lady-length, a savage fiber falling to their shoulders; and in their ears gold rings glinted. Whether plenipotentiaries from the pearl-floored palace of Poseidon or mariners merely, Viking-tressed seamen out of the Gothic North languishing after a long and barberless voyage, they are included permanently in my memory's curio cabinet: an object to be revolved in the light that way and this, like those crystal lozenges with secretive carvings sealed inside.

After consideration, "Thunder on Cobra Street" does become decipherable. On the Heights there is no Cobra Street, though a street exists that suits the name, a steep downhill incline leading to a dark sector of the dockyards. Not a true part of the Heights neighborhood, it lies, like a serpent at the gates, on the outmost periphery. Seedy hangouts, beer-sour bars and bitter candy stores mingle among the eroding houses, the multi-family dwellings that architecturally range from time-blackened brownstone to magnified concepts of Mississippi privy.

Here, the gutters are acrawl with Cobras; that is, a gang of "juvenile" delinquents: COBRA, the word is stamped on their sweat shirts, painted, sometimes in letters that shine with a fearful phosphorescence, across the backs of their leather jackets. The steep street is within their ugly estate, a bit of their "turf," as they term it; an infinitesimal bit, for the Cobras, a powerful cabala, cast owning eyes on acres of metropolitan terrain. I am not brave—*au contraire;* quite frankly these fellows, may they be twelve years old or twenty, set my heart thumping like a sinner's at Sunday meeting. Nevertheless, when it has been a matter of convenience to pass through this section of their domain, I've compelled my nerves to accept the challenge.

On the last venture, and perhaps it will remain the last, I was carrying a good camera. The sun was unseen in a sky that ought to either rumble or rain. Rackety children played skip-rope, while a lamppost-lot of idle elders looked on, dull-faced and drooping: a denim-painted, cowboy-booted gathering of Cobras. Their eyes, their asleep sick insolent eyes, swerved on me as I climbed the street. I crossed to the opposite curb; then *knew*, without needing to verify it, that the Cobras had uncoiled and were sliding toward me. I heard them whistling; and the children hushed, the skip-rope ceased swishing. Someone—a pimpled purple birthmark bandit-masked the lower half of his face—said, "Hey yuh, Whitey, lem-meseeduhcamra." Quicken one's step? Pretend not to hear? But every alternative seemed explosive. "Hey, Whitey, hey yuh, takemuhpitchawant-cha?"

Thunder salvaged the moment. Thunder that rolled, crashed down the street like a truck out of control. We all looked up, a sky ripe for storm stared back. I shouted, "Rain! Rain!" and ran. Ran for the Heights, that safe citadel, that bourgeois bastion. Tore along the Esplanade—where the nice young mothers were racing their carriages against the coming disaster. Caught my breath under the thrashing leaves of troubled elms, rushed on: saw the flower-wagon man struggling with his thunder-frightened horse. Saw, twenty yards ahead, then ten, five, then none, the yellow house on Willow Street. Home! And happy to be.

Probably the finest personal essay ever written about New York is the one by E. B. White that first appeared in 1949 and is reprinted in full below. For many lovers of the city it has become the definitive tribute.

E. B. White

A distinguished stylist, subtle humorist, and the author of two children's classics, *Stuart Little* (1945) and *Charlotte's Web* (1952), E. B. White has been writing both light and serious pieces for *The New Yorker* since its early days. His collections of essays include *Is Sex Necessary*, written with James Thurber; *Quo Vadimus?*, *One Man's Meat*, *The Second Tree from the Corner*, and *The Points of My Compass*. He has also written a large number of witty poems and with his wife, Katherine S. White, is the coeditor of *A Sub-Treasury of American Humor*. His revision of William Strunk, Jr.'s *The Elements of Style*, published in 1959, has become a standard reference work. E. B. White was born in Mount Vernon, New York, in 1899 and has lived in Maine for many years.

Here Is New York

On any person who desires such queer prizes, New York will bestow the gift of loneliness and the gift of privacy. It is this largess that accounts for the presence within the city's walls of a considerable section of the population; for the residents of Manhattan are to a large extent strangers who have pulled up stakes somewhere and come to town, seeking sanctuary or fulfillment or some greater or lesser grail. The capacity to make such dubious gifts is a mysterious quality of New York. It can destroy an individual, or it can fulfill him, depending a good deal on luck. No one should come to New York to live unless he is willing to be lucky.

New York is the concentrate of art and commerce and sport and religion and entertainment and finance, bringing to a single compact arena the gladiator, the evangelist, the promoter, the actor, the trader and the merchant. It carries on its lapel the unexpungeable odor of the long past, so that no matter where you sit in New York you feel the vibrations of great times and tall deeds, of queer people and events and undertakings. I am sitting at the moment in a stifling hotel room in 90-degree heat, halfway down an air shaft, in midtown. No air moves in or out of the room, yet I am curiously affected by emanations from the immediate surroundings. I am twenty-two blocks from where Rudolph Valentino lay in state, eight blocks from where Nathan Hale was executed, five blocks from the publisher's office where Ernest Hemingway hit Max Eastman on the nose, four miles from where Walt Whitman sat sweating out editorials for the Brooklyn Eagle, thirty-four blocks from the street Willa Cather lived in when she came to New York to write books about Nebraska, one block from where Marceline used to clown on the boards of the Hippodrome, thirty-six blocks from the spot where the historian Joe Gould kicked a radio to pieces in full view of the public, thirteen blocks from where Harry Thaw shot Stanford White, five blocks from where I used to usher at the Metropolitan Opera and only a hundred and twelve blocks from the spot where Clarence Day the Elder was washed of his sins in the Church of the Epiphany (I could continue this list indefinitely); and for that matter I am probably occupying the very room that any number of exalted and somewise memorable characters sat in, some of them on hot, breathless afternoons, lonely and private and full of their own sense of emanations from without.

When I went down to lunch a few minutes ago I noticed that the man sitting next to me (about eighteen inches away along the wall) was Fred Stone. The eighteen inches were both the connection and the separation that New York provides for its inhabitants. My only connection with Fred Stone was that I saw him in *The Wizard of Oz* around the beginning of the century. But our waiter felt the same stimulus from being close to a man from Oz, and after Mr. Stone left the room the waiter told me that when he (the waiter) was a young man just arrived in this country and before he could understand a word of English, he had taken his girl for their first theater date to *The Wizard of Oz*. It was a wonderful show, the waiter recalled—a man of straw, a man of tin. Wonderful! (And still only eighteen inches away.) "Mr. Stone is a very hearty eater," said the waiter thoughtfully, content with this fragile participation in destiny, this link with Oz.

New York blends the gift of privacy with the excitement of participation; and better than most dense communities it succeeds in insulating the individual (if he wants it, and almost everybody wants or needs it) against all enormous and violent and wonderful events that are taking place every minute. Since I have been sitting in this miasmic air shaft, a good many rather splashy events have occurred in town. A man shot and killed his wife in a fit of jealousy. It caused no stir outside his block and got only small mention in the papers. I did not attend. Since my arrival, the greatest air show ever staged in all the world took place in town. I didn't attend and neither did most of the eight million other inhabitants, although they say there was quite a crowd. I didn't even hear any planes except a couple of westbound commercial airliners that habitually use this air shaft to fly over. The biggest ocean-going ships on the North Atlantic arrived and departed. I didn't notice them and neither did most other New Yorkers. I am told this is the greatest seaport in the world, with six hundred and fifty miles of water front, and ships calling here from many exotic lands, but the only boat I've happened to notice since my arrival was a small sloop tacking out of the East River night before last on the ebb tide when I was walking across the Brooklyn Bridge. I heard the *Queen Mary* blow one midnight, though, and the sound carried the whole history of departure and longing and loss. The Lions have been in convention. I've seen not one Lion. A friend of mine saw one and told me about him. (He was lame, and was wearing a bolero.) At the ballgrounds and horse parks the greatest sporting spectacles have been enacted. I saw no ballplayer, no race horse. The governor came to town. I heard the siren scream, but that was all there was to that—an eighteen-inch margin again. A man was killed by a falling cornice. I was not a party to the tragedy, and again the inches counted heavily.

I mention these merely to show that New York is peculiarly constructed to absorb almost anything that comes along (whether a thousand-foot liner out of the East or a twenty-thousand-man convention out of the West) without inflicting the event on its inhabitants; so that every event is, in a sense, optional, and the inhabitant is in the happy position of being able to choose his spectacle and so conserve his soul. In most metropolises, small and large, the choice is often not with the individual at all. He is thrown to the Lions. The Lions are overwhelming; the event is unavoidable. A cornice falls, and it hits every citizen on the head, every last man in town. I sometimes think that the only event that hits every New Yorker on the head is the annual St. Patrick's Day parade, which is fairly penetrating—the Irish are a hard race to tune out, there are 500,000 of them in residence, and they have the police force right in the family.

The quality in New York that insulates its inhabitants from life may simply weaken them as individuals. Perhaps it is healthier to live in a community where, when a cornice falls, you feel the blow; where, when the governor passes, you see at any rate his hat.

I am not defending New York in this regard. Many of its settlers are probably here merely to escape, not face, reality. But whatever it means, it is a rather rare gift, and I believe it has a positive effect on the creative capacities of New Yorkers—for creation is in part merely the business of forgoing the great and small distractions.

Although New York often imparts a feeling of great forlornness or for-sakenness, it seldom seems dead or unresourceful; and you always feel that either by shifting your location ten blocks or by reducing your fortune by five dollars you can experience rejuvenation. Many people who have no real independence of spirit depend on the city's tremendous variety and sources of excitement for spiritual sustenance and maintenance of morale. In the country there are a few chances of sudden rejuvenation—a shift in weather, perhaps, or something arriving in the mail. But in New York the chances are endless. I think that although many persons are here from some excess of spirit (which caused them to break away from their small town), some, too, are here from a deficiency of spirit, who find in New York a protection, or an easy substitution.

There are roughly three New Yorks. There is, first, the New York of the man or woman who was born here, who takes the city for granted and accepts its size and its turbulence as natural and inevitable. Second, there is the New York of the commuter—the city that is devoured by locusts each day and spat out each night. Third, there is the New York of the person who was born somewhere else and came to New York in quest of something. Of these three trembling cities the greatest is the last—the city of final destination, the city that is a goal. It is this third city that accounts for New York's high-strung disposition, its poetical deportment, its dedication to the arts, and its incomparable achievements. Commuters give the city its tidal restlessness; natives give it solidity and continuity; but the settlers give it passion. And whether it is a farmer arriving from Italy to set up a small grocery store in a slum, or a young girl arriving from a small town in Mississippi to escape the indignity of being observed by her neighbors, or a boy arriving from the Corn Belt with a manuscript in his suitcase and a pain in his heart, it makes no difference: each embraces New York with the intense excitement of first love, each absorbs New York with the fresh eyes of an adventurer, each generates heat and light to dwarf the Consolidated Edison Company.

The commuter is the queerest bird of all. The suburb he inhabits has no essential vitality of its own and is a mere roost where he comes at day's end to go to sleep. Except in rare cases, the man who lives in Mamaroneck or Little Neck or Teaneck, and works in New York, discovers nothing much about the city except the time of arrival and departure of trains and buses, and the path to a quick lunch. He is desk-bound, and has never, idly roaming in the gloaming, stumbled suddenly on Belvedere Tower in the Park, seen the ramparts rise sheer from the water of the pond, and the boys along the shore fishing for minnows, girls stretched out negligently on the shelves of the rocks; he has never come suddenly on anything at all in New York as a loiterer, because he has had no time between trains. He has fished in Manhattan's wallet and dug out coins, but has never listened to Manhattan's breathing, never awakened to its morning, never dropped off to sleep in its night. About 400,000 men and women come charging onto the Island each week-day morning, out of the mouths of tubes and tunnels. Not many among them have ever spent a drowsy afternoon in the great rustling oaken silence of the reading room of the Public Library, with the book elevator (like an old water wheel) spewing out books onto the trays. They tend their furnaces in Westchester and in Jersey, but have never seen the furnaces of the Bowery, the fires that burn in oil drums on zero winter nights. They may work in the financial district downtown and never see the extravagant plantings of Rockefeller Center—the daffodils and grape hyacinths and birches and the flags trimmed to the wind on a fine morning in spring. Or they may work in a midtown office and may let a whole year swing round without sighting Governors Island from the sea wall. The commuter dies with tremendous mileage to his credit, but he is no rover. His entrances and exits are more devious than those in a prairie-dog village; and he calmly plays bridge while buried in the mud at the bottom of the East River. The Long Island Rail Road alone carried forty million commuters last year; but many of them were the same fellow retracing his steps.

The terrain of New York is such that a resident sometimes travels farther, in the end, than a commuter. Irving Berlin's journey from Cherry Street in the lower East Side to an apartment uptown was through an alley and was only three or four miles in length; but it was like going three times around the world.

A poem compresses much in a small space and adds music, thus heightening its meaning. The city is like poetry: it compresses all life, all races and breeds, into a small island and adds music and the accompaniment of internal engines. The island of Manhattan is without any doubt the greatest human concentrate on earth, the poem whose magic is comprehensible to millions of permanent residents but whose full meaning will always remain elusive. At the feet of the tallest and plushiest offices lie the crummiest slums. The genteel mysteries housed in the Riverside Church are only a few blocks from the voodoo charms of Harlem. The merchant princes, riding to Wall Street in their limousines down the East River Drive, pass within a few hundred yards of the gypsy kings; but the princes do not know they are passing kings, and the kings are not up yet anyway —they live a more leisurely life than the princes and get drunk more consistently.

New York is nothing like Paris; it is nothing like London; and it is not Spokane multiplied by sixty, or Detroit multiplied by four. It is by all odds the loftiest of cities. It even managed to reach the highest point in the sky at the lowest moment of the depression. The Empire State Building shot twelve hundred and fifty feet into the air when it was madness to put out as much as six inches of new growth. (The building has a mooring mast that no dirigible has ever tied to; it employs a man to flush toilets in slack times; it has been hit by an airplane in a fog, struck countless times by lightning, and been jumped off of by so many unhappy people that pedestrians instinctively quicken step when passing Fifth Avenue and 34th Street.)

Manhattan has been compelled to expand skyward because of the absence of any other direction in which to grow. This, more than any other thing, is responsible for its physical majesty. It is to the nation what the white church spire is to the village—the visible symbol of aspiration and faith, the white plume saying that the way is up. The summer traveler swings in over Hell Gate Bridge and from the window of his sleeping car as it glides above the pigeon lofts and back yards of Queens looks southwest to where the morning light first strikes the steel peaks of midtown, and he sees its upward thrust unmistakable: the great walls and towers rising, the smoke rising, the heat not yet rising, the hopes and ferments of so many awakening millions rising—this vigorous spear that presses heaven hard.

It is a miracle that New York works at all. The whole thing is implausible. Every time the residents brush their teeth, millions of gallons of water must be drawn from the Catskills and the hills of Westchester. When a young man in Manhattan writes a letter to his girl in Brooklyn, the love message gets blown to her through a pneumatic tube—*pfft*—just like that. The subterranean system of telephone cables, power lines, steam pipes, gas mains and sewer pipes is reason enough to abandon the island to the gods and the weevils. Every time an incision is made in the pavement, the noisy surgeons expose ganglia that are tangled beyond belief. By rights New York should have destroyed itself long ago, from panic or fire or rioting or failure of some vital supply line in its circulatory system or from some deep labyrinthine short circuit. Long ago the city should have experienced an insoluble traffic snarl at some impossible bottleneck. It should have perished of hunger when food lines failed for a few days. It should have been wiped out by a plague starting in its slums or carried in by ships' rats. It should have been overwhelmed by the sea that licks at it on every side. The workers in its myriad cells should have succumbed to nerves, from the fearful pall of smoke-fog that drifts over every few days from Jersey, blotting out all light at noon and leaving the high offices suspended, men groping and depressed, and the sense of world's end. It should have been touched in the head by the August heat and gone off its rocker.

Mass hysteria is a terrible force, yet New Yorkers seem always to escape it by some tiny margin: they sit in stalled subways without claustrophobia, they extricate themselves from panic situations by some lucky wisecrack, they meet confusion and congestion with patience and grit—a sort of perpetual muddling through. Every facility is inadequate—the hospitals and schools and playgrounds are overcrowded, the express highways are feverish, the unimproved highways and bridges are bottlenecks; there is not enough air and not enough light, and there is usually either too much heat or too little. But the city makes up for its hazards and its deficiencies by supplying its citizens with massive doses of a supplementary vitamin—the sense of belonging to something unique, cosmopolitan, mighty and unparalleled.

To an outlander a stay in New York can be and often is a series of small embarrassments and discomforts and disappointments: not understanding the waiter, not being able to distinguish between a sucker joint and a friendly saloon, riding the wrong subway, being slapped down by a bus driver for asking an innocent question, enduring sleepless nights when the street noises fill the bedroom. Tourists make for New York, particularly in summertime—they swarm all over the Statue of Liberty (where many a resident of the town has never set foot), they invade the Automat, visit radio studios, St. Patrick's Cathedral, and they window shop. Mostly they have a pretty good time. But sometimes in New York you run across the disillusioned—a young couple who are obviously visitors, newlyweds perhaps, for whom the bright dream has vanished. The place has been too much for them; they sit languishing in a cheap restaurant over a speechless meal.

The oft-quoted thumbnail sketch of New York is, of course: "It's a wonderful place, but I'd hate to live there." I have an idea that people from villages and small towns, people accustomed to the convenience and the friendliness of neighborhood over-the-fence living, are unaware that life in New York follows the neighborhood pattern. The city is literally a composite of tens of thousands of tiny neighborhood units. There are, of course, the big districts and big units: Chelsea and Murray Hill and Gramercy (which are residential units), Harlem (a racial unit), Greenwich Village (a unit dedicated to the arts and other matters), and there is Radio City (a commercial development), Peter Cooper Village (a housing unit), the Medical Center (a sickness unit) and many other sections each of which has some distinguishing characteristic. But the curious thing about New York is that each large geographical unit is composed of countless small neighborhoods. Each neighborhood is virtually self-sufficient. Usually it is no more than two or three blocks long and a couple of blocks wide. Each area is a city within a city within a city. Thus, no matter where you live in New York, you will find within a block or two a grocery store, a barbershop, a newsstand and shoeshine shack, an ice-coal-and-wood cellar (where you write your order on a pad outside as you walk by), a dry cleaner, a laundry, a delicatessen (beer and sandwiches delivered at any hour to your door), a flower shop, an undertaker's parlor, a movie house, a radio-repair shop, a stationer, a haberdasher, a tailor, a drugstore, a garage, a tearoom, a saloon, a hardware store, a liquor store, a shoe-repair shop. Every block or two, in most residential sections of New York, is a little main street. A man starts for work in the morning and before he has gone two hundred yards he has completed half a dozen missions: bought a paper, left a pair of shoes to be soled, picked up a pack of cigarettes, ordered a bottle of whiskey to be dispatched in the opposite direction against his home-coming, written a message to the unseen forces of the wood cellar, and notified the dry cleaner that a pair of trousers awaits call. Homeward bound eight hours later, he buys a bunch of pussy willows, a Mazda bulb, a drink, a shine—all between the corner where he steps off the bus and his apartment. So complete is each neighborhood, and so strong the sense of neighborhood, that many a New Yorker spends a lifetime within the confines of an area smaller than a country village. Let him walk two blocks from his corner and he is in a strange land and will feel uneasy till he gets back.

Storekeepers are particularly conscious of neighborhood boundary lines. A woman friend of mine moved recently from one apartment to another, a distance of three blocks. When she turned up, the day after the move, at the same grocer's that she had patronized for years, the proprietor was in ecstasy—almost in tears—at seeing her. "I was afraid," he said, "now that you've moved away I wouldn't be seeing you any more." To him, *away* was three blocks, or about seven hundred and fifty feet.

I am, at the moment of writing this, living not as a neighborhood man in New York but as a transient, or vagrant, in from the country for a few days. Summertime is a good time to re-examine New York and to receive again the gift of privacy, the jewel of loneliness. In summer the city contains (except for tourists) only die-hards and authentic characters. No casual, spotty dwellers are around, only the real article. And the town has a somewhat relaxed air, and one can lie in a loincloth, gasping and remembering things.

I've been remembering what it felt like as a young man to live in the same town with giants. When I first arrived in New York my personal giants were a dozen or so columnists and critics and poets whose names appeared regularly in the papers. I burned with a slow steady fever just because I was on the same island with Don Marquis, Heywood Broun, Christopher Morley, Franklin P. Adams, Robert C. Benchley, Frank Sullivan, Dorothy Parker, Alexander Woollcott, Ring Lardner and Stephen Vincent Benét. I would hang around the corner of Chambers Street and Broadway, thinking: "Somewhere in that building is the typewriter that archy the cockroach jumps on at night." New York hardly gave me a living at that period, but it sustained me. I used to walk quickly past the house in West 13th Street between Sixth and Seventh where F.P.A. lived, and the block seemed to tremble under my feet—the way Park Avenue trembles when a train leaves Grand Central. This excitation (nearness of giants) is a continuing thing. The city is always full of young worshipful beginners—young actors, young aspiring poets, ballerinas, painters, reporters, singers—each depending on his own brand of tonic to stay alive, each with his own stable of giants.

New York provides not only a continuing excitation but also a spectacle that is continuing. I wander around, re-examining this spectacle, hoping that I can put it on paper. It is Saturday, toward the end of the afternoon. I turn through West 48th Street. From the open windows of the drum and saxophone parlors come the listless sounds of musical instruction, monstrous insect noises in the brooding field of summer. The Cort Theater is disgorging its matinee audience. Suddenly the whole block is filled with the mighty voice of a street singer. He approaches, looking for an audience, a large, cheerful Negro with grand-opera contours, strolling with head thrown back, filling the canyon with uninhibited song. He carries a long cane as his sole prop, and is tidily but casually dressed—slacks, seersucker jacket, a book showing in his pocket.

This is perfect artistic timing; the audience from the Cort, where *The Respectful Prostitute* is playing, has just received a lesson in race relations and is in a mood to improve the condition of the black race as speedily as possible. Coins (mostly quarters) rattle to the street, and a few minutes of minstrelsy improves the condition of one Negro by about eight dollars. If he does as well as this at every performance, he has a living right there. New York is the city of opportunity, they say. Even the mounted cop, clumping along on his nag a few minutes later, scans the gutter carefully for dropped silver, like a bird watching for spilt grain.

It is seven o'clock and I re-examine an exspeakeasy in East 53rd Street, with dinner in mind. A thin crowd, a summer-night buzz of fans interrupted by an occasional drink being shaken at the small bar. It is dark in here (the proprietor sees no reason for boosting his light bill just because liquor laws have changed). How dark, how pleasing; and how miraculously beautiful the murals showing Italian lake scenes—probably executed by a cousin of the owner. The owner himself mixes. The fans intone the prayer for cool salvation. From the next booth drifts the conversation of radio executives; from the green salad comes the little taste of garlic. Behind me (eighteen inches again) a young intellectual is trying to persuade a girl to come live with him and be his love. She has her guard up, but he is extremely reasonable, careful not to overplay his hand. A combination of intellectual companionship and sexuality is what they have to offer each other, he feels. In the mirror over the bar I can see the ritual of the second drink. Then he has to go to the men's room and she has to go to the ladies' room, and when they return, the argument has lost its tone. And the fan takes over again, and the heat and the relaxed air and the memory of so many good little dinners in so many good little illegal places, with the theme of love, the sound of ventilation, the brief medicinal illusion of gin.

Another hot night I stop off at the Goldman Band concert in the Mall in Central Park. The people seated on the benches fanned out in front of the band shell are attentive, appreciative. In the trees the night wind stirs, bringing the leaves to life, endowing them with speech; the electric lights illuminate the green branches from the under side, translating them into a new language. Overhead a plane passes dreamily, its running lights winking. On the bench directly in front of me, a boy sits with his arm around his girl; they are proud of each other and are swathed in music. The cornetist steps forward for a solo, begins, "Drink to me only with thine eyes. . . ." In the wide, warm night the horn is startlingly pure and magical. Then from the North River another horn solo begins— the *Queen Mary* announcing her intentions. She is not on key; she is a half tone off. The trumpeter in the bandstand never flinches. The horns quarrel savagely, but no one minds having the intimation of travel injected into the pledge of love. "I leave," sobs Mary. "And I will pledge with mine," sighs the trumpeter. Along the asphalt paths strollers pass to and fro; they behave considerately, respecting the musical atmosphere. Popsicles are moving well. In the warm grass beyond the fence, forms wriggle in the shadows, and the skirts of the girls approaching on the Mall are ballooned by the breeze, and their bare shoulders catch the lamplight. "Drink to me only with thine eyes." It is a magical occasion, and it's all free.

On week ends in summer the town empties. I visit my office on a Saturday afternoon. No phone rings, no one feeds the hungry IN-baskets, no one disturbs the papers; it is a building of the dead, a time of awesome suspension. The whole city is honeycombed with abandoned cells—a jail that has been effectively broken. Occasionally from somewhere in the building a night bell rings, summoning the elevator—a special fire-alarm rings. This is the pit of loneliness, in an office on a summer Saturday. I stand at the window and look down at the batteries and batteries of offices across the way, recalling how the thing looks in winter twilight when everything is going full blast, every cell lighted, and how you can see in pantomime the puppets fumbling with their slips of paper (but you don't hear the rustle), see them pick up their phone (but you don't hear the ring), see the noiseless, ceaseless moving about of so many passers of pieces of paper: New York, the capital of memoranda, in touch with Calcutta, in touch with Reykjavik, and always fooling with something.

In the café of the Lafayette, the regulars sit and talk. It is busy yet peaceful. Nursing a drink, I stare through the west windows at the Manufacturers Trust Company and at the red brick fronts on the north side of Ninth Street, watching the red turning slowly to purple as the light dwindles. Brick buildings have a way of turning color at the end of the day, the way a red rose turns bluish as it wilts. The café is a sanctuary. The waiters are ageless and they change not. Nothing has been modernized. Notre Dame stands guard in its travel poster. The coffee is strong and full of chicory, and good.

Walk the Bowery under the El at night and all you feel is a sort of cold guilt. Touched for a dime, you try to drop the coin and not touch the hand, because the hand is dirty; you try to avoid the glance, because the glance accuses. This is not so much personal menace as universal—the cold menace of unresolved human suffering and poverty and the advanced stages of the disease alcoholism. On a summer night the drunks sleep in the open. The sidewalk is a free bed, and there are no lice. Pedestrians step along and over and around the still forms as though walking on a battlefield among the dead. In doorways, on the steps of the savings bank, the bums lie sleeping it off. Standing sentinel at each sleeper's head is the empty bottle from which he drained his release. Wedged in the crook of his arm is the paper bag containing his things. The glib barker on the sight-seeing bus tells his passengers that this is the "street of lost souls," but the Bowery does not think of itself as lost; it meets its peculiar problem in its own way—plenty of gin mills, plenty of flophouses, plenty of indifference, and always, at the end of the line, Bellevue.

A block or two east and the atmosphere changes sharply. In the slums are poverty and bad housing, but with them the reassuring sobriety and safety of family life. I head east along Rivington. All is cheerful and filthy and crowded. Small shops overflow onto the sidewalk, leaving only half the normal width for passers-by. In the candid light from unshaded bulbs gleam watermelons and lingerie. Families have fled the hot rooms upstairs and have found relief on the pavement. They sit on orange crates, smoking, relaxed, congenial. This is the nightly garden party of the vast Lower East Side—and on the whole they are more agreeable-looking hot-weather groups than some you see in bright canvas deck chairs on green lawns in country circumstances. It is folksy here with the smell of warm flesh and squashed fruit and fly-bitten filth in the gutter, and cooking.

At the corner of Lewis, in the playground behind the wire fence, an open-air dance is going on—some sort of neighborhood affair, probably designed to combat delinquency. Women push baby carriages in and out among the dancers, as though to exhibit what dancing leads to at last. Overhead, like banners decorating a cotillion hall, stream the pants and bras from the pulley lines. The music stops, and a beautiful Italian girl takes a brush from her handbag and stands under the street lamp brushing her long blue-black hair till it shines. The cop in the patrol car watches sullenly.

The Consolidated Edison Company says there are eight million people in the five boroughs of New York, and the company is in a position to know. As in every dense community, virtually all races, all religions, all nationalities are represented. Population figures are shifty—they change almost as fast as one can break them down. It is safe to say that about two million of New York's eight million are Jews—roughly one in four. Among this two million who are Jewish are, of course, a great many nationalities— Russian, German, Polish, Rumanian, Austrian, a long list. The Urban League of Greater New York estimates that the number of Negroes in New York is about 700,000. Of these, about 500,000 live in Harlem, a district that extends northward from 110th Street. The Negro population has increased rapidly in the last few years. There are half again as many Negroes in New York today as there were in 1940. There are about 230,000 Puerto Ricans living in New York. There are half a million Irish, half a million Germans. There are 900,000 Russians, 150,000 English, 400,000 Poles, and there are quantities of Finns and Czechs and Swedes and Danes and Norwegians and Latvians and Belgians and Welsh and Greeks, and even Dutch, who have been here from away back. It is very hard to say how many Chinese there are. Officially there are 12,000, but there are many Chinese who are in New York illegally and who don't like census takers.

The collision and the intermingling of these millions of foreign-born people representing so many races and creeds and nationalities make New York a permanent exhibit of the phenomenon of one world. The citizens of New York are tolerant not only from disposition but from necessity. The city has to be tolerant, otherwise it would explode in a radioactive cloud of hate and rancor and bigotry. If the people were to depart even briefly from the peace of cosmopolitan intercourse, the town would blow up higher than a kite. In New York smolders every race problem there is, but the noticeable thing is not the problem but the inviolate truce. Harlem is a city in itself, and being a city Harlem symbolizes segregation; yet Negro life in New York lacks the more conspicuous elements of Jim Crowism. Negroes ride subways and buses on terms of equality with whites, but they have not yet found that same equality in hotels and restaurants. Professionally, Negroes get on well in the theater, in music, in art and in literature; but in many fields of employment the going is tough. The Jim Crow principle lives chiefly in the housing rules and customs. Private owners of dwellings legally can, and do, exclude Negroes. Under a recent city ordinance, however, apartment buildings that are financed with public moneys or that receive any tax exemption must accept tenants without regard to race, color or religion.

To a New Yorker the city is both changeless and changing. In many respects it neither looks nor feels the way it did twenty-five years ago. The elevated railways have been pulled down, all but the Third Avenue. An old-timer walking up Sixth past the Jefferson Market jail misses the railroad, misses its sound, its spotted shade, its little aerial stations, and the tremor of the thing. Broadway has changed in aspect. It used to have a discernible bony structure beneath its loud bright surface; but the signs are so enormous now, the buildings and shops and hotels have largely disappeared under the neon lights and letters and the frozen-custard façade. Broadway is a custard street with no frame supporting it. In Greenwich Village the light is thinning: big apartments have come in, bordering the Square, and the bars are mirrored and chromed. But there are still in the Village the lingering traces of poesy, Mexican glass, hammered brass, batik, lamps made of whisky bottles, first novels made of fresh memories—the old Village with its alleys and ratty one-room rents catering to the erratic needs of those whose hearts are young and gay.

Grand Central has become honky-tonk, with its extradimensional advertising displays and its tendency to adopt the tactics of a travel broker. I practically lived in Grand Central Terminal at one period (it has all the conveniences and I had no other place to stay) and the great hall seemed to me one of the more inspiring interiors in New York, until Lastex and Coca-Cola got into the temple.

All over town the great mansions are in decline. Schwab's house facing the Hudson on Riverside is gone. Gould's house on Fifth Avenue is an antique shop. Morgan's house on Madison Avenue is a church administration office. What was once the Fahnestock house is now Random House. Rich men nowadays don't live in houses; they live in the attics of big apartment buildings and plant trees on the setbacks, hundreds of feet above the street.

There are fewer newspapers than there used to be, thanks somewhat to the late Frank Munsey. One misses the *Globe,* the *Mail,* the *Herald;* and to many a New Yorker life has never seemed the same since the *World* took the count.

Police now ride in radio prowl cars instead of gumshoeing around the block swinging their sticks. A ride in the subway costs ten cents, and the seats are apt to be dark green instead of straw yellow. Men go to saloons to gaze at televised events instead of to think long thoughts. It is all very disconcerting. Even parades have changed some. The last triumphal military procession in Manhatten simply filled the city with an ominous and terrible rumble of heavy tanks.

The slums are gradually giving way to the lofty housing projects—high in stature, high in purpose, low in rent. There are a couple of dozens of these new developments scattered around; each is a city in itself (one of them in the Bronx accommodates twelve thousand families), sky acreage hitherto untilled, lifting people far above the street, standardizing their sanitary life, giving them some place to sit other than an orange crate. Federal money, state money, city money and private money have flowed into these projects. Banks and insurance companies are in back of some of them. Architects have turned the buildings slightly on their bases, to catch more light. In some of them, rents are as low as eight dollars a room. Thousands of new units are still needed and will eventually be built, but New York never quite catches up with itself, is never in equilibrium. In flush times the population mushrooms and the new dwellings sprout from the rock. Come bad times and the population scatters and the lofts are abandoned and the landlord withers and dies.

New York has changed in tempo and in temper during the years I have known it. There is greater tension, increased irritability. You encounter it in many places, in many faces. The normal frustrations of modern life are here multiplied and amplified—a single run of a cross-town bus contains, for the driver, enough frustration and annoyance to carry him over the edge of sanity: the light that changes always an instant too soon, the passenger that bangs on the shut door, the truck that blocks the only opening, the coin that slips to the floor, the question asked at the wrong moment. There is greater tension and there is greater speed. Taxis roll faster than they rolled ten years ago—and they were rolling fast then. Hackmen used to drive with verve; now they sometimes seem to drive with desperation, toward the ultimate tip. On the West Side Highway, approaching the city, the motorist is swept along in a trance—a sort of fever of inescapable motion, goaded from behind, hemmed in on either side, a mere chip in a millrace.

The city has never been so uncomfortable, so crowded, so tense. Money has been plentiful and New York has responded. Restaurants are hard to get into; businessmen stand in line for a Schrafft's luncheon as meekly as idle men used to stand in soup lines. (Prosperity creates its bread lines, the same as depression.) The lunch hour in Manhattan has been shoved ahead half an hour, to 12:00 or 12:30, in the hopes of beating the crowd to a table. Everyone is a little emptier at quitting time than he used to be. Apartments are festooned with No Vacancy signs. There is standing-room-only in Fifth Avenue buses, which once reserved a seat for every paying guest. The old double-deckers are disappearing—people don't ride just for the fun of it any more.

At certain hours on certain days it is almost impossible to find an empty taxi and there is a great deal of chasing around after them. You grab a handle and open the door, and find that some other citizen is entering from the other side. Doormen grow rich blowing their whistles for cabs; and some doormen belong to no door at all—merely wander about through the streets, opening cabs for people as they happen to find them.

By comparison with other less hectic days, the city is uncomfortable and inconvenient; but New Yorkers temperamentally do not crave comfort and convenience—if they did they would live elsewhere.

The subtlest change in New York is something people don't speak much about but that is in everyone's mind. The city, for the first time in its long history, is destructible. A single flight of planes no bigger than a wedge of geese can quickly end this island fantasy, burn the towers, crumble the bridges, turn the underground passages into lethal chambers, cremate the millions. The intimation of mortality is part of New York now: in the sound of jets overhead, in the black headlines of the latest edition.

All dwellers in cities must live with the stubborn fact of annihilation; in New York the fact is somewhat more concentrated because of the concentration of the city itself, and because, of all targets, New York has a certain clear priority. In the mind of whatever perverted dreamer might loose the lightning, New York must hold a steady, irresistible charm.

It used to be that the Statue of Liberty was the signpost that proclaimed New York and translated it for all the world. Today Liberty shares the role with Death. Along the East River, from the razed slaughterhouses of Turtle Bay, as though in a race with the spectral flight of planes, men are carving out the permanent headquarters of the United Nations—the greatest housing project of them all. In its stride, New York takes on one more interior city, to shelter, this time, all governments, and to clear the slum called war. New York is not a capital city—it is not a national capital or a state capital. But it is by way of becoming the capital of the world. The buildings, as conceived by architects, will be cigar boxes set on end. Traffic will flow in a new tunnel under First Avenue. Forty-seventh Street will be widened (and if my guess is any good, trucks will appear late at night to plant tall trees surreptitiously, their roots to mingle with the intestines of the town). Once again the city will absorb, almost without showing any sign of it, a congress of visitors. It has already shown itself capable of stashing away the United Nations—a great many of the delegates have been around town during the past couple of years, and the citizenry has hardly caught a glimpse of their coattails or their black Homburgs.

This race—this race between the destroying planes and the struggling Parliament of Man—it sticks in all our heads. The city at last perfectly illustrates both the universal dilemma and the general solution, this riddle in steel and stone is at once the perfect target and the perfect demonstration of nonviolence, of racial brotherhood, this lofty target scraping the skies and meeting the destroying planes halfway, home of all people and all nations, capital of everything, housing the deliberations by which the planes are to be stayed and their errand forestalled.

A block or two west of the new City of Man in Turtle Bay there is an old willow tree that presides over an interior garden. It is a battered tree, long suffering and much climbed, held together by strands of wire but beloved of those who know it. In a way it symbolizes the city: life under difficulties, growth against odds, sap-rise in the midst of concrete, and the steady reaching for the sun. Whenever I look at it nowadays, and feel the cold shadow of the planes, I think: "This must be saved, this particular thing, this very tree." If it were to go, all would go—this city, this mischievous and marvelous monument which not to look upon would be like death.

The South

BALTIMORE

———❖———

Baltimore has always been a city of mixed identity. Geo-
graphically situated in the North, it has always thought of
itself as part of the South. At the turn of the century, Balti-
more had a large population of substantial German fami-
lies, among them H. L. Mencken's. His cigar-making fa-
ther and uncle provided him with the gemütlichkeit *of his*
memories. If ever a worldly and sharp-tongued commenta-
tor permitted himself any sentimentality, it was Mencken
in dealing with his native city. The portrait is irresistible.
As he recalls it, Baltimore emerges warm, tolerant, and
alive to the new currents of cultural and intellectual
excitement.

H. L. Mencken

It is difficult to assess H. L. Mencken's (1880–1956) contributions to American literature and the American language. As a master polemicist, editor of the influential *Smart Set* and *The American Mercury* together with George Jean Nathan, and author of the scholarly *American Language,* he was a major voice among the writers of his time. One's fondest memories of Mencken as a human being come from his delightful autobiography, which appeared in three volumes: *Happy Days,* 1940, from which the selection below is taken; *Newspaper Days,* 1941; and *Heathen Days,* 1943.

from Happy Days

The city into which I was born in 1880 had a reputation all over for what the English, in their real-estate advertising, are fond of calling the amenities. So far as I have been able to discover by a labored search of contemporary travel-books, no literary tourist, however waspish he may have been about Washington, Niagara Falls, the prairies of the West, or even Boston and New York, ever gave Baltimore a bad notice. They all agreed, often with lubricious gloats and gurgles, (*a*) that its indigenous victualry was unsurpassed in the Republic, (*b*) that its native Caucasian females of all ages up to thirty-five were of incomparable pulchritude, and as amiable as they were lovely, and (*c*) that its home-life was spacious, charming, full of creature comforts, and highly conducive to the facile and orderly propagation of the species.

There was some truth in all these articles, but not, I regret to have to add, too much. Perhaps the one that came closest to meeting scientific tests was the first. Baltimore lay very near the immense protein factory of Chesapeake Bay, and out of the bay it ate divinely. I well recall the time when prime hard crabs of the channel species, blue in color, at least eight inches in length along the shell, and with snow-white meat almost as firm as soap, were hawked in Hollins street of Summer mornings at ten cents a dozen. The supply seemed to be almost unlimited, even in the polluted waters of the Patapsco river, which stretched up fourteen miles from the bay to engulf the slops of the Baltimore canneries and fertilizer factories. Any poor man could go down to the banks of the river, armed with no more than a length of stout cord, a home-made net on a pole, and a chunk of cat's meat, and come home in a couple of hours with enough crabs to feed his family for two days. Soft crabs, of course, were scarcer and harder to snare, and hence higher in price, but not much. More than once, hiding behind my mother's apron, I helped her to buy them at the door for two-and-a-twelfth cents a piece. And there blazes in my memory like a comet the day when she came home from Hollins market complaining with strange and bitter indignation that the fishmongers there—including old Harris, her favorite—had begun to *sell* shad roe. Hitherto, stretching back to the first settlement of Baltimore Town, they had always thrown it in with the fish. Worse, she reported that they had now entered upon an illegal combination to lift the price of the standard shad of twenty inches—enough for the average family, and to spare—from forty cents to half a dollar. When my father came home for lunch and heard this incredible news, he predicted formally that the Republic would never survive the Nineteenth Century.

Terrapin was not common eating in those days, any more than it is in these, but that was mainly because few women liked it, just as few like it today. It was then assumed that their distaste was due to the fact that its consumption involved a considerable lavage with fortified wines, but they still show no honest enthusiasm for it, though Prohibition converted many of them into very adept and eager boozers. It was not, in my infancy, within the reach of the proletariat, but it was certainly not beyond the bourgeoisie. My mother, until well past the turn of the century, used to buy pint jars of the picked meat in Hollins market, with plenty of rich, golden eggs scattered through it, for a dollar a jar. For the same price it was possible to obtain *two* wild ducks of respectable if not royal species— and the open season ran gloriously from the instant the first birds wandered in from Labrador to the time the last stragglers set sail for Brazil. So far as I can remember, my mother never bought any of these ducks, but that was only because the guns, dogs and eagle eye of my uncle Henry, who lived next door, kept us oversupplied all Winter.

Garden-truck was correspondingly cheap, and so was fruit in season. Out of season we seldom saw it at all. Oranges, which cost sixty cents a dozen, came in at Christmas, and not before. We had to wait until May for strawberries, asparagus, fresh peas, carrots, and even radishes. But when the huge, fragrant strawberries of Anne Arundel county (pronounced Ann'ran'l) appeared at last they went for only five cents a box. All Spring the streets swarmed with hucksters selling such things: they called themselves, not hucksters, but Arabs (with the first *a* as in *day*), and announced their wares with loud, raucous, unintelligible cries, much worn down by phonetic decay. In Winter the principal howling was done by colored men selling shucked oysters out of huge cans. In the dark backward and abysm of time their cry must have been simply "Oysters!", but generations of Aframerican larynxes had debased it to "Awneeeeeee!", with the final *e*'s prolonged until the vendor got out of breath. He always wore a blue-and-white checked apron, and that apron was also the uniform of the colored butlers of the Baltimore gentry when engaged upon their morning work—sweeping the sidewalk, scouring the white marble front steps, polishing up the handle of the big front door, and bragging about their white folks to their colleagues to port and starboard.

Oysters were not too much esteemed in the Baltimore of my youth, nor are they in the Baltimore of today. They were eaten, of course, but not often, for serving them raw at the table was beyond the usual domestic technic of the time, and it was difficult to cook them in any fashion that made them consonant with contemporary ideas of elegance. Fried, they were fit only to be devoured at church oyster-suppers, or gobbled in oyster-bays by drunks wandering home from scenes of revelry. The more celebrated oyster-houses of Baltimore—for example, Kelly's in Eutaw street— were patronized largely by such lamentable characters. It was their playful custom to challenge foolishlooking strangers to wash down a dozen raw Chincoteagues with half a tumbler of Maryland rye: the town belief was that this combination was so deleterious as to be equal to the kick of a mule. If the stranger survived, they tried to inveigle him into eating another dozen with sugar sprinkled on them: this dose was supposed to be almost certainly fatal. I grew up believing that the only man in history who had ever actually swallowed it and lived was John L. Sullivan.

There is a saying in Baltimore that crabs may be prepared in fifty ways and that all of them are good. The range of oyster dishes is much narrower, and they are much less attractive. Fried oysters I have just mentioned. Stewed, they are undoubtedly edible, but only in the sorry sense that oatmeal or boiled rice is edible. Certainly no Baltimorean not insane would argue that an oyster stew has any of the noble qualities of the two great crab soups—shore style (with vegetables) and bisque (with cream). Both of these masterpieces were on tap in the old Rennert Hotel when I lunched there daily (years after the term of the present narrative) and both were magnificent. The Rennert also offered an oyster pot-pie that had its points, but the late Jeff Davis, manager of the hotel (and the last public virtuoso of Maryland cookery), once confessed to me that its flavor was really due to a sly use of garlic. Such concoctions as panned and scalloped oysters have never been eaten in my time by connoisseurs, and oyster fritters (always called flitters in Baltimore) are to be had only at free-for-all oyster-roasts and along the wharves. A roasted oyster, if it be hauled off the fire at the exact instant the shell opens, is not to be sniffed at, but getting it down is a troublesome business, for the shell is too hot to be handled without mittens. Despite this inconvenience, there are still oyster-roasts in Baltimore on Winter Sunday afternoons, and since the collapse of Prohibition they have been drawing pretty good houses. When the Elks give one they hire a militia armory, lay in a thousand kegs of beer, engage 200 waiters, and prepare for a mob. But the mob is not attracted by the oysters alone; it comes mainly to eat hot-dogs, barbecued beef and sauerkraut and to wash down these lowly victuals with the beer.

The greatest crab cook of the days I remember was Tom McNulty, originally a whiskey drummer but in the end sheriff of Baltimore, and the most venerated oyster cook was a cop named Fred. Tom's specialty was made by spearing a slice of bacon on a large fork, jamming a soft crab down on it, holding the two over a charcoal brazier until the bacon had melted over the crab, and then slapping both upon a slice of hot toast. This titbit had its points, I assure you, and I never think of it without deploring Tom's too early translation to bliss eternal. Fred devoted himself mainly to oyster flitters. The other cops rolled and snuffled in his masterpieces like cats in catnip, but I never could see much virtue in them. It was always my impression, perhaps in error, that he fried them in curve grease borrowed from the street railways. He was an old-time Model T flat-foot, not much taller than a fire-plug, but as big around the middle as a load of hay. At the end of a busy afternoon he would be spattered from head to foot with blobs of flitter batter and wild grease.

It was the opinion of my father, as I have recorded, that all the Baltimore beers were poisonous, but he nevertheless kept a supply of them in the house for visiting plumbers, tinners, cellar-inspectors, tax-assessors and so on, and for Class D social callers. I find by his bill file that he paid $1.20 for a case of twenty-four bottles. His own favorite malt liquor was Anheuser-Busch, but he also made occasional experiments with the other brands that were then beginning to find a national market: some of them to survive to this day, but the most perished under Prohibition. His same bill file shows that on December 27, 1883, he paid Courtney, Fairall & Company, then the favorite fancy grocers of Baltimore, $4 for a gallon of Monticello whiskey. It retails now for from $3 to $3.50 a *quart*. In those days it was always straight, for the old-time Baltimoreans regarded blends with great suspicion, though many of the widely-advertised brands of Maryland rye were of that character. They drank straight whiskey straight, disdaining both diluents and chasers. I don't recall ever seeing my father drink a high-ball; the thing must have existed in his day, for he lived on to 1899, but he probably regarded its use as unmanly and ignoble. Before every meal, including breakfast, he ducked into the cupboard in the dining-room and poured out a substantial hooker of rye, and when he emerged he was always sucking in a great whiff of air to cool off his tonsils. He regarded this appetizer as necessary to his well-being. He said that it was the best medicine he had ever found for toning up his stomach.

How the stomachs of Baltimore survived at all in those days is a pathological mystery. The standard evening meal tended to be light, but the other two were terrific. The repertoire for breakfast, beside all the known varieties of pancake and porridge, included such things as ham and eggs, broiled mackerel, fried smelts, beef hash, pork chops, country sausage, and even—God help us all!—what would now be called Welsh rabbit. My father, save when we were in the country, usually came home for lunch, and on Saturdays, with no school, my brother Charlie and I sat in. Our favorite Winter lunch was typical of the time. Its main dishes were a huge platter of Norfolk spots or other pan-fish, and a Himalaya of corncakes. Along with this combination went succotash, buttered beets, baked potatoes, string beans, and other such hearty vegetables. When oranges and bananas were obtainable they followed for dessert—sliced, and with a heavy dressing of grated cocoanut. The calorie content of two or three helpings of such powerful aliments probably ran to 3000. We'd all be somewhat subdued afterward, and my father always stretched out on the dining-room lounge for a nap. In the evening he seldom had much appetite, and would usually complain that cooking was fast going downhill in Baltimore, in accord with the general decay of human society. Worse, he would warn Charlie and me against eating too much, and often he undertook to ration us. We beat this sanitary policing by laying in a sufficiency in the kitchen before sitting down to table. As a reserve against emergencies we kept a supply of ginger snaps, mushroom crackers, all-day suckers, dried apricots and solferino taffy in a cigar-box in our bedroom. In fear that it might spoil, or that mice might sneak up from the cellar to raid it, we devoured this stock at frequent intervals, and it had to be renewed.

The Baltimoreans of those days were complacent beyond the ordinary, and agreed with their envious visitors that life in their town was swell. I can't recall ever hearing anyone complain of the fact that there was a great epidemic of typhoid fever every Summer, and a wave of malaria every Autumn, and more than a scattering of smallpox, especially among the colored folk in the alleys, every Winter. Spring, indeed, was the only season free from serious pestilence, and in Spring the communal laying off of heavy woolen underwear was always followed by an epidemic of colds. Our house in Hollins street, as I first remember it, was heated by Latrobe stoves, the invention of a Baltimore engineer. They had mica windows (always called isinglass) that made a cheery glow, but though it was warm enough within the range of that glow on even the coldest Winter days, their flues had little heat to spare for the rooms upstairs. My brother and I slept in Canton-flannel nightdrawers with feathers above us and underneath, but that didn't help us much on January mornings when all the windows were so heavily frosted that we couldn't see outside. My father put in a steam-heating plant toward the end of the eighties—the first ever seen in Hollins street—, but such things were rare until well into the new century. The favorite central heating device for many years was a hot-air furnace that was even more inefficient than the Latrobe stove. The only heat in our bathroom was supplied from the kitchen, which meant that there was none at all until the hired girl began to function below. Thus my brother and I were never harassed by suggestions of morning baths, at least in Winter. Whenever it was decided that we had reached an intolerable degree of grime, and measures were taken to hound us to the bathroom, we went into the vast old zinc-lined tub together, and beguiled the pains of getting clean by taking toy boats along. Once we also took a couple of goldfish, but the soap killed them almost instantly.

At intervals of not more than a month in Winter a water-pipe froze and burst, and the whole house was cold and clammy until the plumbers got through their slow-moving hocus-pocus. Nothing, in those days, seemed to work. All the house machinery was constantly out of order. The roof sprang a leak at least three times a year, and I recall a day when the cellar was flooded by a broken water-main in Hollins street, and my brother and I had a grand time navigating it in wooden washtubs. No one, up to that time, had ever thought of outfitting windows with fly-screens. Flies overran and devoured us in Summer, immense swarms of mosquitoes were often blown in from the swamps to the southwest, and a miscellany of fantastic moths, gnats, June-bugs, beetles, and other insects, some of them of formidable size and pugnacity, buzzed around the gas-lights at night.

We slept under mosquito canopies, but they were of flimsy netting and there were always holes in them, so that when a mosquito or fly once got in he had us all to himself, and made the most of it. It was not uncommon, in Summer, for a bat to follow the procession. When this happened my brother and I turned out with brooms, baseball bats and other weapons, and pursued the hunt to a kill. The carcass was always nailed to the backyard fence the next morning, with the wings stretched out as far as

possible, and boys would come from blocks around to measure and admire it. Whenever an insect of unfamiliar species showed up we tried to
capture it, and if we succeeded we kept it alive in a pill-box or baking-
powder can. Our favorite among pill-boxes was the one that held Wright's
Indian Vegetable Pills (which my father swallowed every time he got into
a low state), for it was made of thin sheets of wood veneer, and was thus
more durable than the druggists' usual cardboard boxes.

Every public place in Baltimore was so furiously beset by bugs of all
sorts that communal gatherings were impossible on hot nights. The very
cops on the street corners spent a large part of their time slapping mosquitoes and catching flies. Our pony Frank had a fly-net, but it operated only
when he was in motion; in his leisure he was as badly used as the cops.
When arc-lights began to light the streets, along about 1885, they attracted so many beetles of gigantic size that their glare was actually obscured. These beetles at once acquired the name of electric-light bugs, and
it was believed that the arc carbons produced them by a kind of spontaneous generation, and that their bite was as dangerous as that of a tarantula.
But no Baltimorean would ever admit categorically that this Congo-like
plague of flying things, taking one day with another, was really serious, or indeed a plague at all. Many a time I have seen my mother leap up
from the dinner-table to engage the swarming flies with an improvised
punkah, and heard her rejoice and give humble thanks simultaneously
that Baltimore was not the sinkhole that Washington was.

These flies gave no concern to my brother Charlie and me; they seemed
to be innocuous and even friendly compared to the chiggers, bumble-bees
and hornets that occasionally beset us. Indeed, they were a source of
pleasant recreation to us, for very often, on hot Summer evenings, we
would retire to the kitchen, stretch out flat on our backs on the table, and
pop away at them with sling-shots as they roosted in dense clumps upon
the ceiling. Our favorite projectile was a square of lemon-peel, roasted by
the hired girl. Thus prepared, it was tough enough to shoot straight and
kill certainly, but when it bounced back it did not hurt us. The hired
girl, when she was in an amiable mood, prepared us enough of these mis-
siles for an hour's brisk shooting, and in the morning she had the Red
Cross job of sweeping the dead flies off the ceiling. Sometimes there were
hundreds of them, lying dead in sticky windrows. When there were horse-
flies from the back alley among them, which was not infrequently, they
leaked red mammalian blood, which was an extra satisfaction to us. The
stables that lined the far side of the alley were vast hatcheries of such flies,
some of which reached a gigantic size. When we caught one we pulled off

its wings and watched it try idiotically to escape on foot, or removed its legs and listened while it buzzed in a loud and futile manner. The theory taught in those days was that creatures below the warm-blooded level had no feelings whatever, and in fact rather enjoyed being mutilated. Thus it was an innocent and instructive matter to cut a worm into two halves, and watch them wriggle off in opposite directions. Once my brother and I caught a turtle, chopped off its head, and were amazed to see it march away headless. That experience, in truth, was so astonishing as to be alarming, and we never monkeyed with turtles thereafter. But we got a good deal of pleasure, first and last, out of chasing and butchering toads, though we were always careful to avoid taking them in our hands, for the juice of their kidneys was supposed to cause warts.

At the first smell of hot weather there was a tremendous revolution in Hollins street. All the Brussels carpets in the house were jimmied up and replaced by sleazy Chinese matting, all the haircloth furniture was covered with linen covers, and every picture, mirror, gas bracket and Rogers group was draped in fly netting. The carpets were wheelbarrowed out to Steuart's hill by professional carpet beaters of the African race, and there flogged and flayed until the heaviest lick yielded no more dust. Before the mattings could be laid all the floors had to be scrubbed, and every picture and mirror had to be taken down and polished. Also, the lace curtains had to come down, and the ivory-colored Holland shades that hung in Winter had to be changed to blue ones, to filter out the Summer sun. The lace curtains were always laundered before being put away—a formidable operation involving stretching them on huge frameworks set up on trestles in the backyard. All this uproar was repeated in reverse at the ides of September. The mattings came up, the carpets went down, the furniture was stripped of its covers, the pictures, mirrors and gas brackets lost their netting, and the blue Holland shades were displaced by the ivory ones. It always turned out, of course, that the flies of Summer had got through the nettings with ease, and left every picture peppered with their calling cards. The large pier mirror between the two windows of the parlor usually got a double dose, and it took the hired girl half a day to renovate it, climbing up and down a ladder in the clumsy manner of a policeman getting over a fence, and dropping soap, washrags, hairpins and other gear on the floor.

The legend seems to prevail that there were no sewers in Baltimore until after the World War, but that is something of an exaggeration. Our house in Hollins street was connected with a private sewer down the alley in the rear as early as I have any recollection of it, and so were many other houses, especially in the newer parts of the town. But I should add that we also had a powder room in the backyard for the accommodation of laundresses, whitewashers and other visiting members of the domestic faculty, and that there was a shallow sink under it that inspired my brother and me with considerable dread. Every now and then some child in West Baltimore fell into such a sink, and had to be hauled out, besmeared and howling, by the cops. The one in our yard was pumped out and fumigated every Spring by a gang of colored men who arrived on a wagon that was called an O.E.A.—*i.e.*, odorless excavating apparatus. They discharged this social-minded duty with great fervor and dispatch, and achieved non-odoriferousness, in the innocent Aframerican way, by burning buckets of rosin and tar. The whole neighborhood choked on the black, greasy, pungent smoke for hours afterward. It was thought to be an effective preventive of cholera, smallpox and tuberculosis.

All the sewers of Baltimore, whether private or public, emptied into the Back Basin in those days, just as all those of Manhattan empty into the North and East rivers to this day. But I should add that there was a difference, for the North and East rivers have swift tidal currents, whereas the Back Basin, distant 170 miles from the Chesapeake capes, had only the most lethargic. As a result it began to acquire a powerful aroma every Spring, and by August smelled like a billion polecats. This stench radiated all over downtown Baltimore, though in Hollins street we hardly ever detected it. Perhaps that was due to the fact that West Baltimore had rival perfumes of its own—for example, the emanation from the Wilkins hair factory in the Frederick road, a mile or so from Union Square. When a breeze from the southwest, bouncing its way over the Wilkins factory, reached Hollins street the effect was almost that of poison gas. It happened only seldom, but when it happened it was surely memorable. The householders of the vicinage always swarmed down to the City Hall the next day and raised blue hell, but they never got anything save promises. In fact, it was not until the Wilkinses went into the red and shut down their factory that the abomination abated—and its place was then taken, for an unhappy year or two, by the degenerate cosmic rays projected from a glue factory lying in the same general direction. No one, so far as I know, ever argued that these mephitic blasts were salubrious, but it is a sober fact that town opinion held that the bouquet of the Back Basin was. In proof thereof it was pointed out that the clerks who sweated all Summer in the little coops of offices along the Light street and Pratt street wharves were so remarkably long-lived that many of them appeared to be at least 100 years old, and that the colored stevedores who loaded and unloaded the Bay packets were the strongest, toughest, drunkenest and most thieving in the whole port.

The Baltimore of the eighties was a noisy town, for the impact of iron wagon tires on hard cobblestone was almost like that of a hammer on an anvil. To be sure, there was a dirt road down the middle of every street, kept in repair by the accumulated sweepings of the sidewalks, but this cushioned track was patronized only by hay-wagons from the country and like occasional traffic: milk-men, grocery deliverymen and other such regulars kept to the areas where the cobbles were naked, and so made a fearful clatter. In every way, in fact, city life was much noiser then than it is now. Children at play were not incarcerated in playgrounds and policed by hired ma'ms, but roved the open streets, and most of their games involved singing or yelling. At Christmas time they began to blow horns at least a week before the great day, and kept it up until all the horns were disabled, and in Summer they began celebrating the Fourth far back in June and were still exploding fire-crackers at the end of July. Nearly every house had a dog in it, and nearly all the dogs barked more or less continuously from 4 a.m. until after midnight. It was still lawful to keep chickens in backyards, and many householders did so. All within ear range of Hollins street appeared to divide them as to sex in the proportion of a hundred crowing roosters to one clucking hen. My grandfather Mencken once laid in a coop of Guineas, unquestionably the noisiest species of *Aves* known to science. But his wife, my step-grandmother, had got in a colored clergyman to steal them before the neighbors arrived with the police.

In retired by-streets grass grew between the cobblestones to almost incredible heights, and it was not uncommon for colored rag-and-bone men to pasture their undernourished horses on it. On the steep hill making eastward from the Washington Monument, in the very heart of Baltimore, some comedian once sowed wheat, and it kept on coming up for years thereafter. Every Spring the Baltimore newspapers would report on the prospects of the crop, and visitors to the city were taken to see it. Most Baltimoreans of that era, in fact, took a fierce, defiant pride in the bucolic aspects of their city. They would boast that it was the only great seaport on earth in which dandelions grew in the streets in Spring. They believed that all such vegetation was healthful, and kept down chills and fever. I myself once had proof that the excess of litter in the streets was not without its value to mankind. I was riding the pony Frank when a wild thought suddenly seized him, and he bucked me out of the saddle in the best manner of a Buffalo Bill bronco. Unfortunately, my left foot was stuck in the stirrup, and so I was dragged behind him as he galloped off. He had gone at least a block before a couple of colored boys stopped him. If the cobblestones of Stricker street had been bare I'd not be with you today. As it was, I got no worse damage than a series of harsh scourings running from my neck to my heels. The colored boys took me to Reveille's livery-stable, and stopped the bloodshed with large gobs of spider web. It was the hemostatic of choice in Baltimore when I was young. If, perchance, it spread a little tetanus, then the Baltimoreans blamed the mercies of God.

WASHINGTON, D.C.

"Capital of Miserable Huts," "The Mudhole," "Wilderness City" were some of the epithets flung at the nation's capital in the early years of its existence. It was to remain little more than a collection of official buildings and the President's residence surrounded by muddy roads until after the Civil War, when the Union victory gave new impetus to the creation of a dignified and beautiful capital. But even by the 1880s, it was still something of a frontier town. Two contrasting aspects of the city during those years—the casual morality of its transients during the housing shortage, and the pretentious social life of its newly rich and powerful—are described below by a Washington correspondent of the period.

Frank Carpenter

Frank Carpenter (1855–1924) was born into a prominent Mansfield, Ohio, banking family. After receiving a B.A. and an M.A. from Wooster University, he began a long and successful career as a journalist. In 1877 he became the Washington correspondent for the Cleveland *Leader*. In 1888 he left the capital and traveled everywhere for the next thirty-six years, writing hundreds of nationally syndicated articles and many books, including a series of widely used *Readers* for young people about foreign countries. His Washington pieces were collected from the family scrapbooks by his daughter Frances into the book *Carp's Washington* (1960), from which the following selection is taken.

from Carp's Washington

Within the past two days the season of 1882–1883 has opened. The hotels are filling up, and scores of strangers are wearing out the soles of their shoes looking up comfortable quarters for the winter. Washington is a city of boardinghouses, and of all cities which charge extraordinary prices for very ordinary board, it bears the palm. Every man, woman, and company holding property here expects to feast off the newcomers. The city plans to make, during the few months of a session of Congress, enough to keep itself alive during all the rest of the year.

The coming season promises to be one of the liveliest, both socially and politically. Nearly every desirable house in the fashionable localities has been rented. New buildings are going up rapidly but the demand is far in excess of the supply. The rent for furnished rooms is fully one hundred per cent higher than in Cleveland. The two in which I live are of moderate size, on the second floor of a three-story brick on F Street, near the Ebbitt House. They are fairly well furnished, and some Congressman or politician would gladly pay one hundred dollars a month for them. In my search for living quarters I saw others at forty and fifty dollars, shabbily furnished, and a full mile from the Capitol. These were without board, and so dreary that their occupants would be in danger of suicide from the blues.

The hotels are being refitted and repainted. The hotel men say they never saw a brighter outlook at this period of the year. They have received enough letters inquiring for rooms to have disposed of their whole space, and they predict that more people will be in Washington this winter than ever before.

There is little doubt that this is true. It is a new session of Congress with a change of party power. The Democrats have the House and it will be a long session. The lobbyists have already arrived in swarms. It is a session preceding a national election, and the politicians will be busy keeping their pots boiling.

The prices at the Washington hotels are much higher than those for private board. It would take the best part of a Congressman's salary to pay his board and whisky bills, if he did not take a room high up under the roof and leave his family at home. One New York Congressman paid last year six hundred dollars a week for his rooms at one of the hotels here, and his extras made his monthly bills run into the thousands.

The hotel scenes of the capital present many strange features. These are different at the different houses. The Arlington, on Fifteenth Street near the White House, is staid and quiet, high priced and eminently respectable. The Ebbitt, the Riggs, and the Willard are the homes of the politicians and the centers of gossip. Their lobbies and reading rooms are large, and filled every night from five o'clock until eleven with a crowd of politicians, statesmen, and strangers, all jabbering away about the Government, society, and public men. All classes, and all sorts of characters meet in the Washington hotel of an evening. Now a newspaper correspondent, his whole frame an interrogation point, comes in, looks over the crowd, glances at the register, and either stops to interview some statesman or rushes away to some other source of news.

The Westerners stay more at the National, the Metropolitan, and the other hotels near the Capitol. These houses have an atmosphere all their own, and their billiard rooms especially are worth a visit. I have seen fifteen tables going at one time in one hotel, and a hundred men, many of them Congressmen, sitting in a line on the chairs along the wall, watching the play as though they were Monte Carlo gamblers and had money to win on each stroke of the cue.

They use plenty of tobacco at these Washington hotels. The floor of an office is often made a general spittoon; where if one dropped a coin, he would want to put on a glove before picking it up. Our national habit of tobacco-spitting reigns supreme in these hotels filled with the Westerners. Their marble floors often look as though walnuts had been hulled on them and the stains left wet on their bright, polished surfaces.

.   .   .

In respect to the social relation, Washington is one of the wickedest cities of its size in the country. It is natural it should be so for the bulk of the population here are transients. They are away from home; most are far from their families; many have but few friends and acquaintances.

There are thousands of young unmarried people in the government departments whose work ends at four o'clock and does not begin again until nine the next morning. Time hangs heavy on their hands, and associations, not of the best, are often contracted to make it pass. The large number of unmarried men, or married men away from their wives—together with the fact that most of them have money in their pockets—make the capital a great resort for the demimonde. Many a female clerk, losing her position, devoid of family and friends, drifts into their number in order to keep body and soul together.

In no other city are such affairs carried on more openly. The following advertisements, which I clip from a half dozen issues of the *Star* newspaper, show that here no bones are made about them.

> WANTED—A FURNISHED ROOM in a quiet family, for gentleman and lady; board for lady only; no questions. Address "Prompt," Star Office.
>
> WANTED—ROOM BY A GENTLEMAN of elegant habits, stranger in the city, but located here for a year; would like room or rooms and board in home of a discreet young widow, where he can enjoy all the comforts of a home. Address, in entire confidence, G. R., Star Office.
>
> WANTED—A PLEASANT FURNISHED ROOM, heated, to be used occasionally, where no questions will be asked. Address E. H., Star Office.
>
> WANTED—By two sisters, two large unfurnished rooms, where no questions will be asked. Address E. H., Star Office.
>
> PERSONAL—A widow lady desires a gentleman to assist her financially. Mrs. B. C., Star Office.
>
> PERSONAL—A widow of culture desires the acquaintance of a liberal gentleman between 45 and 50. Address Mrs. L. Meredith, Star Office.
>
> PERSONAL—A young widow desires position as housekeeper for a widower of means. Mrs. M. Smith, Star Office.

I might repeat a hundred such advertisements, for they appear daily in the Washington papers. Here, as in all big cities, the advertising sheets of the press are full of stories for those who read between the lines.

Washington is like no other city in the world. It is a living curiosity, made up of the strangest and most incongruous elements. There is a fairy-tale sense of instability about it. As with the palace of Aladdin which flew away in the night, one feels that this city could easily vanish and that he could wake up some morning to find himself stranded on the empty Potomac Flats. The city looks as if it had sprung up in a morning, or rather as if a whirlwind had picked up some great town, mixed the big houses up with the little ones, then cast the whole together in one miscellaneous mass, keeping intact only the city streets.

These Washington streets are the finest in the country. Broad and smooth, made of black asphaltum as hard as stone, they are kept as clean as your parlor floor. The street cleaner is a character whom you will seldom find out of Washington. He rides a great machine whose roller is covered with hundreds of stiff little twigs, arranged in a spiral. As the horses pull the machine along, the roller turns, and the broomlike twigs sweep the dust and dirt off to the side where they are gathered up and carted away.

I never saw such a machine before, and it could not well be used on other than asphalt streets. It makes a whirring noise as it goes along, raising a great dust, which is kept out of the air by the covering frame. Several such machines move daily over the streets here, with the result that Washington is the cleanest city in the Union.

But Washington houses are all jumbled together. A five-story palace that cost originally a million dollars rubs elbows with a shanty costing a few hundreds, just as the owner of the one crowds the owner of the other on the Washington sidewalks. The shanty says to the palace, "This is a free country. We are equals. You are nothing but a house. And all your fine trimmings make you no better than me; I am a house too. My master may be bigger than yours during the next administration; then perhaps I shall be built up, and you'll be sold for that mortgage which you know very well is now on your roof."

The small houses and the big ones are all equal here. So are the men. Fine clothes have little to do with making the man here in Washington, and the rugged Westerner, clad in his homespun, can get as good credit at the hotels as the New York dandy with his broadcloth coat and his diamond stud. The most simply clad are often the richest and the most powerful.

Editor Battelle, of Toledo, told me the other day that this city reminds him of one vast boardinghouse. Most of its people do not really live in it; they merely stay for a time. So it is that only a few own property, and that the renting class is so large. Thousands make their homes in suites of rooms, taking their meals in restaurants, or having them sent in by caterers.

The Washington caterer is a curious character. He is usually a colored gentleman, who supplies families and single boarders with meals at so much a month. Twenty dollars per person is the average price. For that he will bring your breakfast and dinner in a square tin box to your rooms, every morning and evening for thirty days.

The caterer's box is about two feet square. Fitted inside it are shelves of grated iron like those of the oven of a cooking stove. The box opens at one end and the victuals are placed hot on its shelves. The box then is closed tight for carrying, but although his horse trots fast, the caterer may have to come a long way, and the soup will often need reheating on your own little stove.

The dinner my caterer brought me last night was hardly up to the usual standard, but I had soup, roast beef and roast mutton, fresh lettuce and asparagus, macaroni, white potatoes and sweets, warm apple sauce, sliced oranges and lemon pie.

To my mind, this is not the most pleasant way in which to eat. Sometimes the coffee spills upon the beefsteak; the salt and the pepper get into the preserves or the sugar. Often a knife is forgotten, or a napkin fails to put in appearance. After trying a caterer for a week or so, the roomer often becomes disgusted. Then he goes back to the boardinghouse table of gossip, or takes refuge in one of the numerous restaurants which are found in every quarter of the city. Many a Congressman eats nowhere else.

Washington has the most reasonable streetcar system in the United States. There are two-cent, three-cent, and five-cent fares. I know of no other place where you can get about more easily. There are hundreds of horse-cars, and the transfer system is such that you can go all over the city for one fare, or at the farthest for two.

Some of the streetcar scenes in Washington are as amusing as those in the theaters of another city. The greatest of the great ride in streetcars here. It is not unusual to find yourself wedged in between a Senator whose oratory brings thousands out to hear him, and a General whose deeds will live in history as long as time lasts. Today your companion may be a noted lawyer, tomorrow you may hobnob and chat, if you will, with a member of the President's Cabinet.

I rode home from the Capitol last night in a car in which there were half a dozen Justices of the Supreme Court. Off the bench, they are as jolly a lot of fellows as you could meet anywhere. They had left their gowns in the disrobing room, and they came into the car in overcoats and mufflers. Stanley Matthews, who led the procession, took his seat up near the fare box, and during the trip he bobbed up and down putting in fares and getting their change for the people behind him.

In addition to the streetcars, there is a line of herdic cabs in operation which charge the same fares and which carry great numbers of passengers. The first of these were small affairs with seats for six or eight. Large ones, longer than the biggest omnibus, have been more lately put into service, and they are both comfortable and elegant.

These herdics are boxlike compartments with glass windows and doors at the back, mounted on wheels. They are comfortably cushioned and handsomely finished in rich olive green. The driver sits up in front and handles his horses with skilled hands and a loud voice. To pay the fare each passenger walks to the front of the compartment and drops his nickel into a slot.

One of these herdic lines which runs from the Capitol into the fashionable Northwest section of the city, is more patronized by noted men than are the higher-priced private vehicles. The herdics, in all, carried 1,300,-000 passengers last year. They are proving so profitable that a new line is to be put on within a few weeks. The smooth streets of Washington are especially adapted to such vehicles, which have surely come to stay.

The more expensive two-wheeled hansom cabs also roll over the Washington streets in great numbers. They accommodate two persons and their charges are seventy-five cents an hour, or twenty-five cents a trip. The driver sits on a small seat, high at the back, and looks over the roof of the cab. His reins stretch well above his passengers' heads to the horse's bit. The glass doors in the front of the cab may be opened wide so that nothing impedes the view of the thoroughfare.

There is a bill now in Congress which may give Washington a cable-car line. Such cable street railroads, I predict, will be largely used here some day. The climate is right for them. The magnificent distances of the capital call for them. When they come, they will bring suburban property in great demand, increasing many times the values of the outlying territories.

Last week I spent a few days in New York, in order to take myself out of the ruts of Washington do-less-ness, and to find out what the people of other sections of the country are thinking. Washington City is the poorest place in the United States from which to judge the temper of the nation. Its citizens have a different outlook on life than those of the individual states, and its atmosphere is artificial and enervating.

In New York everything throbs with the chase for the almighty dollar; you catch the spirit of intense energy which pervades every corner of the metropolis. In Washington often pleasure takes precedence over work. The surroundings tend to deaden, rather than quicken you into activity.

On Broadway a streetcar will not wait for you if you are not just at its stopping point. It goes on and you must stand there until the next car comes along. In Washington people a block away signal the cars by waving their hands or their umbrellas. Then they walk to the car at a leisurely pace, while the drivers wait patiently and the horses rest. I have seen herdics as well as cars stop for as much as two minutes, and no passenger objected.

In New York, if an eighty-cent legal-tender dollar of the past was rolled along the sidewalk, everyone on the street would make a rush for it. In Washington it would be watched with interest; the people would wonder why it was rolling and where it came from before they would make the effort to pick it up. In New York the chief talk is of money; in Washington gossip and great men are the leading subjects. In New York a fall in stocks sets all tongues buzzing; in Washington, if a bureau chief loses his job, the same result is accomplished.

New York is a city of things, as well as of money. Washington is a city of persons. A friend said to me today, "In New York you can see almost any *thing* you want to see, while in Washington you can see almost any great man."

Yet, on the whole, Washington is the pleasanter place in which to live. With all its great men, there is more opportunity for a nobody to become somebody than in the great whirlpool of New York, which seethes and boils, which keeps the poor and the moderately well-to-do at the bottom, and which allows to be seen in the foreground only those who have already made their millions or their fame.

. . . .

The extravagances of the past social season would make Andrew Jackson turn over in his grave, and the economical soul of John Adams quiver with indignation at the wicked waste in the circles of Washington's high life. President Adams could not have swallowed his oatcake and lemonade if he had read about a luncheon like that given by Mrs. Senator Stanford, at which Pacific Coast ladies ate from china plates that cost a hundred dollars apiece and drank tea from a pot of solid gold.

The dinners of Washington could not be more expensive if their pepper and salt were grains of gold dust. They make one think of the Roman epicure, Apicius, with his banquets of nightingales' tongues. Just to glance at their bills of fare is to make your mouth water.

Mrs. Stanford's luncheon took two and a half hours to serve. Its twelve courses consisted of raw oysters, consommé in cups, baked bass and potatoes, macaroni, roast beef and tomatoes, Roman punch, brown squab, salad, olives and cheese, fresh strawberries and cream, charlottes, ices, coffee and sweets! Still, it was only a luncheon. The dainty eaters put it all away quite easily, in spite of their hearty breakfasts and the fact that their dinner is their main meal.

At the dinner that Secretary of the Navy Whitney gave for the Honorable Joseph Chamberlain and Sir Charles Tupper recently, many courses of English, as well as American, dishes were featured. There were English hares, dressed with truffles and mushrooms, and American wild turkey, stuffed with roast chestnuts. The terrapin was served in small silver saucepans, with long handles and removable silver lids, engraved with a W. Then came cheese soufflé, canvasback duck, ice cream, café mousse, and coffee.

It is not in their food alone, however, that these Washington dinners are remarkable. The serving and preparation of the table are quite as important. At state dinners at the White House the table is a veritable bouquet, both cook and gardener proving themselves to be artists. The cook sculptures his figures in sugary confections; the gardener creates monumental floral decorations. Corsage bouquets are always found at the plates of the ladies, and not long ago these were all orchids, which are by no means a poor man's flower.

Take the decorations at Mrs. Leland Stanford's dinner for Mrs. Grant! The center of the table was covered with an old-gold satin scarf, bordered with blue plush, and embroidered with patterns of begonia leaves. Along the table were silver vases filled with Jacqueminot roses, and tall silver candelabra, for each of which a silver brick was consumed in the making. The names of the guests were on cards upon which were painted the flowers of California.

At a recent reception at Mrs. Senator Hearst's, the walls and mirrors were draped with rose-colored silk, and the mantels were decorated with poinsettia blossoms and Annunciation lilies. In a doorway between the parlor and the ballroom there was an umbrella covered with California moss, sprayed over with carnations, with a pendant fringe of gilded cypress cones. In the back parlor, the mantels were draped with Nile green silk, held up with bunches of silver and gold pine cones, with pampas grass suspended in the center.

The hall and the library were filled with palms and calla lilies, and the tower room off the main parlor was fragrant with roses on tables and stands. And yet the man who owns this house began life in poverty. I doubt not the day has been when he thought the prettiest flowers in the world were the potato blossoms on his father's farm in Missouri.

A curious feature of the wining and dining of Washington is the craze for giving entertainments of special colors. It is not necessary that these hues should match the dress or the hair of the hostess. A Senator's redheaded daughter might, of course, have a white tea in honor of the horse which is supposed always to accompany her. But seriously, these colored dinners, luncheons, and teas are worthy of comment. I was invited to a pink tea last week, to an orange reception the week before, and I have even attended blue and purple affairs.

Not long ago Miss Bacon, the daughter of Representative Bacon of New York, gave a red luncheon at which the shades of the candles and glass globes were red, the bread and baked potatoes were tied with red ribbon, and a cushion of red tulips formed the centerpiece. The souvenirs were Japanese bon-bons with dwarf red roses springing from their tops. Even the ice cream was red, in the form of strawberries in little red candy hampers.

The most elaborate of all was the violet dinner which Mr. and Mrs. Roswell P. Flower gave last night. There were violets everywhere, and violet color predominated in the decorations. Bowls of the fragrant purple flowers were set on the mantels, and even the fireplaces were filled with masses of stevia and violets. On the center of the damask tablecloth, on a strip of old Duchess lace, stood a filigree silver basket overflowing with purple blossoms. A broad violet satin ribbon ran in a zigzag pattern up and down the long table, while great heaps of violets at each end proved to be made up of corsage bouquets, one for each lady, with her name painted in gold on the long violet ribbons which tied it. The cheese straws and cakes were tied with violet ribbons, and the entire dinner service was of violet and gold. The only variation was in the men's boutonnieres, which were lilies of the valley and Jacqueminot rosebuds.

An innovation at the recent luncheon of a Western representative's wife has caused much comment. The hostess placed before each guest a little cup filled with red, white, and black beans, announcing that the one who guessed nearest the correct number would receive a prize. Mrs. Stanford, who guessed two hundred, won.

The cost of entertaining is constantly on the increase here in Washington, and the days when a Congressman could entertain like a prince on his five thousand a year have long since gone by. Today you cannot get any kind of a housemaid for less than three or four dollars a week, and the good women cooks command twenty dollars a month. French chefs are paid from a hundred a month up, and it is a poor coachman who does not receive his dollar a day with board.

It is well known that Washington hostesses hire the china for their large balls and receptions. Almost every china store in this town has stocks of plain white dishes which go out and come back many times during the social season. I asked one of these merchants why the dishes used for this purpose were so plain.

"It is not because people like them," he explained, "but because their guests cannot so easily tell that this is the same china they ate from the day before at another house. Suppose you were to notice some brightly ornamented Japanese plates at Mrs. Senator B's tea. Then the next afternoon you were served cakes upon exactly the same kind of plates at Mrs. Representative C's. You might remark to a friend that Japanese dishes were all the rage here in Washington, but she would shake her head and whisper into your ear the one damning word 'hired.' "

The President gave his second White House evening reception of the year just this week, and a thousand bare backs and bare necks gleamed under the gaslight of the East Room's magnificent chandeliers. A thousand men were in danger of colds in their claw-hammer coats, and the archdemon Pneumonia had plenty of chance to pick out his victims.

Washington, more and more, apes the courts of Europe, and a fair share of the sixty billion dollars which the *World Almanac* says the United States is now worth, is put into the dress of its people. We are lavishing fortunes on clothes. There is enough silk worn here every winter to carpet a whole state; there are pearls by the bushel, and diamonds by the peck.

At the White House the other night there were at least five hundred women wearing diamonds of various sizes. I counted fifty pairs of solitaire earrings whose stones were as big as the end of my thumb, and thirty diamond stars and pendants any one of which would buy a large farm. One brunette beauty, dressed in a flowing red gown, had by actual count eighty-five diamonds on her person. Some of these, set in bracelets and rings, were not unusually large, but the solitaires in her ears were as big as hazelnuts. She shook at least five thousand dollars this way and that every time she moved her head.

Jewels are worn here not only by the young and beautiful but by the middle-aged and the wrinkled. The day of the old-fashioned grandmother has passed, and you will not see one old lady in a lace cap. The older the woman, the more giddy she seems to be. She cuts her dresses an inch lower at the bust for every extra ten years, and I blush for the fair sex when I look at the décolleté corsages and fat bare backs of the powdered old dames.

I do not believe the charge that some of these fine ladies of Washington hire their jewelry, just as they hire the china for their entertainments. Of course much that is worn now is shoddy and cheap, and half the brilliants you see at the White House receptions are surely rhinestones. The gems worn by Senators' wives and other millionaires' daughters are supposed to be pure. But who can tell? The fact that such highly placed females wear them would, if they were paste, make them pass for real.

By all odds the finest collection of real diamonds is that of Mrs. Leland Stanford, who wears a dozen different sets every season. She has some amazing stones, as big as pigeons' eggs, which once belonged to Queen Isabella of Spain. Another set of clear yellow diamonds glow like golden fire under the gas flames of the East Room, and she owns still a third, made up of purest blue-white stones, which shine even brighter. The gossips say Mrs. Stanford keeps her sixty different diamond rings on a string of common black tape.

Mrs. Senator Jones of Nevada owns some of the most elegant pearls seen in Washington. One of her choicest possessions is a necklace of large, perfect pearls with a splendid diamond pendant made to represent an oyster shell. A single exceptionally fine pearl is affixed to this glittering shell on the spot where a pearl in an oyster is usually found.

The Washington nabobs are a strange conglomeration. Some have the bluest of blue blood in their veins, education acquired in the best of schools, and manners polished by long sojourns in Europe. Such persons have, as a rule, many friends among the great public figures of the day, and have little trouble about getting into the swim.

There is, however, another class who have nothing but their money to recommend them. Their vulgar ostentation marks them as nouveau riche, and when you meet them at large receptions you have no difficulty in recognizing them. Many use bad grammar; the men cannot avoid mentioning their wealth; and the women, whether their figures make it advisable or not, dress in the most extravagant extremes of fashion. Stories of the crudities of such people are legion.

There is one lady whom I shall call Madame Newrich, whose husband has made a fortune in trade, and who has installed his family in a splendid mansion here in Washington. Not long ago Madame Newrich sat at a formal dinner party beside one of the most noted generals of the late war. The General, himself none too careful of his table manners, used the point of his knife to convey a bit of food from his plate to his mouth. His dinner companion gave him a nudge in the ribs.

"I beg your pardon, General," she said in a loud whisper, "but when my husband makes a social blunder, he is glad to have me correct him. I know your wife, at least, will thank me when I tell you not to eat with your knife. People in Washington are queer. They eat only with their forks and their spoons."

The General looked at the busybody with astonishment. He said not a word, but turned away to talk with his neighbor on the other side.

The great charm of society in Washington is that it is not entirely founded on wealth. Its principal interest comes from the fact that the most important and successful men in all branches of activity come here. Instead of there being one lion to roar at a party, there may be ten or twenty or thirty. So many men and women of brains and brilliance give Washington gatherings a sparkle that is found nowhere else, except perhaps in the capitals of Europe. There is a frankness and simplicity and a lack of snobbishness as regards wealth and fashion. While there are extravagant displays in the homes of the rich, these are no more frequented by people of real importance than are the more modest establishments of the officials of moderate means.

Washington hostesses, in the main, depend upon their own gifts for entertaining. There are no one or two great caterers such as hold sway in New York. Nor are there any social dictators who decide who shall be and who shall not be invited to parties. It would be hard to imagine any of the important families here turning over their invitation lists to some social agent to blue-pencil. Washington has been called provincial, and in many ways it is, but it has today the only real cosmopolitan society in the United States.

The officers of the retired Army and Navy forces are always in great demand. One of the old stand-bys is General Van Vliet. You will find him at every reception, at nearly every big dinner. You may have heard the story of how General Sherman, who is nearly as constant a dinner-goer as General Van Vliet, one night forgot at which house he was scheduled to dine. Seeing Van Vliet walk past his door in full dress, Sherman decided to follow him, being sure that the General would lead him to the right party. He was not disappointed.

Like many another member of Washington society, General Van Vliet is able to change his politics at will. During Arthur's Administration he was such a strong Republican that now it is surprising to find him thick as thieves with the Democrats. Everybody likes Van Vliet, and the excuse is made for him that no Army man should hold any political views. The day after Cleveland was inaugurated, the General called at the White House to tell Colonel Lamont how he and the President should conduct the Administration's social program. After he had finished speaking, one of the other visitors spoke up.

"And pray how long have you been a Democrat, General?" he asked, smiling.

"Since yesterday noon," was the old gentleman's unruffled reply.

KNOXVILLE

———◆———

Snugly situated in the valley between the Smoky Mountains and the Cumberlands, Knoxville remained a serene nineteenth-century city well into the 30s. The contemporary world intruded during the Roosevelt Administration, when Knoxville became the headquarters for the TVA, which brought with it new people with new ways of doing things. Even greater changes came with the development of nearby Oak Ridge. The city as it was in 1915 is recaptured in the two selections below: the poetic evocation of Agee, and the more objective recollection of Joseph Wood Krutch.

Joseph Wood Krutch

The essayist, critic, and editor Joseph Wood Krutch was born in
Knoxville in 1893. As a professor at Columbia and the drama critic
for *The Nation* for many years, he had considerable influence on a
generation of students and theatergoers. His interest in philosophy,
the sources of culture, and man's relation to nature is expressed in his
many books, among which the best known are *The Modern Temper*
(1929), *The Measure of Man* (1954), and *Human Nature and the Human Condition* (1959). He is the editor of *The Gardener's World,* an
anthology of writing on the pleasures of making things grow. The selection below is from his autobiography, *More Lives Than One,* published in 1962.

from More Lives Than One

Since I left it in 1915 when I was twenty-one years old I have visited it
many times, but for shorter and shorter periods at greater and greater
intervals. Each time that I go I see less that I recognize, fewer and fewer
people I know. Spiritually as well as physically it seems very little like the
town that was once my world, and the last time I was there I met only one
person on the street who recognized me.

No doubt most former inhabitants of most towns have had a similar
experience, but Knoxville has undergone the effect not only of the forces
which have transformed most towns but of some very special ones as well.
As the administrative seat of the TVA it grew by leaps and bounds both
in population and in the awareness of the world. Then, about fifty miles
away, the mysterious community of Oak Ridge sprang into being to become in effect a suburb.

My Knoxville was, on the contrary, a town of only a little more than
thirty thousand and carried on with Chattanooga the inevitable running
quarrel concerning which was the larger and the more progressive. But
only toward the end of my stay there did the new race of Rotarians and
"boosters" begin to develop the new techniques of local chauvinism. Such
importance as the town had it owed chiefly to the fact that it was the
county seat and the home of the University, and, as such, quite superior
to less sophisticated towns, especially to Maryville to which visiting comic
actors always made dutiful, slighting reference under instruction from the
local stage manager.

The farmers of the surrounding country drove their wagons in at night, slept in them in the public square, and were ready the next morning individually to offer for sale a few bushels of green beans, a few pounds of homemade butter, a few dressed chickens, and a dishpan of lye hominy covered with a piece of cheesecloth to keep it moist. I can still see my father moving from wagon to wagon, snapping the beans to discover which were freshest, bending the breastbones of the chickens to find the youngest.

Many terms, the very origin of which had probably been forgotten, were still universally used. The train which was ultimately to carry me away to New York was always referred to as "the Vestibule"—a survival, I suppose, from the days when only the most important trains had their rear platforms enclosed. A short line over which a sort of donkey engine pulled a few cars to a community some five miles away was "the dummy" and the subject of what may well have been, after Mother Goose, the first specimen of the poetic art I ever learned by heart. I supposed at the time that it had been composed by a local bard but it was actually, I believe, widely current and merely adapted to each local scene by a change of the two proper names:

> Some folks say that the Dummy won't run
> But I done seen what the Dummy's done done.
> It left Fountain City at half-past one
> And got into Knoxville at the settin' of the sun.

Probably few still living inhabitants of Knoxville now remember the odd terminology which was once taken for granted, but in the hills not far away so many Seventeenth Century words still linger that a local physician repeated to me only a few years ago the reply given by a patient who was asked the origin of a badly swollen ankle: "Well, Doc, I just hunkered down, it creeled, and then it poned up 'til I thought hit was agoin' to beal." All but one of the strange words is, I believe, to be found in large dictionaries. Translation: "I squatted on my heel, it twisted, and swelled up so much I thought it might ulcerate."

Social distinctions in Knoxville were real enough and already based rather more on wealth than on family, but at least everyone knew, and spoke to, nearly everyone else. Very few boys were sent away to preparatory schools and only comparatively few from the richest or most pretentious families attended either the one private school for boys or the corresponding one for girls. The latter was called with fine Victorian effect, "The East Tennessee Female Institute." Most of us went to the public schools where the chief distinction between the more and the less respectable group was that by the middle of May members of the less respectable began to appear barefooted in the classroom. We others waited until we could ceremoniously remove our shoes and stockings immediately on returning home after the last day of classes. None except the children of self-consciously superior parents put shoes on again except for dress-up occasions, especially Sundays.

Another odd social distinction, then probably valid in most communities and, for all I know, still prevalent, concerned the acceptable ways in which a boy might earn money. Only ragamuffins sold newspapers in the center of town. But to have a "route" along which papers were delivered daily was more than permissible. It was, indeed, something to be proud of. If all of this suggests a Norman Rockwell magazine cover the fact is that these so popular works of art do actually represent the United States of half a century ago more truly than they do even country or small-town life today.

• • •

Of the influence of my remarkably understanding, sympathetic, loving, and sensibly indulgent parents and of my two brothers I shall have to speak presently, but at the moment I cannot help stressing the extent to which my parents fitted the pattern. They were well enough educated by the modest standards of the community but "intellectual ferment" was hardly part of its prevailing atmosphere. The whole of Europe and America was living in the afterglow of Nineteenth Century complacency and awareness of such preliminary stirrings of doubt, dissatisfaction, and anxieties as affected intellectual centers had hardly reached Knoxville despite the presence of the quietly traditional state university. Those who read current books read Harold McGrath, George Barr McCutcheon, Owen Wister, John Fox, Jr., and perhaps, if they were unusually intellectual, the novelist Winston Churchill. But it was only by accident and after I had got into college that I so much as heard of H. G. Wells and Bernard Shaw.

Few if any Knoxville children were ever "overstimulated." The public school system (and I believe the two private schools also) were so traditional that they had all but forgotten what the tradition was supposed to be about. We did learn to read and write, as many present-day pupils do not, and we were exposed to those "classics" which had somehow become entrenched in the schools: Two plays of Shakespeare, Milton's *Minor*

Poems, Sir Roger de Coverley, and *Silas Marner.* I thought they all were unmitigated bores as did, I suspect, my teacher. Yet I did voluntarily learn by heart a few lines of Milton and I well remember that the first impulse I ever had to write anything was in imitation of the Sir Roger de Coverley papers. In fact, I think it would not be stretching a point to say that the character of the Spectator, who had embraced observation and reporting as his role in life, first made that seem to me an attractive one, and I may have been at that moment first encouraged towards the "detachment," rather than the "commitment," for which I have often been blamed in our own more stirring times.

Except that we were exposed—though no more than exposed—to a few enduring works of literature instead of being allowed, as in some modern schools, to write "reports" on whatever trash we happened to favor, the school system was about as bad as possible. In these pre-Deweyian days no one had ever heard of "progressive methods," and it was only about the time when I went to college that Professors of Education began to appear there. One of the principal functions of the school system was to provide a livelihood for worthy spinsters and widows who might otherwise have become a charge upon the community. They got their jobs exclusively on the basis of need and respectability, and they were assigned to whatever grade in the elementary school or to whatever subject in the high school happened to offer a vacancy at the moment.

The result was not always happy either for teacher or pupil. The former were often nervous wrecks as a result of their brave struggle to do something for which they had neither gift nor preparation. The latter often got a rather odd idea of the nature of learning. Under my high school teacher of history I memorized a textbook, paragraph by paragraph, each of which I promptly forgot when, for the next day, I memorized the succeeding paragraphs. I was taught physics by an elderly spinster who had not the faintest idea what a scientific principle was and who, to my great delight but also perhaps to the detriment of my modesty, used to call upon me to explain Archimedes' Law or to perform one of the experiments which, in her hands, never came off, partly because she didn't know what they were supposed to demonstrate. The Latin teacher, a rather pathetic spinster, was the only member of the high school faculty who had a genuine interest, however slight, in her subject and she was just sufficiently concerned with its declining popularity to say to me when I announced that I was dropping it in my senior year: "Et tu, Brute!" Yet she taught Latin not as a language, however dead, but as a sort of cryptogram we were expected to solve with the aid of the vocabulary at the back of the book and the useful footnotes explaining the more unusual constructions.

. . .

I have no nostalgia for my childhood and I do not idealize the kind of lives Knoxvillians lived in my day. Adults and children alike were unadventurous both physically and intellectually. Their world was thoroughly provincial and lacked stimulation as well as excitement. But I cannot help remembering at the same time how relatively free it was from both the public and the private pressures, tensions, and anxieties of today. Civilization did not seem to be threatened, and the pattern of individual lives was more firmly established. We are now accustomed to see our world as a concatenation of "problems"; few living before World War I took any such view of it. Most people were less anxious to keep up with the Joneses and had no installment payments to meet. They "entertained" seldom, spent much more time alone at home with their own families and, except for the professional theater, had few public amusements. But there were also many fewer demands on their time.

Children were expected to amuse themselves and did not have to be provided with "something to do." Since they walked to school their mothers did not spend hours a day transporting them to classes or to the scene of extracurricular activities. Neither was it expected that they would attend meetings of the P.T.A. or the League of Women Voters. I don't think I ever heard this or that required as "a civic duty," and "being a good citizen" was little more than a matter of obeying the law.

For all these reasons middle-class people had more leisure, or at least lived in a more leisurely fashion, than they do today. But there was also another, perhaps even more important, reason why they could do so, and it has to be faced. Though they had comparatively few of what we call "labor-saving devices" they had the greatest labor-saving device of all, namely servants—almost invariably black.

During my childhood only a few of the wealthiest "kept a carriage." But because domestic servants were paid so little—a few dollars a week—everyone not actually poverty-stricken had at least one as a matter of course. My own family never dreamed of aspiring to a carriage but I had a colored nurse and my mother took "someone in the kitchen" for granted. Today it is precisely the other way around. A family must be poor indeed if it does not own an automobile while many who belong definitely to the class called "rich" run their houses with no more than part-time servants.

It is often remarked that the Good Life of the Athenian citizen had slavery as its necessary condition. Similarly, the merely comfortable life of my Knoxville was based upon a less harsh version of the same institution. Tennessee was not the deep south, but neither I nor anyone else ever thought of "a Negro problem" or supposed that the modus vivendi which seemed accepted without reservation by both groups need ever be disturbed. If any lynchings occurred or if, indeed, any overt acts of violence disturbed the peace of "race relations" I do not remember them. Whether or not the Negroes actually believed themselves to be natural inferiors I do not know, but they accepted with apparent cheerfulness and often with humor the assumption that they were.

What is now called "Uncle Tomism" was very nearly universal. Somehow I have always remembered as typical a little incident which occurred when, as an adolescent, I stopped near the market square to have my shoes shined by a peripatetic Negro youth. A policeman passed by and the boy, perhaps my own age, looked up with a cheery, "Mornin', Captain." Then after the policeman had passed he said to me with a conspiratorial grin: "He's only a lieutenant but I always ups 'em one."

In those days "white supremacy" worked, for the most part, smoothly, however wrong it may have been. And when I read today the hysterical protests against Negro jokes, Jewish jokes, and other "stereotypes" as it is fashionable to call them, I am reminded of a curious cultural phenomenon characteristic of Knoxville in my day and very revealing of the attitude of the Negroes themselves.

In the one legitimate theater Negroes were admitted only to the third or "peanut gallery" which was usually empty or nearly so. But every September the theatrical season was opened by Al G. Field's Minstrels, a company of white performers who blacked their faces to sing, dance, and crack jokes, all in terms of a "stereotype." On that night the peanut gallery was always full of Negroes howling with delight. Far from considering the performance an insult, they regarded it as a compliment. This was the one day of the year when they and their culture were given formal recognition. And though it may be true, as many will no doubt insist, that the fact merely demonstrates the completeness of the degradation which they had accepted, they certainly did not themselves see it that way. In 1962 Al G. Field's Minstrels would probably seem naïve to the whites, offensive to the colored people.

Like the white citizens of today's Knoxville, the children of these Negroes have lost something as well as gained something. For them, too, life has now become a series of problems. They have exchanged a possibly degrading acceptance of things as they are for anxiety, anger and a corroding sense of wrong. Because of them tomorrow may be better; today is, in some ways, worse.

James Agee

Since his premature death, James Agee (1909–1955) has been increasingly recognized as one of America's uniquely gifted writers. He was born in Knoxville and was graduated from Yale. His first published book was the volume of poetry *Permit Me Voyage*. He was sent by *Fortune* magazine to gather material on sharecropper life, and when the results were found unsuitable for magazine use, they appeared in the book *Let Us Now Praise Famous Men* (1941). Generally ignored at the time of its publication, it is now recognized as a major work. His film criticism for *The Nation, Time, Life,* and *Partisan Review* has been collected in *Agee on Film.* Towards the end of his life he worked on movie scripts, including *The African Queen* and *The Quiet One.* His posthumously published *A Death in the Family* (1957) and the play adapted from it both won Pulitzer Prizes. The selection below first appeared in *Partisan Review* in 1938 and has since been set to music by Samuel Barber and choreographed by Alvin Ailey.

Knoxville: Summer of 1915

We are talking now of summer evenings in Knoxville, Tennessee in the time that I lived there so successfully disguised to myself as a child. It was a little bit mixed sort of block, fairly solidly lower middle class, with one or two juts apiece on either side of that. The houses corresponded: middle-sized gracefully fretted wood houses built in the late nineties and early nineteen hundreds, with small front and side and more spacious back yards, and trees in the yards, and porches. These were softwooded trees, poplars, tulip trees, cottonwoods. There were fences around one or two of the houses, but mainly the yards ran into each other with only now and then a low hedge that wasn't doing very well. There were few good friends among the grown people, and they were not poor enough for the other sort of intimate acquaintance, but everyone nodded and spoke, and even might talk short times, trivially, and at the two extremes of the general or the particular, and ordinarily next door neighbors talked quite a bit when they happened to run into each other, and never paid calls. The men were mostly small businessmen, one or two very modestly executives, one or two worked with their hands, most of them clerical, and most of them between thirty and forty-five.

But it is of these evenings, I speak.

Supper was at six and was over by half past. There was still daylight,

278

shining softly and with a tarnish, like the lining of a shell; and the carbon lamps lifted at the corners were on in the light, and the locusts were started, and the fire flies were out, and a few frogs were flopping in the dewy grass, by the time the fathers and the children came out. The children ran out first hell bent and yelling those names by which they were known; then the fathers sank out leisurely in crossed suspenders, their collars removed and their necks looking tall and shy. The mothers stayed back in the kitchen washing and drying, putting things away, recrossing their traceless footsteps like the lifetime journeys of bees, measuring out the dry cocoa for breakfast. When they came out they had taken off their aprons and their skirts were dampened and they sat in rockers on their porches quietly.

It is not of the games children play in the evening that I want to speak now, it is of a contemporaneous atmosphere that has little to do with them: that of the fathers of families, each in his space of lawn, his shirt fishlike pale in the unnatural light and his face nearly anonymous, hosing their lawns. The hoses were attached at spigots that stood out of the brick foundations of the houses. The nozzles were variously set but usually so there was a long sweet stream of spray, the nozzle wet in the hand, the water trickling the right forearm and the peeled-back cuff, and the water whishing out a long loose and low-curved cone, and so gentle a sound. First an insane noise of violence in the nozzle, then the still irregular sound of adjustment, then the smoothing into steadiness and a pitch as accurately tuned to the size and style of stream as any violin. So many qualities of sound out of one hose; so many choral differences out of those several hoses that were in earshot. Out of any one hose, the almost dead silence of the release, and the short still arch of the separate big drops, silent as a held breath, and the only noise the flattering noise on leaves and the slapped grass at the fall of each big drop. That, and the intense hiss with the intense stream; that, and that same intensity not growing less but growing more quiet and delicate with the turn of the nozzle, up to that extreme tender whisper when the water was just a wide bell of film. Chiefly, though, the hoses were set much alike, in a compromise between distance and tenderness of spray (and quite surely a sense of art behind this compromise, and a quiet, deep joy, too real to recognize itself), and the sounds therefore were pitched much alike; pointed by the snorting start of a new hose; decorated by some man playful with the nozzle; left empty, like God by the sparrow's fall, when any single one of them desists; and all, though near alike, of various pitch; and this in unison. These sweet pale streamings in the light lift out their pallors and

their voices all together, mothers hushing their children, the hushing un-
naturally prolonged, the men gentle and silent and each snaillike withdrawn into the quietude of what he singly is doing, the urination of huge
children stood loosely military against an invisible wall, and gently happy
and peaceful, tasting the mean goodness of their living like the last of
their suppers in their mouths; while the locusts carry on this noise of hoses
on their much higher and sharper key. The noise of the locust is dry, and
it seems not to be rasped or vibrated but urged from him as if through a
small orifice by a breath that can never give out. Also there is never one
locust but an illusion of at least a thousand. The noise of each locust is
pitched in some classic locust range out of which none of them varies
more than two full tones; and yet you seem to hear each locust discrete
from all the rest, and there is a long, slow, pulse in their noise, like the
scarcely defined arch of a long and high set bridge. They are all around in
every tree, so that the noise seems to come from nowhere and everywhere
at once, from the whole shell heaven, shivering in your flesh and teasing
your eardrums, the boldest of all the sounds of night. And yet it is habitual to summer nights, and is of the great order of noises, like the noises of
the sea and of the blood her precocious grandchild, which you realize you
are hearing only when you catch yourself listening. Meantime from low in
the dark, just outside the swaying horizons of the hoses, conveying always
grass in the damp of dew and its strong green-black smear of smell, the
regular yet spaced noises of the crickets, each a sweet cold silver noise
threenoted, like the slipping each time of three matched links of a small
chain.

But the men by now, one by one, have silenced their hoses and drained
and coiled them. Now only two, and now only one, is left, and you see
only ghostlike shirt with the sleeve garters, and sober mystery of his mild
face like the lifted face of large cattle enquiring of your presence in a
pitch-dark pool of meadow; and now he too is gone; and it has become
that time of evening when people sit on their porches, rocking gently and
talking gently and watching the street and the standing up into their
sphere of possession of the trees, of birds hung havens, hangars. People go
by; things go by. A horse, drawing a buggy, breaking his hollow iron
music on the asphalt: a loud auto: a quiet auto: people in pairs, not in a
hurry, scuffling, switching their weight of aestival body, talking casually,
the taste hovering over them of vanilla, strawberry, pasteboard and
starched milk, the image upon them of lovers and horsemen, squared with
clowns in hueless amber. A street car raising its iron moan; stopping;

belling and starting, stertorous; rousing and raising again its iron increasing moan and swimming its gold windows and straw seats on past and past and past, the bleak spark crackling and cursing above it like a small malignant spirit set to dog its tracks; the iron whine rises on rising speed; still risen, faints; halts; the faint stinging bell; rises again, still fainter; fainting, lifting, lifts, faints forgone: forgotten. Now is the night one blue dew.

Now is the night one blue dew, my father has drained, he has coiled the hose.
Low on the length of lawns, a frailing of fire who breathes.
Content, silver, like peeps of light, each cricket makes his comment over and over in the drowned grass.
A cold toad thumpily flounders.
Within the edges of damp shadows of side yards are hovering children nearly sick with joy of fear, who watch the unguarding of a telephone pole.
Around white carbon corner lamps bugs of all sizes are lifted elliptic, solar systems. Big hardshells bruise themselves, assailant: he is fallen on his back, legs squiggling.
Parents on porches: rock and rock. From damp strings morning glories: hang their ancient faces.
The dry and exalted noise of the locusts from all the air at once enchants my eardrums.

On the rough wet grass of the back yard my father and mother have spread quilts. We all lie there, my mother, my father, my uncle, my aunt, and I too am lying there. First we were sitting up, then one of us lay down, and then we all lay down, on our stomachs, or on our sides, or on our backs, and they have kept on talking. They are not talking much, and the talk is quiet, of nothing in particular, of nothing at all in particular, of nothing at all. The stars are wide and alive, they seem each like a smile of great sweetness, and they seem very near. All my people are larger bodies then mine, quiet, with voices gentle and meaningless like the voices of sleeping birds. One is an artist, he is living at home. One is a musician, she is living at home. One is my mother who is good to me. One is my father who is good to me. By some chance, here they are, all on this earth; and who shall ever tell the sorrow of being on this earth, lying, on quilts, on the grass, in a summer evening, among the sounds of the night. May God bless my people, my uncle, my aunt, my mother, my good father, oh, remember them kindly in their time of trouble; and in the hour of their taking away.

After a little I am taken in and put to bed. Sleep, soft smiling, draws me unto her: and those receive me, who quietly treat me, as one familiar and well-beloved in that home: but will not, oh, will not, not now, not ever; but will not ever tell me who I am.

MEMPHIS

The picture of Memphis that emerges below is one that no white writer could have drawn. Richard Wright's early life there is a sharp reminder that the charm and cruelty of Southern cities have always been inseparable. Wright was among the young blacks who quickly learned their place in the repressive system. He was also one of those who was not willing to endure that repressive fate and moved on to what appeared to be a more tolerant North.

Richard Wright

Richard Wright (1908–1960) was born near Natchez, Mississippi, and died in Paris. He was among those who thought, for a short time, that Communism might be his answer. In a chapter of *The God That Failed* he describes his disillusionment. Probably Wright's leading literary success, in addition to *Black Boy,* published in 1945 and from which the selection below was taken, was *Native Son,* which became an international best-seller and then was successfully adapted for the stage.

from Black Boy

While wandering aimlessly about the streets of Memphis, gaping at the tall buildings and the crowds, killing time, eating bags of popcorn, I was struck by an odd and sudden idea. If I had attempted to work for an optical company in Jackson and had failed, why should I not try to work for an optical company in Memphis? Memphis was not a small town like Jackson; it was urban and I felt that no one would hold the trivial trouble I had had in Jackson against me.

I looked for the address of a company in a directory and walked boldly into the building, rode up in the elevator with a fat, round, yellow Negro of about five feet in height. At the fifth floor I stepped into an office. A white man rose to meet me.

"Pull off your hat," he said.

"Oh, yes, sir," I said, jerking off my hat.

"What do you want?"

"I was wondering if you needed a boy," I said. "I worked for an optical company for a short while in Jackson."

"Why did you leave?" he asked.

"I had a little trouble there," I said honestly.

"Did you steal something?"

"No, sir," I said. "A white boy there didn't want me to learn the optical trade and ran me off the job."

"Come and sit down."

I sat and recounted the story from beginning to end.

"I'll write Mr. Crane," he said. "But you won't get a chance to learn the optical trade here. That's not our policy."

I told him that I understood and accepted his policy. I was hired at

284

eight dollars per week and promised a raise of a dollar a week until my wages reached ten. Though this was less than I had been offered for the café job, I accepted it. I liked the open, honest way in which the man talked to me; and, too, the place seemed clean, brisk, businesslike.

I was assigned to run errands and wash eyeglasses after they had come from the rouge-smeared machines. Each evening I had to take sacks of packages to the post office for mailing. It was light work and I was fast on my feet. At noon I would forgo my lunch hour and run errands for the white men who were employed in the shop. I would buy their lunches, take their suits out to have them pressed, pay their light, telephone, and gas bills, and deliver notes for them to their stenographer girl friends in near-by office buildings. The first day I made a dollar and a half in tips. I deposited the money I had left from my trip and resolved to live off my tips.

I was now rapidly learning to contain the tension I felt in my relations with whites, and the people in Memphis had an air of relative urbanity that took some of the sharpness off the attitude of whites toward Negroes. There were about a dozen white men in the sixth-floor shop where I spent most of my time; they varied from Ku Klux Klanners to Jews, from theosophists to just plain poor whites. Although I could detect disdain and hatred in their attitudes, they never shouted at me or abused me. It was fairly easy to contemplate the race issue in the shop without reaching those heights of fear that devastated me. A measure of objectivity entered into my observations of white men and women. Either I could stand more mental strain than formerly or I had discovered deep within me ways of handling it.

When I returned to Mrs. Moss's that Monday night, she was surprised that I had changed my plans and had taken a new job. I showed her my bankbook and told her my plan for saving money and bringing my mother to Memphis. As I talked to her I tried to tell from her manner if Bess had said anything about what had happened between us, but Mrs. Moss was bland and motherly as always.

Bess avoided me, refusing to speak when we were alone together; but when her mother was present, she was polite. A few days later Mrs. Moss came to me with a baffled look in her eyes.

"What's happened between you and Bess?" she asked.

"Nothing," I lied, burning with shame.

"She don't seem to like you no more," she said. "I wanted you-all to kinda hit it off." She looked at me searchingly. "Don't you like her none?"

I could not answer or look at her; I wondered if she had told Bess to give herself to me.

"Well," she drawled, sighing, "I guess folks just have to love each other naturally. You can't make 'em." Tears rolled down her cheeks. "Bess'll find somebody."

I felt sick, filled with a consciousness of the woman's helplessness, of her naïve hope. Time and again she told me that Bess loved me, wanted me. She even suggested that I "try Bess and see if you like her. Ain't no harm in that." And her words evoked in me a pity for her that had no name.

Finally it became unbearable. One night I returned home from work and found Mrs. Moss sitting by the stove in the hall, nodding. She blinked her eyes and smiled.

"How're you, son?" she asked.

"Pretty good," I said.

"Ain't you and Bess got to be friends or something yet?"

"No ma'am," I said softly.

"How come you don't like Bess?" she demanded.

"Oh, I don't know." I was becoming angry.

"It's 'cause she ain't so bright?"

"No, ma'am. Bess's bright," I lied.

"Then how come?"

I still could not tell her.

"You and Bess could have this house for your home," she went on. "You-all could bring up your children here."

"But people have to find their own way to each other," I said.

"Young folks ain't got no sense these days," she said at last. "If somebody had fixed things for me when I was a gal, I sure would've taken it."

"Mrs. Moss," I said, "I think I'd better move."

"Move then!" she exploded. "You ain't got no sense!"

I went to my room and began to pack. A knock came at the door. I opened it. Mrs. Moss stood in the doorway, weeping.

"Son, forgive me," she said. "I didn't mean it. I wouldn't hurt you for nothing. You just like a son to me."

"That's all right," I said. "But I'd better move."

"No!" she wailed. "Then you ain't forgive me! When a body asks forgiveness, they means it!"

I stared. Bess appeared in the doorway.

"Don't leave, Richard," she said.

"We won't bother you no more," Mrs. Moss said.

I wilted, baffled, sorry, ashamed. Mrs. Moss took Bess's hand and led her away.

I centered my attention now upon making enough money to send for my mother and brother. I saved each penny I came by, stinting myself on food, walking to work, eating out of paper bags, living on a pint of milk and two sweet rolls for breakfast, a hamburger and peanuts for lunch, and a can of beans which I would eat at night in my room. I was used to hunger and I did not need much food to keep me alive.

I now had more money than I had ever had before, and I began patronizing secondhand bookstores, buying magazines and books. In this way I became acquainted with periodicals like *Harper's Magazine,* the *Atlantic Monthly,* and the *American Mercury.* I would buy them for a few cents, read them, then resell them to the bookdealer.

Once Mrs. Moss questioned me about my reading.

"What you reading all them books for, boy?"

"I just like to."

"You studying for law?"

"No, ma'am."

"Well, I reckon you know what you doing," she said.

Though I did not have to report for work until nine o'clock each morning, I would arrive at eight and go into the lobby of the downstairs bank —where I knew the Negro porter—and read the early edition of the Memphis *Commercial Appeal,* thereby saving myself five cents each day, which I spent for lunch. After reading, I would watch the black porter perform his morning ritual: he would get a mop, bucket, soap flakes, water, then would pause dramatically, roll his eyes to the ceiling and sing out:

"Lawd, today! Ahm still working for white folks!"

And he would mop until he sweated. He hated his job and talked incessantly of leaving to work in the post office.

The most colorful of the Negro boys on the job was Shorty, the round, yellow, fat elevator operator. He had tiny, beady eyes that looked out between rolls of flesh with a hard but humorous stare. He had the complexion of a Chinese, a short forehead, and three chins. Psychologically he was the most amazing specimen of the southern Negro I had ever met. Hard-headed, sensible, a reader of magazines and books, he was proud of his race and indignant about its wrongs. But in the presence of whites he would play the role of a clown of the most debased and degraded type.

One day he needed twenty-five cents to buy his lunch.

"Just watch me get a quarter from the first white man I see," he told me as I stood in the elevator that morning.

A white man who worked in the building stepped into the elevator and waited to be lifted to his floor. Shorty sang in a low mumble, smiling, rolling his eyes, looking at the white man roguishly.

"I'm hungry, Mister White Man. I need a quarter for lunch."

The white man ignored him. Shorty, his hands on the controls of the elevator, sang again:

"I ain't gonna move this damned old elevator till I get a quarter, Mister White Man."

"The hell with you, Shorty," the white man said, ignoring him and chewing on his black cigar.

"I'm hungry, Mister White Man. I'm dying for a quarter," Shorty sang, drooling, drawling, humming his words.

"If you don't take me to my floor, you will die," the white man said, smiling a little for the first time.

"But this black sonofabitch sure needs a quarter," Shorty sang, grimacing, clowning, ignoring the white man's threat.

"Come on, you black bastard, I got to work," the white man said, intrigued by the element of sadism involved, enjoying it.

"It'll cost you twenty-five cents, Mister White Man; just a quarter, just two bits," Shorty moaned.

There was silence. Shorty threw the lever and the elevator went up and stopped about five feet shy of the floor upon which the white man worked.

"Can't go no more, Mister White Man, unless I get my quarter," he said in a tone that sounded like crying.

"What would you do for a quarter?" the white man asked, still gazing off.

"I'll do anything for a quarter," Shorty sang.

"What, for example?" the white man asked.

Shorty giggled, swung around, bent over, and poked out his broad, fleshy ass.

"You can kick me for a quarter," he sang, looking impishly at the white man out of the corners of his eyes.

The white man laughed softly, jingled some coins in his pocket, took out one and thumped it to the floor. Shorty stooped to pick it up and the white man bared his teeth and swung his foot into Shorty's rump with all the strength of his body. Shorty let out a howling laugh that echoed up and down the elevator shaft.

"Now, open this door, you goddamn black sonofabitch," the white man said, smiling with tight lips.

"Yeeeess, siiiiir," Shorty sang; but first he picked up the quarter and put it into his mouth. "This monkey's got the peanuts," he chortled.

He opened the door and the white man stepped out and looked back at Shorty as he went toward his office.

"You're all right, Shorty, you sonofabitch," he said.

"I know it!" Shorty screamed, then let his voice trail off in a gale of wild laughter.

I witnessed this scene or its variant at least a score of times and I felt no anger or hatred, only disgust and loathing. Once I asked him:

"How in God's name can you do that?"

"I needed a quarter and I got it," he said soberly, proudly.

"But a quarter can't pay you for what he did to you," I said.

"Listen, nigger," he said to me, "my ass is tough and quarters is scarce."

I never discussed the subject with him after that.

Other Negroes worked in the building: an old man whom we called Edison; his son, John; and a night janitor who answered to the name of Dave. At noon, when I was not running errands, I would join the rest of the Negroes in a little room at the front of the building overlooking the street. Here, in this underworld pocket of the building, we munched our lunches and discussed the ways of white folks toward Negroes. When two or more of us were talking, it was impossible for this subject not to come up. Each of us hated and feared the whites, yet had a white man put in a sudden appearance we would have assumed silent, obedient smiles.

To our minds the white folks formed a kind of superworld: what was said by them during working hours was rehashed and weighed here; how they looked; what they wore; what moods they were in; who had outdistanced whom in business; who was replacing whom on the job; who was getting fired and who was getting hired. But never once did we openly say that we occupied none but subordinate positions in the building. Our talk was restricted to the petty relations which formed the core of life for us.

But under all our talk floated a latent sense of violence; the whites had drawn a line over which we dared not step and we accepted that line because our bread was at stake. But within our boundaries we, too, drew a line that included our right to bread regardless of the indignities or degradations involved in getting it. If a white man had sought to keep us from obtaining a job, or enjoying the rights of citizenship, we would have bowed silently to his power. But if he had sought to deprive us of a dime, blood might have been spilt. Hence, our daily lives were so bound up with trivial objectives that to capitulate when challenged was tantamount to surrendering the right to life itself. Our anger was like the anger of children, passing quickly from one petty grievance to another, from the memory of one slight wrong to another.

"You know what the bastard Olin said to me this morning?" John would ask, biting into a juicy hamburger.

"What?" Shorty would ask.

"Well, I brought him his change from paying his gas bill and he said: 'Put it here in my pocket; my hands are dirty,' " John said. "Hunh . . . I just laid the money on the bench besides him. I ain't no personal slave to him and I'll be damned if I'll put his *own* money in his *own* pocket."

"Hell, you're right," Shorty would say.

"White folks just don't think," old man Edison would say.

"You sure got to watch 'em," Dave, the night janitor, would say. (He would have slept in the room on a cot after his night's cleaning; he would be ready now to keep a date with some girl friend.)

"Falk sent me to have his suit pressed," I would say. "He didn't give me a penny. Told me he would remember it on payday."

"Ain't that some nerve?" John would say.

"You can't eat his memories," Shorty would say.

"But you got to keep on doing them favors," old man Edison would say. "If you don't, they won't like you."

"I'm going north one of these days," Shorty would say.

We would all laugh, knowing that Shorty would never leave, that he depended too much upon the whites for the food he ate.

"What would you do up north?" I would ask Shorty.

"I'd pass for Chinese," Shorty would say.

And we would laugh again. The lunch hour would pass and we would go back to work, but there would be in our faces not one whit of the sentiment we had felt during the hour of discussion.

One day I went to the optical counter of a department store to deliver a pair of eyeglasses. The counter was empty of customers and a tall, florid-faced white man looked at me curiously. He was unmistakably a Yankee, for his physical build differed sharply from that of the lanky Southerner.

"Will you please sign for this, sir?" I asked, presenting the account book and the eyeglasses.

He picked up the book and the glasses, but his eyes were still upon me.

"Say, boy, I'm from the North," he said quietly.

I held very still. Was this a trap? He had mentioned a tabooed subject and I wanted to wait until I knew what he meant. Among the topics that southern white men did not like to discuss with Negroes were the following: American white women; the Ku Klux Klan; France, and how Negro soldiers fared while there; Frenchwomen; Jack Johnson; the entire northern part of the United States; the Civil War; Abraham Lincoln; U. S. Grant; General Sherman; Catholics; the Pope; Jews; the Republican party; slavery; social equality; Communism; Socialism; the 13th, 14th, and 15th Amendments to the Constitution; or any topic calling for positive knowledge or manly self-assertion on the part of the Negro. The most accepted topics were sex and religion. I did not look at the man or answer. With one sentence he had lifted out of the silent dark the race question and I stood on the edge of a precipice.

"Don't be afraid of me," he went on. "I just want to ask you one question."

"Yes, sir," I said in a waiting, neutral tone.

"Tell me, boy, are you hungry?" he asked seriously.

I stared at him. He had spoken one word that touched the very soul of me, but I could not talk to him, could not let him know that I was starving myself to save money to go north. I did not trust him. But my face did not change its expression.

"Oh, no, sir," I said, managing a smile.

I was hungry and he knew it; but he was a white man and I felt that if I told him I was hungry I would have been revealing something shameful.

"Boy, I can see hunger in your face and eyes," he said.

"I get enough to eat," I lied.

"Then why do you keep so thin?" he asked me.

"Well, I suppose I'm just that way, naturally," I lied.

"You're just scared, boy," he said.

"Oh, no, sir," I lied again.

I could not look at him. I wanted to leave the counter, yet he was a white man and I had learned not to walk abruptly away from a white man when he was talking to me. I stood, my eyes looking away. He ran his hand into his pocket and pulled out a dollar bill.

"Here, take this dollar and buy yourself some food," he said.

"No, sir," I said.

"Don't be a fool," he said. "You're ashamed to take it. God, boy, don't let a thing like that stop you from taking a dollar and eating."

The more he talked the more it became impossible for me to take the dollar. I wanted it, but I could not look at it. I wanted to speak, but I could not move my tongue. I wanted him to leave me alone. He frightened me.

"Say something," he said.

All about us in the store were piles of goods; white men and women went from counter to counter. It was summer and from a high ceiling was suspended a huge electric fan that whirred. I stood waiting for the white man to give me the signal that would let me go.

"I don't understand it," he said through his teeth. "How far did you go in school?"

"Through the ninth grade, but it was really the eighth," I told him. "You see, our studies in the ninth grade were more or less a review of what we had in the eighth grade."

Silence. He had not asked me for this long explanation, but I had spoken at length to fill up the yawning, shameful gap that loomed between us; I had spoken to try to drag the unreal nature of the conversation back to safe and sound southern ground. Of course, the conversation was real; it dealt with my welfare, but it had brought to the surface of day all the dark fears I had known all my life. The Yankee white man did not know how dangerous his words were.

(There are some elusive, profound, recondite things that men find hard to say to other men; but with the Negro it is the little things of life that become hard to say, for these tiny items shape his destiny. A man will seek to express his relation to the stars; but when a man's consciousness has been riveted upon obtaining a loaf of bread, that loaf of bread is as important as the stars.)

Another white man walked up to the counter and I sighed with relief.

"Do you want the dollar?" the man asked.

"No, sir," I whispered.

"All right," he said. "Just forget it."

He signed the account book and took the eyeglasses. I stuffed the book into my bag and turned from the counter and walked down the aisle, feeling a physical tingling along my spine, knowing that the white man knew I was really hungry. I avoided him after that. Whenever I saw him I felt in a queer way that he was my enemy, for he knew how I felt and the safety of my life in the South depended upon how well I concealed from all whites what I felt.

One summer morning I stood at a sink in the rear of the factory washing a pair of eyeglasses that had just come from the polishing machines whose throbbing shook the floor upon which I stood. At each machine a white man was bent forward, working intently. To my left sunshine poured through a window, lighting up the rouge smears and making the factory look garish, violent, dangerous. It was nearing noon and my mind was drifting toward my daily lunch of a hamburger and a bag of peanuts. It had been a routine day, a day more or less like the other days I had spent on the job as errand boy and washer of eyeglasses. I was at peace with the world, that is, at peace in the only way in which a black boy in the South can be at peace with a world of white men.

Perhaps it was the mere sameness of the day that soon made it different from the other days; maybe the white men who operated the machines felt bored with their dull, automatic tasks and hankered for some kind of excitement. Anyway, I presently heard footsteps behind me and turned my head. At my elbow stood a young white man, Mr. Olin, the immediate foreman under whom I worked. He was smiling and observing me as I cleaned emery dust from the eyeglasses.

"Boy, how's it going?" he asked.

"Oh, fine, sir!" I answered with false heartiness, falling quickly into that nigger-being-a-good-natured-boy-in-the-presence-of-a-white-man pattern, a pattern into which I could now slide easily; although I was wondering if he had any criticism to make of my work.

He continued to hover wordlessly at my side. What did he want? It was unusual for him to stand there and watch me; I wanted to look at him, but was afraid to.

"Say, Richard, do you believe that I'm your friend?" he asked me.

The question was so loaded with danger that I could not reply at once. I scarcely knew Mr. Olin. My relationship to him had been the typical relationship of Negroes to southern whites. He gave me orders and I said, "Yes, sir," and obeyed them. Now, without warning, he was asking me if I thought that he was my friend; and I knew that all southern white men fancied themselves as friends of niggers. While fishing for an answer that would say nothing, I smiled.

"I mean," he persisted, "do you think I'm your friend?"

"Well," I answered, skirting the vast racial chasm between us, "I hope you are."

"I am," he said emphatically.

I continued to work, wondering what motives were prompting him. Already apprehension was rising in me.

"I want to tell you something," he said.

"Yes, sir," I said.

"We don't want you to get hurt," he explained. "We like you round here. You act like a good boy."

"Yes, sir," I said. "What's wrong?"

"You don't deserve to get into trouble," he went on.

"Have I done something that somebody doesn't like?" I asked, my mind frantically sweeping over all my past actions, weighing them in the light of the way southern white men thought Negroes should act.

"Well, I don't know," he said and paused, letting his words sink meaningfully into my mind. He lit a cigarette. "Do you know Harrison?"

He was referring to a Negro boy of about my own age who worked across the street for a rival optical house. Harrison and I knew each other casually, but there had never been the slightest trouble between us.

"Yes, sir," I said. "I know him."

"Well, be careful," Mr. Olin said. "He's after you."

"After me? For what?"

"He's got a terrific grudge against you," the white man explained. "What have you done to him?"

The eyeglasses I was washing were forgotten. My eyes were upon Mr. Olin's face, trying to make out what he meant. Was this something serious? I did not trust the white man, and neither did I trust Harrison. Negroes who worked on jobs in the South were usually loyal to their white bosses; they felt that that was the best way to ensure their jobs. Had Harrison felt that I had in some way jeopardized his job? Who was my friend: the white man or the black boy?

"I haven't done anything to Harrison," I said.

"Well, you better watch that nigger Harrison," Mr. Olin said in a low, confidential tone. "A little while ago I went down to get a Coca-Cola and Harrison was waiting for you at the door of the building with a knife. He asked me when you were coming down. Said he was going to get you. Said you called him a dirty name. Now, we don't want any fighting or bloodshed on the job."

I still doubted the white man, yet thought that perhaps Harrison had really interpreted something I had said as an insult.

"I've got to see that boy and talk to him," I said, thinking out loud.

"No, you'd better not," Mr. Olin said. "You'd better let some of us white boys talk to him."

"But how did this start?" I asked, still doubting but half believing.

"He just told me that he was going to get even with you, going to cut you and teach you a lesson," he said. "But don't you worry. Let me handle this."

He patted my shoulder and went back to his machine. He was an important man in the factory and I had always respected his word. He had the authority to order me to do this or that. Now, why would he joke with me? White men did not often joke with Negroes, therefore what he had said was serious. I was upset. We black boys worked long hard hours for what few pennies we earned and we were edgy and tense. Perhaps that crazy Harrison was really after me. My appetite was gone. I had to settle this thing. A white man had walked into my delicately balanced world and had tipped it and I had to right it before I could feel safe. Yes, I would go directly to Harrison and ask what was the matter, what I had said that he resented. Harrison was black and so was I; I would ignore the warning of the white man and talk face to face with a boy of my own color.

At noon I went across the street and found Harrison sitting on a box in the basement. He was eating lunch and reading a pulp magazine. As I approached him, he ran his hand into his pocket and looked at me with cold, watchful eyes.

"Say, Harrison, what's this all about?" I asked, standing cautiously four feet from him.

He looked at me a long time and did not answer.

"I haven't done anything to you," I said.

"And I ain't got nothing against you," he mumbled, still watchful. "I don't bother nobody."

"But Mr. Olin said that you came over to the factory this morning, looking for me with a knife."

"Aw, naw," he said, more at ease now. "I ain't been in your factory all day." He had not looked at me as he spoke.

"Then what did Mr. Olin mean?" I asked. "I'm not angry with you."

"Shucks, I thought *you* was looking for me to cut me," Harrison explained. "Mr. Olin, he came over here this morning and said you was going to kill me with a knife the moment you saw me. He said you was mad at me because I had insulted you. But I ain't said nothing about you." He still had not looked at me. He rose.

"And I haven't said anything about you," I said.

Finally he looked at me and I felt better. We two black boys, each working for ten dollars a week, stood staring at each other, thinking, comparing the motives of the absent white man, each asking himself if he could believe the other.

"But why would Mr. Olin tell me things like that?" I asked.

Harrison dropped his head; he laid his sandwich aside.

"I . . . I . . ." he stammered and pulled from his pocket a long, gleaming knife; it was already open. "I was just waiting to see what you was gonna do to me . . ."

I leaned weakly against a wall, feeling sick, my eyes upon the sharp steel blade of the knife.

"You were going to cut me?" I asked.

"If you had cut me, I was gonna cut you first," he said. "I ain't taking no chances."

"Are you angry with me about something?" I asked.

"Man, I ain't mad at nobody," Harrison said uneasily.

I felt how close I had come to being slashed. Had I come suddenly upon Harrison, he would have thought I was trying to kill him and he would have stabbed me, perhaps killed me. And what did it matter if one nigger killed another?

"Look here," I said. "Don't believe what Mr. Olin says."

"I see now," Harrison said. "He's playing a dirty trick on us."

"He's trying to make us kill each other for nothing."

"How come he wanna do that?" Harrison asked.

I shook my head. Harrison sat, but still played with the open knife. I began to doubt. Was he really angry with me? Was he waiting until I turned my back to stab me? I was in torture.

"I suppose it's fun for white men to see niggers fight," I said, forcing a laugh.

"But you might've killed me," Harrison said.

"To white men we're like dogs or cocks," I said.

"I don't want to cut you," Harrison said.

"And I don't want to cut you," I said.

Standing well out of each other's reach, we discussed the problem and decided that we would keep silent about our conference. We would not let Mr. Olin know that we knew that he was egging us to fight. We agreed to ignore any further provocations. At one o'clock I went back to the factory. Mr. Olin was waiting for me, his manner grave, his face serious.

"Did you see that Harrison nigger?" he asked.

"No, sir," I lied.

"Well, he still has that knife for you," he said.

Hate tightened in me. But I kept a dead face.

"Did you buy a knife yet?" he asked me.

"No, sir," I answered.

"Do you want to use mine?" he asked. "You've got to protect yourself, you know."

"No, sir. I'm not afraid," I said.

"Nigger, you're a fool," he spluttered. "I thought you had some sense! Are you going to just let that nigger cut your heart out? His boss gave *him* a knife to use against *you!* Take this knife, nigger, and stop acting crazy!"

I was afraid to look at him; if I had looked at him I would have had to tell him to leave me alone, that I knew he was lying, that I knew he was no friend of mine, that I knew if anyone had thrust a knife through my heart he would simply have laughed. But I said nothing. He was the boss and he could fire me if he did not like me. He laid an open knife on the edge of his workbench, about a foot from my hand. I had a fleeting urge to pick it up and give it to him, point first into his chest. But I did nothing of the kind. I picked up the knife and put it into my pocket.

"Now, you're acting like a nigger with some sense," he said.

As I worked Mr. Olin watched me from his machine. Later when I passed him he called me.

"Now, look here, boy," he began. "We told that Harrison nigger to stay out of this building and leave you alone, see? But I can't protect you when you go home. If that nigger starts at you when you are on your way home, you stab him before he gets a chance to stab you, see?"

I avoided looking at him and remained silent.

"Suit yourself, nigger," Mr. Olin said. "But don't say I didn't warn you."

I had to make my round of errands to deliver eyeglasses and I stole a few minutes to run across the street to talk to Harrison. Harrison was sullen and bashful, wanting to trust me, but afraid. He told me that Mr. Olin had telephoned his boss and had told him to tell Harrison that I had planned to wait for him at the back entrance of the building at six o'clock and stab him. Harrison and I found it difficult to look at each other; we were upset and distrustful. We were not really angry at each other; we knew that the idea of murder had been planted in each of us by the white men who employed us. We told ourselves again and again that we did not agree with the white men; we urged ourselves to keep faith in each other. Yet there lingered deep down in each of us a suspicion that maybe one of us was trying to kill the other.

"I'm not angry with you, Harrison," I said.

"I don't wanna fight nobody," Harrison said bashfully, but he kept his hand in his pocket on his knife.

Each of us felt the same shame, felt how foolish and weak we were in the face of the domination of the whites.

"I wish they'd leave us alone," I said.

"Me too," Harrison said.

"There are a million black boys like us to run errands," I said. "They wouldn't care if we killed each other."

"I know it," Harrison said.

Was he acting? I could not believe in him. We were toying with the idea of death for no reason that stemmed from our own lives, but because the men who ruled us had thrust the idea into our minds. Each of us depended upon the whites for the bread we ate, and we actually trusted the whites more than we did each other. Yet there existed in us a longing to trust men of our own color. Again Harrison and I parted, vowing not to be influenced by what our white boss men said to us.

The game of egging Harrison and me to fight, to cut each other, kept up for a week. We were afraid to tell the white men that we did not believe them, for that would have been tantamount to calling them liars or risking an argument that might have ended in violence being directed against us.

One morning a few days later Mr. Olin and a group of white men came to me and asked me if I was willing to settle my grudge with Harrison with gloves, according to boxing rules. I told them that, though I was not afraid of Harrison, I did not want to fight him and that I did not know how to box. I could feel now that they knew I no longer believed them.

When I left the factory that evening, Harrison yelled at me from down the block. I waited and he ran toward me. Did he want to cut me? I backed away as he approached. We smiled uneasily and sheepishly at each other. We spoke haltingly, weighing our words.

"Did they ask you to fight me with gloves?" Harrison asked.

"Yes," I told him. "But I didn't agree."

Harrison's face became eager.

"They want us to fight four rounds for five dollars apiece," he said. "Man, if I had five dollars, I could pay down on a suit. Five dollars is almost half a week's wages for me."

"I don't want to," I said.

"We won't hurt each other," he said.

"But why do a thing like that for white men?"

"To get that five dollars."

"I don't need five dollars that much."

"Aw, you're a fool," he said. Then he smiled quickly.

"Now, look here," I said. "Maybe you *are* angry with me . . ."

"Naw, I'm not." He shook his head vigorously.

"I don't want to fight for white men. I'm no dog or rooster."

I was watching Harrison closely and he was watching me closely. Did he really want to fight me for some reason of his own? Or was it the money? Harrison stared at me with puzzled eyes. He stepped toward me and I stepped away. He smiled nervously.

"I need that money," he said.

"Nothing doing," I said.

He walked off wordlessly, with an air of anger. Maybe he will stab me now, I thought. I got to watch that fool . . .

For another week the white men of both factories begged us to fight. They made up stories about what Harrison had said about me; and when they saw Harrison they lied to him in the same way. Harrison and I were wary of each other whenever we met. We smiled and kept out of arm's reach, ashamed of ourselves and of each other.

Again Harrison called to me one evening as I was on my way home.

"Come on and fight," he begged.

"I don't want to and quit asking me," I said in a voice louder and harder than I had intended.

Harrison looked at me and I watched him. Both of us still carried the knives that the white men had given us.

"I wanna make a payment on a suit of clothes with that five dollars," Harrison said.

"But those white men will be looking at us, laughing at us," I said.

"What the hell," Harrison said. "They look at you and laugh at you every day, nigger."

It was true. But I hated him for saying it. I ached to hit him in his mouth, to hurt him.

"What have we got to lose?" Harrison asked.

"I don't suppose we have anything to lose," I said.

"Sure," he said. "Let's get the money. We don't care."

"And now they know that we know what they tried to do to us," I said, hating myself for saying it. "And they hate us for it."

"Sure," Harrison said. "So let's get the money. You can use five dollars, can't you?"

"Yes."

"Then let's fight for 'em."

"I'd feel like a dog."

"To them, both of us are dogs," he said.

"Yes," I admitted. But again I wanted to hit him.

"Look, let's fool them white men," Harrison said. "We won't hurt each other. We'll just pretend, see? We'll show 'em we ain't dumb as they think, see?"

"I don't know."

"It's just exercise. Four rounds for five dollars. You scared?"

"No."

"Then come on and fight."

"All right," I said. "It's just exercise. I'll fight."

Harrison was happy. I felt that it was all very foolish. But what the hell. I would go through with it and that would be the end of it. But I still felt a vague anger that would not leave.

When the white men in the factory heard that we had agreed to fight, their excitement knew no bounds. They offered to teach me new punches. Each morning they would tell me in whispers that Harrison was eating raw onions for strength. And—from Harrison—I heard that they told him I was eating raw meat for strength. They offered to buy me my meals each day, but I refused. I grew ashamed of what I had agreed to do and wanted to back out of the fight, but I was afraid that they would be angry if I tried to. I felt that if white men tried to persuade two black boys to stab each other for no reason save their own pleasure, then it would not be difficult for them to aim a wanton blow at a black boy in a fit of anger, in a passing mood of frustration.

The fight took place one Saturday afternoon in the basement of a Main Street building. Each white man who attended the fight dropped his share of the pot into a hat that sat on the concrete floor. Only white men were allowed in the basement; no women or Negroes were admitted. Harrison and I were stripped to the waist. A bright electric bulb glowed above our heads. As the gloves were tied on my hands, I looked at Harrison and saw his eyes watching me. Would he keep his promise? Doubt made me nervous.

We squared off and at once I knew that I had not thought sufficiently about what I had bargained for. I could not pretend to fight. Neither Harrison nor I knew enough about boxing to deceive even a child for a moment. Now shame filled me. The white men were smoking and yelling obscenities at us.

"Crush that nigger's nuts, nigger!"

"Hit that nigger!"

"Aw, fight, you goddamn niggers!"

"Sock 'im in his f—k—g piece!"

"Make 'im bleed!"

I lashed out with a timid left. Harrison landed high on my head and, before I knew it, I had landed a hard right on Harrison's mouth and blood came. Harrison shot a blow to my nose. The fight was on, was on against our will. I felt trapped and ashamed. I lashed out even harder, and the harder I fought the harder Harrison fought. Our plans and promises now meant nothing. We fought four hard rounds, stabbing, slugging, grunting, spitting, cursing, crying, bleeding. The shame and anger we felt for having allowed ourselves to be duped crept into our blows and blood ran into our eyes, half blinding us. The hate we felt for the men whom we had tried to cheat went into the blows we threw at each other. The white men made the rounds last as long as five minutes and each of us was afraid to stop and ask for time for fear of receiving a blow that would knock us out. When we were on the point of collapsing from exhaustion, they pulled us apart.

I could not look at Harrison. I hated him and I hated myself. I clutched my five dollars in my fist and walked home. Harrison and I avoided each other after that and we rarely spoke. The white men attempted to arrange other fights for us, but we had sense enough to refuse. I heard of other fights being staged between other black boys, and each time I heard those plans falling from the lips of the white men in the factory I eased out of earshot. I felt that I had done something unclean, something for which I could never properly atone.

NEW ORLEANS

---◆---

New Orleans is a magic place to people from other parts of the country. There's no other city that can boast so colorful a combination of traditions—French, Spanish, Negro; an old aristocracy with a strong foreign flavor; the Mardi Gras carnivals, once considered the most beautiful and elaborate in the world; the early years of jazz that produced music and performers known throughout the world. Two different voices speak below of contrasting aspects of the city in the early years of the century: Louis Armstrong's New Orleans is the background for his informal musical education at funerals and picnics; Hamilton Basso remembers the French Quarter before it became a tourist attraction.

Hamilton Basso

Hamilton Basso (1904–1964), studied law at Tulane University, then switched to reporting for the New Orleans *Item* and later for the *Times Picayune*. He was on the staff of *The Nation* in the 30s, and was an associate editor of *The New Yorker* from 1943 until his death. Among his best-known novels are *Days before Lent* and *The View from Pompey's Head*. With his wife, he coedited *The World from Jackson Square,* an anthology of writing about his native city.

A New Orleans Childhood
The House on Decatur Street

Finding myself in New Orleans recently—a pleasant place to be and one that I get to as often as I can—I decided to have another look at the French Quarter. I say "another look" because I have been looking at the French Quarter, off and on, for well over forty years. It is where I come from. I was born in the Quarter and spent the first ten years of my life there. Then my family moved to another part of New Orleans, but I continued to spend a good deal of time in the section, because my father's parents still lived there. They had always lived in the Quarter, and it never occurred to them to live anywhere else. Certainly it never occurred to them or to me that the Quarter would someday become one of the principal tourist attractions in the United States, or that one of its main thoroughfares, Bourbon Street, would turn into as noisy a stretch of pavement as can be found this side of Hong Kong. This last trip to New Orleans was my first in several years, and I had not paid much attention to the Quarter on my two or three previous stopovers, so this time, largely because of what I had been reading about my old neighborhood in the magazines, I was curious to see for myself just what had happened to it. A lot had happened, I found, and the most unattractive part of it had happened to Bourbon Street. What they say about that particular bit of Dixie, it saddens me to report, is mostly true.

Bourbon Street runs the length of the Quarter, which is fourteen blocks long and seven blocks wide, and once was all there was to New Orleans. When French was generally spoken in the city, it used to be known as Le Vieux Carré. This translates into English as the Old Quadrangle. Nowadays, some local-color enthusiasts in New Orleans go rather out of their way to refer to the section as Le Vieux Carré—a tendency especially no-

ticeable among those whose Gallic tradition has its roots in Kansas or
South Dakota—but I think we can let that pass. We can also let pass the
street signs that have been put up since my day—signs that read "Rue de
Chartres" and "Rue Royale," for instance. There was never that kind of
self-conscious Gallicizing in the Quarter when I lived there. Some of the
older members of the French-speaking households might call a thoroughfare a *rue* in the bosom of the family, but in public a street was always
called a street. My suspicion is that if any of these worthies had walked
forth one morning in their alpaca coats and bombazine dresses and seen
their streets labelled *rues* they would have concluded, not without testi-
ness, that those American late-comers in the city administration were trying to have some ill-mannered fun at their expense.

Many tourists think it is amusing that a convivial street like Bourbon
should have the same name as a whiskey (I must say I have managed to
keep from being bowled over by the coincidence), and a lot of them appear to be under the impression that the street was named after the beverage. The facts are otherwise. The street arrived first. The whiskey made
its appearance in Bourbon County, Kentucky—a state that I wouldn't
want to offend, God knows, but the truth of the matter is that hardly
anybody ventured into it before 1750, and the whiskey didn't really start
flowing until a couple of decades later. Bourbon Street was in business
long before that. It was one of the first streets laid out in New Orleans,
back around 1718, and it was christened in honor of the royal house of
France.

The street we lived on during my childhood was Decatur Street—
named after Stephen Decatur, the naval hero—which is parallel to Bourbon, and three blocks from it. We lived between Barracks Street, which
was called that because it was where the French troops had had their
barracks, and Hospital Street (now Governor Nicholls Street), on which
the first hospital in New Orleans had stood. We were only two blocks
from the Mississippi River, which was half a mile wide here, and we were
even closer to the United States Mint. There was naturally a kind of
wonder attached to the river, where ships from all over the world mingled
with our little ferryboats, and old men fished for catfish in the sun. The
austere, gray Mint was still in operation during my childhood, and as
soon as I was able to take in the fact that money was coined there, I
regarded it with awe. Pennies were the coins I knew most about in those
days—they bore the very Grecian profile of an Indian in a war bonnet, on
the band of which was inscribed the word "LIBERTY"—and in the matter of wealth my imagination never went further than them. I used to

have a dream in which I would light upon a small cache of pennies, blazing like the sun, and though the dream frequently repeated itself, I was always too overcome by my find to count up how much it amounted to—about twenty cents, I would guess. I stopped having that dream before we moved away from the Quarter, but even now when I am given pennies in change I go through them, hoping to find an Indian-head.

Bourbon Street had nothing that could compete with the river or the Mint, and my immediate neighborhood was much more entertaining in my eyes. Besides, Bourbon Street was then pretty much a residential street —no streets in the Quarter were completely residential, then or ever— while Decatur Street was given over to shopkeepers. My father's father was one of these—at least, to begin with. He had opened a shoe store on Decatur Street in the early eighteen-eighties, and in time he prospered sufficiently to branch out into what would nowadays be called a small industry. Somewhere around 1890, he bought a few machines and set up a shoe factory behind the store. It was a modest operation during my childhood, employing no more than six men, two of them cobblers who made shoes to order, but when the workmen were bustling amidst a complicated arrangement of whirring belts and spinning wheels, I found the factory just as impressive as many years later I was to find Willow Run.

The building was quite large—large enough to house the store, the factory, and all of us besides. Built during the Spanish occupation of New Orleans, or shortly thereafter, it was L-shaped, consisted of three stories and an attic, and had the customary wrought-iron balconies—extremely simple ones compared to some of the others in the Quarter—and the customary courtyard in the rear. My grandparents lived on the floor above the store and the factory, and my parents and I lived on the floor above that. There were six rooms on each floor, and the living quarters were reached by a stairway spiralling up from a door that gave on the street. The ascending curves were contained in a high, shadowy well, whose walls, I remember, were always damp. I have forgotten how many steps there were, but our quarters seemed a long way up.

While I was still quite young, my grandfather roofed the courtyard over with a glass skylight, to provide more space for the factory, but I can recall how the courtyard looked before then, with my grandmother's flower garden, a pair of scraggly banana trees, and a jagged line of broken bottles cemented onto the top of the rear wall, which was about fifteen feet high. This was the Quarter's way of burglar-proofing, and there were few courtyards that were not similarly protected. The glass fragments on our wall always seemed rather ominous to me, telling of the danger that lurked in the outside world, but when the sun shone on them and brought out their colors—brown and green and garnet and blue—I thought they were beautiful. The impression they made must have gone deep, for I have never since seen a stained-glass window—not even in Notre Dame—without being reminded of them.

Apart from the broken bottles, what I remember best about the courtyard is one of its tenants—an alligator who lived in it for a time. We always had rather curious pets in our family, and the alligator was one of them. He was a present. My grandfather had a close friend who grew rice in the lower part of Louisiana, not far from the Gulf of Mexico, and he used to keep us supplied with the bounty of that part of the country—sacks of fresh oysters, braces of wild duck, rail birds, an occasional sea turtle, and, somewhere along the line, the alligator. A kind man, he thought the creature might amuse me. I thought so, too, when I first heard he was coming, but that was pure ignorance. I had a lot to learn about alligators.

My mother tells me that ours was a relatively small specimen, only three feet long, but to me he seemed enormous. I didn't like his looks much, either, and, for me, he took on the role of the enemy in our midst. We had four other pets at the time: a parrot, who was a splendid conversationalist and could sing part of a march; two canaries; and a bright South American bird, given us by a sea captain we knew. I had heard tales about the cruel appetite of alligators, and I began to fear for the birds—particularly the parrot, a special friend of mine. The other birds were caged, but he had the run of the courtyard, and he thought he owned the place. I had visions of him tangling with the intruder, briefly asserting his rights, and then disappearing, with one last squawk, into the darkness of the alligator's maw. Feeling the need of outside help, I began to mention the parrot in my prayers.

I soon found that I need not have bothered. The alligator, as lazy and torpid as most of his kind, lay motionless for days at a time. The parrot, strutting about the courtyard and eating sunflower seeds within an inch of his ugly head, never gave him a thought, and neither, after a time, did I, except to reflect occasionally on what a big disappointment he was. He became simply another object in the courtyard. Then he vanished, leaving not a trace. One evening he was in the courtyard, and the next morning he wasn't. There weren't any holes or crevices he could have crawled through, and all the doors had been locked and barred for the night. We had a fine mystery on our hands. I didn't care two cents about that large lizard, and in my heart I knew it, but I wasn't going to miss the chance of making a scene, so I insisted that everybody look for him. Work was held up that morning while my grandfather led an alligator hunt, delivering commands in English, French, and Italian, and my mother, who has never been able to stand the thought of any creature in distress, wandered about the courtyard calling "Here, alligator! Here, alligator!" in a troubled, anxious way that moved even me. But the alligator was gone! I was enjoying the excitement, and, to prolong it, I suggested that we call in the police, but my grandfather and my father were cool to the idea. We never did find out what happened to the alligator; our best guess was that some pilferer had managed to scale the rear wall of the courtyard, braving the wicked barrier of glass, and had carried him off. If that was the case, the fellow must have wanted an alligator pretty badly.

All the other families in our block lived, as we did, over their places of business. Many of them had pets, too—mockingbirds, Brazilian finches, cardinals, macaws. Nor was my alligator the only unusual one. There were also a monkey and a squirrel, and—no less unusual in New Orleans, where the thermometer often hovers around a hundred during the summer—a huge St. Bernard. He belonged to a widow, Mrs. Wallansbach (whose name, like the names of all the other people mentioned in this chronicle, I have changed). A number of German families moved to Louisiana in the early seventeen-hundreds, and Mrs. Wallansbach's husband, a restaurateur, was a descendant of one of them. After his death, which occurred before I had a chance to know him, Mrs. Wallansbach sold the restaurant, but she continued to live above it. I can remember her only vaguely—a pair of steel-rimmed spectacles and a bun of reddish hair— and I doubt whether I would remember her at all if it were not for the St. Bernard, which accompanied her everywhere and was one of the attractions of our neighborhood. The French Market—the largest market in New Orleans, and very much like Les Halles, in Paris—was a few blocks away from us on Decatur Street, and whenever Mrs. Wallansbach went shopping there, the business of the day came to a standstill as everybody stopped to admire the St. Bernard. I felt privileged to be on intimate terms with such a spectacular animal. It was his size that appealed to me, not his personality. I knew that our parrot was more talented and more affectionate—he liked to perch on my shoulder and nibble my ear, whereas the St. Bernard resisted all my attempts at playfulness—but the sheer bulk of the dog made up for his lack of other qualities. Mrs. Wallansbach often let me lead him—or, rather, be led by him—on his evening stroll around the Mint, and I enjoyed nothing better, for then I was at the very center of attention.

Mrs. Wallansbach was a good friend of my grandparents, and I often dropped in to visit her. I was generally accompanied on these calls by my closest friend, a recently arrived little French girl named Hélène Rouillard. Hélène's mother and father had died of yellow fever shortly after they reached New Orleans, and Hélène, an only child, had been adopted by the Wilsons, who kept a bookstore across the street from us. Since Hélène and I were the only small children on the block, we were much in each other's company. Hélène knew hardly any English at first, but we managed to get along. What entranced me most about her was her wooden shoes, the first sabots I had ever seen. Hélène could do anything in them—run, jump, even skip rope—and their hollow clack soon became one of the accustomed sounds of our street. My mother recalls that she could usually tell where Hélène and I were, and even what we were up to, by the clatter of those shoes. After a while, the process of Americanization set in, and Hélène put aside her sabots. For me, she was never again quite the same girl.

We were great droppers-in, we two. We had both houses to roam about in, along with our courtyard and the luxuriant walled garden that lay behind the Wilsons' bookstore, but more often than not we went visiting. We were greatly spoiled, and I am afraid we sometimes made nuisances of ourselves. One of our favorite ports of call was the blacksmith shop around the corner on Hospital Street, facing the Mint. It could not have been as smoky and cavernous as I now remember it, or the sparks as dazzling, or the horses as spirited, or the smith as grimy and gigantic, but of the rings that he used to make for us from horseshoe nails, I am altogether sure: They were masterpieces. After leaving the smithy, Hélène and I would often descend upon the two maiden Valvan sisters, who were milliners. We could count on a bonbon from them, since they both had a passion for sweets, and they thought Hélène was so chic that they let her model hats. We would then drop in on Mr. Gallardo, the baker; visit Peter, the gunsmith; admire the wares in Mr. Mayer's jewelry store; and pass the time of day with Mr. and Mrs. Scheidemann, who owned a crockery shop.

Mr. Scheidemann, a grave, slow-spoken man with heavy shoulders and a bald head, seemed to me to be slightly more than mortal. I had learned from family conversations that it was his habit to spend the late-afternoon hours in the courtyard writing poetry, and even though all I knew about poetry was Mother Goose, and perhaps the first few lines of "Paul Revere's Ride," this dedication of Mr. Scheidemann's set him apart in my eyes. I had only to listen to my grandfather or Mr. Wilson to know that it was no mean thing to be a poet. There was something, I gathered, called "the life of the mind." It interested me, this life of the mind, and I felt a great curiosity to see it close up. What did a poet do when he was writing poetry? How did he look? Did he speak his lines out loud, or what? There came a time when I simply had to find out. Late one afternoon, I left the Wilsons' garden, where Hélène and I had been catching dragonflies, and instead of going straight home as I had told her I would, I went down the street and stole into the passage that led to the Scheidemann's courtyard. The long corridor was shadowy, with crates of china piled against the walls, and since this was no conventional visit but deliberate espionage, I was thrilled by my own recklessness. Tiptoeing to the end of the corridor, I peered into the courtyard. Mr. Scheidemann was sitting in a wicker chair, in his suspenders. He was smoking a cigar and had a small writing pad on his knee. I spied on him for what seemed like an hour, and nothing happened. Mr. Scheidemann just sat there, smoking his cigar. It was a disappointing experience, but it had its value. It taught me that poetry can't be hurried, and that a poet may be a bald-headed man in suspenders, smoking a cigar.

Among the few events that really shook me in those days was the death of an animal with whom I was acquainted, and I was particularly sobered when Mrs. Wallansbach's St. Bernard gave up the ghost. He had been so large and was now so humbled, and my world, as it always did when somebody or something was removed from it, seemed smaller and emptier than before. Then, too, when it came to animals, I felt that there was a great unfairness about the mystery beyond the grave. I knew where dead people went—to Heaven—and it troubled me that no such harbor had been provided for dead animals. I trusted my elders, and hoped they were right when they said that even the smallest creature was sure to be looked after, but since they could not tell me *how*, or guarantee that there were angelic presences in the shapes of horses, dogs, cats, and parrots, the notion of unfairness persisted. I never brooded for very long, of course. I was as resilient as most children, and anyway I knew how risky it was to question the wisdom of Our Merciful Father. When somebody presently gave Hélène a mallard duckling, it expanded my universe just as the death of the St. Bernard had contracted it. I quickly recovered from the loss of my towering friend.

Mrs. Wallansbach had a harder time of it. Though I was too young to know it then, I can see now that she gave the St. Bernard all her affection, except the part of it which in her kindliness she saved for Hélène and me. Unable to bear the thought of losing him completely, she called in a taxidermist and commissioned him to stuff the animal. Needless to say, I wanted to know all the details of the procedure, which sounded fascinating, and I was puzzled by the strange expression that crossed the faces of my parents and grandparents when I brought the matter up. Eventually, it became clear to me that they had certain reservations about the propriety of stuffing a household pet, but I still thought it was a fine thing for Mrs. Wallansbach to do, and so did Hélène. The mallard duckling was beginning to pall a little, for it didn't seem to comprehend that it was supposed to follow us wherever we went, and we were impatient for the day when we would see the St. Bernard again.

The day came about a month later. Hélène was in bed with the measles, and I had gone on a shopping expedition with my mother. On the way home, we ran into Mrs. Wallansbach. She invited me to stop in and visit with her, and I immediately knew the reason for the invitation. The St. Bernard had come back. I followed Mrs. Wallansbach up the stairs and into her parlor. The slatted blinds of the long windows that opened on her balcony had been drawn against the sun, and there in a corner, where the shadows were deepest, stood the St. Bernard. Looming even larger than in life, he stood motionless on his stiff legs, staring up at me with blank, dismaying eyes. Mrs. Wallansbach asked me if I didn't want to pat him, and I felt I had to, but I declined the glass of lemonade that she offered me. I stopped dropping in on Mrs. Wallansbach after that, and there has been something of a barrier between St. Bernards and me ever since.

Compared to this street and these people, Bourbon Street didn't amount to much. My grandfather owned a building on it, which he used as a warehouse, and sometimes I would go there with him. The building was thought to have been a barracks when New Orleans and the rest of the Louisiana Territory were ruled by Spain, and some of the windows had iron bars. Our family doctor was on Bourbon Street, too—a small, lively Creole gentleman who kept goldfish and always smelled of snuff— and I would have to go and see him every now and then, usually in connection with my tonsils. But the only real interest Bourbon Street had for me, and that only indirectly, was the French Opera House. The two cobblers who worked for my grandfather, Mr. Fisher and Mr. Auchin, used to make shoes for the troupes that appeared there.

New Orleans naturally went in for opera—first light opera and then grand opera, too. As early as 1810 there were three theatres in the Quarter given over to musical dramas of one kind or the other, and long before I knew the date of the Louisiana Purchase or the fact that General P. G. T.

Beauregard, another French Quarter resident, had ordered the firing on Fort Sumter and thus started the Civil War, I was aware that Jenny Lind and Adelina Patti had sung in New Orleans in the eighteen-fifties. It was sometimes hard for me to be sure where the past ended and the present began, so great was their overlapping. There were a number of things relatively remote from me in which I felt I had a personal stake—the great yellow-fever epidemics, for instance, since my grandfather and my grandmother had lived through several of them. Because of my grandfather's shoe factory I felt that I had a personal stake in everything that had ever happened in the French Opera House.

The building, which was one of the handsomest in the Quarter, was erected in 1859, but it did not come into its full glory until the years between 1890 and 1910. My father always insisted that the opera heard there was better than any ever presented by the Metropolitan in New York. I cannot vouch for his opinion, since my few visits to the French Opera House took place before I reached the age of appreciation. I do know that my father was a man of great local pride, and he tended to view anything—even people, I'm afraid—that came out of New Orleans as automatically superior. In this, I might add, he resembled a substantial portion of the population.

The Opera House was still going strong when I lived in the Quarter. My grandparents sometimes attended performances, and my father was a true devotee. My own link with the opera, however, came through Mr. Fisher and Mr. Auchin. Because of an arrangement my grandfather had with the management, he could always get them a pass to the upper gallery. Mr. Fisher did not go very often, but Mr. Auchin, like my father, rarely missed a performance. Though I find it hard to recall what Mr. Fisher looked like—all I am sure of is that he had a goatee and blue eyes —Mr. Auchin appears plainly before me whenever I come across a picture of Gustave Flaubert. Most of what I know about opera, which isn't much, I learned from Mr. Fisher and Mr. Auchin. I hung around them often, but never so steadily as when they were working on the shoes for the opera company. Their workbenches assumed a gala look then. The shoes were made with satin uppers, and bright squares of satin, of every imaginable hue, would be scattered about like small, dazzling flags; there was one particular shade of scarlet that burns in my memory as the most beautiful color I have ever seen.

It was something of a disappointment to my father, especially after he acquired a phonograph, that I did not appreciate the music of the operas as much as I might have. But I partly made up for that deficiency by my enjoyment of the plots, nearly all of which Mr. Fisher and Mr. Auchin, between them, knew to the last incident. Mr. Auchin was a superb story-teller. To be sure, he had the habit of lapsing into French at the most exciting moments, but he was very patient when I lost the drift, as I soon did, and he had to repeat himself in English. One year, he made the shoes for "Faust," and over his workbench, he told me, bit by bit, what happens when you make a pact with the Devil. Mr. Auchin never called Mephistopheles Mephistopheles. He knew the scoundrel for what he was, and was not going to get fancy. In those days, the Devil was much in my thoughts. My grandfather took a scornful view of him, as did my father, but Mr. Auchin, who attended early Mass every Sunday at the St. Louis Cathedral and was considerably more conservative, saw the Devil exactly as my friend Hélène had told me she did—horned, cloven-hoofed, and pitchforked, chalking up the black marks and coldly awaiting the day when he could settle his accounts. I was caught in the middle. I was eager to side with my father and grandfather, since the Devil was the last person I wanted hovering in the background, and I listened very hard when they said that the Devil merely stood for evil, which lurked in every crack and crevice of the world, and particularly in the heart of man. Mr. Auchin and Hélène, though, had Authority on their side. Pulled first one way and then the other, I took a long time to make up my mind. Though I hoped that my father and grandfather were right, and though they seemed quite able to look out for themselves, no matter what, I decided to take no chances. Hélène and Mr. Auchin, plus Authority, won out.

Mr. Auchin told the story of "Faust" so vividly that I asked my father to take me to it. Since I had never asked to go to the opera before, he was pleased to detect in me what he regarded as the first stirrings of a musical turn of mind. The truth of the matter was, however, that I was spurred by the same impulses that had caused me to sneak into Mr. Scheidemann's courtyard. I wanted to see the Devil at his devilry, just as I had wanted to see a poet at his poetry. The evening was not a success. I had never been so disappointed in anybody as I was in that Devil. Compared to the fellow introduced into my mythology by Mr. Auchin and Hélène, he couldn't have frightened a sick cat. When he first appeared in a puff of smoke, I thought he was sensational and expected great things of him, but he never came through; he was even less convincing than the maskers who paraded in his guise on Mardi Gras. As far as I was concerned, Mr. Auchin's shoes were the best part of the show. My father had to shush me throughout the first act, and for the rest of the evening I had a hard time keeping awake.

I never went to the opera with my father again. As he later admitted, he was driven to the conclusion that the vaudeville bills at the Orpheum Theatre were more in my line. They were, too. My father and I did not get together on the subject of music until I awoke to the appeal of jazz. He was able to appreciate jazz as much as he appreciated opera, and, of course, it had the further advantage of being a native New Orleans product. Here I do not think that his patriotism led him astray. Jazz was then first making itself unmistakably heard—in street parades, on marches back from the cemeteries after Negro funerals, on trucks that used to drive through the streets hung with signs advertising some coming event—usually a prizefight—and the sound of creation filled the air. New Orleans jazz needs no testimonial from me, but those, I swear, were the days.

The French Opera House was destroyed by fire in 1919. My father had moved us from Decatur Street several years before—my sister Mary had arrived, and we needed more room—and when my grandfather died, in 1917, we sold the factory and the old house, and my last family tie with the Quarter was broken. Our new house was in a middle-class neighborhood on the "uptown" side of Canal Street—New Orleans' main thoroughfare, which divides the city in two—and although I eventually got more or less used to our new surroundings, especially after I entered high school and began to make a new set of friends, I don't think I ever really felt at home there. I'm sure my father never did. He had grown up in the French Quarter, and in spirit he never left it. The day after the fire at the French Opera House, my father came home early and took me down to see the charred ruins of the building in which I had spoiled his enjoyment of "Faust." He was silent and subdued, and I was then old enough to understand that he was thinking of the past and all that was in the past, and of how it could never be again.

I understood my father's feelings even better on my recent trip to New Orleans. Around eight o'clock one evening, I walked over to Decatur Street. It was the first time I had been there in more than twenty-five years. All my former friends were gone, I knew—Hélène, the Wilsons, the Misses Valvan, Mr. and Mrs. Scheidemann, Mrs. Wallansbach, Peter the gunsmith, and Mr. Gallardo the baker. Our old house was still standing, and as large as I remembered it, but it was barred and shuttered and empty, falling into ruin, and the whole block had a similarly derelict appearance. The only lighted buildings were several of those mean, shabby bars to be found in waterfront districts all over the world. One bar had taken the place of the Wilsons' bookstore. As I stood before it, I found myself shaking my head.

At that, though, I liked what has happened to Decatur Street better than I liked what has happened to Bourbon Street. It is lined with one cabaret after another, and apparently the tourists find them attractive, for there are always throngs of them on the street. I don't want to give the impression that I have anything against tourists, because I haven't, and it is perhaps foolish of me, simply because I used to have my tonsils looked at on Bourbon Street and because it was part of my childhood in other ways, to object to its bars and strip-tease emporiums, and to its silly pretense of old-world romanticism. I do object, though—strongly. I don't like to see all the walls come tumbling down.

After leaving Decatur Street, I had a cup of coffee in the French Market and then a drink in a non-tourist bar, and, at about nine o'clock, I strolled over to Bourbon Street. Even at that early hour, business was thriving. A line of more than a hundred people was waiting to witness the performance of a lady who calls herself the Cat Girl, and I noticed that the Wildcat Girl, the Cupcake Girl, the Tassel Girl, and twenty or so more were also getting a play. These, of course, were only the featured performers, with star billing. I have no idea of the number of other, uncapitalized girls who were less conspicuously stashed away. Each of the divinities who grace Bourbon Street has a barker in her retinue. These attendants stand at the doors of the temples, and it is evidently one of their duties, when they sight a likely customer, to open the doors for an instant, permitting a glimpse of the rites within.

All this activity—the tourists touring, the barkers barking, the doors opening, the ladies exposing more pink and powdered flesh than ever Rubens got around to painting in his whole industrious lifetime—takes place to the accompaniment of jazz. On the whole, I did not think that it was good jazz, and some of it sounded terrible, but I am getting to be cross and irritable and after my visit to Decatur Street was perhaps not in a very responsive mood. I went by the parking lot where the French Opera House used to stand, and then, a block or so farther on, a whole series of doors began opening as I passed. Through one, I saw a lady standing on a bar, who appeared to be in danger of losing her skirt. A moment later, I came upon two small, white-haired gentlemen talking on the curb. One look at them—their sober clothes, their coloring, the general hang of their appearance—and I knew that they were not far from their homes. They could have been two of our neighbors on Decatur Street. Paying not the slightest attention to their surroundings, or to the blare of noise that welled up all about them, they were talking most earnestly. Their speech had an unmistakable French Quarter accent—a way of pronunciation greatly tempered by the several foreign languages that have long been used there, though less today than formerly—and I was able to catch a few sentences as I strolled past. They were talking about the Holy Name Society's picnic the following Sunday. Suddenly, I felt much better about everything. The Quarter was not yet lost. It was being defended, and at its center it still held fast.

Louis Armstrong

Famous everywhere for his trumpet-playing, his scat-singing, and his personal charm, Louis Armstrong was born in New Orleans on the 4th of July in 1900 and began his professionl career there. He went to Chicago and then to New York, where he joined Fletcher Henderson's band in 1924. The recordings he made between 1925 and 1932 have been a source of ideas and inspiration for performers ever since. He has appeared in many films, and has been sent on good-will tours to South America and Africa by the State Department. The selection below is taken from his autobiography, *Satchmo: My Life in Jazz*, published in 1954.

Storyville Days and Nights

Arthur Brown was one of my playmates at school. He was a quiet, good-looking youngster with nice manners and a way of treating the girls that made them go wild about him. I admired the way he played it cool. He was going with a girl who had a little brother who was very cute. Too cute, I would say, since he was always playing with a pistol or a knife. We did not pay much attention to the kid, but one day when he was cleaning his gun he pointed it at Arthur Brown saying "I am going to shoot." Sure enough, he pulled the trigger; the gun was loaded and Arthur Brown fell to the ground with a bullet in his head.

It was a terrible shock. We all felt so bad that even the boys cried.

When Arthur was buried we all chipped in and hired a brass band to play at his funeral. Beautiful girls Arthur used to go with came to the funeral from all over the city, from Uptown, Downtown, Front o' Town and Back o' Town. Every one of them was weeping. We kids, all of us teen-agers, were pallbearers. The band we hired was the finest I had ever heard. It was the Onward Brass Band with Joe "King" Oliver and Emanuel Perez blowing the cornets. Big tall Eddy Jackson booted the bass tuba. A bad tuba player in a brass band can make work hard for the other musicians, but Eddy Jackson knew how to play that tuba and he was the ideal man for the Onward Brass Band. Best of all was Black Benny playing the bass drum. The world really missed something by not digging Black Benny on that bass drum before he was killed by a prostitute.

It was a real sad moment when the Onward Brass Band struck up the funeral march as Arthur Brown's body was being brought from the church to the graveyard. Everybody cried, including me. Black Benny beat the bass drum with a soft touch, and Babe Mathews put a handkerchief under his snare to deaden the tone. "Nearer, My God, to Thee" was played as the coffin was lowered into the grave.

As pallbearers, Cocaine Buddy, Little Head Lucas, Egg Head Papa, Harry Tennison and myself wore the darkest clothes we had, blue suits for the most part. Later that same year Harry Tennison was killed by a hustling gal of the honky-tonks called Sister Pop. Her pimp was named Pop and was well known as a good cotch player. Pop did not know anything about the affair until Sister Pop shot Harry in the brain with a big forty-five gun and killed him instantly. Later on Lucas and Cocaine Buddy died natural deaths of TB.

The funerals in New Orleans are sad until the body is finally lowered into the grave and the Reverend says, "ashes to ashes and dust to dust." After the brother was six feet under ground, the band would strike up one of those good old tunes like "Didn't He Ramble?" and all the people would leave their worries behind. Particularly when King Oliver blew that last chorus in high register.

Once the band starts, everybody starts swaying from one side of the street to the other, especially those who drop in and follow the ones who have been to the funeral. These people are known as the "second line" and they may be anyone passing along the street who wants to hear the music. The spirit hits them and they follow along to see what's happening. Some follow only a few blocks, but others follow the band until the whole affair is over.

Wakes are usually held when the body is laid out in the house or the funeral parlor. The family of the deceased usually serves a lot of coffee and cheese and crackers all night long so that the people who come to sing hymns over the corpse can eat and drink to their heart's delight. I used to go to a lot of wakes and lead off with a hymn. After everybody had joined in the chorus, I would tiptoe on into the kitchen and load up on crackers, cheese and coffee. That meal always tasted specially good. Maybe it was because that meal was a freebie and didn't cost me anything but a song— or I should say, a hymn.

There was one guy who went to every wake in town. It did not matter whose wake it was. In some way he would find out about it and get there, rain or shine, and lead off with a hymn. When I got old enough to play in the brass band with good old-timers like Joe Oliver, Roy Palmer, Sam Dutrey and his brother Honore, Oscar Celestin, Oak Gasper, Buddy Petit, Kid Ory and Mutt Carey and his brother Jack, I began noticing this character more frequently. Once I saw him in church looking very sad and as if he was going to cry any minute. His clothes were not very good and his pants and coat did not match. What I admired about him was that he managed to look very presentable. His clothes were well pressed and his shoes shined. Finally I found out the guy was called Sweet Child.

For some time funerals gave me the only chance I had to blow my cornet. The war had started, and all the dance halls and theaters in New Orleans had been closed down. A draft law had been passed and every-body had to work or fight. I was perfectly willing to go into the Army, but they were only drafting from the age of twenty-one to twenty-five and I was only seventeen. I tried to get into the Navy, but they checked up on my birth certificate and threw me out. I kept up my hope and at one enlistment office a soldier told me to come back in a year. He said that if the war was still going on I could capture the Kaiser and win a great, big prize. "Wouldn't that be swell," I thought. "Capture the Kaiser and win the war." Believe me, I lived to see that day.

Since I did not have a chance to play my cornet, I did odd jobs of all kinds. For a time I worked unloading the banana boats until a big rat jumped out of a bunch I was carrying to the checker. I dropped that bunch and started to run. The checker hollered at me to come back and get my time, but I didn't stop running until I got home. Since then bananas have terrified me. I would not eat one if I was starving. Yet I can remember how I used to love them. I could eat a whole small ripe bunch all by myself when the checker could not see me.

Every time things went bad with me I had the coal cart to fall back on, thanks to my good stepfather Gabe. I sure did like him, and I used to tease Mayann about it.

"Mama, you know one thing?" I would say. "Papa Gabe is the best step-pa I've ever had. He is the best out of the whole lot of them."

Mayann would kind of chuckle and say:

"Aw, go on, you Fatty O'Butler."

That was the time when the moving-picture actor Fatty Arbuckle was in his prime and very popular in New Orleans. Mayann never did get his name right. It sounded so good to me when she called me Fatty O'Butler that I never told her different.

I would stay at the coalyard with father Gabe until I thought I had found something better, that is something that was easier. It was hard work shoveling coal and sitting behind my mule all day long, and I used to get awful pains in my back. So any time I could find a hustle that was just a little lighter, I would run to it like a man being chased.

The job I took with Morris Karnoffsky was easier, and I stayed with

him a long time. His wagon went through the red-light district, or Storyville, selling stone coal at a nickel a bucket. Stone coal was what they
called hard coal. One of the reasons I kept the job with Morris Karnoffsky
was that it gave me a chance to go through Storyville in short pants. Since
I was working with a man, the cops did not bother me. Otherwise, they
would have tanned my hide if they had caught me rambling around that
district. They were very strict with us youngsters and I don't blame them.
The temptation was great and weak-minded kids could have sure messed
things up.

As for me I was pretty wise to things. I had been brought up around the
honky-tonks on Liberty and Perdido where life was just about the same as
it was in Storyville except that the chippies were cheaper. The gals in my
neighborhood did not stand in cribs wearing their fine silk lingerie as
they did in Storyville. They wore the silk lingerie just the same, but
under their regular clothes. Our hustlers sat on their steps and called to
the "Johns" as they passed by. They had to keep an eye on the cops all the
time, because they weren't allowed to call the tricks like the girls in Storyville. That was strictly a business center. Music, food and everything else
was good there.

All of the cribs had a small fireplace. When our wagon passed by, the
girls would holler out to Morris and tell him to have his boy bring in
some coal. I would bring them whatever they ordered, and they would
generally ask me to start a fire for them or put some coal on the fire that
was already burning. While I was fixing the fire I couldn't help stealing a
look at them, which always sent me into a cold sweat. I did not dare say
anything, but I had eyes, and very good ones at the time, and I used them.
It seemed to me that some of the beautiful young women I saw standing
in those doorways should have been home with their parents.

What I appreciated most about being able to go into Storyville without
being bothered by the cops, was Pete Lala's cabaret where Joe Oliver had
his band and where he was blowing up a storm on his cornet. Nobody
could touch him. Harry Zeno, the best-known drummer in New Orleans,
was playing with him at the time. What I admired most about Zeno was
that no matter how hard he played the sporting racket, he never let it
interfere with his profession. And that's something the modern-day musician has to learn. Nothing ever came between Harry Zeno and his drums.

There were other members of Joe Oliver's band whose names have become legendary in music. The world will never be able to replace them,
and I say that from the bottom of my heart. These musicians were Buddy
Christian, guitar (he doubled on piano also); Zoo Robinson, trombone;

Jimmy Noone, clarinet; Bob Lyons, bass violin; and last but not least, Joe Oliver on the cornet. That was the hottest jazz band ever heard in New Orleans between the years 1910 and 1917.

Harry Zeno died in the early part of 1917 and his funeral was the largest ever held for any musician. Sweet Child, by the way, was at this funeral too, singing away as though he was a member of Zeno's lodge. The Onward Brass Band put him away with those fine, soothing funeral marches.

Not long after Zeno died, talk started about closing down Storyville. Some sailors on leave got mixed up in a fight and two of them were killed. The Navy started a war on Storyville, and even as a boy I could see that the end was near. The police began to raid all the houses and cabarets. All the pimps and gamblers who hung around a place called Twenty-Five, while their chicks were working, were locked up.

It sure was a sad scene to watch the law run all those people out of Storyville. They reminded me of a gang of refugees. Some of them had spent the best part of their lives there. Others had never known any other kind of life. I have never seen such weeping and carrying-on. Most of the pimps had to go to work or go to jail, except a privileged few.

A new generation was about to take over in Storyville. My little crowd had begun to look forward to other kicks, like our jazz band, our quartet and other musical activities.

Joe Lindsey and I formed a little orchestra. Joe was a very good drummer, and Morris French was a good man on the trombone. He was a little shy at first, but we soon helped him to get over that. Another shy lad was Louis Prevost who played the clarinet, but how he could play once he got started! We did not use a piano in those days. There were only six pieces: cornet, clarinet, trombone, drums, bass violin and guitar, and when those six kids started to swing, you would swear it was Ory and Oliver's jazz band.

Kid Ory and Joe Oliver got together and made one of the hottest jazz bands that ever hit New Orleans. They often played in a tail gate wagon to advertise a ball or other entertainments. When they found themselves on a street corner next to another band in another wagon, Joe and Kid Ory would shoot the works. They would give with all that good mad music they had under their belts and the crowd would go wild. When the other band decided it was best to cut the competition and start out for another corner, Kid Ory played a little tune on his trombone that made the crowd go wild again. But this time they were wild with laughter. If you ever run into Kid Ory, maybe he will tell you the name of the tune. I don't dare write it here. It was a cute little tune to celebrate the defeat of the enemy. I thought it screamingly funny and I think you would too.

Kid knew how much Joe Oliver cared for me. He also knew that, great as he was, Joe Oliver would never do anything that would make me look small in the eyes of the public. Oftentimes when our band was on the street advertising a lawn party or some other entertainment, our tail wagon would run into the Ory-Oliver band. When this happened Joe had told me to stand up so that he would be sure to see me and not do any carving. After he saw me he would stand up in his wagon, play a few short pieces and set out in another direction.

One day when we were advertising for a ball we ran into Oliver and his band. I was not feeling very well that day and I forgot to stand up. What a licking those guys gave us. Sure enough when our wagon started to leave, Kid Ory started to play that getaway tune at us. The crowd went mad. We felt terrible about it, but we took it like good sports because there was not any other band that could do that to us. We youngsters were the closest rivals the Ory band had.

I saw Joe Oliver the night of the day he had cut in on us.

"Why in hell," he said before I could open my mouth, "didn't you stand up?"

"Papa Joe, it was all my fault. I promise I won't ever do that again."

We laughed it all off, and Joe bought me a bottle of beer. This was a feather in my cap because Papa Joe was a safe man, and he did not waste a lot of money buying anybody drinks. But for me he would do anything he thought would make me happy.

At that time I did not know the other great musicians, such as Jelly Roll Morton, Freddie Keppard, Jimmy Powlow, Bab Frank, Bill Johnson, Sugar Johnny, Tony Jackson, George Fields and Eddy Atkins. All of them had left New Orleans long before the red-light district was closed by the Navy and the law. Of course, I met most of them in later years, but Papa Joe Oliver, God bless him, was my man. I often did errands for Stella Oliver, his wife, and Joe would give me lessons for my pay. I could not have asked for anything I wanted more. It was my ambition to play as he did. I still think that if it had not been for Joe Oliver, jazz would not be what it is today. He was a creator in his own right.

Mrs. Oliver also became attached to me and treated me as if I were her own son. She had a little girl by her first marriage named Ruby, whom I knew when she was just a little shaver. She is married now and has a daughter who will be married soon.

One of the nicest things Joe Oliver did for me when I was a youngster was to give me a beat-up old cornet of his which he had blown for years. I prized that horn and guarded it with my life. I blew on it for a long, long time before I was fortunate enough to get another one.

Cornets were much cheaper then than they are today, but at that they cost sixty-five dollars. You had to be a big-shot musician making plenty of money to pay that price for a horn. I remember how such first-rate musicians as Hamp Benson, Kid Ory, Zoo French, George Brashere, Joe Petit and lots of other fellows I played with beamed all over when they got new horns. They acted just as though they had received a brand-new Cadillac.

I got my first brand-new cornet on the installment plan with "a little bit down" and a "little bit now and then." Whenever my collector would catch up with me and start talking about a "little bit now," I would tell him:

"I'll give you-all a little bit *then,* but I'm damned if I can give you-all a little bit *now.*"

Cornet players used to pawn their instruments when there was a lull in funerals, parades, dances, gigs and picnics. Several times I went to the pawnshop and picked up some loot on my horn. Once it was to play cotch and be around the good old hustlers and gamblers.

I can never stop loving Joe Oliver. He was always ready to come to my rescue when I needed someone to tell me about life and its little intricate things, and help me out of difficult situations. That is what happened when I met a gal named Irene, who had just arrived from Memphis, Tennessee, and did not know a soul in New Orleans. She got mixed up with a gambler in my neighborhood named Cheeky Black who gave her a real hard time. She used to come into a honky-tonk where I was playing with a three-piece combo. I played the cornet; Boogus, the piano; and Sonny Garbie, the drums. After their night's work was over, all the hustling gals used to come into the joint around four or five o'clock in the morning. They would ask us to beat out those fine blues for them and buy us drinks, cigarettes, or anything we wanted.

I noticed that everyone was having a good time except Irene. One morning during an intermission I went over to talk to her and she told me her whole story. Cheeky Black had taken every nickel she had earned and she had not eaten for two days. She was as raggedy as a bowl of slaw. That is where I came in with my soft heart. I was making a dollar and twenty-five cents a night. That was a big salary in those days—if I got it; some nights they paid us, and some nights they didn't. Anyway, I gave Irene most of my salary until she could get on her feet.

That went on until she and Cheeky Black came to the parting of the ways. There was only one thing Irene could do: take refuge under my wing. I had not had any experience with women, and she taught me all I know.

We fell deeply in love. My mother did not know this at first. When she did find out, being the great little trouper she was, she made no objections. She felt that I was old enough to live my own life and to think for myself. Irene and I lived together as man and wife. Then one fine day Irene was taken deathly sick. As she had been very much weakened by the dissipated life she had led, her body could not resist the sickness that attacked her. Poor girl! She was twenty-one, and I was just turning seventeen. I was at a loss as to what to do for her.

The worst was when she began to suffer from stomach trouble. Every night she groaned so terribly that she was nearly driving me crazy. I was desperate when I met my fairy godfather, Joe Oliver. I ran into him when I was on my way to Poydras Market to get some fish heads to make a cubie yon for Irene the way Mayann had taught me how to cook it. Papa Joe was on his way to play for a funeral.

"Hello, kid. What's cooking?" he asked.

"Nothing," I said sadly.

Then I told him about Irene's sickness and how much I loved her.

"You need money for a doctor? Is that it?" he said immediately. "Go down and take my place at Pete Lala's for two nights."

He was making top money down there—a dollar and a half a night. In two nights I would make enough money to engage a very good doctor and get Irene's stomach straightened out. I was certainly glad to make the money I needed so much and I was also glad to have a chance to blow my cornet again. It had been some time since I had used it.

"Papa Joe," I said, "I appreciate your kindness, but I do not think I am capable of taking your place."

Joe thought for a moment and then he said:

"Aw, go'wan and play in my place. If Pete Lala says anything to you, tell him I sent ya."

As bad as I actually needed the money I was scared to death. Joe was such a powerful figure in the district that Pete Lala was not going to accept a nobody in his place. I could imagine him telling me so in these very words.

When I went there the next night, out of the corner of my eye I could see Pete coming before I had even opened my cornet case. I dumbed up and took my place on the bandstand.

"Where's Joe?" Pete asked.

"He sent me to work in his place," I answered nervously.

To my surprise Pete Lala let me play that night. However, every five minutes he would drag his club foot up to the bandstand in the very back of the cabaret.

"Boy," he would say, "put that bute in your horn."

I could not figure what on earth he was talking about until the end of the evening when I realized he meant to keep the mute in. When the night was over he told me that I did not need to come back.

I told Papa Joe what had happened and he paid me for the two nights, anyway. He knew how much I needed the money, and besides that was the way he acted with someone he really liked.

Joe quit Pete Lala's when the law began to close down Storyville on Saturday nights, the best night in the week. While he was looking for new fields he came to see Irene and me, and we cooked a big pot of good gumbo for him. Irene had gotten well, and we were happy again.

The year 1917 was a turning point for me. Joe Lindsey left the band. He had found a woman who made him quit playing with us. It seemed as though Joe did not have much to say about the matter; this woman had made up Joe's mind for him. In any case, that little incident broke up our little band, and I did not see any more of the fellows for a long time, except when I occasionally ran into one of them at a gig. But my bosom pal Joe Lindsey was not among them.

When I did see Joe again he was a private chauffeur driving a big, high-powered car. Oh, he was real fancy! There was a good deal of talk about the way Joe had left the band and broken up our friendship to go off with that woman. I told them that Joe had not broken up our friendship, that we had been real true friends from childhood and that we would continue to be as long as we lived.

Everything had gone all right for Seefus, as we called Joe, so long as he was just a poor musician like the rest of us. But there's a good deal of truth in the old saying about all that glitters ain't gold. Seefus had a lot of bad luck with that woman of his. In the first place she was too old for him, much too old. I thought Irene was a little too old for me, but Seefus went me one better—he damn near tied up with an old grandma. And to top it off he married the woman. My God, did she give him a bad time! Soon after their marriage she dropped him like a hot potato. He suffered terribly from wounded vanity and tried to kill himself by slashing his throat with a razor blade. Seeing what had happened to Joe, I told Irene that since she was now going straight, she should get an older fellow. I was so wrapped up in my horn that I would not make a good mate for her. She liked my sincerity and she said she would always love me.

After that I went to the little town of Houma, La.—where the kid we called Houma, at the Home, came from—to play in a little band owned by an undertaker called Bonds. He was so nice to me that I stayed longer than I had planned. It was a long, long time before I saw Irene or Joe Lindsey, but I often thought about them both.

Things had not changed much when I returned to New Orleans. In my quarter I still continued to run across old lady Magg, who had raised almost all the kids in the neighborhood. Both she and Mrs. Martin, the schoolteacher, were old-timers in the district. So too was Mrs. Laura—we never bothered about a person's last name—whom I remember.

Whenever one of these three women gave any of us kids a spanking we did not go home and tell our parents because we would just get another one from them. Mrs. Magg, I am sure, is still living.

When I returned from Houma I had to tell Mrs. Magg everything that had happened during the few weeks I was there. Mr. Bonds paid me a weekly salary, and I had my meals at his home, which was his undertaking establishment. He had a nice wife and I sure did enjoy the way she cooked those fresh butter beans, the beans they call Lima beans up North. The most fun we had in Houma was when we played at one of the country dances. If the hall was only half full I used to have to stand and play my cornet out of the window. Then, sure enough, the crowd would come rolling in. That is the way I let the folks know for sure that a real dance was going on that night. Once the crowd was in, that little old band would swing up a breeze.

Being young and wild, whenever I got paid at the end of a week, I would make a beeline for the gambling house. In less than two hours I would be broker than the Ten Commandments. When I came back to Mayann she put one of her good meals under my belt, and I decided never to leave home again. No matter where I went, I always remembered Mayann's cooking.

One day some of the boys in the neighborhood thought up the fantastic idea to run away from home and hobo out to get a job on a sugar-cane plantation. We rode a freight train as far as Harrihan, not over thirty miles from New Orleans. I began to get real hungry, and the hungrier I got, the more I thought about those good meat balls and spaghetti Mayann was cooking the morning we left. I decided to give the whole thing up.

"Look here, fellows," I said, "I'm sorry, but this don't make sense. Why leave a good home and all that good cooking to roam around the country without money? I am going back to my mother on the next freight that passes."

And believe me, I did. When I got home Mayann did not even know that I had lit out for the cane fields.

"Son," she said, "you are just in time for supper."

I gave a big sigh of relief. Then I resolved again never to leave home unless Papa Joe Oliver sent for me. And I didn't either.

I don't want anyone to feel I'm posing as a plaster saint. Like everyone I have my faults, but I always have believed in making an honest living. I was determined to play my horn against all odds, and I had to sacrifice a whole lot of pleasure to do so. Many a night the boys in my neighborhood would go uptown to Mrs. Cole's lawn, where Kid Ory used to hold sway. The other boys were sharp as tacks in their fine suits of clothes. I did not have the money they had and I could not dress as they did, so I put Kid Ory out of my mind. And Mayann, my sister Mama Lucy, and I would go to some nickel show and have a grand time.

The Middle West

CLEVELAND

————◆————

*At the time of World War I, Cleveland was the sixth
largest city in the United States and the most important
manufacturing city in Ohio. With jobs plentiful in war
industries, masses of Negroes migrated to Cleveland. In the
selection below, taken from* The Langston Hughes Reader,
*published in 1958, the author describes his first brush with
discrimination in the city.*

Langston Hughes[*]

My Most Humiliating
Jim Crow Experience

It happened in Cleveland years ago when I was in High School, and the Great Migration of Negroes from the South during World War I was at its height. Jim Crow, new to Cleveland in most public places, was beginning to raise its ugly head.

Our High School French class had gone to see a matinee performance of the late great Sarah Bernhardt, with her wooden leg, in Cleopatra's death scene, where the asp stings her in the bosom. The magic of Sarah's famous golden voice still rings in my ears.

But of that afternoon, there is an even more vivid memory. Following the performance, with one of my white classmates, a Polish-American boy, I went across the street from the theatre into one of Cleveland's large cafeterias. Its self-service and low prices appealed to our school-boy pocket-books. Its long cases and counters and steam-tables loaded with appetizing food whetted our appetites. We took our trays and got in line. My white school-mate was just in front of me.

We passed around in front of the colorful green salads, the sweet, good looking desserts, the white and pink and chocolate frosted cakes, the long steam-table with its soups and vegetables and meats. Each of us selected our foods, and stopped with our trays before the cashier's desk. She rang up my friend's bill, he paid her, and passed on to seek a table.

But when the white woman looked at me and then down at my tray, I thought she would never stop striking the keys on the cash register. It rang and rang and rang. The amount it registered on the black and white tabs behind its glass strip became larger and larger. Finally the cashier pulled out a check and flung it on my tray. It was *Eight Dollars and Sixty-Five Cents!*

My friend's check had been only about forty-five or fifty cents. I had selected about the same amount of food. I looked in amazement at the cashier.

"Why is mine so much?" I asked.

"That is just what you will pay if you eat in here," said the cashier.

* See biographical note on page 172.

"But I don't have that much food," I said.

"That is what you will pay to eat it," said the cashier, her face growing more and more belligerent, her skin turning red and her eyes narrowing. I could see the hatred in her face.

"But it doesn't cost that much," I said.

"Pay your check—or else put your tray down and leave it," she shouted. "You are holding up the line. That's what it costs if you want to eat!"

I put my tray down and left it there in front of her. I had not run into anything like that before in Cleveland, but I know it was because I was colored. I went up to the table where my white classmate was eating and said, "Come on, let's get out of here. They won't let me eat in this place."

He was astonished, and it took a long time to explain it to him, because he did not know that such things went on in this democratic land that his parents had travelled way across the sea to find. But neither one of us made any protest. We were only fifteen or sixteen, and we did not know what to say. He and I both were embarrassed.

Some years later a large group of Communists picketed that same restaurant and others like it in Cleveland. Negro and white workers together went in and insisted on service for all. In that way they broke down the color line and ended that kind of un-American Jim Crow in the downtown cafeterias in Cleveland. I do not believe such an incident would happen to a High School boy there today. At least, I hope not. Such things are harder to take when one is young.

COLUMBUS

In 1910, Columbus, Ohio was a city of 181,000 people, the state capital, the home of Ohio State University, and an important manufacturing center. However, in his reminiscence "The Figgerin' of Aunt Wilma" James Thurber has caught the flavor of what was essential to older and smaller American cities: close human connection between all its citizens. Anonymity and impersonality may be the hallmark of present-day urban life, but Thurber reminds us that in the not-too-distant past, personal contact existed in all the necessary functions. Groceries were not purchased in a huge depersonalized supermarket and bought ready packaged, untouched by human hands, but in a most personal manner from a neighborhood storekeeper with whom one had a distinct and unique relationship. Thurber memorializes one of the most attractive aspects of the city as it was— the rich individual character of neighborhood life. Those contemporary cities where such life has already disappeared are so much the poorer.

James Thurber

James Thurber (1894–1961) was born in Columbus, went to Ohio State University—which provided him with the materials for his well-known play "The Male Animal"—and started his career as a reporter. As a result of a meeting with E. B. White, he joined the staff of *The New Yorker*, where he achieved fame both as an artist and a writer. His drawings of the battles between the sexes, the fables involving beast and man, his picture of the modern Everyman, Walter Mitty—all these and more are an enduring joy. The selection below comes from *Thurber Country*, published in 1953.

The Figgerin' of Aunt Wilma

When I was a boy, John Hance's grocery stood on the south side of Town Street, just east of Fourth, in the Central Market region of Columbus, Ohio. It was an old store even then, forty-five years ago, and its wide oak floor boards had been worn pleasantly smooth by the shoe soles of three generations of customers. The place smelled of coffee, peppermint, vinegar, and spices. Just inside the door on the left, a counter with a rounded glass front held all the old-fashioned penny candies—gumdrops, licorice whips, horehound, and the rest—some of them a little pale with age. On the rear wall, between a barrel of dill pickles and a keg of salt mackerel in brine, there was an iron coffee grinder, whose handle I was sometimes allowed to turn.

Once, Mr. Hance gave me a stick of Yucatan gum, an astonishing act of generosity, since he had a sharp sense of the value of a penny. Thrift was John Hance's religion. His store was run on a strictly cash basis. He shared the cost of his telephone with the Hays Carriage Shop, next door. The instrument was set in a movable wooden cubicle that could be whirled through an opening in the west wall of the store. When I was ten, I used to hang around the grocery on Saturday afternoons, waiting for the telephone to disappear into the wall. Then I would wait for it to swing back again. It was a kind of magic, and I was disappointed to learn of its mundane purpose—the saving of a few dollars a month.

Mr. Hance was nearly seventy, a short man with white hair and a white mustache and the most alert eyes that I can remember, except perhaps Aunt Wilma Hudson's. Aunt Wilma lived on South Sixth Street and always shopped at Mr. Hance's store. Mr. Hance's eyes were blue and capable of a keen concentration that could make you squirm. Aunt Wilma had black agate eyes that moved restlessly and scrutinized everybody with bright suspicion. In church, her glance would dart around the congregation seeking out irreverent men and women whose expressions showed that they were occupied with worldly concerns, or even carnal thoughts, in the holy place. If she lighted on a culprit, her heavy, dark brows would lower, and her mouth would tighten in righteous disapproval. Aunt Wilma was as honest as the day is long and as easily confused, when it came to what she called figgerin', as the night is dark. Her clashes with Mr. Hance had become a family legend. He was a swift and competent calculator, and nearly fifty years of constant practice had enabled him to add up a column of figures almost at a glance. He set down his columns swiftly on an empty paper sack with a stubby black pencil. Aunt Wilma, on the other hand, was slow and painstaking when it came to figgerin'. She would go over and over a column of numbers, her glasses far down on her nose, her lips moving soundlessly. To her, rapid calculation, like all the other reckless and impulsive habits of men, was tainted with a kind of godlessness. Mr. Hance always sighed when he looked up and saw her coming into his store. He knew that she could lift a simple dollar transaction into a dim and mystic realm of confusion all her own.

I was fortunate enough to be present one day in 1905 when Mr. Hance's calculating and Aunt Wilma's figgerin' came together in memorable single combat. She had wheedled me into carrying her market basket, on the ground that it was going to be too heavy for her to manage. Her two grandsons, boys around my own age, had skipped out when I came to call at their house, and Aunt Wilma promptly seized on me. A young'un, as she called everybody under seventeen, was not worth his salt if he couldn't help a body about the house. I had shopped with her before, under duress, and I knew her accustomed and invariable route on Saturday mornings, when Fourth Street, from Main to State, was lined with the stands of truck gardeners. Prices were incredibly low in those days, but Aunt Wilma questioned the cost, the quality, and the measure of everything. By the time she had finished her long and tedious purchases of fresh produce from the country, and we had turned east into Town Street and headed for Mr. Hance's store, the weight of the market basket was beginning to pain my arm. "Come along, child, come along," Aunt Wilma snapped, her eyes shining with the look of the Middle Western housewife engaged in hard but virtuous battle with the wicked forces of the merchandising world.

I saw Mr. Hance make a small involuntary gesture with his right hand as he spied Aunt Wilma coming through the door. He had just finished with a customer, and since his assistant was busy, he knew he was in for it. It took a good half hour for Aunt Wilma to complete her shopping for groceries, but at length everything she wanted was stacked on the counter in sacks and cans and boxes. Mr. Hance set deftly to work with his paper sack and pencil, jotting down the price of each article as he fitted it into the basket. Aunt Wilma watched his expert movements closely, like a hostile baseball fan waiting for an error in the infield. She regarded adroitness in a man as "slick" rather than skillful.

Aunt Wilma's purchases amounted to ninety-eight cents. After writing down this sum, Mr. Hance, knowing my aunt, whisked the paper bag around on the counter so that she could examine his addition. It took her some time, bending over and peering through her glasses, to arrive at a faintly reluctant corroboration of his figgerin'. Even when she was satisfied that all was in order, she had another go at the column of numbers, her lips moving silently as she added them up for the third time. Mr. Hance waited patiently, the flat of his hands on the counter. He seemed to be fascinated by the movement of her lips. "Well, I guess it's all right," said Aunt Wilma, at last, "but everything *is* so dear." What she had bought for less than a dollar made the market basket bulge. Aunt Wilma took her purse out of her bag and drew out a dollar bill slowly and handed it over, as if it were a hundred dollars she would never see again.

Mr. Hance deftly pushed the proper keys of the cash register, and the red hand on the indicator pointed to $.98. He studied the cash drawer, which had shot out at him. "Well, well," he said, and then, "Hmm. Looks like I haven't got any pennies." He turned back to Aunt Wilma. "Have you got three cents, Mrs. Hudson?" he asked.

That started it.

Aunt Wilma gave him a quick look of distrust. Her Sunday suspicion gleamed in her eyes. "*You* owe *me two* cents," she said sharply.

"I know that, Mrs. Hudson," he sighed, "but I'm out of pennies. Now, if you'll give me three cents, I'll give you a nickel."

Aunt Wilma stared at him cautiously.

"It's all right if you give him three cents and he gives you a nickel," I said.

"Hush up," said Aunt Wilma. "I'm figgerin'." She figgered for several moments, her mouth working again.

Mr. Hance slipped a nickel out of the drawer and placed it on the counter. "There is your nickel," he said firmly. "Now you just have to give me three cents."

Aunt Wilma pecked about in her purse and located three pennies, which she brought out carefully, one at a time. She laid them on the counter beside the nickel, and Mr. Hance reached for them. Aunt Wilma was too quick for him. She covered the eight cents with a clean hand. "Wait, now!" she said, and she took her hand away slowly. She frowned over the four coins as if they were a difficult hand in bridge whist. She ran her lower lip against her upper teeth. "Maybe if I give you a dime," she said, "and take the eight cents . . . It is *two* cents you're short, ain't it?"

Mr. Hance began to show signs of agitation. One or two amused customers were now taking in the scene out of the corners of their eyes. "No, no," said Mr. Hance. "That way, you would be making me a present of seven cents!" This was too much for Aunt Wilma. She couldn't understand the new and preposterous sum of seven cents that had suddenly leaped at her from nowhere. The notion that she was about to do herself out of some money staggered her, and her eyes glazed for a moment like a groggy prizefighter's. Neither Mr. Hance nor I said anything, out of fear of deepening the tangle. She made an uncertain move of her right hand and I had the wild thought that she was going to give Mr. Hance one of the pennies and scoop up the seven cents, but she didn't. She fell into a silent clinch with the situation and then her eyes cleared. "Why, of *course!*" she cried brightly. "I don't know what got into me! You take the eight cents and give me a dime. Then I'll have the two cents that's coming to me." One of the customers laughed, and Aunt Wilma cut him down with a swift glare. The diversion gave me time to figure out that whereas Mr. Hance had been about to gain seven cents, he was now going to lose a nickel. "That way, *I* would be making *you* a present of *five* cents, Mrs. Hudson," he said stiffly. They stood motionless for several seconds, each trying to stare the other down.

"Now, here," said Mr. Hance, turning and taking her dollar out of the still open cash drawer. He laid it beside the nickel and the pennies. "Now, here," he said again. "You gave me a dollar three, but you don't owe me a dollar three—you owe me five cents less than that. Here is the five cents." He snatched it up and handed it to her. She held the nickel between thumb and forefinger, and her eyes gleamed briefly, as if she at last comprehended the peculiar deal, but the gleam faded. Suddenly she handed him his nickel and picked up her dollar and her three cents. She put the pennies back in her purse. "I've rung up the ninety-eight cents, Mrs. Hudson," said Mr. Hance quickly. "I must put the dollar back in the till." He turned and pointed at the $.98 on the indicator. "I tell you what. If you'll give me the dollar, I'll give you the nickel and we'll call it square." She obviously didn't want to take the nickel or give up the dollar, but she did, finally. I was astounded at first, for here was the penny-careful Mr. Hance knocking three cents off a bill, but then I realized he was afraid of losing the dollar and was willing to settle for the lesser of two evils.

"Well," said Aunt Wilma irritably, "I'm sure I don't know what you're trying to do."

I was a timid boy, but I had to plunge into the snarl, if only on behalf of the family honor. "Gee, Aunt Wilma," I told her, "if you keep the nickel, he's giving you everything for ninety-five cents."

Mr. Hance scowled hard at me. He was afraid I was going to get him in deeper than he already was. "It's all right, son," he said. "It's all right." He put the dollar in the till and shoved the drawer shut with a decisive bang, but I wasn't going to give up.

"Gee whiz, Aunt Wilma," I complained, "you still owe him three cents. Don't you see that?"

She gave me the pitying glance of a superior and tired intelligence. "I never owed him three cents in my life," she said tartly. "He owes me two cents. You stay out of things you don't understand."

"It's all right," said Mr. Hance again, in a weary voice. He was sure that if she scrabbled in her purse again for the three pennies, she would want her dollar back, and they would be right where they had started. I gave my aunt a look of disenchantment.

"Now, wait!" she cried suddenly. "Maybe I have the exact change! I don't know what's got into me I didn't think of that! I think I have the right change after all." She put back on the counter the nickel she had been clutching in her left hand, and then she began to peck at the coins in her purse and, after a good minute, arranged two quarters, four dimes, Mr. Hance's nickel, and three pennies on the counter. "There," she said, her eyes flashing triumph. "Now you give me my dollar back."

Mr. Hance sighed deeply, rang out the cash drawer by pushing "No Sale," and handed her the dollar. Then he hastily scraped up the change, deposited each coin in its proper place in the till, and slammed the drawer shut again. I was only ten, and mathematics was not my best study, but it wasn't hard to figure that Mr. Hance, who in the previous arrangement had been out three cents, was now out five cents. "Good day, Mrs. Hudson," he said grimly. He felt my sympathetic eyes on him, and we exchanged a brief, knowing masculine glance of private understanding.

"Good day, Mr. Hance," said Aunt Wilma, and her tone was as grim as the grocer's.

I took the basket from the counter, and Mr. Hance sighed again, this time with relief. "Goodbye, goodbye," he said with false heartiness, glad to see us on our way. I felt I should slip him the parsley, or whatever sack in the basket had cost a nickel.

"Come on, child," said Aunt Wilma. "It's dreadfully late. I declare it's taken hours to shop today." She muttered plaintively all the way out of the store.

I noticed as I closed the door behind us that Mr. Hance was waiting on a man customer. The man was laughing. Mr. Hance frowned and shrugged.

As we walked east on Town Street, Aunt Wilma let herself go. "I never heard of such a thing in all the born days of my life," she said. "I don't know where John Hance got his schooling, if he got any. The very idea— a grown man like that getting so mixed up. Why, I could have spent the whole day in that store and he'd never of figgered it out. Let him keep the two cents, then. It was worth it to get out of that store."

"*What* two cents, Aunt Wilma?" I almost squealed.

"Why, the two cents he still owes me!" she said. "I don't know what they teach you young'uns nowadays. Of course he owes me two cents. It come to ninety-eight cents and I give him a dollar. He owed me two cents in the beginning and he still owes me two cents. Your Uncle Herbert will explain it to you. Any man in the world could figger it out except John Hance."

I walked on beside her in silence, thinking of Uncle Herbert, a balding, choleric man of high impatience and quick temper.

"Now, you let *me* explain it to your Uncle Herbert, child," she said. "I declare you were as mixed up as John Hance was. If I'd of listened to you and given him the three cents, like you said, I'd never of got my dollar back. He'd owe me five cents instead of two. Why, it's as plain as day."

I thought I had the solution for her now, and I leaped at it. "That's right, Aunt Wilma," I almost yelled. "He owed you a nickel and he gave you the nickel."

Aunt Wilma stabbed me with her indignation. "I gave *him* the nickel," she said. "I put i. on the counter right there under your very eyes, and you saw him scoop it up."

I shifted the market basket to my left arm. "I know, Aunt Wilma," I said, "but it was *his* nickel all the time."

She snorted. "Well, he's got his precious nickel, ain't he?" she demanded. I shifted the basket again. I thought I detected a faint trace of uneasiness in her tone. She fell silent and quickened her cadence, and it was hard for me to keep up with her. As we turned south into Sixth Street, I glanced up and saw that she was frowning and that her lips were moving again. She was rehearsing the story of the strange transaction for Uncle Herbert. I began to whistle. "Hush up, child," she said. "I'm figgerin'."

Uncle Herbert was sitting in the living room, eating an apple. I could tell from his expression that he was in one of his rare amiable moods. Aunt Wilma grabbed the basket away from me. "Now, you let me explain it to your uncle," she said. "You wait till I get back." She sailed out of the room on her way to the kitchen.

A little breathlessly, I told Uncle Herbert the saga of Aunt Wilma's complicated financial quandary. He was chuckling when she came back into the room.

Uncle Herbert's amusement nettled her. "The boy got it wrong," she said accusingly. "He didn't tell it right. He was ever' bit as mixed up as John Hance." Uncle Herbert's chuckle increased to full and open laughter. Aunt Wilma glared at him until he subsided.

"Now, Herbert, you listen to me," she began, but he cut in on her.

"If Hance ever gives you that two cents he owes you, Wilma," he said, "I tell you what you have to do to square accounts. Someday you're going to have to give him a dime for three cents." He began to laugh again.

Aunt Wilma Hudson stared at each of us in turn, with a look of fine, cold scorn, and then she raised both her hands and let them fall helplessly. "I declare," she said, "I don't know how the world gets along with the men runnin' it."

MANSFIELD

Paul M. Angle

Paul M. Angle, born in Mansfield, Ohio, in 1900, is a historian and an authority on the Civil War. Angle started to work in his father's grocery store in 1910, and though Mansfield was a very small city at that time, with a population of not more than twenty thousand, the flourishing grocery store may be considered typical of thousands of others scattered across the country in the 1920s. The following selection originally appeared in *American Heritage* in August, 1963.

My Father's Grocery Store

As I remember, I was nine years old when my father decided that the time had come for me to "help out" in his grocery store. The year was 1910, and the place was Mansfield, Ohio. Twelve years would pass before I escaped completely from that thralldom.

In the beginning my duties were as small as I was: taking an occasional deposit to the bank and obtaining change, collecting small accounts, and delivering orders to customers who lived nearby and wanted a few groceries in a hurry. I also scrubbed the mold—it was harmless—from the hams and sides of bacon that hung in our back room, and from "Lebanon bologna," a wonderful smoked summer sausage which we bought in barrels, if you please, from a maker in Lebanon, Pennsylvania.

I do not remember the amount of my pay, but I suspect that I was doing a little work for the allowance I would have received in any case. And I had one compensation enjoyed by no other youngster in town. My father loved baseball, and every day the team was in town, except Saturdays and Sundays, we were in the bleachers. (On Saturdays we had too much business in the store; and on Sundays, in our family, we went only to church.) I can still remember Mansfield's first baseman, Zeke Reynolds; a third baseman named Tim Flood who had an arm about as strong as an old maid's; and a pitcher, Jeff Holmquist, who once went twenty-seven straight innings, won his game, and retired from baseball with a permanently ruined arm.

As time passed I became a kind of junior clerk, waiting on customers when my father and the two clerks were busy, putting up orders, and packaging the many commodities that we bought in bulk. (Packaging in the modern supermarket appalls me, and I cannot reconcile myself to the lavish use of paper bags. We never used one if we could avoid it. Did the

340

customer want to carry home a purchase of six or eight articles? We sold him a basket.) There was sugar, granulated, powdered, light brown, and dark brown, to be put up in two-pound and five-pound bags; an insecticide called Slug Shot, which we sold in one-pound packages; and coffee—always coffee.

Coffee deserves special mention. My father sold Chase & Sanborn's coffees almost exclusively. We carried the premium Seal Brand, which even then came in tins, but our big seller was a Santos that we sold under the private brand of Angle's Lunch Coffee. (Twenty-five cents a pound when I first remember it.) We received it in sixty-pound bags direct from Boston, ground it in our own mill, and packaged it in purple glazed-paper bags supplied by Chase & Sanborn. We also carried Mocha, Java, and Maleberry Java in the bean. Try to find any of the three in stores today.

Tea, too, was a bulk commodity. Although we stocked Lipton's, Salada, and Chase & Sanborn's Orange Pekoe in packages, most of the tea was ladled out of a row of big canisters which stood on a shelf behind the coffee mill. We had four: one each for young hyson, oolong, gunpowder, and spider-leg Japan. In comparison with coffee we sold little tea, so incoming shipments were infrequent. But they were exciting occasions. Tea was shipped then, and may be still, in big cubic containers of paper-lined lead foil. These were covered with straw matting, bound with split bamboo, and marked with Chinese and Japanese characters. Foreign foods were no novelty in our store—we had sardines from France, Portugal, and Norway; condiments and jams from England and Scotland; grapes and raisins from Spain; bulk olives from Italy—but here, in the great packages of tea, was the mysterious East. Nothing quite equalled them.

I am sure that the store's volume, in coffee and tea, was insignificant by today's standards, but fifty years ago it was large enough to deserve careful cultivation. Every Christmas brought a substantial gift from Chase & Sanborn: an inlaid tea caddy, a silver coffee service, a silver tray. These were cherished, not so much as possessions but as evidences of a relationship that somehow seemed to transcend the merely commercial.

Our own packaging of sugar, coffee, tea, and other commodities was prevailing trade practice. The grocery store of 1912 bore a far closer resemblance to the store of 1882, when my father first entered the business, than it did to the store of 1921, the last year of which I have direct knowledge.

In 1912 we still sold many kinds of food in bulk only. On the floor stood paper-lined bushel baskets containing navy beans, marrowfat beans, kidney beans, lima beans, dried peas, split peas, oatmeal, and rolled oats. (Oatmeal and rolled oats are not the same.) We had tubs of salt mackerel and kegs of sour, dill, and sweet pickles. Cheese came only in wheels or bricks and was not, thank God, processed. In the summer, if sales were slow, oil would begin to ooze from the last segment of a wheel of Herkimer. A day or two later maggots would appear, and simultaneously, through some kind of telepathy, our one customer who would buy cheese only when it had maggots in it. (I always wondered whether he ate maggots and all or picked them out first, but I am sure his cheese was unsurpassed in richness and pungency.)

There were times when selling bulk goods meant hard work. Vinegar, for instance. Because ours was a "quality" store we stocked vinegar in bottles—cider vinegar, tarragon, and white wine—but most of what we sold was drawn from a barrel into containers which our customers supplied.

Tapping the barrel took both skill and muscle. A full barrel weighed well over two hundred pounds. The first step in the procedure was to swing it up on end, pry out the wooden stopper, and drive in the spigot, making sure that it was turned off. Then we had to work the barrel onto a low cradle, with the spigot at the bottom of the front end and the bung at the top of the barrel.

Next came the turn of an ingenious tool. The bung starter, made of hard wood, had a head something like the head of an axe and a narrow, flat haft with just the right amount of spring to it. One hammered on the barrel around the bung, which gradually loosened. It was then wrapped in a piece of burlap and fitted lightly into the bunghole. The burlap was porous enough to admit the air that was needed before the vinegar would flow from the spigot, and yet dense enough to keep out flies and insects— or most of them.

Incidentally, in my youth the bung starter was the barkeeper's favorite weapon. Most whiskey was sold from barrels, so at least one was to be found behind every bar. Time after time, when the unmistakable sounds of riot came from the saloon next door, I have looked on the scene from the safety of the rear entrance—our store and the saloon shared a back porch—and watched one of the Wolf brothers in magnificent action, conquering the field with a bung starter. By the time the police arrived, only an ambulance was needed.

One other lively memory centers on the next-door saloon. The local breweries sold beer on credit, but every Monday morning each saloon had to pay its bill in full. A collector saw to that. By long-standing custom, he bought one for the house when the bill was paid. But here the rules were strict: the "house" meant only the customers who were present when the collector came through the swinging doors. There were five saloons around the public square on which our store was situated, and every Monday morning some artful maneuvering took place.

About ten o'clock a dozen barflies would emerge from Schmutzler's and head tentatively for the Park Saloon. Julius Weber, the collector for Renner & Weber's Brewery, would tag along behind with great deliberation. When three-fourths of the distance had been covered Mr. Weber would veer sharply to the right and head at top speed for Wolf Brothers'. Instantly the pack would change course, but Mr. Weber usually won. And so did Mr. Bricker, the collector for Mansfield's other brewery.

To return to the scoops and balance-weight scales and paper bags. . . . Selling bulk goods, as I have indicated, was trade practice, but with my father it was also the result of a strong conviction. Bulk goods, he believed —and with reason—were just as good as those that came already packaged, and always cheaper. Why make the customer pay an unnecessary premium?

Take Argo starch as an example. For many years he refused to handle it. I can still hear him say: "I have bulk starch just as good as Argo, and I can sell it at half the price." In time we came to stock Premium soda crackers and Uneeda biscuits in packages, but he always preferred to sell the Premium crackers from the tins in which they came and the Uneeda biscuits from their characteristic cottonwood boxes. (I wonder what he would think today of radishes and green onions in cellophane bags. I know what he would think—and I can almost hear him snort.)

By the time I was gently but firmly led to work, my father had been in the grocery business for almost thirty years. In his own boyhood, the same persuasion that he exercised on me had taken him into his father's grocery store, and the result was a determination to escape from it at whatever cost. The price was apprenticeship as a carriage painter.

After four years he became a master painter, armed with a certificate of competence and good character. (The document is one of my most cherished possessions.) Finding no work at his home in southern Pennsylvania, he started west, making his way, after a few months, to Mansfield, Ohio, where he had relatives. There he found work at his trade, but he was injudicious enough to fall in love with the daughter of a prominent grocer. He married the daughter, started to work in the store, and in 1882, when his father-in-law decided to go into the wholesale business, bought it.

His first act was characteristic. The store, A. W. Remy & Son, was well-known. My father immediately took down the sign. While the removal was in progress Louis Freundlich, Mansfield's leading clothing merchant, walked up.

"John," he said, "you're making a mistake. Remy's is a well-known, respected name. Operate under it."

"Mr. Freundlich," my father replied, "maybe I'll succeed and maybe I'll fail, but whatever I do, I'll do under my own name."

John Angle had just that kind of quiet courage. He was a prohibition-ist by strong conviction. The saloon next door served a light lunch—not free, but costing no more than ten or fifteen cents. It consisted of sand-wiches and soup. Although the soup was made in a wash boiler, it was good—bean soup, split pea, or vegetable. (My father always maintained that it was purposely overseasoned so that it would lead to another beer.) Most of the ingredients for the lunch came from our store.

One day a friend came in with one of the local-option petitions that the Mansfield drys regularly and vainly circulated. (Mansfield had a large German population, and the good burghers had no intention of giving up their schnapps and beer. They didn't, until compelled to by the Eight-eenth Amendment and the Volstead Act. It is ironic that the first federal Prohibition commissioner should have been Honest John Cramer, a Mansfielder.)

"John," my father's friend said, "I don't suppose you will want to sign this on account of the boys next door"—pointing to the saloon—"but I thought I'd give you a chance."

"Let me have it," my father replied, and immediately affixed his fine bold signature. The Wolf brothers, be it recorded to their credit, conti-nued to buy split peas and cabbage and tomatoes as if nothing had hap-pened.

The Wolfs were only two of our rather incongruous customers. Three or four doors away stood Brunk's tailor shop. There worked Mr. Men-dlich—ten hours a day five days a week, and until nine at night on Satur-days. We could always count on Mr. Mendlich on Saturday night. His first stop, after work, was Wolf Brothers', where he bought two bottles of beer. Next came Angle's Grocery. Mr. Mendlich was an Austrian with a rudimentary knowledge of English.

"Da feesh," he would say, and whoever was waiting on him would fetch a quarter-pound of dried herring, "blind robbins" in our parlance. "Brod," "kase," and two or three other standard items followed—the list never varied. Mr. Mendlich, obviously, was preparing for a Saturday night lunch, his one pleasure of the week. He was a very small man, no more than four and a half feet tall, and always neatly dressed in heavy, old-fashioned European woolens; he was always pleasant and deferential. Forty-five years ago I thought him funny. Today I look on him as an admirable citizen and a complete gentleman.

And there was Phoebe Wise. Phoebe was as much a part of Mansfield's history as Johnny Appleseed, the Dowie Elders, and Senator John Sherman, and more romantic than any of them. She was a recluse who lived a short distance out of town and quite near the Ohio State Reformatory. The story was—whether true or not I never knew—that when Phoebe was a young woman she had a lover of whom her father disapproved violently. The young man could not call at the house, and had to see Phoebe surreptitiously. One night the reformatory siren wailed to announce the escape of a prisoner. Soon afterward there was a noise in the bushes near the Wise house. Phoebe's father took his shotgun and fired in the direction of the sound. Later, when he investigated, he found the dead body of his daughter's lover. Thereafter, Phoebe dressed only in the clothing she had assembled for a trousseau, and left the house only when need compelled her to.

One summer afternoon I stood in front of the store, disgustedly watching two country boys cut capers for the benefit of their girls. One had a bottle of evil-smelling medicine, which he insisted on poking under all noses. Phoebe Wise approached, dressed as always in her 1880 finery. "Hey, Phoebe!" the boy with the bottle called out. Phoebe, though slightly "touched," had dignity, and everyone treated her with consideration. "Hey, Phoebe!" the boy repeated. "What does this smell like?" Phoebe sniffed the bottle gravely, and then commented with deliberation: "To me it smells just like horse-piss." The boys and their girls retreated in red-faced confusion and Phoebe, unperturbed, made her purchases.

At the opposite end of the social and economic scale were two other customers, Mr. Leiter and Peter Scholl. Mr. Leiter was an aristocrat; at least he lived on Park Avenue, the fashionable street, and enjoyed an independent income. But the income was Mrs. Leiter's, and she was not noted for her liberality. When she sent Mr. Leiter shopping, she gave him the exact change that he would need.

Now Mrs. Leiter was a vegetarian, and so, perforce, was her husband. Yet, in the store he always managed to sidle up to the meat slicer, eyes open for any nubbin of summer sausage or slice of boiled ham that might be lying there. He thought that he snitched these morsels and wolfed them without our knowledge. We pitied Mr. Leiter. Had we known when he was coming I think we would have been prepared with something more substantial than the usual scraps.

Peter Scholl was an aristocrat, but a real one. He owned the Independent Oil Company, a distributing firm; lived in one of Mansfield's great Victorian houses; and was driven back and forth to work every day by a liveried coachman behind two of the finest bays I have ever seen. He was tall, portly, and florid, with waxed mustaches, and winter and summer he wore a Homburg and a Prince Albert coat. In appearance he resembled Bismarck, but not in manner. When he stopped at the store to buy French sardines packed in olive oil and vegetables—a delicacy that seems to have disappeared from American groceries—or greengage plums in heavy syrup, or peaches in brandy, he would deal only with my father, to whom he was as deferential as he would have been to Bismarck himself.

Peter Scholl knew, of course, that my father was his customer, although a very small one, but I wonder whether the owner of the Independent Oil Company ever knew the strength of John Angle's loyalty. We had a kerosene tank from which we sold a few gallons a week. The kerosene came from Peter Scholl's company. At intervals a Standard Oil salesman would try to get the business, small as it was. Whatever the inducement—a big discount, a new tank free—it was rejected with contempt.

I wish I could say that all the "carriage trade" customers were like Peter Scholl. A few were so insufferable that they aroused prejudices in me from which I have never escaped—prejudices which, in fact, I cherish. They were the ones who drove around in White Steamers, belonged to the country club, played golf, said "marasheeno" instead of "maraskeeno" and "tomahto" instead of "tomayto," were alternately imperious and condescending with all of us at the store, and rarely paid their bills on time. I have never joined a country club, I gave up golf after one brief whirl, I say "maraskeeno" and "tomayto," I treat clerks with courtesy, and I pay my bills promptly. . . . Page a psychiatrist.

In happy contrast were the Canarys. Tom Canary was a "white-wing"— he swept up the horse droppings from the streets around the square. His route took him past the store, and he frequently stopped to place an order. Whenever possible, I delivered it, because I found the sight of old Mrs. Canary smoking a corncob pipe endlessly fascinating. To this day, I have seen no other woman indulge in this pleasure.

Mrs. Canary smoked Five Brothers tobacco. I doubt that the brand is still on the market. And what, I wonder, has happened to some of our other steady sellers—Star Brand plug, Red Band and Mail Pouch scrap, fine-cut under any name, and Bull Durham and Duke's Mixture? I say nothing of cigarettes: in Ohio the seller had to pay a stiff license fee, and the demand, before World War I, was too small to justify our handling them.

I look back, with mixed feelings, on another element of our business: the sale of Fourth of July fireworks. We stocked heavily: torpedoes, fire-crackers, cannon crackers ranging in length from two to twelve inches, grasshoppers, Roman candles, sky rockets, pinwheels, fountains, and rela-tively harmless sparklers. Part of our stock was displayed in the front win-dows of the store and part on sidewalk tables. Since the clerks and my father were usually busy inside, I took care of the sidewalk.

There, for ten days, I would alternate between excitement and fear. To sell fireworks was fun, but to watch men paw through Roman candles with one hand while the other hand held a lighted cigar—that was not fun. Moreover, the mild admonitions of a twelve-year-old boy had little influ-ence on adults. We escaped accident only through good luck.

This was the bad side of fireworks; the good side came out on Fourth of July night. Since my father was able to buy at cost, he always laid in for his family a more lavish assortment of fireworks than anyone else in the neighborhood. On the whole, it was his show. The children, under close surveillance, were allowed to wave sparklers, and the older ones were trusted with an occasional Roman candle, but it was my father who nailed the pinwheels to the fine hard maples that bordered the street in front of our house and fired the sky rockets from a specially constructed trough. The display was memorable, and no one was ever hurt.

The Fourth of July, in my boyhood, had only two rivals in the calendar of events. One was the annual grocers' picnic. The great day approached at snail's speed, but it never failed to arrive. At 7 A.M. the town's grocers and clerks, their wives and families, with heavily laden picnic baskets, boarded a Baltimore & Ohio special train for Sandusky, fifty miles north on Lake Erie. By nine o'clock the train had reached its destination, and everyone ran up the gangplank of the old side-wheeler that plied between the city and Cedar Point, three miles across the bay.

Fifty years ago the Point was paradise. (It may still be.) For excitement it offered a huge roller coaster; for the "fast" set it provided a dance hall and wine rooms, where the very good wines of the Lake Erie islands could be bought by the glass; but for everyone from the land-locked city of Mansfield the great attraction was a marvelous beach sloping so gently that even small children could wade far out in safety. Here our family spent most of the day, the women dressed in middy blouses with long sleeves, baggy bloomers, and long black stockings; the men and boys almost as amply clothed. (I wonder where we changed. I don't remember bathhouses.)

About dusk, and all too soon, came departure time. Once more the trip across the bay, then the boarding of the B&O special. Many of the picnickers, tired out because unaccustomed to sun and water and stuffed with the contents of the baskets, would curl up to sleep. They rarely succeeded. There were always some who had underestimated the strength of the island wines or overestimated their own capacities, so the return trip was at best noisy, and at worst marked by a few brawls. But these were incidents readily overlooked even by our abstinent family. Nothing could mar the pleasures of the grocers' picnic. Even the weather was beneficent. I do not remember a rainy day.

The other great day was Christmas, which I suppose I looked forward to with especial zest because it was my birthday. But for the joys of Christmas I paid a price. There were two hundred Christmas trees to be boxed, and I was a helper, though not a willing one. My father had discovered years before my time that by nailing trees in boxes, which served as standards, he could get larger sales and higher prices. All year long he saved the fine white pine packing cases in which all canned goods were delivered. The trees would arrive about the time my Christmas vacation began, and from then until the twenty-fourth of December I would be busy with hammer and saw.

I was fatuous enough to think that I would escape this chore when I went to college. I didn't. I sometimes suspect that boxing Christmas trees, like my experience with some of Mansfield's elite, left me with a psychosis. Never since have I touched the simplest carpenter's tools except under urgent necessity.

The Christmas-tree trade was my last experience with the grocery store. In fact, my days as a clerk ended with the summer of 1917, after I had finished my junior year in high school. For three months I worked full-time. I opened the store at 6 A.M. A few minutes later the truck gardener appeared, his wagon loaded with vegetables of a freshness rarely encountered today: green onions, green turnips, kohlrabi (who now knows kohlrabi?), radishes (especially the slender white icicles), carrots, leaf lettuce, green and wax beans that really snapped, peas in pods that crackled when opened—all pulled no later than the preceding afternoon. As the summer advanced, sweet corn came on the market—first the Early Evergreen, then the scraggly but delicious Golden Bantam with its big yellow kernels in four double rows and the wonderful Country Gentleman whose kernels didn't grow in rows, and finally the large white Stowell's Evergreen, lord of all the sweet corns. No hybrids these, but the true varieties, with a flavor and a succulence lost forever.

All summer there were berries: strawberries, blackberries, black raspberries, red raspberries, and huckleberries shipped from the Cumberland Valley of Pennsylvania, my father's boyhood home. These were his special care. For hours each day he would stand at a counter, turning each quart from its original wooden box into a new one. In the process he would pick out any that were soft or moldy. At the same time the larger ones managed to land on top, and somehow the thirty-two quarts of the standard crate became thirty-four quarts. In the winter, by similar necromancy, the contents of a container of bulk oysters expanded in the same proportion.

The vegetables, the berries, the tomatoes, the cantaloupe and watermelons, the peaches and pears and plums and early apples that appeared before the end of the summer, were offered for sale not inside the store but in front of it. The fruits were displayed in bushel baskets, berries and garden vegetables were ranged on long tables, and watermelons made a row near the curb.

In the winter the same outdoor tables held smoked sausage and fresh sausage in the gut—far superior to the stuff that comes in cloth bags— pudding meat, souse, and head cheese, all produced by local farmers. Spring saw the tables loaded with sassafras root and Richland County maple syrup, at least the equal of the more famous products from the Western Reserve and Vermont.

My working day, that summer of 1917, lasted from 6 A.M. until 6 P.M. Until 6 P.M., that is on Tuesday, Wednesday, Thursday, and Friday. On Monday, for some historic reason which no one remembered, we stayed open until 9 P.M.; on Saturday until 11 P.M. My father, as reluctant a riser as I am, arrived at the store between 7:30 and 8 o'clock in the morning. Even in my time he had given up the Monday night stint—there was little business—but on Saturday night he stayed to shut up shop. This meant balancing the cash register, computing his personal grocery bill for the week, making a final inspection, and examining the fruits and berries to see whether there were any which could not be expected to survive until Monday. Those which looked doubtful he took home, and on Sunday afternoon my mother converted them into preserves or canned them.

Arriving home about midnight, my father embarked on a program that never varied. First, he bathed and shaved in preparation for church the following morning. Then he dressed, at least to the extent of trousers and undershirt. Next, he addressed himself to a snack. If oysters were in season, he would have half a pint raw, seasoned with vinegar and salt and pepper. For the rest of the year his preference was cove oysters (in cans) or his best sardines. Following the first course came half of one of the pies my mother had baked that morning, and then three or four cups of coffee. The food gone, he read the *Saturday Evening Post* until, in spite of the coffee, he found himself nodding. And so to bed. I doubt that the most ardent concert-goer, the most dedicated devotee of the theatre, ever found more pleasure in music or the stage than my father derived from his simple Saturday indulgences.

The pre-supermarket grocery store called for long hours and hard work. Ours, at least, yielded only a modest return. The peak of my father's earnings came during and after World War I, when he netted, without charging anything for his own services, about $5,000 a year. In the 1920's, chain-store competition began to hurt. Business dropped off, yet he managed, with the invaluable aid of my mother, who worked harder even than he did, to maintain a large house, feed the family well, and bring the last of eight children to maturity. When he sold the store in 1939, after fifty-seven years, it was no forced sale, but one dictated by an arthritic condition which made long hours on his feet impossible. And I am proud to say that all his bills were paid, and that he ended up with a small surplus.

TOLEDO

The Toledo that Kenneth Rexroth knew in 1918 was a wide-open town where gambling houses, burlesque shows, and brothels opened their doors to teen-agers. Even the Boy Scout troop he belonged to when he was thirteen had its share of extramural gang leaders. Rexroth describes his life as a tough youngster on his own, running a popcorn business, terrorizing the rich kids, and unexpectedly participating in the spectacular Willys-Overland strike that turned a part of the city into a battlefield. The selection below is from An Autobiographical Novel, *published in 1966.*

Kenneth Rexroth

Poet, painter, translator, and critic, Kenneth Rexroth is a spectacular autodidact. He was born in Indiana in 1905, supported himself from the time he dropped out of high school, moved to Chicago's bohemian district when he was sixteen, and joined the IWW. He knew the jazz, Negro, radical, and artistic world of the 20s in New York and San Francisco. Rexroth was one of the first abstract painters in America, and has written books of essays and poetry as well as translations from Chinese and other languages.

from An Autobiographical Novel

One of the things that gave Toledo, Ohio, its special character in those days was that it was a sanctuary, like the monastic properties in London in the Middle Ages. Extradition was extremely difficult. You could commit a crime somewhere else and run to Toledo and as long as you behaved yourself, it took all hell to get you out. This meant that the crooks policed the town. It was no place to stick up a grocery store or prowl houses. You might find yourself full of holes in the gutter. This meant also that the town was wide open. There were whorehouses all over the place. On the best corner in town, above the drugstore where I ran my popcorn machine, was a whorehouse that ran as wide open as the Farmers' Market. I was a great favorite of the girls and ran intimate errands and sold them lots of popcorn. Gambling was wide open and I often called for my father at cardrooms with no thought that I was doing anything unusual.

There were several burlesque shows and nobody ever stopped me from attending them. It is true that I was already very tall and was beginning to acquire that look of misleading maturity which was possibly to keep me alive through my adolescence. In a dim light I might have been mistaken for a smooth-faced, very young man—but I didn't look all that old, even though I did wear long pants, something few little boys did in those days.

I am sure that in no other city in America could I have come and gone into brothels, cardrooms, and burlesque shows without question. I did better than run errands for the biggest burlesque show; I sold them, each evening before we both began business, all the popcorn and roasted peanuts left over from the night before—at a tremendous discount, of course, but still we both made money and I always had fresh popcorn and peanuts at no loss.

352

Possibly it was this connection with the adult world of hustlers that led me to change my friends among the children. The street we lived in was a dividing line between rich and poor neighborhoods. The kids I have been describing all lived in the rich neighborhood, on a group of streets whose names ended in "wood"—Collingwood, Cherrywood, Oakwood, and so forth. In the other direction the streets ran downhill to the Libby-Owens Glass plant, a number of foundries and small factories, and then to the creek bottoms and off to the right, to the Willys-Overland plant. Here the poor kids lived.

The first one I met in the Boy Scout troop. He was a dwarf, or rather a red-haired midget with a large head, and around the Boy Scouts he conducted himself with grave, impeccable decorum. His name was Meade Somers. Why Meade belonged to the Boy Scouts, I have no idea. Possibly because his other life was not enough to satisfy his extraordinary intelligence. Although we were only little boys, I look back on him as one of the most intelligent people I have ever known. His other life certainly provided plenty of satisfactions. He was the leader of a gang of perhaps fifteen kids ranging in age from ten to eighteen. Although he was younger than the majority of boys in the gang and a midget, his leadership was never questioned. He was by far the brainiest and the toughest and incomparably the most cool. Nothing fazed him.

We used to go on our bicycles on pilfering expeditions in drugstores and groceries all over town. We did a regular business in hot bicycles and automobile accessories. Meade had discovered that during the busy times of the day the most unattended cash registers were to be found in small garages, for everybody would be busy underneath a car. He used to take another boy whom he could leave outside riding up and down, ringing his bicycle bell continuously, and yelling, "Bang, bang, bang, here come the cops!" at the top of his lungs. Meade would coolly walk in, punch the key of the largest denomination on the cash register, clean it out into a paper sack, get on his bicycle, and ride coolly and slowly away.

The gang had one inflexible rule: if you got caught, you got kicked out. So it, too, was a sort of Eagle Scout troop. By definition, as they say, it consisted of kids who didn't get caught. Whenever anybody started doing anything really dangerous, Meade put his foot down. Some of the older boys were expelled one day for rolling drunks, which Meade considered tempting fate. Everybody in the gang had his girl and the sexual relations were much like those that prevailed among the rich kids, except that they were much tougher and never promiscuous. Every new member, male or female, was "initiated," but after that, you paired off and stayed with

your partner or you got kicked out. There was no homosexuality whatever, nor were there any public orgies of the sort the rich kids went in
for.

I suppose I was a sort of traitor to my class, because I became assistant
brain and under my guidance we drove the rich kids out of almost all
their activities around town and along the creek and confined them to
their own neighborhood. We took over the Village and spent our time
drinking homemade beer we had stolen from our parents' cellars, roasting
potatoes and wienies, stewing up oilcans full of slum gullion, spooning
with our girls, and plotting devilment. We also took over the swimming
hole.

At this time I acquired a nickname which I was never to lose among
hustlers. To this day many people in the San Francisco Tenderloin and
the Fillmore district call me Duke. I never told anybody that back home
in Toledo or Chicago or wherever I came from last that people called me
Duke. It always reappeared spontaneously; just as certain people in the
underworld are always called Blackie or Whitey or Kid, some are called
Duke. It's no great compliment. The most affected girl in a whorehouse is
usually called Duchess. There is a slightly different type who, in the words
of Engels, has also cut himself loose from the upper classes, who is invariably called Professor. A few people, down the years, have called me Professor. Possibly I occupy that ambiguous category between Duke and Professor for which there is no name.

At the swimming hole there was a pest whom we had inherited from the
rich kids—the first adult male homosexual I had ever seen. He had been
more than welcome among the rich kids, to whom he used to give dimes.
Dimes didn't mean anything to us, and Meade decided that he should be
charged a dollar. After he had thought it over for a few days, he raised the
price to five dollars and finally decided to chase the homosexual away
altogether. So he delegated the four biggest kids in the gang to get rid of
him. Meade and I didn't go swimming that afternoon. He was a strong
disbeliever in violence and taught me never to be around when it took
place.

We also terrorized the rich kids who worked as caddies at the golf
course in Ottawa Park. Within a short time we all became bored with
caddying, so we sold the jobs back to the rich kids and confined ourselves,
whenever we came and went through Ottawa Park, to using the holes in
the golf course as privies. I realize now that the boys of this gang were
strongly affected by their fathers' ideas. They were reflecting the general

radicalization of the working class at the end of the First War. Their universal term of contempt and abuse was "bushwa," which we believed was French for bullshit. Meade seemed to operate on the principle that anyone who didn't work hard in a factory for a living was a rascal, and that the children of the middle class were idiots. Curiously enough, the boys in the gang never made any attempt to take away the rich kids' girls; in fact, they had even more contempt for them than they did for the boys. My girl, whom I had brought along with me, was known as Duchess and was just barely tolerated. Meade used to say that she was immoral. He never explained what he meant, but I think he had an infallible nose for what was really a budding fashionable country-club sexuality.

The gang took up a lot of time and consumed a lot of mental energy. So Meade and I, and Duchess, and Meade's girl Red used to relax just like Al Capone, by going fishing. Just like Al Capone we had our own private fishing preserve that no one else ever touched. On the outskirts of the city there was a large cemetery. It was beautifully landscaped around two small lakes. At some time or other these lakes had been stocked with pan fish, perch, blue gills, sunfish, bullheads, carp, yellow catfish, and even a few pike. The place was patrolled during the day, but the nightwatchman was terrified of the dead and never went out of his little house. So we used to go in at night, shine a couple of flashlights on the water, and carry away a gunnysack full of fish. My father and grandmother were greatly pleased with the fish dinners, but though my father begged me to take him with me, I never told him where we went.

One of the finest adventures that my association with this gang involved me in was the Willys-Overland strike. This took place shortly before the Armistice and was one of the most bitterly fought strikes of the time. Who led it, I don't know. Possibly the IWW. It had all the characteristics of a strike under revolutionary leadership—a big rank-and-file strike committee, soup kitchens, a mass picket line, dozens of soapboxers. The kids of the strikers got jobs as runners. This was a necessity because the plant covered a good many acres and the mass picket lines were concentrated at several gates, considerable distances apart. We went on our bicycles carrying messages from one picket captain to another, general orders from the strike committee, bundles of bulletins, and big sacks of sandwiches. The National Guard was called out and set up machine guns inside the plant and sentries with bayonets at the gates. I became quite a hero, but I can't remember exactly what I did. I can remember bicycling furiously past the administration building, convinced that I was going to be blown off my bicycle by a hail of machine-gun bullets, but what it was all about, I do not know. That night I was introduced at the mass meeting and everybody cheered and clapped.

A few days later the strike came to its climax in the most spectacular battle I was ever to see in my years in the labor movement. Tear gas had just come in and I believe the Army loaned a supply of canisters to the city police. The mayor ordered the mass picketing stopped, and the strikers, of course, ignored the order.

The next day the street in front of the main gate was a solid mass of cops, stretched for more than a block past the next factory, the De Vilbis Atomizer plant. First were a couple of platoons of mounted police, armed with long sticks like the lathis that the British used on the Indians. Behind them were foot police and amongst them a detail of tear-gas hurlers. The mounted police rode very slowly toward the gate, pushing the strikers back a foot at a time with the breasts of their horses, but not using their sticks. The strike committee was prepared for them. They had gone up to the carbarns across the street and taken the junked poles—whole pine trees rotted out at the base and presumably stacked up with the rest of the junk to be sold as firewood. Each pole was manned by about eight heavyweight Slav and Hungarian strikers, and they were planted behind the picket line, just in front of the bridge across Ten-Mile Creek, invisible to the cops, who were a couple of blocks higher up the street.

Now, as the street (Cherry Street, I believe it was) went down the hills to the bridge it passed between cut banks about thirty feet high, so there was a narrow canyon rising straight out of the sidewalks. When the strikers had been pushed away from the main gates, a mounted police officer fired a shot in the air and shouted a proclamation ordering them to disperse. Instead, the picket line surged back against the horses and the mounted police charged, swinging their lathis. The picket line ran back toward the bridge and the cops were drawn down into the canyon, between the masses of strikers on the sidewalks. The picket line opened up and the boys with the poles came through. When this happened the tear-gas detail hurled the canisters over the heads of the mounted police into the front ranks of the strikers. Unfortunately, scientific warfare had not reached the point it was to achieve in World War II. There was a gas detail, but there were no meteorologists in the police force, and a couple of hundred cops had not noticed that the wind was blowing in their faces.

The pandemonium was indescribable. The horses were enveloped in clouds of tear gas, which made them scream with the bloodcurdling scream of horses in a fire and they took off up the steep banks, spilling their riders, as the boys with the poles, with wet handkerchiefs wrapped round their faces, charged.

Considerable time passed before order was restored. The cops were shooting in all directions but lucky for us they didn't shoot one another or anybody else. I think a few strikers got flesh wounds, but they were hauled away to safety and the only serious damage was done to the horses, some of whom broke their legs on the cut bank and had to be shot. When the battle was at its height, out the gate came the U.S. Army on the run with fixed bayonets and the strikers vanished like snowflakes or Sitting Bull's Indians after the Battle of the Little Big Horn. A few strikers who had been thrown into the muck of the creek were fished out and locked up. The press exploded and demanded that everybody in the union be tried for attempted murder, but a few days later the strike was settled.

This was my first strike and, except for the poor horses, that I can still hear screaming, certainly my most enjoyable. When I look back on it one of the most significant things, it seems to me, is that at the age of twelve or thirteen, like all of Engels' "Members of the upper class who cut themselves loose from their own class and go over to the workers," I got on the payroll. I started off in the labor movement as a pie-card artist.

INDIANAPOLIS

———◆———

*Indianapolis at the turn of the century could have been
called the very archetype of the average size American city.
Small enough to maintain close ties with the surrounding
country, large enough to receive an invigorating stream of
visitors from the East, Indianapolis was a magnet for the
bright and ambitious young Indiana farm lads. Unlike Chicago, the Indiana metropolis had a stable, almost restful
character. Booth Tarkington's Penrod could only have
grown up in Indianapolis, rather than in a larger city. Yet
the picture of Indianapolis drawn in the selections below
is far more than merely sentimental and nostalgic. Both
authors participated in politics—Tarkington in the Indiana state legislature and Bowers as an American diplomat, and their writing is sharply conscious of social and
class distinctions.*

Booth Tarkington

Booth Tarkington (1867–1946) was born in Indianapolis and served in the Indiana state legislature before he became a novelist. He was enormously popular throughout his long career, although his greatest success was his early novel *Penrod,* written in 1914. *The Magnificent Ambersons,* from which this selection is taken, was published in 1918 and became the subject of a movie directed by Orson Welles in 1941.

from The Magnificent Ambersons

Major Amberson had "made a fortune" in 1873, when other people were losing fortunes, and the magnificence of the Ambersons began then. Magnificence, like the size of a fortune, is always comparative, as even Magnificent Lorenzo may now perceive, if he has happened to haunt New York in 1916; and the Ambersons were magnificent in their day and place. Their splendour lasted throughout all the years that saw their Midland town spread and darken into a city, but reached its topmost during the period when every prosperous family with children kept a Newfoundland dog.

In that town, in those days, all the women who wore silk or velvet knew all the other women who wore silk or velvet, and when there was a new purchase of sealskin, sick people were got to windows to see it go by. Trotters were out, in the winter afternoons, racing light sleighs on National Avenue and Tennessee Street; everybody recognized both the trotters and the drivers; and again knew them as well on summer evenings, when slim buggies whizzed by in renewals of the snow-time rivalry. For that matter, everybody knew everybody else's family horse-and-carriage, could identify such a silhouette half a mile down the street, and thereby was sure who was going to market, or to a reception, or coming home from office or store to noon dinner or evening supper.

During the earlier years of this period, elegance of personal appearance was believed to rest more upon the texture of garments than upon their shaping. A silk dress needed no remodelling when it was a year or so old; it remained distinguished by merely remaining silk. Old men and governors wore broadcloth; "full dress" was broadcloth with "doeskin" trousers; and there were seen men of all ages to whom a hat meant only that rigid, tall silk thing known to impudence as a "stove-pipe." In town and country these men would wear no other hat, and, without self-consciousness, they went rowing in such hats.

Shifting fashions of shape replaced aristocracy of texture: dressmakers, shoemakers, hatmakers, and tailors, increasing in cunning and in power, found means to make new clothes old. The long contagion of the "Derby" hat arrived: one season the crown of this hat would be a bucket; the next it would be a spoon. Every house still kept its bootjack, but high-topped boots gave way to shoes and "congress gaiters"; and these were played through fashions that shaped them now with toes like box-ends and now with toes like the prows of racing shells.

Trousers with a crease were considered plebeian; the crease proved that the garment had lain upon a shelf, and hence was "ready-made"; these betraying trousers were called "hand-me-downs," in allusion to the shelf. In the early 'eighties, while bangs and bustles were having their way with women, that variation of dandy known as the "dude" was invented: he wore trousers as tight as stockings, dagger-pointed shoes, a spoon "Derby," a single-breasted coat called a "Chesterfield," with short flaring skirts, a torturing cylindrical collar, laundered to a polish and three inches high, while his other neckgear might be a heavy, puffed cravat or a tiny bow fit for a doll's braids. With evening dress he wore a tan overcoat so short that his black coat-tails hung visible, five inches below the overcoat; but after a season or two he lengthened his overcoat till it touched his heels, and he passed out of his tight trousers into trousers like great bags. Then, presently, he was seen no more, though the word that had been coined for him remained in the vocabularies of the impertinent.

It was a hairier day than this. Beards were to the wearers' fancy, and things as strange as the Kaiserliche boar-tusk moustache were commonplace. "Side-burns" found nourishment upon childlike profiles; great Dundreary whiskers blew like tippets over young shoulders; moustaches were trained as lambrequins over forgotten mouths; and it was possible for a Senator of the United States to wear a mist of white whisker upon his throat only, not a newspaper in the land finding the ornament distinguished enough to warrant a lampoon. Surely no more is needed to prove that so short a time ago we were living in another age!

. . . At the beginning of the Ambersons' great period most of the houses of the Midland town were of a pleasant architecture. They lacked style, but also lacked pretentiousness, and whatever does not pretend at all has style enough. They stood in commodious yards, well shaded by left-over forest trees, elm and walnut and beech, with here and there a line of tall sycamores where the land had been made by filling bayous from the creek. The house of a "prominent resident," facing Military Square, or National Avenue, or Tennessee Street, was built of brick upon a stone foundation, or of wood upon a brick foundation. Usually it had a "front porch" and a "back porch"; often a "side porch," too. There was a "front hall"; there was a "side hall"; and sometimes a "back hall." From the "front hall" opened three rooms, the "parlour," the "sitting room," and the "library"; and the library could show warrant to its title—for some reason these people bought books. Commonly, the family sat more in the library than in the "sitting room," while callers, when they came formally, were kept to the "parlour," a place of formidable polish and discomfort. The upholstery of the library furniture was a little shabby; but the hostile chairs and sofa of the "parlour" always looked new. For all the wear and tear they got they should have lasted a thousand years.

Upstairs were the bedrooms; "mother-and-father's room" the largest; a smaller room for one or two sons, another for one or two daughters; each of these rooms containing a double bed, a "washstand," a "bureau," a wardrobe, a little table, a rocking-chair, and often a chair or two that had been slightly damaged downstairs, but not enough to justify either the expense of repair or decisive abandonment in the attic. And there was always a "spare-room," for visitors (where the sewing-machine usually was kept), and during the 'seventies there developed an appreciation of the necessity for a bathroom. Therefore the architects placed bathrooms in the new houses, and in the older houses tore out a cupboard or two, set up a boiler beside the kitchen stove, and sought a new godliness, each with its own bathroom. The great American plumber joke, that many-branched evergreen, was planted at this time.

At the rear of the house, upstairs, was a bleak little chamber, called "the girl's room," and in the stable there was another bedroom, adjoining the hayloft, and called "the hired man's room." House and stable cost seven or eight thousand dollars to build, and people with that much money to invest in such comforts were classified as the Rich. They paid the inhabitant of "the girl's room" two dollars a week, and, in the latter part of this period, two dollars and a half, and finally three dollars a week. She was Irish, ordinarily, or German, or it might be Scandinavian, but never native to the land unless she happened to be a person of colour. The man or youth who lived in the stable had like wages, and sometimes he, too, was lately a steerage voyager, but much oftener he was coloured.

After sunrise, on pleasant mornings, the alleys behind the stables were gay; laughter and shouting went up and down their dusty lengths, with a lively accompaniment of curry-combs knocking against back fences and stable walls, for the darkies loved to curry their horses in the alley. Darkies always prefer to gossip in shouts instead of whispers; and they feel that profanity, unless it be vociferous, is almost worthless. Horrible phrases were caught by early rising children and carried to older people for definition, sometimes at inopportune moments; while less investigative children would often merely repeat the phrases in some subsequent flurry of agitation, and yet bring about consequences so emphatic as to be recalled with ease in middle life.

. . . They have passed, those darky hired-men of the Midland town; and the introspective horses they curried and brushed and whacked and amiably cursed—those good old horses switch their tails at flies no more. For all their seeming permanence they might as well have been buffaloes —or the buffalo laprobes that grew bald in patches and used to slide from the careless drivers' knees and hang unconcerned, half way to the ground. The stables have been transformed into other likenesses, or swept away, like the woodsheds where were kept the stove-wood and kindling that the "girl" and the "hired-man" always quarrelled over: who should fetch it. Horse and stable and woodshed, and the whole tribe of the "hired-man," all are gone. They went quickly, yet so silently that we whom they served have not yet really noticed that they are vanished.

So with other vanishings. There were the little bunty street-cars on the long, single track that went its troubled way among the cobblestones. At the rear door of the car there was no platform, but a step where passengers clung in wet clumps when the weather was bad and the car crowded. The patrons—if not too absent-minded—put their fares into a slot; and no conductor paced the heaving floor, but the driver would rap remindingly with his elbow upon the glass of the door to his little open platform if the nickels and the passengers did not appear to coincide in number. A lone mule drew the car, and sometimes drew it off the track, when the passengers would get out and push it on again. They really owed it courtesies like this, for the car was genially accommodating: a lady could whistle to it from an upstairs window, and the car would halt at once and wait for her while she shut the window, put on her hat and cloak, went downstairs, found an umbrella, told the "girl" what to have for dinner, and came forth from the house.

The previous passengers made little objection to such gallantry on the part of the car: they were wont to expect as much for themselves on like occasion. In good weather the mule pulled the car a mile in a little less than twenty minutes, unless the stops were too long; but when the trolley-car came, doing its mile in five minutes and better, it would wait for nobody. Nor could its passengers have endured such a thing, because the faster they were carried the less time they had to spare! In the days before deathly contrivances hustled them through their lives, and when they had no telephones—another ancient vacancy profoundly responsible for leisure—they had time for everything: time to think, to talk, time to read, time to wait for a lady!

They even had time to dance "square dances," quadrilles, and "lancers"; they also danced the "racquette," and schottisches and polkas, and such whims as the "Portland Fancy." They pushed back the sliding doors between the "parlour" and the "sitting room," tacked down crash over the carpets, hired a few palms in green tubs, stationed three or four Italian musicians under the stairway in the "front hall"—and had great nights!

But these people were gayest on New Year's Day; they made it a true festival—something no longer known. The women gathered to "assist" the hostesses who kept "Open House"; and the carefree men, dandified and perfumed, went about in sleighs, or in carriages and ponderous "hacks," going from Open House to Open House, leaving fantastic cards in fancy baskets as they entered each doorway, and emerging a little later, more carefree than ever, if the punch had been to their liking. It always was, and, as the afternoon wore on, pedestrians saw great gesturing and waving of skin-tight lemon gloves, while ruinous fragments of song were dropped behind as the carriages rolled up and down the streets.

"Keeping Open House" was a merry custom; it has gone, like the all-day picnic in the woods, and like that prettiest of all vanished customs, the serenade. When a lively girl visited the town she did not long go unserenaded, though a visitor was not indeed needed to excuse a serenade. Of a summer night, young men would bring an orchestra under a pretty girl's window—or, it might be, her father's, or that of an ailing maiden aunt—and flute, harp, fiddle, 'cello, cornet, and bass viol would presently release to the dulcet stars such melodies as sing through "You'll Remember Me," "I Dreamt That I Dwelt in Marble Halls," "Silver Threads Among the Gold," "Kathleen Mavourneen," or "The Soldier's Farewell."

They had other music to offer, too, for these were the happy days of "Olivette" and "The Mascotte" and "The Chimes of Normandy" and "Giroflé-Girofla" and "Fra Diavola." Better than that, these were the days of "Pinafore" and "The Pirates of Penzance" and of "Patience." This last was needed in the Midland town, as elsewhere, for the "aesthetic movement" had reached thus far from London, and terrible things were being done to honest old furniture. Maidens sawed what-nots in two, and gilded the remains. They took the rockers from rocking-chairs and gilded the inadequate legs; they gilded the easels that supported the crayon portraits of their deceased uncles. In the new spirit of art they sold old clocks for new, and threw wax flowers and wax fruit, and the protecting glass domes, out upon the trashheap. They filled vases with peacock feathers, or cat-tails, or sumach, or sunflowers, and set the vases upon mantelpieces and marble-topped tables. They embroidered daisies (which they called "marguerites") and sunflowers and sumach and cat-tails and owls and peacock feathers upon plush screens and upon heavy cushions, then strewed these cushions upon floors where fathers fell over them in the dark. In the teeth of sinful oratory, the daughters went on embroidering: they embroidered daisies and sunflowers and sumach and cat-tails and owls and peacock feathers upon "throws" which they had the courage to drape upon horsehair sofas; they painted owls and daisies and sunflowers and sumach and cat-tails and peacock feathers upon tambourines. They hung Chinese umbrellas of paper to the chandeliers; they nailed paper fans to the walls. They "studied" painting on china, these girls; they sang Tosti's new songs; they sometimes still practised the old, genteel habit of lady-fainting, and were most charming of all when they drove forth, three or four in a basket phaeton, on a spring morning.

Croquet and the mildest archery ever known were the sports of people still young and active enough for so much exertion; middle-age played euchre. There was a theatre, next door to the Amberson Hotel, and when Edwin Booth came for a night, everybody who could afford to buy a ticket was there, and all the "hacks" in town were hired. "The Black Crook" also filled the theatre, but the audience then was almost entirely of men who looked uneasy as they left for home when the final curtain fell upon the shocking girls dressed as fairies. But the theatre did not often do so well; the people of the town were still too thrifty.

They were thrifty because they were the sons or grandsons of the "early settlers," who had opened the wilderness and had reached it from the East and the South with wagons and axes and guns, but with no money at all. The pioneers were thrifty or they would have perished: they had to store away food for the winter, or goods to trade for food, and they often feared they had not stored enough—they left traces of that fear in their sons and grandsons. In the minds of most of these, indeed, their thrift was next to their religion: to save, even for the sake of saving, was their earliest lesson and discipline. No matter how prosperous they were, they could not spend money either upon "art," or upon mere luxury and entertainment, without a sense of sin.

Against so homespun a background the magnificence of the Ambersons was as conspicuous as a brass band at a funeral. Major Amberson bought two hundred acres of land at the end of National Avenue; and through this tract he built broad streets and cross-streets; paved them with cedar block, and curbed them with stone. He set up fountains, here and there, where the streets intersected, and at symmetrical intervals placed cast-iron statues, painted white, with their titles clear upon the pedestals: Minerva, Mercury, Hercules, Venus, Gladiator, Emperor Augustus, Fisher Boy, Stag-hound, Mastiff, Greyhound, Fawn, Antelope, Wounded Doe, and Wounded Lion. Most of the forest trees had been left to flourish still, and, at some distance, or by moonlight, the place was in truth beautiful; but the ardent citizen, loving to see his city grow, wanted neither distance nor moonlight. He had not seen Versailles, but, standing before the Fountain of Neptune in Amberson Addition, at bright noon, and quoting the favourite comparison of the local newspapers, he declared Versailles outdone. All this Art showed a profit from the start, for the lots sold well and there was something like a rush to build in the new Addition. Its main thoroughfare, an oblique continuation of National Avenue, was called Amberson Boulevard, and here, at the juncture of the new Boulevard and the Avenue, Major Amberson reserved four acres for himself, and built his new house—the Amberson Mansion, of course.

This house was the pride of the town. Faced with stone as far back as the dining-room windows, it was a house of arches and turrets and girdling stone porches: it had the first porte-cochère seen in that town. There was a central "front hall" with a great black walnut stairway, and open to a green glass skylight called the "dome," three stories above the ground floor. A ballroom occupied most of the third story; and at one end of it was a carved walnut gallery for the musicians. Citizens told strangers that the cost of all this black walnut and wood-carving was sixty thousand dollars. "Sixty thousand dollars for the wood-work *alone!* Yes, sir, and hardwood floors all over the house! Turkish rugs and no carpets at all, except a Brussels carpet in the front parlour—I hear they call it the 'reception-room.' Hot and cold water upstairs and down, and stationary washstands in every last bedroom in the place! Their sideboard's built right into the house and goes all the way across one end of the dining room. It isn't walnut, it's solid mahogany! Not veneering—solid mahogany! Well, sir, I presume the President of the United States would be tickled to swap the White House for the new Amberson Mansion, if the Major'd give him the chance—but by the Almighty Dollar, you bet your sweet life the Major wouldn't!"

The visitor to the town was certain to receive further enlightenment, for there was one form of entertainment never omitted: he was always patriotically taken for "a little drive around our city," even if his host had to hire a hack, and the climax of the display was the Amberson Mansion. "Look at that greenhouse they've put up there in the side yard," the escort would continue. "And look at that brick stable! Most folks would think that stable plenty big enough and good enough to live in; it's got running water and four rooms upstairs for two hired men and one of 'em's family to live in. They keep one hired man loafin' in the house, and they got a married hired man out in the stable, and his wife does the washing. They got box-stalls for four horses, and they keep a coupay, and some new kinds of fancy rigs you never saw the beat of! 'Carts' they call two of 'em—'way up in the air they are—too high for me! I guess they got every new kind of fancy rig in there that's been invented. And harness— well, everybody in town can tell when Ambersons are out driving after dark, by the jingle. This town never did see so much style as Ambersons are putting on, these days; and I guess it's going to be expensive, because a lot of other folks'll try to keep up with 'em. The Major's wife and the daughter's been to Europe, and my wife tells me since they got back they make tea there every afternoon about five o'clock, and drink it. Seems to me it would go against a person's stomach, just before supper like that, and anyway tea isn't fit for much—not unless you're sick or something. My wife says Ambersons don't make lettuce salad the way other people do; they don't chop it up with sugar and vinegar at all. They pour olive oil on it with their vinegar, and they have it separate—not along with the rest of the meal. And they *eat* these olives, too: green things they are, something like a hard plum, but a friend of mine told me they tasted a good deal like a bad hickory-nut. My wife says she's going to buy some; you got to eat nine and then you get to like 'em, she says. Well, I wouldn't eat nine bad hickory-nuts to get to like *them,* and I'm going to let these olives alone. Kind of a woman's dish, anyway, I suspect, but most everybody'll be makin' a stagger to worm through nine of 'em, now Ambersons brought 'em to town. Yes, sir, the rest'll eat 'em, whether they get sick or not! Looks to me like some people in this city'd be willing to go crazy if they thought that would help 'em to be as high-toned as Ambersons. Old Aleck Minafer—he's about the closest old codger we got—he come in my office the other day, and he pretty near had a stroke tellin' me about his daughter Fanny. Seems Miss Isabel Amberson's got some kind of a dog—they call it a Saint Bernard—and Fanny was bound to have one, too. Well, old Aleck told her he didn't like dogs except rat-terriers, because a rat-terrier cleans up the mice, but she kept on at him, and finally he said all right she could have one. Then, by George! she says Ambersons *bought* their dog, and you can't get one without paying for it: they cost from fifty to a hundred dollars up! Old Aleck wanted to know if I ever heard of anybody buyin' a dog before, because, of course, even a Newfoundland or a setter you can usually get somebody to give you one. He says he saw some sense in payin' a nigger a dime, or even a quarter, to *drown* a dog for you, but to pay out fifty dollars and maybe more—well, sir, he like to choked himself to death, right there in my office! Of course everybody realizes that Major Amberson is a fine business man, but what with throwin' money around for dogs, and every which and what, some think all this style's bound to break him up, if his family don't quit!"

One citizen, having thus discoursed to a visitor, came to a thoughtful pause, and then added, "Does seem pretty much like squandering, yet when you see that dog out walking with this Miss Isabel, he seems worth the money."

"What's she look like?"

"Well, sir," said the citizen, "she's not more than just about eighteen or maybe nineteen years old, and I don't know as I know just how to put it—but she's kind of a *delightful* lookin' young lady!"

Claude Bowers

Claude Bowers (1878–1958), born in Indiana, historian and diplomat, is probably best known for his studies of Thomas Jefferson. This selection comes from his autobiography, *My Life*, published in 1962. Always closely identified with the Democratic party, he was Ambassador to Spain and Chile.

from My Life

When we settled in Indianapolis in 1891 it had a population of from ninety to a hundred thousand. Aside from its size, it differed from the average Indiana county seat mainly in that it had been planned, as was Washington. The streets are arranged in a gridiron pattern, cut diagonally by four long avenues radiating from the Circle, the plaza in the heart of the business district. During the greater part of the 1890s the center of the Circle was enclosed by a high wooden fence, behind which the Soldiers' and Sailors' Monument was slowly rising to its ultimate height of 284 feet. The chairman of the Monument Commission was the father of a friend of mine, and when the shaft was almost completed I was permitted to walk to the top. This was a distinction, since few were allowed behind the fence.

Transportation was by little horse-drawn streetcars, all converging at the transfer station—which was nothing more than an abandoned street-car—at the corner of Washington and Illinois streets. The cars were without conductors, and the passengers were supposed to drop their fares into a slot inside, which connected with the money box beside the driver up front. Many times I was to see the car stopped between streets for the driver sharply to remind a tricky passenger that he had neglected to deposit his nickel. Around this time the first electric streetcar appeared, going up Massachusetts Avenue to College Avenue. It was the only decent way to travel on Massachusetts Avenue, which was unpaved and often deep in mud.

On the ground floor of Tomlinson's Hall, on Delaware Street, was the market, where the butchers had their stalls and where farmers brought their produce fresh on market mornings. All housewives, from high to low, did their own marketing, the more prosperous driving to the market with a servant to carry their baskets to the carriage. On market mornings one would almost certainly meet most of one's acquaintances there.

368

The hall above, the largest in the city, was the scene of political rallies and state conventions all through the Nineties. In that hall I heard the greatest American orators of the time. There many times I heard Bryan's moving eloquence, and Bourke Cockran thundering against "free silver" and imperialism with a brilliance that would have been notable in the St. Stephen's of the days of Fox, Pitt and Sheridan. There, too, I listened to the polished periods of William C. P. Breckinridge, the "silver-tongued orator of the Blue Grass," to the wit and humor of Chauncey M. Depew, and to the thrilling oratory of Albert J. Beveridge that could have been set to music.

The city had the charm of a large country town. There was nothing then beyond Sixteenth Street. The three most fashionable streets were Meridian, Pennsylvania and Delaware, all of them tree-lined, with their fine old houses, most of them brick, built in the days when people demanded spaciousness. These homes were usually set back from the street in wide lawns shaded by tall forest trees, and on summer afternoons passers-by could see the members of the households sitting in rocking chairs far back in the grounds, the women with their sewing or knitting, the men with their newspapers. The autonomous community of Woodruff Place had been fantastically conceived twenty years before—eighty suburban acres, with wide drives in the center of which were park strips for flowers, grass, fountains, fancy urns and bad statuary. In this sylvan retreat Booth Tarkington was to place *The Magnificent Ambersons.*

The country-town touch of the proud little capital could be seen especially on Saturday nights, when the stores stayed open and the streets downtown were thronged with people bent on buying, or merely on mingling with their neighbors, and when a band gave concerts from the balcony of the leading store. All in all, it was a comfortable, homey community, with no pushing or shoving, where the people lived normal lives and where businessmen went home for lunch and in the evening found time and inclination to read the *News* and to stroll across velvety lawns to their neighbors' to exchange views on what they read.

In those days it was the custom of the greatest artists of the stage to close their New York engagements in early spring and gallantly fare forth across the continent. In my boyhood in Indianapolis I saw all the great actors and actresses in all the great plays at the English Theater on the Circle. This had been built in 1880 and had opened with Lawrence Barrett in *Hamlet,* followed by Sarah Bernhardt in *Camille.* The Indianapolitans were enthusiastic devotees of the play. When a brilliant artist was to appear, it was usual to find the play itself on the reading tables of the

homes before it was given on the stage. Outstanding new plays like
Rostand's *Cyrano de Bergerac* created real excitement. When Mansfield
appeared in Indianapolis during his first season in the role, there was an
intense competition for seats. It was winter, but, in spite of sleet, rain and
a biting wind, by late afternoon of the day before the tickets were to go on
sale there was already a line of people stretching from the box office on
the Circle to Meridian Street and for a block up that thoroughfare. Some
of those who stood shivering in the storm throughout that bitter night
suffered the penalty of pneumonia, and I know of one who died from the
effects of the night's hardships. We boys went to the gallery, entering
through an alley that was packed back to Meridian Street, and since gallery seats could not be reserved, the congestion in the alley was dense. All
who availed themselves of the gallery seats were not boys, but I am sure
that the great proportion of the galleryites carried to the play a finer
background for appreciation than was generally found in the pit and the
boxes.

Ours was a churchgoing town, and I am afraid there was something
puritanical and prudish in its stern resentment of the coarse or suggestive,
and its definition of the indecent would seem ridiculous today. I recall the
reaction when Sadie Martinot, a French actress, appeared in a comedy
called *The Turtle*. It was understood to be immoral, and the press edito-
rially urged the people to show their disapproval by staying home. Paxton
Hibben and I went to the Circle and, having made sure that no respectable person saw us, sneaked in and found seats in the pit. But when the
theater began to fill, we noted with amusement that the most staid of the
city's matrons were arriving, looking a bit flustered as they glanced about
and found friends, equally embarrassed. We were delighted when a
woman who was a friend of Pax's mother found her seat to be beside him
and blushed prettily. When the play was over, we were astonished to find
the carriages of the most fashionable in Indianapolis congesting the
Circle.

Now, *The Turtle* was really inane and, judged by present standards,
positively puritanic. The most "immoral" scene was that in which the
naughty lady of the play disrobed behind a screen and hung her lingerie
on it in sight of the horrified—and delighted—audience. We observed
that the more sedate ladies pretended not to look, but out of the corner of
their eyes they missed nothing. But unfortunately for their pose, the boys
in the gallery, by their obscene screams, put special emphasis on the
dreadful scene.

In Anna Held's first American season she took Indianapolis by storm, though one of our foremost citizens was moved to wrath when the little actress, her protruding breasts none too completely covered, leaned far over into the box where he sat with his wife, and with outstretched arms and languishing looks, sang:

> *"Oh, won't you come and play wiz me?*
> *I've got such a nice little way wiz me!"*

It was this appearance of Anna Held's that introduced me to the awesome mysteries of the stage door. Pax Hibben had laboriously wrought a sonnet in French expressing his adoration and asking for an autographed photograph, and had sent it to her private car. That afternoon a messenger with a package from Miss Held appeared at the Hibben home, requesting payment for delivery, but the family was out and a servant refused it. In the evening when Pax learned of the tragedy he was beside himself with rage and demanded the immediate discharge of the servant. To placate him and save the servant, his mother helped him write an explanatory note in French, and Pax and I found our way to the stage door and, by means of a ten-cent cigar, bribed the doorman to deliver it. To our joy he returned with an invitation to go backstage, and we soon found ourselves standing beside the little charmer in the wings, not a little embarrassed by her state of undress. Pale and trembly, the infatuated Pax poured forth his explanation in a French no Frenchwoman could have understood, and the smiling lady replied in an English never before heard on land or sea. We had got nowhere when Miss Held's cue called her to the stage, and the picture never was delivered.

I always remember with affection the gallery of the English Theater, which seems to this day a place of magic. From there I looked down on Bernhardt, on Mansfield, on Irving and Terry in *The Merchant of Venice* and *The Bells*, on Modjeska in *Macbeth* more than once, on Ada Rehan at her best, on Mrs. Fiske in her famous roles. I recall vividly, as though the scene actually were before me, Maude Adams frisking like a sprite over the moonlit stage in *The Little Minister*, Sothern and Julia Marlowe playing their famous Shakespearean roles, and the latter in *When Knighthood Was in Flower*. The thrill of the night I saw Nat Goodwin and Maxine Eliot in *Nathan Hale* abides. John Drew, the perfect gentleman, was always a delight, though I doubt that *Rosemary* would seem so sweet and charming in this scoffing age.

DETROIT

---◆---

The future of Detroit—and of mass production techniques everywhere—was determined in 1899, the year that Henry Ford opened his first factory. Since then, the city has become the world's largest automobile manufacturing center. Detroit has had an uneasy history, for the immigrants who came from everywhere to take their places on the assembly lines have turned it into a contemporary cauldron. The city has known bitter labor struggles, bloody riots, and spectacular growth—all because of the Tin Lizzie. In the selection below, the French writer Céline presents the dehumanization of the Ford worker in words that recall the images of Chaplin's Modern Times.

Louis-Ferdinand Céline

The only European represented in this anthology is the French writer Louis-Ferdinand Céline (1894–1961), about whom Trotsky said, "Céline walked into great literature as other men walk into their own homes." Although his major works first appeared in the 1930s, his influence as an unremitting pessimist and as the observer of the evil and insanity of urban life, continues to be felt by a younger generation of writers. During a controversial lifetime that included a medical career, adventures in Africa, and collaboration with the Nazis during World War II, Céline visited the United States several times. During the 1920s, he took a job at the Ford Motor Company, and it is this experience that he describes in the selection below. It is taken from *Journey to the End of the Night*, published in English in 1934. The translator is John H. P. Marks.

from Journey to the End of the Night

People said to me in the street what the sergeant had said to me in the forest. "There you are," they said; "straight ahead. You can't go wrong."

And I came in fact to a group of great squat buildings full of windows, through which you could see, like a cage full of flies, men moving about, but only just moving, as if they were contending very feebly against Heaven knows what impossibility. So this was Ford's? And then all about one, and right up to the sky itself, the heavy many-sided roar of a cataract of machines, shaking, revolving, groaning, always about to break down and never breaking down.

"So here we are," said I to myself. "It's not very exciting. . . ." It was even worse than everywhere else. I went closer, to a door where it said on a slate that there were men wanted.

I wasn't the only one waiting. One of the others in the queue told me that he'd been there two days and was still in the same place. He'd come from Yugoslavia, this goat, to get a job. Another down-and-out addressed himself to me; he said he'd come to take a foreman's job just because he felt like it—a madman, a bluffer.

Hardly any one spoke English in this crowd. They gazed at one another distrustfully, like animals used to being thrashed. A urinous, sweaty smell rose from their ranks, like at the hospital. When they talked to you, you avoided their mouths, because the poor already smell of death inside.

It was raining on our little army, as we stood very close together in

373

single file under the eaves. People looking for jobs can be packed together very tight. What he liked about Ford's, an old Russian confided in me, was that they took on anybody and anything. "Only look out," he advised me, "don't miss a day here, because if you do they'll throw you out in a jiffy and in another two two's they'll have put one of those mechanical things in your place, they're always handy; and then if you want to come back, you're out of luck." He spoke good Parisian, this Russian; he'd been a taxi-driver for years but then they'd shot him out after a cocaine affair at Bezons and in the end, playing *zanzi* with a fare at Biarritz, he'd staked his taxi and lost it.

It was true what he'd said about their taking on anybody at Ford's. He hadn't lied. I didn't believe him, though, because tramps are very apt to talk a lot of hooey. There's a point of poverty at which the spirit isn't with the body all the time. It finds the body really too unbearable. So it's almost as if you were talking to the soul itself. And a soul's not properly responsible.

They had us stripped, of course, to start with. The examination took place in a sort of laboratory. We filed slowly through. "You're in terrible shape," the assistant informed me, as I came up, "but that doesn't matter." And I'd been afraid they might refuse to give me the job because of the fevers I'd had in Africa, as soon as they noticed, if by any chance they prodded my liver. But not at all; they seemed very pleased to find invalids and wrecks in our little lot.

"In the job you'll have here, it won't matter what sort of a mess you're in," the examining doctor assured me at once.

"So much the better," I replied; "but you know, sir, I'm an educated man and I once studied medicine myself. . . ."

He at once gave me a dirty look. I realized that I'd again gone and put my foot in it, to my own disadvantage.

"Your studies won't be any use to you here, my lad. You haven't come here to think, but to go through the motions that you'll be told to make. . . . We've no use for intellectuals in this outfit. What we need is chimpanzees. Let me give you a word of advice: never say a word to us about being intelligent. We will think for you, my friend. Don't forget it."

He was right to warn me. It was better that I should understand their way of doing things and know what to expect. I'd made enough silly mistakes in the past to last me another ten years at least. I meant to be taken for a good little worker from now on. When we'd put on our clothes again, we were sent off in slow-moving single files and hesitant groups towards the places where the vast crashing sound of the machines came from. The whole building shook, and oneself from one's soles to one's ears was possessed by this shaking, which vibrated from the ground, the glass panes and all this metal, a series of shocks from floor to ceiling. One was turned by force into a machine oneself, the whole of one's carcass quivering in this vast frenzy of noise, which filled you within and all around the inside of your skull and lower down rattled your bowels, and climbed to your eyes in infinite, little, quick unending strokes. As you went along, you lost your companions. You gave them a little smile when they fell away, as if it was all the greatest fun in the world. You couldn't speak to them any longer or hear them. Each time, three or four stayed behind around a machine.

You resist, though, all the same; you find it difficult to dislike your own substance; you long to stop it all and be able to think about it and hear your heart beating clearly within you; but now it's impossible. It can't stop. Disaster is in this unfortunate steel trap, and we, we're spinning round in it with the machines, and with the earth itself. All one great whirling thing. And a thousand little wheels, and hammers never falling at one time, their thunders crowding one against the other, some of them so violent that they spread sort of silences around themselves which make you feel a little better.

The little bucking trolley car loaded with metal bits and pieces strives to make headway through the workmen. Out of the light! They jump aside to let the hysterical little thing pass along. And hop! There it goes like a mad thing, clinking on its way amid belts and flywheels, taking the men their rations of fetters.

The workmen bending solicitously over the machines, eager to keep them happy, are a depressing sight; one hands them the right-sized screws and still more screws, instead of putting a stop once and for all to all this smell of oil, and this vapour which burns your throat and your eardrums from inside.

It isn't shame which makes them hang their heads. You give in to noise as you give in to war. You let yourself drift to the machines with the three ideas you have left aflutter somewhere behind your forehead. And it's all over. . . . Everywhere you look now, everything you touch, is hard. And everything you still manage to remember something about has hardened like iron and lost its savour in your thoughts.

You've become old, all of a sudden,—disgustingly old. Life outside you must put away; it must be turned into steel too, into something useful. You weren't sufficiently fond of it as it was, that's why. So it must be made into a thing, into something solid. By Order.

I tried to speak to the foreman, shouting into his ear. He answered by grunting like a pig, and merely made signs to show me, very patiently, the extremely simple job I should be engaged on from then onwards, forever. My minutes and hours, the rest of my time, would be spent like the rest of them here, in passing small bolts to the blind man next to me who sorted them out in size, sorted them out now as he had been sorting them out for years, the same bolts. I was very bad at it from the start. No one blamed me at all, but after three days on this first job, I was moved on, a failure already, to trailing around with the little trolley of nuts and oddments which went coasting along from one machine to another. There I left three, here a dozen, yonder only five. No one spoke to me. One only lived in a sort of suspense between stupefaction and frenzy. Nothing mattered except the continuous feeding of the several thousand machines which ordered all these men about.

When at six o'clock everything stops, you carry the noise away in your head. I had a whole night's noise and smell of oil in mine, as if I'd been fitted with a new nose, a new brain for evermore.

So by dint of renunciation, bit by bit I became a different man—a new Ferdinand. All the same, the wish to see something of the people outside came back to me. Certainly not any of the hands from the factory; my mates were mere echoes and whiffs of machinery like myself, flesh shaken up for good. What I wanted was to touch a real body, a body rosy and alive, in real, soft, silent life.

CHICAGO

Each of the authors who writes about Chicago in this section illumines one special characteristic of the city, and in four of the five selections presented, an aspect of the city is described that may possibly be as true today as it was in the past.

Curiously enough, both Frank Norris's Laura and Mary Ellen Chase see pre-World War I Chicago through the fresh eyes of a young girl visiting Chicago for the first time. Although The Pit is set perhaps fifteen years earlier than Miss Chase's story, both selections convey the feeling of intense activity, the almost breathless quality of the rushing crowds in the streets. The two girls come from placid small towns and both are stunned by the power of the city. For who can doubt that the same reaction occurs anew each time the innocent visitor first visits the mighty capital of the Midwest?

Theodore Dreiser presents still another side of Chicago and one that neither Norris's Laura nor young Miss Chase could possibly have imagined. Dreiser describes a red-light district that is vivid and real in a period before such life had to be discreetly hidden.

Jane Addams's description of immigrant slum life will not seem strange to those who know the contemporary ghettos in so many of our large cities, although some sixty years separate us from the time she describes. Possibly the most important difference is that very few social workers today would have Miss Addams's confidence that time and good will will result in an end to the problems of the poor.

George Ade is the only writer in this section who de-

scribes an aspect of city life that has completely disappeared. The old colorful horse-drawn vehicles he remembers were almost gone at the beginning of the century. Certainly to-day there are very few city dwellers who can remember anything more than the old milk wagons and perhaps an itinerant scissors-grinder.

Jane Addams

Pioneer social worker, militant reformer, and tireless propagandist for world peace, Jane Addams (1860–1935) was born in Cedarville, Illinois. After a trip abroad during which she met some of the early settlement-house workers in England, she returned to the United States and established Hull-House in 1889 on Chicago's West Side. It became the most distinguished social work center in the country as well as the headquarters for civic and legal reform.

Miss Addams was one of the founders and the first president of the Women's International League for Peace and Freedom, and she shared in the Nobel Peace Prize in 1931. The selection below is from her *Twenty Years at Hull House,* published in 1910.

The Professor "Masurek" of whom she speaks is Thomas Masaryk, who eventually became the first President of Czechoslovakia; Dr. Dewey is the educator John Dewey and Dr. Du Bois is W. E. B. Du Bois, the Negro reformer and professor.

from Twenty Years at Hull-House

From our very first months at Hull-House we found it much easier to deal with the first generation of crowded city life than with the second or third, because it is more natural and cast in a simpler mold. The Italian and Bohemian peasants who live in Chicago, still put on their bright holiday clothes on a Sunday and go to visit their cousins. They tramp along with at least a suggestion of having once walked over plowed fields and breathed country air. The second generation of city poor too often have no holiday clothes and consider their relations a "bad lot." I have heard a drunken man in a maudlin stage, babble of his good country mother and imagine he was driving the cows home, and I knew that his little son who laughed loud at him, would be drunk earlier in life and would have no such pastoral interlude to his ravings. Hospitality still survives among foreigners, although it is buried under false pride among the poorest Americans. One thing seemed clear in regard to entertaining immigrants; to preserve and keep whatever of value their past life contained and to bring them in contact with a better type of Americans. For several years, every Saturday evening the entire families of our Italian neighbors were our guests. These evenings were very popular during our first winters at Hull-House. Many educated Italians helped us, and the house became known as a place where Italians were welcome and where

national holidays were observed. They come to us with their petty law-
suits, sad relics of the *vendetta,* with their incorrigible boys, with their
hospital cases, with their aspirations for American clothes, and with their
needs for an interpreter.

An editor of an Italian paper made a genuine connection between us
and the Italian colony, not only with the Neapolitans and the Sicilians of
the immediate neighborhood, but with the educated *connazionali*
throughout the city, until he went south to start an agricultural colony in
Alabama, in the establishment of which Hull-House heartily coöperated.

Possibly the South Italians more than any other immigrants represent
the pathetic stupidity of agricultural people crowded into city tenements,
and we were much gratified when thirty peasant families were induced to
move upon the land which they knew so well how to cultivate. The starting of this colony, however, was a very expensive affair in spite of the fact
that the colonists purchased the land at two dollars an acre; they needed
much more than raw land, and although it was possible to collect the
small sums necessary to sustain them during the hard time of the first two
years, we were fully convinced that undertakings of this sort could be
conducted properly only by colonization societies such as England has
established, or, better still, by enlarging the functions of the Federal Department of Immigration.

An evening similar in purpose to the one devoted to the Italians was
organized for the Germans, in our first year. Owing to the superior education of our Teutonic guests and the clever leading of a cultivated German
woman, these evenings reflected something of that cozy social intercourse
which is found in its perfection in the fatherland. Our guests sang a great
deal in the tender minor of the German folksong or in the rousing spirit
of the Rhine, and they slowly but persistently pursued a course in German history and literature, recovering something of that poetry and romance which they had long since resigned with other good things. We
found strong family affection between them and their English-speaking
children, but their pleasures were not in common, and they seldom went
out together. Perhaps the greatest value of the Settlement to them was in
placing large and pleasant rooms with musical facilities at their disposal,
and in reviving their almost forgotten enthusiasms. I have seen sons and
daughters stand in complete surprise as their mother's knitting needles
softly beat time to the song she was singing, or her worn face turned rosy
under the hand-clapping as she made an old-fashioned courtsey at the
end of a German poem. It was easy to fancy a growing touch of respect in
her children's manner to her, and a rising enthusiasm for German litera-

ture and reminiscence on the part of all the family, an effort to bring together the old life and the new, a respect for the older cultivation, and not quite so much assurance that the new was the best.

This tendency upon the part of the older immigrants to lose the amenities of European life without sharing those of America, has often been deplored by keen observers from the home countries. When Professor Masurek of Prague gave a course of lectures in the University of Chicago, he was much distressed over the materialism into which the Bohemians of Chicago had fallen. The early immigrants had been so stirred by the opportunity to own real estate, an appeal perhaps to the Slavic land hunger, and their energies had become so completely absorbed in money-making that all other interests had apparently dropped away. And yet I recall a very touching incident in connection with a lecture Professor Masurek gave at Hull-House, in which he had appealed to his countrymen to arouse themselves from this tendency to fall below their home civilization and to forget the great enthusiasm which had united them into the Pan-Slavic Movement. A Bohemian widow who supported herself and her two children by scrubbing, hastily sent her youngest child to purchase, with the twenty-five cents which was to have supplied them with food the next day, a bunch of red roses which she presented to the lecturer in appreciation of his testimony to the reality of the things of the spirit.

An overmastering desire to reveal the humbler immigrant parents to their own children lay at the base of what has come to be called the Hull-House Labor Museum. This was first suggested to my mind one early spring day when I saw an old Italian woman, her distaff against her homesick face, patiently spinning a thread by the simple stick spindle so reminiscent of all southern Europe. I was walking down Polk Street, perturbed in spirit, because it seemed so difficult to come into genuine relations with the Italian women and because they themselves so often lost their hold upon their Americanized children. It seemed to me that Hull-House ought to be able to devise some educational enterprise, which should build a bridge between European and American experiences in such wise as to give them both more meaning and a sense of relation. I meditated that perhaps the power to see life as a whole is more needed in the immigrant quarter of a large city than anywhere else, and that the lack of this power is the most fruitful source of misunderstanding between European immigrants and their children, as it is between them and their American neighbors; and why should that chasm between fathers and sons, yawning at the feet of each generation, be made so unnecessarily cruel and impassable to these bewildered immigrants? Suddenly I looked up and saw the old woman with her distaff, sitting in the sun on the steps of a tenement house. She might have served as a model for one of Michael Angelo's Fates, but her face brightened as I passed and, holding up her spindle for me to see, she called out that when she had spun a little more yarn, she would knit a pair of stockings for her goddaughter. The occupation of the old woman gave me the clew that was needed. Could we not interest the young people working in the neighboring factories, in these older forms of industry, so that, through their own parents and grandparents, they would find a dramatic representation of the inherited resources of their daily occupation. If these young people could actually see that the complicated machinery of the factory had been evolved from simple tools, they might at least make a beginning towards that education which Dr. Dewey defines as "a continuing reconstruction of experience." They might also lay a foundation for reverence of the past which Goethe declares to be the basis of all sound progress.

My exciting walk on Polk Street was followed by many talks with Dr. Dewey and with one of the teachers in his school who was a resident at Hull-House. Within a month a room was fitted up to which we might invite those of our neighbors who were possessed of old crafts and who were eager to use them.

We found in the immediate neighborhood, at least four varieties of these most primitive methods of spinning and three distinct variations of the same spindle in connection with wheels. It was possible to put these seven into historic sequence and order and to connect the whole with the present method of factory spinning. The same thing was done for weaving, and on every Saturday evening a little exhibit was made of these various forms of labor in the textile industry. Within one room a Syrian woman, a Greek, an Italian, a Russian, and an Irishwoman enabled even the most casual observer to see that there is no break in orderly evolution if we look at history from the industrial standpoint; that industry develops similarly and peacefully year by year among the workers of each nation, heedless of differences in language, religion, and political experiences.

And then we grew ambitious and arranged lectures upon industrial history. I remember that after an interesting lecture upon the industrial revolution in England and a portrayal of the appalling conditions throughout the weaving districts of the north, which resulted from the hasty gathering of the weavers into the new towns, a Russian tailor in the audience was moved to make a speech. He suggested that whereas time had done much to alleviate the first difficulties in the transition of weaving from hand work to steam power, that in the application of steam to sewing we are still in the first stages, illustrated by the isolated woman who tries to support herself by hand needlework at home until driven out by starvation, as many of the hand weavers had been.

The historical analogy seemed to bring a certain comfort to the tailor as did a chart upon the wall, showing the infinitesimal amount of time that steam had been applied to manufacturing processes compared to the centuries of hand labor. Human progress is slow and perhaps never more cruel than in the advance of industry, but is not the worker comforted by knowing that other historical periods have existed similar to the one in which he finds himself and that the readjustment may be shortened and alleviated by judicious action; and is he not entitled to the solace which an artistic portrayal of the situation might give him? I remember the evening of the tailor's speech that I felt reproached because no poet or artist has endeared the sweaters' victim to us as George Eliot has made us love the belated weaver, Silas Marner. The textile museum is connected directly with the basket weaving, sewing, millinery, embroidery, and dressmaking constantly being taught at Hull-House, and so far as possible with the other educational departments; we have also been able to make a collection of products, of early implements, and of photographs which are full of suggestion. Yet far beyond its direct educational value, we prize it because it so often puts the immigrants into the position of teachers, and we imagine that it affords them a pleasant change from the tutelage in which all Americans, including their own children, are so apt to hold them. I recall a number of Russian women working in a sewing-room near Hull-House, who heard one Christmas week that the House was going to give a party to which they might come. They arrived one afternoon when, unfortunately, there was no party on hand and, although the residents did their best to entertain them with impromptu music and refreshments, it was quite evident that they were greatly disappointed. Finally it was suggested that they be shown the Labor Museum—where gradually the thirty sodden, tired women were transformed. They knew how to use the spindles and were delighted to find the Russian spinning frame. Many of them had never seen the spinning wheel, which has not penetrated to certain parts of Russia, and they regarded it as a new and wonderful invention. They turned up their dresses to show their homespun petticoats; they tried the looms; they explained the difficulty of the old patterns; in short, from having been stupidly entertained, they themselves did the entertaining. Because of a direct appeal to former experiences, the immigrant visitors were able for the moment to instruct their American hostesses in an old and honored craft, as was indeed becoming to their age and experience.

In some such ways as these have the Labor Museum and the shops pointed out the possibilities which Hull-House has scarcely begun to develop, of demonstrating that culture is an understanding of the long-established occupations and thoughts of men, of the arts with which they have solaced their toil. A yearning to recover for the household arts something of their early sanctity and meaning, arose strongly within me one evening when I was attending a Passover Feast to which I had been invited by a Jewish family in the neighborhood, where the traditional and religious significance of woman's daily activity was still retained. The kosher food the Jewish mother spread before her family had been prepared according to traditional knowledge and with constant care in the use of utensils; upon her had fallen the responsibility to make all ready according to Mosaic instructions that the great crisis in a religious history might be fittingly set forth by her husband and son. Aside from the grave religious significance in the ceremony, my mind was filled with shifting pictures of woman's labor with which travel makes one familiar; the Indian women grinding grain outside of their huts as they sing praises to the sun and rain; a file of white-clad Moorish women whom I had once seen waiting their turn at a well in Tangiers; south Italian women kneeling in a row along the stream and beating their wet clothes against the smooth white stones; the milking, the gardening, the marketing in thousands of hamlets, which are such direct expressions of the solicitude and affection at the basis of all family life.

There has been some testimony that the Labor Museum has revealed the charm of woman's primitive activities. I recall a certain Italian girl who came every Saturday evening to a cooking class in the same building in which her mother spun in the Labor Museum exhibit; and yet Angelina always left her mother at the front door while she herself went around to a side door because she did not wish to be too closely identified in the eyes of the rest of the cooking class with an Italian woman who wore a kerchief over her head, uncouth boots, and short petticoats. One evening, however, Angelina saw her mother surrounded by a group of visitors from the School of Education, who much admired the spinning, and she concluded from their conversation that her mother was "the best stick-spindle spinner in America." When she inquired from me as to the truth of this deduction, I took occasion to describe the Italian village in which her mother had lived, something of her free life, and how, because of the opportunity she and the other women of the village had to drop their spindles over the edge of a precipice, they had developed a skill in spinning beyond that of the neighboring towns. I dilated somewhat on the freedom and beauty of that life—how hard it must be to exchange it all for a two-room tenement, and to give up a beautiful homespun kerchief for an ugly department store hat. I intimated it was most unfair to judge her by these things alone, and that while she must depend on her daughter to learn the new ways, she also had a right to expect her daughter to know something of the old ways.

That which I could not convey to the child but upon which my own mind persistently dwelt, was that her mother's whole life had been spent in a secluded spot under the rule of traditional and narrowly localized observances, until her very religion clung to local sanctities,—to the shrine before which she had always prayed, to the pavement and walls of the low vaulted church,—and then suddenly she was torn from it all and literally put out to sea, straight away from the solid habits of her religious and domestic life, and she now walked timidly but with poignant sensibility upon a new and strange shore.

It was easy to see that the thought of her mother with any other background than that of the tenement was new to Angelina and at least two things resulted; she allowed her mother to pull out of the big box under the bed the beautiful homespun garments which had been previously hidden away as uncouth; and she openly came into the Labor Museum by the same door as did her mother, proud at least of the mastery of the craft which had been so much admired.

A club of necktie workers formerly meeting at Hull-House, persistently resented any attempt on the part of their director to improve their minds. The president once said that she "wouldn't be caught dead at a lecture," that she came to the club "to get some fun out of it," and indeed it was most natural that she should crave recreation after a hard day's work. One evening I saw the entire club listening to quite a stiff lecture in the Labor Museum and to my rather wicked remark to the president that I was surprised to see her enjoying a lecture, she replied, that she did not call this a lecture, she called this "getting next to the stuff you work with all the time." It was perhaps the sincerest tribute we have ever received as to the success of the undertaking.

The Labor Museum continually demanded more space as it was enriched by a fine textile exhibit lent by the Field Museum, and later by carefully selected specimens of basketry from the Philippines. The shops have finally included a group of three or four women, Irish, Italian, Danish, who have become a permanent working force in the textile department which has developed into a self-supporting industry through the sale of its homespun products.

These women and a few men, who come to the museum to utilize their European skill in pottery, metal, and wood, demonstrate that immigrant colonies might yield to our American life something very valuable, if their resources were intelligently studied and developed. I recall an Italian, who had decorated the doorposts of his tenement with a beautiful pattern he had previously used in carving the reredos of a Neapolitan church, who was "fired" by his landlord on the ground of destroying property. His feelings were hurt, not so much that he had been put out of his house, as that his work had been so disregarded; and he said that when people traveled in Italy they liked to look at wood carvings but that in America "they only made money out of you."

Sometimes the suppression of the instinct of workmanship is followed by more disastrous results. A Bohemian, whose little girl attended classes at Hull-House, in one of his periodic drunken spells had literally almost choked her to death, and later had committed suicide when in delirium tremens. His poor wife, who stayed a week at Hull-House after the disaster until a new tenement could be arranged for her, one day showed me a gold ring which her husband had made for their betrothal. It exhibited the most exquisite workmanship, and she said that although in the old country he had been a goldsmith, in America he had for twenty years shoveled coal in a furnace room of a large manufacturing plant; that whenever she saw one of his "restless fits," which preceded his drunken periods, "coming on," if she could provide him with a bit of metal and persuade him to stay at home and work at it, he was all right and the time passed without disaster, but that "nothing else would do it." This story threw a flood of light upon the dead man's struggle and on the stupid maladjustment which had broken him down. Why had we never been told? Why had our interest in the remarkable musical ability of his child, blinded us to the hidden artistic ability of the father? We had forgotten that a long-established occupation may form the very foundations of the moral life, that the art with which a man has solaced his toil may be the salvation of his uncertain temperament.

There are many examples of touching fidelity to immigrant parents on the part of their grown children; a young man, who day after day, attends ceremonies which no longer express his religious convictions and who makes his vain effort to interest his Russian Jewish father in social problems; a daughter who might earn much more money as a stenographer could she work from Monday morning till Saturday night, but who quietly and docilely makes neckties for low wages because she can thus abstain from work Saturdays to please her father; these young people . . . through many painful experiences have reached the conclusion that pity, memory, and faithfulness are natural ties with paramount claims.

This faithfulness, however, is sometimes ruthlessly imposed upon by immigrant parents who, eager for money and accustomed to the patriarchal authority of peasant households, hold their children in a stern bondage which requires a surrender of all their wages and concedes no time or money for pleasures.

There are many convincing illustrations that this parental harshness often results in juvenile delinquency. A Polish boy of seventeen came to Hull-House one day to ask a contribution of fifty cents "towards a flower piece for the funeral of an old Hull-House club boy." A few questions made it clear that the object was fictitious, whereupon the boy broke down and half defiantly stated that he wanted to buy two twenty-five cent tickets, one for his girl and one for himself, to a dance of the Benevolent Social Twos; that he hadn't a penny of his own although he had worked in a brass foundry for three years and had been advanced twice, because he always had to give his pay envelope unopened to his father; "just look at the clothes he buys me" was his concluding remark.

Perhaps the girls are held even more rigidly. In a recent investigation of two hundred working girls it was found that only five per cent had the use of their own money and that sixty-two per cent turned in all they earned, literally every penny, to their mothers. It was through this little investigation that we first knew Marcella, a pretty young German girl who helped her widowed mother year after year to care for a large family of younger children. She was content for the most part although her mother's old-country notions of dress gave her but an infinitesimal amount of her own wages to spend on her clothes, and she was quite sophisticated as to proper dressing because she sold silk in a neighborhood department store. Her mother approved of the young man who was showing her various attentions and agreed that Marcella should accept his invitation to a ball, but would allow her not a penny towards a new gown to replace one impossibly plain and shabby. Marcella spent a sleepless night and wept bitterly, although she well knew that the doctor's bill for the children's scarlet fever was not yet paid. The next day as she was cutting off three yards of shining pink silk, the thought came to her that it would make her a fine new waist to wear to the ball. She wistfully saw it wrapped in paper and carelessly stuffed into the muff of the purchaser, when suddenly the parcel fell upon the floor. No one was looking and quick as a flash the girl

picked it up and pushed it into her blouse. The theft was discovered by
the relentless department store detective who, for "the sake of the example," insisted upon taking the case into court. The poor mother wept
bitter tears over this downfall of her "frommes Mädchen" and no one had
the heart to tell her of her own blindness.

I know a Polish boy whose earnings were all given to his father who
gruffly refused all requests for pocket money. One Christmas his little sisters, having been told by their mother that they were too poor to have any
Christmas presents, appealed to the big brother as to one who was earning
money of his own. Flattered by the implication, but at the same time
quite impecunious, the night before Christmas he nonchalantly walked
through a neighboring department store and stole a manicure set for one
little sister and a string of beads for the other. He was caught at the door
by the house detective as one of those children whom each local department store arrests in the weeks before Christmas at the daily rate of eight
to twenty. The youngest of these offenders are seldom taken into court
but are either sent home with a warning or turned over to the officers of
the Juvenile Protective Association. Most of these premature law breakers
are in search of Americanized clothing and others are only looking for
playthings. They are all distracted by the profusion and variety of the
display, and their moral sense is confused by the general air of open-
handedness.

These disastrous efforts are not unlike those of many younger children
who are constantly arrested for petty thieving because they are too eager
to take home food or fuel which will relieve the distress and need they so
constantly hear discussed. The coal on the wagons, the vegetables displayed in front of the grocery shops, the very wooden blocks in the loosened street paving are a challenge to their powers to help out at home. A
Bohemian boy who was out on parole from the old detention home of the
Juvenile Court itself, brought back five stolen chickens to the matron for
Sunday dinner, saying that he knew the Committee were "having a hard
time to fill up so many kids and perhaps these fowl would help out." The
honest immigrant parents, totally ignorant of American laws and municipal regulations, often send a child to pick up coal on the railroad tracks
or to stand at three o'clock in the morning before the side door of a restaurant which gives away broken food, or to collect grain for the chickens
at the base of elevators and standing cars. The latter custom accounts for
the large number of boys arrested for breaking the seals on grain freight
cars. It is easy for a child thus trained to accept the proposition of a junk

dealer to bring him bars of iron stored in freight yards. Four boys quite recently had thus carried away and sold to one man, two tons of iron.

Four fifths of the children brought into the Juvenile Court in Chicago are the children of foreigners. The Germans are the greatest offenders, Polish next. Do their children suffer from the excess of virtue in those parents so eager to own a house and lot? One often sees a grasping parent in the court, utterly broken down when the Americanized youth who has been brought to grief clings as piteously to his peasant father as if he were still a frightened little boy in the steerage.

Many of these children have come to grief through their premature fling into city life, having thrown off parental control as they have impatiently discarded foreign ways. Boys of ten and twelve will refuse to sleep at home, preferring the freedom of an old brewery vault or an empty warehouse to the obedience required by their parents, and for days these boys will live on the milk and bread which they steal from the back porches after the early morning delivery. Such children complain that there is "no fun" at home. One little chap who was given a vacant lot to cultivate by the City Garden Association, insisted upon raising only popcorn and tried to present the entire crop to Hull-House "to be used for the parties," with the stipulation that he would have "to be invited every single time." Then there are little groups of dissipated young men who pride themselves upon their ability to live without working, and who despise all the honest and sober ways of their immigrant parents. They are at once a menace and a center of demoralization. Certainly the bewildered parents, unable to speak English and ignorant of the city, whose children have disappeared for days or weeks, have often come to Hull-House, evincing that agony which fairly separates the marrow from the bone, as if they had discovered a new type of suffering, devoid of the healing in familiar sorrows. It is as if they did not know how to search for the children without the assistance of the children themselves. Perhaps the most pathetic aspect of such cases is their revelation of the premature dependence of the older and wiser upon the young and foolish, which is in itself often responsible for the situation because it has given the children an undue sense of their own importance and a false security that they can take care of themselves.

On the other hand, an Italian girl who has had lessons in cooking at the public school, will help her mother to connect the entire family with American food and household habits. That the mother has never baked bread in Italy—only mixed it in her own house and then taken it out to the village oven—makes all the more valuable her daughter's understanding of the complicated cooking stove. The same thing is true of the girl who learns to sew in the public school, and more than anything else, perhaps, of the girl who receives the first simple instruction in the care of little children,—that skillful care which every tenement-house baby requires if he is to be pulled through his second summer. As a result of this teaching I recall a young girl who carefully explained to her Italian mother that the reason the babies in Italy were so healthy and the babies in Chicago were so sickly, was not, as her mother had firmly insisted, because her babies in Italy had goat's milk and her babies in America had cow's milk, but because the milk in Italy was clean and the milk in Chicago was dirty. She said that when you milked your own goat before the door, you knew that the milk was clean, but when you bought milk from the grocery store after it had been carried for many miles in the country, you couldn't tell whether or not it was fit for the baby to drink until the men from the City Hall who had watched it all the way, said that it was all right.

Thus through civic instruction in the public schools, the Italian woman slowly became urbanized in the sense in which the word was used by her own Latin ancestors, and thus the habits of her entire family were modified. The public schools in the immigrant colonies deserve all the praise as Americanizing agencies which can be bestowed upon them, and there is little doubt that the fast-changing curriculum in the direction of the vacation-school experiments, will react still more directly upon such households.

It is difficult to write of the relation of the older and most foreign-looking immigrants to the children of other people,—the Italians whose fruit-carts are upset simply because they are "dagoes," or the Russian peddlers who are stoned and sometimes badly injured because it has become a code of honor in a gang of boys to thus express their derision. The members of a Protective Association of Jewish Peddlers organized at Hull-House, related daily experiences in which old age had been treated with such irreverence, cherished dignity with such disrespect, that a listener caught the passion of Lear in the old texts, as a platitude enunciated by a man who discovers in it his own experience, thrills us as no unfamiliar phrases can possibly do. The Greeks are filled with amazed rage when their very name is flung at them as an opprobrious epithet. Doubtless these difficulties would be much minimized in America, if we faced our own race problem with courage and intelligence, and these very Mediterranean immigrants might give us valuable help. Certainly they are less conscious than the Anglo-Saxon of color distinctions, perhaps because of their traditional familiarity with Carthage and Egypt. They listened with respect and enthusiasm to a scholarly address delivered by Professor Du Bois at Hull-House on a Lincoln's birthday, with apparently no consciousness of that race difference which color seems to accentuate so absurdly, and upon my return from various conferences held in the interest of "the advancement of colored people," I have had many illuminating conversations with my cosmopolitan neighbors.

The celebration of national events has always been a source of new understanding and companionship with the members of the contiguous foreign colonies not only between them and their American neighbors but between them and their own children. One of our earliest Italian events was a rousing commemoration of Garibaldi's birthday, and his imposing bust presented to Hull-House that evening, was long the chief ornament of our front hall. It called forth great enthusiasm from the *connazionali* whom Ruskin calls, not the "common people" of Italy, but the "companion people" because of their power for swift sympathy.

A huge Hellenic meeting held at Hull-House, in which the achievements of the classic period were set forth both in Greek and English by scholars of well-known repute, brought us into a new sense of fellowship with all our Greek neighbors. As the mayor of Chicago was seated upon the right hand of the dignified senior priest of the Greek Church and they were greeted alternately in the national hymns of America and Greece, one felt a curious sense of the possibility of transplanting to new and crude Chicago, some of the traditions of Athens itself, so deeply cherished in the hearts of this group of citizens.

The Greeks indeed gravely consider their traditions as their most precious possession and more than once in meetings of protest held by the Greek colony against the aggressions of the Bulgarians in Macedonia, I have heard it urged that the Bulgarians are trying to establish a protectorate, not only for their immediate advantage, but that they may claim a glorious history for their "barbarous country." It is said that on the basis of this protectorate, they are already teaching in their schools that Alexander the Great was a Bulgarian and that it will be but a short time before they claim Aristotle himself, an indignity the Greeks will never suffer!

To me personally the celebration of the hundredth anniversary of Mazzini's birth was a matter of great interest. Throughout the world that day Italians who believed in a United Italy came together. They recalled the hopes of this man who, with all his devotion to his country, was still more devoted to humanity and who dedicated to the workingmen of Italy, an appeal so philosophical, so filled with a yearning for righteousness, that it transcended all national boundaries and became a bugle call for "The Duties of Man." A copy of this document was given to every school child in the public schools of Italy on this one hundredth anniversary, and as the Chicago branch of the Society of Young Italy marched into our largest hall and presented to Hull-House an heroic bust of Mazzini, I found myself devoutly hoping that the Italian youth, who have committed their future to America, might indeed become "the Apostles of the fraternity of nations" and that our American citizenship might be built without disturbing these foundations which were laid of old time.

George Ade

Born in Indiana, George Ade (1866–1944) joined the *Chicago Morning News*—later to become the *Chicago Record*—in 1890. He soon began to write unsigned features called "Stories of the Streets and of the Town." In 1898 he embarked on his "Fables in Slang" which were syndicated throughout the country and eventually brought him wealth and fame. He was also a successful playwright. The selection below was first printed as a Chicago newspaper column.

Vehicles Out of the Ordinary

Anyone who keeps his eyes open can find a number of strange vehicles in Chicago, but he must go out into the districts where the people live, and not confine his observations to the down-town district. In the crowded business streets the trucks, delivery wagons and hansom cabs are about the only types to be seen.

At a corner in the southwestern part of the city the evangelist's wagon was drawn up alongside the board walk and a small crowd had collected to listen to the music and read the inscriptions. The vehicle was something like a fancy farm wagon with a canopy top to it, except that the sideboards were not so high. It was drawn by two horses, and the driver sat in a broad seat at the front. Behind him was the organ, which was built as a part of the wagon, being joined to the floor and the sideboards. The scriptural quotations were painted on red cloth curtains concealing the back part of the wagon, where there were two or three chairs. When the curtains were removed and the canopy moved out of the way the back part of the wagon became a rostrum, or pulpit.

The man at the organ played some introductory chords and sang a hymn in a robust voice loud enough for out-door use, and the evangelist made an exhortation.

Then the driver clucked at his horses and said "Getep" and the portable church was driven to another corner and the services were repeated.

On many of the less pretentious streets the waffle man with his squatty wagon is a familiar and welcome sight. His establishment on wheels is drawn by a patient horse, who is always more willing to stop than he is to start. The wagon, which is of a dull red color, is mounted on low wheels.

The waffle man does his own driving, for his gasoline stove is at the front of the wagon. His cooking utensils, batter, and the rest of the kitchen outfit are kept in shelves at the front, while at the back there is a flat counter where the customers may be served. Sometimes he rings a bell and again he will keep up a mournful, monotonous wail of "Wa-a-a-fles; wa-a-a-fles."

The waffle booth on the corner or the handcart of the "levee" district has been familiar for a long time, but the waffle wagon which supplies families is a thing of recent date.

The old cobbler and his traveling shop are known on many of the streets in the northwestern section of the city. He has a covered wagon, which is fitted up inside with all that is needed in a repair shop. The driver, who is as old and grizzled as the cobbler, labors to keep the horse going, and shouts "Old Shoes to mend!" The venerable cobbler saves rent and gets plenty of work, for the children know him and wait for him, a dozen or more gathering around his queer vehicle to watch him put on the half soles.

The sandwich wagon or "buffet car" is common enough, especially on the south side between Van Buren and 12th streets, and on the west along Halsted and Madison streets. There are a few along North Clark Street, and now and then one may be found even in the remote districts, especially around the parks or any resort where people congregate of an evening. It was the sandwich wagon that popularized the "ham and egg sandwich," an oily luxury which has been taken up by many of the restaurants.

At first the wagons served only sandwiches, but with growing competition they have introduced cold-meat lunches, baked beans, coffee, hot corn on the cob and other delicacies. If one is not troubled with a false pride one can get a good warm lunch at low prices and stand on the curbstone while he eats it. Occasionally there will be seen a buffet car with a little counter in the back end of it. At the counter are three stools, so that at least three customers may sit while they are being served.

The average sandwich car to be found in State Street has numerous windows decorated with tempting advertisements. The oil or gasoline stove is banked about with loaves of bread, the carcasses of chickens and great knobs of ham. "Albert" or "Charley," or whatever may be the name on the illuminated sign, wears a white jacket and a white cap and takes a professional pride in turning a piece of ham without putting the fork to it.

As a rule, each of these wagons has a "stand" where it remains from an early hour in the evening until the last customers go home, sometimes the break of day. The horse is not kept "hitched up" all night, but is in shelter near at hand, and when there are no more 10-cent pieces in sight he and the "buffet car" disappear.

An intelligent Italian, whose "territory" covers the residence streets far up on the north side, owns a street piano. It is one of the large kind, mounted on a cart platform. Until quite lately he had to employ another Italian to go with him and help pull the thing. This was not always easy work, especially if the street happened to be rough or a trifle slippery. Therefore, to save himself labor and avoid paying an extra salary, he bought a small donkey, which now does all the hard work. This little animal soon became throroughly acquainted with his duties. He stands perfectly still when commanded to do so, although the command is in Italian, a new language to him. His head hangs down, his eyes close and the ears droop in a melancholy way until the piano begins to pound out "The Blue Bells of Scotland." As soon as those familiar strains are heard he lifts his head and prepares to move, because he knows that is the last piece in the repertory.

The fish-peddler's vehicle is nothing more than a box mounted on two wheels, with a pair of shafts in front and a place behind for the peddler to stand. The driver stands back of the box, in which the fish are packed in ice. When a customer calls him all he has to do is say "Whoa," lift up the lid, haul out a fish and weigh it with his spring scales.

Another strange peddler has a wagon with a hayrack on top and makes his living by selling sheaves of straw and sacks of corn-husks, which are used as bedding in many quarters where foreign laborers reside.

The lemonade wagon and the confectionery store on wheels were common enough in the World's Fair neighborhood last year, but there is an air of novelty about the tin-type "gallery" on wheels now jumping from one vacant lot to another.

Advertising agents are responsible for many of the weird vehicles on the streets. They send out Roman chariots to advertise a new chewing gum, and one of them rather overdid it by having a red-headed woman drive four white horses abreast.

Every one in Chicago must have seen at one time or another those two huge bill-boards, joined at the top, mounted on four small wheels and drawn by a team of shaggy donkeys not much larger than jack rabbits.

It will be conceded that the moving van is the most majestic vehicle to be seen, while from an artistic standpoint the gilded pie wagon has no rival. Then there is the fancy little steam boiler on wheels which is used in blowing out the stopped-up pipes.

Every summer the suburbs are visited by strolling gypsies who make homes in the big gaudy caravans. It would be an interesting procession— one made up of the queer vehicles in Chicago.

Frank Norris

Frank Norris (1870–1902) was born in Chicago and died at the age of thirty-two after an operation for appendicitis. He is best remembered today as one of the first American writers in the naturalist tradition and as the author of *McTeague, The Octopus,* and *The Pit,* from the last of which the next selection is taken. He is the only author in this anthology who is represented with selections from two different novels. The second selection is from *McTeague* and describes San Francisco city life.

from The Pit

Their car, or rather their train of cars, coupled together in threes, in Chicago style, came, and Landry escorted them down town. All the way Laura could not refrain from looking out of the windows, absorbed in the contemplation of the life and aspects of the streets.

"You will give yourself away," said Page. "Everybody will know you're from the country."

"I am," she retorted. "But there's a difference between just mere 'country' and Massachusetts, and I'm not ashamed of it."

Chicago, the great grey city, interested her at every instant and under every condition. As yet she was not sure that she liked it; she could not forgive its dirty streets, the unspeakable squalor of some of its poorer neighbourhoods that sometimes developed, like cancerous growths, in the very heart of fine residence districts. The black murk that closed every vista of the business streets oppressed her, and the soot that stained linen and gloves each time she stirred abroad was a never-ending distress.

But the life was tremendous. All around on every side, in every direction the vast machinery of Commonwealth clashed and thundered from dawn to dark and from dark till dawn. Even now, as the car carried her farther into the business quarter, she could hear it, see it, and feel in her every fibre the trepidation of its motion. The blackened waters of the river, seen an instant between stanchions as the car trundled across the State Street bridge, disappeared under fleets of tugs of lake steamers, of lumber barges from Sheboygan and Mackinac, of grain boats from Duluth, of coal scows that filled the air with impalpable dust, of cumbersome schooners laden with produce, of grimy rowboats dodging the prows and paddles of the larger craft, while on all sides, blocking the horizon, red in

colour and designated by Brobdingnag letters, towered the hump-
shouldered grain elevators.

Just before crossing the bridge on the north side of the river she had
caught a glimpse of a great railway terminus. Down there below, rectilinear, scientifically paralleled and squared, the Yard disclosed itself. A system of grey rails beyond words complicated opened out and spread im-
measurably. Switches, semaphores, and signal towers, stood here and
there. A dozen trains, freight and passenger, puffed and steamed, waiting
the word to depart. Detached engines hurried in and out of sheds and
roundhouses, seeking their trains, or bunted the ponderous freight cars
into switches; trundling up and down, clanking, shrieking, their bells filling the air with the clangour of tocsins. Men in visored caps shouted
hoarsely, waving their arms or red flags; drays, their big dappled horses,
feeding in their nose bags, stood backed up to the open doors of freight
cars and received their loads. A train departed roaring. Before midnight
it would be leagues away boring through the Great Northwest, carrying
Trade—the lifeblood of nations—into communities of which Laura had
never heard. Another train, reeking with fatigue, the air brakes screaming, arrived and halted, debouching a flood of passengers, business men,
bringing Trade—a galvanizing elixir—from the very ends and corners of
the continent.

Or, again, it was South Water Street—a jam of delivery wagons and
market carts backed to the curbs, leaving only a tortuous path between
the endless files of horses, suggestive of an actual barrack of cavalry. Provi-
sions, market produce, "garden truck" and fruits, in an infinite welter of
crates and baskets, boxes and sacks, crowded the sidewalks. The gutter
was choked with an overflow of refuse cabbage leaves, soft oranges, decay-
ing beet tops. The air was thick with the heavy smell of vegetation. Food
was trodden under foot, food crammed the stores and warehouses to
bursting. Food mingled with the mud of the highway. The very dray
horses were gorged with an unending nourishment of snatched mouthfuls
picked from backboard, from barrel top, and from the edge of the sidewalk. The entire locality reeked with the fatness of a hundred thousand
furrows. A land of plenty, the inordinate abundance of the earth itself
emptied itself upon the asphalt and cobbles of the quarter. It was the
Mouth of the City, and drawn from all directions, over a territory of immense area, this glut of crude subsistence was sucked in, as if into a rapa-
cious gullet, to feed the sinews and to nourish the fibres of an immeasurable colossus.

Suddenly the meaning and significance of it all dawned upon Laura.

The Great Grey City, brooking no rival, imposed its dominion upon a reach of country larger than many a kingdom of the Old World. For thousands of miles beyond its confines was its influence felt. Out, far out, far away in the snow and shadow of northern Wisconsin forests, axes and saws bit the bark of century-old trees, stimulated by this city's energy. Just as far to the southward pick and drill leaped to the assault of veins of anthracite, moved by her central power. Her force turned the wheels of harvester and seeder a thousand miles distant in Iowa and Kansas. Her force spun the screws and propellers of innumerable squadrons of lake steamers crowding the Sault Sainte Marie. For her and because of her all the Central States, all the Great Northwest roared with traffic and industry; sawmills screamed; factories, their smoke blackening the sky, clashed and flamed; wheels turned, pistons leaped in their cylinders; cog gripped cog; beltings clasped the drums of mammoth wheels; and converters of forges belched into the clouded air their tempest breath of molten steel.

It was Empire, the resistless subjugation of all this central world of the lakes and the prairies. Here, midmost in the land, beat the Heart of the Nation, whence inevitably must come its immeasurable power, its infinite, infinite, inexhaustible vitality. Here, of all her cities, throbbed the true life—the true power and spirit of America; gigantic, crude with the crudity of youth, disdaining rivalry; sane and healthy and vigorous; brutal in its ambition, arrogant in the new-found knowledge of its giant strength, prodigal of its wealth, infinite in its desires. In its capacity boundless, in its courage indomitable; subduing the wilderness in a single generation, defying calamity, and through the flame and the débris of a commonwealth in ashes, rising suddenly renewed, formidable, and Titanic.

Laura, her eyes dizzied, her ears stunned, watched tirelessly.

"There is something terrible about it," she murmured, half to herself, "something insensate. In a way, it doesn't seem human. It's like a great tidal wave. It's all very well for the individual just so long as he can keep afloat, but once fallen, how horribly quick it would crush him, annihilate him, how horribly quick, and with such horrible indifference! I suppose it's civilization in the making, the thing that isn't meant to be seen, as though it were too elemental, too—primordial; like the first verses of Genesis."

The impression remained long with her, and not even the gaiety of their little supper could altogether disperse it. She was a little frightened —frightened of the vast, cruel machinery of the city's life, and of the men who could dare it, who conquered it. For a moment they seemed, in a sense, more terrible than the city itself—men for whom all this crash of conflict and commerce had no terrors. Those who could subdue it to their purposes, must they not be themselves more terrible, more pitiless, more brutal? She shrank a little. What could women ever know of the life of men, after all? Even Landry, extravagant as he was, so young, so exuberant, so seemingly innocent—she knew that he was spoken of as a good business man. He, too, then had his other side. For him the Battle of the Street was an exhilaration. Beneath that boyish exterior was the tough coarseness, the male hardness, the callousness that met the brunt and withstood the shock of onset.

Theodore Dreiser

Theodore Dreiser (1871–1945) was born in Terre Haute, Indiana, and did his best writing against the background of city life. Perhaps this may have been because he had worked as a newspaperman in Saint Louis, Chicago, Pittsburgh, and New York.

The selection presented here is from *Dawn*, which was published in 1931 and is characteristic Dreiser: the kind of strong, frank prose that was attacked as "coarse" in an earlier day. Incidentally, it was Frank Norris in 1914, an editor with a leading American publisher, who accepted Dreiser's first novel, *Sister Carrie*, for publication. When the publisher read the manuscript on his return from Europe, he was shocked at its tone and content and attempted to cancel the contract given to Dreiser. He failed in this, and the book was printed in a cheap edition of one thousand but never distributed, advertised, or displayed. It has since come to be recognized as one of the classics of American naturalism.

from Dawn

. . . Chicago red light streets as we ventured into them after dark—as has always been the custom—were as typical of the raw, brawling force of sex, and particularly of this hardy city, as anything could be. For cheek by jowl with immense manufacturing buildings which were springing up on every hand—tall fourteen- and sixteen-story buildings which were then already the marvel of America, and unknown to New York among other things—were the low brick residences formerly the homes of conservative citizens who had long since moved before the encroaching manufacturing and sales life of the city. In one way, too, these were quiet, dark streets, with here and there only patches of shabby frame dwellings devoted to saloons, pool-rooms, stores, rooming houses and the like, whereas for the rest, they were prowled over and through by hungry and seeking or, as we now say, sex-starved men, from all parts of America, really. But so minutely as seen before these taller, newer buildings, great sky-scrapers dark and silent and now towering shadow-like above these rows of houses with their red or pink fan-lights over the door and occasionally a name emblazoned: invariably that of a woman. (Might it not as well have been *Aphrodite?*) Policemen too, here and there to be seen,—grafters and henchmen, belike—and, on occasion, robbers—and along with all this a line of cabs in one or another section, the scene resembling an etching.

And throughout all, a muffled sound of activity; the feet of men coming out of or going into houses or swinging along the street in groups or pairs, and talking in low tones, and occasionally a woman crossing from one section to another.

It was an old picture, but to me, then, exciting. We set out after a dinner at Rector's, a basement restaurant then gaining considerable fame, and wandered into this region, looking for the signal lights over the doors. Although insisting he had never been here before, still O'Connor seemed familiar enough with the process of discovery and entry, for saying: "Let's look in here!" he knocked at a door and was at once admitted by a Negro maid, who remarked cheerfully: "Come right in, boys!" I recall well the flaring red plush curtains that divided the front room from another in the rear, the tall gilt mirrors, the bright gilt chairs, and the upright piano, at which, no sooner were we seated, a blasé youth, entering from the rear room, seated himself and began to play, but without paying any attention to us whatever. And as actresses entering upon a stage and from a rear room set off by heavy plush curtains—from which had been issuing sounds of laughter and conversation—presently came several girls, detached portions apparently, of a larger group of men and women already congregated there.

"Hello, boys!" Even yet I can hear the voice of the meaty German girl who approached me. She was clad in a pink silk chemise, with stockings to match, her yellow hair piled in a high spiral at the back of her head, her fat, gross face apparently glowing with health. "How you like this costume?" she asked, stepping forward, moving her lips suggestively, and leaning over and pressing against me the better to impress—or should I say infect—me with her charm. A slimmer, more graceful girl, in evening dress, had already approached O'Connor and in his lap was being fondled by him.

I confess that as coarse and gross as all this was, there was still a vigorous, healthy reality about it which quite intrigued me. It smacked so of vigor and lust and hunger and a kind of brainless mad reward for the brainless mad ills of this world from which no healthy male or female is really ever wholly free. To my hungry sex sense then, how reviving and at the same time torturing, this consciousness of the value of potency as well as youth and means! Ah, to have all! Not be as I was—impoverished and impotent! At the very same time and in spite of this, I was luxuriated as might one who is cold, say, and permitted to enjoy a fire. Really, I think I was so enraptured by this particular and generic phase of life, or this particular showy setting of it, that its various and often crude details did not trouble me at all. For here a woman was a woman, provided she was plump and rosy. Her mental characteristics or tendencies were of no particular import. It was her form, that mystic geometric formula which something has invented and which when contemplated by the eye of man inflames his passions. I say "invented," for I think man really is an invention, a schemed-out machine, useful to a larger something which desires to function through him as a machine, be that air, fire, water, electricity, cosmic rays, or what you will. At any rate, and most assuredly, man is no self-propelling body by any means; air and water and heat and other things most certainly make him go. As a flying machine may to-day be operated by invisible rays, so man. A part of the motivating power, perhaps, enters through the eye, another part through the mouth, the nose; touch is responsible for some reactions, and so it goes. But certainly one of the geometric formulae which causes man to act, to energize or procreate in the very necessary process which the continuation of human life on earth compels, is the form of a woman, and its energizing force is communicated through the eye. What humorous master decided on this double mechanism which a man and a woman constitute, and why?

Be that as it may, and just at that time, a woman was a woman to me, a pretty girl a charming implement for effecting sex delight. I fondled this offering of the fates, regardless of the fact that she was as dull and coarse as any girl might well be, and was thrilled by the discovery that she had nothing on save this pink chemise, that I was in contact with her rounded solid flesh. Ecstasized sensorially, yet also made to remember that I had no money and no potency wherewith to entertain her, I accepted the snuggling and its effect about as a man eats a meal, knowing he cannot pay for it. And this was all the more emphasized by an early inquiry on the part of the girl as to whether I did not want to go upstairs, and since I did not, by the additional inquiry of a colored maid who came to ask what we wished to drink—cigars, beer, wine, or what? Cigars at fifty cents each, beer at a dollar the bottle, alleged champagne at five dollars but of American make and very bad, presumably cultivated cider.

Since I could not pay the price that was demanded by this girl—five dollars for a single relationship—I was about to extricate myself by pretending to be dissatisfied, when O'Connor, coming over to me, signalled: "Come on!" and then, *sotto voce:* "You don't want that!" To smooth matters, we each took a cigar off the tray, which he paid for, and affecting a serenity and indifference which I did not feel, we set forth again.

"There's nothing worth while in there," was his comment as we went down the steps, myself wondering why after all the girls he knew and played with in Bloomington, he should choose to come here. "They're just tough, vulgar bitches," he went on. But just the same, my mind was full of the wonder of being able to join issues with such a plump piece of pastry as I had just released, of being able to spend hours in such meaty, perfumed embraces.

There were thereafter other houses, and into several of these we entered, O'Connor paying as we did so. (I still wonder why.) And before we were through, I had become almost expert in sampling these beauties (exteriorly, at least) the while maintaining a seemingly judicial and undetermined state of mind. For I found, and that quickly, that it would not do to seem appreciative or inclined to any one girl, lest one failed of an excuse to depart. At the same time, what a beggar I felt! How cheap! With each additional entrance and exit I grew more and more disgusted with myself than with anything I saw, and wanted much to get away. As for O'Connor, with his money and aplomb and determined and critical selective sense, he was by no means abashed. For, as he said, when he found what he wanted, he would stay, and not before. Hence, while remote and non-committal, as I could see, he, like myself, was looking these several candidates over and sensualizing at his ease. Yet presently, and as I saw, he did find one who seemed to attract him, and so stayed. And although he urged me to do the same, offering me bills wherewith to continue my search, I refused. The whole process for me had been ruined for the want of independent means.

And though looked at askance and even frowned upon by maid and "professor"—as the musician was called—at last I made my way out. Yet not without some expense. For although O'Connor had paid for most, I presently had spent three dollars for three bottles of beer—my financial limit, and more. In consequence, depressed by this experience, I decided to go no more—would not see O'Connor any more on this trip, and managed so.

Afterwards, I thought—some years afterwards, though—what spindling beginners we must have seemed to those women, accustomed as they were to politicians, priests, and that heavy type of businessman who comes with a roll of money and a solid, matter-of-fact conception of these mundane pleasures! How trivial! But then again, the thought of these women receiving all and sundry staggered me. For although one could not really see the man ahead of one or the man behind, still there he was. And you shared only functionally in what could be no more than a machine process. More, the same girls approached me as every other with a pretense of

special interest—an affectation of a fresh delight with you, me. And so—
not only a little pathetic, but worse, a farce, really.

But how ridiculous! Astounding!

Surely somewhere must be forces of intelligence that look on and laugh,
as we do at comic toys. But where, oh, where is the toy-maker who makes
us? And can it be that he is ashamed to show us his face?

Mary Ellen Chase

Mary Ellen Chase was born in Blue Hill, Maine, in 1887 and has
written about her native state with affectionate insight in such novels
as *Mary Peters* and *Silas Crockett*. She has been a teacher as well as
a writer for the major part of her life. Her classroom activities started
in country schools and took her to Smith College in 1926, where,
until her retirement in 1955, she was one of the most popular professors.

In addition to her novels, essays, and stories for children, Miss
Chase has written books about England and several volumes of autobiography. From one of these, *A Goodly Fellowship*, published in
1939, the selection below is taken.

from A Goodly Fellowship

I was sitting up in my berth and peering from the window the next morning long before it was light enough to see. The flat expanse of country,
with the harvest already cut and with corn stacked in golden huts upon
the shorn ground, was as fascinating to my eyes when it had once come
into vision as the tumbling Berkshire hills. It made up in newness what it
lacked in beauty. I suddenly remembered how Stevenson in *Across the
Plains* had named as beautiful the words *Ohio, Indiana, Illinois.* Now
they seemed beautiful to me also although I had never thought of them in
that way before.

When we at last swept through the sordid outskirts of Chicago in the
early afternoon, I was well-nigh exhausted even more from excitement
than from Middle Western heat. But my fervor knew no lessening, and I
pinned on one of my father's large handkerchiefs in almost painful curiosity and agitation. The elderly gentleman promised by the Bible Institute was awaiting me, similarly marked. I thought even then, I remember,
that I should have recognized him without his handkerchief since, among
all the many persons on the platform, he alone could have emerged from
a Bible Institute.

He conducted me with a benevolent and, I felt, faintly disapproving air
to the elevated railroad, and I staggered after him bearing my suit-case,
which he did not offer to carry and which I was too embarrassed to give to
any importuning porter, not being sure of them and their ways. Once we
had landed within the Bible Institute and I had been shown my very hot
and somewhat musty room, I decided that benevolence and faint disap-

proval were two of the current attitudes of that institution. By the time I
had eaten my supper in company with others of its inmates, I had added
to these, suspicion and a very unattractive zeal.

My mother was quite right in assuming that I should be safe within its
doors. Surely no one would enter it who was not compelled by inner or by
outer force to do so! It was a place devoted to one purpose, namely the
saving of souls, and even to me, whose religious background had been
extremely simple, not to say fervent at times, it was the most embarrassing
of hostels. All the dozen or so young women whom it housed were training to be evangelists, as I learned to my great confusion at supper when
two of them asked me if I had made the great decision. Upon my vowing
hastily and stoutly that I had, their suspicion of me somewhat relaxed for
the moment, but their zeal was fired to anecdotal vigor by their very relief.

I stayed two weeks in the Bible Institute. It was the only place I have
ever known which grew increasingly unpalatable from constant association. I never quite knew whether to admire or to dislike the single-
minded young women, who, when they were not at prayer, at oral testi-
monials, or at Bible study, went about doing good; but I think my only
genuine emotion toward them and their activities was an extreme sense of
embarrassment. We never had quite enough to eat, I remember, although
perhaps my hunger partly resulted from the uncomfortable knowledge
that everyone but me was dedicated to the principle that man does not
live by bread alone. Before we sat down to each scanty meal, we sang a
hymn with a chorus which said,

"O to be nothing, nothing!"

Since I had come to Chicago with the express purpose of being something,
I found this hymn exceedingly irritating. I think I regarded it with super-
stition as well, fearing that the thrice-daily repetition of its refrain might
result in my becoming precisely nothing at all!

We had nightly prayer circles at which my presence was tacitly expected
and my habitual silence the cause of renewed suspicion. This atmosphere
of constant petition with which the entire establishment was redolent got
somewhat on my nerves, not to say my conscience, especially since the only
praying of which I was capable throughout the fortnight was of a most
selfish and anti-social nature, namely that I might get a job.

Had I not, indeed, like St. Paul been intent only upon "this one
thing," had I not been tormented by fears lest I should fail therein, I
might conceivably have become interested in the Bible Institute and in

the study of its strange, tenacious, fervid minds. But the more intent I became upon my own future as the jobless days went on, the more its curious existence seemed a law unto itself and quite divorced from life outside its grimy, comfortless walls. I learned, however, that it was known elsewhere. For when Mr. B. F. Clark, the manager of the teachers' agency which held my future in its hands, asked me upon the occasion of my first call upon him where I was living in Chicago, and I told him, he rose from his chair and cried, "My God!"

I shall always remember my first visit to Mr. Clark's office in Steinway Hall on Van Buren Street. He told me some years afterwards that he remembered it, too, in fact that it had always stood him in good stead as a source of amusement when he needed entertainment in his thoughts. I am sure that no young teacher from Maine had ever before journeyed jobless to Chicago to cast herself upon his mercy. I am sure, too, that he was quite unprepared to meet such eager ingenuousness in a young woman, even in those days when artlessness was still not uncommon among the young.

I went to see him the first morning after my arrival in Chicago, when I had ascertained from the most worldly of the Bible students how I should get to Van Buren Street. I went on the street-car since I did not dare essay the elevated railroad by myself, and I carried my suit-case with me. I do not know just why I thus encumbered myself. Perhaps I was still conscious of my mother's adjurations to keep my most valuable possessions with me as much as possible in such a city. But I think rather that I needed a generous receptacle for more letters of recommendation and for the themes which I had written in college and which, I thought, might give added proof to Mr. Clark that I knew something about the teaching of English.

When I had once reached Van Buren Street with my suit-case and had taken the elevator to the eleventh floor of Steinway Hall, I was in a frightful state of nervous excitement, which did not lessen upon my discovery that no one of a dozen young women in a dozen different offices had ever so much as heard of me. After a long wait during which the furious beating of my heart sent added blood to my already very red cheeks, I was, however, ushered, still with my suit-case, into the presence of him upon whose probably long since forgotten suggestion I had come to Chicago. Mr. Clark, seeing my suit-case, quite naturally thought I had only just arrived; and when I explained that it contained documents which might be of interest to him, he leaned back in his chair and laughed long and loudly.

He was a small, round man of perhaps fifty, with intensely blue round eyes set in a very smooth, pink face. He had brushy white hair parted in the middle, and he was dressed in a light gray suit with a red tie. As I stood there much embarrassed before him, I thought of George Meredith, who had recently died and who, I had read somewhere, favored light gray suits with red ties. For a moment I thought self-consciously of impressing Mr. Clark by the comparison and then thought better of it.

I asked instead whether he really thought I should get a position, and I remember that he said he felt sure of it, since he could not allow some school to be deprived of me. I took this as a compliment at the moment and felt much encouraged, although later I realized that another meaning lurked within his words. My heart leaped at his next announcement.

"Let me see," he said. "There may be something this minute. What about Mason City, Iowa? They want a Latin teacher."

My heart fell as quickly as it had risen.

"I'm afraid Iowa is beyond the Mississippi, isn't it?" I said.

"Why the Mississippi?" asked Mr. Clark, fumbling among other papers on his desk. "It's a nice river. Got anything against it?"

"No," said I. "It's only that my mother would prefer me not to go beyond the Mississippi unless it's really necessary."

Mr. Clark laughed again. I could see that our interview was unusual to him in many respects. Then he told me with great encouragement that he felt reasonably sure some opening this side of the Mississippi would put in an appearance before many days had passed. I in turn assured him that with his permission I should look in at the office every morning at this hour, and he did not seem to object to my proposal.

The morning of my first visit to Mr. Clark is also memorable to me because of a somewhat terrifying as well as humorous accident which befell me before I was again safely within the walls of the Bible Institute. There is always, I think, an element of pathos in inexperience and the mishaps which it often calls down upon itself, humorous as such mishaps may be. Perhaps for this very reason much of the humor of today lacks a kind of mellowness since inexperience has become so relatively impossible in an age like our own.

I had lived all of my twenty-two years in the country and in the most countrified country at that. The college which I attended was a country college, situated in a small town, the nearest city being the inconsiderable one of Bangor. I knew nothing of great cities and their ways, and had I not been so eager to enjoy my new freedom to its limit and to learn all that I could about my new surroundings, I should have felt terrified by Chicago, its dirt, its uproar, and its frenzied rush.

Strange and frightening as everything seemed to me, however, I determined upon leaving Mr. Clark's office on Van Buren Street to walk to the Bible Institute. I was impelled to do so by a variety of desires: to make my next letter home as dramatic and interesting as possible; to see what Chicago was really like; to avoid another street-car since in the first I had felt extremely self-conscious and ill at ease; and above all else to postpone as long as possible my re-entry into the Bible Institute. Even with my suit-case the distance did not seem long to me when the impatient door-man at Steinway Hall had explained to me with many pointings of a scornful finger the requisite blocks west and the turn northward.

I reached Dearborn Street with no disaster and turned northward. The day was warm, and I took my time, seemingly the only person, I thought, on the street who was not in a hurry. There was and still is, unless I am mistaken, a bridge on Dearborn Street which crosses the Chicago River. The structure of this bridge meant nothing to me, but I lingered thereon, being fascinated by the filthy water of the river and by a peculiar craft coming upstream. This struck me, I remember, as odd since there was obviously no way by which it might proceed beyond the bridge. I walked on slowly, studying the steady progress of the boat, when I was startled by the blowing of whistles and the apparent haste of everyone but me. Whether I was hidden by the iron uprights of the bridge from the sight of the men responsible for its manipulation, I do not know; but by the time I had come to my senses and was hurrying to reach the other side, I felt to my horror the solid boards beneath my feet begin to rise in the air and to place me and my suit-case in an ever-increasingly precarious position at an angle of some forty-five degrees.

Terrified as I was at this angle, which, I surmised, must steadily increase toward ninety degrees, I had sense enough now to realize quickly the connection between the bridge and the boat. Since the bridge had parted in its middle and was rising in the air to allow the passage of the boat, I knew that it was destined to come down again. I had not come to Chicago to meet my death, and I instantly decided upon the only way to avoid it. I wedged my suit-case between two of the iron supports which met at an angle and somehow cast myself upon it with my arms clinging to whatever there was to cling to. I would hold on, I determined, with all my strength until the bridge once again assumed its normal position, when I would extricate myself and walk off with what dignity I could muster.

But by the time my decisions were made and I was placed in my desperate position, the men in charge of this curious feat of engineering had spotted me. There were shouts, more blowing of whistles, the gathering of a crowd on the nearer bank of the river. The boat backed downstream; the bridge began to descend. I felt it slowly dropping backward behind me. It clanged and bumped into position; and I was lifted to my feet by two policemen who had run onto the bridge from the nearer pavement.

Once on the street I found myself the center of a strange assortment of men and women, many with foreign faces, who, used to such bridges as this, had been awaiting its normal behavior in order to cross the river. I instantly recognized that my courage in the face of danger meant nothing whatever to them. They thought I was either mad or senseless and were curiously waiting to discover which.

The bigger policeman, who had not relinquished his hold upon me, began at once to question me.

"Young woman," he screamed, "are you tired of life? Just what do you mean by not heeding signals?"

I explained as best I could, while the crowd increased and I wanted terribly to die, that I had never before seen such a bridge and that I had not understood the connection between the signals and myself.

"Will you kindly tell us," asked the other policeman, who still held my suit-case, looking upon it occasionally with disdain and scorn, "who you are and where on earth you hail from?"

I strove to hold back my nervous tears as I gave my name and the state of my kindly engendure, which at that moment I devoutly wished I had never left.

The crowd howled with unkind amusement and repeated the howl when, upon further harsh inquiry, I was obliged to tell where I was staying in the city; I thought for some terrible moments that I was not to be allowed to proceed on my way unattended by the law; but my obvious innocence and the sight of my tears apparently convinced the policemen that I was truthful, if a fool, and they at last let me go.

A kind-faced woman walked five blocks with me. She insisted upon carrying my suit-case, and, although I could not speak a word to her, I have always felt toward her a gratitude which I have felt toward few persons before or since.

The Bible Institute for the only time during my stay in Chicago looked good to me when I had once reached it. I hurried to my room to burst into tears of utter humiliation upon my miserable bed. For days I suffered paroxysms of dread lest my exploit appear in the papers and reach the round, blue eyes of Mr. Clark, who would then and there decide that such ignorance deserved no confidence. But apparently, I concluded, when I again felt safe, it was of importance only as a story to be told as a joke by all the strange and awful people who had witnessed it.

It was months before I saw that it had its humorous aspects, not, indeed, until it had been received with high amusement by friends whom I was soon to make. Most of them, I think, never really believed the story in spite of my asseverations. But it was so true in every detail that it even now reappears in certain dreams of terror. For when in the night I find myself, like De Quincey, jeered at by monsters in human form, I know that far back somewhere in my mind the Dearborn Street bridge still stands, flanked by Chinamen and negroes and two burly policemen, and that I, even in my sleep, am searching somewhere for a kind-faced woman to thank her after many years.

I have often since wondered exactly what I did during that fortnight in Chicago. I think it was a period not of action so much as of certain concentrated and extremely limited states of mind. I was too beset by fear and uncertainty to read much, as I should otherwise have done. My bodily frame attended prayer circles and went occasionally under the chaperonage of the elderly gentleman with the handkerchief to hysterical, revivalistic gatherings in certain undesirable portions of the city; but my mind rarely accompanied it. I am sure I walked miles on bridgeless streets and along the Lake front, hopeful at times, at others fearful. I grew thin during that fortnight, partly from scanty, ill-cooked meals, mostly from anxiety.

But at last on an afternoon early in September Mr. Clark summoned me to Van Buren Street, and I went in a fever of excitement. He said, while I stood opposite him trembling with hope, that a certain school in Wisconsin had been so favorably impressed by a letter concerning me that its headmistresses wished to see me. They wanted a teacher of history who would assist in English. Above everything else they wanted one who knew and liked the country. The school, Mr. Clark, said, was a rather unusual boarding-school known as the Hillside Home School; and although its mistresses preferred a teacher with more experience than mine, he thought it might afford the very place for me. He said that with my approval he would inform the Lloyd-Jones sisters that I would arrive at Spring Green, Wisconsin, which was the nearest town to Hillside, on the following afternoon at six o'clock.

I presume I walked back to the Bible Institute on ordinary pavements, but they were to me high and wide pathways toward my future. The dirty city which had terrified and humiliated me seemed clothed in light, shining and kind. I caught myself smiling at strangers on the street who, surprised, smiled shyly back at me. I was now freed from anxiety and fear, for in my new resiliency I had not a doubt in my mind that, whoever the Lloyd-Jones sisters were, they were as eagerly awaiting me as I was awaiting them. This assurance prompted me to pack my trunk before supper so that, when I was once engaged to teach at the Hillside Home School, I might not have to return to Chicago at all. I would then, I thought, write the Bible Institute to send it after me so that I might never again have to climb its steps to peal its clanging, dissonant bell.

I remember that at supper that night I asked boldly for another piece of cake and a second helping of custard. The horrified silence which greeted my request was broken at last by the most serious of the would-be evangelists, who offered me her portion, which she assured me she did not want. I do not think I even demurred at accepting it or blushed at my temerity. For I was leaving this odd house where the desire of everyone was to be nothing and embarking on my way where I was to be something at last.

MILWAUKEE

At the turn of the century, Milwaukee was a bilingual city with a heavy German accent on the beer, the customs, the cultural activities, and the newspapers. The immigrant population was highly literate, made up mostly of the informed middle-class that fled from the revolutionary turmoil in Middle Europe, and by 1910—the time described in both selections below—it supported five German-language newspapers out of a total of eleven.

Both Edna Ferber and Ernest Meyer were involved in the journalistic life of the city but in quite different ways. Miss Ferber came to Milwaukee when she was eighteen to make her way as a reporter for the Journal, *and she describes her adventures as a pioneering "sob sister" who was paid fifteen dollars a week to cover stories all over town. Ernest Meyer's father was an editorial writer for* Germania, *and from the description of the family's life at the time, they might just as well have been living in "the old country."*

Edna Ferber

One of America's most successful novelists, Edna Ferber was born in Kalamazoo, Michigan, and spent her early working years as a reporter in the Middle West. Her first fiction dealt with the new "career" women who were beginning to make their way in business. In 1924 she won the Pulitzer Prize for *So Big*, and in 1926 she published *Show Boat*, which turned into the perennially popular operetta with music by Jerome Kern. Later novels include *Cimarron* and *Saratoga Trunk*. Together with George S. Kaufman, Miss Ferber wrote many successful plays, including *Dinner at Eight* and *Stage Door*. The selection below is from her autobiography, *A Peculiar Treasure*, published in 1960.

from A Peculiar Treasure

They put me on the Schandein case there on the Milwaukee Journal. A good deal of the time I didn't know what they were talking about. But I sat in the courtroom with Cook, the Journal court and police reporter, taking it all down and telephoning it in, for it was hot stuff, and the Milwaukee papers were getting out special editions on it. The Schandein case had started, innocently enough, seemingly, as a private squabble about a will in one of the wealthy Milwaukee beer-brewing families. But in turning over these legal matters they were found to give off a frightful stench. Medical, clinical, sexual terms rose like a miasma from the witness stand. I was being initiated into big-town reporting with a vengeance. That was why they had so hurriedly sent for me. The regular woman reporter, who wrote under the name of Jean Airlie, was away on vacation when the Schandein case broke. Campbell, the managing editor, had liked my stuff as Appleton correspondent. I was put in as an emergency stop-gap to get what was known as the woman's angle. If they were taken aback at the appearance of a wide-eyed kid they said nothing but hurled me into the nauseating mess and I waded through it. Milwaukee's aristocracy was made up of brewing families. They lived in vast stone or brick houses on Grand Avenue, the lawns decorated with iron deer, with pergolas, gazebos, and painted dwarfs patterned after those we now know in Snow White. The social gathering place for these clans was the old Germania Club. Names such as Pabst, Schlitz, Uhlein, Schandein were Milwaukee's Royal Family titles, and some of these were present in the courtroom or were pulled into the case. The Milwaukee papers were delirious with joy.

The Milwaukee of that time was as German as Germany. There actually were to be seen signs in the windows of shops on the almost solid German South Side which read, "Hier wird Englisch gesprochen." Of the four hundred thousand population, surely three fourths were German or Polish. There was a distinctly foreign flavor about the city—its architecture, its tempo, the faces of its people, its food, its solid dowdy matrons. Victor Berger, the Socialist, was a growing influence. When you were sent to interview him he was given to mild attempts at cheek-pinching, but then, mine was a plump pink cheek and politics is a dusty business. I didn't resent it.

Arrived, I made straight for a boarding house that had been recommended to me as cheap, clean, good. On fifteen dollars a week I couldn't be too luxurious. Kahlo's turned out to be a gold mine, for I used it, complete, in my first novel, Dawn O'Hara, written four years later. Kahlo's was a decent three-story brick house directly across from the pleasant Courthouse Square. I never have seen anyone work with such a fury of energy as the lean gaunt Mrs. Kahlo. She cooked, cleaned, showed rooms, managed the place. Her hair was skewered in a tight knob that seemed to pull the skin away from her eyes. She wore clean gingham, and I never saw her without an apron and rolled-up sleeves. Herr Kahlo, true to the tradition of boarding-house ladies' husbands, was the ornamental end of the partnership. I never saw him work, except that occasionally you might behold him setting a very special dish—an Apfel Pfannkuchen or an extra wienerschnitzel—before a favored guest, with a flourish. He wore bright blue suits, sported a waxed Kaiser Wilhelm mustache, ushered the guests to their places in the dining room or sat chatting with them at table, a sociable glass of beer at his elbow. Perhaps he did the marketing. Certainly the food was excellent and plentiful enough to have been bought by one who liked good living and easy going.

Except for an occasional trip to Chicago I never had been away from home alone over a period of more than a few days. I wasn't lonely or apprehensive for a moment. I was enormously exhilarated. Every move was adventure. My first room at Kahlo's seemed fabulously luxurious, but my grandeur was only temporary. My permanent room, commensurate with my purse, was unavailable for the moment, and I was therefore regally lodged in temporary quarters. It turned out that my permanent bedroom, much lower-priced, could be reached only by passing through the kitchen. I didn't mind. It was a clean-scoured kitchen, full of fine smells. This room of mine boasted a fireplace in which I rather furtively took to burning bits of wood, old magazines and newspapers, lolling romantically before the brief blaze, until the fire-engine company dashed up and I discovered that I was about to burn the house down, the fireplace and chimney being intended more for ornament than use. I made up my mind that if ever I built a house I'd have a fireplace in practically every room. (The house is just built. And there they are. Life is truly a wonderful thing.) I never had had a bedroom to myself. This first one looked like a ballroom. My scant wardrobe was lost in the vast clothes closet with its forest of bristling hooks. This, I felt, was Life. This was the Girl Reporter in her proper setting.

At Kahlo's, as at home in Appleton, dinner was served at noon, supper at night. That held true in most Milwaukee households. Milwaukee businessmen, other than those owning the big department stores on Grand Avenue and Wisconsin Street, locked their shops at noon, went home to a huge hot dinner, then composed themselves for an hour's nap on the sofa, the open sheets of the day's Germania spread over their faces to keep the flies away.

Kahlo's dining room might have been a pension in Berlin or Munich. I put on a fresh shirtwaist and went down to supper. A roar of guttural conversation stopped as I entered the dining room. It was not that the Kahlo boarders were struck dumb by my beauty. It was their disconcerting way of taking stock of a newcomer. In silence Herr Kahlo ushered me to my solitary table. Forks were suspended in mid-air, spectacles turned like searchlights upon me, knobby foreheads glistened in my direction.

"Wer ist das?"

"Nichts schönes."

"Hm. Neues Mädchen. Hi, Karl! Etwas neues!"

I understand German. Not flattering.

They were, for the most part, engineers imported from Germany, employed in the huge works of the Allis Chalmers Company in South Milwaukee; in the Cutler-Hammer Company, or any of a dozen big steel works or engineering plants in and about Milwaukee. They had bulging foreheads, their hair was shaved or worn en brosse, many of them wore beards and thick spectacles, their neckties were echt Deutsch, they were brilliant technicians, they were the worst-mannered lot I'd ever encountered. An occasional engineering wife was meek, deferential and frumpy. Supper was buttery, German and good. Kalter aufschnitt with kartoffel salat, or wienerschnitzel with Germanfried. The floor was carpetless and clean, there was a stand of hardy potted plants in the bay window, the walls were ornamented with colored pictures showing plump bare-armed serving girls being chucked under the chin by mustached lieutenants in splendid uniforms. The men drank beer with their meals and read the Milwaukee Staats-Zeitung and the Germania.

One heard practically no English spoken. Herr Kahlo had assured me that, while he spoke English very well, still, in Milwaukee, "it gives meistens German." It did give mostly German, indeed.

After supper I went upstairs and wrote home a ten-page letter bursting with description.

That first glimpse of the Milwaukee Journal office was disillusioning. They were even then erecting a new building on Fourth Street, just off Grand Avenue. The present building was a ramshackle dirty brick affair on Michigan and Milwaukee streets. As at the Crescent office we were here jumbled together in a heap. The city room was dark, dusty, crowded. The city editor, the sporting editor, reporters, stenographers worked amidst incredible racket and seeming confusion. I thought it was wonderful.

At that time the Milwaukee Journal was a very yellow bulletin afternoon paper. Edition after edition rolled off the presses from eleven in the morning until three in the afternoon. When something enormous broke in the way of news there were later editions. To this day my brain is freshest between the hours of eight and three. After three it seems to click off as though extinguished by an electric switch. That comes of working during my formative years on an afternoon paper. A fiction writer trained on a morning paper usually finds his mind keenest at night.

It was a good training course, that paper, but brutal. My fifteen a week did not come unearned. Three or four of the staff stood out as definite characters. Campbell, the managing editor, turned out to be not only Scotch, but dour. His name was Henry, but I always spoke of him as Haggis (behind his back). Lou Simonds, the city editor, could have gone on in a play just as he was, complete. He was young, massive, powerful; a slave driver. He wore a green eyeshade, a blue shirt with no collar, his sleeves were rolled above his great elbows, his pink face was always smeared with ink or lead. In one mighty fist he usually carried a wad of copy paper, his pants were inadequately sustained by a leather belt out of whose precarious clutch they appeared always on the verge of slipping. This, together with his rather portly stomach, gave his costume a vaguely Egyptian effect.

He swore fluently, but not offensively. Nothing he did was offensive, for he was a really superb fellow and a great newspaperman. His method was nerve-racking. When you came in with a hot story he would stand over your typewriter with a huge pair of desk scissors in his hand, and as you wrote he snipped the typed bits off your machine and thrust them at the waiting copy boy to be rushed to the composing room. If you delayed a split second he yelled, "Hell, what d'you think this is—a weekly! Come on, now. Get it out!"

The paper was a miracle of condensation. It used the bulletin method. Most stories were worth a stick or two only. A stick is a printer's metal frame holding type. There was a saying in the Journal office that a murder rated one stick, a massacre two. By noon, when the city room was crackling with typewriters at which the reporters sat turning out their morning's grist, you would hear Simonds' bellow above the din: "Keep it down now, fellas! . . . Boil it! . . . Shave it! Na-a-a, Cook, don't get fancy. . . . Heh, waddy yuh think this is—a weekly!"

On the copy desk Distelhorst's blue pencil slashed like a Turk's scimitar. You learned to make one word do duty for ten. You began to search your very vitals for the right first word for that first paragraph. It was a city-room rule that the gist of your story must be packed into that first paragraph, and the paragraph must be brief. When I ceased to be a reporter and became a writer of fiction I found the habit of condensation so fixed that fifteen hundred or two thousand words covered any short-story idea I might have. The stories contained in my first book of short stories, Buttered Side Down, could only have been written by an ex-newspaper reporter.

By far the most picturesque and altogether engaging person about the Journal office was the little sports editor, Wallie Rowland. Wallie was much more than sports editor—he was a sort of unofficial general guiding spirit, though he would have denied this fact. He knew every inch of the newspaper business from the delivery alley to the office of Niemann, the proprietor of the Journal. He signed his stuff Brownie, and he was known all over Wisconsin. Thin, small-boned, swarthy, of Welsh descent, curly black hair, enormous black eyes in a sallow pointed face. His face was somber until he smiled his peculiarly winning smile, which transformed him. The women in the office all cooed over Wallie, but he played no favorites. Even Edith Crombie, the society editor, an old society gal herself, who came in daily at the elegant hour of eleven wafting a delicate scent into the gritty city room and wearing always the most immaculate of lemon chamois gloves, condescended to Wallie, though she spoke to no one else. Wallie called her Edie and slapped her English tweed shoulders and she beamed frostily. At the age of six Wallie had sold papers on a downtown corner. Then he got a Journal job as office boy.

Half the time he had slept at night on a pile of old papers and sacks in a warm corner of the pressroom. Occasionally he would be sent out with the photographer to carry the tripod and pretty soon he himself was staff photographer. He knew more ball players, fighters and horsemen than the sports editor himself. He never went out of the building that he didn't come back with a story. He used to take a hand in the sports department on rush days. He became sports editor. He could operate a linotype, he could act as managing editor in Campbell's absence, and did. His conversation was droll, wise, witty, laconic. He was partial to gaudy habiliments. His shirts, ties, socks and shoes bordered on the fantastic, but in the office he wore a disreputable out-at-elbows coat that was little more than a ragged bundle of tobacco burns, mucilage spots and ink. His office visitors were likely to be battered gentlemen with cauliflower ears, husky voices, brown derbies, and noses that swerved in odd directions, unexpectedly. Also ladies very bright as to hair and general color effect. He kept a revolver, loaded, in his desk drawer and had a disconcerting way of twirling it absent-mindedly on one forefinger as he sat back in his swivel chair, his feet propped high. No one knew what risky devious paths intersected little Wallie's life that he should have this grim weapon of defense; but it wasn't there for fun.

When we collected dimes and quarters for a devil's-food cake sent round from the Princess Restaurant it always was cut in Wallie's office, the portions firmly dissected with a piece of string held taut. He never drank. He smoked a virulent pipe whose bowl was shaped like a miniature automobile. There came to me more knowledge, warmth and companionship from my association with Wallie Rowland than from anyone I had ever known until that time. In my first novel, Dawn O'Hara, he appears in the romantic (I hope) character of Blackie.

Fortunately the Journal office was within walking distance of Kahlo's. By eight or eight-thirty I was at work. I stayed almost four years on the paper, doing a man-size job which, at the end, pretty well wrecked my health for a year, and which certainly has affected it in all the years thereafter. I loved every minute of it, and I'd do it all over again.

It was part of my duties to cover the morning nine-o'clock police court with Cook, when the dirt of the streets was swept in from the night before. In the foul-smelling room off the courtroom there always was huddled a motley pitiable crew of petty criminals, prostitutes, drunks, pickpockets, vagrants; all the flotsam and jetsam of the night streets in a town of four or five hundred thousand.

Thirty days. Thirty days. Thirty days. The judge rapped it out, monotonously. The bedraggled girls had the paint and mascara of the night before on their unwashed faces and stale cheap perfume emanated from the crushed finery. The faces of the men had the blank and secret look of those who have learned the prison lesson of keeping their mouths shut and their sensibilities from registering anything but sullen resentment. Outside corridors and courtroom benches were usually crowded with weeping or voluble relatives or hangers-on, or shyster lawyers. I was not yet nineteen, I had lived most of my life in the small-town atmosphere, mine was an intelligent middle-class family of taste. My year and a half on the Appleton Crescent had been a kindergarten. Now I was smack up against the real school of life.

That daily morning police court was—and is—a terrible indictment of civilized society. Vaguely I sensed this. Once, in the very beginning, when I spoke a word of pity or remonstrance a tobacco-chewing bailiff said, "Aw, don't worry yourself about them there. They earn it easy."

"They do not!" I snapped, feeling very superior. He laughed.

Juvenile court was another assignment. In these stories we were, humanely enough, forbidden to use the names of first-offense minors. The phrase "sob sister" to describe a newspaper woman feature writer had come in. Juvenile court stories were sob-sister stuff. About an old courtroom in daily use there is a distinctive smell that, to one accustomed to it, cannot be mistaken. It is an odor of unwashed bodies, unaired garments, tobacco, dust, and despair or fright. For the human body gives off certain odors under various emotions, as the glands function. The courtroom smell is the smell of the underprivileged; the worried poor folks smell.

It was a fine breaking-in for me—the Schandein case. After that anything to which I was assigned seemed mild and fragrant. In those first days Cook and I covered the case turn and turn about; he would be out in the corridor telephoning his stuff into the waiting office while I held the fort. When he returned I dashed to the telephone to dictate my story to the waiting stenographer. I had to make a reasonably coherent and smooth-running story out of my hastily scribbled notes. I was blithely ignorant of the meaning of much of the testimony.

Today city newspapers pool their stories. There is practically no such thing as a scoop. The Richard Harding Davis days when reporters beat or scooped one another have vanished before a central news office from which a story is dealt out to each paper, all of one cut. But in my Journal days it was every man for himself. It made newspaper life exciting and newspaper jobs precarious. Underpaid, overworked, it was (and perhaps still is) one of the most exhilarating occupations in the world.

Strangely enough, though Milwaukee was full of beer gardens, ranging all the way from the famous Schlitz's Palm Garden to any little saloon backroom, none of these was the favorite rendezvous of Milwaukee's newspaper fraternity. After the Press Club (men only) it was Martini's that claimed their patronage. Though the name has a racy sound, Martini's was nothing more than a little German bakery and coffee house over on East Water Street. I described it at length in Dawn O'Hara. It was a part of the newspaper life of my Milwaukee. The shop occupied the front, facing the street. The café was behind this. Before noon the pastry trays began to come up. No real meals were served. One could have only cakes and coffee or chocolate. The newspaper and theatrical people began to drop in at four in the afternoon or thereabouts. Milwaukee had clung to the old-country custom of coffee and cakes in midafternoon. Mr. and Mrs. Martini were Alsatians. That flaky confection, custard or cream-filled, known the world over as a Napoleon, was called a Bismarck at Martini's. There were acres of cakes and kuchens—coffee rings, bund-kuchen, apple, plum, apricot kuchens, cream-filled horns (hörnchen, in German; similar in shape to the French croissant, but richer). Practically every edible thing in Milwaukee was filled or ornamented with whipped cream. They put cream in the marinated herring, cream in the sauerkraut, in the soup. Their figures were frightful. In the back room were small marble-topped tables, a huge stove glowed in the middle of the room in winter, on the wall were racks holding German newspapers and magazines: Jugend, Die Woche, Fliegende Blätter. Chess games went on indefinitely. Oceans of coffee and rich chocolate topped with whipped cream were consumed, together with tons of buttery cakes. Here you found the afternoon newspapermen when their day's grist was in, and the morning newspapermen fortifying themselves for the night's work. The actors and actresses from the Pabst Theater German stock company had tables sacred to their use. These were a vivacious and picturesque crew, frumpy, voluble, self-absorbed.

Your coffee or chocolate was served you, but you armed yourself with plate and fork and foraged for your own pastries. Here at Martini's I spent many a late afternoon hour with Wallie. The reporters on the German newspapers seemed to live there.

Martini's has gone grand. The massive crockery (you could just manage to get your lips over the thick cup edge) has become china, the old East Water Street stand (even that is now North Water) has been abandoned. Like many pleasant institutions, it went with the war.

Somehow, I made out on my fifteen a week. Free theater tickets often came my way through the office. My clothes were made in Appleton. My room with board came to about eight dollars a week. I simply did without most things. What I could not afford—and what could I not afford!—I simply ignored. About every two or three weeks I went home to Appleton by train, a distance of over one hundred miles. Sometimes I had enough money for this trip; sometimes I hadn't. But I had to see my invalid father; he counted on my coming. At such times I committed the only deliberately dishonest act of which I have been consciously guilty. I would buy a twenty-five-cent parlor-car seat ticket on the five-o'clock train and take my place grandly in green plush luxury. When the conductor came round I would hand him the parlor-car ticket with a dollar bill neatly folded beneath. Years later I sent the Northwestern Railroad what I thought I owed them. But perhaps they still can put me in jail. It was pleasant to be with my father, my mother and sister for twenty-four hours, but it was good to be back at work on Monday. I liked my new independence. Appleton, outside my own family, had lost much interest for me.

Ernest Meyer

Following in his father's tradition as a newspaperman, Ernest Meyer (1894–1952) worked for the old Socialist *Leader* in Milwaukee and was managing editor of the Madison *Capital Times*. He came to New York in the 1930s to write a column called *As the Crow Flies* for the New York *Post*. He wrote many magazine stories, among them the one that follows, which appeared in the *American Mercury* in August 1933. He also wrote two memoirs: *Yellow Back,* an account of his life in a camp for conscientious objectors during World War I, and *Bucket Boy,* his newspaper reminiscences.

Twilight of a Golden Age

When my father came to Milwaukee in 1887 there were five daily German newspapers and only two in English. The grocery and apothecary shops of the town, especially on the North and West Sides, had signs stuck in their windows reading: "English Spoken Here." Things had changed a good bit by 1910, what with the new generation forgetting their *Muttersprache,* the Poles coming closer and closer from the South Side, and the Jews buying up the once palatial homes of the burghers in Walnut street, but the old flavor still permeated the city.

We live in a double flat, nicknamed the Germania. This is because the five men who dwell in it, whether as householders or as boarders, all work in the editorial rooms of the *Germania,* the German evening newspaper. My father is the editorial writer, and with us room Kurt Pabst, a reporter, and Dr. Guido Schmidt, the telegraph editor. Pabst is short and skinny, with flaxen whiskers, and he spends almost every night of his life playing solitaire for vast, imaginary sums in his room. He takes the game very seriously. Sometimes he comes rushing in all excited. "*Herrgott!* I owe the bank $2,600! Has anybody ever seen such luck?"

Dr. Schmidt, who holds a Berlin Ph.D., has an enormous red Kaiser Wilhelm mustache which he ties up each night in a *Bartbinde*. He wears a choker collar and clicks his heels when he greets you. He is a Prussian, and the other Germans in the house make fun of him, for they are from Bavaria or Hanover, and don't take life so seriously. They hope he will lose his stance some day and trip on the tails of his cutaway, but he never does.

Upstairs lives the life of the house. He is Dolfee Doellinger, police reporter. He has a bullet head of close-cropped red hair, and a tooth-brush mustache, and is a man of extraordinary inventions. Once he found a muddy chemise under a bush in Juneau Park, and with nothing else to work on constructed a murder mystery so amazing, so crammed with dark surmises that readers of the *Germania* gasped for a week and reporters for the other newspapers cried: "Fake!" Now and then we are alarmed late at night by a fusillade of shots upstairs. It is only Dolfee shooting mice in the hallway. Then he comes down, dressed in a nightgown and top-hat, sits gravely at our piano, and plays with stubby, fat but masterful fingers.

He keeps a birthday book, and in it has the name and birthday of every city official, ward-heeler, policeman, and saloonkeeper in town. It is a slim day, indeed, in which he does not find four or five entries. So he makes the rounds, slaps Schultz, Schmidt, Sullivan and Blenski on the back and congratulates them boisterously on the great occasion. Schmidt, Schultz, Sullivan and Blenski, pleased that someone has remembered their birthday, promptly invite him to drink, and he comes home at night full of conscious rectitude and lager.

This is Monday night, and the men are at *Skat* in the kitchen. I am cramming for a high-school exam in an adjoining room, and the sound of their voices reaches me in a quiet monotone: "*Nullo . . . Passe . . . Passe . . . Null ouvert . . . Schippen Solo . . . Passe . . . Schneider. . . ."*

During a pause, my father's voice calls my name. I go into the kitchen. Nobody looks up at me; they are scowling soberly at their cards—even Dolfee, with a Turkish fez perched rakishly on his red thatch. There is a bucket on the table, and next to it a dime. I pick up the bucket and dime and steal out. I walk over to Gustav Ziegenstein's saloon, which, ironically enough, is on Cold Spring avenue. There is nobody at the bar, but Gustav and an old crony are playing chess at a corner table. They glance at me briefly, and continue with their problem. I do not dare disturb Gustav, for he has a short temper when he is bothered at chess, especially by children. I pluck a large pretzel from the bowl on the bar and munch it, while I admire for the hundredth time the enormous painting of Custer's Last Fight which covers half of the end wall.

At length Gustav moves his bishop, snorts "*Guarde!*" and rises to wait on me. He rinses the bucket, then holds it under the spurting tap, and Gettelman's Dark Brew makes a pleasing, drumming sound as it hits the bottom of the pail.

"Ten cents worth please. And father says, *bitte gut messen.*"

"Hm. *Skat* tonight, I suppose?"

"Yes. Every Monday night."

"Who is playing by your house?"

I name the players. At the mention of Dolfee, Gustav looks up angrily from under his white, tufty eyebrows.

"Dot loafer!" he cries. "Dot *Halunke!* I haf a goot mind to put in der beer some paprika!"

Gustav doesn't like Dolfee. Gustav, indeed, hasn't forgiven Dolfee since the time of Halley's comet. The papers were naturally full of the comet, and a cracked scientist prophesied that the earth would pass through its tail, and we might all be gassed. Everybody was uneasy, and especially Gustav. Dolfee learned of his tremors, and decided to have some fun. He read him imaginary extracts from newspapers telling the exact time of doom. He pointed out that he could not take his stock with him to Heaven, and Gustav, pale, shaking, agreed that was so. On the night before the Great Doom, scared out of his wits, poor Gustav gave away all his stock. The whole neighborhood was there, led by Dolfee in a monk's cassock and carrying a hymnal. . . . The next day Gustav still lived, though not so happily.

I take my pail and return home. The four are in the midst of a difficult play. My father nods his thanks, and I place the bucket next to the row of steins. I return to my chemistry book, and the monotone of *Nullo . . . Passe . . . Tournee* mingles till bedtime with the symbols for sulphuric acid and sodium chloride.

Tuesday there's always the *Männerchor*. There are nearly a hundred *Gesangvereine* in the city, and every Milwaukeean who makes pretensions to the Higher Life must belong to one, whether he can sing or not. As for me, I can't sing, but on Tuesday night I leave home with my brother-in-law, and we pick up Willie Eckhardt in the next block and take a trolley car to North avenue and Twenty-ninth street. There is a saloon there run by a man named August, and on the second floor is a meeting hall that our *Männerchor* rents from August for a dollar a night.

It is pretty well crowded when we arrive. There are forty men, young and old. Most of the bassos are enormously stout, though the fellow with the deepest voice is Weizenpfeffer, who is a skinny stringbean with a great, bobbing Adam's apple. He can boom like a bull fiddle and everybody envies him, for there is a tradition that a bull-fiddle voice indicates masculine virility. The first tenors always look a little bit sheepish, though they're strapping fellows enough.

Our director is already there, fussily waiting for the late-comers. If rehearsals fail to start on time the top of his bald head grows beet-red. He is a choleric man, with a black mustache and bright eyes that bore right through one when he is enraged. His name is Schildkrot, and in his home he is a martinet. He works himself and his family furiously; he directs three singing societies, two orchestras and a string quartette, and he's always dashing from one to the other with a worn brief-case spilling with scores. He boasts that his son, fifteen years old, can play the 'cello, trombone, fiddle and xylophone, and that his daughter, eighteen, can play the bass viol, harp, piano and violin.

I went to their home once and found that it was true that Rudy and Helga could really play all these instruments, very excellently, too, but I had never met such unhappy children. Rudy's lower lip was pulled down in a perpetual pout, and Helga, who was beautiful, with long black braids coiled at the nape of her neck, had the restless eyes of a caged lynx. They practised five hours a day, and on a good many nights each week were called out to give public or private concerts, for they were famous as child prodigies.

While Schildkrot was still our director, Rudy ran away to Texas and played the trombone for a medicine show, and not a month later Helga eloped with a dashing Hungarian who happened at the time to be directing a band in a Chestnut street palm-garden. Herr Direktor Schildkrot was laid low by the double blow, but soon recovered, and with awful imprecations swore that the children should never enter his house again. During this time he was more bristly and beet-headed than ever, and he rarely laughed. But when, a year or so later, Helga bobbed up with a boy baby, he forgave her in a really noble speech. Helga was rarely seen in public after that; she preferred sitting home, playing the 'cello, and the Herr Direktor was late at a good many rehearsals because he lingered so long in the nursery tooting a toy horn for the baby. He was no longer so choleric as he had been in the past, so we were all very glad for Helga's baby.

But these things happened later. Tonight Herr Schildkrot is in a dour mood. We are ten minutes late in getting started, and he launches a torrent of abuse at poor Kranzel, the youngest second tenor, who slinks downcast to his place. The scores have been passed out, and Schildkrot taps smartly with his baton on the metal music stand. We are singing "Hans und Liesel," and launch forth with a booming

> *Und der Hans schleicht umher,*
> *Truebe Augen, blasse Wangen. . . .*

but we are interrupted by a sharp crack of the baton, and find the Herr Direktor clawing the air with his hands.

"Miserable!" he roars. "*Takt falsch!* And it should be *moderato,* not *crescendo. Himmel!* You are singing about a love-sick boy with pale cheeks, and you roar like a pack of lions in mating time. *Dummkopfe!* Now, begin again, please."

He gives us the pitch, and we're off once more. We struggle through the stanza again and again, lashed by the Herr Direktor's caustic tongue. We are close-packed in the little hall. It is growing very hot, even though it is Winter and the windows are open. At last we sing the song to his satisfaction, and the Herr Direktor allows us five minutes' pause while we tumble down the stairs to August's bar and lap up beer with thirsty throats. The Herr Direktor does not come with us: it would not be dignified for a man in his position. But August's bartender fetches him a stein upstairs, and it leaves him a bit milder.

Then we fight our way through "Gebet vor der Schlacht," and when the last solemn verse is ended we visit August again. We sing—or think we sing—with more spirit, more abandonment as the evening wears on, and when the two hours are up and the Herr Direktor collects his scores and goes home, we adjourn to August's for good—and then we really sing. Such singing! It brings tears to our eyes; it makes our bosoms swell with the sense of high accomplishment; we feel that we are serving Art with noble passion.

"*Ach,*" booms Weizenpfeffer, "that last song was perfect! There is no other *Männerchor* in Milwaukee that can sing it with such feeling."

We believe him. He is lank as a stringbean, but he has the deepest basso in town, and such men speak the truth.

On Wednesday night there is always a performance at the Pabst Theater. To miss it is unthinkable. We buy season tickets, and from October to May go each Wednesday to sink in red plush and weep and laugh. There is no better stock company anywhere in America; the players come direct from the Berlin Stadttheater, and are renewed each year with fresh talent. On Saturday and Sunday nights they put on frothy stuff—light operas, comedies, farces and such—but on Wednesdays they don their buskins and tread the stage in graver measures. Goethe, Schiller, Shakespeare, Hauptmann, Sudermann, Strindberg, Ibsen, von Hoffmansthal, Hebbel, Schnitzler, Molnar,—what a roster of great names, great plays, what nights to be remembered!

Tonight everyone feels especially expectant. We are going to see the first part of the "König Heinrich" trilogy. It is ponderous, it is slow-moving, but it is heroic and soul-filling—a dramatic joint of beef. It begins with the young prince, and it ends with the pilgrimage of the beaten King to Canossa to hunger three days in the cold and beg his boon of the Pope. It has fifteen acts, and will take three nights.

Later on we will hear of an upstart modernist named O'Neil whose plays run into two performances, crammed into a matinée and evening, and we will remember the three fat nights of "König Heinrich" and chuckle to ourselves. What has the English stage to offer that can match it? *Himmel,* don't you know that Shaw's "Pygmalion" was produced for the first time in America, not in English but in German—and in this same red-plush old Pabst Theater? Yes, that is so, even though it is difficult, to say the least, for a German heroine to speak London cockney.

So we settle in our seats in the balcony amid a buzz of chatter. Everyone knows everyone else, for this is subscriber's night. Every Wednesday we know exactly who will sit to our right, to our left, and behind and in front of us. Yet each Wednesday we shake hands solemnly with our neighbors and launch a cannonade of small talk as if we had not seen them in seven years.

"*Ach,* Frau Braunschweig. It is so good to see you again. I really must come and call on you one day."

"On my next *Kaffeeklatsch,* Frau Beyer, I shall most certainly call you on the telephone. You have never tried my *Blitzkuchen.* And how is your Waldemar's rheumatism?"

There is a running about, as people flit up and down the aisles to shake hands with old cronies, former sweethearts, business friends. Only Old Hermann Suelze doesn't budge. Hermann weighs perhaps 300 pounds. He bulks prodigiously on an aisle seat. He subscribes each year to two seats, to take care of the overflow.

There is a certain constraint, or self-consciousness, in the lower boxes. Here sit the élite, the great ones, who are patrons of the theater and yearly contribute large sums to it so that Milwaukee may have a playhouse of which one can boast. That fine dame in white satin, for instance —well, she inherited her wealth from a man who came to Milwaukee half a century ago and laid the foundation of his fortune by brewing each day three barrels of lager beer and peddling them himself in a wheelbarrow. Too bad the poor barrow-pusher isn't here tonight to see the grand theater which his money helps support, and to feast his eyes on the dame in white satin. But no man lives forever.

The curtain rises. Everybody is glad that Konrad Bolton and Berthold Sprotte are cast in major rôles. They are favorites, but every member of the company is well-loved. They are all great actors, but there is nothing highty-tighty about them. They make friends everywhere; they have often been to our house, where they sang and joked, while I stood goggle-eyed in admiration at the chesty Berthold, who only a week before I had seen murdered in "Macbeth." There he was, eating a Bismarck herring as lively as you please.

In the long intermission, all the men arise and file downstairs to the buffet, while the women and children remain behind and fill the theater with their shrill voices. In the buffet there is Pabst on tap, and an excellent free lunch. Two minutes before the curtain rises a bell clangs, and the men file upstairs again, wiping their mustaches.

After the performance it is the women's turn. The men must go with them then to Martini's, a block from the theater. It is a confectioner's shop, specializing in *Schaumtorte, Apfelkuchen, Marzipan,* thick chocolate with whipped cream, and strong coffee. During the day old men play chess at the little tables, but they clear out for the Wednesday night invasion. After a bit, some of the actors come in, and the groups at the tables fight for the honor of claiming them. The long, narrow room throbs with talk; little screams of laughter cut through the haze of cigar smoke.

And there, of all people, is the giant Berthold. Not a moment ago he had paced the stage in ermine, heaping regal wrath on the head of the prince, and here he is booming his big laugh while he plucks a fragile pastry from a tray carried by a red-cheeked waitress. I stare in amazement. He is winking at her. The King is flirting with a commoner!

On Thursday when I return from high-school Mother says: "Go into the cellar, child, and find a sack. Then take a car to Steinmeyer's and see if you can buy some red cabbage. I need about eight large, firm heads. If Steinmeyer has none, go to all the stores in State and Chestnut streets until you have your eight heads."

"Eight heads of cabbage is an awful lot," I say.

"Fritz von Pagel is coming," she replies simply. "He has just come to town, and he telephoned me he would like to have supper with us. He is bringing everything else, but he was unable to find red cabbage. And that, you know, is his *Leibgericht.*"

Fritz von Pagel! What a feast there will be tonight, then. The thought lends agility to my heels, and I dash for the sack, thinking of that great and mysterious man. He is enormous, with a shaved head and keen eyes behind his glasses. While he was still in Germany he and his three brothers inherited a great landed estate. What luxury after the stern discipline of *Gymnasium!* The four brothers lived like feudal barons. They entertained often and lavishly. They bought blooded horses. They bought regal furnishings. Money flowed like sand through their fingers. Soon they had spent everything, down to the last copper. They pawned what remained of their property and sailed for America. In the next twenty years one of the brothers became an affluent public official. Another committed suicide. A third ended as a sheepherder in Montana. And Fritz—

Well, Fritz was sometimes up and sometimes down. He was a promoter of great enterprises. Sometimes they failed, and he lived on a crust; sometimes they succeeded, and he regained his lost flesh. At such times he bought gifts. Once he gave my mother a huge, gold-plated, filigree four-poster bed, much too fine for any of us, though it was a thing to show off to the neighbors. Another time he brought a set of Haviland China, exquisitely hand-decorated with the von Pagel crest.

Just now he was up high and talked in millions. With Chicago and Milwaukee capital he was promoting a huge irrigation enterprise in the Western desert. He made flying visits to Milwaukee, and always came to eat with us, bringing loads of edibles, for he hated the stuff they served in hotels. And such small portions!

So I find my sack and joyfully take the trolley car to Steinmeyer's. But they have no red cabbage. It is just out of season. I go to Schultz's. Schultz has two precious heads, and he takes a personal interest in my quest. He realizes it is most important.

"Eight heads! Hm! Well, I'll give you these two, and I'll call up Braun and Zwillig and Ebers. You just wait."

He comes back from the telephone triumphant. Braun has three heads and Zwillig has three more. I dash off at top speed and collect them. At length I have my eight heads, round and firm and shining, and board the trolley again with the sack over my shoulder.

When I reach home, there is Fritz von Pagel. He has just driven up in a cab, and mother is helping him unload a heap of things. I help. A whole baked ham, fresh from Dernehl's ovens. A great frosted potato-cake. Cans of caviar, *Sardellen*, anchovies and smoked goose-breast. A Liederkranz cheese, very fragrant. A wooden box of *fromage de Brie*, more so. A straw-covered flask of chianti. A bottle of port. A large pumpernickel.

Enough for an army, I think. But mother knows better. Once Fritz, in one of his Milwaukee ventures, boarded with us.

"And the *Rotkraut!*" he asks anxiously when we have carried everything into the house.

"I got it downtown," I say proudly. "Eight heads. I went to three stores."

Fritz beams at me, rubbing his hands. His shaved head, set atop his great shoulders and paunch, looks like an egg balanced on a pumpkin.

"Now, that is fine," he says. "You have done well. For months out West I have dreamed of your mother's red cabbage. So, then, here is something for you."

He fishes into his coat pocket and hands me a package. There is a necktie in it. Made from a real rattlesnake skin. I thank him and dash out to show it to Willie Eckhardt, who has nothing half so astonishing.

When I return, supper is ready. It lasts all evening. Now and then there is a pause, then everybody starts again. Father, the two boarders and Fritz von Pagel shine with bliss; and I and my two sisters wait impatiently for the potato-cake. Mother has cooked the eight red cabbages in two big iron pots, flavoring them with apples, a bit of bacon, and the right dash of vinegar. The bowls of long, glistening shreds vanish one after the other; the cabbage melts in your mouth. The ham is almost gone. The caviar, *Sardellen,* anchovies and smoked goose-breast were mere palate-ticklers before the meal really started. It is incredible, but the platters are at last all clean, and Fritz von Pagel is still alive, and almost purring. Then the cake goes, too, and mother brings pots of coffee and the cheese and pumpernickel.

Fritz von Pagel leans back, lights a cigar and ruminates aloud.

"When such meals are no more, men will be no more," he says. "What women our modern men are already becoming! Who were the biggest and bravest men? The Vikings! And such eaters! Ah, when I read of their feasts my eyes go dim with sadness and my mouth puckers with desire. America is becoming a race of *Waschweiber.* Look, I have seen with my own eyes what is happening. In the big cities they are starting something new—cafeterias, they call them; maybe you have one of these horrors even in Milwaukee. You run in a line, like a machine, and pick food hastily from the shelves. And what food! Colored salads, a little leaf of lettuce with a *Happchen* of potato-salad on it. Or maybe a dozen peas. Imagine! A real man can eat half a head of lettuce and a pint of vinegar just as an entrée, a mere mouthful. I tell you, the thing is serious. It may well be fatal. On twelve peas you cannot raise even a race of rabbits. *Abscheulich!*"

He stares moodily into his glass of chianti, then brightens.

"*Nu*—let us drink a toast to cabbages—and Kings!"

The men clink glasses. Mother comes in to clear the debris from the great table. She gathers the empty bowls and platters. A little mournfully,

I think. Perhaps she had thought there would be a little warmed-over cabbage for tomorrow's lunch.

On Sunday afternoon the whole family goes to hear Christian Bach's orchestra at the West Side Turnerhalle. It is not proper to miss it; besides, it costs only fifteen cents on a season ticket, and the music fits in with the slumbrous Sabbath feeling that follows a dinner of *Knödel* and *Sauerbraten*. It is that kind of music, soothing and sensible—and not the type of Gershwin *staccato* that never helped a man digest an honest meal.

Also, the setting is meant for relaxation. There are tables and chairs on the floor, and when we come in the hall is already misty with cigar smoke that drifts in layers in the shafts of light from the high windows. A door off to one end leads into the long barroom, and from it bustle waiters laden with steins, while from a kitchen in the rear waitresses bring trays of coffee and cakes for the women and children.

The air is comforting with the fragrance of hops, coffee and tobacco. Combined with the music of Suppé and Strauss it induces a benign expansiveness in which one feels like taking the world to one's bosom, even including Old Petrus Grimm, who sits alone at a table with his dour eyes fastened on his beer-mug. Petrus is the neighborhood bear, and everybody blames his bitterness on a blighted romance in the Old Country, though it is more likely due to liver and gout.

Up on the stage, Christian Bach does well with his thirty-five men. Direktor Bach is old and very short, but agile, which is a bad thing when the tempo is swift or he works to coax the woodwinds into nobler effort. At such times his wig turns half way around on his head and protrudes at such a curious angle that few can blame the children for tittering, even though such levity is sternly rebuked. The musicians have learned not to smile at these crises, for Herr Bach has a peppery temper. Besides, they are fond of him. He has been teaching them music since they were in knee-pants, and his son, Hugo, a splendid 'cellist, will carry on after him, and so on and on, world without end.

This thought is at the back of our minds: the thought of continuity, of tradition, of certain tomorrows bringing their certain, well-savored joys. But during the intermission Old Petrus brings his beer-mug and his melancholy slanting eyebrows over to our table and sits with us, and then we are no longer sure of anything. My parents and my sisters and I stir a little uneasily, for Petrus makes us feel somehow insecure.

"Look," he says, waving his hand to the balcony above us. "Once more it is empty."

We look, and sure enough there are only half a dozen people sitting up there. We remember when the benches were well filled, mostly with young couples who liked to sit in the shadows listening to the dreamy music and holding hands.

"That is what we're coming to," mourns Old Petrus, stroking his beard. "Where are the young people this afternoon? Are they here, listening to decent music? No. They are in the nickel-shows. *Ach,* imagine such trash-heaps! And now, I am told, they are building one even on our North Side. Our children will forget our language, our music, our art; these concerts are dying already, and soon they will close the German Theater and our turnerhalls, and all because we let our young people go to the nickel-shows just to see one funny fellow hit another funny fellow with a pie in the face."

We laugh, but when the music begins again we grow thoughtful. Can it be that Old Petrus is right? Who are upholding the traditions; who are the leaders in the old ways? We think of Christian Bach, Brosius, our venerable gymnastics teacher; Heine, the artist who gives me lessons Saturdays, and a dozen others. All old men, creaking a bit. Already the new generation is walking strange paths; yearly the theater deficit grows larger; the loud, brassy cabarets with their barbaric cocktails are drawing young patrons from the Widow Heiser's mellow tavern. And in the rooms of the Deutscher Club one hears, alack, more and more a tongue that should be alien to its corridors. Maybe Old Petrus is right.

But *Teufel!* That is only the gossip of old women, male and female. This glorious life will endure; it is built too solidly to be destroyed by innovation. Thus we think when, on Sunday night, we gather at the tables of Mamma Memmler's *Gasthaus* in Sherman street. It is across the street from Schlitz Park, where, in Summertime, music flows from the bandstand and an old blind horse drags the carousel round and round and round. Tonight the snow lies deep on the pavilion tops, and the park gates are locked, but in Mamma Memmler's place everything is laughter and light. The walls are gaily painted with troubadours, fat monks, and mottoes: *Gut Heil! . . . Es Lebe das Leben! . . . Wer nicht liebt Wein, Weib und Gesang. . . .* And in a prominent place is hung the framed original copy of a poem by Eugene Field, written in that very place when the rascal tarried in Milwaukee years ago. The poem is about Mamma Memmler's two daughters, who were beautiful children then. They are young women now, and still beautiful, and I adore them, Clara and Meta.

The tables are crowded. I know everyone; each has a *Stammtisch,* and they are here every Sunday. There is the artists' table, where Heine, Lorenz and Peters call for their Riesling. There is the musicians' group, with our *Männerchor* director resting for the first time in a week, and near it is the actors' table, where Berthold Sprotte hoists a stein and sings a comic song, while his wife, the contralto, hums an accompaniment. And there is the newspaper men's table, with Dolfee Doellingen wearing his Turkish fez, and the seven-Prussian frown of Dr. Guido Schmidt melted into a laugh that shakes the tips of his Kaiser mustache.

All are here; all fit into the pattern of the good week. Here is where the loose laurels are gathered into a crown to fit Bacchus. The taps at the little bar fizz; Mamma Memmler brings on the lunch—a whole roast porker tonight—and the platter is saluted by a salvo of hochs. I sit at the table with Clara and Meta, playing dominoes badly, for the sisters are distractingly beautiful. The air grows heavy with smoke. Some one throws open a window.

I look out at the frozen trees and pavilion tops in the park across the street. The dome of the bandstand looks like a white helmet sticking above the fence. There is snow everywhere, heavy and glittering under the corner lamps, and strangely friendly.

KANSAS CITY
(*Missouri*)

———◆———

*Kansas City, Missouri, was a city that grew up fast. In 1860
it had a population of about 4500. By 1905 it had already
become the Gateway to the Southwest, a major metropolis
of 250,000, humming with river and rail activities. "As a
multiple railway terminus," says Virgil Thomson, recalling
his Kansas City boyhood, "it offered welcome equally to
old Confederates, to business families from Ohio and New
England, to German farmers, brewers from Bavaria, cattlemen from Colorado and the West, to miners, drummers. . . ." His list goes on and on and is a catalog of the
transient America of the period.*

*Among the travelers who came to Kansas City in 1905
were Edward Dahlberg and his mother, who established
herself as a lady barber in a shop near the Grand Opera
House downtown. Her customers included businessmen
and politicians, one of whom, according to the author, was
the young Harry Truman.*

Edward Dahlberg

Edward Dahlberg had an itinerant childhood that took him from
Boston, where he was born in 1900, to Louisville, Memphis, New
Orleans, and by the time he was six, to Kansas City, Missouri, which
is the setting for his first novel, *Bottom Dogs*. From the time it was
published in England in 1929, with an introduction by D. H. Lawrence, it has been known to a small faithful group of admirers. Dahlberg has achieved wider recognition in recent years as a critic and
teacher. His autobiography, *Because I Was Flesh* (1963), from which
the selection below is reprinted, was described by Alfred Kazin as
"one of the few important American books published in our day."

from Because I Was Flesh

In 1905 they came to Kansas City; it was a wide-open town; there were
more sporting houses and saloons than churches. The stews were as far out
as Troost Avenue. When a bachelor or a stale codger was in sore need of
easing himself, he looked about for a sign in the window which said:
Transient Rooms or *Light Housekeeping*. A brakeman on the M-K-T
knew where he could get a glass of beer for a nickel, which also entitled
him to a free lunch of hard-boiled eggs with pretzels and Heinz ketchup.
The streets were cobblestoned hills, and their names were April songs of
feeling: Walnut, Locust, Cherry, Maple, Spruce and Oak.

The town was not a senseless Babel: the wholesale distillers were on
Wyandotte, the commission houses stood on lower Walnut, hustlers for a
dollar an hour were on 12th and pimps loitered in the penny arcades
between 8th and 5th on Main Street. If one had a sudden inclination for
religion he could locate a preacher in a tented tabernacle of Shem beneath the 8th Street viaduct, and if he grew weary of the sermons, there
was a man a few yards away who sold Arkansas diamonds, solid gold cuff
links, dice, and did card tricks. Everybody said that vice was good for
business, except the Christian Scientists and the dry Sunday phantoms
who lived on the other side of the Kaw River in Kansas City, Kansas.

The great Missouri River on which Kansas City, Missouri, lay, once
known as the *Concepción* in honor of the Virgin Mary, was as dissolute as
the inhabitants. There was a lusty steamboat trade on the Missouri, and
freighters plied between St. Louis, Kansas City and New Orleans. Country boys from Topeka and Armourdale came to Kansas City to get work in

the stockyards and in the Armour and Swift packing houses; and chicks, with rosy, jocular rumps, arrived in hordes from St. Joseph and Joplin.

One could take a nickel streetcar ride to Swope or Fairmount Parks; on an Indian summer evening, when the crickets sang in the tall, speared grass or in the oak branches, workmen in trade-union denims and overalls sat on the porches to take the air and say hello to a switchman or an acquaintance who had a job in the West Bottoms.

When business was dead and the Dog Star had parched the melons, dried up the heifers and the white leghorns, and prices were high, many blamed William Howard Taft. In the Teddy Roosevelt days butter had been eighteen cents a pound, milk was five cents a quart and eggs were ten cents a dozen.

When Lizzie came to Kansas City there was one lady barbershop on Walnut which was three doors from the ticket office of the Burlington Railroad. The proprietor of the place was a round-shouldered, cranky man barber who had an interest in the barber college located on Delaware Street. After six weeks of training at the barber college a green farm girl would be hired as an apprentice; she received no wages for the first three months and had to depend upon tips from customers. Usually no more than seventeen years of age, she attracted a great deal of trade. A stockman or a smart drummer from out of town would rather get a manicure from a lady barber than go to the Orpheum for an evening of big-time vaudeville. The odor of witch hazel, hair tonic and face powder, and the motions of the girls, who wore tight corsets, inflamed an old rounder. When a railroader got into the chair of a country trollop, he felt that he would perish from pleasure when she removed the lather from his jaw with her small finger.

These farm girls were as wild as Semiramis; but if they found out that they had a clumsy simpleton on their hands or an indefatigable curmudgeon who had already used up a wife with a hanging udder and five children, they would make him cough up a few hundred dollars. They did not care very much about an ordinary masher or a codger but they would support a curly-haired Adonis who knew how to chew Spearmint gum and smoke Turkish Hassan cigarettes with the air of one who had had enough amours to have set Ilium on fire.

No lecher was so intolerable as a skinflint. A lady barber took the greatest delight in being courted although she had no thought of a wedding. She liked to go to a good show, say to the Gillis Theatre for a wild West performance; if she craved refinement she preferred *Beverly of Graustark* or a swell burlesque at the Grand Opera House. Supper at an oyster house and a night at Electric Park were exciting; when a city alderman or the owner of a big livery stable took a girl out to Cliff Drive for a buggy ride, she talked about it for a whole week.

It was the time when women went to law for heart balm, and when breach-of-promise suits were exceedingly popular. A lady in sound health, who had locked all her hopes of marriage in her breast, had no hesitation in divulging them in court if she felt a man had been so low and rotten as to deceive her. There was hardly a judge sitting on the bench who was so callous as not to have considerable feeling for the delicacy of her heart. If a bachelor was foolhardly enough to be seen with a woman in public, or worse, to take an embittered spinster of thirty to Swope Park, and after that denied he was engaged to her, he was undone. He was sure to be seethed in the marriage-pot, and should he prove too tough for boiling except in some illicit hotel room, he was compelled to pay for the honor of the woman he had never desecrated. A good many such triflers, or just dead beats who had gotten into woman trouble of this sort, vanished or crossed the state line and found employment in Kansas City, Kansas, so that their wages could not be garnisheed. Fast women, and ladies with the subtlest principles, preferred to speculate in men rather than risk their savings in wildcat oil or second mortgages.

There were six barber chairs in the shop on Walnut Street; a cuspidor, shaped like an Etruscan amphora, stood within reach of a man in a barber chair who wanted to spit the brown juice of his chewing tobacco into it. A shave was five cents and a haircut a dime; a good tipper gave a girl an extra ten cents for a close shave.

Lizzie was given the last chair because she had a long, Jewish nose; turned-up gentile noses were very much in style, and a dapper man who wore suspenders and was as neat as a pin and had a fine position in a meat-packing house or at the Union Depot would go mad over a barber girl with a snub nose. Quite a few embezzlers would skip town with a warm, Grecian-nosed trull from Joplin. The prettiest chits were put up front to draw in transients who happened to pass by and who had never heard of a lady barber.

The shop opened at seven in the morning to catch railroaders on their way to the yards or big loafy-faced men who auctioned off horses and mules in livery stables near the stockyards. The girls rushed to their chairs when a locomotive engineer dropped in; anybody who worked for the Santa Fe or the Burlington was rumored to be a good spender.

The barbershop was an emporium for talk, easy, warm joshing, and expectorating in the brass spittoons. Lizzie knew how to keep a customer in his place, and on occasion cut a man with her razor or dug her scissors into his ear because he had his hand on her thigh instead of underneath the haircloth.

Often the shop did not close till nine o'clock at night. She took the boy to a Catholic parochial school to learn German because she wanted him to be cultured. The school did not let out till late and that kept him off the streets.

She had to work on a commission basis, and her wages, including tips, were seven to eight dollars a week. Cutting hair and shaving cowhands, grouches and town loafers for fourteen hours was no picnic, she told her boy. Most of the time she had to stand on her feet. The man barber would not allow the help to sit, even when the place was empty on dull, rainy days. A woman seated in her chair with crossed legs or lounging on the mahogany settee looked bad and attracted the wrong kind of trade. He was particularly strict in July and August, which he claimed were the two worst months for temptation; a man was teased more in summer than in any other season. He warned the barber girls not to spit, wriggle in their bustles as they stood by their chairs and called out: "You're next, sir," or make squeaking, sensual noises with their patent-leather shoes when they stepped over to the basin to soak a towel in hot water. Smoking was positively forbidden; sporting women were easily recognized because they smoked Sweet Caporals. He cautioned the girls not to chew gum and make loud, clucking sounds with their tongues, and he would not keep a lady barber who went to the water closet too often; he said that flushing the toilet during business hours raised disorderly feelings in the customers.

He expected a barber girl to keep occupied all the time. When no one was in her chair, she had to cut the *Kansas City Star* into small square sheets on which the lather was wiped. She had to sharpen her razor on a hone and then ply it to and fro on the leather strop. There were the shaving mugs and the hairbrushes to be washed out in boiling water and the combs to be disinfected in Lysol.

Some proprietors of the genteel barbershops on Baltimore Street were thinking of raising prices because the cheaper chin-scrapers were giving the trade a bad name. People said that barber tools were dirty and carried such contagious diseases as dandruff, scarlet fever, barber's itch, boils, pimples and water on the knee. Horse swappers and common teamsters who sat on empty fruit crates in the big livery stables and swore and guffawed all afternoon claimed that one could get the pox or the clap from an unsanitary hair clipper, eyebrow tweezer or hairbrush. This kind of loose chatter could start a panic, and the owner of the place on Walnut was so uneasy that he changed the name of it to The Sanitary Barbershop.

The girls were flighty and easily discouraged, and if a lady barber thought she could not please the trade she took off her apron and quit. A lady barber was in the dumps all day if a customer had been short-tempered with her. She liked to coo into the ear of the man in her chair: "Sir, do you part your hair in the middle, or on the side? What a lady-killer's pompadour you have! How about some tonic? Or let me rub pomade into your scalp and give you a stiff hair brushing." But if he gave her a short answer: "Just leave it dry, lady, I'm in a hurry," she wept or took the afternoon off.

Lizzie rented a furnished bedchamber in a rock-ribbed house on McGee near Admiral Boulevard. McGee was a poor humble street, lined with elms, maples and oaks—what bread and meat there is in the sight of a living, green tree. There were many yards and vacant lots covered with tangled grass and rough, acrid sunflowers, and the latticed porches and sun-fed wooden steps were a comfort to people.

On her feet all day, except for a few minutes to take a quick bite or when the owner ran out for a bowl of chili, she would sink into the oak rocker as soon as she returned to the lodginghouse. She unlaced her high-top shoes, worked herself out of the corset, and removed her beige cotton stockings.

The child slept, graved in the large double bed. When she was so worn out she wondered how she would make ends meet, and then she looked about to find something to do so that she could banish such weak thoughts. She hunted for her pince-nez glasses, which she had laid on the floor, picked up a curling iron or tried to mend the yellowing corset cover.

Virgil Thomson

Composer, critic, and teacher, Virgil Thomson was born in Kansas City, Missouri, in 1896, went to Harvard and taught there as a young man, when he was also music critic for the Boston *Transcript*. From 1925 to 1934 he worked and studied in Paris, where his friendship with Gertrude Stein resulted in the use of her text for his opera *Four Saints in Three Acts* (1934). In 1936 he was appointed director of the Federal Music Project in New York. For many years he was music critic for the New York *Herald Tribune*. Among his best-known scores are those for the documentary films *The Plough that Broke the Plains, The River,* and *Louisiana Story.*

from Virgil Thomson

To anyone brought up there, as I was, "Kansas City" always meant the Missouri one. When you needed to speak of the other you used its full title, Kansas-City-Kansas; and you did not speak of it often, either, or go there unless you had business. Such business was likely to be involved with stockyards or the packing houses, which lay beyond the Kansas line in bottom land. The Union Depot, hotel life, banking, theaters, shopping —all the urbanities—were in Missouri.

So was open vice. One block on State Line Avenue showed on our side nothing but saloons. And just as Memphis and St. Louis had their Blues, we had our *Twelfth Street Rag* proclaiming joyous low life. Indeed, as recently as the 1920s H. L. Mencken boasted for us that within the half mile around Twelfth and Main there were two thousand second-story hotels. We were no less proud of these than of our grand houses, stone churches, and slums, our expensive street railways and parks, and a political machine whose corruption was for nearly half a century an example to the nation.

Kansas, the whole state, was dry. And moralistic about everything. There was even an anticigarette law. Nearly till World War II, one bought "coffin nails" under the counter and paid five cents more per pack than in Missouri. Though Kansas had always been a Free State and supported right in Kansas-City-Kansas a Negro college, most of our colored brethren preferred Missouri, where life was more fun. The truth is that Kansas was Yankee territory, windy and dry, with blue laws on its books; and the women from there wore unbecoming clothes and funny hats.

442

As for the food, a touring musician described a hotel steak with "I drew my knife across it, and it squeaked." As late as 1948, motoring west with the painter Maurice Grosser, I caused him to drive in one day from Slater, in Saline County, Missouri, to Colorado Springs, 714 miles, by insisting one must not eat or sleep in Kansas. He had yielded, he thought, to mere Missouri prejudice. But when we stopped once for coffee and a hamburger (safe enough), and noticing under a fly screen some darkish meringue-topped pies I asked the waitress what kind they were, she replied, "Peanut butter," he says I turned and simply said, "You see?"

I learned in my grown-up years how beautiful Kansas can be in the middle and west, an ocean of mud in winter and of wheat in summer, with a rolling ground swell underneath and a turbulent sky above, against which every still unbroken windmill turns like a beacon. I came also in those later years to respect her university at Lawrence, especially for music, and to read her free-speaking editors, William Allen White of Emporia, Ed Howe of Atchison. I have wished merely to point out here, in telling what life was like on the Missouri side, that any Southern child from there inevitably grew up making fun of Kansas.

Such fun, of course, was chiefly made in private. Publicly our city was for tolerance. As a multiple railway terminus, it offered welcome equally to old Confederates, to business families from Ohio and New England, to German farmers, brewers from Bavaria, cattlemen from Colorado and the West, to miners, drummers, and all railroaders, to Irish hod carriers, Jewish jewelers, New York investors, and Louisiana lumberjacks, to school teachers, music teachers, horse showers, horse doctors, to every species of doctor and clergyman and to many a young male or female fresh off the farm. In such a cosmopolis mutual acceptance was inevitable. So also was a certain exclusiveness, based on contrasts in manners, morals, and religion.

. . .

Beyond our residential neighborhood there were forays into the great world of downtown, of department stores with their smells of dress goods and with their stools that one could whirl around on. I was taken every October to the Carnival parade and carried home by my father sound asleep. But the greatest adventure was going to the depot to meet somebody, usually my grandmother. For this we traveled either on a cable car that went over a cliff and down a steep incline or on an electric one that went through that same cliff in a black tunnel. At the depot itself there were men with megaphones singing lists of railroad lines and towns and numbered tracks. As for the trains, their engines looked so powerful, in motion or at rest, that I did not dare go near them without holding tightly to my father's hand. Even thus, my fear was awful. There was no identity at all between these monstrous machines and their toy images that I cuddled every night in bed.

DES MOINES

County seat, state capital, and centrally located, Des Moines, Iowa, was chosen during a year of the early 1920s as the reunion city for one of the great pageants of the past: the annual meeting of the veterans of the Grand Army of the Republic. Their ranks were thinning, but there were still plenty of old soldiers on hand to make an impressive showing. They came with their drum corps, their families, and their memories to the big city that had been little more than a fort when the Civil War started. At the time of the festivities described below, MacKinlay Kantor was one of the young Des Moines citizens enthralled by these living guardians of the republic. An older Iowa witness was the publisher of a farm journal—Henry Wallace—who went on to become a Vice-President of the United States.

MacKinlay Kantor

MacKinlay Kantor was born in 1904 and began his writing career as a reporter on an Iowa newspaper edited by his mother. Many of his successful novels deal with the Civil War: *Long Remember* (1934), *Arouse and Beware* (1936), and *Andersonville* (1955), which was later turned into a stirring play. *Glory for Me* (1945), a novel about the return of three servicemen after World War II, became the popular film *The Best Years of Our Lives*, for which Kantor also wrote the adaptation. The selection below is from his reminiscences, *The Day I Met a Lion*, published in 1968.

from The Day I Met a Lion

. . . It is 1922, and the place is Des Moines. More than twenty thousand strangers have come to town. These include not only throngs of Civil War veterans, but Daughters of Union Veterans, Sons of Union Veterans, Women's Relief Corps, Ladies of the GAR . . . all the acolytes, all the attendants, eager wives and grandchildren.

It is September, the traditional month for the reunion. Sun falls kindly as a summer sun but without its hurt. From their train windows as they approach, stealing across river valleys or down them, the visitors can see that woods are bright in patches with the red of vines already turned. There is a perfume of corn and oaks in the country air.

The Polk County Courthouse has been made into a general headquarters . . . there's room to maneuver in, there. Halls and lobbies roar with human triumph, with muttered campaigns. People are passing out cards and posters. *Vote for Smith for Commander-in-Chief . . . J. D. MacTavish, Our New Commander . . . Nugent from Nebraska.* Why should it mean so much to be elected to a high post in the organization? Ah, but it does, it does.

Bob Spunner, picturesque with white Buffalo Bill hair, mustache, and imperial— He has had his picture taken for the eleventh time since the encampment began, and is even now telling an admiring throng of high-schoolers that he will be one hundred years old on his next birthday.

Twelve feet away, Eben Collins, once of the 16th Vermont, is breaking into righteous wrath, peering over his shoulder and then turning to wave a purple-veined fist in front of Harry Kuppner ex-68th Pennsylvania.

"That old Spunner is lying again! Listen to him! He ain't a hundred years old any more than I am! I remember hearing him at the Encampment a couple of years ago, telling folks he was just about to be *ninety*. I tell you, he ought to be *exposed* as a *fake!*"

"Oh, don't pay no attention to him, Ebe. He's just weak in the head."

On the stairway leading to the second floor, a ladies' quartette is singing. The women wear gowns of identical pattern, but varying in shade, and each has a red-white-and-blue scarf, and is bedizened with badges relating to her membership in the Daughters of Union Veterans. This quartette is an institution. The Girls, as they are called, have been singing at Encampments for many years. They have their own nickname proudly flourished . . . we'll call them the Columbus Canaries, or perhaps the Aberdeen Angels, or the Kalamazoo Korus. It doesn't matter. They seem to have more teeth than most women of their years . . . but they practice that untrained harmony of people who love to sing for singing's sake.

> *Tenting tonight, tenting tonight,*
> *Tenting on the old camp ground. . . .*

They own a rival in the shape of Aloysius Boyle of Brooklyn, New York, who some fifty-nine years ago fought on the Union left with the Irish Brigade on that glaring July second at Gettysburg. Mr. Boyle loves to sing, himself, and has done so consistently at every Encampment since he first began to attend in 1888. During the evenings he is apt to burst into Chauncey Olcott ballads without any urging at all, but now a patriotic number is suggested by the activity of the ladies' quartette.

In eagerness Mr. Boyle does not wait for their applause to die down. He has established himself seven steps on the stairway above the ladies, and is holding one hand over his heart and one extended toward the crowd. His seamed pink face is alive with compassion, the silver hair around his pink scalp stands out like a halo.

> *While the shot and shell were screaming upon the battlefield,*
> *The boys in blue were fighting, their Country's flag to shield—*

A yell of fifes, a bombardment of drums like thunder beyond the gates of Heaven: these serve to drown Mr. Boyle out, and to make his eventual speech about his own designation as an "Irish nightingale" fall on deafened ears. The Pasadena Drum Corps has tuned up outside the main entrance. People go flocking around. The Pasadena Drum Corps is noted, has long been noted.

Still, there are those snobs among the National Association of Civil War Musicians who demand that the Pasadena Drum Corps be placed at the *end* of the annual parade, "so's they won't disturb the rest of us. They got those blame fifes in the key of C! Everybody else has got B-flat!"

B-flat or C, it matters not at the moment. They are playing *The Raw Recruit* as if the entire military past, present, and future of the United States of America depends on it. The crowd falls back, laughing in a storm. The Pasadena Drum Corps has decided to march through the door and play *inside,* and this they are doing. The elderly graystone building quivers in its roots.

'Way over across town, at the State House, shuttling bands of veterans and other visitors are sightseeing. They wander happily from cannon to cannon on the spacious grounds. Uncle Mel Gartway sits resting on a concrete ledge, surrounded by a flock of schoolgirls. The children are in awe of his empty sleeve and the badge which proclaims his one-time participation in warfare with the 13th U.S. Infantry; and awed as by a miracle when their teacher points out the Congressional Medal worn by Mr. Gartway.

He shows off a polished lead Minié ball which hangs from his watch chain.

"Weighs just an ounce. Or used to. . . . I reckon some of the weight has wore off by now. But that was the reason they had to take off my arm. 'Twas at Vicksburg, nineteenth of May, Eighteen sixty-three. . . ."

Back across the river, at Sixth and Walnut, the Michigan Drum Corps has tuned up, and the Michigan Drum Corps is something to hear. They are nearly forty strong, and they boast a snare drummer—a squat, solemn, bearded man—who can beat the Long Roll for a full three minutes without tiring, and does so without even being asked. With a hundred others, Mr. George Warner Young, local insurance man, and Mr. Harvey Ingham, local editor, stand entranced in the crowd. So do the Reverend Frank Chalmers McKean, local Presbyterian, and Mr. Henry A. Wallace, local farm journal publisher. They will all be late at their offices, coming from lunch, but nobody cares. This is more important than being on time.

Tribes of children congregate everywhere, following the veterans like *Kinderleine* lured by the Pied Piper. Truancies rise to a new high this week, but at least it is rumored that the schools will close officially for the grand parade.

Fresh-faced housewives, members of one of the local Ladies' Aid societies, are progressing slowly along the sidewalk, laden with baskets of home-baked cookies which are being lightened with speed. "For veterans only," they cry, shaking their heads at other hands extended hopefully. "Sorry. Veterans only."

Fat old Werner Larsen, one-time 1st Minnesota, wants to know how many cookies he can have. He is awarded two big thick brown ones. "My wife used to call these hermits," he says wistfully, "when she was alive. And—do I get a kiss, lady, to go along with 'em?" Yes.

The little bearded man from Michigan has finished his Long Roll, and finished the jig he does along with it. The street is resounding with shouted requests from the thickening crowds. "Play *Yankee Doodle.*" "Hey, mister! Play *The Girl I Left Behind Me!*" "Play *Marching Through Georgia!*"

"*Marching Through Georgia,*" says one gray-haired raw-boned fifer to another. "They don't seem to realize that wasn't written till after the War."

"*Girl's* all right, and so's *Yankee Doodle,* but they're chestnuts. Let's give 'em something regular. *Eighteen Twelve* or *Gilderoy.*"

But—

"*Village Quickstep,*" calls the Fife Major, and holds his instrument aloft in signal. The music begins . . . long slow movement first. It was popular as a guard-mount during the War.

(I remember starting to play it on my fife, at an Encampment of United Confederate Veterans, in Richmond in 1932. I had been ensconced with some shaggy North Carolinians who demanded, "Give us a tune." So I began to play, and the next minute was threatened by a long-haired gentleman from Arkansas who descended with waving cane. "Stop that damn Yankee quickstep!" We became fast friends within the hour. Mr. Reeley and I exchanged annual letters for years following. Until the day I received that inevitable missive from a niece: "I am sorry to have to tell you . . .")

Let us walk, let us push our way along sidewalks and go into the street itself. Traffic moves at a crawl . . . old soldiers are limping everywhere. Old ladies, too. All the local children underfoot . . .

A drum corps from Pittsburgh is playing in front of the Savery Hotel, a drum corps from Massachusetts in front of the Kirkwood. We might eventually elbow our way to the counter of a narrow restaurant near Third and Grand—one called the Bon Ton Cafe—and try to sustain ourselves with a cup of coffee. Mr. Gust Zanias is the proprietor. With a wide grin, Mr. Zanias is contemplating three veterans of the 5th New Jersey Volunteers—the only ones who could find each other at this Encampment, although there are believed to be others of their comrades around. They have laboriously counted out change, to pay for their late midday dinner. "No check, Pop," says Gust. "Not for you folks, not here today. No check."

Des Moines has taken the visitors to its heart, just as Grand Rapids will do in 1934, and Rochester in 1935, and Washington itself in 1936. Not so many in the Michigan Drum Corps in 1936 . . . not so many in the Pasadena Drum Corps. What you might call a corporal's guard from all the GAR drum corps, even with Sons of Union Veterans helping out. And fat Bert Child, National Secretary, marching slowly in the lead, no longer able to beat his drum. . . .

What about the little fellow who used to play the Long Roll? You know . . . he kind of danced around while he played it?

Oh, yes, I mind him well. But he's gone. Gone for years.

It is 1922 again. A clear morning, not too warm. Maybe there is an imagined smell of hickory nuts along with native coal smoke in the air . . . Jonathan apples are ripening in orchards north of town.

Locust Street is a pulsating river of black slouch hats and ragged whiskers. Uncle Mac McGeehan slides his shriveled wrist inside the thong of his bass-drum club, preparing to pound long and heartily.

We find the beauty of bugles here . . . tarnished brass fringe dangles heavily from treasured flags. And some infirm among the color-bearers will allow sturdy Boy Scouts to lift the weighty staffs instead. But others will never yield, they won't give up the chore. Arms are strained, shoulders bent and aching . . . the stirrup in which the flagstaff rests grows hard and hurtful. But they will not give up. Never, never. They go tottering on, and applause roars like a waterfall.

Herein is apology for nothing. This is the patrolling of a valiant Past.

We have but to stop and think, and recognize that there must be dullards and cheats and even cowards somewhere in the unsteady ranks—men who treated their wives with cruelty, who were stupid with their children —men who lied, and stole from their partners, and are yet alive and talkative about war careers which are from first to last an extravagant falsehood.

Yea, there are bound to be a few of those.

But in the main we know also that here we are observing Thanksgiving Day and Ground-Hog Day and Arbor Day and Memorial Day. Here marches the grease and greenness of an elder America.

Because we own illusions, captivating and vigorous ones. Our illusions have not been washed away (a nation grows more confused in each hour that its illusions are drowned).

Drums continue steady, strong as a lumberman's heartbeat. Fifes shrill out their messages of *Jefferson and Liberty* and *O, Lassie, Art Thou Sleeping Yet?*

We consider the blue-coated sire who sat calmly with his newspaper in the Fort Des Moines Hotel lobby an hour ago. His scanty beard was black, his hair black as a crow's wing. And people said, "Oh, he can't be a Veteran. He must be one of the Sons."

So we went up and asked him. He put down his paper with tranquility, and smiled a welcome and a dismissal. "Ninety-three years old next November," he said. "Never took no water in my whiskey."

. . . And we know that their late enemies possess the same bliss and assurance: those men who wear tiny Maltese crosses in everyday coat buttonholes, just as the Grand Army men wear a coin of reddish-bronze.

There are the words of General Stephen D. Lee resounding from a Southern city, years before, when he spoke of angels "with things like chevrons on their wings." Stephen Dill Lee asked his rhetorical questions out of a regional heart, as proud as these activating the hoary ranks before us, from our own Upper-Mississippi or Upper-Ohio or Upper-Hudson areas.

"When the pale sergeant comes, we shall listen for voices in the upper air, saying, 'Welcome, Comrade. Do they love us still in Dixie?' "

Oh indeed, they loved them down in Dixie. And we Yankees loved our own dark-jacketed throngs through all the years they marched, until they were only a trickle and then but a memory.

But it seemed that the very act of gazing upon them conferred a Degree in Patriotism, an ability to weather the future scorn of people who hold that it is essential to consider the honor of some other State before we consider our own. People who declare that the Flag is a mask held in front of a façade of trickery and deceit. . . .

Forty-five years are vanished. We worship in the glory of September. Drumsticks press their fervor against taut skin of the drums, the lame feet shuffle on, and we follow in rapture.

MINNEAPOLIS

Minneapolis during the Depression was the scene of some of the sharpest labor struggles ever seen in this country. Charles Rumford Walker's American City, *published in 1937 and from which this selection was taken, remains a brilliant study of how this conflict culminated in the violent Minneapolis general truck-driver's strike of 1934. In the context of the economic despair of the Depression years, Walker makes clear why so many thought that such strikes were the inevitable beginnings of a new kind of social order. There is little trace of the old militant and dedicated labor movement in today's Minneapolis. Like most other large American cities, it has been largely concerned in recent years with the problems of growth and expansion to the suburbs.*

Charles Rumford Walker

Charles Rumford Walker was born in Concord, New Hampshire, in 1893. After graduating from Yale, he went to work in an open-hearth steel mill near Pittsburgh in 1919 to gather material for his first book, *Steel,* published in 1922. He has continued his observations of the industrial scene and in 1962 published *Technology and Civilization.*

from American City

The city of Minneapolis is a man in his late thirties who made a tremendous success at twenty-five. His parentage is mixed and racial differences quarrel in his veins. Ideas, too, and emotions thwart each other in his head. He is not quite sure of himself. And yet—he is pugnacious and still young with plenty of blood in him. His friends wonder where he is going next.

Minneapolis isn't like any other city. Not like New York. It's not cosmopolitan. Nor is it like, say Detroit. Detroit is like a big company town —held down to the belt and the sales talk. Minneapolis is far more varied and more headstrong. Nor is it like Pittsburgh, which is crowded and smoky and tough like the steel it makes. Nothing like Kansas City, which has tried to be like Boston. Nor like Boston—St. Paul is proverbially the Boston of the Middle West. Minneapolis is like none of them. And yet, it shares the American common denominator with each of them.

Minneapolis is an imperial city at the headwaters of the Mississippi—half way between east and west America—strategic to the plains of Minnesota, the Dakotas, parts of Montana and Wisconsin. Looking down from the Foshay tower one sees the gorge of the Mississippi, broad levees for river traffic, and an incredible web of railroad trackage, with shining arteries disappearing into the East and West. Along the river banks and elsewhere are tall tubular elevators like watch towers fortifying the flour mills.

Every city is supposed to have a personality, evident and appreciable to sentient persons—visitor or native alike. Minneapolis is no exception.

Physically and financially the city is close to the soil. She is a farmers' city. Her leading industry, milling, grinds his grain. The bulk of her commerce is with the agricultural empire surrounding—almost invading—her. Farmers come to her from all over the Northwest to sell grain and vegetables, to market butter fat, and to borrow money. You see them with their produce in the market; you see them on the streets of Minneapolis, in their overalls. And in high boots, with sunburned faces, eating in her restaurants; or over in St. Paul in the state office building, in the governor's chamber, dirt farmers with *bona fide* Minnesota manure on their boots, singly or in delegations telling the legislature, telling the governor what to do. Democrat, Republican, Farmer-Labor—the farmer is one-half of economics and two-third of politics in Minnesota. He contributes all he can to the personality of Minneapolis. But he doesn't dominate it.

Minneapolis does not look at the farmer as he looks at himself—or at Minneapolis. He looks warily at Minneapolis as "the city," as the home of the grain exchange, as the Wall Street of the Northwest. She looks at the farmer eagerly and with calculation as her best customer. For despite substantial manufactures, Minneapolis is at bottom a city of commerce and transportation, in fact as well as in spirit. Not only does the citadel of warehouses tell you that, but you breathe it in the atmosphere of her streets and her market place: those rows of semitrailers backed up to eight freight depots, the trucks on meat row and fish row, and the *fleets* of trucks loading at the city's 991 wholesalers, or moving out of the city with everything from safety pins to cultivators to the villages and farms of the Northwest.

As with most persons, blood is a basic component of personality with all the racial inheritances it carries. Along the streets of Minneapolis, in factories and offices, singing their own songs in cafés, are fair-haired, blue-eyed Scandinavians who have come from Copenhagen, Stockholm, Oslo, to Minneapolis, the Norse capital of America. Fifty-six per cent of Minnesota's population is foreign born. Plenty of the Norse languages and German are still spoken, especially in the market with farmers driving in from Chaska, or Mankato or Faribault or Cloquet. Or the Scandinavian guttural makes over Middle Western Americanese. *Skoal!* at Norse beer joints. Herring and Swedish bread at "A bit o' old Sweden," the café in north Minneapolis.

This is the Northland. Last winter the thermometer stayed under twenty below zero for two months. In the Minneapolis Club, where descendants of New Englanders foregather, they lean to whiskey as a fuel in winter, and gin fizzes to cool them off in the summer. In the rest of Minneapolis—mostly—the beverage for both purposes is beer. The drys never got a real foothold in the Northland. Statistics show that Minnesota drinks more beer in a year than Kansas does in a decade. Swing music has invaded Minneapolis, infecting the nimble-jointed, but Minneapolis still has a dozen public dance halls advertising "Old-Fashioned Dances." Anglo-Saxon, French-Canadian, and Scandinavian youth all like to dance the Swedish schottische.

Scandinavian influence bites deeper than the old customs. The governor of Minnesota for six years was Floyd Bjorsterne Olson. All over Minneapolis are co-operative oil stations, stores, and factories. Over in St. Paul the Farmers' Union Central Exchange displays a row of shiny red tractors with a "co-op" label on each. Like beer and the schottische, the ubiquitous "co-op" and the Norse governor are part of the city's personality.

Today there are Olsons and Petersons and Andersons in Minnesota politics. But look over the names of the bankers, or railroad directors, or the owners of the flour mills or timber lands. They are Walker, Weyerhauser, Pillsbury, Crosby, Bennett, Washburn. The Pillsburys came from New Hampshire, the Washburns and Crosbys from Maine; most of the "first families" came from New England, direct or via Ohio or Iowa. The rosters of the Minneapolis and the Woodhill Country Club contain no Norse names. Didn't the melting pot work in Minnesota, or hasn't there been time yet for a vertical infiltration? The city is a split personality.

I lived in Minneapolis in a two-story six-room house with a neat lawn around it, a sprinkler, and a garage. There are maybe fifty thousand houses like mine in Minneapolis, besides, of course, the larger ones. I don't mean that everybody has one. There are a few apartments and there are tiny cottages on the outskirts and flop houses and dollar-a-week flats around Bridge Square. But architecturally they overflow the city. (It is said that fifty-six per cent of Minneapolitans own their own homes.)

Builders transmute a regional quality into sticks and stones in spite of themselves. And the thousands of blocks of residential Minneapolis share with most American cities the peculiar mediocrity of the "brown era." Six rooms to ten rooms, one-family or duplex, gambrel roof or plain, the line of the roof and the proportion of parts are unfailingly wrong. And the colors are ugly ones from the drab brown side of the palette. Of course Minneapolis is no different from other American cities in her predilection for the brown heterodox house, except that—very fortunately having fewer tenements—she has more houses. The streets of Minneapolis are beautiful in the summer because they are broad, and the number of trees, hedges, and sprinkled lawns are phenomenal. Only when the leaves fall and the gardens and lawns freeze does the drab era exhibit itself nakedly.

Minneapolis is close to the soil. And though some of her citizens have forgotten it, she is close to her recent beginnings in the pioneer west.

Seventy-five years ago Minneapolis was a village of a dozen shacks near the Falls of St. Anthony. Her inhabitants busied themselves shooting elk and Indians. Men and cities that mature slowly have different personalities from those who grow up fast, or skip stages to an early success.

There is still plenty of room in the city—more than in most—with its boulevards, its lakes, and its half wild parks; room for the bank president and the garage mechanic to go swimming or skating or fishing within the city limits. Though the bank president goes to Lake Minnetonka or the pool at Woodhill and the mechanic to Lake Harriet, which is closer to the six-room houses. And outside the city, lots of room in Minnesota with its "10,000 lakes" for picnics and week-end fishing. So that space, perhaps, is one thing which gives an air of freedom, real or imagined, to the personality of the city. Something apart from the geography contributes, too: the faces of men and women on the streets, farmers in overalls and workers in shirt sleeves on Hennepin Avenue, or jostling against business men in the legislative halls across the river, and on the steps of the Capitol.

In Minneapolis, cultural bases are melting in spots and freezing in others.

An evangelist copying Coughlin adopts the radio in an anti-vice campaign. He adds, "What Minneapolis needs to be rid of far more than the gangsters are the Dunne brothers." (The Dunne brothers are insurgent Minneapolis labor leaders.)

Two old people, she in her sixties, he at seventy-four, stop going to church. They join the Townsend movement and play cards and eat ice cream at Townsend sociables. Every night they pray that God will inspire Congress to vote them $200 a month.

Floyd Bjornsterne Olson, governor of Minnesota, addresses the unemployed from the steps of the State Capitol. He says if Capitalism cannot prevent a recurrence of depressions, he hopes "the present system of government goes right down to hell!" The unemployed citizens of Minnesota cheer.

The "Citizens' Alliance," representing eight hundred Minneapolis employers, meets in honor of the ideals which built the city. The speaker talks about the economic system under which the eight hundred employers live. "In the first place it is somewhere between 20,000 and 40,000 years old," he says; ". . . it cannot be hurried."

The Greek Orthodox Church holds its synod in Minneapolis, affirming belief in a sixteen-hundred-year-old ritual.

In the Unitarian Parish House, the Theatre Union of Minneapolis plays "Squaring the Circle," a Soviet comedy, to an applauding audience.

The day I settled into my comfortable six-room house on Harriet Avenue, a lady came to the door and said she was from the "Welcome Wagon." She welcomed me to the city, and offered me food samples from the grocer and the baker. I thanked her. Sitting in my parlor—and unofficially—she confided to me that conditions in the city were terrible. She hinted that radicals and racketeers had established a malign dictatorship.

A few days later I was in the office of a grain merchant, scion of one of the "empire builders" of the Northwest. "In 1934, the Communist leaders of the truck drivers' strike captured the streets of the city. They even put strikers in as traffic officers!" he told me. "After the next election we shall put all the Communists and criminals who are ruining the city in jail."

Floyd Bjornsterne Olson, first Farmer-Labor governor in the United States, died in August, 1936. A rabbi, a Lutheran minister and a Catholic priest preached a sermon over him. Governor La Follette of Wisconsin delivered the funeral oration. He had the largest funeral in the history of the Northwest.

A descendant of one of Minneapolis' pioneers sums it up: "My grandfather was a banker in a small town in Minnesota," he says. "In those days you could make a loan on a man's face. And it was good security. It isn't any more. *Something has slipped.*"

In 1849 Minneapolis was a sawmill town on the Falls of St. Anthony. In sixty years, a vast explosion of economic energy—remarkable in human history—had made the city what it is today, what 50,000 annual convention delegates see, what the Civic and Commerce Association describes . . .

But beneath the surface, sometimes puncturing it, the city is restless, and in ferment, defiant to the new, defiant to the old, puzzled, explosive, trying to hold on to itself, trying to break loose and go places. Where?

The Employment Stabilization Research Institute, staffed with economists from the University of Minnesota, predicts that: "Barring some unforeseen, fortuitous circumstance, Minnesota faces the prospect of a decline in industry, bringing in its trail a decline in the standard of living . . . an increasing tax burden . . . a growing unemployed population."

"If the rest of the country," says one native of Minneapolis, who is an officer of the strongest trade union in the Northwest, "had the workers as well organized as in Minneapolis, I'd like to see the Fascists start something. Today—if they wanted to—the workers of Minneapolis could seize power."

"A Republican administration," says a business man of energy and vision, "will restore our liberties, jail our agitators, and give us peace and prosperity. We have a fine city, intelligent leaders, and hidden in our soil and laboratories are the seeds of an industrial expansion we have hardly tapped. The future is bright."

OKLAHOMA CITY

———◆———

Now America's largest city in land area—it covers about
630 square miles—Oklahoma City was settled almost over-
night in 1889 when the Territory was opened to home-
steaders. From the beginning it had a sizeable Negro popu-
lation, and eventually it became one of the jazz centers in
the Southwest. Before he began to concentrate on writing,
music was the moving force in Ralph Ellison's life, and in
the selection below he describes his native city as the source
of inspiration for both. For a boy sensitive to how his world
sounded and looked, Oklahoma City provided a marvelous
diversity in the 1920s: Indians, blues singers, elegant old
ladies, and "the churches, the schoolyards, the barber shops,
the cotton-picking camps; places where folklore and gossip
thrived."

Ralph Ellison

Ralph Ellison was born in Oklahoma City in 1914, studied music at Tuskegee Institute, and has made literature his major preoccupation in recent years. His first novel, *Invisible Man* (1952), was an immediate success and has become a classic work on the Negro in America. He is the author of many short stories and critical essays. The selection below is from the collection *Shadow and Act*, published in 1964.

from Shadow and Act

Negro Oklahoma City was starkly lacking in writers. In fact, there was only Roscoe Dungee, the editor of the local Negro newspaper and a very fine editorialist in that valuable tradition of personal journalism which is now rapidly disappearing; a writer who in his emphasis upon the possibilities for justice offered by the Constitution anticipated the anti-segregation struggle by decades. There were also a few reporters who drifted in and out, but these were about all. On the level of *conscious* culture the Negro community was biased in the direction of music.

These were the middle and late twenties, remember, and the state was still a new frontier state. The capital city was one of the great centers for southwestern jazz, along with Dallas and Kansas City. Orchestras which were to become famous within a few years were constantly coming and going. As were the blues singers, Ma Rainey and Ida Cox, and the old bands like that of King Oliver. But best of all, thanks to Mrs. Zelia N. Breaux, there was an active and enthusiastic school music program through which any child who had the interest and the talent could learn to play an instrument and take part in the band, the orchestra, the brass quartet. And there was a yearly operetta and a chorus and a glee club. Harmony was taught for four years and the music appreciation program was imperative. European folk dances were taught throughout the Negro school system, and we were also taught complicated patterns of military drill.

I tell you this to point out that although there were no incentives to write, there was ample opportunity to receive an artistic discipline. Indeed, once one picked up an instrument it was difficult to escape. If you chafed at the many rehearsals of the school band or orchestra and were drawn to the many small jazz groups, you were likely to discover that the jazzmen were apt to rehearse far more than the school band; it was only that they seemed to enjoy themselves better and to possess a freedom of imagination which we were denied at school. And once one learned that the wild, transcendent moments which occurred at dances or "battles of music," moments in which memorable improvisations were ignited, depended upon a dedication to a discipline which was observed even when rehearsals had to take place in the crowded quarters of Halley Richardson's shoeshine parlor. It was not the place which counted, although a large hall with good acoustics was preferred, but what one did to perfect one's performance.

If this talk of musical discipline gives the impression that there were no forces working to nourish one who would one day blunder, after many a twist and turn, into writing, I am misleading you. And here I might give you a longish lecture on the Ironies and Uses of Segregation. When I was a small child there was no library for Negroes in our city, and not until a Negro minister invaded the main library did we get one. For it was discovered that there was no law, only custom, which held that we could not use these public facilities. The results were the quick renting of two large rooms in a Negro office building (the recent site of a pool hall), the hiring of a young Negro librarian, the installation of shelves and a hurried stocking of the walls with any and every book possible. It was, in those first days, something of a literary chaos.

But how fortunate for a boy who loved to read! I started with the fairy tales and quickly went through the junior fiction; then through the Westerns and the detective novels, and very soon I was reading the classics— only I didn't know it. There were also the Haldeman Julius Blue Books, which seem to have floated on the air down from Girard, Kansas; the syndicated columns of O. O. McIntyre, and the copies of *Vanity Fair* and the *Literary Digest* which my mother brought home from work—how could I ever join uncritically in the heavy-handed attacks on the so-called Big Media which have become so common today?

There were also the pulp magazines and, more important, that other library which I visited when I went to help my adopted grandfather, J. D. Randolph (my parents had been living in his big rooming house when I was born), at his work as custodian of the law library of the Oklahoma State Capitol. Mr. Randolph had been one of the first teachers in what became Oklahoma City; and he'd also been one of the leaders of a group who walked from Gallatin, Tennessee, to the Oklahoma Territory. He was a tall man, as brown as smoked leather, who looked like the Indians with whom he'd herded horses in the early days.

And while his status was merely the custodian of the law library, I was to see the white legislators come down on many occasions to question him on points of law, and often I was to hear him answer without recourse to the uniform rows of books on the shelves. This was a thing to marvel at in itself, and the white lawmakers did so, but even more marvellous, ironic, intriguing, haunting—call it what you will—is the fact that the Negro who knew the answers was named after Jefferson Davis. What Tennessee lost, Oklahoma was to gain, and after gaining it (a gift of courage, intelligence, fortitude and grace), used it only in concealment and, one hopes, with embarrassment . . .

In the loosely structured community of that time, knowledge, news of other ways of living, ancient wisdom, the latest literary fads, hate literature—for years I kept a card warning Negroes away from the polls, which had been dropped by the thousands from a plane which circled over the Negro community—information of all kinds, found its level, catch-as-catch can, in the minds of those who were receptive to it. Not that there was no conscious structuring—I read my first Shaw and Maupassant, my first Harvard Classics in the home of a friend whose parents were products of that stream of New England education which had been brought to Negroes by the young and enthusiastic white teachers who staffed the schools set up for the freedmen after the Civil War. These parents were both teachers and there were others like them in our town.

But the places where a rich oral literature was truly functional were the churches, the schoolyards, the barbershops, the cotton-picking camps; places where folklore and gossip thrived. The drug store where I worked was such a place, where on days of bad weather the older men would sit with their pipes and tell tall tales, hunting yarns and homely versions of the classics. It was here that I heard stories of searching for buried treasure and of headless horsemen, which I was told were my own father's versions told long before. There were even recitals of popular verse, "The Shooting of Dan McGrew," and, along with these, stories of Jesse James, of Negro outlaws and black United States marshals, of slaves who became the chiefs of Indian tribes and of the exploits of Negro cowboys. There was both truth and fantasy in this, intermingled in the mysterious fashion of literature.

Writers, in their formative period, absorb into their consciousness much that has no special value until much later, and often much which is of no special value even then—perhaps, beyond the fact that it throbs with affect and mystery and in it "time and pain and royalty in the blood" are suspended in imagery. So, long before I thought of writing, I was claimed by weather, by speech rhythms, by Negro voices and their different idioms, by husky male voices and by the high shrill singing voices of certain Negro women, by music; by tight spaces and by wide spaces in which the eyes could wander; by death, by newly born babies, by manners of various kinds, company manners and street manners; the manners of white society and those of our own high society; and by inter-racial manners; by street fights, circuses and minstrel shows; by vaudeville and moving pictures, by prize fights and foot races, baseball games and football matches. By spring floods and blizzards, catalpa worms and jack rabbits; honeysuckle and snapdragons (which smelled like old cigar butts); by sunflowers and hollyhocks, raw sugar cane and baked yams; pigs' feet, chili and blue haw ice cream. By parades, public dances and jam sessions, Easter sunrise ceremonies and large funerals. By contests be-tween fire-and-brimstone preachers and by presiding elders who got "laughing-happy" when moved by the spirit of God.

I was impressed by the expert players of the "dozens" and certain noto-rious bootleggers of corn whiskey. By jazz musicians and fortunetellers and by men who did anything well; by strange sicknesses and by interest-ing brick or razor scars; by expert cursing vocabularies as well as by ex-alted praying and terrifying shouting, and by transcendent playing or singing of the blues. I was fascinated by old ladies, those who had seen slavery and those who were defiant of white folk and black alike; by the enticing walks of prostitutes and by the limping walks affected by Negro hustlers, especially those who wore Stetson hats, expensive shoes with well-starched overalls, usually with a diamond stickpin (when not in hock) in their tieless collars as their gambling uniforms.

And there were the blind men who preached on corners, and the blind men who sang the blues to the accompaniment of washboard and guitar, and the white junkmen who sang mountain music and the famous huck-sters of fruit and vegetables.

And there was the Indian-Negro confusion. There were Negroes who were part Indian and who lived on reservations, and Indians who had children who lived in towns as Negroes, and Negroes who were Indians and traveled back and forth between the groups with no trouble. And Indians who were as wild as wild Negroes and others who were as solid and steady as bankers. There were the teachers, too, inspiring teachers and villainous teachers who chased after the girl students, and certain female teachers who one wished would chase after young male students. And a handsome old principal of military bearing who had been blem-ished by his classmates at West Point when they discovered on the eve of graduation that he was a Negro. There were certain Jews, Mexicans, Chinese cooks, a German orchestra conductor and an English grocer who owned a Franklin touring car. And certain Negro mechanics—"Cadillac Slim," "Sticks" Walker, Buddy Bunn and Oscar Pitman—who had so assimilated the automobile that they seemed to be behind a steering wheel even as they walked the streets or danced with girls. And there were the whites who despised us and the others who shared our hardships and our joys.

There is much more, but this is sufficient to indicate some of what was present even in a segregated community to form the background of my work, my sense of life.

OMAHA

❦

Omaha in the years before World War I had a population that was more than half foreign-born. Nevertheless, one is struck by the similarity with other Midwest cities, particularly Indianapolis as pictured by Claude Bowers and James Thurber's Columbus, both represented in this anthology.

Charles W. Morton

Charles W. Morton was born in Omaha in 1899 and after working as a Boston newspaperman became the associate editor of *The Atlantic Monthly* and was associated with the magazine for almost thirty years. He also wrote *How to Deal with Women and Other Vicissitudes*, 1951. The following selection is from *It Has Its Charms*, published in 1966.

from It Has Its Charms

Home, as nearly as I can judge it some sixty years later, was divided about equally into three parts: family, school, and summers. Geographically, home was Omaha, Nebraska, a much rawer frontier city at the turn of the century than it chose to think itself. It never occurred to me that we could or should live anywhere else, or that our manner of living was at all different from that of families everywhere. True, there were families in Omaha who lived far more splendidly than we did, who lived in big houses and kept their own horses and were driven to church of a Sunday by their own coachmen in gleaming carriages, open or closed, according to the weather, while we used trolley cars during the week and went for our Sunday drive in vehicles hired from Gorman's Livery Stable, on Leavenworth Street, just below 28th. Equally true, there were children who came to school in ragged overalls and strange, foreign-looking outer clothing in the wintertime; children who were dirty and a few—whom we regarded with curiosity and some awe—who consistently stank, quite strongly and, oddly enough, quite differently, one from another. But these variables meant nothing at all to us as schoolchildren; in fact, we were solidly instructed, at home as well as in school, that money or clothes or family had no bearing on our individual worth as Americans: all we had to do was to study hard, mind our manners, and thus prepare ourselves for the great things which would inevitably fall to us in consequence.

National origins were likewise to be ignored, and this could hardly have been otherwise in a community so filled with first-generation immigrants—Scandinavians, Poles, Bohemians, Germans, Anglo-Saxons—that it would have been impossible to envision any preferred group. We took for granted such names as Swoboda, Ruszika, Kuehne, Hostettler, Sjoberg, Gustafson, Spiesburger, Reznicek, Dowling, Rourke, Cohn, Berquist, and such. I do not recall any Negro in my class at Park School, but I believe race would have received the same indifference as religion: a private affair and of interest to nobody else. The preachment was put to us daily that religious discrimination in benighted Europe had caused the forebears of all of us to seek out the New World and to settle in the very heart of it—Nebraska. Here, whatever one's religion might be, it was his by choice and not compulsion, and we must never forget that freedom of choice was the great principle on which we should always live.

The acceptance of these ideas by the children of Park School was total, and I have often tried to account for the immense authority and prestige which the teachers enjoyed in propounding them, and indeed in asserting anything else, from the sounds of the alphabet to the multiplication table. The teacher was a person set apart and distinctly above, incapable of error, always to be believed and obeyed, the natural source of knowledge. I do not recall any child being rude to the teacher, no matter what other misbehavior might have occurred in the classroom. It would have been insufficient to say that we were docile or tractable; we were a devoted band of scholars, disciples following a stern mistress. When the fourth-grade teacher, a Miss Stapenhorst, left us to become a bride, we wept openly. I think the feeling was that here we were, just coming to grips with the rudiments of English grammar, and how could we ever expect to master them without the all-wise (and beautiful) Miss Stapenhorst?

The general climate of an Omaha public school, then, was one of hard work, carried on with great seriousness. Classes were large, thirty or more children in a single room and taught in all subjects by a single teacher; yet, as a reasonably bright boy with a fairly large and early reading background, I had all I could do to keep abreast of the rest of the class. I worked hard, and so did everyone else. The main reason, underlying what might seem today a phenomenal state of affairs, was, I believe, quite simple.

At least half the children were first-generation Americans; their parents had known only too bitterly the poverty, and the consequent lack of education, in Europe. Now laid before them was not only a free education but the same free education that all other American children would get, rich and poor alike, and the child was going to get it, and get it for all it was worth, or the immigrant parents would deal with the child accordingly. The pressure of home and school combined was irresistible, for along with the yearning for their children's advancement, these parents brought the traditional respect of the European for the teacher, the learned person.

I have no idea what traumas my classmates—or for that matter I myself

—may have suffered in so hard-driving and competitive an interval. Perhaps some innate talents among us failed of disclosure by a process that was nothing more nor less than the three R's; yet many of my classmates grew up to become influential members of the community, and to me all subsequent classroom experiences seemed light exercise in comparison with the obligations imposed by the public schools of Omaha, Nebraska.

I make some point of the egalitarian spirit of the school, since it carried over into our after-school play and most of our social exchanges. If we inclined to make up our games and friendships from within the neighborhood, on account of mere accessibility, the only ruling standard was congeniality, and it did not matter who a child's parents were, or what he wore, or what he lived in: granted any mutual liking at all, he was welcome, fully equal, and indeed superior if he had the qualities to make him so.

So it was that a good cross-section of us went to the same dancing school, went with our parents to the Orpheum on Friday nights (no school, so sleep late the next morning), and occasionally to the Boyd Theater to savor what had been a Broadway hit only a year or two earlier.

The dancing school was conducted by a Mr. Chambers in a sizable ballroom in the basement of a building at 25th and Farnam Streets. His daughter, Halcyon, assisted him in our instruction and, as I recall her, was very nearly as proficient as Fred and Adele Astaire, the star pupils of the class, no older than we were, friendly and attractive, but so fantastically accomplished as to seem more a part of the adult world than of ours. Mr. Chambers, a slim, graying man with tightly curly hair, always gave off a powerful aroma of cloves; as my mother said darkly of him: he Drinks. Even so, he taught us the two-step, the waltz, the schottische (which remains to me only as a name), and the elements of a stilted ballroom etiquette, but for good measure we plugged away, also, at reels and "fancy dancing"; this took us through clog dancing and what we were assured were the traditional national dances of various lands—Spain, Holland, Scotland, Ireland—to appropriate piano accompaniments. The only two that I could ever get through from start to finish were the Dutch wooden-shoe bit and a "rube" dance to the tune of "Reuben, Reuben, I've Been Thinking," the first with hands on hips and a certain amount of jump-ups and heel-clacking, and the latter's comic overtones supplied by a deadpan, hands-in-the-pockets routine. I cannot fairly say that I ever drew heavily on this repertory in later life, but there have been occasions when, in liquor, I have obliged with a stylized hornpipe or a double-shuffle and buck-and-wing.

Friday nights at the Orpheum gave us eight or ten years of big-time vaudeville, which afforded during its heyday a representative sampling of the entertainment world. They were the only outings of that sort to which my father would condescend; we always had the same seats—my father, my mother, and my sister who was three years my senior and ruled most of our joint doings with an iron hand.

The program followed a rigid pattern, beginning with the emergence of the orchestra into the pit, much string-plucking, tooting, tuning, and promising sounds of making ready, after which the leader would appear, a rotund, ruddy little man, with oily black hair parted in the center, who combined the functions of conductor and first violin, nodding and turning toward various members of the orchestra as he played. I am sure they would have played just as smoothly without him, but he was a fixture, well regarded by the Orpheum audience and always greeted by solid applause. He tucked a white silk handkerchief into his collar, tapped his men to the alert with a few whacks of his bow, threw back his head and— off they all went into The Overture: Zampa, Poet and Peasant, Ballet Egyptian, Light Cavalry, Waltz of the Flowers, Under the Double Eagle, Siamese Patrol, Coppelia, a noble assortment. Our favorite was "Morning" from Peer Gynt, which the drummer enlivened as the piece warmed up by blowing all sorts of cheepings, trills, and warblings. I believe these were his own idea and not Grieg's, for my sister and I exchanged disgusted glances years later when the Boston Pops Orchestra failed to greet that same dawn with even a single twitter of bird-calling. The Orpheum conductor's name was either Huster or Schuster—Alvin Schuster, as I have it. "Little Mr. Schuster," my mother called him; she was given to diminutives, and it was always "the little egg man" or "the little man at the circulating library" or "Little Mr. Resnicek"—this last a brawny neighborhood butcher who must have weighed at least 200 pounds.

After little Mr. Schuster had taken two or three bows and graciously included his men in acceptance of the applause, the program usually began with acrobats, or a cycling act, jugglers, or wire-walking—something calling for no great mental investment by the audience, and it usually ended with an offering of the same sort, an act that could withstand an audience's settling in or groping for its wraps and overshoes preparatory to leaving. The high point of the evening was "the skit"—a one-act play spotted midway through the show and often a vehicle for some celebrated stage personality. The great chiller among all skits was *The Drums of Oudh*, a melodrama of mounting tension, played throughout to the sullen beat of offstage native drumming, which became almost impercep-

tibly more and more menacing and culminated in a great hullabaloo
when the final charge of the loud-drumming and bloodthirsty natives was
broken up by the English garrison, who produced a real honest-to-god
Gatling gun and cranked out with it an ear-splitting victory that left the
Orpheum Theater in a haze of black-powder smoke.

Variety was of course the essence of vaudeville; its comedians, musicians, vocalists, magicians, and playlets were as popular in the music halls
of London and the provinces as they were in Omaha or the Antipodes or
New York. Vaudeville was the great regional equalizer of its time, and I
am still mindful of the evening when I was first on my own in New York
as a schoolboy and attended the "Sunday Night Concert" at the Winter
Garden. Theaters were closed on Sundays, but behind this euphemism a
"sacred concert," i.e., a vaudeville performance, was permitted at the
Winter Garden. Smoking was allowed, also, a racy state of theatergoing
indeed, with an ashtray on the back of every seat, and my expectations
were of the loftiest. But I was scandalized to find myself watching a program of acts long familiar to me in the Orpheum at home, listening to the
same jokes, and seeing the supposedly sophisticated New York audience
falling out of its chairs at comedy routines that had been only so-so even
when they were new. My uninformed reaction to the whole evening was
one of disgust: these Easterners should get on to themselves and move out
where vaudeville was at least up to date, even if they couldn't smoke
during the performance.

Omaha, like most Middle Western cities, was laid out in squares, the
numbered streets running north and south and the streets with names,
more or less perpendicular to the Missouri River, east and west. Most of
its houses were of wood, economically square and thus requiring a mini-
mum of roof and exterior surface area, and altogether without blandish-
ment. Uptown Omaha, in short, was a succession of straight streets lined
with ugly houses on meager lots, the ordinary dimensions of a lot being 50
by 135 feet, although some home-owners bought an additional adjoining
lot for more room and as a hopeful long-term investment. The summer
heat was unkind to lawns and flowers, but a surprisingly large number of
trees shaded the older streets.

The houses became larger and more pretentious in what was called the
West Farnam neighborhood, but the still newer section known as Dundee, a little farther west, had clung to the fifty-foot lot through most of its
development before finally indulging itself in a few curved streets and
more spacious home sites. The city and with it anything like a smooth

pavement ended abruptly at Fairacres, atop the next ridge west of Dundee, and beyond lay the open rolling countryside, largely treeless save for the cottonwoods and poplars screening the small farmhouses from the fierce winds. Fairacres was the city's first neighborhood to possess houses with several acres of grounds and some variety of landscaping for each; it remained an outpost of not more than ten or a dozen houses throughout the uneasy '20s, but it has long since been leapfrogged by miles of nondescript "developments," replacing with row on row of standardized houses the cornfields of an earlier day.

For children, the great lack was anything like a water playground, a beach, a pool. West of the city on the road to Millard was a pasture through which wandered a small muddy stream. Here and there it had cut through the yellow clay soil deeply enough to provide us with a slide of six or eight feet, down the wet clay and into a shallow pool. It was only a seasonal resource, a dry gully for most of the year, but when it was wet it was prized accordingly. More dependable and more hazardous was a deep pool, below an abandoned railroad trestle, where some wayward trickle from the Missouri had collected, not far from the branch trolley line that went to East Omaha. Like that of the parent river, the water here was the color of rich *café au lait,* but that was true of most natural swimming holes of the region. What finally estranged us from the place was the arrival of a middle-aged citizen one day who stripped on the trestle, produced a bar of yellow soap, and gave himself a bath in "our" pool, amid widening rings of suds. He then proceeded to launder, with much rubbing and rinsing, the union suit of long underwear that he had just taken off. It seemed to us too crass a use of what we had dimly counted a sporting and recreational location: the pool was only thirty or forty feet in diameter—too small for ourselves and the man's underwear and suds. We never went back there again. The Missouri itself had no place whatever in our lives; its banks were treacherous and its currents even more so. We rarely saw the river, except when crossing the bridge to Iowa, for its vast floodings and shifting channels made it useless to all but a few duck hunters and squatters.

Downtown Omaha's shopping district, even with its office buildings, hotels, banks, and such, was in retrospect surprisingly small, some twenty-five square blocks or so, extending from 14th Street on the east to about 20th Street, and from Dodge Street at the north to Howard at the south. The buildings were utilitarian, most of them so stark and uninteresting that the eye tended to take them all in together as a harmonious whole in their uniform ugliness, without really looking at any one of them. One knew them by the enterprises they housed: Bennett's, the Bee Building, the Omaha National Bank Building, Browning & King, Drexel's shoe store, and of course J. L. Brandeis ("The Largest Department Store Between Chicago and Denver"), Benson & Thorne ("The Liliputian Bazar"), Myers & Dillon, the first drugstore in the city to serve a "Brownstone Front": chocolate sauce on chocolate ice cream with chopped nuts on top!

Some sort of boundary line seemed to obtain at 14th Street, especially at the intersection of 14th and Douglas, a rallying point and the uptown limit for a neighborhood of nickelodeons, employment agencies, cheap saloons, pawn shops, and pitchmen, thronged in fair weather by the stockhands, farmers, and itinerants whose business or holidays had brought them to town. The more prosperous ranchers and farmers stayed farther uptown at the Rome or the Castle, two hotels on a trolley line to South Omaha and its stockyards and packing houses, and one saw them of an evening occupying rows of rocking chairs on the broad sidewalks outside their lodgings.

The pitchmen always drew large and round-eyed crowds. Most dashing among them was one whose pitch was backed by an anatomical chart, lighted at night by kerosene flares, and who must have done very well selling "medicine"—a white powder—at $1 a can. It was harmless, he shouted, and to prove it he would toss a pinch of it down his throat at intervals, but its effects were salutary beyond belief: "Just like yah old mother used to give the house its spring cleaning, that, friends, is what yah need and what yah get from this re-mark-a-ble Ginseng Compound." And why was ginseng so expensive? Simply this: the Chinese worshiped it as god . . . oldest civilization . . . inventors of gunpowder . . . long before Gutenberg printed with movable type . . . etc. Thanks, friends, and tomorrow you'll be thanking me. Another man, while King C. Gillette was still struggling for a place in the sun, sold great quantities of a straight razor at $1 each. Its peculiar virtue, he argued, was that its blade was *magnetized,* and to prove it he would dip the blade into a box of pins and hold the razor aloft to show clusters of pins adhering to it. His clincher was a harrowing account of the infections to be picked up in the ordinary barber shop, the worst of which began with "bumps on yah face" and eventually disclosed itself as "that dr-r-read disease, the ba-a-hba's ITCH," this last word being shouted at the peak of his oratorical register.

The Douglas Street area never seemed so sordid and forbidding as Chicago's skid row; it had, rather, a carnival atmosphere of garish lights and catchpenny entertainments, and its drunks were more likely to be asleep in their rooming houses or at tables in the back rooms of saloons than along the curb. Farther east and a bit north, between the so-called whole- sale district and the river, was a red-light district covering several blocks through which we used to walk briskly as small boys, wondering what could lie behind all the mysterious rumors about the charms of the neigh- borhood, and not a little alarmed by the unaccountable remarks of the slatternly women sitting in the doorways or on the ramshackle porches of their crumbling houses. Our other occasional foray into a world still be- yond our ken was to a matinee at the Krug, the older and lowlier of Omaha's two burlesque theaters, where for 10 cents a head we could sit in the gallery and see the latest weekly offering by one of the two major burlesque "wheels," which covered the country with their highly stylized shows, just as the Orpheum Circuit, Pantages, and others did with vaude- ville. I have lost the names of most of the productions and their star per- formers, but I can recall distinctly "The Tailor-Made Girls" and the opening chorus of their show:

> *"We . . . are the Tailor-Made Girls,*
> *Tiddy-boom, tiddy-boom, tiddy-boom . . ."*

By around 1908 the transition from horse-drawn vehicles was scarcely begun. The automobile was still for recreational purposes, and each new make that we saw—and there were hundreds of different ones on the streets, even in a small city like Omaha—received our closest scrutiny. A ride in any self-propelled car was exhilarating; each had its own distinc- tive smells and sounds; but our own Sunday afternoon "drive" was still in a surrey from Gorman's, which limited severely the range of our travels. Our usual route was via "The Boulevard," which led in a southeasterly direction to a long bridge across the railroad yards known as "The Via- duct." Here we would pause to rest the horses, while my sister and I could watch the trains—a magic word—perhaps only a switch engine or two shifting freight and cattle cars, but sometimes a big double-header freight, with a booster engine behind the caboose, or a long passenger train, bound for Denver or Billings or Cheyenne—my father usually knew where. At the far end of The Viaduct was one of the city's three principal breweries, and here we always stopped at a loading platform where a man in a leather apron brought out foaming glasses of beer for my parents. We then drove smartly home, for the livery-stable horses were always keener on the return than on the way out, while my father tipped his derby hat and exchanged bows with most of the other drivers on The Boulevard.

The parking lot of that period was the livery stable, and there were big stables and blacksmiths' shops downtown as well as in the residential neighborhoods. Farmers who had come to town only for the day in their heavy unsprung wagons hitched their big teams along the curb. The only springs in such a rig were under the driver's seat, where in bad weather the farmer, wearing a buffalo-skin coat and swathed in buffalo robes, tried to keep warm but occasionally had to clamber down and walk beside the team to get his circulation back. The ranchers and some of the farmers wore ankle-length beaver coats, sometimes with beaver lining as well, a warm, impossibly heavy garment and relatively inexpensive, for the beavers were regarded as a nuisance in the cattle country and I believe there was at one time even a bounty on them.

Of all the horse-drawn vehicles, the most sinister and the most fascinating to us was the "deadanimal-wagon," very wide, with high wooden sides, its bed so low as barely to clear the ground, which went about on call to haul away any horse that had died on the street. Our greatest interest was to find out whether the wagon was empty or horrifyingly loaded, which we could do by rushing out and having a quick peek through the crack in its tailgate. Not even a dog so compelled our sympathy as did the horse, and the sight of a dead horse on the street, or a glimpse of it in the deadanimal-wagon brought small children to the point of tears.

My mother, in a wonderfully non-interfering way, was a constantly reassuring presence.

.   .   .

It would be hard for me to exaggerate the staunchness of my mother's endorsement of us, a thick-and-thin position which she held imperturbably and without regard to what others thought of us. The complaint that we were "spoiled" she took with good-humored indifference, but in more serious issues she was a formidable defender. One of my guiltiest recollections concerns a neighbor whose house, a block from ours, we passed on the way to school. A long picket fence fronted the place and from a position safely behind the fence an aging, portly, and insanely disagreeable fox terrier screeched and snarled at every passer-by, child or adult. It was the sort of dog that brings a postman to a state of nerves, and if a child walking past happened to run a stick along the fence pickets the animal went into an ecstasy of rage.

I was about seven years old on this occasion, running my stick along the fence and finding the fox terrier in full voice, when an upstairs window was raised and a woman leaned out. She had moved too quickly to put anything more on, and she was wearing a corset and, with a tendency to bulge out of it, a corset cover. She began shouting at us. It would have been easy to dissuade us more affably, I feel certain, but her anger was almost as provocative as her dog's.

I was moved to reply. "Shut up, *fat!*" I shouted. The window went down, slam.

My sister and I and our constant companion Ed Dowling, who lived a block away, were summoned to the principal's office at the Park School the next afternoon. The teachers were, as I have said, respected by the children, by Miss Eveleth, the principal, was an awesome power, invoked only in grave situations. She gave us a stern account of our sins, and bade us accompany her to the offended neighbor and apologize then and there. It was a trying experience, and I am sure we must have presented a woe-begone appearance to my mother, when Miss Eveleth brought us home, perhaps an hour after our usual time.

My mother said she had been worried about our nonappearance. Miss Eveleth intended, I suppose, to make sure that our parents were fully apprised of our conduct. "I am afraid this is a sad little party," Miss Eveleth began, and she went on through the whole grisly tale.

I cannot recall ever seeing my mother discountenanced, least of all by anything to do with my sister and me. She waited until Miss Eveleth completed her story. I remember being astonished by the potency of the defense my mother brought to bear in our behalf. Her manner was gla-cial: the principal had erred, she had made a serious mistake in not bring-ing us home and consulting my mother before forcing us to apologize to this woman, a family whose name my mother did not know; this was a highhanded action and inexcusable. As to the merits of the case itself, the dog was a notorious nuisance in the neighborhood and annoyed the chil-dren, making our walk to school and back a hardship, if not dangerous. As for women who shouted at small children, my mother felt comment was unnecessary. She would consult my father that evening as to what further action she might wish to take. Good afternoon, Miss Eveleth.

The episode became something of a family joke, but my mother never forgot Miss Eveleth's behavior. " '*A sad little party,*' indeed," she would say indignantly, repeating the words of the misguided principal. "The very idea!"

My mother once took me on a small shopping tour in a light buggy provided by Gorman's. The horse was named Frank (our Sunday team were named Maude and Cob); he had a somewhat lumbering gait and

476 OMAHA

interfered badly. I was about six years old and allowed to "drive" by holding the ends of the reins, below my mother's grasp of them; but this time, through an excess of trust in poky old Frank, I was allowed to drive in reality. Frank was clattering away down a slight grade when he got tangled up with himself and down he went, sliding to a stop but leaving the buggy and ourselves unharmed.

I was sure that Frank had fallen on account of some driving lapse of mine, and when I got out and saw his bright red blood on the pavement, I burst into roars of grief. Huddled with his legs every which way, Frank showed no disposition to stand up. He seemed to me to be dying and I felt that I had killed him. My mother was having none of this: she was disgusted with Frank, who got to his feet once again when my mother gave a tug on his bridle, while a helpful passerby gave him a smart kick in the rump. Frank, it transpired, had only skinned his knee, but I was saddened for days by the recollection of his wound.

More exciting even than the deadanimal-wagon was the occasional procession through the neighborhood of "movers," a word which, in this connection, I have never encountered elsewhere. There would be an ecstatic shout, "Here come some *movers*," as they passed along our street on their way somewhere else. They were, I suppose, failed homesteaders, or about to fail again as homesteaders or farmers: a procession, single file, headed by a boy of perhaps our own age mounted on a fractious-looking stockhorse, followed by a decrepit wagon or two, sagging under a load of beaten-up household effects, bedsprings, washboilers, chairs, and pathetic sundries; a surrey drawn by one or two horses and driven in rather a proprietary way by the father, head of the family, with the elder females, surrounded by more belongings, in the rear seat. Perhaps there would be another wagon, driven by a suntanned girl no older than ourselves, two or three dogs trotting alongside and fully capable of standing off any nonsense from our neighborhood pets, several young horses running loose (which the movers were whispered to have stolen), and another boy of school age bringing up the rear, sometimes a boy riding bareback, simply for lack of a saddle, but impressing us with his disdainful mastery of his mount. For our part we stood at the curb gaping, marveling at the responsibilities assumed by the movers' children, wondering where they would sleep that night, and hoping that some such portion of high adventure might one day be ours. We were far beneath the notice of the movers' children, who rode by with never so much as a wave of the hand. Occasionally there were Indians who came along in outfits even more bedraggled than those of the movers, and one saw Indians downtown at times; but for the most part Indians were seen only in the waiting rooms of doctors' offices, sitting stolidly in a cloud of body odors so heavy as to seem almost visible and seeking relief from their endemic disease, trachoma.

The West

The West

SAN FRANCISCO

---◆---

San Francisco as seen by Norris's McTeague at the begin-
ning of the century and the same city seen by John Dos
Passos forty years later during World War II are two differ-
ent worlds. But the common denominator for this great
cosmopolitan center, ever since its founding in 1776 as a
Spanish military presidio and mission, is its uniquely
beautiful setting of steep hills leading to the Golden Gate
and San Francisco Bay.

  San Francisco has always attracted writers from every-
where; Norris and Dos Passos were but two who came and
recorded their impressions. More recently the beat and
hippie movements put down their first roots in San Fran-
cisco.

Frank Norris[*]

from McTeague

The street never failed to interest him. It was one of those cross streets peculiar to Western cities, situated in the heart of the residence quarter, but occupied by small tradespeople who lived in the rooms above their shops. There were corner drug stores with huge jars of red, yellow, and green liquids in their windows, very brave and gay; stationers' stores, where illustrated weeklies were tacked upon bulletin boards; barber shops with cigar stands in their vestibules; sad-looking plumbers' offices; cheap restaurants, in whose windows one saw piles of unopened oysters weighted down by cubes of ice, and china pigs and cows knee deep in layers of white beans. At one end of the street McTeague could see the huge power-house of the cable line. Immediately opposite him was a great market; while farther on, over the chimney stacks of the intervening houses, the glass roof of some huge public baths glittered like crystal in the afternoon sun. Underneath him the branch post-office was opening its doors, as was its custom between two and three o'clock on Sunday afternoons. An acrid odor of ink rose upward to him. Occasionally a cable car passed, trundling heavily, with a strident whirring of jostled glass windows.

On week days the street was very lively. It woke to its work about seven o'clock, at the time when the newsboys made their appearance together with the day laborers. The laborers went trudging past in a straggling file—plumbers' apprentices, their pockets stuffed with sections of lead pipe, tweezers, and pliers; carpenters, carrying nothing but their little pasteboard lunch baskets painted to imitate leather; gangs of street workers, their overalls soiled with yellow clay, their picks and long-handled shovels over their shoulders; plasterers, spotted with lime from head to foot. This little army of workers, tramping steadily in one direction, met and mingled with toilers of a different description—conductors and "swing men" of the cable company going on duty; heavy-eyed night clerks from the drug stores on their way home to sleep; roundsmen returning to the precinct police station to make their night report, and Chinese market gardeners teetering past under their heavy baskets. The cable cars began

[*] See biographical note on page 397.

to fill up; all along the street could be seen the shop keepers taking down their shutters.

Between seven and eight the street breakfasted. Now and then a waiter from one of the cheap restaurants crossed from one sidewalk to the other, balancing on one palm a tray covered with a napkin. Everywhere was the smell of coffee and of frying steaks. A little later, following in the path of the day laborers, came the clerks and shop girls, dressed with a certain cheap smartness, always in a hurry, glancing apprehensively at the power-house clock. Their employers followed an hour or so later—on the cable cars for the most part—whiskered gentlemen with huge stomachs, reading the morning papers with great gravity; bank cashiers and insurance clerks with flowers in their buttonholes.

At the same time the school children invaded the street, filling the air with a clamor of shrill voices, stopping at the stationers' shops, or idling a moment in the doorways of the candy stores. For over half an hour they held possession of the sidewalks, then suddenly disappeared, leaving behind one or two stragglers who hurried along with great strides of their little thin legs, very anxious and preoccupied.

Towards eleven o'clock the ladies from the great avenue a block above Polk Street made their appearance, promenading the sidewalks leisurely, deliberately. They were at their morning's marketing. They were handsome women, beautifully dressed. They knew by name their butchers and grocers and vegetable men. From his window McTeague saw them in front of the stalls, gloved and veiled and daintily shod, the subservient provision-men at their elbows, scribbling hastily in the order books. They all seemed to know one another, these grand ladies from the fashionable avenue. Meetings took place here and there; a conversation was begun; others arrived; groups were formed; little impromptu receptions were held before the chopping blocks of butchers' stalls, or on the sidewalk, around boxes of berries and fruit.

From noon to evening the population of the street was of a mixed character. The street was busiest at that time; a vast and prolonged murmur arose—the mingled shuffling of feet, the rattle of wheels, the heavy trundling of cable cars. At four o'clock the school children once more swarmed the sidewalks, again disappearing with surprising suddenness. At six the great homeward march commenced; the cars were crowded, the laborers thronged the sidewalks, the newsboys chanted the evening papers. Then all at once the street fell quiet; hardly a soul was in sight; the sidewalks were deserted. It was supper hour. Evening began; and one by one a multitude of lights, from the demoniac glare of the druggist's windows to the dazzling blue whiteness of the electric globes, grew thick from street corner to street corner. Once more the street was crowded. Now there was no thought but for amusement. The cable cars were loaded with theatregoers—men in high hats and young girls in furred opera cloaks. On the sidewalks were groups and couples—the plumbers' apprentices, the girls of the ribbon counters, the little families that lived on the second stories over their shops, the dressmakers, the small doctors, the harness makers— all the various inhabitants of the street were abroad, strolling idly from shop window to shop window, taking the air after the day's work. Groups of girls collected on the corners, talking and laughing very loud, making remarks upon the young men that passed them. The *tamale* men appeared. A band of Salvationists began to sing before a saloon.

Then, little by little, Polk Street dropped back to solitude. Eleven o'clock struck from the power-house clock. Lights were extinguished. At one o'clock the cable stopped, leaving an abrupt silence in the air. All at once it seemed very still. The ugly noises were the occasional footfalls of a policeman and the persistent calling of ducks and geese in the closed market. The street was asleep.

John Dos Passos

John Dos Passos is one of America's most original and important writers, and his influence as an innovator in stylistic techniques has been acknowledged not only at home, but also by a whole generation of French novelists, among them Camus and Sartre. Born in Chicago in 1896, he went to Harvard and became a newspaper correspondent after World War I. His interest in the events that shape history has taken him all over the world—to Spain during the Civil War, to Mexico, to the Near East, and his novels reflect his concern with individual liberties as they are affected by clashing ideologies. Among his most important works are *Manhattan Transfer* (1925), and *USA* (1938).

His journalistic travels during World War II took him to San Francisco. His impressions of that city as it appeared in 1944 are taken from an article he wrote at the time for *Harper's* Magazine.

San Francisco Looks West

If you happen to be endowed with topographical curiosity the hills of San Francisco fill you with an irresistible desire to walk to the top of each one of them. Whoever laid the town out took the conventional checkerboard pattern of streets and without the slightest regard for the laws of gravity planked it down blind on an irregular peninsula that was a confusion of steep slopes and sandhills. The result is exhilarating. Wherever you step out on the street there's a hilltop in one direction or the other. From the top of each hill you get a view and the sight of more hills to the right and left and ahead that offer the prospect of still broader views. The process goes on indefinitely. You can't help making your way painfully to the top of each hill just to see what you can see. I kept thinking of what an old French seaman said to me once, describing with some disgust the behavior of passengers on a steamboat: *"Le passager c'est comme le perroquet, ça grimpe toujours."*

This particular morning was a windy morning, half sun and blue sky and half pearly tatters of fog blowing in from the Pacific. Before day it had been raining. I had started out from a steamy little lunchroom where I had eaten a magnificent breakfast of eighteen tiny wheat cakes flanked by broiled bacon and washed down by fresh-made coffee. They still know how to cook in old San Paco's town. In my hand was a list of telephone numbers to call and of men to go to see in their offices. It was nine o'clock,

484

just the time to get down to work. Instead of turning down in the direction of offices and the business part of town, I found I had turned the other way and was resolutely walking up the nearest hill.

This one is Nob Hill, I know that. I remember it years ago when there were still gardens on it and big broken-paned mansions of brown stone, and even, if I remember right, a few wind-bleached frame houses with turrets and scalelike shingles imitating stone and scrollsaw woodwork round the porches. Now it's all hotels and apartment houses, but their massive banality is made up for by the freakishness of the terrain. At the top, in front of the last of the old General-Grant-style houses, I stop a second to get my breath and to mop the sweat off my eyebrows.

Ahead of me the hill rises higher and breaks into a bit of blue sky. Sun shines on a block of white houses at the top. Shiny as a toy fresh from a Christmas tree, a little cable car is crawling up it. Back of me under an indigo blur of mist are shadowed roofs and streets and tall buildings with wisps of fog about them, and beyond, fading off into the foggy sky, stretches the long horizontal of the Bay Bridge.

Better go back now and start about my business. The trouble is that down the hill to the right I've caught sight of accented green roofs and curved gables painted jade green and vermilion. That must be Chinatown. Of course the thing to do is to take a turn through Chinatown on the way down toward the business district. I find myself walking along a narrow street in a jungle of Chinese lettering, interpreted here and there by signs announcing Chop Suey, Noodles, Genuine Chinese Store. There are ranks of curio stores, and I find myself studying windows full of Oriental goods with as much sober care as a small boy studying the window of a candy store. The street tempts you along. Beyond the curio shops there are drug stores, groceries giving out an old drenched smell like tea and camphor and lychee nuts, vegetable stores, shops of herb merchants that contain very much the same stock of goods as those Marco Polo saw with such wonder on his travels. In another window there are modern posters: raspberry-and-spinach-tinted plum-cheeked pin-up girls and stern lithographs of the Generalissimo; a few yellowing enlargements of photographs of eager-looking young broad-faced men in cadets' uniforms. The gilt lettering amuses the eye. The decorative scroll-work of dragons and lotus flowers leads you along. You forget the time wondering how to size up the smooth Chinese faces. At the end of the street I discover that an hour has passed and that I have been walking the wrong way all the time.

I come out into a broad oblique avenue full of streetcars and traffic. Suddenly the Chop Suey signs are gone and now everything is Spaghetti, Pizza, Ravioli, Bella Napoli, Grotta Azzura, blooming in painted signs along the housefronts. There are Italian bakeries and pastry shops breathing out almond paste and anise. In small bars men sit talking noisily as they drink black coffee out of glasses. Restaurants smell of olive oil and spilled wine. I cross the street and at the top of another hill catch a glimpse of a white tower shaped like a lighthouse. That must be Signal Hill.

As I walk up through a shabby light-gray cheerful quarter where all the doorbells have Italian and Spanish names, and where the air out of doorways smells of garlic and floor polish and there begin to be pots of geraniums on the tops of scaly walls that conceal small gardens, or carnations now and then on a window sill, it suddenly feels like the quiet streets back of Montmartre or, so many years ago, Marseilles. I reach the top of Signal Hill just in time to take refuge in the tower from a spat of driving rain.

From the tower I look down into a swirl of mist, shot with lights and shadows like the inside of a shell, that pours in from the ocean. Now and then the hurrying mist tears apart long enough to let me see wharves crowded with masts and derricks or an expanse of bright ruffled water— and once, rank on rank of sullen-looking gray freighters at anchor. Two young men in khaki are standing beside me, squinting to see through the rain-spattered glass.

"Boy, it won't be long now," says one.

"You mean before we are stuck down in the hold of one of those things."

"You said it." They notice that I am listening. They exchange reproachful looks and their mouths shut up tight and they move away.

When I leave the tower the sun is beginning to burn through dazzling whiteness. There is blue in the puddles on the paved parking place on top of the hill. It has become clear that this isn't any day to call up telephone numbers or to pester people in their offices. It is a day to walk round the town. And the first thing to do is to get a look out through the Golden Gate.

I plunged down the hill in the direction of the harbor, lost my bearings in a warehouse section, found myself beside a little stagnant inner harbor packed with small motor fishing boats painted up Italian style; and then took a freshly painted cable car to the top of another hill. I got off and set out along a street of frame houses that seemed to be leading me in the direction of the ocean. The houses were all alike, painted cream color, with jutting bay windows and odd little columns on each side of the front door. I walked on and on through the pleasant mild sunlight, expecting to see the ocean from the top of each rise.

Eventually the sight of a hill steeper than the rest, topped with green shrubbery and tall gray pillars of blooming eucalyptus trees, made me change my course. From up there you must be able to see the ocean and the Golden Gate and everything. I got up to the top, puffing after a stiff climb. The hilltop was a park. All the city and the Bay clear to Oakland and the bridges and the hills opened out in every direction at my feet. But not the Golden Gate, though I could see the high straw-colored hills beyond. And toward the ocean there was only a bright haze.

An old Mexican was raking fallen eucalyptus leaves and scaled-off bark into a bonfire that trailed stinging sharp tonic-flavored smoke across the path. At the very summit of the path, cut off from the wind by a hedge of shiny-leaved privet, four whiskered old men were seated round a green board table playing cribbage. It was quiet and sunny up there. The billowing blue smoke cut them off from the city. There is something very special about the smell of burning eucalyptus leaves. In the light fragrant air of the late morning the old men sat in relaxed attitudes of passionless calm. They held their cards with the detachment of gods on Olympus. They weren't smoking. They weren't talking. No one was in any hurry to get along with the game. Their pleasure wasn't in the sun or the air or the immense view. Maybe it was just in being alive, in the gentle ambrosial coursing of the blood through their veins, in the faint pumping of the heart. That may have been what the Greeks meant when they wrote about the shadowless painless pleasures of the spirits in the Elysian Fields.

I had stopped in my tracks to look at the four old men, and they all four looked up at me and craned their necks at the same moment. They showed such startled surprise at seeing me standing in the path that I might have been a spook from another world. Maybe I was. I hurried off down into the city again.

Eventually I had to ask my way to the ocean. Somebody said I ought to take a car to the Cliff House. Somewhere in the back of my memory there was connected with that name a park on a cliff, full of funny beer-garden statuary under pines—and the disappointment as a child of not being able to spot a sea lion among the spuming rocks off the headland. The streetcar, a full-sized normal streetcar, rattled along through a suburban section of low stucco houses and across wide boulevards planted with palms, described an S through pines down a steep slope, and finally came to rest in a decrepit barn beside a lunch counter. I stepped out onto a road that curved down the steep slope to the old square white restaurant, and farther round the headland to the broad gray beach, where slow rollers very far apart broke and growled and slithered inland in a swirl of gray water and were sucked back in spume.

I went out and leaned over the parapet of the observation platform. The blue-gray Pacific was clear far out to where a fog bank smudged the horizon. Coming round from the Golden Gate—which I still couldn't catch sight of—a gray patrol boat showed white teeth as it chewed its way seaward into the long swells. Still no black heads of sea lions bobbing around Seal Rocks. . . . A few gulls circled screaming over the platform.

Beside me three very black G.I.'s stood in a huddle staring out at the ocean. Farther along two sailors had their backs turned to the view and were watching with envious looks a boy and girl in sweaters and slacks who looked like high-school kids, and were giggling and horsing and pushing each other around. A sergeant of Marines, very snappy in his greens, strutted out of the building that houses the slot machines; a girl with a blue handkerchief tied round her yellow head was holding onto his arm with both hands. For a couple of minutes the two of them stared hard out to sea as if their eyes could pierce the fog bank. Then they hurried back indoors to the slot machines.

Leaning on the parapet over the hushed and heaving expanse of misted indigo that marks for most Americans the beginning of the Pacific Ocean, I wondered what these two had been thinking. I suppose there's the same question in all our minds when we look westward over the Pacific. Beyond the immense bulge of the world, is the ocean ours or is it theirs? When we've made it ours, what will we want to do with it? The young men in uniform know they are going to have the answer to that question printed on their hides. No wonder they keep their lips tight pressed when they stare out toward the western horizon.

In the restaurant on the level above, the tables are all full but the eaters are very quiet. There are many family parties. Old people and middle-aged people brooding around a young man or woman in uniform.

At the table next to mine there's a white-haired man and woman and a stoutish lady with pixie frames on her glasses who's evidently a doting female relative and seems to be somewhat in the way. They don't take their eyes off a first lieutenant in khaki with a close-cropped black bullet head and ruddy cheeks who looks barely old enough to be in high school.

The minute you see them you know that the old people have come to say good-by. Maybe it's their last meal together. They are all trying to be very self-possessed. The father is always starting to tell little jokes and neglecting to finish them. They keep forgetting where the salt cellar is on the table. The mother handles the plate of rolls when she passes it round as if it were immensely breakable. They fork the food slowly into their mouths. None of them knows what he is eating. All their motions are very careful and precise as if they feared the slightest false move would break the fragile bonds that are holding the day together for them. The slightest fumble, and these last few hours will be spilt and lost.

It's very different at the table between mine and the window. There a slender young Air Force major, with dark curly hair already thinning on either side of a high forehead, is taking out a strikingly pretty dark-haired girl. She might be his sister. There's something slightly similar about the way the two of them are built, about the way the nostrils are set in their noses. Or she might be his girl or his wife or just the right chance acquaintance. They have had cocktails and oysters. The waiter is bringing them a bottle in a bucket of ice. They have ordered abalone steaks. They aren't saying much but their eyes are shining and they keep looking at each other and at the wine glasses and at the food on their plates and at the fog bank creeping toward them across the black ocean as if they'd never seen anything in the least like these things before. They think they are alone in the restaurant. It's not so much that they are smiling at each other as that smiles are bubbling up all around them. Time, you can see, stands still for them.

Better get going. I had begun to feel lonely. The rest of my lunch didn't have much flavor to it. Coming out of the restaurant, the fog pressed clammy against my face. I turned up my coat collar and went shuffling up the hill toward the streetcar line. My coat felt suddenly out at the elbows. Everything about me felt shabby and frayed. Maybe it is that there are many things a civilian in wartime feels out of.

LOS ANGELES

◆━━◆

*Los Angeles sees itself as the Megalopolis of the future;
it is therefore fitting that the final selection in this book
comes from Christopher Rand's* Los Angeles: The Ultimate
City, *published in 1967. The key word is "ultimate" of
course, and Mr. Rand's book has the same definitive quality that characterizes E. B. White's* Here Is New York, *also
represented in this anthology.*

Christopher Rand

Christopher Rand was born near Salisbury, Connecticut, in 1912, and died in 1968. For over twenty years before his death he contributed some sixty-five travel articles to *The New Yorker,* all extraordinarily perceptive accounts of cities the world over.

from Los Angeles: The Ultimate City

Los Angeles may be the ultimate city of our age. It is the last station, anyway, of the Protestant outburst that left northern Europe three centuries ago and moved across America: the last if only because with it the movement has reached the Pacific. There are other cities on our West Coast, but none so huge or dynamic as Los Angeles, or so imbued with the Northern wilfulness in battling nature. L.A., as its people often call it, is the product to a rare degree of technology. Though built on a near-desert, it is the most farflung of the world's main cities now, and probably the most luxuriously materialistic. It is also—apart from the big "underdeveloped" cities, with their shantytown outskirts—the fastest growing in population. With its hinterland, of Southern California, it is gaining nearly a thousand inhabitants a day, and is expected to go on gaining indefinitely. The Angelenos, its people, are prone to live in the future and to project their statistics forward; the visitor hears them talk more about 1980 than about next year. "This is an optimistic city," a friend here told me recently. "If something is built wrong it doesn't matter much. Everyone expects it to be torn down and rebuilt in a decade or two." It will all have been straightened out, that is, in the 1980 city, which will also be half as large again as the present one.

The physical Los Angeles is hard to define because the concept is a flexible one, depending on who is talking and what about. Strictly or politically speaking, there are both a City and a County of Los Angeles. The City is grotesque in shape; it stretches about forty miles from north to south, but is riddled with enclaves along the way, and its main body is connected with its seaport, San Pedro, by a long corridor, half a mile wide, recalling that between ancient Athens and the Piraeus. By contrast L.A. County is shaped normally enough; the County includes the City, the enclaves within it, and a considerable hinterland, much of this wild mountains. And then there is what the statisticians call Greater Los Angeles: an area of more than four thousand square miles, with a population

491

of more than nine million, that takes in Los Angeles County; Orange
County, a super-suburb to L.A.'s southeast, and parts of Riverside, Ven-
tura, and San Bernadino counties, to the east and north. Most Angelenos
include Orange County when talking about their city. Some include other
bits of hinterland as well, and a few go so far, in certain contexts, as to
put in Santa Barbara, 90 miles up the coast, and San Diego, 120 miles
down it. Projections for the end of this century place a continuous megalopolis, centered on L.A., along this 210-mile stretch (and inland over the
mountains and valleys). In the optimistic, futuristic mood prevailing
here, one can easily see this projection, which almost coincides with what
is now called Southern California, as Los Angeles itself; and people sometimes talk as if it were that. They also talk as if it were, or would be, the
greatest city in the world.

.   .   .

One way to view Los Angeles is as a machine. All modern cities are machines, but L.A. is more so than the others. It is a humming, smoking,
ever-changing contraption, with mechanics incessantly working at it, trying to make improvements and to get the bugs out. Being a populous near-
desert, it depends crucially on imported water. It is also under threat
from floods, fires, and earthquakes, to which its technological daring
makes it especially vulnerable. Because of its scatteredness, furthermore,
it is concerned, day in and day out, with keeping a transport system moving at high speed. And finally it must deal with the waste products, the
smog, and other obscenities, that its operations throw off.

.   .   .

The L.A. freeways, another case of technological pioneering, are linked
with the passion for owner-driven cars. Los Angeles is an autopia, to borrow a name from one of Disneyland's attractions. It is the only city I have
lived in, in the U.S. or abroad, where I have needed a car of my own;
elsewhere I have used the public transport—buses, subways, taxis—and
felt free as a bird while walking, without any parking problem, between
them. But L. A., as already noted, feels that freedom lies in driving oneself;
the emphasis is less on the onus of parking, or of wrestling with the traffic,
than on the power to whizz off in the direction of one's choice.

Cars are also looked on as toys or status symbols in L.A., and I have
seen more sports cars, more Lincolns, even more Rolls-Royces there than
anywhere else. Cars are respected there. I remember coming back to
America in 1956, after two or three years in India. I stayed for a while on

the East Coast then and heard much grumbling about Detroit's new products, which had been getting bigger in my absence and sprouting tail-fins; my Eastern friends thought the tail-fins absurd and felt that the bigness crowded the streets unnecessarily. Then I passed on to Southern California and found no such resentments; people there didn't mind the tailfins—some even liked them—and they thought the cars' new claims to space were justified. And space has been provided: new wide streets and freeways, plus untold new acres of parking lots, have been laid out in L.A.; the old downtown section is now two-thirds given over to streets and parking. The City's expanding colleges and universities, most of whose students and faculty commute by car, are also pressed for space; they are faced with becoming islands amid seas of parking lots unless they build multi-storied garages. UCLA—the University of California at Los Angeles—is building seven such garages, and plans to accommodate ten thousand cars by 1969; meanwhile, though, it is engaged in town-and-gown squabbles over student parking in the streets.

Restaurants in L.A. must have plenty of parking space available, and so must shops and offices. If I go to an office on Wilshire Boulevard, to meet someone for lunch, he will see to it that my car is parked without expense, much as a host in old rural England would have seen to the stabling of my horse. If I go to an office on business, my car is likewise usually stabled as a part of the transaction. Big L.A. offices tend to have their own parking places; small ones have arrangements with commercial lots; the receptionists of these smaller firms can "validate" a visitor's claim check when he steps in the door. Some big firms also have motor pools from which their employees draw vehicles for traveling on business in the city, without using their own gas and tires.

One way or another, a member of the L.A. middle class should have his (or her) four wheels to be effective, and few but the very poor—the Negroes, Mexicans, old people, and less fortunate students—are without them. These poor may ride on buses, but preferably for short hauls only, as a citywide bus trip takes up hours. There is no other cheap way to move unless one counts walking, which is thought eccentric, is seldom adequate for the time and distance involved, and is not encouraged by the city's layout: some streets have no sidewalks along them; many others are dreary stretches scaled to the automobile; and in some sections, furthermore, pedestrians risk being picked up as vagrants unless they are carrying canes, leading dogs, or otherwise demonstrating a leisure-class status.

Taxicabs exist in Los Angeles, but they aren't prominent in the city's life; one seldom notices them. And in 1964 it was discovered that all, or nearly all, of the local taxis had long had their meters rigged to their customers' disadvantage. I haven't heard of such wholesale rigging in any other American city, and I suspect it got by in L.A. because the permanent residents weren't much affected—taxis being mainly for transients and newcomers not initiated into the local culture.

Apart from owner-driven cars, in fact, the most approved vehicles for local travel in L.A. are helicopters, which also go well with the big distances and love of machinery. Helicopter travel is coming up fast in the city. Movie stars are carried to work by helicopters; local firms use helicopters to shuttle their people from one plant or office to another; and so on. Helicopter noise in the sky is becoming a nuisance, and public complaints are heard about it. Helicopter landing pads have also become important. Most of the new high-rise office buildings have pads on top of them, and at least one local architect is specializing in solving the problems these entail: the support of extra weight on the roofs, for instance; the isolation of the helicopters' extra noise; and the safeguarding of buildings against destructive harmonics that helicopter vibrations might set up.

L.A. is probably the most helicopter-oriented city in the world, but still that is nothing beside its auto-orientation. Not all Angelenos are good drivers, but most are, and the poor ones are held in contempt. Individually the Angelenos are disciplined to driving by practice from childhood up; and as a mass they are disciplined to it by the L.A. police force, which rides herd on them. L.A. has one of the most efficient police forces of all time (however insensitive it may be toward human minorities). With car-owners it seldom raises its voice or is unreasonable, but it is always there, lurking under a billboard or knifing down a freeway on a motorcycle. If a driver transgresses it pounces inexorably, writing out his ticket with fairness and with an authority from which there is little or no escape. And thus the skilled and disciplined corps of motorists, obedient to autopia's imperatives, has been shaped. An Angeleno who cannot join it is in a bad way. I know a youth here, the son of a friend, who is a fine boy, but through some block can't pass his driving test. As a result he is miserable, a drag on everyone. He simply isn't with it.

·   ·   ·

Culture is a much discussed subject in Los Angeles now, with L.A. often being compared to San Francisco. This comparison may turn up whether the culture in question is High Culture—community patronage of the arts—or the lower-case culture that simply means the people's way of life. Much is being heard about High Culture especially, for L.A. has been putting on a burst of activity. In 1964 an ambitious new Music Center was opened in the city's old downtown section; then in '65 a new Art Museum was opened part way out from there, on Wilshire Boulevard, the city's main axis; these and similar developments have been hailed in the L.A. press, in speeches and in conversation, and one feels that the local mood must be rather like that of New York in the heyday of Ward McAllister and the Astor and Vanderbilt families. Huge amounts of money are coming into town, and civic leaders are striving to convert it into something less crass, more praiseworthy. There is a defensiveness in their efforts, reflecting all the years in which L.A. has been scorned by other cities as a hick town. San Francisco is one of those other cities, and this enters into the present rivalry.

The two places have remarkably different histories, for all that they are in the same state. San Francisco has always had a superb harbor, and for more than a century the city has done a profitable business as a commercial, banking, and managerial center. The Gold Rush of '49 gave it a good start. The gold was actually mined or panned a hundred miles inland from San Francisco, but it came out through the city and was there detached from its owners, in large part, by merchants, saloon-keepers, lawyers, and others who had a better notion of how to conserve wealth. Thus San Francisco changed from a frontier settlement to a capitalist center almost overnight. It was further helped by the booming of the Comstock Lode, in Nevada, in the 1860's. The Comstock, a silver bonanza, was *two* hundred miles inland, but it likewise gave its all, or nearly that, toward building San Francisco up; either the new Comstock mines were developed by San Francisco capital, or if some lucky noncapitalist struck it rich in them, he would most likely move to San Francisco and add his winnings to the general stake. From that time on the place had a regional near-monopoly of mining money and knowhow. With some Eastern help San Francisco leadership opened up the later Western mines—copper, nickel, or whatever—and went on to develop much of the Western lumbering and farming businesses too. The city grew richer and richer, almost without direct effort: without anything so squalid, say, as a big local industry.

As a port, San Francisco had been cosmopolitan from the outset, and now the spending of its rich men made it ever more so. Well back in the nineteenth century French chefs were being imported, European musicians were being summoned to play, and San Francisco families were

making international marriages. Perhaps these things were done gaudily
in the early days, but they grew more quiet as the decades passed, and by
the 1930's, when I lived in San Francisco for a while, the process had
become mellow and seemly. The city had a good symphony orchestra by
then; three good museums; a reputable population of writers and artists;
many good restaurants; a couple of excellent universities in its suburbs;
and an upper class consisting of bankers, lawyers, refined merchants, and
other sedentary people steeped in the cultivated life. "San Francisco is to
Los Angeles in the twentieth century," a student of California has told
me, "exactly as Boston was to New York in the nineteenth. I mean exactly. There is no difference." This statement may oversimplify things,
but still it gives an idea.

Not till well into this century did L.A. get started as a city, and then
its first big moneymaking activities verged on the ludicrous: one was the
movie industry, then thought so trashy; another was the digging of oil
wells in the midst of human settlements. The place became a laughing-
stock of other cities, San Francisco included. Much of San Francisco's
early population build-up, coming largely by sea, had been recruited
from the East Coast or abroad; and later on additions of like origin were
attracted there. L.A., in contrast, built its population up from overland
arrivals, which meant Middle Westerners (and secondarily Southeastern-
ers). Even today Middle Westerners dominate the L.A. immigration
stream. A recent survey, based on the 1960 census, showed that most newcomers of that vintage had been born in Minnesota, Iowa, Missouri, the
Dakotas, Nebraska, or Kansas, though they tended to have come to California, circuitously, via Ohio, Indiana, Illinois, Michigan, or Wisconsin.
Either way, they were Midwesterners, a people well stereotyped in American folklore—as being mainly derived, for instance, from Low Church
Protestant stock; as having been puritan and materialistic to start with; as
having had their aversion to the colorful intensified by small-town Midwest life; as having been tellingly portrayed by Sinclair Lewis; and as
being squares, from the North European countries of the rectilinear flags
(whose greatest modern prophet has perhaps been Piet Mondrian, the
rectilinear painter). In the Midwest they planted their squareness on the
landscape: gridirons on the settlements; rectangular fields, farms, towns,
counties, and states on the open country. And coming to L.A. they have
planted it wherever possible; an L.A. teenager can spend half his waking
life now on or in concrete rectangles, such as tennis courts, highways, and
swimming-pools.